KU-286-653

Florida

THE ROUGH GUIDE

There are more than one hundred Rough Guide titles
covering destinations from Amsterdam to Zimbabwe

Forthcoming titles include
Chile • Indonesia • New Orleans • Toronto

Rough Guide Reference Series
Classical Music • European Football • The Internet • Jazz
Opera • Reggae • Rock Music • World Music

Rough Guide Phrasebooks
Czech • Egyptian Arabic • French • German • Greek
Hindi & Urdu • Hungarian • Indonesian • Italian • Japanese
Mandarin Chinese • Mexican Spanish • Polish • Portuguese
Russian • Spanish • Swahili • Thai • Turkish • Vietnamese

Rough Guides on the Internet
www.roughguides.com

ROUGH GUIDE CREDITS

Text editor: Andrew Taber

Series editor: Mark Ellingham

Editorial: Martin Dunford, Jonathan Buckley, Jo Mead, Kate Berens, Amanda Tomlin, Ann-Marie Shaw, Paul Gray, Chris Schüler, Helena Smith, Judith Bamber, Kieran Falconer, Orla Duane, Olivia Eccleshall, Ruth Blackmore, Sophie Martin, Jennifer Dempsey, Sue Jackson, Geoff Howard, Claire Saunders, Anna Sutton Gavin Thomas (UK); Andrew Rosenberg (US)

Production: Susanne Hillen, Andy Hilliard, Link Hall, Helen Ostick, James Morris, Julia Bovis, Michelle Draycott, Cathy Edwards

Cartography: Melissa Flack, Maxine Burke, Nichola Goodliffe

Picture research: Eleanor Hill

Online editors: Alan Spicer, Kate Hands (UK); Geronimo Madrid (US)

Finance: John Fisher, Celia Crowley, Neeta Mistry, Katie Miesiaczek

Marketing & Publicity: Richard Trillo, Simon Carloss, Niki Smith (UK); Jean-Marie Kelly, SoRelle Braun (US)

Administration: Tania Hummel, Alexander Mark Rogers

ACKNOWLEDGEMENTS

Loretta Chilcoat: I would like to thank Michelle Abram, the Greater Miami CVB, Brent Mundt, Hostelling International, Stacie Faulds, the Greater Fort Lauderdale CVB, Raymond Hawkins, Wayne Wilson, Larry Ataniso, Peter Neufeldt, Colin Raynor, "Uncle Bob" Robe, Uncle Frank and Aunt Helen, Squeezle Snr. and Adrian C. At Rough Guides, my gratitude goes to Tania Hummel for her unyielding patience during the rental car fiasco, and Martin Dunford and Andrew Taber for accepting the natural disasters I seem to attract.

Rona Gindin: Special thanks to Michelle Baumann, Pam Brandon and the other publicists at Disney for graciously accepting my relentless stream of questions; to Jan Johnson at the River Ranch for her hospitality and the funky swamp-buggy ride. Especially, love and thanks to co-researchers Michael, Josh (5) and Ryan (1) for their blatantly honest appraisals of sights visited during our frequent weekend voyages.

Neil Roland: Huge thanks to all the fantastically helpful tourist offices, especially: the Sarahs and Rainy Moran at McCluskey for the Florida Keys; Patricia Rice of Van Zandt for Sarasota; Alexandra Owen in Bradenton; Witt Tuttle in St Petersburg; Tracy Louthain in Tallahassee; and Sheilah Bowman in Pensacola. Also big thanks to Tanya Nigro and Colin Brodie at Tourism Florida; Andrew Taber for sympathetic and encouraging editing. For their essential friendship and frequent acts of random kindness: Kevin Naff, Stan Cohen, Bill Hooz, Sam Koskey, Jamie Hunt, and especially Sara, for so much.

Thanks also to Cathy Edwards for typesetting, Melissa Flack for maps and Gillian Armstrong for proofreading.

PUBLISHING INFORMATION

This fourth edition published January 1999 by Rough Guides Ltd, 62–70 Shorts Gardens, London WC2H 9AB.

Distributed by the Penguin Group:

Penguin Books Ltd, 27 Wrights Lane, London W8 5TZ.

Penguin Books USA Inc., 375 Hudson Street, New York 10014, USA.

Penguin Books Australia Ltd, 487 Maroondah Highway, PO Box 257, Ringwood, Victoria 3134, Australia.

Penguin Books Canada Ltd, 10 Alcorn Avenue, Toronto, Ontario, Canada M4V 1E4.

Penguin Books (NZ) Ltd, 182–190 Wairau Road, Auckland 10, New Zealand.

Typeset in Linotron Univers and Century Old Style to an original design by Andrew Oliver.

Printed in England by Clays Ltd, St Ives plc.

Illustrations in Part One and Part Three by Edward Briant.

Illustrations on p.1 by Tommy Yamaha; and p.369 by Henry Iles.

© The Rough Guides Ltd 1999

No part of this book may be reproduced in any form without permission from the publisher except for the quotation of brief passages in reviews.

416pp – Includes index.

A catalogue record for this book is available from the British Library.

ISBN 1-85828-403-1

The publishers and authors have done their best to ensure the accuracy and currency of all the information in *The Rough Guide to Florida*; however, they can accept no responsibility for any loss, injury, or inconvenience sustained by any traveler as a result of information or advice contained in the guide.

Florida

THE ROUGH GUIDE

written and researched by
**Loretta Chilcoat, Rona Gindin,
Neil Roland and Mick Sinclair**

with additional contributions from
Adrian Curry

THE ROUGH GUIDES

THE ROUGH GUIDES

TRAVEL GUIDES • PHRASEBOOKS • MUSIC AND REFERENCE GUIDES

 We set out to do something different when the first Rough Guide was published in 1982. Mark Ellingham, just out of university, was traveling in Greece. He brought along the popular guides of the day, but found they were all lacking in some way. They were either strong on ruins and museums but went on for pages without mentioning a beach or taverna. Or they were so conscious of the need to save money that they lost sight of Greece's cultural and historical significance. Also, none of the books told him anything about Greece's contemporary life – its politics, its culture, its people, and how they lived.

So, with no job in prospect, Mark decided to write his own guidebook; one that aimed to provide practical information that was second to none, detailing the best beaches and the hottest clubs and restaurants, while also giving hard-hitting accounts of every sight, both famous and obscure, and providing up-to-the-minute information on contemporary culture. It was a guide that encouraged independent travelers to find the best of Greece, and was a great success, getting shortlisted for the Thomas Cook travel guide award,

and encouraging Mark, along with three friends, to expand the series.

The Rough Guide list grew rapidly and the letters flooded in, indicating a much broader readership than had been anticipated, but one which uniformly appreciated the Rough Guide mix of practical detail and humor, irreverence and enthusiasm. Things haven't changed. The same four friends who began the series are still the caretakers of the Rough Guide mission today: to provide the most reliable, up-to-date and entertaining information to independent-minded travelers of all ages, on all budgets.

We now publish a hundred titles and have offices in London and New York. The travel guides are written and researched by a dedicated team of more than a hundred authors, based in Britain, Europe, the USA and Australia. We have also created a unique series of phrasebooks to accompany the travel series, along with an acclaimed series of music guides, and a best-selling pocket guide to the Internet and World Wide Web. We also publish comprehensive travel information on our Web site:

www.roughguides.com

HELP US UPDATE

We've gone to a lot of effort to ensure that this edition of *The Rough Guide to Florida* is accurate and up-to-date. However, places get "discovered"; telephone numbers change; restaurants, hotels and other tourist facilities raise prices or lower standards. If you feel we've got it wrong or left something out, we'd like to know, and if you can remember the address, price, the time, the phone number, so much the better.

We'll credit all contributions, and send a copy of the next edition (or any other Rough Guide if you prefer) for the best letters.

Please mark letters: "Rough Guide Florida" and send to:
Rough Guides Ltd, 62–70 Shorts Gardens, London WC2H 9AB, or Rough Guides, 375 Hudson St, 9th Floor, New York, NY 10014.

Or send email to: mail@roughguides.co.uk

Online updates about this book can be found on Rough Guides' Web site at **www.roughguides.com**

LIST OF MAPS

MAP SYMBOLS

Interstate	Museum
US Highway	Historic House
State Highway	Public Gardens
Secondary State Highway	Lighthouse
Track	Marshland
Trail	Information Centre
Railway	Post Office
Ferry route	Wall
State border	Building
Chapter division boundary	Church
River	Cemetery
Airport	National/State Park
Hotel	Park
Campsite	Indian Reservation
Picnic area	Beach

CONTENTS

Introduction viii

PART THREE CONTEXTS 369

INTRODUCTION

The cut-rate package trips and photos of tanning flesh and Mickey Mouse that fill the pages of glossy holiday brochures ensure that everyone has an image of **Florida** – but seldom one that's either accurate or complete. Pulling 35 million visitors each year to its beaches and theme parks, the aptly nicknamed "sunshine state" is devoted to the tourist trade, yet it's also among the least-understood parts of the US, with a history, character and diversity of landscape unmatched by any other region. Beyond the palm-fringed sands, hiking and canoeing trails wind through little-known forests and rivers, and the famed beaches themselves can vary wildly over a short distance – hordes of copper-toned ravers are often just a frisbee's throw from a deserted, pristine strand coveted by wildlife-watchers. Variations continue inland, where smart, modern cities are rarely more than a few miles away from steamy, primeval swamps.

In many respects, Florida is still evolving. Socially and politically, it hasn't stayed still since the earliest days of US settlement: stimulating growth has always been the paramount concern, and with a thousand people a day moving to the booming state, it's currently the fourth most populous place in the nation. The changing demographics have begun eroding the traditional Deep South conservatism and are overturning the common notion that Florida is dominated by retirees. In fact, the new Floridians tend to be a younger breed, working energetically to shape not only the future of Florida but that of the whole US. Immigration from outside the country is also on the increase, with Spanish- and French-Creole-speaking enclaves providing a reminder of geographic and economic ties to Latin America and the Caribbean. These links have proven almost as influential in raising the state's material wealth over the past decade as the arrival of huge domestic businesses, including sections of the film industry that have opted for central Florida in preference to Hollywood.

Florida does, however, have a number of problems to contest with, the most pressing of which is its growing reputation for crimes against (and even murders of) tourists. While the authorities have devised schemes to reduce such attacks, it is an inescapable fact that visitors are an inviting target for both opportunist and organized criminals. Statistically, it's highly unlikely that you'll become a victim, but you should be wary at all times and pay heed to the safety tips given throughout the book. On the home front, the state is struggling to provide enough houses, schools and roads for its growing population; levels of poverty in the rural areas can be severe; and in an increasingly multi-ethnic society, racial tensions frequently surface. Expanding towns without jeopardizing the environment is another hot issue; large amounts of land are under state or federal protection, and there are signs that the conservation lobby is gaining the upper-hand. Nevertheless, uncontrolled development is posing serious ecological problems – not least to the Everglades.

Where to go and when

Heat-induced lethargy is no excuse not to get out and explore the different facets of Florida, as the state is compact enough to be toured easily and quickly. The essential stop is **Miami**, whose addictive, cosmopolitan vibe is enriched by its large Hispanic population, and where the much-photographed Art Deco district of **Miami Beach** provides an unmistakable backdrop for the state's liveliest night clubs.

From Miami, a simple journey south brings you to the **Florida Keys**, a hundred-mile string of islands of which each has something to call its own, be it sport fishing, coral-reef diving, or a unique species of dwarf deer. The single road spanning the Keys comes

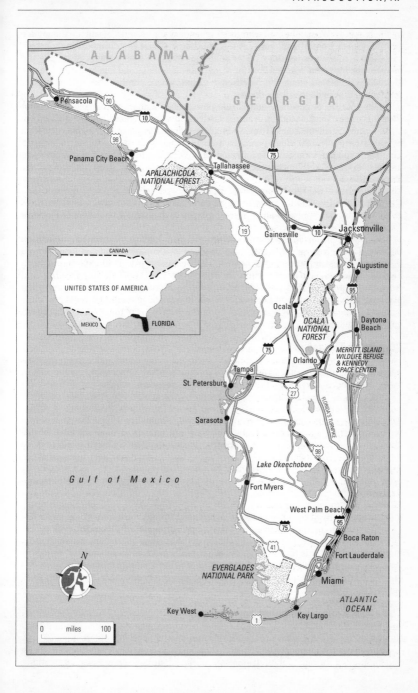

to a halt at **Key West**, a blob of land that's legendary for its sunsets and anything-goes attitude. North from Miami, much of the **Southeast Coast** is a disappointingly urbanized strip – commuter territory better suited for living in than visiting. Alongside the busy towns, however, beaches flow for many unbroken miles and finally escape the residential stranglehold along the **Northeast Coast**, where communities are often subservient to the sands that flank them.

When you tire of beachlife and ocean views, make a short hop inland to **Central Florida**, whose verdant terrain features cattle farms, grassy hillsides, and isolated villages beside expansive lakes. The sole but rather dramatic disruption to this rural idyll is **Walt Disney World**, which practices tourism on the scale of the infinite. If you're in the mood, you can indulge in its ingenious fix of escapist fun; if not, the upfront commercialism may well encourage you to skip north to the deep forests of the **Panhandle**, Florida's link with the Deep South – or to the art-rich towns and sunset-kissed beaches of the **West Coast**. Explore these at your leisure as you progress steadily south to the **Everglades**, a massive, alligator-filled swathe of sawgrass plain, mangrove islands and cypress swamp, which provides as definitive a statement of Florida's natural beauty as you'll encounter.

Cost-wise, it makes little difference **when** you visit. Intense, year-round competition for your dollar gives rise to tremendous bargains in accommodation and food, though prices are lowest off-season (see below). The best-value plan is to explore northern Florida in March and move south in April – or vice versa during October and November. However, it is also worth considering Florida's climatic variations when planning your trip; winter in northern Florida is unsuitable for beach holidays, while summer in the south is plagued by high humidity, with many of the natural areas infested by mosquitoes.

Climate and seasons

Florida is split into **two climatic zones**: subtropical in the south and warm temperate – like the rest of the southeastern US – in the north. More importantly for the visitor, these two zones determine the state's **tourist seasons**, which are different for Florida's southern and northern halves and have a great effect on costs (see above).

Anywhere **south of Orlando** experiences very mild winters (November to April), with pleasantly warm temperatures and a low level of humidity. This is the peak period for tourist activity, with prices at their highest and crowds at their thickest. It also marks the best time to visit the inland parks and swamps. The southern summer (May to October) seems hotter than it really is (New York is often warmer) because of the extremely high humidity, relieved only by afternoon thunderstorms and sometimes even hurricanes (the southern section of Florida was devastated by **Hurricane Andrew** in August 1992, and, to a lesser degree, Hurricane Georges in September 1998); at this time of year you'll be lucky to see a blue sky. Lower prices and fewer tourists are the rewards for braving the mugginess, though mosquitoes can render the natural areas off-limits. Winter is the off-peak period **north of Orlando**; in all probability, the only chill you'll detect is a slight nip in the evening air, though it's worth bearing in mind that at this time of year, the sea is really too cold for swimming, and snow has been known to fall in the Panhandle. The northern Florida summer is when the crowds arrive, and when the days – and the nights – can be almost as hot and sticky as southern Florida.

The Florida sun: sunbathing and sunburn

Any visitor with sensitive skin should bear in mind that Florida shares a latitude with the Sahara Desert; the power of the Florida **sun** should never be underestimated.

Time spent outdoors should be planned carefully at first, especially between 11am and 2pm, when the sun is at its strongest. A powerful **sunscreen** is essential; anything with an SPF of less than 25 is unlikely to offer the necessary protection. Light-colored, loose-fitting, lightweight clothes should protect any parts of your body not accustomed to direct sunlight. Wear a hat with a wide brim, carry sunglasses, and keep to the shaded side of the street. Drink plenty of **fluids** (but not alcohol) to prevent dehydration – public drinking-water fountains are provided for this purpose; iced tea is the best drink for cooling off in a restaurant.

AVERAGE DAYTIME TEMPERATURES (°F)											
	Jan	Feb	Mar	Apr	May	Jun	Jul	Aug	Sep	Oct	Nov	Dec
Miami	68	69	71	74	78	81	82	84	81	78	73	70
Key West	69	71	74	77	80	83	85	85	84	80	75	72
Orlando	61	63	66	72	78	82	82	82	81	75	67	61
Tampa	60	61	66	72	77	81	82	82	81	75	67	62
Tallahassee	53	56	63	68	72	78	81	81	77	74	66	59
Jacksonville	52	55	61	67	73	79	82	81	78	70	62	55
Pensacola	52	55	60	67	74	80	81	81	78	70	60	54

PART ONE

THE
BASICS

GETTING THERE FROM BRITAIN AND IRELAND

There's never been a better time for British travelers to go to Florida. Price wars between airlines on transatlantic routes are hotter than ever, and many operators are tossing in car rental and accommodation for only a little over the regular airfare. Comparatively few airlines fly non-stop from the UK to Florida, but many have one-stop links, and connections from other US airports are plentiful. Innumerable charter flights from all over the UK to major holiday centers such as Orlando throw up even more low-cost options.

FLIGHTS

Although you can fly to the US from many of Britain's regional airports, the only **non-stop scheduled** flights to Florida are from London, and all of these land either at Miami or, less often, Orlando. The **flight time** is around eight hours, leaving London around midday and arriving during the afternoon (local time). The return journey is slightly shorter, leaving in the early evening and flying through the night to arrive in London around breakfast time.

Specialist agents (see p.4) can offer cut-price seats on direct **charter flights**. These are particularly good value if you're traveling from a British city other than London, though they tend to be limited to the summer season, be restricted to so-called "holiday destinations," and have fixed departure and return dates. Brochures are available in most high street travel agents, or contact the specialists direct.

Many more routings use direct **one-stop** flights to Florida (a flight may be called "direct" even if it stops on the way, provided it keeps the same *flight number* throughout its journey). Obviously, these take a few hours longer than non-stop flights but can be more convenient (and sometimes cheaper) if you're not aiming specifically for Miami or Orlando. All the state's cities and large towns have airports – the other major one is Tampa – with good links from other US cities.

FLIGHTS FROM BRITAIN

The following carriers operate **scheduled flights** to Florida from London (all use Gatwick airport unless otherwise stated).

Air Canada (☎ 0990/247226) Daily from Heathrow via Toronto to Miami and other Florida airports.

American Airlines (☎0181/572 5555) Daily non-stop to Miami from Heathrow; one-stop flights to most other Florida airports, usually via Dallas.

British Airways (☎0345/222 111) Daily non-stop to Miami from Heathrow; 1–2 daily via Miami or Orlando to Tampa; 4 weekly non-stop to Miami; daily non-stop to Orlando; daily to Charlotte from Gatwick then onwards by USAir to most major Florida airports.

Continental (☎0800/776464) Daily via Newark to most Florida airports.

Delta ✈☎0800/414767) Daily to Orlando, connecting with all other Florida airports; also daily via Atlanta to most Florida airports.

Northwest (☎0990/561000) Daily via Detroit to Orlando and (via Orlando) to Miami.

United (☎0845/ 8444777) Daily to Miami from Heathrow (via Washington or Chicago).

Virgin Airlines (☎0800/747747) 4–5 weekly non-stop to Miami; daily to Orlando.

Alternatively, you could take a flight to New York or **another city** on the northern East Coast and travel on from there – this won't save any money overall but is an idea if you want to see more of the country before reaching Florida. Again, agents have the cheapest offers.

FARES

Whenever and however you go, the most expensive time to fly is **high season**, between June and August and a week either side of Christmas; April, May, September and October are slightly less pricey, and November to March is considered **low season** – cheaper still. It's important to remember, however, that high season in the UK is the low season – the least costly and least busy time – in south Florida, so the extra you might spend on a summer flight may be offset by cheaper deals once you're on the ground. Seasons in north Florida, however, match those of the UK. For more on the seasonal variations across Florida, see the Introduction.

Before booking a flight, **shop around** for the best price: scan the travel ads in the Sunday papers, in London's *Time Out* and giveaway magazines, or phone the airlines or one of the agents mentioned below. The details we've given are the latest available, but are sure to have undergone at least subtle changes by the time you read them.

A basic round-trip **economy-class ticket** will cost between £280 for a midweek flight in low season and £570 for a weekend flight in high season. Economy round-trips have no restrictions regarding length of stay, but changing your return date after booking entails a penalty of £100. **Standby** deals (tickets which you pay for in advance without specifying precise travel dates), and **APEX** round-trips, which have to be booked 14, 21 or 30 days in advance for a stay of at least a week, are £100–150 more expensive than economy fares if bought directly from the airline. However, cut-rate APEX tickets are what you're likely to find offered by **agents** such as STA Travel or Campus (addresses below), who always have the lowest fares, with special reductions for students and anyone under 26.

FLIGHT AGENTS AND SPECIALIST TOUR OPERATORS IN BRITAIN

LOW-COST FLIGHT AGENTS

Campus Travel, 52 Grosvenor Gardens, London SW1 (☎0171/730 2101). Also many other branches around the country.

Council Travel, 28A Poland St, London W1 (☎0171/437 7767).

STA Travel, 86 Old Brompton Rd, London SW7 (☎0171/361 6262). Offices nationwide.

Trailfinders, 42–50 Earls Court Rd, London W8 (☎0171/937 5400).

Travel Cuts, 295 Regent St, London W1 (☎0171/255 2082).

SPECIALIST TOUR OPERATORS

Airtours, Helmshore, Rossendale, Lancs BB4 4NB (☎01706/260000).

AmeriCan + Worldwide Travel, 45 High St, Tunbridge Wells, Kent TN1 1XL (☎01892/511894).

American Adventures, 64 Mount Pleasant Avenue, Tunbridge Wells (☎01892512700).

Bon Voyage, 18 Bellevue Rd, Southampton, Hants SO1 2AY (☎01703/330332).

British Airways Holidays, Astral Towers, Betts Way, London Rd, Crawley, W Sussex RH10 2XA (☎01293/723110).

Contiki Travel, Wells House, 15 Elmfield Rd, Bromley, Kent BR1 1LS (☎0181/2906422).

Explore Worldwide, 1 Frederick St, Aldershot, Hants GU11 1LQ (☎01252/319448).

Greyhound, Sussex House, London Rd, East Grinstead, West Sussex RH19 1LD (☎01342/317317).

Premier Holidays, Westbrook, Milton Rd, Cambridge CB4 1YQ (☎01223/355977).

Transatlantic Vacations, 3A Gatwick Metro Center, Balcombe Rd, Horley, Surrey RH6 9GA (☎01293/774441).

TrekAmerica, 4 Waterperry Court, Middleton Road, Banbury, Oxon OX16 8QG (☎01295 256 777).

Unijet, "Sandrocks," Rocky Lane, Haywards Heath, West Sussex RH16 4RH (☎0870/ 5114 114).

Virgin Holidays, The Galleria, Station Rd, Crawley, West Sussex RH10 1WW (☎01293/617181).

Through an agent, provided your plans are flexible and you hunt around, you can often make savings of £100–200 on regular fares, bringing prices down to around £300–350 for a weekend flight in high season. Also watch for short-term offers from the major airlines – which can cut fares to any east-coast US city to as low as £220 round-trip.

Many agents and airlines offer **"open jaw"** deals whereby you fly into one US city and out through another. These won't save money if you're sticking to Florida but you could, for example, combine New York with Miami for around £380.

Finally, around £100 can be cut from the cheaper fares if you travel as a **courier**. Most of the major courier firms, such as CTS Ltd (☎0171/351 0300), DHL (☎0181/890 9393) and Polo Express (☎0181/759 5838) – see the *Yellow Pages* for others – offer cheap round-trip flights as payment for delivering a package or documents; for example, the fee for a round-trip flight to Miami could be as low as £150. As a courier, you may be required to sacrifice your baggage allowance, but the companies usually do their best to accommodate you. The envelope/parcel need only be delivered to a name waiting at your destination airport, meaning you can get right on with your trip.

PACKAGES

Packages – fly-drive, flight-accommodation deals and guided tours (or a combination of all three) – can be a good way of skirting potential problems once you're in Florida and they usually work out cheaper than arranging the same trip yourself. The drawbacks are the loss of flexibility and the fact that flight-accommodation schemes often use hotels in the mid-range to expensive bracket – cheaper accommodation is almost always readily available. There are a great many packages to choose from and your high-street travel agent will have plenty of brochures and information.

FLIGHT AND ACCOMMODATION DEALS

There's really no end of **flight and accommodation packages** to all the major coastal areas and Orlando, and although you can always do things cheaper independently, you won't be able to do the *same* things cheaper – in fact the equivalent room booked by itself will probably be a lot more expensive. STA Travel (address on p.4) offers a package deal which includes flight and $15-a-night hostel accommodation (bear in mind

few Florida towns boast hostels, see "Accommodation" p.27).

Any number of tour operators offer other, costlier deals. Of these, Virgin Holidays has the cheapest and widest selection, averaging £400–500 per person for a week, inclusive of return flight and car rental. See also "Accommodation," p.28, for details of pre-booked accommodation schemes.

FLY-DRIVE DEALS

Fly-drive deals, which combine car rental with a flight booking, can be extremely good value, and should certainly be considered before booking a flight and car rental separately. In fact, many airlines offer seven days' car rental at little, if any, extra cost above booking a flight to Florida with them. British Airways, for example, can set you up with a week's car rental and a return flight to Miami or Orlando for £315–489 depending on the time of year. If you're not aiming for these major centers, several American airlines have even cheaper deals based on smaller Florida cities.

The most obvious drawback of fly-drive deals is that the quoted prices are usually based on four adults sharing a car (and, obviously, each booking a flight with the airline involved); two people traveling together will often face a £20 surcharge. Scan a handful of brochures for the deal which suits you best – and be sure to read the small print. Renting a car for longer than seven days can usually be arranged with a minimum of fuss for as little as £23 per week for a compact car (ideal for two people); around £33 for a mid-sized vehicle.

Other important facts to consider when looking for a fly-drive deal are the unavoidable extra expenses such as the Collision Damage Waiver, the Florida surcharge and the cost of fuel, and the fact that under-25s may face problems renting a car in the US (although a pre-arranged booking should prevent this). For complete details on these matters and full car rental and driving facts, see "Getting around."

TOURING AND ADVENTURE PACKAGES

Geographical isolation and scorching summer temperatures mean that Florida tends to miss out on the specialist **touring and adventure trips** that cover much of the rest of the US. Nonetheless, TrekAmerica is one UK-based company that does include Florida. An eight-day trip (winter only) costs £339; a fourteen-day excursion leaving from Miami goes for £442 regardless of the time of year; and a fourteen-day "Atlantic Dream" trek from New York to Miami via Orlando will set you back £468. Other operators worth contacting include Contiki and AmeriCan Adventures, whose brochures can be found in youth- and student-oriented travel outlets. Once you're in Florida, tours of much shorter length, often just a day or two, can usually be arranged on the spot – details are given throughout the Guide.

FLIGHTS FROM IRELAND

It's not possible to fly non-stop from Ireland to Florida, though Aer Lingus and Delta have services from Dublin and Shannon via New York or Atlanta for IR£500–550. If you're under 26 or a student, the cheapest flights from Eire to Florida are through USIT (see below), which offers a return fare of IR£420 with Northwest via London.

AIRLINES AND FLIGHT AGENTS IN IRELAND

AIRLINES

Aer Lingus
Belfast ☎0645 737747; Dublin and Limerick ☎01/474239; Cork ☎021/327155.

Delta Airlines
Belfast ☎01232/480526; Dublin ☎1800/768080.

FLIGHT AGENTS

American Holidays, Lombard House, Lombard St, Belfast 1 (☎01232/238762); 38 Pearse St, Dublin 2 (☎01/679 8800).

Apex Travel, 59 Dame St, Dublin 2 (☎01/671 5933).

Flight Finders International, 13 Baggot St Lower, Dublin 2 (☎01/676 8326).

Joe Walsh Tours, 8–11 Baggot St, Dublin (☎01 6622222).

Thomas Cook, 11 Donegall Place, Belfast (☎01232/554455); 118 Grafton St, Dublin (☎01/677 1721).

USIT, Fountain Center, Belfast BT1 6ET (☎01232/324073); Aston Quay, Dublin 2 (☎01 602 1600); other branches nationwide.

GETTING THERE FROM NORTH AMERICA

Getting to Florida from anywhere else in North America is never a problem, as the region is well serviced by air, rail and road networks. Every major and most minor US airlines fly to Florida, where Miami is the main hub, closely followed by Orlando and Tampa. Flying remains the quickest but most expensive way to travel; taking the train is a close second; traveling by bus is much less costly but also the slowest and least comfortable mode of transport.

BY AIR

Prices are similar no matter which airline you choose; variations in cost are more dependent on the conditions governing the ticket – whether it's

AIRLINES IN NORTH AMERICA

Air Canada ☎1-800/776-3000; in Canada call diectory assistance for local toll-free numbers

Air Tran Airways ☎1-800/825-8538

American Airlines ☎1-800/433-7300

America West Airlines ☎1-800/235-9292

Canadian Airlines ☎1-800/426-7000; ☎1-800/665-1177 in Canada

Continental Airlines ☎1-800/525-0280

Delta ☎1-800/221-1212 in the US; in Canada, call directory assistance for local toll-free numbers

Kiwi Airlines ☎1-800/538-5494

Midwest Express ☎1-800/452-2022

Northwest/KLM ☎1-800/225-2525

Tower Air ☎1-800/221-2500; 1-718/553-8500

TWA ☎1-800/221-2000

United Airlines ☎1-800/241-6522

US Airways ☎1-800/428-4322

Note that the **Canadian toll-free directory assistance number** is ☎1-800/555-1212

---

fully refundable, the time and day (midweek is always cheaper than weekends) and most importantly the **time of year** you travel.

Booking directly with an airline tends to be expensive, although it is the best way to take advantage of any car rental and accommodation deals they may offer in conjunction with a flight (see "Packages," p.5). Price-wise, the best outlets for plane tickets are the **specialist operators** such as STA and Council Travel (see p.4), primarily aimed at students but able to offer competitively priced fares to everybody.

Of the **major carriers**, Delta and American Airlines have the best links with the state's many smaller regional airports. You can expect to pay in the region of $175–225 from New York or from Chicago. From LA the lowest fare is going to be around $275. Of the **smaller airlines**, Tower Air has direct flights from New York to Miami and Fort Lauderdale. The least expensive round-trip ticket, subject to availability, is $184 to Miami or $164 to Fort Lauderdale. Kiwi, based in Newark and New York, services Orlando, Miami and West Palm Beach. Fares range from $110–$160 each way, and depend more on availability and advance booking requirements than seasonal adjustments. You can also take advantage of Kiwi's deal with Avis, which entitles you to a reduction in the cost of car rental. Midwest Express flies from Milwaukee to Orlando throughout the year; flights to Fort Lauderdale, Fort Myers and Tampa are scheduled for mid-December to mid-April only. Air Tran Airways, based in Atlanta, has flights to Jacksonville, Fort Lauderdale, Fort Myers, Fort Walton Beach, Orlando, Tampa and We.t Palm Beach from a number of Southern, Mid-Western

and East Coast Cities. Their round-trip fare from La Guardia Airport in New York to Jacksonville is around $210.

From **Canada**, Air Canada flies direct from Toronto to Miami and Tampa; from Montreal the company has direct flights to Fort Lauderdale and Miami; and, in the spring only, flights from Toronto embark for Fort Myers and West Palm Beach. Canadian Airlines fly Toronto and Montréal to Miami; from Toronto only they fly to Fort Lauderdale, Fort Myers, Tampa and Sarasota. American Airlines consistently offers the most economical fares, with flights from Toronto to Miami, Orlando and Fort Lauderdale plus several other Florida cities. They also fly to Miami from Vancouver. American Airlines' best deal is its weekend round-trip flights from Toronto or Montréal to Miami for CDN$315. Otherwise, their lowest round-trip fare from either city is, at the time of writing, CDN$357; from Vancouver to Miami, expect to pay at least $CDN513.

Again, the place to find the lowest-priced fares is a **specialist flight agent**, such as Travel Cuts. If your plans are very flexible, scanning the travel pages of your local newspaper may turn up some bargains; though be sure to read the small print – many seemingly attractive deals are dependent on two people traveling together and using specified hotel accommodation.

BY CAR

How feasible it is to **drive** to Florida naturally depends on where you live and how much time you have. If you're aiming for the tourist hot-spots like Orlando, you may enjoy a few days passing through the relaxing scenery of the southeast

DISCOUNT AGENTS IN NORTH AMERICA

Council Travel, 205 E 42nd St, New York, NY 10017 (☎1-800/226-8624 or 212/822-2700). Other offices include: 530 Bush St, Suite 700, San Francisco, CA 94108 (☎415/421-3473); 10904 Lindbrook Drive, Los Angeles, CA 90024 (☎310/208-3551); 1138 13th St, Boulder, CO 80302 (☎303/447-8101); 3300 M St NW, 2nd Floor, Washington, DC 20007 (☎202/337-6464); 1153 N Dearborn St, Chicago, IL 60610 (☎312/951-0585); 273 Newbury St, Boston, MA 02116 (☎617/266-1926). Nationwide specialists in student travel.

STA Travel, 10 Downing St, New York, NY 10014 (☎1-800/777-0112; 212/627-3111). Other offices include: 7202 Melrose Ave, Los Angeles, CA 90046 (☎213/934-8722); 51 Grant Ave, San Francisco, CA 94108 (☎415/391-8407); 297 Newbury St, Boston, MA 02115 (☎617/266-6014); 429 S Dearborn St, Chicago, IL 60605 (☎312/786-9050); 3730 Walnut St, Philadelphia, PA 19104 (☎215/382-2928); 317 14th Ave SE, Minneapolis, MN 55414 (☎612/615-1800). Worldwide specialists in independent travel.

Travel Cuts, 187 College St, Toronto, ON M5T 1P7 (416/979-2406). Other offices include: 180 MacEwan Student Center, University of Calgary, Calgary, AB T2N 1N4 (☎403/282-7687); 12304 Jasper Av, Edmonton, AB T5N 3K5 (☎403/488-8487); 1613 Rue St Denis, Montréal, PQ H2X 3K3 (☎514/843-8511); 555 W 8th Ave, Vancouver, BC V5Z 1C6 (☎604/822-6890); University Center, University of Manitoba, Winnipeg MB R3T 2N2 (☎204/269-9530). Canadian student travel organization.

before and after your trip. From the northeast or midwest, reckon on around 26 hours of actual driving to get to Florida; from the West Coast you'll probably need 40 hours behind the wheel.

BY TRAIN

A few years ago, the deregulation of the airline industry helped make domestic air travel as cheap as train travel. In an effort to win back business, **Amtrak** (contactable on a nationwide toll-free number ☎1-800/USA RAIL) has sharpened up its act all round: raising comfort levels, offering better food, introducing "Thruway" buses to link with its trains, and launching new services – most recently the Los Angeles–Miami *Sunset Limited* route. Consequently, traveling to Florida by train can be enjoyable and relaxing, if not particularly inexpensive.

From **New York**, the *Silver Meteor* and the *Silver Star* traverse the eastern seaboard daily to Miami via Orlando, while the *Silver Palm* takes a detour at Jacksonville and continues to Miami via Tampa. Fares range from $148 (the discounted fare, subject to availability) to $406 for a round-trip ticket, and the journey from New York takes between 26 and 29 hours. From **Los Angeles** to Orlando, the *Sunset Limited* crosses the southerly reaches of the US in a three-day journey. The lowest discounted round-trip fare varies according to season from $306-$558.

If you really can't bear to be parted from your car and you live within driving distance of Lorton, Virginia (just south of Washington DC), the **Florida Auto Train** will carry you and your vehicle to Sanford, near Orlando. The journey time is 16–17 hours and passenger fares range from $85 to $169 each way; depending on its size, your vehicle will cost an additional $143–296 each way.

All the above involve overnight travel. To spare yourself a restless night fidgeting in your seat, AMTRAK offers a choice of sleeping accomodations. To give you an idea of the price range, two nights on the *Sunset Limited* in an "economy sleeper," essentially a narrow bed that pulls down from the wall, will set you back an extra $414; a family room will cost you $672; and a deluxe bedroom (for two) starts at $777.

BY BUS

Long-distance travel on **Greyhound** buses (☎1-800/231-2222) can be an endurance test but is at least the cheapest form of public transport to the Sunshine State. Also, if you have the time and inclination to include a few stopovers on the way, you'll find that Greyhound operates a more comprehensive service than do planes or trains (they also reach all but the smallest Florida towns). Scan your local newspaper or call your local Greyhound station for special fares, which are periodically offered, and remember that midweek travel is marginally cheaper than traveling on weekends.

Otherwise, the lowest round-trip fare from either Chicago or New York to Miami is currently $118; no refunds allowed. A more flexible ticket (allowing an 85% refund) costs $172. From LA to Miami the cheaper fare is, once again, $118 and the more flexible one $225.

PACKAGES

Pick up the travel section of any newspaper and you'll see dozens of Florida **package deals** on offer. These come in all shapes and sizes, and are designed to appeal to a multitude of budgets and interests. Most, however, simply offer a week or two in the Florida sun for a single price – from around $550 per person per week (from New York) or $750 (from LA) – inclusive of round-trip flights and accommodation.

Besides independent operators catering to specialist interests, package deals are also offered by most airlines and by Amtrak.

GETTING THERE FROM AUSTRALIA & NEW ZEALAND

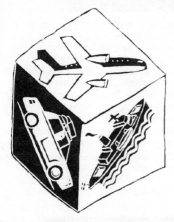

Because of the enormous distance, there are no direct flights to Florida from Australia or New Zealand. Travelers should fly to Los Angeles or San Francisco – the main points of entry to the US – and make their way from there. Of the airlines, United Airlines, Air New Zealand and Qantas are the best at arranging trouble-free connecting services through to Miami and Orlando.

Fares vary throughout the year according to season: low season for flights to the US is Feb–March and Oct 16–Nov 30; mid season is Jan 16–31, April–May and Sept 1–Oct 15; high season is Dec 1–Jan 15 and Jun–Aug. Your local travel agent will give you information on the latest deals; student and under-26 deals, where available, are about ten percent cheaper.

From Australia there are **direct flights** to LA and San Francisco five times weekly from Sydney, Melbourne and Brisbane on Air New Zealand (A$1699 low season/A$2399 high season), daily from Cairns, Brisbane, Sydney, Adelaide and Melbourne on Qantas (A$1799/2499), and daily from Sydney on United Airlines (A$1899/2499).

You can include a Pacific **stopover**, if you want, with Air New Zealand (from major eastern Australian cities via Auckland; A$1750/2299). For around A$1899/2399, you can fly Cathay Pacific (via Hong Kong from Sydney & Brisbane); Malaysia Airlines (from Sydney via Kuala Lumpur); Qantas (from major eastern Australian cities via Hawaii or Auckland and Papeete); and Air Pacific (from Sydney via Fiji). The best deal is consistently with Japan Airlines (from Cairns, Brisbane and Sydney A$1550/1880), but includes a night's stopover in Tokyo; Tokyo accommodation is included in the fare. Other airlines with several indirect flights a week from major Australian airports are Korean Airlines (A$1799/2199) and Singapore Airlines (A$2099/2899).

From New Zealand there are no direct flights through to Florida. As with Australia, you're looking at a fare to Los Angeles or San Francisco and then an add-on. The best direct deals to LA and San Francisco are from Auckland; add about NZ$100 for departures from Christchurch and Wellington. Daily flights are operated by Air New Zealand for around NZ$1899/2899 while United Airlines and Qantas are both around NZ$2199/2899.

Flights to LA via their homeports are operated several times a week by JAL and Korean Airlines (both NZ$1999/2399); Malaysia Airlines via Kuala Lumpur (NZ$2099/2699); and Air Pacific via Fiji (NZ$1950/2899).

AIRLINES IN AUSTRALIA

Air New Zealand, Australia (☎13/2476); New Zealand (☎09/357 3000).

Air Pacific, Australia (☎02/9957 0150 or 1-800/230 150); New Zealand (☎09/379 2404).

Cathay Pacific, Australia (☎13/1747); New Zealand (☎09/379 0861).

Delta Air Lines, Australia (☎02/9262 1777 or 1-800/251 878); New Zealand (☎09/379 3370).

Japan Airlines, Australia (☎02/9272 1111); New Zealand (☎09/379 9906).

Korean Airlines, Australia (☎02/9262 6000); New Zealand (☎09/307 3687).

Malaysia Airlines, Australia (☎13/2627); New Zealand (☎09/373 2741).

Northwest Airlines, Australia (☎02/9231 6333).

Qantas, Australia (☎13/1211); New Zealand (☎09/357 8900 or ☎800/808 767).

Singapore Airlines, Australia (☎13/1011); New Zealand (☎09/379 3209).

United Airlines, Australia (☎13/1777); New Zealand (☎09/379 3800).

FLIGHT AGENTS IN AUSTRALIA

Anywhere Travel, 345 Anzac Parade, Kingsford, Sydney (☎02/9663 0411).

Budget Travel, 16 Fort St, Auckland (☎09/366 0061 or 0800/808 040).

Destinations Unlimited, 3 Milford Rd, Milford, Auckland (☎09/373 4033).

Flight Centers Australia: Circular Quay, Sydney, plus branches nationwide (☎13/1600 for information). New Zealand: National Bank Towers, 205–225 Queen St, Auckland (☎09/209 6171); Shop 1M, National Mutual Arcade, 152 Hereford St, Christchurch (☎03/379 7145); 50–52 Willis St, Wellington (☎04/472 8101); other branches nationwide.

STA Travel, Australia: 732 Harris St, Ultimo, Sydney; 256 Flinders St, Melbourne (☎13/1776 for information). New Zealand: Travelers' Center, 10 High St, Auckland (☎09/309 0458); 233 Cuba St, Wellington (☎04/385 0561); 223 High St, Christchurch (☎03/379 9098); other branches nationwide.

Thomas Cook, Australia: 175 Pitt St, Sydney; 330 Collins St, Melbourne; plus branches in other state capitals (☎13/1771 for information and locations). New Zealand: 96 Anzac Ave, Auckland (☎09/379 3920).

Tymtro Travel, Level 0, 130 Pitt St. Sydney, (☎02/9223 2211 OR ☎1300/652 969)

Trailfinders, 91 Elizabeth St, Brisbane (☎07/3229 0887)

SPECIALIST TOUR OPERATORS IN AUSTRALIA

The Adventure Specialists, Floor 1, 69 Liverpool Street, Sydney (☎02/261 292).

Adventure World, 73 Walker St, Sydney (☎02/956 7766); 8 Victoria Ave, Perth (☎09/221 2300); 101 Great South Rd, Remuera, Auckland (☎09/524 5118).

American Travel Center, 2nd Floor, 262 Adelaide St, Brisbane (☎07/3221 4788).

Padi Travel Network, 4/372 Eastern Valley Way, Chatswood, NSW (☎1-800 678 100).

Sydney International Travel, 75 King St, Sydney (☎02/9299 8000).

United Vacations, Level 4, Challis House, 4 Martin Place, Sydney (☎13/1884).

Wiltrans, Level 10, 189 Kent St, Sydney (☎02/9255 0899).

GAY AND LESBIAN

Pride Travel, 254 Bay St, Brighton, Melbourne (☎03/9596 3566 or 1-800/061 427); Sydney (☎1-800 808 696).

Silke's Travel, 263 Oxford St, Darlinghurst, Sydney (☎02/9380 5835).

Once in LA, adding on a return fare to destinations in Florida costs around US$380. Various coupon deals, valid within the continental US, are available with your main ticket. A minimum purchase of three usually applies, for example *AA*'s Coupon Pass costs $US330 for the first three, and between US$60 and US$100 for subsequent tickets (maximum of ten).

Round-the-World deals from Australasia include Cathay Pacific-UA's "Globetrotter," ANZ-KLM-Northwest's "World Navigator," and Quantas-BA's "Global Explorer," all of which offer similar packages of six stopovers worldwide, with additional stopovers (around A/NZ$100 each) and limited backtracking for A$2599/$3299;NZ$3189/$3699. More US-oriented, but only available in Australia, is Singapore-TWA's "Easyworld" fare, allowing unlimited backtracking within the US (flat rate A$3150). For unlimited flexibility, *UA*, in conjunction with a variety of airlines, also offers an unrestricted RTW fare for around A/NZ$4500/4800. In addition, some airlines combine their regular services at a discounted rate, although these are generally more restrictive; Air France-Qantas is by far the cheapest, allowing three stops in each direction from A$1699/NZ$2099.

VISAS AND RED TAPE

VISAS

To visit the US for a period of less than ninety days, citizens of Austria, Andorra, Belgium, Britain, Brunei, Denmark, Finland, France, Germany, Iceland, Ireland, Italy, Japan, Liechtenstein, Luxembourg, Monaco, the Netherlands, New Zealand, Norway, San Marino, Spain, Sweden and Switzerland need a **full passport** and a **visa waiver form**. The latter will be provided either by your travel agent or by the airline during check-in or on the plane, and must be presented to immigration on arrival. Prospective visitors from Australia and all other parts of the world not mentioned above must have a valid passport and a **non-immigrant visitor's visa**. To obtain a visa, fill in the application form available at most travel agents and send it with a full passport to your nearest US Embassy or Consulate. Visas are not issued to convicted criminals. You'll need to give precise dates of your trip and declare that you're not intending to live or work in the US (if you are intending to do either of these things, see "Staying on," p.47).

IMMIGRATION CONTROLS

During the flight, you'll be handed an **immigration form** (and a customs declaration: see below), which must be filled out and, after landing, given up at immigration control. Part of the form will be attached to your passport, where it must stay until you leave, when an immigration or airline official will detach it.

On the form you must give details of where you are staying on your first night (if you don't know write "touring") and the date you intend to **leave** the US. You should also be able to prove that you have enough **money** to support yourself while in the US ($300–400 per week is

---

Canadian citizens are in a particularly privileged position when it comes to crossing the border into the US. Although it is possible to enter the States without your passport, you should really have it with you on any trip that brings you as far as Florida. Only if you plan to stay for more than ninety days do you need a visa.

Bear in mind that if you cross into the States in your car, trunks and passenger compartments are subject to spot searches by US Customs personnel, though this sort of surveillance is likely to decrease as remaining tariff barriers fall over the next few years. Remember, too, that Canadians are legally barred from seeking gainful employment in the US.

US EMBASSY AND CONSULATES IN CANADA

Embassy: 100 Wellington St, Ottawa, ON K1P 5T1 (☎613/238-5335).

Consulates:

Suite 1050, 615 Macleod Trail SE, Calgary, AB T2G 4T8 (☎403/266-8962).

Suite 910, Cogswell Tower, Scotia Square, Halifax, NS B3J 3K1 (☎902/429-2481).

455 Rene Levesque Blvd, Montréal, QC H2Z 1Z2

(☎514/398-9695).

1 St Genevieve St, 2 Place Dufferin, PO Box 939, Québec City, QC G1R 4T9 (☎418/692-2095).

360 University Ave, Toronto, ON M5G 1S4 (☎416/595-1700).

1095 West Pender St, Vancouver, BC V6E 4E9 (☎604/685-4311).

US EMBASSY AND CONSULATES ELSEWHERE

Australia
Moonhah Place, Canberra (☎62/733 711).
Denmark
Dag Hammerskjöld Allé 24, 2100 Copenhagen (☎35 55 31 44).
Eire
42 Elgin St, Ballsbridge, Dublin (☎01/688 8777).
Netherlands
Museumplein 19, Amsterdam (☎020/790 321).
New Zealand
29 Fitzherbert Terrace, Thorndon, Wellington (☎4/722 068).

Norway
Drammensveien 18, Oslo (☎22 44 85 50).
Sweden
Strandvägan 101, Stockholm (☎08/783 5300).
UK
5 Upper Grosvenor St, London W1 (☎0171/499 7010).

3 Regent Terrace, Edinburgh EH7 5BW (☎0131/556 8315).

Queens House, 14 Queen St, Belfast BT1 6EQ (☎01232/328239).

considered sufficient) as anyone revealing the slightest intention of working while in the country is likely to be refused admission. You may also experience difficulties if you admit to being HIV positive or having TB.

CUSTOMS

Customs officers will relieve you of your customs declaration and ask if you have any fresh foods. You'll also be asked if you've visited a farm in the last month: if you have, your shoes may well be taken away for inspection.

The **duty-free allowance** if you're over 17 is 200 cigarettes and 100 cigars and, if you're over 21, a liter of spirits.

As well as foods and anything agricultural, it's also **prohibited** to carry into the country any articles from North Korea, Cuba, Iran, Iraq, Libya, Serbia or Montenegro, obscene publications, lottery tickets, chocolate liqueurs or pre-Columbian artefacts. Anyone caught carrying drugs into the country will not only face prosecution but be entered in the records as an undesirable and probably denied entry for all time. If you take prescription medicines, it may be a good idea to carry

a letter from a doctor stating the exact nature of the pills you are carrying, in order to ease your passage through Customs.

EXTENSIONS AND LEAVING

The date stamped on the form in your passport is the **latest** you're legally entitled to stay. Leaving a few days after may not matter, especially if you're heading home, but more than a week or so can result in a protracted – and generally unpleasant – interrogation from officials, which may cause you to miss your flight and be denied entry to the US in the future and your American hosts and/or employer to face legal proceedings.

Although not a foolproof method, one of the simplest ways to stay on is to make a quick trip to the Bahamas: the least costly way to do this is as a $100 day-trip with Seascape Ltd (☎1-800/327-7400), one of many cruise companies operating between Miami and Fort Lauderdale to the Bahamas and the Caribbean – its ads are in all the local newspapers. When you re-enter the US, you may be searched, so make sure you don't have a US library card or anything else that might indicate you have an unofficial, semi-permanent

US address; your diary may also be examined. All being well, you'll routinely have a new leaving date stamped in your passport.

Alternatively, you can do things the official way and get an **extension** before your time is up. This can be done by going to the nearest **US Immigration and Naturalization Service (INS)** office (in Miami at 7880 Biscayne Blvd, ☎305/536 5741; other addresses will be under the "Federal Government Offices" listings at the front of the phone book). They will automatically assume that you're working illegally and it's up to you to convince them otherwise. Do this by providing evidence of ample finances and, if possible, an upstanding American citizen to vouch for your worthiness. Obviously you'll also have to explain why you didn't plan for the extra time initially – saying your money lasted longer than you expected, or that a close relative is coming over, are well-worked excuses.

HEALTH AND INSURANCE

HEALTH

If you have a serious **accident** while in Florida, emergency medical services will get to you quickly and charge you later. For **emergencies** or ambulances, dial ☎911 (or whatever variant may be on the information plate of the pay phone). If you have an accident but don't require an ambulance, we've listed casualty departments in the Guide; ditto for **dental treatment**.

Should you need to see a **doctor**, lists can be found in the *Yellow Pages* under "Clinics" or "Physicians and Surgeons." A basic consultation fee is $50–100, payable in advance. Medication isn't cheap either – keep receipts for all you spend and claim it back on your insurance policy when you return.

Many **minor ailments** can be remedied using the fabulous array of potions and lotions available in **drugstores**. Foreign visitors should bear in mind that many pills available over the counter at home need a prescription in the US and that local brand names can be confusing; ask for advice at the **pharmacy** in any drugstore.

Travelers from Europe do not require **inoculations** to enter the US.

INSURANCE

Though not compulsory, **travel insurance** is *essential* for **foreign travelers**. The US has no national health system and you can lose an arm and a leg (so to speak) having even minor medical treatment. Bank and credit cards (particularly American Express) often have certain levels of medical or other insurance included, especially if you use them to pay for your trip.

If you plan to participate in water sports or do some hiking or skiing, you'll probably have to pay an extra premium; check carefully that any insurance policy you are considering will cover you in case of an accident. Note also that very few insurers will arrange on-the-spot payments in the event of a major expense or loss; you will usually be reimbursed only after going home. In all cases of loss or theft of goods, you will have to contact the local police to have a report made out so that your insurer can process the claim.

BRITISH COVER

Most **travel agents** and tour operators will offer you insurance when you book your flight or holiday, and some will insist you take it. These policies are usually reasonable value, though as ever, you should check the small print. Good value policies include Endsleigh, who charge around £35 for three weeks to cover life, limb and luggage (with a 25 percent reduction if you

TRAVEL INSURANCE COMPANIES IN THE UK

Campus Travel or **STA** (see p.4 for addresses)

Endsleigh Insurance, 97–107 Southampton Row, London WC1B 4AG (☎0171/436 4451).

Frizzell Insurance, Frizzell House, County Gates, Bournemouth, Dorset BH1 2NF (☎01202/292333).

Columbus Travel Insurance, 17 Devonshire Square, London EC2M 4SQ (☎0171/375 0011)

forego luggage insurance). Columbus does an annual multi-trip policy, which offers twelve months' cover for £89 with a maximum single trip duration of 60 days. Their Globetrotter Policy for backpackers is the cheapest, at £26 for up to four weeks, though this does not cover baggage or missed departures.

If you feel the cover is inadequate, or you want to compare prices, any travel agent, **insurance broker** or **bank** should be able to help. If you have a good "all risks" home insurance policy it may well cover your possessions against loss or theft even when overseas, and many private medical schemes also cover you when abroad – make sure you know the procedure and the helpline number.

On all policies, read the small print to ensure the cover includes a sensible amount for medical expenses – this should be at least £1,000,000, which will cover the cost of an air ambulance to fly you home in the event of a serious injury or hospitalization.

NORTH AMERICAN COVER

Before buying an insurance policy, **North American travelers** should check that they're not already covered for health charges or costs by their current **health insurance**. If, in the event of an accident or illness, you are unable to use a phone or are required to pay the practitioner immediately, save all the **forms** to support a claim for subsequent reimbursement. Remember that time limits may apply when making claims after the fact, so promptness in contacting your insurer is highly advisable. Holders of official **student/teacher/youth cards** are entitled to accident coverage and hospital in-patient benefits – the annual membership is far less than the cost of comparable insurance. **Students** may also find that their student health coverage extends during the vacations and for

one term beyond the date of last enrollment. **Bank and credit cards** (particularly American Express) often provide certain levels of medical or other insurance, and travel insurance may also be included if you use a major credit or charge card to pay for your trip. **Homeowners' or renters'** insurance often covers theft or loss of documents, money and valuables while you are on holiday.

After exhausting the possibilities above, you might want to contact a specialist **travel insurance** company; your travel agent can usually recommend one, or see the box below.

Travel insurance **policies** vary: some are comprehensive while others cover only certain risks (accidents, illnesses, delayed or lost luggage, cancelled flights, etc). In particular, ask whether the policy pays medical costs up front or reimburses you later. For policies that include lost or stolen luggage, check exactly what's covered, and make sure the per-article limit will cover your most valuable possessions.

The best **premiums** are usually to be had through student/youth travel agencies – STA policies, for example, come in two forms: with or without medical coverage. The current rates are $45/$35 (for up to 7 days); $60/$45 (8-15 days); $110/$85 (1 month); $140/$115 (45 days); $165/$135 (2 months); $50/$35 (for each extra month). If you're planning to do any "dangerous sports" (skiing, mountaineering, etc), be sure to ask whether these activities are covered: some companies levy a surcharge.

Most North American travel policies apply only to items lost, stolen or damaged while in the custody of an identifiable, responsible third party – hotel porter, airline, luggage consignment, etc. Even in these cases you will have to contact the local police within a certain time limit to have a complete report made out so that your insurer can process the claim.

TRAVEL INSURANCE COMPANIES IN NORTH AMERICA

Access America ☎1-800/284-8300

Carefree Travel Insurance ☎1-800/323-3149

Desjardins Travel Insurance – Canada only ☎1-800/463-7830

STA Travel ☎1-800/777-0112

Travel Guard ☎1-800/826-1300

Travel Insurance Services ☎1-800/937-1387

AUSTRALASIAN COVER
Most **travel insurance** is put together by the airlines in conjunction with insurance companies (see box below). They are all comparable in premium and coverage. Adventure sports are covered, with the exception of mountaineering with ropes, bungy jumping (some policies), and unassisted diving without an Open Water license – check the policy first. A typical insurance policy will cost A$190/NZ$220 for one month, A$270/NZ$320 for two months and A$330/NZ$400 for three months.

> **TRAVEL INSURANCE COMPANIES IN AUSTRALASIA**
>
> **Cover More**, Level 9, 32 Walker St, North Sydney (☎02/9202 8000; toll-free 1800/251 881).
>
> **Ready Plan**, 141–147 Walker St, Dandenong, Victoria (toll-free ☎1800/337 462); 10th Floor, 63 Albert St, Auckland (☎09/379 3208).

COSTS, MONEY AND BANKS

To help with planning your Florida vacation, this book contains detailed price information for lodging and eating throughout the region. Unless otherwise stated, the hotel price codes given (explained on p.27) are for the cheapest double room in high season, exclusive of any local taxes which may apply, while meal prices include food only and not drinks or tip. Naturally, as time passes after the publication of the book, you should make allowances for inflation.

Even when the exchange rate is at its least advantageous (see box below), most visitors find virtually everything – accommodation, food, petrol, cameras, clothes and more – to be better value in the US than it is at home. However, if you're used to traveling in the less expensive countries of Europe, let alone in the rest of the world, you shouldn't expect to scrape by on the same minuscule budget once you're in the US.

Your biggest single expense is likely to be **accommodation**. Few hotel or motel rooms in cities cost under $30 – around $50 is more usual – and rates in rural areas are little cheaper. Although hostels offering dorm beds – usually for $12–15 – exist, they are not widespread and in any case represent only a very small saving for two or more people traveling together. Camping, of course, is cheap, ranging from free to perhaps $18 per night, but is rarely practical in or around the big cities.

As for **food**, $10 a day is enough to get you an adequate life-support diet, while for a daily budget of around $20 you can dine pretty well. Beyond this, everything hinges on how much sightseeing, taxi-taking, drinking and socializing you do. Much of any of these – especially in a major city – and you're likely to be going through upwards of $50 a day.

The rates for **traveling** around using buses, trains and even planes, may look cheap on paper, but costs soon mount up. For a group of two or more, **renting a car** can be a very good investment.

Sales tax of 6 percent is added to virtually everything you buy in shops, but it isn't part of the marked price.

TRAVELERS' CHECKS

US dollar travelers' checks are the best way to carry money, for both American and foreign visitors; they offer the great security of knowing that lost or stolen checks will be replaced. You should have no problem using the better-known checks, such as American Express and Visa, in shops,

MONEY: A NOTE FOR FOREIGN TRAVELERS

Regular upheaval in the world's money markets causes the relative value of the **US dollar** against the currencies of the rest of the world to vary considerably. Generally speaking, one **pound sterling** will buy between $1.45 and $1.80; one **Canadian dollar** is worth between 76¢ and $1; one **Australian dollar** is worth between 67¢ and 88¢; and one **New Zealand dollar** is worth between 55¢ and 72¢.

Notes and coins

US currency comes in **notes** worth $1, $5, $10, $20, $50 and $100, plus various larger (and rarer) denominations. Confusingly, all are the same size and same green color, making it necessary to check each note carefully. The dollar is made up of 100 cents in **coins** of 1 cent (known as a **penny**), 5 cents (a **nickel**), 10 cents (a **dime**) and 25 cents (a **quarter**). Very occasionally you might come across **JFK half-dollars** (50¢), **Susan B. Anthony dollar coins**, or a **two-dollar note**. Change (quarters are the most useful) is needed for buses, vending machines and telephones, so always carry plenty.

Each of the two main networks operates a toll-free line to let customers know the location of their nearest ATM; *Plus System* is ☎1-800/THE-PLUS, *Cirrus* is ☎1-800/4CI-RRUS.

kind of plastic. In addition, hotels and car rental companies will ask for a card either to establish your credit-worthiness, or as security, or both. Even in these dark days for credit buying, some people still get funny about cash.

With Mastercard or Visa it is also possible to **withdraw cash** at any bank displaying relevant stickers, or from appropriate automatic teller machines (**ATMs**). Diners Club cards can be used to cash personal checks at Citibank branches. American Express cards can only get cash, or buy travelers' checks, at American Express offices (check the *Yellow Pages*) or from the travelers' check dispensers at most major airports. Most **Canadian** credit cards issued by hometown banks will be honored in the US, as will other credit cards issued abroad.

Thanks to relaxation in interstate banking restrictions, American holders of **ATM cards** from out of state are likely to discover that their cards work in the machines of select Florida banks (check with your bank before you leave home). Not only is this method of financing safer, but at around only a dollar per transaction it's economical as well. Foreign travelers can also use their ATM cards, as long as they're linked to international networks such as Cirrus and Plus – though it's important to check the latest details with your credit card company before departing, as otherwise the machine may simply gobble up your plastic friend. Overseas visitors should also bear in mind that fluctuating exchange rates may result in spending more (or less) than expected than when the item eventually shows up on a statement.

restaurants and filling stations (don't be put off by "no checks" signs, which only refer to personal checks). Be sure to have plenty of the $10 and $20 denominations for everyday transactions.

Major Florida banks – such as Bank of America, Barnett, First Florida, Southeast and Sun – will (with considerable fuss) change travelers' checks in **other currencies** and foreign currency. Commission rates tend to be lower at exchange bureaux like Deak-Perera and Thomas Cook; airport exchange offices can also be reasonable. Hotels rarely, if ever, change money.

Banking hours in Florida are generally 10am until 3pm Monday to Thursday and 10am to 5pm on Fridays.

PLASTIC MONEY AND CASH MACHINES

If you have a **Visa**, **Mastercard** (known elsewhere as **Access**), **Diners Club**, **Discover** or **American Express** card you really *shouldn't* leave home without it. Almost all stores, most restaurants and many services will take some

For **emergency phone numbers** to call if your checks (and/or credit cards) should be stolen, see p.36.

EMERGENCIES

If you're flat broke and at your wits' end as to what to do, there are a few alternatives before making a meal of yourself to the local alligators. Assuming you know someone who is prepared to send you money in a crisis, the quickest way is to have them take the cash to the nearest **Western Union** office (information on ☎1-800/325-6000 in the US; ☎0800/833833 in the UK; toll-free ☎1 800/649 565 in Australia; and ☎09/302 0143 in New Zealand), and have it instantaneously wired to the office nearest you, subject to the deduction of a ten percent commission. **American Express MoneyGram** (☎1-800/543-4080) offers a similar service.

It's also possible to have money wired directly from a bank in your home country to a bank in the US, though this is somewhat less reliable because it involves two separate institutions. If you go this route, the person wiring the funds to you will need to know the routing number of the bank the funds are being wired to. Having money wired from home is never convenient or cheap, and should only be considered a last resort.

If you have a few days' leeway, a cheaper method is to have a postal money order sent through the mail; these are exchangeable at any post office. The equivalent for foreign travelers is the **international money order**, for which you need to allow up to seven days in the international air mail before arrival. An ordinary check sent from overseas takes two to three weeks to clear.

Foreign travelers in difficulties have the option of throwing themselves on the mercy of their nearest national consulate, which will – in the worst cases – repatriate you, but will never, under any circumstances, lend you money.

COMMUNICATIONS: TELEPHONES AND POST

Visitors from overseas tend to be impressed by the speed and efficiency of communications in the US, and for the most part, Florida conforms to this high standard. However, a laid-back attitude is ingrained in certain areas (notoriously so in the Florida Keys), which can frustrate travelers who have yet to adjust to the local pace.

TELEPHONES

Florida's **telephones** are run by several companies, the largest being Southern Bell, all of which are linked to the *AT&T* network.

Public telephones invariably work and are easily found – on street corners, in railway and bus stations, hotel lobbies, bars, restaurants – and they take 25¢, 10¢ and 5¢ coins. The cost of a **local call** from a public phone varies according to the actual distance being called. The minimum is 25¢ for the first three minutes and a further 10¢ for each additional three minutes – when necessary, a voice will come on the line telling you to pay more.

More expensive are **non-local calls** ("zone calls"), to numbers within the same area code (commonly, vast areas are covered by a single code) but costing much more and sometimes requiring you to dial 1 before the seven-digit number. Pricier still are **long-distance calls** (ie to a different area code), for which you'll need plenty of change. If you still owe money at the end of the call, the phone will ring immediately and you'll be asked for the outstanding amount (if you don't cough up, the person you've been calling will get the bill). Non-local calls and long-distance calls are far cheaper if made between 6pm and 8am, and calls from **private phones** are always much cheaper than those from public phones.

Making telephone calls from **hotel rooms** is usually more expensive than from a payphone (and there are usually payphones in hotel lobbies). On the other hand, some budget hotels offer free local calls from rooms – ask when you check in. An increasing number of phones accept **credit cards** – simply swipe the card through the slot and dial. Another way to avoid the necessity of carrying copious quantities of change everywhere is to obtain an **AT&T charge card** (information on ☎1-800/874-4000 ext 359), for which you have to have an American credit card.

USEFUL NUMBERS

Emergencies ☎911; ask for the appropriate emergency service: fire, police or ambulance

Local directory information ☎411

Long-distance directory information ☎1 (Area Code)/555-1212

Directory enquiries for toll-free numbers ☎1-800/555-1212

Operator ☎0

FLORIDA AREA CODES

305 Miami, the Florida Keys and the southern section of the Southeast Coast.

407 Orlando and surrounds and the central section of the East Coast.

850 All the Panhandle east of and including Tallahassee.

904 Most of the Northeast Coast, North Central Florida, and some of the northern parts of the West Coast.

941 Most of the West Coast and parts of South Central Florida.

INTERNATIONAL TELEPHONE CALLS

International calls can be dialed direct from private or (more expensively) public phones. You can get assistance from the **international operator** (☎1-800/874-4000), who may also interrupt every three minutes asking for more money, and call you back for any money still owed immediately after you hang up. One alternative is to make a **collect call** (to "reverse the charges"); dialing ☎1-800/445-5667 will connect you with an operator in Britain.

The **cheapest rates** for international calls to Europe are between 6pm and 7am, when a direct-dialed three-minute call will cost roughly $5.

In **Britain**, it's possible to obtain a free **BT Chargecard** (☎0-800/800 838). All calls from overseas can be charged to your quarterly domestic account; from Florida, you contact the British operator via AT&T, and your call is charged at standard payphone rates.

The telephone code to dial **TO the US** from the outside world (excluding Canada) is 1.

To make international calls **FROM the US**, dial 011 followed by the country code:

Australia 61	**Germany** 49
Denmark 45	**Ireland** 353

Netherlands 31	**Sweden** 46
New Zealand 64	**United Kingdom** 44

Many government agencies, car rental firms, hotels and other services have **toll-free numbers**, for which you don't have to pay anything: these numbers always have the prefix ☎1-800. Some lines, such as ☎1-800/577-HEAT to get the latest on the Miami Heat basketball team, employ the letters on the push-button phones as part of their "number."

MAIL SERVICES

Post offices are usually open Mon–Fri 9am–5pm and Sat 9am–noon, and there are blue **mail boxes** on many street corners. Ordinary **mail within the US** costs 32¢ for a letter weighing up to an ounce; addresses must include the **zip code** (postal code), as well as the sender's address on the envelope. **Air mail** between Florida and Europe generally takes about a week to arrive. Postcards, aerograms and letters weighing up to half an ounce (a single sheet) cost 60¢.

Letters can be sent c/o **General Delivery** (what's known elsewhere as **poste restante**) to any post office in the country but *must* include the post office's zip code and will only be held for thirty days before being returned to sender – so make sure there's a return address on the envelope. If you're receiving mail at someone else's address, it should include "c/o" and the regular occupant's name; otherwise it, too, is likely to be returned.

Rules on sending **parcels** are very rigid: packages must be in special containers bought from post offices and sealed according to their instructions, which are given at the start of the Yellow Pages. To send anything out of the country, you'll need a **customs declaration form**, available from a post office. Postal rates for sending a parcel weighing up to 1lb are $9.75 to Europe, $11.20 to Australasia.

TELEGRAMS AND FAXES

To send a **telegram** (sometimes called "a wire") don't go to a post office but to a Western Union office (listed in the *Yellow Pages*). Credit card holders can dictate their message over the phone.

For domestic telegrams ask for a **mailgram**, which will be delivered to any address in the country the following morning. **International telegrams** are slightly cheaper than the cheapest international phone call: one sent during the day from Florida should arrive at its overseas destination the next morning.

Public **fax** machines, which may require your credit card to be "swiped" through an attached device, are found at photocopy centers and, occasionally, in bookshops.

INFORMATION, MAPS AND THE MEDIA

Advance information for a trip to Florida can be obtained by post from the Florida Tourist Board at 126 W Van Buren Street, Tallahassee, Florida 32399-2000 (☎850/487-1462); Canadian travelers can call Travel USA at $2 per minute (☎900/451-4050). Once in Florida, you'll find most large towns have at least a Convention and Visitors Bureau ("CVB;" usual hours Mon–Fri 9am–5pm, Sat 9am–1pm), offering detailed information on the local area and discount coupons for food and accommodation, but unable to book hotel or motel rooms.

In addition there are **Chambers of Commerce** almost everywhere; these are designed to promote local business interests, but are more than

---

FLORIDA TOURISM OFFICES OVERSEAS

US Travel and Tourism Administration (**USTTA**) offices are located all over the world, usually sharing the buildings of US embassies or consulates. They tend to provide fairly basic brochures; for detailed advice it's better to contact Florida direct.

UK
Florida Tourism 18–24 Westbourne Grove, London W2 (☎0171/727 1661). An information-by-phone hotline. Calls cost 39–45p per minute. Information packets available if you write to Florida Tourism, at BH&P, Darby House, Merstham, Redhill, Surrey RH1 3DN. Allow up to four weeks for parcel to arrive.

Australia
4 Cliff St, Milsons Point, Sydney, NSW 2061 (☎612/957 3144).

Denmark
Dag Hammerskjöld Allé 24, 2100 Copenhagen (☎31 42 31 44).

Ireland
Queen's House, 14 Queen St, Belfast BT1 6EQ (☎0232/228239).

Netherlands
Museumplein 19, Amsterdam (☎020/790 321).

Norway
Drammensveien 18, Oslo (☎22 44 85 50).

Sweden
Strandvägan 101, Stockholm (☎08/783 53000).

happy to provide travelers with local maps and information. Most communities have local **free newspapers** (see "Media" below) carrying news of events and entertainment – the most useful of which we've detailed in the Guide.

Drivers entering Florida will find **Welcome Centers**, fully stocked with information leaflets and discount booklets, at two points: on Hwy-231 at Campbellton, near the Florida–Alabama border and off I-75 near Jennings, just south of the Florida–Georgia line. More convenient for arrivals on I-10 are the **visitor information centers** at Pensacola and Tallahassee, detailed later in the Guide.

MAPS

CVBs and Chambers of Commerce give away an excellent **free map** of the whole state (though the *Official Transportation Map* does not, as its name suggests, detail public transport routes). If you're planning to drive or cycle (see "Getting around") through rural areas, use DeLorme's highly detailed 120-page *Florida Atlas & Gazetteer* ($12.95). The best commercially available **city plans** are published by Rand-McNally (see box on p.21).

Local **hiking** maps are available at ranger stations in state and national parks either free or for $1–2 and some camping shops carry a supply. For traveling around more of the US, the *Rand McNally Road Atlas* is a good investment, covering the whole country plus Canada and Mexico.

Members of the American Automobile Association (AAA) and its overseas affiliates (such as both the AA and the RAC in Britain) can also benefit from their maps and general assistance. They're based at 1000 AAA Drive, Heathrow, FL 32746-5063 (☎1-800/336-4357); further offices all across the state are listed in local phone books.

MEDIA

The best-read of **Florida's newspapers** is the *Miami Herald*, providing in-depth coverage of state, national and world events; the *Orlando Sentinel* and *Tampa Tribune* are not far behind

and, naturally enough, excel at reporting their own areas. **Overseas newspapers** are often a preserve of specialist bookshops, though you will find them widely available in major tourist areas.

Every community of any size has at least a few **free newspapers**, found in street-distribution bins or just lying around in piles. It's a good idea to pick up a full assortment: some simply cover local goings-on, others provide specialist coverage of interests ranging from long-distance cycling to getting ahead in business – and the classified and personal ads can provide hours of entertainment. Many of them are also excellent sources for bar, restaurant and nightlife information, and we've mentioned the most useful titles in the Guide.

TELEVISION

Florida's **TV** is pretty much the standard network sitcom and talk-show barrage you get all over the country, with frequent interruptions for hard-sell commercials.

Game shows fill up most of the morning schedule; around lunchtime you can take your pick of any of a dozen daily soaps. Slightly better are the **cable networks**, to which you'll have access in most hotels and include the around-the-clock news of CNN and MTV"'s non-stop circuit of mainstream pop videos.

Especially in the south, Spanish-language stations service the Hispanic communities.

RADIO

Most of Florida's **radio** stations stick to the usual commercial format of retro-rock, classic pop, country, or easy-listening.

In general, except for news and chat, the occasional fire-and-brimstone preacher, and Latin and Haitian music, stations on the AM band are best avoided in favor of the FM band, in particular the public and college stations on the air in Tallahassee, Gainesville, Orlando, Tampa and Miami, found on the left of the dial (88–92FM). These invariably provide diverse and listenable programming, whether it be bizarre underground rock or abstruse literary discussions, and they're also good sources for local nightlife news.

MAPS AND TRAVEL BOOK SUPPLIERS

AUSTRALIA

The Map Shop, 16a Peel St, Adelaide (☎08/8231 2033).

Bowyangs, 372 Little Burke St, Melbourne (☎03/9670 4383).

Perth Map Center, 891 Hay St, Perth (☎08/9322 5733).

Travel Bookshop, Shop 3, 175 Liverpool St, Sydney (☎02/9261 8200).

Worldwide Maps and Guides, 187 George St, Brisbane (☎07/3221 4330).

CANADA

Open Air Books and Maps, 25 Toronto St, M5R 2C1 (☎416/363-0719).

Ulysses Travel Bookshop, 4176 St-Denis, Montreal H2W 2M5 (☎514/843 9447).

World Wide Books and Maps, 1247 Granville St, Vancouver V6Z 1G3 (☎604/687-3320).

IRELAND

Easons Bookshop, 40 O'Connell St, Dublin 1 (☎01/873 3811).

Fred Hanna's Bookshop, 27–29 Nassau St, Dublin 2 (☎01/677 1255).

Hodges Figgis Bookshop, 56–58 Dawson St, Dublin 2 (☎01/677 4754).

Waterstone's, Queens Bldg, 8 Royal Ave, Belfast BT1 1DA (☎01232/247355).

NEW ZEALAND

Specialty Maps, 58 Albert St, Auckland (☎09/307 2217).

UK

Daunt Books, 83 Marylebone High St, London W1 (☎0171/224 2295).

John Smith and Sons, 57–61 St Vincent St, Glasgow G2 5TB (☎0141/221 7472).

National Map Center, 22–24 Caxton St, London SW1 (☎0171/222 4945).

Stanfords*, 12–14 Long Acre, London WC2 (☎0171/836 1321); 52 Grosvenor Gardens, London SW1W 0AG; 156 Regent St, London W1R 5TA.

The Travel Bookshop, 13–15 Blenheim Crescent, London W11 2EE (☎0171/229 5260).

***Note**: Maps by **mail or phone order** are available from Stanfords; ☎0171/836 1321.

USA

Book Passage, 51 Tamal Vista Blvd, Corte Madera, CA 94925 (☎415/927-0960).

The Complete Traveler Bookstore, 3207 Fillmore St, San Francisco, CA 92123 (☎415/923-1511).

The Complete Traveler Bookstore, 199 Madison Ave, New York, NY 10016 (☎212/685-9007).

Elliot Bay Book Company, 101 S Main St, Seattle, WA 98104 (☎206/624-6600).

Forsyth Travel Library, 226 Westchester Ave, White Plains, NY 10604 (☎1-800/367-7984).

Map Link Inc., 30 S La Patera Lane, Unit 5, Santa Barbara, CA 93117 (☎805/692-6777).

The Map Store Inc., 1636 ISt NW, Washington, DC 20006 (☎202/628-2608).

Phileas Fogg's Books & Maps, #87 Stanford Shopping Center, Palo Alto, CA 94304 (☎1-800/533-FOGG).

Rand McNally*, 444 N Michigan Ave, Chicago, IL 60611; (☎312/321-1751); 150 E 52nd St, New York, NY 10022 (☎212/758-7488); 595 Market St, San Francisco, CA 94105 (☎415/777-3131).

Travel Books & Language Center, 4437 Wisconsin Ave, Washington, DC 20016 (☎1-800/220-2665).

Sierra Club Bookstore, 6014 College Ave, Oakland, CA 94618 (☎510/658-7470).

Traveler's Bookstore, 22 W 52nd St, New York, NY 10019; (☎212/664-0995).

***Note**: Rand McNally now has more than twenty stores across the US; call (☎1-800/333-0136 ext 2111) for the nearest store or for direct mail maps.

GETTING AROUND

Travel in the surprisingly compact state of Florida is rarely difficult or time-consuming. Crossing between the east and west coasts, for example, takes only a couple of hours and even the longest possible trip – between the western extremity of the Panhandle and Miami – can just about be accomplished in a day. With a car you'll have no problems at all, but traveling by public transport requires adroit forward planning: cities and larger towns have bus links – and, in some cases, an infrequent train service – but many rural areas and some of the most enjoyable sections of the coast are sadly off-limits to non-drivers.

BUSES

Buses are the cheapest way to travel. The only long-distance service is Greyhound, which links all major cities and many smaller towns. In isolated areas buses are fairly scarce, sometimes only appearing once a day, if at all – so plot your route with care. Between the big cities, buses run around the clock to a fairly full timetable, stopping only for meal breaks (almost always fast-food dives) and driver change-overs. Greyhound, though not luxurious, is bearable and it's feasible occasionally to save on a night's accommodation by traveling overnight and sleeping on the bus. Any sizeable community will have a Greyhound station; in smaller places the local post office or gas station doubles as the stop and ticket office. In the Florida Keys, the bus makes scheduled stops but can also be flagged down anywhere along the Overseas Highway.

Fares – for example $37 one way between Miami and Orlando – are expensive but not staggeringly so and can sometimes be reduced by traveling on weekdays (except Fridays).

Remarkably, in 1993 Greyhound stopped publishing **timetables**, with the exception of condensed summaries of nationwide services – which obviously makes detailed route planning for Florida extremely difficult. The only toll-free information service is in Spanish (☎1-800/531-5332); otherwise information can be obtained from local terminals. The phone numbers for the larger Greyhound stations are given in the Guide.

It's handy to know that a fair-sized chunk of the Southeast Coast can be covered for very little money (if also very slowly) using **local buses**, which connect neighboring districts. It's possible, for example, to travel from Miami to West Palm Beach for under $3, but doing so takes all day and three changes of bus – the Tri-Rail (see below) covers the same route for even less.

BY TRAIN AND TRI-RAIL

A much less viable way of getting about is by **train** (run by Amtrak). Florida's railroads were built to service the boom towns of the Twenties and, consequently, some rural nooks have rail links as good as the modern cities. The actual trains are clean and comfortable, with most routes in the state offering two services a day. In some areas, Amtrak services are extended by buses, usable only in conjunction with the train.

Fares are not particularly cheap – $51 one way between Miami and Orlando is typical.

> For **Amtrak** information: ☎1-800/USA RAIL
> For **Tri-Rail** information: ☎1-800/TRI RAIL

THE TRI-RAIL

Designed to reduce road traffic along the congested Southeast Coast, the elevated **Tri-Rail** system came into operation in 1989, ferrying commuters between Miami and West Palm Beach with twelve stops on the way. The single-journey flat fare is a very cheap $2.50; the only drawback is the fact that almost all services run during rush hours – meaning a very early start, or an early evening arrival.

BY PLANE

Provided your plans are flexible and you use the special cut-rate fares which are regularly advertised in local newspapers, off-peak **plane** travel within Florida is not much more expensive than taking a bus or train – and will also, obviously, get you there more quickly. Typical cut-rate one-way fares are around $75 for Miami–Orlando and $120 for Miami–Tallahassee; full fares are much higher.

For toll-free airline numbers, see p.7.

DRIVING AND CAR RENTAL

As a major vacation destination, Florida is one of the cheapest places in the US in which to **rent** a car, thanks to a very competitive market. Drivers are supposed to have held their licenses for at least one year (though this is rarely checked), and people under 25 may very well encounter problems or restrictions when renting. If you are under 25, always call ahead.

Car rental companies will also expect you to have a credit card; if you don't have one they

ADVANCE PLANNING FOR OVERSEAS TRAVELERS

All the main American airlines (and British Airways in conjunction with USAir) offer **air passes** for visitors who plan to fly a lot within the US: these have to be bought in advance, and in the UK are usually sold with the proviso that you cross the Atlantic with the relevant airline. All the deals are broadly similar, involving the purchase of at least three **coupons** (for around £160; around £55 for each additional coupon), each valid for a flight of any duration in the US.

The Visit USA scheme entitles foreign travelers to a 30 percent discount on any full-priced US domestic fare, provided you buy the ticket before you leave home – but this isn't a wise choice for travel within Florida, where full-priced fares are very high.

Greyhound Ameripasses

Foreign visitors intending to travel virtually every day by bus (which is unlikely), or to venture further around the US, can buy a Greyhound **Ameripass**, offering unlimited travel within a set time limit, before leaving home: most travel agents can oblige. In the UK, they cost £75 (4-day), £85 (5-day), £110 (7-day), £170 (15-day), £230 (30-day) or £330 (60-day). Note that the 4-day pass is valid only Monday–Thursday. Greyhound's office is at Sussex House, London Road, East Grinstead, West Sussex RH19 1LD (☎01342/317317). It is no longer possible to buy extensions in the US.

The first time you use your pass, it will be dated by the ticket clerk (this becomes the commencement date of the ticket), and your destination is written on a page which the driver will tear out and keep as you board the bus. Repeat this procedure for every subsequent journey.

Amtrak rail passes

Rail travel can't get you around all Florida, but overseas travelers have a choice of three **rail passes**. The least expensive, the **East Region Pass**, available in 15- and 30-day forms, costs £128 (£156 June–September 7th) and £159 (£194) respectively. Alternatively, the **National Pass** entitles you to travel throughout the US, again for 15 or 30 days, for a price of £178 (£266 June–September 7th) or £234 (£334) respectively. By combining rail with some other form of travel, you could take advantage of the 30-day **Coastal Pass**, permitting unlimited train travel on the country's east and west coasts; this pass costs £141 (£172 June–September 7th). There is no 15-day option on the Coastal Pass.

On production of a passport issued outside the US or Canada, the passes can be bought at Amtrak stations in the US. In the UK, you can buy them from Amtrak's UK agent, Destination Marketing Limited, Molasses House, Clove Hitch Key, Plantation Wharf, London SW11 3TN (☎0171 253 9009).

Car rental

UK nationals can **drive** in the US on a full UK driving license (International Driving Permits are not regarded as sufficient). Fly-drive deals are good value if you want to **rent** a car (see p.5), though you can save up to 60 percent simply by booking in advance with a major firm (Holiday Autos guarantee the cheapest rates). You can choose not to pay until you arrive, but make sure you take a written confirmation of the quoted price with you. Remember that it's safer not to rent a car straight off a long transatlantic flight; and that standard rental cars have **automatic transmissions**.

It's also easier and cheaper to book RVs (see overleaf) in advance from Britain. Most travel agents who specialize in the US can arrange RV rental, and usually do it cheaper if you book a flight through them as well. A price of £400 for a five-berth van for a fortnight is fairly typical.

CAR RENTAL COMPANIES

IN THE UK
Alamo ☎0870/600 0008
Avis ☎0990/900500
Budget ☎0800/181181
Dollar (Eurodollar) ☎0990/365365
Hertz ☎0990/996699
Holiday Autos ☎0990/300400

IN NORTH AMERICA
Alamo ☎1-800/354-2322
Avis ☎1-800/331-1212
Budget ☎1-800/527-0700
Dollar ☎1-800/421-6868
Hertz ☎1-800/654-313; in Canada ☎1-800/263-0600
Holiday Autos ☎1-800/422-7737
National ☎1-800/CAR-RENT
Rent-A-Wreck ☎1-800/535-1391
Thrifty ☎1-800/367-2277

IN AUSTRALIA
Avis ☎02/93539000
Budget ☎13/2848
Hertz ☎13/3039
Renault Eurodrive ☎02/9299 3344

IN NEW ZEALAND
Avis ☎09/525 1982
Budget ☎09/275 2222
Fly and Drive Holidays ☎09/529 3709
Hertz ☎0800/655 955

IN IRELAND
Avis ☎353/21281111
Budget Rent-A-Car ☎01232/230700
Europcar ☎01232/450904 or 01232/423444
Hertz ☎01/ 676 7476
Holiday Autos ☎01/454 9090

may let you leave a hefty **deposit** (at least $200) but don't count on it. The likeliest tactic for getting a good deal is to phone the major firms' toll-free 800 numbers for their best rates – most will try to beat the offers of their competitors, so it's worth haggling.

In general, the lowest rates are available at the airport branches. Always be sure to get free unlimited mileage and be aware that leaving the car in a different city than the one in which you rent it may incur a **drop-off charge** of as much as $200 – though many firms do not charge drop-off fees within Florida.

Alternatively, a number of **local** companies rent out new – and not so new – vehicles; in Miami try Alva (☎305/4444-3923) or Inter-America Car Rental (☎305/871-3030; in Fort Lauderdale, Florida Auto Rental (☎305/764-1008). Other companies are listed in the Yellow Pages. Rates in Miami range from $25 to $40 a day, and $130 to $165 a week with unlimited mileage. Again, you should always check that free mileage is included in the rental cost.

When you rent a car, read the small print carefully for details on **Collision Damage Waiver (CDW)**, a form of insurance which often isn't included in the initial rental charge but is well worth considering. This specifically covers the car that you are driving yourself – you are in any case

insured for damage to other vehicles. At $9 to $12 a day, it can add substantially to the total cost, but without it you're liable for every scratch to the car – even those that aren't your fault. Some credit card companies (AMEX for example) offer automatic CDW coverage to anyone using their card to pay in full for the rental; read the fine print beforehand in any case. You'll also be charged a **Florida surcharge** of $2 per day.

If you decide to hire a bottom-of-the-range model, when you go to pick up the vehicle you will invariably be asked if you want to **upgrade** to a better quality car for an apparently small extra charge. Although it may sound like a good deal, bear in mind two things: firstly, if the company has already hired out all of their bottom-of-the-range cars, they are duty-bound to give you a better car at no extra charge (a fact that they will not necessarily inform you of before asking you to upgrade); secondly, the mark-up price for a better-quality car is quoted at a daily rate, which may sound reasonable at first but quickly escalates when totalled for your entire trip, and does not include extras such as tax.

When collecting your car, ensure that it has a **full tank** of gas, as this is part of the agreement. Likewise, you are expected to return the car with a full tank, and if you don't you will probably end up paying for a whole tank even if you left it half full. Again, check the terms. Finally, check to see if it is cheaper to arrange car hire and insurance from your own country rather than waiting until you reach the US.

RENTING AN RV

Besides cars, Recreational Vehicles or **RVs** – those huge juggernauts that rumble down the highway complete with multiple bedrooms, bathrooms and kitchens – can be rented from around $300 per week for a basic camper on the back of a pickup truck. These are good for groups or families traveling together, but they can be quite unwieldy on the road.

Rental outlets are not as common as you might expect, as people tend to own their own RVs. On top of the rental fees you have to take into account mileage charges, the cost of gas (some RVs do twelve miles to the gallon or less) and any drop-off charges. In addition, it is rarely legal simply to pull up in an RV and spend the night at the roadside; you are expected to stay in designated RV parks – some of which charge $35 per night.

The Recreational Vehicle Rental Association, 3251 Old Lee Highway, Fairfax, VA 22030 (☎703/591-7130 or ☎1-800/336-0355) publishes a newsletter and a directory of rental firms. A couple of the larger companies offering RV rentals are Cruise America (☎1-800/327-7799) and Go! Vacations (☎1-800/845-9888).

ROADS

The best roads for covering long distances quickly are the wide, straight and fast **Interstate Highways**, usually at least six lanes and always prefixed by "I" (for example I-95) – marked on maps by a red, white and blue shield bearing the number. Even-numbered Interstates usually run east–west and those with odd numbers north–south.

A grade down are the **State** and **US highways** (for example Hwy-1), sometimes divided into scenic off-shoots such as Hwy-A1A, which runs parallel to Hwy-1 along Florida's east coast. There are a number of **toll roads**, by far the longest being the 318-mile **Florida's Turnpike**; tolls range from 25¢ to $6 and are often graded according to length of journey – you're given a distance marker when you enter the toll road and pay the appropriate amount when you leave. You'll also come across **toll bridges**, usually charging 10–25¢ to cross, sometimes as much as $3.

Even major roads in cities are technically state or US highways but are better known by their local name. Part of Hwy-1 in Miami, for instance, is more familiarly known as Biscayne Boulevard. Rural areas also have much smaller **County Roads** (given as **Routes** in the Guide, such as Route 78 near Lake Okeechobee); their number is preceded by a letter denoting their county.

RULES OF THE ROAD

Although the law says that drivers must keep up with the flow of traffic, which is often hurtling along at 70mph, the official **speed limit** in Florida is 55mph (65mph on some Interstate stretches), with lower signposted limits – usually around 30–35mph – in built-up areas. A **minimum speed limit** of 40mph also applies on many Interstates and highways. There are no spot fines; if you get a ticket for **speeding**, your case will come to court and the size of the fine will be at the discretion of the judge; $75 is a rough minimum. If **the police** do flag you down, don't get out of the car and don't reach into the glove compartment as they may think you have a gun. Simply sit still with your hands on the wheel; when questioned, be polite and don't attempt to make jokes.

Apart from the obvious fact that Americans **drive on the right**, various rules may be unfamiliar to **foreign drivers**. US law requires that any **alcohol** be carried unopened in the trunk of the car; it's illegal to make a **U-turn** on an Interstate or anywhere where a single unbroken line runs along the middle of the road; to **park on a highway**; and for front-seat passengers to ride without fastened **seatbelts.** At junctions, you can turn right on a red light if there is no traffic approaching from the left; and some junctions are **four-way stops**: a crossroads where all traffic must stop before proceeding in order of arrival.

It can't be stressed too strongly that **Driving Under the Influence (DUI)** is a very serious offence. If a police officer smells alcohol on your breath, he/she is entitled to administer a breath, saliva or urine test. If you fail, they'll lock you up with other inebriates in the "drunk tank" of the nearest jail until you sober up – and, controversially, in some parts of the state they're empowered to suspend your driving license immediately. Your case will later be heard by a judge, who can fine you $200 or in extreme (or repeat) cases, imprison you for thirty days.

AMERICAN DRIVING TERMS

Antennae	Aerial
Divided Highway	Dual carriageway
Fender	Bumper/Car wing
Freeway	Limited access motorway
Gas(oline)	Petrol
Hood	Bonnet
No standing	No parking or stopping
Parking brake	Hand brake
Parking lot	Carpark
Speed zone	Area where speed limit decreases
Stickshift	Gear stick/manual transmission
Trunk	Boot
Turn-out	Lay-by
Windshield	Windscreen

PARKING

Parking meters are common in cities; their charge for an hour ranges from 25¢ to $1. **Parking lots** generally charge $2 an hour, $6 per day. If you park in the wrong place (such as within ten feet of a fire hydrant) your car is likely to be towed away or **wheel-clamped**; a sticker on the windscreen will tell you where to pay the $30 fine. Whenever possible, **park in the shade**; if you don't, you might find the car too hot to touch when you return to it – temperatures inside cars parked in the full force of the Florida sun can reach 140°F.

BREAKDOWN

If you **break down** in a rented car, there'll be an emergency number pinned to the dashboard. Otherwise you should sit tight and wait for the Highway Patrol or State Police, who cruise by regularly. Raising the hood of your car is recognized as a call for assistance, though women traveling alone should, obviously, be wary of doing this. Another tip, for women especially, is to rent a **mobile telephone** from the car hire agency – you often only have to pay a nominal amount until you actually use it, but having a phone can be reassuring and even a potential life-saver.

HITCHING

Where it's legal, **hitching** may be the cheapest way to get around but it is also the most unpredictable and potentially very dangerous, especially for women traveling alone. Small country roads are your best bet: in rural areas it's not uncommon for the locals to get around by thumb. One place *not* to

hitch is Miami; not only is this illegal, but if you do take the risk, the chances are you'll be lucky to live to regret it. Anywhere else, observe the general common-sense rules on hitching: make sure you sit next to a door that's unlocked, keep your luggage within reach, refuse the ride if you feel unsure of the driver and demand to be let out if you become suspicious of his/her intentions.

Hitching is illegal not only in Miami but also on the outskirts of many other cities; indeed it is always prohibited to wait for a lift by standing on the road (as opposed to beside it on the pavement or grass verge) or by a freeway entrance sign – rules which are enforced. On Interstates, thumb from the entrance ramps only. Another, slightly less risky, technique is to strike up a conversation with likely-looking drivers in roadside diners or gas stations. Safer still is to scrutinize the **"ride boards"** on university campuses, though drivers found this way will usually expect a contribution towards fuel costs.

CYCLING

Cycling is seldom a good way to get around the major cities (with the exception of some sections of Miami), but many smaller towns are quiet enough to be pleasurably explored by bicycle, there are many miles of marked **cycle paths** along the coast, and long-distance **bike trails** crisscross the state's interior. Cycling is gaining popularity among Floridians, too, and a free monthly magazine, *Florida Bicyclist*, is aimed at the growing band of devoted pedallers; find it in bookshops and bike shops or on street corners.

Bikes can be **rented** for $8–15 a day, $30–55 a week, from many beach shops and college campuses, some state parks and virtually any place where cycling is a good idea; outlets are listed in the Guide.

For **long-distance** cycling – anything over thirty miles a day – you'll need a good-quality, all-terrain, multi-gear bike, preferably with wide touring tires. For safety and visibility, wear a brightly colored **helmet** and cycling **gloves** (available from most bike shops). Keep your water-bottle filled and drink from it frequently to avoid dehydration – don't forget the power of the Florida sun.

The best **cycling areas** are in North Central Florida, the Panhandle and in parts of the Northeast Coast. By contrast, the southeast coastal strip is heavily congested and many south

Florida inland roads are narrow and dangerous. Wherever you cycle, avoid the heaviest traffic – and the midday heat – by doing most of your pedalling before 10am.

For free biking information and detailed maps ($2–15) of cycling routes, write to the State Bicycle Program, Florida Department of Transportation, 605 Suwanee Street, Tallahassee, FL 32399-0450 (☎805/488-3111). You can get the same maps from most youth hostels; the Florida AYH also publishes the AYH Bicycle Hospitality Directory, a list of local cycling enthusiasts willing to host bike-mad visitors overnight (PO Box 533097, Orlando, FL 32853-3097).

ACCOMMODATION

Accommodation costs inevitably account for a significant proportion of the expenses for any traveler in Florida, though as ever in the US you usually get good value for what you pay. If you're on your own, it's possible to pare costs by sleeping in dormitory-style hostels, where a bed can cost from $12 to $15. Youth hostels in Florida, however, are surprisingly few and far between, with just two affiliated to the IYHA (International Youth Hostel Association, (in Key West and Clearwater) for the whole west coast; there's also a non-affiliated hostel just outside the Everglades. Groups of two or more will find it little more expensive to stay in the far more plentiful motels and hotels, where basic rooms away from the major cities typically cost anything upwards of $40 a night. Many hotels will set up a third single bed for around $5–10 on top of the regular price, reducing costs for three people sharing. By contrast, the lone traveler will have a hard time of it: "singles" are usually double rooms at an only slightly reduced rate. Prices quoted by hotels and motels are almost always for the actual room rather than for each person using it.

Motels are plentiful on the main approach roads to cities, around beaches and by the main road junctions in country areas. High-rise **hotels** predominate along the popular sections of the coast and are sometimes the only accommodation in city centers. In major cities **campgrounds** tend to be on the outskirts, if they exist at all.

ACCOMMODATION PRICE CODES

It's a fact of Florida life that the plain-and-simple motel room, which costs $30 on a weekday in low season, is liable to cost two or three times that amount on a weekend in high season. To further complicate matters, high and low season vary depending on whether you're in north or south Florida (see Introduction), and some establishments that depend on business travelers for their trade (such as those in downtown areas, distanced from the nearest beach) will actually be cheaper on weekends than on weekdays. Local events – such as a Space Shuttle launch on the Space Coast, or Spring Break in Panama City Beach – can also cause prices to increase dramatically.

Throughout the book, we've graded accommodation prices according to the cost of the least expensive double room throughout most of the year – but do allow for the fluctuations outlined above.

① up to $30	③ $45–60	⑤ $80–100	⑦ $130–180
② $30–45	④ $60–80	⑥ $100–130	⑧ $180+

Wherever you stay, you'll be expected to **pay in advance**, at least for the first night and perhaps for further nights too, particularly if it's high season and the hotel's expecting to be busy. Payment can be in cash or in dollar travelers' checks, though it's more common to give your credit card number and sign for everything when you leave. **Reservations** are only held until 5pm or 6pm unless you've told the hotel you'll be arriving late. Most of the larger chains have an advance booking form in their brochures and will make reservations at another of their premises for you.

Since cheap accommodation in the cities and on the popular sections of the coast is snapped up fast, always book ahead whenever possible, using the suggestions in this book.

HOTELS AND MOTELS

While **motels** and **hotels** essentially offer the same things – double rooms with bathroom, TV and phone – motels are often one-off affairs run by their owners and tend to be cheaper (typically $30–45) than hotels ($45–75), which are likely to be part of a nationwide chain. All but the cheapest motels and hotels have pools for guests' use and many offer cable TV and free local phone calls. Under $60, rooms tend to be similar in quality and features; spend $60–70 in rural areas or $80–100 in the cities and you get more luxury – a larger room and often additional facilities such as a tennis court, gym and golf course. Paying over $150 brings all the above, plus a fabulous ocean view, en-suite jacuzzi and all imaginable upmarket trappings.

HOTEL DISCOUNT VOUCHERS

Many of the higher-rung hotel chains offer **prepaid discount vouchers**, which in theory save you money if you're prepared to pay in advance. To take advantage of such schemes, British travelers must purchase the vouchers in the UK, at a usual cost of between £30 and £60 per night for a minimum of two people sharing. However, it's hard to think of a good reason to buy them; you may save a nominal amount on the fixed rates, but better-value accommodation is not exactly difficult to find in the US, and you may well regret the inflexibility imposed upon your travels. Most UK travel agents will have details of the various voucher schemes; the cheapest is the "Go As You Please" deal offered by Days Inn (☎01483/440480 in Britain).

Alternatively, there are a number of unexciting but dependable budget-priced chain hotels, which, depending on location, cost around $30-50; the cheapest are *Days Inn, Econo Lodge, Hampton Inns, Knights Inns* and *Red Carpet Inns*. Higher up the scale are mid-range chains like *Best Western, Howard Johnson's* (now usually abbreviated to HoJo's), *TraveLodge* and *La Quinta* – though if you can afford their prices (usually $75–125), there's normally somewhere nicer to stay.

On your travels you'll also come across resorts, which are motels or hotels equipped with a restaurant, bar and private beach – on average these cost $70–110; and efficiencies, which are motel rooms adapted to offer cooking facilities – ranging from a stove squeezed into a corner to a fully equipped kitchen – usually for $10–15 above the basic room rate.

Since inexpensive diners are everywhere, very few hotels or motels bother to offer **breakfast**, though there's a trend towards providing free coffee (from paper cups) and sticky buns on a self-service basis from the lobby.

OTHER DISCOUNTS AND RESERVATIONS

During **off-peak periods** many motels and hotels struggle to fill their rooms and it's worth **haggling** to get a few dollars off the asking price. Staying in the same place for more than one night will bring further reductions. In addition, pick up the many **discount coupons** that fill tourist information offices and welcome centers (see p.19), and look out for the free *Traveler Discount Guide*. Read the small print, though: what appears to be an amazingly cheap room rate sometimes turns out to be a per-person charge for two people sharing and limited to midweek.

When it's worth blowing cash on somewhere really atmospheric we've said as much in the Guide. Bear in mind the most upmarket establishments have all manner of services that may appear to be free but for which you will be expected to tip in a style commensurate with the hotel's status – see "Tipping" in "Directory."

BED AND BREAKFAST

The American attitude to holiday accommodation differs from the British in that characterful, old villas converted into bed and breakfasts are often not recommended by visitor centers if they lack the amenities of more modern and more mundane motels. Most towns throughout Florida have a

---

BED AND BREAKFAST AGENCIES

For a list of inns in various areas, contact one or several of the following:

A&A Bed & Breakfast of Florida Inc PO Box 1316, Winter Park, FL 32790 (☎407/628-3222).

B&B Scenic Florida PO Box 3385, Tallahassee, FL 32315-3385 (☎850/386-8196).

Bed'n'Breakfast Central Gulf Coast PO Box 9515, Pensacola, FL 32513-3222 (☎850/438-796).

Bed & Breakfast East Coast PO Box 1373, Marathon, FL 33050 (☎305/743-4118).

Bed & Breakfast of Volusia County PO Box 573, DeLeon Springs, FL 32028 (☎904/985-5068).

Florida Suncoast Bed & Breakfast PO Box 12, Palm Harbor, FL 33563 (☎941/784-5118).

IBN booking centers

Australia (Sydney) ☎02/9261 1111.
Canada (Ontario) ☎1-800/663 5777.
UK (London) ☎0171 836 1036
New Zealand (Auckland) ☎9/3092802

---

so-called historic section, and it is worth driving around to discover bed and breakfasts in the most serene surroundings. Even the larger establishments tend to have less than ten rooms, sometimes without TV and phone but always with flowers, stuffed cushions and an almost contrived homely atmosphere; others may just be a couple of furnished rooms in someone's home.

While always including a huge and wholesome breakfast (five courses are not unheard of), prices vary greatly: anything from $45 to $200 depending on location and season; most cost between $60 and $80 per night for a double. Bear in mind, too, that most are booked well in advance, making it sensible to contact either the inn directly (details are given throughout the Guide), or one of the agents below, at least a month ahead – longer in high season.

YS AND HOSTELS

At around $12 (a few dollars more for non-members) per night per person, **hostels** are clearly the cheapest accommodation option other than camping. There are two main kinds of cheap, hostel-like accommodation in the US: *YMCA/YWCA* hostels (known as *"Ys"*), offering accommodation for both sexes or, in a few cases, women only; and official *AYH* youth hostels. In Florida you'll find **AYH youth hostels** in Miami Beach, Daytona Beach, St Augustine, Fort Lauderdale, Key West, Orlando and Clearwater near St Petersburg. You can make reservations through the International Booking Network (IBN) and for a small booking fee, the Hostelling International association in

your home country can reserve accommodation before leaving home. This has the advantage of putting a confirmation slip in your hand, which you won't have if telephone booking long distance once in the United States.

Particularly if you're traveling in high season, it's advisable to book ahead through one of the specialist travel agents or international youth hostel offices. Some hostels will allow you to use a sleeping bag, though officially they should (and many do) insist on a sheet sleeping bag, which can usually be rented at the hostel. The maximum stay at each hostel is technically three days, though this is again a rule that is often ignored if there's space. Few hostels provide meals, but most have cooking facilities, and there's sometimes a curfew of around midnight: alcohol, smoking and, of course, drugs are banned.

The informative *American Youth Hostel (AYH) Handbook* ($5) is available from hostels in the US, or direct from the AYH national office: 733 15th Street NW, Suite 840, Washington DC 20005 (☎202/783-6161). Specific hostel information for Florida can be had from the Florida Council, PO Box 533097, Orlando, FL 32853-3097 (☎407/649-8761).

For overseas hostelers, the *International Youth Hostel Handbook* provides a full list of hostels. In Britain; it's available from the Youth Hostel Association headquarters/shop, at 14 Southampton Street, London WC2 (☎0171/836 1036), where you can also buy a year's IYHF membership for £9 (£3 if you're under 18).

CAMPING

Florida **campgrounds** range from the primitive (a flat piece of ground that may or may not have a water tap) to others that are more like open-air hotels with shops, restaurants and washing facilities. Naturally, prices vary according to amenities, ranging from nothing at all for the most basic plots to up to $35 a night for something comparatively luxurious. There are plenty of campgrounds but often plenty of people intending to use them: take special care over plotting your route if you're camping during public holidays or weekends, when many sites will be either full or very crowded. By contrast, some of the more basic campgrounds in state and national parks will often be completely empty midweek. For camping in the wilderness, there's a nightly charge of $1.50 payable at the area's administrative office.

Privately run campgrounds are everywhere, their prices range from $8 to $35 and the best are listed throughout the Guide; for a fuller list, write for the free *Florida Camping Directory* to the Florida Campground Association, 1638 Plaza Drive, Tallahassee, FL 32308-5364 (☎850/656-8878).

State parks – there are over 300 in Florida – are often excellent places to camp; sites cost $5–20 for up to four people sharing. Never more than half the space is reserved, the rest goes on a first-come first-served basis (bear in mind that park offices close at sunset; you won't be able to camp there if you arrive later). Reservations can be made within two months of arrival by phone

only, and stays are limited to fourteen days. Reservations won't be held after 5pm unless previously arranged. If you're doing a lot of camping in state parks, get the two free leaflets, *Florida State Parks Camping Reservations Procedures* and *Florida State Parks Fees Schedule* from any state park office, or by writing to the Department of Natural Resources, Division of Recreation and Parks, 3900 Commonwealth Boulevard, Tallahassee, FL 32399 (☎850/488-9872).

Similarly priced campgrounds exist in National Parks and National Forests – see the details throughout the Guide, or contact the National Park Service, PO Box 2416, Tallahassee, FL 32316 (☎904/222-1167) and the US Forest Service, Suite 4061, 227 N Bronough Street, Tallahassee, FL 32301 (☎850/681-7265).

However desolate it may look, much of undeveloped Florida is, in fact, private land and rough camping is illegal. For permitted rough camping, see "The Backcountry," p.37.

FOOD AND DRINK

Fresh fish and seafood are abundant all over Florida, as is the high-quality produce of the state's cattle farms – served as ribs, steaks and burgers – and junkfood is as common as anywhere else in the country. But the choice of what to eat is influenced by where you are. In the northern half of the state, the accent is on wholesome cooking – traditional Southern dishes such as grits, cornbread and fried chicken. As you head south through Florida, this gives way to the most diverse and inexpensive gathering of Latin American and Caribbean cuisines to be found anywhere in the US – you can feast on anything from curried goat to mashed plantains and yucca.

BREAKFAST

Florida has a mass of restaurants, fast-food outlets, cafés and coffee shops on every main street, all trying to outdo one another with their cut-price daily specials. In every town mentioned in this book you'll find reviews of the full range of eating options.

For the price (on average $3–5) breakfast makes a good-value, very filling start to the day. Go to a **diner**, **café** or **coffee shop**, all of which are very similar and usually serve breakfast until at least 11am (though some continue all day) – though there are special deals at earlier times, say 6–8am, when the price may be even less.

LUNCH AND SNACKS

The Florida workforce takes its lunch-break between 11.30am and 1.30pm, during which hours all sorts of low-cost **set menus** and all-you-can-eat specials are on offer – generally excellent value. Chinese restaurants, for example, frequently have help-yourself rice and noo-dles or dim sum feasts for $4–6, and many Japanese restaurants give you a chance to eat sushi much more cheaply ($6–8) than usual. Most Cuban restaurants and fishcamps (see "Dining Out," below) are exceptionally well priced all the time and you can get a good-sized lunch in one for $4–5. **Buffet restaurants** – most of which also serve breakfast and dinner – are found in most cities and towns; $6–8 lets you pig out as much as you can from a wide variety of hot dish-es. A chain version, *Shoney's*, turns up through-out the state.

As you'd expect, there's also pizza; count on paying $5–7 for a basic two-person pizza at national chains and local outlets. If it's a warm day and you can't face hot food, find a deli (see below) with a salad bar, where you can help your-self for $3. Frozen yogurt or ice cream may be all you feel like eating in the midday heat: look for exotic versions made with mango and guava sold by Cuban vendors.

SNACKS

For **quick snacks**, many **supermarket deli counters** do ready-cooked meals for $3–4, as well as a range of **salads** and **sandwiches**. Filled **bagels** are also common, while **street stands** sell hot dogs, burgers or a slice of pizza for around $1: in Miami, **Cuban fast-food stands** serve crispy pork sandwiches and other spicy snacks for $2–3, and most shopping malls have ethnic fast-food stalls, often pricier than street stands but usually with edible and filling fare. Bags of fresh oranges, grapefruit and water-melons are often sold from the roadside in rural areas, as are **boiled peanuts** – a dollar buys a steaming bagful. Southern fast-food chains like *Popeye's Famous Fried Chicken* and *Sonny's Real Pit Bar-B-Q* and Mexican outlets such as *Taco Bell*, will satisfy your hunger for $3–4, but are only marginally better than the inevitable **burger chains**. **Coffee shops** appear all through Florida, providing a huge array of basic cooking in relaxed surroundings.

FREE FOOD AND BRUNCH

Some **bars** are used as much by diners as drinkers, who fill up on the free **hors d'oeuvres** laid out by a lot of city bars between 5 and 7pm Monday to Friday – an attempt to nab the com-muting classes before they head off to the sub-urbs – and sometimes by beachside bars to grab beach-goers before they head elsewhere for the evening. For the price of a drink you can stuff yourself on chilli, seafood or pasta.

Brunch is another deal to look out for: indulged in on weekends (usually Sunday) between 11am and 2pm. For a set price ($8 and up) you get a light meal (or even a groaning buffet) and a variety of complimentary cocktails or champagne. We've listed the most interesting venues in the Guide.

DINING OUT

Even if it sometimes seems swamped by the more fashionable regional and ethnic cuisines, traditional **American cooking** is found all over Florida. Portions are big and you start with **salad**, eaten before the main course arrives; look out for **heart of palm** salad, based around the delicious vegetable at the heart of the sable palm tree. Main dishes are dominated by enormous **steaks**, **burgers**, piles of **ribs** or half a **chick-en**. Vegetables include french fries or a baked potato, the latter commonly topped with sour cream and chives.

Southern cooking makes its presence felt throughout the northern half of the state. Vegetables such as **okra**, **collard greens**, **black-eyed peas, fried green tomatoes** and fried **eggplant** are added to staples such as fried chicken, roast beef and **hogjaw** – meat from the mouth of a pig. Meat dishes are usual-ly accompanied by **cornbread** to soak up the thick gravy poured over everything; with fried fish, you'll get **hush puppies** – fried corn balls with tiny bits of chopped onion. Okra is also used in **gumbo** soups, a feature of **Cajun** cooking, which originated in nearby Louisiana as a way of using up leftovers. A few (usually expensive) Florida restaurants specialize in Cajun food but many others have a few Cajun items (such as red beans and rice and hot and spicy shrimp and steak dishes) on their menu.

Don't be shocked to see **alligator** on menus: most of the meat comes from alligator farms, which cull a certain number each year. The tails are deep-fried and served in a variety of styles – none of which make much of a mark on the bland, chicken-like taste. **Frogs' legs** also crop up occasionally.

Regional nouvelle cuisine of the Californian kind is far too pretentious and expensive for the typical Floridian palate, although some restaurants in the larger cities do extraordinary and inspired things with local fish and the produce of the citrus farms, creating small but beautifully presented and highly nutritious affairs for around $40 a head.

Almost wherever you eat you'll be offered Key Lime Pie as a dessert, a dish which began life in the Florida Keys, made from the small limes that grow there. The pie is similar to lemon meringue but with a sharper taste. Quality varies greatly; take local advice to find a good outlet and your tastebuds will tell you why many swear by it.

FISH AND SEAFOOD

Florida excels with **fish and seafood** – which is great news for non-meat eaters. Even the shabbiest restaurant is likely to have an excellent selection, though fish comes freshest and cheapest at **fishcamps**, rustic places right beside the river where your meal was swimming just a few hours before; a fishcamp lunch or dinner will cost around $5–9. **Catfish** tends to top the bill, but you'll also find **grouper**, **dolphin** (the fish not the mammal, sometimes known by its Hawaiian name, **mahimahi**), **mullet**, **tuna** and **swordfish**, any of which (except catfish, which is nearly always fried) may be boiled, grilled, fried or "blackened" (charcoal-grilled). Of **shellfish**, the tender claws of **stone crabs**, eaten dipped in butter, raise local passions during their mid-October to mid-May season; **spiny** (or **"Florida"**) **lobster** is smaller and more succulent than its more famous Maine rival; **oysters** can be extremely fresh (the best come from Apalachicola) and are usually eaten raw (though best avoided during summer, when they carry a risk of food poisoning) – many restaurants have special **"raw bars,"** where you can also consume meaty **shrimp**, in regular and jumbo sizes. One crustacean you can't eat raw is the very chewy **conch** (pronounced "konk"); abundant throughout the Florida Keys, they usually come deep-fried as fritters served up with various sauces, or as a chowder-like soup.

ETHNIC CUISINE

Florida's **ethnic cuisines** become increasingly exotic the further south you go. In Miami, **Cuban food** is extremely easy to find and can be very good value. Most Cuban dishes are meat-based: frequently pork, less often beef or chicken, always fried (including the skin, which becomes a crispy crackling) and usually heavily spiced, served with a varying combination of yellow or white rice, black beans, plantains (a sweet, banana-like vegetable) and yucca (cassava) – a potato-like vegetable completely devoid of taste. Seafood crops up less often, most deliciously in thick soups, such as *sopa de mariscos* – shellfish soup. Unpretentious Cuban diners serve a filling lunch or dinner for under $6, though a growing number of upmarket restaurants will charge three times as much for identical food. In busy areas, many Cuban cafés have street windows where you buy a thimble-sized cup of sweet and rich *café Cubano* – Cuban coffee – for 50–75¢, strong enough to make your hair stand on end; the similarly priced *café con leche*, coffee with warm milk or cream, is strictly for the unadventurous and regarded by Cubans as a children's drink. If you want a cool drink in Miami, look out for roadside stands offering *coco frio* – coconut milk sucked through a straw directly from the coconut, for $1.

Although nowhere near as prevalent as Cuban cooking, foods from other parts of the Caribbean and Latin America are easily located around Miami: Haitian food is the latest craze, but Argentinian, Colombian, Nicaraguan, Peruvian, Jamaican and Salvadorean restaurants also serve the city's diverse migrant populations – at very affordable prices.

Other ethnic cuisines turn up all around the state, too. Chinese food is everywhere and often very cheap, as is Mexican, though many Mexican restaurants are more popular as places to knock back margaritas than for eating in; Japanese is more expensive; Italian food is popular but can be expensive once you leave the simple pastas and explore the more gourmet-inclined Italian regional cooking that's catching on fast in the major cities. French food, too, is widely available, though always pricey, the cuisine of social climbers and power-lunchers and rarely found outside the larger cities. Thai, Korean and Indonesian food is similarly city-based, though usually cheaper; Indian restaurants, on the other hand, are thin on the ground just about everywhere and often very expensive. More plentiful are well-priced, family-run Greek restaurants, and a smattering of Minorcan places are evidence of one of Florida's earliest groups of European settlers.

Whatever and wherever you eat, service will always be enthusiastic and excellent. Foreign travelers should note that this is mainly due to the American system of tipping, on which the staff depend for the bulk (and sometimes all) of their earnings. You should always top up the bill by 15–20 percent; not to tip at all is severely frowned upon. The only exceptions to this rule are trendy, South Beach-type restaurants, which sometimes add a service charge to the bill. Many (not all) restaurants accept payment in the form of credit/charge cards: if you use one, a space will be left to fill in the appropriate tip; travelers' checks are also widely accepted (see p.15).

AMERICAN FOOD TERMS FOR FOREIGN TRAVELERS

A la mode	With ice cream
Au jus	Meat served with a gravy made from its own juices
Biscuit	Scone
BLT	Bacon, lettuce and tomato toasted sandwich
Broiled	Grilled
Brownie	A fudgy, filling chocolate cake
Chips	Potato crisps
Cilantro	Coriander
Clam chowder	A thick soup made with clams and other seafood.
Cookie	Biscuit
Eggplant	Aubergine
English muffin	Toasted bread roll, similar to a crumpet
Frank	Frankfurter (hot dog)
(French) fries	Chips
Gravy	White lard-like sauce poured over biscuits for breakfast
Grits	Ground white corn, served hot with butter, often a breakfast side dish.

Hash browns	Potato chunks or grated potato chips fried in fat
Hero	French-bread sandwich
Hoagie	Another French-bread sandwich
Home fries	Thick-cut fried potatoes
Jello	Jelly
Jelly	Jam
Muffin	Small cake made with bran and/or blueberries
Popsicle	Ice lolly
Potato chips	Crisps
Pretzels	Savory circles of glazed pastry
Seltzer	Fizzy/soda water
Sherbet	Sorbet
Shrimp	Prawns
Sub	Yet another French-bread sandwich
Soda	Generic term for any soft drink
Surf 'n' Turf	Restaurant serving fish and meat
Teriyaki	Chicken or beef, marinated in soy sauce and grilled
Yucca	Cassava
Zucchini	Courgettes

CUBAN SPECIALTIES

Ajiaco criollo	Meat and root vegetable stew
Arroz	Rice
Arroz con leche	Rice pudding
Bocadillo	Sandwich
Chicarones de pollo	Fried chicken crackling
Frijoles	Beans
Frijoles negros	Black beans
Maduros	Fried plantains
Masitoas de puerca	Fried spiced pork
Morros y Christianos	Literally "Moors and Christians", black beans and white rice

Pan	Bread
Pan con lechon	Crispy pork sandwich
Piccadillo	Minced meat, usually beef, served with peppers and olives
Pollo	Chicken
Puerca	Pork
Sopa de mariscos	Shellfish soup
Sopa de plantanos	Meaty, plantain soup
Vaca	Beef
Tostones	Fried mashed plantains

DRINKING

While regular bars in the classic American image do exist in Florida – long, dimly lit counters with a few punters perched on stools before a bartender-cum-guru, and tables and booths for those who don't want to join in the drunken bar-side debates – most drinking is done in restaurant or hotel lounges, at fishcamps (see "Dining Out"), or in "tiki bars," open-sided straw-roofed huts beside a beach or hotel pool. Some beachside bars, especially in Daytona Beach and Panama City Beach, are split-level, multi-purpose affairs with discos and stages for live bands – and take great pride in being the birthplace of the infamous wet T-shirt contest (nowadays sometimes joined by G-string and "best legs" shows), an exercise in unrestrained sexism that shows no signs of declining in popularity among a predominantly late-teen and twenty-something clientele.

To buy and consume alcohol you need to be 21 and could well be asked for ID even if you look much older. Recent clamp-downs have resulted in bars "carding" anyone who looks 30 and under. Licensing laws and drinking hours vary from area to area, but generally alcohol can be bought and drunk in a bar, nightclub or restaurant any time between 10am and 2am. More cheaply, you can usually buy beer, wine or spirits in supermarkets and, of course, liquor stores, from 9am to 11pm Monday to Saturday and from 1pm to 11pm on Sundays. Note that it is illegal to consume alcohol in a car, on most beaches and in all state parks.

BEER

A small band of Florida **micro breweries** (tiny, one-off operations) create interesting beers, though rarely are these sold beyond their own bar or restaurant – such as the **Sarasota Brewing Company** in Sarasota. It's more common for discerning beer drinkers to stick to imported brews, best of which are the Mexican brands Bohemia, Corona, Dos Equis, Superior and Tecate. Don't forget that in all but the more pretentious bars,

COCKTAILS

Bacardi	White rum, lime and grenadine – not the brand name drink	*Manhattan*	Vermouth, whisky, lemon juice and soda
Bellini	Champagne with peach juice	*Margarita*	*The* cocktail to drink in a Mexican restaurant, made with tequila, triple sec, lime juice and limes, and blended with ice to make slush. Served with or without salt. Also available in fruit flavours.
Black Russian	Vodka with coffee liqueur, brown cacao and coke		
Bloody Mary	Vodka, tomato juice, tabasco, Worcester sauce, salt and pepper		
Brandy Alexander	Brandy, brown cacao and cream	*Mimosa*	Champagne and orange juice
Champagne cocktail	Brandy, sugar and champagne	*Mint Julep*	Bourbon, mint and sugar
		Negroni	Vodka or gin, campari and triple sec
Daquiri	Dark rum, light rum and lime, often with banana or strawberry	*Pina Colada*	Dark rum, light rum, coconut, cream and pineapple juice
		Screwdriver	Vodka and orange juice
Harvey Wallbanger	Vodka, galliano, orange juice	*Silk Stocking*	Gin, tequila, white cacao, cream and sugar
Highball	Any spirit plus a soda, water or ginger ale	*Tequila Sunrise*	Tequila, orange juice and grenadine
Kir Royale	Champagne, cassis	*Tom Collins*	Gin, lemon juice, soda and sugar
Long Island Iced Tea	Gin, vodka, white rum, tequila, lemon juice and coke	*Vodka Collins*	Vodka, lemon juice, soda and sugar
Mai-Tai	Dark rum, light rum, cherry brandy, orange and lemon juice	*Whisky Sour*	Bourbon, lemon juice and sugar
		White Russian	Vodka, white cacao and cream

several people can save money by buying a quart or half-gallon **pitcher** of beer. If bar prices are a problem, you can stock up with **six-packs** from a supermarket at $5–7 for domestic, $8–12 for imported brews.

WINE AND SPIRITS

If **wine** is more to your taste, try to visit one of the state's fast-improving **wineries**: several can be toured and their products sampled for free. One of the most successful is Chautauqua Vineyards, in De Funiak Springs in the Panhandle (see p.348). In a bar or restaurant, however, beside a usually threadbare stock of European wines, you'll find a selection from Chile and **California**. *Cabernet Sauvignon* is certainly worth trying – a light, drinkable red; also widespread are the heavier reds – *Burgundy*, *Merlot* and *Pinot Noir*. Among the whites, *Chardonnay* is very dry and full of flavor and generally preferred to *Sauvignon Blanc* or *Fumé Blanc*, though these have their devotees. It's fairly inexpensive: a glass of wine in a bar or restaurant costs from around $2.50, a bottle to $10. Buying a bottle from a supermarket can prove cheaper still.

Spirits generally cost $1.50 a shot. **Cocktails** are extremely popular, especially rich fruity ones consumed while gazing over the ocean or into the sunset. Varieties are innumerable, sometimes specific to a single bar or cocktail lounge, though there are a few standards listed above, any of which will cost $2–5. Cocktails and all other drinks come cheapest during **happy hours** (usually 5–7pm; sometimes much longer) when many are half-price and there might be a buffet thrown in.

PERSONAL SAFETY

No one could pretend that Florida is trouble-free, though outside of the urban centers crime is often remarkably low-key. Even the lawless reputation of murder-a-day Miami is in excess of the truth, though several clearly defined areas are strictly off-limits. At night you should always be cautious – though not unduly frightened – wherever you are. All the major tourist and nightlife areas in cities are invariably brightly lit and well policed. By being careful, planning ahead and taking good care of your possessions, you should, generally speaking, have few real problems.

Foreign visitors tend to report that the police are helpful and obliging when things go wrong, though they'll be less sympathetic if they think you brought the trouble on yourself through carelessness*.

CAR CRIME

Even more than muggings on the street (see below), it's been crimes against tourists driving **rented cars** in Florida that have garnered headlines around the world in recent months and threatened the well-being of the state's number-one industry.

When driving, under no circumstances stop in any unlit or seemingly deserted urban area – and especially not if someone is waving you down and suggesting that there is something wrong with your car. Similarly, if you are "accidentally" rammed by the driver behind, do not stop immediately but drive on to the nearest well-lit, busy and secure area (such as a hotel, toll booth or gas station) and phone the emergency number (☎911) for assistance. Keep your doors locked and windows never more than slightly open (as you'll probably be using

---

*One way you might accidentally break the law is by **jaywalking**. If you cross the road on a red light or anywhere except at an intersection, and are spotted by a cop, you're likely to get a stiff talking-to – and possibly a ticket, leading to a $20 fine.

air conditioning, you'll want to keep them fully closed anyway). Do not open your door or window if someone approaches your car on the pretext of asking directions. Even if the person doing this looks harmless, they may well have an accomplice ready to attack you from behind. Hide any valuables out of sight, preferably locked in the trunk or in the glove compartment (any valuables you don't need for your journey should be left in your hotel safe).

Always take care when planning your route, particularly through urban areas, and be sure to use a reliable map such as the ones we've recommended under "Information, Maps and the Media" (see p.19). Particularly in Miami, local authorities are making efforts to add directions to tourist sights and attractions to road signs, thereby reducing the possibility of visitors unwittingly driving into dangerous areas. Needless to say, you should always heed such directions, even if you think you've located a convenient short cut. Having said all this, it's important not to spend your time in Florida in fear. Outside the problem areas of Miami, there is an easy-going and essentially safe atmosphere on roads throughout the state.

STREET CRIME AND HOTEL BURGLARIES

After car crime, the biggest problem for most travelers in Florida is the threat of **mugging**. It's impossible to give hard and fast rules about what to do if you're confronted by a mugger. Whether to run, scream or fight depends on the situation – but most locals would just hand over their money.

Of course, the best thing is simply to avoid being mugged, and there are a few basic rules worth remembering: don't flash money around; don't peer at your map (or this book) at every street corner, thereby announcing you're a lost stranger; even if you're terrified or drunk (or both), don't appear so; avoid dark streets and never start to walk down one that you can't see the end of; and in the early hours stick to the roadside edge of the pavement so it's easier to run into the road to attract attention.

If the worst happens and your assailant is toting a gun or (more likely) a knife, try to stay calm: remember that he (for this is generally a male pursuit) is probably scared, too. Keep still, don't make any sudden movements – and hand over your money. When he's gone you'll be shocked, but try to find a cab to take you to the nearest police station. Here, report the theft and get a reference number on the report to claim insurance (see "Health and Insurance," p.13) and travelers' check

> ### LOSING YOUR PASSPORT
>
> Few disasters create bigger headaches for foreign travelers than **losing your passport**. You can't get home without it, and it can be an extremely tough process to get a new one. The **British Consulate** in Florida – which can (very grudgingly) issue passports – is in Miami at Suite 2110, S Bayshore Drive, Coconut Grove, FL 33131 (☎305/374-1522). Expect to spend around $40 on fees and waste at least a week. If you are a "Briton in distress," which includes losing your passport, you can call the very helpful British Consulate General in Atlanta, Georgia (☎404 524 5856), who can help organize emergency passports quickly. The office is open Mon–Fri 9am–5pm. Make sure you have at least $50 and photographs of yourself ready.

refunds. If you're in a big city, ring the local Travelers Aid (their numbers are listed in the phone book) for sympathy and practical advice.

Another potential source of trouble is having your hotel room burgled while you're out. Some Orlando area hotels are notorious for this and many such break-ins appear to be inside jobs. Always store valuables in the hotel safe when you go out; when inside keep your door locked and don't open it to anyone who seems suspicious; if they claim to be hotel staff and you don't believe them, call reception on the room phone to check.

LOST TRAVELERS' CHECKS

Lost travelers' checks are a common problem. You should keep a record of the numbers of your checks separately from the actual checks and, if you lose them, ring the issuing company on their toll-free number. They'll ask you for the check numbers, the place you bought them, when and how you lost them and whether it's been reported to the police. All being well, you should get the missing check re-issued within a couple of days – and perhaps an emergency advance to tide you over.

> ### STOLEN TRAVELERS' CHECKS/CREDIT CARDS EMERGENCY NUMBERS
>
> **American Express** (TCs) ☎ 1-800/221-7282; (credit cards) ☎1-800/528-2121
>
> **Diners Card** ☎1-800/968-8300
>
> **Mastercard** (Access) ☎ 1-800/336-8472
>
> **Thomas Cook** ☎1-800/223-7373
>
> **Visa** ☎1-800/627-6811 or ☎1-800/227-6811

THE BACKCOUNTRY

Despite the common notion that Florida is entirely composed of theme parks and beaches, much of the state is undeveloped land containing everything from scrubland and swamps to shady hardwood hammocks and dense forests streaked by gushing rivers. Hiking and canoe trails make the wilderness accessible and rewarding – miss it and you're missing Florida.

The US's protected backcountry areas fall into several potentially confusing categories. State parks are the responsibility of individual states and usually focus on sites of natural or historical significance. National parks are federally controlled, preserving areas of great natural beauty or ecological importance. Florida's three national forests are also federally administered but enjoy much less protection than national parks.

HIKING

Almost all state parks have undemanding **nature trails** intended for a pleasant hour's ramble; anything called a **hiking** or **backpacking trail** – plentiful in state and national parks, national forests and through some unprotected land as part of the 1300-mile **Florida Trail** (intended eventually to run the full length of the state) – requires more thought and planning.

Many hiking trails can be easily completed in a day, the longer ones have rough camping sites at regular intervals (see "Camping," below), and most periodically pass through fully equipped camping areas – giving the option of sleeping in comparative comfort. The best time to hike is from late fall to early spring: this avoids the exhausting heat of the summer and the worst of the mosquitoes (see "Wildlife," below) and reveals a greater variety of animals. While hiking, be extremely wary of the poisonwood tree (ask a park ranger how to identify it); any contact between your skin and its bark can leave you needing hospital treatment – and avoid being splashed by rainwater dripping from its branches. Be sure to carry plenty of drinking water, as well as the obvious hiking prerequisites.

In some areas you'll need a wilderness permit (free or $1) from the local park ranger's or wilderness area administration office, where you should call anyway for maps, general information on the hike and a weather forecast – sudden rains can flood trails in swampy areas. Many state parks run organized hiking trips, details of which are given throughout the Guide. For general hiking information, write for the free *Backpacking in Florida State Parks* to the Florida Department of Natural Resources, 3900 Commonwealth Boulevard, Tallahassee, FL 32393 (☎850/488-0406) and to the Florida Trail Association, PO Box 13708, Gainesville, FL 32604 (☎1-800/343-1882).

CANOEING

One way to enjoy natural Florida without getting blisters on your feet is by **canoeing**. Canoes can be rented for around $12–15 a day wherever conditions are right: the best of Florida's rivers and streams are found in north Central Florida and the Panhandle. Many state and national parks have canoe runs, too; the **Florida Canoe Trails System** comprises 36 marked routes along rivers and creeks, covering a combined distance of nearly a thousand miles.

Before setting off, get a canoeing **map** (you'll need to know the locations of access points and any rough camping sites) and check **weather conditions** and the river's **water level**: a low level can expose logs, rocks and other obstacles; a flooded river is dangerous and shouldn't be canoed; coastal rivers are affected by tides. Don't leave the canoe to **walk on the bank**, as this will cause damage and is likely to be trespassing. When a **motorboat** approaches, keep to the right and turn your bow into the wake. If you're **camping**, do so on a sandbar unless there are designated rough camping areas beside the river. Besides food, carry plenty of drinking water, a first-aid kit, insect repellent and sunscreen.

Several small companies run canoe trips ranging from half a day to a week; they supply the canoe and take you from the end of the route back to where you started. Details are given throughout the Guide; or look out for the free *Canoe Florida* leaflet, available from most state parks and some local tourist information offices. For more on the Florida Canoe Trails System, pick up the free *Florida Recreational Trails System Canoe Trails* (available from the **Department of Natural Resources**, address above).

CAMPING

All hiking trails have areas designated for **rough camping**, with either very limited facilities (a handpump for water, sometimes a primitive toilet) or none at all. Traveling by canoe (see "Canoeing," above), you'll often pass sandbars, which can make excellent overnight stops. It's preferable to cook by stove, but otherwise start **fires** only in permitted areas – indicated by signs – and use deadwood. Where there are no toilets, **bury human waste** at least four inches in the ground and a hundred feet from the nearest water supply and campground. **Burn rubbish** carefully, and what you can't burn, carry away. **Never drink** from rivers and streams, however clear and inviting they may look (you never know what unspeakable acts people – or animals – further upstream have performed in them), or from the state's many natural springs; **water** that isn't from taps should be boiled for at least five minutes or cleansed with a iodine-based purifier before you drink it. Always get advice, maps and a weather forecast from the park ranger's or wilderness area adminstration office – often you'll need to fill in a **wilderness permit**, too and pay a $1.50-a-night **camping fee**.

WILDLIFE

Though you're likely to meet many kinds of **wildlife** on your travels, only mosquitoes and, to a much lesser extent, alligators and snakes, will cause any problems.

From June to November, mosquitoes are a tremendous nuisance and virtually unavoidable in any area close to fresh water. During these months, insect repellent (available for a few dollars in most camping shops and supermarkets) is essential, as is wearing long-sleeved shirts and long trousers. It's rare for mosquitoes to carry diseases, though during 1991 Florida was hit by an outbreak of viral encephalitis, a mosquito-borne disease which can cause paralysis and death. As each generation of mosquitoes dies out during the winter, it's unlikely that this will be repeated – at least not for many years.

The biggest surprise among Florida's wildlife is the apparent docility of alligators – almost always they'll back away if approached by a human (though this is not something you should put to the test) – and the fact that they now turn up all over the place, despite being decimated by decades of uncontrolled hunting. These days, not only is it unlawful to kill alligators (without a license), but feeding one can get you two months in prison and a hefty fine: an alligator fed by a human not only loses its natural fear of people but comes to associate them with food – and lacks the brainpower to distinguish between food and feeder. The only truly dangerous type of alligator is a mother guarding her nest or tending her young. Even then, she'll give you plenty of warning, by showing her teeth and hissing, before attacking.

Like alligators, Florida's snakes don't go looking for trouble, but several species will retaliate if provoked – which you're most likely to do by standing on one. Two species are potentially deadly: the coral snake, which has a black nose and bright yellow and red rings covering its body, and usually spends the daylight hours under piles of rotting vegetation; and the cottonmouth moccasin (sometimes called the water moccasin), dark-colored with a small head, which lives around rivers and lakes. Less harmful, but still worth avoiding, are two types of rattlesnake: the easily identified diamond-back, whose thick body is covered in a diamond pattern, which turns up in dry, sandy areas and hammocks; and the grey-colored pygmy, so small it's almost impossible to spot until it's too late. You're unlikely to see a snake in the wild and snake attacks are even rarer, but if bitten you should contact a ranger or a doctor immediately. It's a wise precaution to carry a snakebite kit, available for a couple of dollars from most camping shops.

For more on Florida's wildlife and its habitats, see "Natural Florida" in Contexts.

WOMEN'S FLORIDA

In the state that invented the wet T-shirt contest and which still promotes itself with photos of bikini-clad models draping themselves around palm trees, first-time visitors may be surprised to find women playing demanding and crucial roles in Florida life – in many respects a mark of the achievements of the women's movement over the past two decades. While the force of feminist politics has dissipated of late, the fact that women's bars, bookstores and support centers – while not on the scale of New York or the West Coast – are well established in the larger cities indicates a continued commitment to female self-determination.

Equally, if not more, effective in this thoroughly capitalist society, are the growing number of women's business organizations seeking ways to further female career advancement and raise (if not destroy) the "glass ceiling" – the invisible sexist barrier halting movement up the corporate ladder. In Florida, some such groups have focused recent efforts on strengthening the female presence in that traditional arena of male-bonding and off-the-record deal-making: the golf course.

Practically speaking, a woman traveling alone in Florida is not usually made to feel conspicuous, or liable to attract unwelcome attention. Outside of Miami and the seedier sections of the other major cities, much of the state can feel surprisingly safe. But as with anywhere, particular care has to be taken at night. Mugging is nowhere near the problem it is in New York, but you can't

relax totally, and should use common sense at all times: walking through unlit, empty streets is never a good idea, and if there's no bus service (and you can afford it), take cabs – if not, an escort. It's true that women who look confident tend not to encounter trouble – those who stand around looking lost and scared are prime targets.

In the major urban centers, provided you listen to advice and stick to the better parts of town, going into bars and clubs alone should pose few problems: there's generally a pretty healthy attitude towards women who do so and your privacy will be respected. Gay and lesbian bars are usually a trouble-free and welcoming alternative.

However, small towns tend not to be blessed with the same liberal or indifferent attitudes towards lone women travelers. People seem to jump immediately to the conclusion that your car has broken down, or that you've suffered some terrible tragedy; in fact, you may get fed up with well-meant offers of help. If your vehicle breaks down in a country area, walk to the nearest house or town for help; on Interstate highways or heavily traveled roads, wait in the car for a police or highway patrol car to arrive. One increasingly available option is to rent a portable telephone with your car, for a small additional charge – a potential life-saver.

Rape statistics in the US are outrageously high, and it goes without saying that you should never hitch alone – this is widely interpreted as an invitation for trouble and there's no shortage of weirdos to give it. Similarly, if you have a car, be careful who you pick up: just because you're in the driving seat doesn't mean you're safe. Avoid traveling at night by public transport – deserted bus stations, if not actually threatening, will do little to make you feel secure – and where possible you should team up with a fellow traveler. There really is security in numbers. On Greyhound buses, follow the example of other lone women and make a point of sitting as near to the front – and the driver – as possible. Should disaster strike, all major towns have some kind of rape counseling service; if not, the local sheriff's office will make adequate arrangements for you to get help, counseling and, if necessary, get you home.

Specific **women's contacts** are listed in the city sections of the Guide, but for good back-up material get hold of *Places of Interest to Women* ($7; Ferrari Publications, PO Box 35575, Phoenix, AZ; ☎602/863-2408), a guide for women traveling in the US, Canada, the Caribbean and Mexico, which is updated annually. And for more detailed country-wide info, read the annual *Index/ Directory of Women's Media* (published by the Women's Institute for the Freedom of the Press, 3306 Ross Place NW, Washington DC 20008), which lists women's publishers, bookshops, theater groups, news services and media organizations and more, throughout the country.

GAY AND LESBIAN FLORIDA

With a thousand people a day moving into the state, it's inevitable that Florida's gay and lesbian communities will grow considerably in the urban areas over the next few years, becoming ever more organized and vocal. At present, the biggest gay and lesbian scene is in Key West, at the tip of the Florida Keys and as far as it is possible to get from the rest of the state. The island town's live-and-let-live tradition has made it a holiday destination favored by American gays and lesbians for decades and many arrivals simply never went home: instead, they've taken up permanent residence and opened guesthouses, restaurants and other businesses – even running gay and lesbian snorkeling and diving trips.

Elsewhere, Miami's fast-expanding network of gay and lesbian resources, clubs and bars – if not as ubiquitous as in New York or on the West Coast – is a major indication of what's to come. There are smaller levels of activity in the other cities, and along developed sections of the coast (where the gay tourist dollar is recognized as being as good as anyone else's) a number of motels and hotels are specifically aimed at gay travelers. Predictably, attitudes to gay and lesbian visitors get progressively worse the further you go from the populous areas. Being open about your sexuality in the rural regions is likely to provoke an uneasy response if not open hostility. Still, even outside the Keys and Miami, there are active and relaxed gay scenes in Pensacola and, to a lesser extent, Tallahassee.

For a complete rundown on local resources, bars and clubs, see the relevant headings in individual cities. Of the national and statewide publications to look out for, by far the best is the free *TWN* (*The Weekly News*; ☎305/757 6333), packed with news, features and ads for Florida's gay bars and clubs. Also worth a look are *Bob Damron's Address Book* (PO Box 11270, San Francisco, CA 94101; $15), a pocket-sized yearbook of nationwide listings of hotels, bars, clubs and resources, available from any gay specialist bookshop, and *Gay Yellow Pages* (Ferrari Publications, PO Box 292, Village Station, New York, NY 100114; $8.95). Specific to Florida, the *Southern Exposure Guide* (☎305/294 6303) is informative for gay and lesbian travelers. *Wire* (☎305/ 538 3111) is good for the South Beach scene, though it is largely male oriented. Specifically lesbian publications are harder to find: the most useful is *Gaia's Guide* (132 W 24th St, New York, NY 10011; $6.95), a yearly international directory with a lot of US information.

For AIDS advice and help, try the South Beach AIDS Project (☎305/532 1033) or the AIDS Hotline (☎800/ 352 2437). In Key West, try the AIDS Help Hotline (☎305/296 6196).

DISABLED TRAVELERS

Travelers with mobility problems or other physical disabilities are likely to find Florida – as with the US generally – to be much more in tune with their needs than any other country in the world. All public buildings must be wheelchair accessible and have suitable toilets, most city street corners have dropped kerbs, and most city buses are able to "kneel" to make access easier and are built with space and handgrips for wheelchair users.

When organizing your holiday, read your travel insurance small print carefully to make sure that people with a pre-existing medical condition are not excluded. A medical certificate of your fitness to travel, provided by your doctor, is also extremely useful; some airlines or insurance companies may insist on it. Make sure that you have extra supplies of perscription drugs – carried with you if you fly – and a prescription including the generic name in case of emergency. Carry spares of any clothing or equipment that might be hard to find; if there's an association representing people with your disability, contact them early in the planning process.

Use your travel agent to make your journey simpler: airline or bus companies can cope better if they are expecting you. With at least a day's notice, domestic airlines within the US, and most transatlantic airlines, can do much to ease a disabled person's journey; wheelchairs can be provided at airports, staff primed to help,

CONTACTS FOR TRAVELERS WITH DISABILITIES

AUSTRALIA
Australian Council for Rehabilitation of the Disabled (ACROD, PO Box 60, Curtin ACT 2605 (☎06/682 4333); 55 Charles St, Ryde (☎02/9809 4488).

IRELAND
Disability Action Group, 2 Annadale Ave, Belfast BT7 3JH (☎01232/91011).
Irish Wheelchair Association, Blackheath Drive, Clontarf, Dublin 3 (☎01/833 8241). A national voluntary organization working with people with disabilities with related services for holidaymakers.

NEW ZEALAND
Disabled Persons Assembly, PO Box 10, 138 The Terrace, Wellington (☎04/472 2626).

UK
Holiday Care Service, 2nd floor, Imperial Building, Victoria Rd, Horley, Surrey RH6 9HW (☎01293/774535). Information on all aspects of travel.
RADAR, 12 City Forum, 250 City Rd, London EC1V 8AS (☎0171/250 3222); Minicom (☎0171/250 4119). A good source of advice on holidays and travel abroad.
Tripscope, The Courtyard, Evelyn Rd, London W4 5JL (☎0181/994 9294). A national telephone information service offering free transport advice.

NORTH AMERICA
Directions Unlimited, 720 N Bedford Rd, Bedford Hills, NY 10507 (☎1-800/533-5343). Tour operator specializing in custom tours for people with disabilities.
Jewish Rehabilitation Hospital, 3205 Place Alton Goldbloom, Montréal, PQ H7V 1R2 (☎514/688-9550). Guidebooks and travel information.
Mobility International USA, PO Box 10767, Eugene, OR 97440 (Voice and TDD: ☎503/343-1284). Information and referral services, access guides, tours and exchange programs. Annual membership $20 (includes quarterly newsletter).
Society for the Advancement of Travel for the Handicapped (SATH), 347 5th Ave, New York, NY 10016 (☎212/447-7284). Non-profit travel-industry referral service that passes queries on to its members as appropriate; allow plenty of time for a response.
Travel Information Service, Moss Rehabilitation Hospital, 1200 West Tabor Rd, Philadelphia, PA 19141 (☎215/456-9600). Telephone information and referral service.
Twin Peaks Press, Box 129, Vancouver, WA 98666 (☎206/694-2462 or 1-800/637-2256). Publisher of the *Directory of Travel Agencies for the Disabled* ($19.95), listing more than 370 agencies worldwide; *Travel for the Disabled* ($19.95); the *Directory of Accessible Van Rentals* ($9.95) and *Wheelchair Vagabond* ($14.95), loaded with personal tips.

and, if necessary, a helper will usually be permitted free travel.

On the ground, the major car rental firms can, given sufficient notice, provide vehicles with hand controls (though these are usually only available on the more expensive makes of vehicle); Amtrak will provide wheelchair assistance at its train stations, adapted seating on board and a 15 percent discount on the regular fare, provided they have 72 hours notice; Greyhound buses, despite the fact that they lack designated wheelchair space, will allow a necessary helper to travel free.

In the Orlando area, B.S. Mini Med specialize in assisting disabled visitors. They provide wheelchair or stretcher transportation from Orlando airport to any Orlando accommodation for $75 and trips within the area – to the Disney parks and other attractions, for example – are charged at $20 plus $2 per mile (for the disabled traveler plus up to eight companions). The company are contactable at 551 Little River Loop, Suite 213, Altamonte Springs, FL 32714 (☎407/296-3460).

Many of Florida's hotels and motels have been built recently, and disabled access has been a major consideration in their construction. Rarely will any part of the property be difficult for a disabled person to reach, and often several rooms are specifically designed to meet the requirements of disabled guests.

The state's major theme parks are also built with disabled access in mind, and attendants are always on hand to ensure that a disabled person gets all the necessary assistance and derives maximum enjoyment from their visit. Even in the Florida wilds, facilities are good: most state parks arrange programs for disabled visitors; the Apalachicola National Forest has a lakeside nature trail set aside for the exclusive use of disabled visitors and their guests; and, in the Everglades National Park, all the walking trails are wheelchair accessible, as is one of the back-country camping sites.

For further information, get the free *Florida Services Directory for Physically Challenged Travelers* from the Florida Division of Tourism (see "Information, Maps and Media" on p.19 for the address). For general information on traveling in the US, contact SATH, the Society for the Advancement of Travel for the Handicapped, 347 Fifth Avenue, Suite 610, New York, NY 10016 (☎212/447-7284).

TRAVELING WITH CHILDREN

Traveling with kids in the United States is relatively problem-free; children are readily accepted – indeed welcomed – in public places across the country and probably nowhere more so than in Florida, where visiting families have long constituted a major part of the state's mighty tourist industry.

Hotels and motels almost without exception welcome children: those in major tourist areas such as Orlando often have a games room (usually of the computer kind) and/or a play area, and allow children below a certain age (usually 14, sometimes 18) to stay free in their parents' room.

In all but the most formal restaurants, young diners are likely to be presented with a kids' menu – liberally laced with hot dogs, dinosaur burgers and ice-cream – plus crayons, drawing-pads and assorted toys.

ACTIVITIES

Most large towns have at least one child-orientated **museum** with plenty of interactive educational exhibits – often sophisticated enough to keep even adults amused for hours. Virtually all museums and other tourist attractions have reduced rates for kids under a certain age.

Florida's theme parks may seem the ultimate in kids' entertainment but in fact are much more geared towards entertaining adults than most people expect. Only Walt Disney World's Magic Kingdom is tailor-made for young kids (though even here, parents are warned that some rides may frighten the very young); adolescents (and adults) are likely to prefer Disney-MGM Studios or Universal Studios.

Away from the blockbusting tourist stops, natural Florida has much to stimulate the young. In the many state parks and in the Everglades National Park, park rangers specialize in tuning formative minds in to the wonders of nature – aided by an abundance of alligators, turtles and all manner of brightly colored birds. A boat trip in dolphin-inhabited waters – several of these are recommended in the Guide – is another likely way to stimulate curiosity in the natural world.

On a more cautious note, adults should take great care not to allow young flesh to be exposed to the Florida sun for too long: even a few minutes' unprotected exposure can cause serious sunburn.

No matter how you go, once you get there be sure to take special care in keeping track of one another – it's no less terrifying for a child to be lost at Walt Disney World than it is for him or her to go missing at the shopping mall. Whenever possible agree a meeting place before you get lost and it's not a bad idea, especially for younger children, to attach some sort of wearable ID card and for toddlers to be kept on reins.

A good idea in a major theme park is to show your child how to find (or how to recognize and ask uniformed staff to take them to) the "Lost Kids Area." This designated space not only makes lost kids easy to locate but provides supervision plus toys and games to keep them amused until you show up. Elsewhere, tell your kids to stay where they are and not to wander; if you get lost, you'll have a much easier time finding each other if you're not all running around anxiously.

GETTING AROUND

Children under two years old **fly** for free – though that doesn't mean they get a seat, a pretty major consideration on long-distance flights – and when aged from two to twelve they are usually entitled to half-price tickets.

Once you're in Florida, traveling by bus may be the cheapest way to go, but it's also the most difficult with kids. Under-2s travel (on your lap) for free; ages 2 to 4 are charged 10 percent of the adult fare, as are any toddlers who take up a seat. Children under 12 years old are charged half the standard fare.

Even if you discount the romance of the railroad, taking the train is by far the best option for long journeys – not only does everyone get to enjoy the scenery, but you can get up and walk around, relieving pent-up energy. Children's discounts are much the same as for bus or plane travel. Recreational Vehicles (RVs) are also a good option for family travel, combining the convenience of built-in kitchens and bedrooms with freedom of the road (see p.25).

Most families choose to travel by car, and while this is the least problematic mode of transport, it's worth planning ahead to assure a pleasant trip. Don't set yourself unrealistic targets if you're hoping to enjoy a driving vacation with your kids. Pack plenty of sensible snacks and drinks; plan stops every couple of hours; arrive at your destination well before sunset; and if you're passing through big cities, avoid traveling during rush hour. Also, it can be a good idea to give an older child some responsibility for route-finding – having someone "play navigator" is good fun, educational and often a real help to the driver. If you're doing a fly-drive vacation, note that car rental companies can usually provide kid's car seats for around $4 a day. You would, however, be advised to take your own, as they are not always available.

SPORTS

Florida is as fanatical about sports as the rest of the US, but what's more surprising is that collegiate sports are often, especially among lifelong Floridians, more popular than their professional counterparts. This is because Florida's professional teams are comparatively recent additions to the sporting scene and have none of the traditions and bedrock support that the state's college sides enjoy. Seventy thousand people attending an intercollege football match is no rarity. Other sports less in evidence include soccer, volleyball, greyhound racing and Jai Alai – the last two chiefly excuses for betting.

PROFESSIONAL SPORTS

BASEBALL

Until April 1993 Florida had no professional **baseball** team of its own. Now they have a world championship team. In 1997, the **Florida Marlins** became the youngest expansion team in history to win the World Series, shelling out millions of dollars to attract star-quality players. After taking the championship, the team slashed its budget, lost most of its marquee names, and is now, unfortunately, at the bottom of the baseball barrel. The Marlins play ball at Joe Robbie Stadium, 16 miles northwest of downtown Miami (box office Mon–Fri 10am–6pm; ☎305/620-25789).

Even if the local pro team is slumping, Florida has long been the home of spring training (Feb and March) for a multitude of professional ball clubs – and thousands of fans plan vacations so that they can watch their sporting heroes going through practice routines and playing in the friendly matches of the Grapefruit League. Much prestige is attached to being a spring training venue and the local community identifies strongly with the team that it hosts – in some cases the link goes back fifty years. Turn up at 10am to join the crowds watching the training (free); of the twenty-odd sides who come to train in Florida, you'll find the country's top teams at the following: the LA Dodgers, Holman Stadium, Vero Beach (☎407/569-4900); the Boston Red Sox, Chain O'Lakes Park, Winter Haven (☎813/293-3900); Detroit Tigers, Marchant Stadium, 2301 Lakeland Hills Blvd, Lakeland (☎813/682-1401); and the Minnesota Twins, Tinker Field, 287 S Tampa Ave, Orlando (☎407/849-6346).

FOOTBALL

Of the state's two professional **football** teams, the **Miami Dolphins** are easily the most successful, appearing five times in the Superbowl and, in 1972, enjoying the only all-win season in NFL history. They too play at the Joe Robbie Stadium (see above; most tickets $30). By contrast, the **Tampa Bay Buccaneers** have fared only moderately well; they're based at 4201 Dale Mabry Highway (☎813/879-BUCS; tickets $15–35).

Much greater fervor is whipped up by the University of Florida's Gators (in Gainesville) and Florida State University's Seminoles (in Tallahassee), both of whom play ten-match seasons in the Southeast Conference – although the Seminoles are planning to join the rival Atlantic Coast Conference. A poor third among the college teams in terms of support but enjoying a record-breaking undefeated home run in 1991, the University of Miami's Hurricanes play in the National College League – which they've won on several occasions. Tickets are $18–35 for professional matches; $12–18 for college games. Further details are given in the Guide.

BASKETBALL

Both the state's two professional **basketball** teams are infants and have yet to make much of a mark: the **Miami Heat** joined the National Basketball Association (NBA) in 1988, followed two years later by **Orlando Magic**. Top among the college sides are Miami University's **Hurricanes**. Tickets for professional games cost $8–26; college games $6–16. Further details are given in the Guide.

ICE HOCKEY

Florida boasts one team in the National Hockey League (NHL): the **Florida Panthers** (☎305/530-4444), who play at the Miami Arena between October and April. Details are given in the Guide.

PARTICIPANT SPORTS

WATER SPORTS

Even non-swimmers can quickly learn to **snorkel**, which is the best way to see one of the state's finest natural assets: the living coral reef that curls around its southeastern corner and along the

Florida Keys. Many **guided snorkeling trips** run to the reef, costing between $15–50 – further details are given throughout the Guide. More adventurous than snorkeling is loading up with air-cylinders to go **scuba diving**. You'll need a **Certified Divers Card** to do this; if you don't already have one you'll be required to take a course, which can last anything from one hour to a day and costs $50–100. Get details from **diving shops**, always plentiful near good diving areas, which can also provide equipment, maps and general information.

When you snorkel or dive, observing a few underwater precautions will increase enjoyment and safety: wear lightweight shoes to avoid treading on jellyfish, crabs, or sharp rocks; don't wear any shiny objects, as these are likely to attract hungry fish such as the otherwise harmless barracuda; never dive alone; always leave your boat by diving into the current – by doing this, the current will help glide you back to the boat later; always display the red and white "diver down" flag. And, obviously, never dive after drinking alcohol.

The same reefs that make snorkeling and diving so much fun cause surfing to be less common than you might expect, limiting it to a few sections of the east coast. Florida's biggest waves strike land between Sebastian Inlet and Cocoa Beach, and surfing tournaments are held here during April and May. Lesser breakers are found at Miami Beach's First Street Beach, Boca Raton's South Beach Park and around the Jacksonville Beaches. Surfboards can be rented from local beach shops for $8–10 a day.

Cutting a (usually) more gentle passage through water, many of the state's rivers can be effortlessly navigated by canoe; these can be rented for around $12–15 a day from most state parks and riverside recreational areas. Additionally, there are a number of long-distance canoe trails and several companies offering inclusive canoe trips; see "The Backcountry" (p.37) for more details.

FISHING

Few things excite higher passions in Florida than **fishing**: the numerous rivers and lakes and the various breeds of catfish, bass, carp and perch that inhabit them bring eager fishermen from all over the US and beyond. Saltwater fishing is no less popular, with barely a coastal jetty in the state not creaking under the strain of weekend anglers. The most sociable way to fish, however, is from a "**party boat**" – a boatload of people putting to sea for a day of rod-casting and boozing; these generally cost $25 and are easily found in good fishing areas. **Sportsfishing** – heading out to deep water to do battle with marlin, tuna and the odd shark – is much more expensive. In the prime sportfishing areas, off the Florida Keys and off the Panhandle around Destin, you'll need around $200 a day for a boat and a guide. To protect fish stocks, a highly complex set of **rules and regulations** governs where you can fish and what you can catch. For the latest facts, get the free *Florida Fishing Handbook* from the **Florida Game and Freshwater Fish Commission**, 620 Meridian Street, Tallahassee, FL 32399-1600 (☎850/488-1960).

FESTIVALS

Someone, somewhere is always celebrating something in Florida, though apart from national holidays, few festivities are shared throughout the region. Instead, there is a disparate multitude of local annual events: art and craft shows, county fairs, ethnic celebrations, music festivals, rodeos, sandcastle-building competitions and many others of every description. The most interesting of these are listed throughout the Guide and you can phone the visitor center in a particular region ahead of your arrival to ask what's coming up. For the main festivities in Miami and Miami Beach see p.110 and in Key West, p.135.

NATIONAL FESTIVALS

As with everywhere else in the US, the most important of the annual **national festivals and holidays** celebrated in Florida is **Independence Day** (July 4), when the entire state grinds to a standstill as people get drunk, salute the flag and partake of firework displays, marches, beauty pageants and more, all in commemoration of the signing of the Declaration of Independence in 1776. **Halloween** (October 31) has no such patriotic overtones – in fact it's not even a public holiday despite being one of the most popular yearly flings. Traditionally, kids run around the streets banging on doors demanding

"trick or treat" and get rewarded with pieces of candy; these days such activity is confined to rural areas, though you will find plenty of evidence of Halloween in cities, with waitresses liable to be disguised as witches or cats and hip city nightspots hosting everyone-dress-in-black specials. More sedate is **Thanksgiving Day** (last Thursday in November), the third big event of the year. This is essentially a domestic affair, when relatives return to the familial nest to stuff themselves with roast turkey in celebration of the first harvest of the Pilgrim Fathers and the start of the European colonization of North America.

The biggest holiday event to hit Florida is the annual Spring Break: a six-week invasion (late February through March and early April) of tens of thousands of students seeking fun in the sun before knuckling down to their summer exams. Times are changing, however: one traditional Spring Break venue, Fort Lauderdale, has successfully encouraged the students to go elsewhere; another, Daytona Beach, is planning to do likewise. Panama City Beach, though, welcomes the carousing collegiates with open arms and Key West – despite its lack of beach – is fast becoming a favorite Spring Break location. If you are in Florida during this time, it'll be hard to avoid some signs of Spring Break – a mob of scantily clad drunken students is a tell-tale sign – and at the busier coastal areas you may well find accommodation costing three times the normal price; be sure to plan ahead.

PUBLIC HOLIDAYS

On both Independence Day and Thanksgiving Day, shops, banks and offices will be closed for the day, as they will on most of the **other public holidays**: New Year's Day; Martin Luther King's Birthday (January 15); President's Day (third Monday in February); Memorial Day (last Monday in May); Labor Day (first Monday in September); Columbus Day (second Monday in October); Veteran's Day (November 11); and Christmas Day. Good Friday is a half-day holiday, though Easter Monday is a full-day holiday.

STAYING ON

Far from being the land of the "newly wed and the nearly dead" as many comedians have described the state, Florida's immaculate climate has persuaded people from all over the US and the rest of the world to arrive in search of a subtropical paradise. The following suggestions for finding work are basic and, if you're not a US citizen, represent the limits of what you can do without the all-important Social Security number (without which legally you can't work at all).

FINDING WORK

Since the federal government introduced fines of up to $10,000 for illegal employees, employers have become understandably choosy about whom they hire. Even the usual **casual jobs** – catering, restaurant and bar work – have tightened up for those without a **Social Security number**. If you do find work it's likely to be of the less visible, poorly paid kind – as washer-upper rather than waiter. **Agricultural work** is always available on Central Florida farms during the October to May citrus harvest; check with the nearest university or college, where noticeboards detail what's available. There are usually no problems with papers in this kind of work, though it often entails working miles from major centers and is wearying "stoop" (continually bending over) labor in blistering heat. If you can stick it out, the pay is often good and comes with basic board and accommodation.

House-cleaning and baby-sitting are also feasible, if not very well-paid options.

FINDING A PLACE TO LIVE

Apartment hunting in Florida is not the nightmare it is in, say, New York: accommodation is plentiful and not always expensive, although the absence of housing associations and co-ops means that there is very little really inexpensive accommodation anywhere except in country areas. Accommodation is almost always rented unfurnished so you'll have to buy furniture; in general, expect to pay $500–600 a month for a studio or one-bedroom apartment, $900–1200 per month for 2–3 bedrooms in Miami, Tampa or Orlando, a lot less in rural areas. Most landlords will expect one month's rent as a deposit, plus one month's rent in advance.

There is no statewide organization for accommodation so you'll have to check out the options in each place. By far the best way to find somewhere is to ask around – often short-term lets come up via word of mouth. Otherwise, rooms for rent are often advertised in the windows of houses and local papers have "Apartments For Rent" sections. In Miami, the best source is *New Times*, although you should also scan the *Miami Herald* classifieds. In Tampa and Orlando check out the *Tampa Tribune* and *Orlando Sentinel* respectively.

OPPORTUNITIES FOR FOREIGN STUDENTS

Foreign students wishing to study in Florida can either try the long shot of arranging a year abroad through their own university, or apply directly to a Florida university (being prepared to stump up the painfully expensive fees)

The Student Exchange Visitor Program, for which participants are given a J-1 visa enabling them to take a job arranged in advance through the program, is not much use since almost all the jobs are at American summer camps – of which the state has none. If you're interested anyway, organizations to contact in the UK include BUNAC (16 Bowling Green Lane, London EC1R OBD; ☎0171/251 3472) or Camp America (37 Queen's Gate, London SW7 5HR; ☎0171/581 7373).

DIRECTORY

ADDRESSES Though foreign visitors can find them confusing at first, American addresses are masterpieces of logic. Generally speaking, roads in built-up areas are laid out to a grid system, creating "blocks": addresses of buildings refer to the block, which will be numbered in sequence from a central point usually somewhere downtown; for example, 620 S Cedar will be six blocks south of this downtown point. In small towns and parts of larger cities, "streets" and "avenues" often run north–south and east–west respectively; streets are usually named (sometimes alphabetically), avenues generally numbered.

CIGARETTES AND SMOKING Smoking is now severely frowned upon in the US, though no government measures have been taken against tobacco advertising. It's possible to spend a month in Florida without ever smelling tobacco; most cinemas are non-smoking, restaurants are usually divided into non-smoking and smoking sections, and smoking is universally forbidden on public transport – including almost all domestic airline flights. Work places, too, tend to be smoke-free zones, so employees are reduced to smoking on the street outside. Cigarettes are, however, still widely sold. A packet of twenty costs around $1.95, though most smokers buy cigarettes by the carton for around $12.

DATES In the American style, the date 6.9.94 means not September 6 but June 9.

DEPARTURE TAX None: airport tax is included in the price of your ticket.

DONATIONS Many museums request donations rather than an admission fee; usually you'll be expected to put $2 or so into the collection as you enter. If you don't, you won't be turned away but will suffer the indignity of being considered a complete cheapskate.

DRUGS Despite the widely accepted fact that much of the marijuana and cocaine consumed in the US arrives through Florida, the state's laws regarding possession of drugs are among the toughest in the country. Recreational drug use is by no means unheard of, but many people, even in the cities, view any kind of drug-taking as an attempt to turn the country over to Satan. Bluntly put, it isn't worth the risk of being caught in possession of any illegal substance in any quantity whatsoever.

ELECTRICITY 110V AC. All plugs are two-pronged and rather insubstantial. Some travel plug adapters don't fit American sockets. British-made equipment won't work unless it has a voltage switching provision.

FLEA MARKETS Beside almost any major road junction, you'll find something touting itself as "Florida's Biggest Fleamarket." The genuinely big ones usually take place on Fridays and weekends, with hundreds of booths selling furniture, household appliances, ornaments, clothes – often hideous and always cheap.

FLOORS The *first* floor in the US is what would be the ground floor in Britain; the *second* floor would be the first floor, and so on.

ID Should be carried at all times. Two pieces should suffice, one of which should have a photo: a passport and credit card(s) are your best bets.

HURRICANES Despite the much publicized onslaught of Hurricane Andrew in August 1992, statistically it's highly improbable that a hurricane will hit during your visit, and even if it does there will be plenty of warning – accurate tracking of potential hurricanes brewing around the Gulf of Mexico and the Caribbean from June to November (regarded as the hurricane season) being a feature of every TV weather bulletin. Local services are well equipped, most buildings are (supposedly) hurricane-proof, evacuation routes are signposted, and even phone books carry tips on how to survive – and since Andrew, and Donna in 1996, Floridians have become much less blasé in their attitude to hurricanes. A more likely source of danger are thunderstorms; see below.

LAUNDROMATS All but the most basic hotels will wash laundry for you, but it'll be a lot cheaper (about $1.50) for a wash and tumble dry in a laundromat – found all over, including many hotels, motels and campgrounds. Take plenty of quarters.

LOTTERY Every few weeks, the state goes potty over the drawing of the winning six-sequence number in the Florida Lottery. Along with millions of others, you can buy as many tickets as you can afford (at a dollar a time) from any shop displaying the lottery sign. The prize sometimes reaches $17 million.

MEASUREMENTS AND SIZES The US has yet to go metric, so measurements are in inches, feet, yards and miles; weight in ounces, pounds and tons. Liquid measurements differ, too: American pints and gallons are about four-fifths of British ones. US clothing sizes can be calculated by subtracting two from British sizes; thus, a British women's size 12 is a US size 10. Shoe sizes are one and a half more than the equivalent British size.

PUBLIC TOILETS Don't exist as such in the city. Bars, restaurants and fast-food outlets are the places to go, though technically you should be a customer.

TAX Be warned that 6 percent sales tax is added to virtually everything you buy in a shop, and is not included in the marked price.

THUNDERSTORMS Subtropical southern Florida has frequent, very localized thunderstorms throughout the summer. Obviously, if possible you should shelter inside a building to avoid being struck by lightning (which, on average, kills eleven people a year). If you're caught in the open, stay away from metallic objects and don't make a dash for your car – most people who are struck are doing this. On the plus side, the air after a storm is refreshingly free of humidity.

TICKETS For music, theater and sports, use Ticketmaster, whose plentiful offices are listed in the phone book and through whom you can buy tickets over the phone with your credit card.

TIME Most of Florida runs on Eastern Standard Time, five hours behind GMT in winter. The

FLORIDA TERMS

Barrier Island A long, narrow island of the kind protecting much of Florida's mainland from coastal erosion, comprising sandy beach and mangrove forest – often blighted by condos (see below).

Condo Short for "condominium", a tall and usually ugly block of (normally) expensive flats, common along the coast and in fashionable areas of cities. Many are rented out for holidays or owned as timeshares.

Cracker Nickname given to Florida farmers from the 1800s, stemming from the sound made by the whip used in cattle round-ups (or possibly from the cracking of corn to make grits). These days it's also a common term for the state's conservative ruralites: surly, insular types who prefer the company of wild hogs to people they don't already know.

Crackerbox Colloquial architectural term for the simple wooden cottage lived in by early Crackers (see above), ingeniously designed to allow the lightest breeze to cool the whole dwelling.

Florida Ice Potentially hazardous mix of oil and water on a road surface following a thunderstorm.

Hammocks Not open-air sleeping places but patches of trees. In the south, and especially in the Everglades, hammocks often appear as "tree islands" above the flat wetlands. In the north, hammocks are larger and occur on elevations between wetlands and pinewoods. All hammocks make excellent wildlife habitats and those in the south are composed of tropical trees rarely seen elsewhere in the US.

Intracoastal Waterway To strengthen coastal defences during World War II, the natural waterways dividing the mainland from the barrier islands (see above) were deepened and extended. The full length, along the east and southwest coasts, is termed the "Intracoastal Waterway".

Key Derived from the word "cay" – literally an island or bank composed of coral fragments.

No see'ems Tiny, mosquito-like insects; near-impossible to spot until they've already bitten you.

Snowbird Term applied to a visitor from the northern US coming to Florida during the winter to escape sub-zero temperatures – usually recognized by their sunburn.

section of the Panhandle west of the Apalachicola River, however, is on Central Standard Time – one hour behind the rest of Florida. British Summer Time runs almost parallel to US Daylight Saving Time – implemented from the last Sunday in April to the last Sunday in October – causing a four-hour time gap for two weeks of the year.

TIPPING You really shouldn't depart a bar or restaurant without leaving a tip of *at least* 15 percent (unless the service is utterly disgusting): it causes a lot of embarrassment and nasty looks and a short paypacket for the waiter/waitress at the end of the week. About the same amount should be added to taxi fares – and round them up to the nearest 50¢ or dollar. A hotel porter should get roughly $1 per item for carrying your baggage to your room. When paying by credit or charge card, you're expected to add the tip to the total bill before filling in the amount and signing.

VIDEOS The standard format used for video cassettes in the US is different from that used in Britain. You cannot buy videos in the US compatible with a video camera bought in Britain.

PART TWO

THE

GUIDE

CHAPTER ONE

MIAMI AND MIAMI BEACH

You tell people you're from Miami and they duck.

Carl Hiaasen.

Far and away the most exciting city in Florida, **Miami** is a stunning and often intoxicatingly beautiful place. Set beside the cool blue waters of Biscayne Bay, with its roads lined by lush tropical foliage, the state's major urban center is awash with sunlight-intensified natural colors and a delicious scent of jasmine. An emergent city with a sharp, contemporary style (and some horrific social problems), there are moments, such as when the downtown skyline glows in the warm night and the beachside palm trees sway in the evening breeze, when a better-looking city is hard to imagine.

The climate and landscape may be near perfect, but it's the people that make Miami unique. In the antithesis of the traditional Anglo-American-dominated US metropolis, half of Miami's two million population is Hispanic, of which the majority are Cubans. They form easily the most visible – and powerful – ethnic group in a city that's home to dozens from all over Latin America and the Caribbean. Spanish is the main language in most areas, and news from Havana, Caracas or Bogota frequently gets more attention than the latest word from Washington. The city is no melting pot, however. Ethnic divisions and tensions are often all too evident. Since the black ghettos first erupted in the Sixties, violent expressions of rage – most recently among Haitians and Puerto Ricans – have been a regular feature of Miami life.

Some sections are still extremely dangerous, but Miami has cleaned itself up considerably since 1980, when it had the highest murder rate in the country. It has also grown rich as a key gateway for US-Latin American trade, to which a glut of expensively designed banks and financial institutions bears witness. Strangely enough, another factor in Miami's revival was the mid-Eighties cop show *Miami Vice*, which was less about crime than designer clothes and subtropical scenery; its featuring of Miami Beach's **Art Deco** district made this a popular location for fashion shoots.

Miami has very little history to look back on. A century ago it was a swampy outpost where a thousand mosquito-tormented settlers commuted by boat around a trading post and a couple of coconut plantations. The arrival of the railroad in 1896 gave Miami its first fixed land link with the rest of the continent, and literally cleared the way for the Twenties property boom, which saw entire communities appearing almost overnight, forming the basis of the modern city.

The Fifties saw **Miami Beach** establishing itself as a celebrity-filled resort area, while at the same time – and with much less fanfare – thousands of Cubans fleeing the successive regimes of Batista and Castro began arriving on mainland Miami. The Sixties and Seventies brought decline, as Miami Beach's celebrity cachet waned and it became a haven for retirees; and the city's tourist industry was damaged still further by the Liberty City riot of 1980, which marked a low point in Miami's black-white relations.

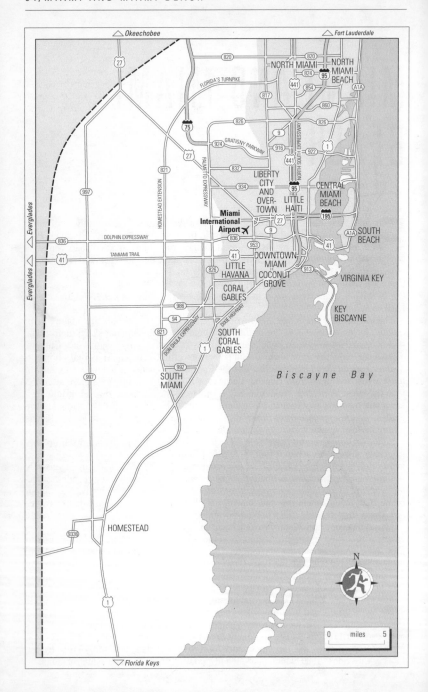

The area code for Miami and Miami Beach is ☎305.

Since then, with the strengthening of Latin American economic links and a younger, more cosmopolitan breed of visitor energizing Miami Beach, the city is enjoying a surge of optimism and affluence – and, as Hispanic immigration into the US drastically alters the demography of the nation, today's Miami could well be a preview of tomorrow's US.

Arrival and information

However and whenever you arrive in Miami, grasping initial bearings will not be difficult. All points of entry are within a few miles of the center, and public transport links are generally reliable. Numerous offices around the city dispense general tourist information and advice.

By air

All passenger **flights** land at Miami International Airport (☎876-7000), a chaotic complex six miles west of downtown Miami. Once through the gate, it's a simple matter to get across the city.

Some of the main **car rental** firms (see "Driving and car rental," p.23) have desks close to the baggage reclaim area and provide free transport to collect a vehicle. Otherwise, you have to grab your luggage, leave the terminal and flag down a bus belonging to your rental company. If you're arriving in Miami after dark, especially after a long flight, consider spending your first night at an airport hotel; the rental parking lots are located in a none-too-safe area, and it can be confusing for first-time visitors to make their way onto the city- or beach-bound highways. **Local buses** depart from several points beside the airport's concourse; take #7 (every 40min; Mon–Fri 5.30am–8.30pm, Sat & Sun 7am–7pm) to downtown Miami (half an hour away), or the "J" bus (every 30min; daily 5.30am–11.30pm) for the slightly longer journey to Miami Beach. "City Bus and Tri-Rail Shuttle" signs opposite the airport's "E" departure gates indicate the bus stop. A short cab ride from the airport will deliver you to the Miami West Greyhound station, with links to other parts of Miami (see below) and beyond.

Quicker, if more expensive than public transport, the **Airporter, SuperShuttle** and **Red Top** minivans (grandly calling themselves "limos") run around the clock and will deliver you to any address in or around Miami for $8–15. Their representatives are easy to spot as you leave the baggage reclaim area. **Taxis** are in plentiful supply outside the airport building; fares are metered and cost around $15 to downtown Miami, $20 to Miami Beach.

By bus

Of several **Greyhound** (☎1/800-231-2222) stations in Miami, the busiest is **Miami West**, near the airport, at 4111 NW 27th Street (☎871-1810). Most Greyhound buses, however, including those to and from Key West, also stop at the **Downtown** station, 700 Biscayne Boulevard (☎379-7403). Fewer services use the city's other Greyhound stations: in **Homestead**, 5 NE Third Avenue (☎247-2040); in **Central Miami Beach**, 7101 Harding Avenue (☎538-0381); and in **North Miami Beach**, 16250 Biscayne Boulevard (☎945-0801). Local bus services are detailed on p.59.

By train and Tri-Rail

The **train** station, 8303 NW 37th Avenue (☎1-800/872-7245), is seven miles northwest of downtown Miami, with an adjacent **Metrorail** stop that provides access to downtown

Miami and beyond; bus #L stops here on its way to Central Miami Beach. The **Tri-Rail** (☎1-800/TRI-RAIL), the cheap commuter service running between Miami and West Palm Beach (see Basics), links directly with the Metrorail at 1149 E 21st Street, also seven miles northwest of downtown Miami. Fares range from $3.50–$9.25. For more information on the Metrorail, see p.58.

By car

Most of the major **roads** into Miami take the form of elevated expressways which – accidents and rush hours permitting – make getting into the city simple and quick, if potentially hair-raising. From the north, **I-95** (also called the **North South Expressway**) streaks over the downtown streets before joining **Hwy-1**, an ordinary road that continues through South Miami. Crossing the Everglades from the west coast, **Hwy-41** (also called the **Tamiami Trail**) enters Miami along SW Eighth Street, and you'll save time by turning off north along the **Florida Turnpike** (coming from the north and skirting the city's western periphery) to reach the **Dolphin Expressway** (**Hwy-836**), which meets I-95 just south of downtown Miami. **Hwy-27**, the main artery from central Florida, becomes the **Robert Frost Expressway** close to the airport and intersects with I-95 just north of the downtown area. The slower, scenic coastal route, **Hwy-A1A**, enters the city at the northern tip of Miami Beach.

Information

Although Miami has no single office devoted to providing tourist **information**, several useful outlets for leaflets, free tourist magazines and general practical advice are dotted around the city. In **downtown Miami**, outside Bayside Marketplace, an information stand is open from 11.30am–8pm; at Miami Beach, the Miami Beach Chamber of Commerce, 1920 Meridian Avenue (Mon–Fri 9am–6pm, Sat & Sun 10am–4pm; ☎672-1270), is a good stop, with a kiosk located at the intersection of Lincoln Road Mall and Washington Avenue (Mon–Fri 9.30am–4pm). Also at **Miami Beach** is the Art Deco Welcome Center, 1001 Ocean Drive, which provides information on South Beach's historic Art Deco district and organizes tours (daily 9am–5pm; ☎672-2014). Useful **Chambers of Commerce** in other districts are detailed throughout the Guide. If you're spending time in **Homestead**, or just passing through, be sure to stop at the area's excellent Visitor Information Center, 160 Hwy-1 (daily 8am–6pm; ☎1-800/388-9669).

Most of the free **maps** are useful for only very basic route finding; it's worth spending $2.50 on the street-indexed *Trakker* map of Miami, available from most newsstands and many shops.

The Friday issue of Miami's only daily **newspaper**, the reputable *Miami Herald* (weekdays 35¢; Sunday edition $1) – which includes the Spanish supplement *El Nuevo Herald* – carries comprehensive weekend entertainment listings.

Getting around

While designed for the car, Miami is a city that's easily navigated and it boasts a comprehensive public transit system that provides a sound alternative for daytime travel.

Driving and car rental

Driving around Miami is practical and a piece of cake, especially once you've got the hang of the one-way street grid system. Traffic in and out of Miami can be heavy, but the city's **expressways** (see "Arrival," above) will carry you swiftly from one area to another. Before setting off on any journey, plan your route carefully so as not to stray accidentally into an unsavory area, and if you do get lost, ask for directions at a gas station. Use ordinary streets and avenues for short journeys only, as they're often clogged

MIAMI MEDIA

Publications

The following are free magazines and newspapers that provide entertainment information about the Greater Miami area. All can be picked up at tourist information centers, street machines or hotels:

Art Deco Tropical ☎534-3884.

Entertainment News & Views ☎576-8566.

El Nuevo Herald ☎376-3535.

Fashion Spectrum ☎534-0084. Glossy fashion magazine.

New Times ☎372-0004. Weekly listings.

Ocean Drive Magazine ☎532-2544. Glossy fashion magazine.

Miami Metro Magazine ☎445-4500. Glossy magazine with local listings.

Sun Post ☎538-9700. Politics and current events newspaper with an insert, "Hype," about the club scene.

Sun Sentinel ☎954/356-4500.

TravelHost ☎866-5850.

Tropical Tribune ☎868-9118.

TWN The Weekly News ☎757-6333. Gay and lesbian newspaper.

TV stations

6 WTVJ NBC

4 WFOR CBS

7 WSVN FOX

10 WPLG ABC

2 WPBT and 17 WLRN PBS

23 WLTV Spanish-language independent (Univision)

33 WBFS Independent (UPN)

34 MDTV Metro Dade TV

Radio stations

WIOD 610 AM. All-talk: phone-ins, entertainment, sports, news.

WINZ 940 AM. All-news format with magazine shows, sports reports, weather and entertainment.

WVUM 90.5 FM. University radio dominated by British indie rock.

WLRN 91.3 FM. In-depth news coverage from National Public Radio (NPR), with educational, political and arts programing.

WTMI 93.1 FM. Classical music by day, jazz after midnight.

WLVE 93.9 FM. Pop, jazz and rock.

WZTA 94.9 FM. Classic Sixties rock.

WFLC 97.3 FM. Adult contemporary rock.

WEDR 99.1 FM. Soul music, with rap and disco.

WMXJ 102.7 FM. Light Oldies.

WHQT 105.1 FM. Black dance music.

WQBA 107.5.FM Spanish contemporary.

WKIS 99.9. FM Country music.

WXDJ 95.7. FM Salsa and merengue.

WPOW 96.5 FM Dance/house music.

by local traffic and may have confusing one-way systems. **Rush hour** (7–9am and 4–6pm) should also be avoided. Driving between Miami and Miami Beach is straightforward using one of six causeways; each well marked and quickly accessed from the main arteries.

There is plenty of provision for **street parking** in Miami, though actually finding an empty space can prove difficult, particularly at night in Coconut Grove and the South Beach. Parking meters are everywhere and usually require 50¢ per half-hour; save every quarter you get, as you'll need vast quantities. Parking at public **parks and beaches** normally costs $2 per day; **parking lots** generally charge $3 an hour, $10 per day. Those in the downtown shopping district charge exorbitant rates, and if you must park in the city, aim for the tiny, reasonably priced parking lot situated across from the Gesu Church (on NE 1st Ave between 2nd and 3rd; $6/day). With the exception of Bayside Marketplace, shopping mall parking lots seldom charge, but may have a two-hour time limit.

Most of the major **car rental** companies have booking desks at the airport and provide free transportation from the terminals to their offices, where your car will be waiting: Alamo, 3355 NW 22nd Street (☎1-800/327-9633); Avis, 2330 NW 37th Street (☎1-800/331-1212); Budget, 3901 NW 38th Street (☎1-800/527-0700); Hertz, 3755 NW 21st Street (☎1-800/654-3131); and Thrifty, 2701 Le Jeune Road (☎1-800/367-2277). Each charges around $25 a day, $150 a week. To rent a car in another part of the city, call and ask for the nearest branch office or look in the phone book. Depending on the fine print, smaller firms can be cheaper. With any company, be wary if you are under 25. Most agencies charge an outrageous underage fee ($25 per day) in addition to the rental fee. Call ahead.

Public transport

An integrated **public transport** network of buses, trains and a monorail run by Metro-Dade Transit covers Miami, making the city easy – if time-consuming – to get around by day. Night travel is much harder, especially in South Beach.

Bus routes cover the entire city, most radiating out from downtown Miami, and run from 4am–2.30am daily. The flat-rate one-way **bus fare** is $1.25, payable on board by dropping the exact amount in change (no notes) into a machine beside the driver. If you need to transfer to another bus, say so when you get on; the driver will give you a free **transfer** ticket, which you hand over to the driver of the next bus. Transfer tickets are route- and time-stamped to prevent you lingering too long between connections or taking a scenic detour (if you do so, you'll be charged the full fare again).

Considerably quicker is the **Metrorail**, a single, elevated railroad that links the northern suburbs with South Miami; trains run every five to fifteen minutes between 5.30am and midnight. Useful stops are Government Center (for the downtown area), Vizcaya, Coconut Grove and Douglas Road or University (for Coral Gables). Stations do, however, tend to be awkwardly situated, and you'll often need to use Metrorail services in conjunction with a bus. One-way **Metrorail fares** are $1.25; buy a token from the machines (insert five quarters) at the station and use it to get through the turnstile. **Transfers between buses and Metrorail** cost 25¢ from the bus driver or a Metrorail station transfer machine.

MIAMI ADDRESSES AND ORIENTATION

Miami's street **naming and numbering system** takes some getting used to. The city splits into quadrants, divided by Flagler Street and Miami Avenue (which intersect downtown). "**Streets**" run east-west and "**avenues**" north-south, their numbers getting higher the further you go from downtown Miami. "**Roads**" are less common and run northwest southeast. Streets and avenues change their compass-point prefix when crossing into a new quadrant. For example, SE First Street becomes SW First Street after crossing Miami Avenue, and NW Second Avenue becomes SW Second Avenue after crossing Flagler Street.

In some areas the pattern varies, most obviously in Coral Gables, where streets have names instead of numbers, and avenues are numbered in sequence from Douglas Avenue.

MAJOR MIAMI BUS ROUTES

From downtown Miami to:

Coconut Grove #48.
Coral Gables #24.
Little Havana #8.
Key Biscayne #B.

Miami Beach #C, #K, or #S (along Alton Rd).
Miami International Airport #7.

Greyhound within Miami, from downtown Miami to:

Homestead (3 daily; 1hr 15min)
Miami Beach (18 daily; 25-45min)

Miami West (18 daily; 15-45min)
North Miami Beach (18 daily; 20-45min)

Downtown Miami is ringed by the **Metromover** (sometimes called the "People Mover"), a monorail loop (6am–midnight) that doesn't cover much ground but gives a bird's-eye view of downtown Miami. The flat fare is 25¢, payable into the machines at the stations. Transfers to Metromover from Metrorail are free; to transfer from Metromover to Metrorail, insert $1 in coins into the turnstile between the respective platforms.

The best way to get around South Beach is via the **Electrowave** – a free, air-conditioned shuttle that runs solely on electricity. The shuttle runs north-south on Washington Avenue, between Seventeenth Street and Fifth Street (Mon–Wed 8am–2am, Thur–Sat 8am–4am, Sun & Holidays 10am–2am; ☎843-9283).

Over **long stays** involving regular public transport use, it's economical to buy a **Metropass**, which gives unlimited rides on all services for a calendar month. The Metropass costs $60 from any shop displaying the Metro-Dade Transit sign, and is on sale from the 20th of each month.

For **information** and **free route maps and timetables**, go to the Transit Service Center (Mon–Fri 7am–6pm) inside the Metro-Dade Center in downtown Miami, or phone ☎770-3131 (Mon–Fri 6am–10pm, Sat & Sun 9am–5pm). Individual route maps and timetables can usually be found on buses.

Besides the official services, **privately run minibuses** (known as "Jitneys") link busy areas for a flat fare of $1. They generally pull up at regular bus stops, but can be waved down practically anywhere. Look for their destination boards on the front. Note that such buses are unregulated and are rarely insured to carry passengers – you travel on them very much at your own risk.

Taxis

Taxis are abundant and often the only way to get around at night without a car. **Fares** average out at $1.80 per mile, hence the trip between the airport and Miami Beach – easily the longest journey you're likely to make – costs around $24; from downtown Miami you'll pay around $11 to Coconut Grove and $15 to Miami Beach. An empty cab will stop if the driver sees you waving, but it's more common to phone: Central Cab (☎532-5555), Metro Taxi (☎888-8888), Yellow (☎444-4444) and Flamingo Taxi (☎885-7000) are all fairly reliable.

Water taxis

If you're in no great hurry, one of the most pleasant ways to get around the city is by **water taxi** (☎954/467-0008). Two routes link to provide an extensive network that stretches from central Miami Beach in the north to Coconut Grove in the south. The **Shuttle Service** (daily 11am–11pm every 15–20min; $3.50 one-way, $6 round-trip, $7.50 all-day pass) runs from the Omni International Mall (north of the Venetian Causeway) to points along the

Miami River (ideal for eating out at the numerous riverside fish restaurants). At Bayside Marketplace you can transfer to the **Beach Service** ($7 one-way, $12 round-trip, $15 all-day pass), with mooring points on the west shore of Miami Beach, Virginia Key (the Seaquarium), Key Biscayne (Crandon Park), Vizcaya and Coconut Grove.

Cycling

Although you won't be able to see all of Miami by **cycling**, Coral Gables and Key Biscayne are perfectly suited to pedal-powered exploration, and there's a fourteen-mile cycle path through Coconut Grove and into South Miami. For details, get hold of the free leaflet *Miami on Two Wheels* from the Greater Miami Convention and Visitors' Bureau, 701 Brickell Ave, Suite 2700 (☎539-3063).

You can **rent a bike** for $12–25 per day from several outlets: in Coconut Grove, Dade Cycle Shop, 3216 Grand Avenue (☎443-6075); or in Key Biscayne, Mangrove Cycles, 260 Crandon Boulevard (☎361-5555). For cruising around Miami Beach, you can beat exorbitant hotel bike-rental charges by going to the Bike Shop, 923 W 39th Street ($5/hr, $20/day; ☎531-4161), or to Cycles on the Beach, 713 Fifth Street (☎673-2055). Miami Beach Bicycle Center, 601 5th St (☎674-0150) arranges guided bicycle tours of the Art Deco district; trips leave on the first and third Sundays of the month and cost $10 for the tour plus $5 for the bike – phone ahead to reserve your place.

Walking tours and rollerblading

Miamians consider **walking** anywhere a bizarre concept, but some of the city's more enjoyable areas are compact enough to cover on foot – though too far apart to walk between. For an informed and entertaining stroll, take one of **Dr Paul George's Walking Tours** (☎375-1625), which are offered in conjunction with the Historical Museum of Southern Florida and look at a number of areas, including downtown Miami, Coconut Grove, Coral Gables, Little Havana, South Beach and the Miami Cemetery. There are 25 different itineraries, and walks last two to three hours and cost $15.

Elsewhere, you shouldn't miss the ninety-minute **Art Deco Walking Tour** of South Miami Beach. A perfect introduction to the area's phenomenal architecture, the tour begins each Saturday at 10.30am and Thursday at 6.30pm from the Art Deco Welcome Center, 1001 Ocean Drive (☎672-2014), and costs $10.

A speedier means of getting around is **rollerblading** or in-line skating, particularly popular in South Beach; see "Listings" for rental (or sales) details.

Bus, boat and helicopter tours

Scores of travel companies run **guided bus tours** around Miami's obvious points of tourist interest, but most are overpriced ($25–40 for a day) and only mildly instructive. Some of the best vehicular tours are operated by the same folks that lead Dr Paul George's Walking Tours (see above); boat ($25), bus ($30) and bike ($15) tours of Miami are available Sept–June. Leaflets for these and other tours are available from any hotel or Chamber of Commerce.

If you prefer water to dry land – and the downtown skyline is undoubtedly most striking from across the water – several small craft moored along the jetty at the Bayside Marketplace offer **boat tours** around Biscayne Bay; check the posted departure times and prices (usually $22 per person for an hour) to find the best deal. One of the longest established is Blackbeard Cruises (☎888-3002), whose ninety-minute trips depart daily at 1pm, 3pm, 5pm, 7pm and 9pm. Other cruises include: Sea Kruz, 300 Alton Rd, Miami Beach Marina (☎538-8300), which has 4–5hr day (1.30pm) and evening (7.30pm) cruises with casino gambling and live music; and Island Queen, Bayside Marketplace (☎379-5119), has an awesome, high-speed boat called the *Bayside Blaster* that zooms up the Government Cut waterway on the weekends.

Accommodation

Finding a place to stay in Miami is only a problem over New Year and important holiday weekends such as Memorial Day and Labor Day. It's small enough that you can stay just about anywhere and not feel isolated, though the lion's share of **hotels** and **motels** are on **Miami Beach**: an ideal base for nightlife, beachlife and seeing the city. Prices vary from $20 to $300, but you can anticipate spending $40–75 during the summer, and $60–100 during the winter (or upwards of $100 per night in the ultra-chic South Beach hotels). **Budget accommodation** is restricted to two **youth hostels** and a fabulous **hostel/hotel** in Miami Beach, and a **campground** miles out in the city's southwest fringe.

Away from Miami Beach, choice is reduced and costs increase. **Downtown Miami** – interesting by day but dull at night – has few affordable rivals to its expense-account chain hotels; distinctive character and architecture make **Coral Gables** appealing, but its rooms are seldom cheap; the stylish high-rise hotels of **Coconut Grove** are a jet-setters' preserve; and in **Key Biscayne** you'll need $100 a night for the plainest ocean-side room. Only in **South Miami**, unremarkable in itself but a feasible base if you're driving, will you find a good assortment of no-frills motels for $40–60 a night. The **airport** area hotels, with just one bargain among them, should only be considered if you're catching a plane at an unearthly hour or arriving late and want to avoid driving into Miami after dark.

During the winter you'd be well advised to **reserve ahead**, either directly or through a travel agent. Between May and November, however, you'll save by going for the best deals on the spot (though you may want to arrange your first night in advance). Don't be afraid to **bargain**, as this can result in a few dollars being lopped off the advertised rate. **Single** rooms are rarely cheaper than **doubles**, and the few exceptions are indicated in "Listings." Prices below are for the winter season; all will be lower during the summer.

Hotels and motels

Downtown Miami

Hampton Inn-Downtown, 2500 Brickell Ave (☎1-800/HAMPTON). A generic but perfectly adequate chain motel, a mile from the center of downtown Miami. ⑤.

Howard Johnson, 110 Biscayne Blvd (☎1-800/654-2000). Very standard chain hotel but the lowest-priced rooms this close to the heart of downtown Miami. ⑤.

Inter-Continental Miami, 100 Chopin Plaza (☎1-800/327-0200). Wicker chairs and a Henry Moore sculpture improve the atmosphere of this multinational chain hotel. Very classy and comfortable. ⑦–⑧.

Best Western Marina Park, 340 Biscayne Blvd (☎1-800/528-1234). A bland exterior shields a personable interior, with views across the Port of Miami and the neighboring parks. ⑥–⑦.

ACCOMMODATION PRICE CODES

All **accommodation prices** in this book have been coded using the symbols below. Note that prices are for the least expensive double rooms in each establishment. For a full explanation see p.27 in Basics.

① up to $30	③ $45-60	⑤ $80-100	⑦ $130-180
② $30-45	④ $60-80	⑥ $100-130	⑧ $180+

Miami River Inn, 118 SW South River Drive (☎325-0045). Most of the buildings making up the inn date to 1908 and provide comfortable accommodation in a unique environment a short walk across the Miami River from the center of town or the Brickell banking district. Rooms have stunning views either of the city or the inn's garden and pool. ④.

Omni International, 1601 Biscayne Blvd (☎1-800/843-6664). Just another hotel catering to wealthy business types. If you can't afford a room, take a peek at the glamorous lobby and subterranean shopping mall. ⑦–⑧.

Coconut Grove

Doubletree at Coconut Grove, 2649 S Bayshore Drive (☎1-800/528-0444). Elegant high-rise with cozy rooms and great views, just a quarter of an hour's walk from the area's cafés and bars. ⑥–⑧.

Grand Bay, 2669 S Bayshore Drive (☎1-800/327-2788) Expense-account elegance all the way. ⑧.

Mayfair House, 3000 Florida Ave (☎1-800/341-0809). Luxury all-suite hotel, complete with rooftop swimming pool. ⑧.

Coral Gables

Biltmore, 1200 Anastasia Ave (☎1-800/727-1926). A landmark, Mediterranean-style hotel that has endured mixed fortunes since it began pampering the rich and famous in 1926. Show up to pace the echoey corridors and sink into the lobby armchairs, even if you can't afford to stay here. ⑦–⑧.

Omni Colonnade, 180 Aragon Ave (☎1-800/533-1337). Marble floors, oriental rugs and brass lamps fill this showpiece of Mediterranean Revival architecture. ⑦–⑧.

Gables Inn, 730 S Dixie Hwy (☎661-7999). Basic but clean and the least expensive in the area. ③.

Place St Michel, 162 Alcazar Ave (☎444-1666). Small, romantic hotel just off the Miracle Mile, with Laura Ashley decor and copious European antiques. Rate includes continental breakfast. ⑤–⑦.

Riviera Courts, 5100 Riviera Drive (☎1-800/368-8602). Simple, homely motel equipped with a pool, close to the University of Miami and Miracle Mile. ③–④.

Key Biscayne

Sheraton Royal, 555 Ocean Drive (☎1-800/334-8484). Upper bracket beachside hotel with all the amenities you can think of, and some good off-season reductions. ⑧.

Silver Sands Oceanfront Motel, 301 Ocean Drive (☎361-5441). Hardly a bargain, but the simple rooms are the cheapest on the island. ⑥.

Sonesta Beach, 350 Ocean Drive (☎1-800/SONESTA). High-rise resort with luxurious rooms, sports facilities, bars and a prime stretch of private beach. ⑦–⑧.

South Miami and Homestead

A1 Budget Motel, 30600 S Dixie Hwy (☎247-7032). Basic and clean, with some non-smoking rooms and a do-it-yourself laundry. ②–③.

Coral Roc, 1100 N Krome Ave (☎247-4010). Unexciting but fully functional motel. ③–④.

Deluxe Inn Motel, 28475 S Dixie Hwy (☎248-5622). Maybe not "deluxe," but good, clean rooms at a fair price. ②–③.

Everglades Motel, 605 S Krome Ave (☎247-4117). A slightly run-down exterior, but the rooms are okay and there's a coin-operated laundry for guests. ②–③.

Best Western Gateway to the Keys, 1 Straus Blvd, Florida City (☎246-5100). One of the most comfortable places to stay hereabouts, and usefully located between the Keys, Miami and the Everglades. ⑤–⑥.

Katy's Place B&B, 31850 SW 195th Ave (☎247-0201). Pleasant bed-and-breakfast with a pool, hot-tub, laundry facilities and home-cooked breakfast. ④–⑤.

Super 8, 1202 N Krome Ave (☎1-800/800-8000). Branch of a plain but cheap motel chain, with clean and reasonably priced rooms. ②–③.

South Miami Beach

Blue Moon, 944 Collins Ave (☎1/800-724-1623). Merv Griffith's newest acquisition is a small, lavish hotel recently remodeled in cool blue and white tones. ⑥–⑧.

Brigham Gardens Guesthouse, 1411 Collins Ave (☎531-1331). Large rooms with either basic or fully equipped kitchens. A tropical garden patio and friendly atmosphere contribute to make this one of the most pleasant places to stay in South Beach. ④–⑥.

Cadet Hotel B&B, 1701 James Ave (☎1/800-43-CADET). A quaint B&B in the heart of South Beach – Clark Gable stayed here. ④.

Cavalier, 1320 Ocean Drive (☎1/800-OUTPOST). Recently opened and completely revamped 1930s Art Deco hotel, now featuring neo-Moorish decor. ⑤–⑥.

Clay, 406 Española Way (☎534-2988). Vintage hotel that functions as the city's only youth hostel (see "Budget Accommodation," below), but has some private rooms. ①–②.

Colony, 736 Ocean Drive (☎1/800-2-COLONY). This beautifully refurbished Art Deco delight is the most photographed hotel in South Beach. ⑤–⑥.

Essex House, 1001 Collins Ave (☎1/800-553-7739). Warm atmosphere and one of the more tastefully restored Art Deco hotels. ④–⑥.

Leslie, 1244 Ocean Drive (☎1-800/OUTPOST). Excellently located on the beachside Art Deco strip, with striking interior design – bright colors and mirrors at crooked angles. Rooms are equipped with tape-player/radios as well as TVs. ⑤–⑥.

Marlin, 1200 Collins Ave (☎1/800-OUTPOST). Eleven costly but cozy suites stunningly decorated with a Caribbean-islands theme, plus a rooftop sun deck. If you can't afford to stay here, at least have a drink at the futuristic bar. ⑥–⑧.

Mermaid, 909 Collins Ave (☎538-5324). Cost-effective rooms – some with kitchenettes – in a Caribbean-style cottage. ③–⑤.

Park Central, 640 Ocean Drive (☎538-1611). Largest of the Art Deco options, and one of the few with a pool. ⑥–⑦.

Raleigh, 1775 Collins Ave (☎534-6300). The 1990s refurbishment aped the original 1940s look, but added state-of-the-art electronics in every room. Probably the best run and currently the most glamorous hotel in South Beach. ⑦–⑧.

Shelley, 844 Collins Ave (☎1/800-414-0612). An original Art Deco hotel with impeccably clean rooms and just across the street from Ocean Drive and the beach. Pastries and juice in the mornings in the lobby. ③–④.

Villa Paradiso, 1415 Collins Ave (☎532-0616). Fully equipped studios and one-bedroom apartments with kitchens, just one block away from the beach. ④–⑥.

Waldorf Towers, 860 Ocean Drive (☎531-7684). Another Art Deco landmark, facing the ocean and right in the throng of the fashionable strip. ⑤–⑥.

Central Miami Beach and Bay Harbor Islands

Alexander, 5225 Collins Ave (☎1-800/327-6121). Well-equipped suites, free champagne on arrival, mattresses adjusted to your desired firmness. You won't want to leave. ⑧.

Eden Roc Resort & Spa, 4525 Collins Ave (☎1-800-327-8337). A landmark on the Beach since the 1950s, this has been refurbished to the last detail and again ranks amongst Miami's most luxurious hotels. Most of the rooms command spectacular views. Besides the two pools there's a health spa offering everything from shiatsu massage to seaweed and salt scrubs. ⑧.

Bay Harbor Inn, 9660 E Bay Harbor Drive, Bay Harbor Islands (☎868-4141). Low-key elegance in an upmarket residential neighborhood a few minutes' walk from the beach and fifteen minutes' drive from downtown. The most attractive rooms are those with views onto Indian Creek, which fronts the inn. ⑤–⑥.

Fontainebleau Hilton, 4441 Collins Ave (☎538-2000). Once the last word in glamour, now elaborately refurbished and seeking to regain its lost esteem; a staff of two thousand attends your every whim. ⑦–⑧.

The Golden Sands, 6910 Collins Ave (☎1-800/932-0333). Nothing flash and mostly filled by package-touring Europeans, but likely to turn up the cheapest deals in this pricey area. ③–④.

North Miami Beach

Blue Mist, 19111 Collins Ave (☎932-1000). The cheapest in Sunny Isles; rooms are basic but most face the ocean. ③–④.

Days Inn, 7450 Ocean Terrace (☎1/800-325-2525). Adequate chain motel with nice pool. ④–⑤.

Paradise Inn, 8520 Harding Ave (☎865-6216). Neatly tucked into Surfside's main street, this is one of the best bargains around. ③.

Thunderbird Resort, 18401 Collins Ave (☎1-800/327-2044). No frills, but handy for both Miami and Fort Lauderdale. Like most hotels around here, you can step straight out of your room into the pool or onto the beach. ④–⑥.

At the airport

Hampton Inn-Miami Airport, 5125 NW 36th St (☎1-800/HAMPTON). Branch of a good-value hotel chain, offering some of the best rates in the airport area. ④.

MIA, Miami International Airport (☎1-800/327-1276). There's no excuse for missing your plane if you stay here; this stylishly designed and fully equipped hotel is located inside the airport, but you'll pay for the convenience. ⑦.

Miami Airways Motel, 5001 36th St (☎883-4700). Easily the cheapest in the area. ②.

Quality Inn, 2373 NW Le Jeune Rd (☎1-800/228-5151). Well-presented chain hotel with a beckoning pool. ④–⑤.

Budget accommodation: youth hostels and camping

Impeccably positioned in the heart of South Beach, the city's AYH **youth hostel**, *Hostel International of Miami Beach*, at the *Clay Hotel*, 406 Española Way (☎534-2988), has beds in small dorms for $10 ($13 for non-IYHA-members), as well as private singles and doubles ($25–35); see "Hotels and motels," above. Also in South Beach, the *Ninth Street Hostel*, 236 Ninth Street (☎534-0268), offers beds in four-person dorms for $12 per person. The newest concept of budget travel has hit South Beach in the form of *Banana Bungalow* (☎1-800-7-HOSTEL), a hostel/hotel with the comforts and con-veniences of both. Boasting a large pool, nightly movies in a plush video room, organized land and water tours, and the cheapest Tiki Bar on the strip, its prices are comparable to local hotels ($40–55 for private rooms, $12–15 for dorm beds), and guests can lounge poolside while playing shuffleboard or gabbing with fellow travelers from around the globe.

Staying at any of the above is certainly preferable to **camping** at *Larry & Penny Thompson Memorial Campground*, 12451 SW 184th Street (☎232-1049), twelve miles southwest of downtown Miami and well away from any bus route; $18 per night, $74 per week.

MIAMI

Despite its relatively small population, **Miami** is a diverse place. Many of its districts are officially cities on their own, and each has a distinctive background and character. Some are compact enough to explore on foot, but you'll need a car, or local buses, to travel between them – though the city doesn't stretch far inland because of the natural barrier of the Everglades swamps, distances between northern and southern reaches are considerable. Beware that the mood within a district can switch dramatically from one block to another, making it easy to stray into hostile territory if you don't stay alert.

The obvious starting point is **downtown Miami**, the small, bustling nerve center of the city. Its streets are lined by garishly decorated shops and filled with a startling cross-section of people, bringing a lively human dimension to an area overlooked by futuristic office buildings. Close to the **downtown area** are regions of marked contrast. Those to the north – with a few exceptions – are run-down and dangerous, infamous for their outbreaks of violent racial unrest. To the south are the international banks signifying Miami's new wealth – and the state-of-the-art residential architecture that comes with it.

Beyond the environs of downtown Miami, the city spreads out in a broad arc to the west and south. The first of Miami's Cubans – who have reshaped the city substantially over the last two decades – settled a few miles west in (what became) **Little Havana**. This is still one of the most enjoyable and intriguing parts of Miami, rich with Latin American looks and sounds but far less solidly Cuban than it used to be. Immediately south, Little Havana's street grid gives way to the spacious boulevards of **Coral Gables**, whose finely wrought Mediterranean architecture – a far cry from cheap pastiches elsewhere – is as impressive now as it was in the Twenties when it set new standards in town planning. South of the downtown area, **Coconut Grove** is mounting a strong bid to become Miami's trendiest quarter; beautifully placed alongside Biscayne Bay, it boasts a plethora of neatly appointed streetside cafés as well as mansions and shops from a bygone era.

Beyond Coconut Grove and Coral Gables, **South Miami** is a lackluster residential sprawl with little of note, fading into farming territory on Miami's southern edge and into the barren expanse of the Everglades to the west. **Key Biscayne** is a more attractive destination: a classy, secluded island community with some beautiful beaches, five miles off the mainland but easily reached by causeway.

Downtown

DOWNTOWN MIAMI is not a place in which to relax: humanity storms down its short streets, rippling the gaudy awnings of countless cut-price electronics, clothes and jewelry stores, easing up only to buy imported newspapers or to gulp down a spicy snack and a mango juice from a fast-food stand.

Since the early Sixties, when newly released Cuban Bay of Pigs veterans came here to spend their US Government back pay, the predominantly Spanish-speaking businesses of the downtown square mile have reaped the benefits of any boost in South or Central American incomes. The recipients pour into Miami airport and move downtown in droves, seeking the goods they can't find at home. Minorities in the throng include dazed-looking European tourists, clean-cut Anglo-Americans with local government jobs, and street people of indeterminate origin dragging their worldly possessions with them. Only some solid US public architecture and whistle-blowing traffic cops remind you that you're still in Florida and not on the main drag of a seething Latin American capital.

The nerve-jangling streets (safe by day), and the feeling they induce of being at the crossroads of the Americas, are reason enough to spend half a day in downtown Miami, but added attractions are an excellent historical collection, a well-stocked library and, rather strangely, an old courthouse filled with works of art. When the street melange becomes too much, you can revive your senses with a quick *café Cubano* in one of the many small Cuban cafés (see "Eating", p.97).

Flagler Street and the Metro-Dade Cultural Center

Nowhere gives a better first taste of downtown Miami than **Flagler Street**, by far the loudest, brightest, busiest strip, and long the area's main attraction. Start at the eastern end by glancing inside the 1938 **Alfred Du Pont Building**, no. 169 E, which now

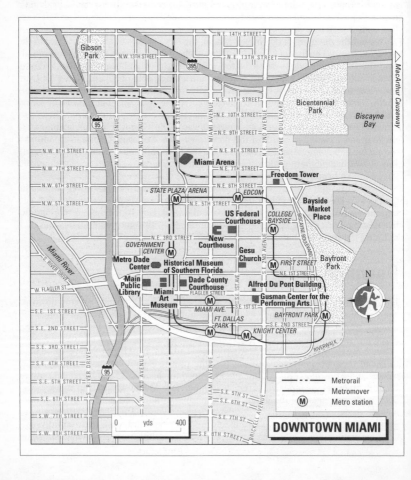

DOWNTOWN MIAMI

houses the Florida National Bank (go up to the first floor); fanciful wrought-iron screens, bulky brass fittings and frescoes of Florida scenes epitomize the decorative style popular with US architects at the end of the Depression.

Nearby, the even less restrained **Gusman Center for the Performing Arts**, no. 174 E, began life in the Twenties as a vaudeville theater, and displays all the exquisitely kitsch trappings you'd expect inside a million-dollar building designed to resemble a Moorish palace. The turrets, towers and intricately detailed columns remain (having escaped demolition in 1972), and a crescent moon still flits across the star-filled ceiling. The only way to get a look at the interior (the exterior is far less interesting) is by buying a ticket for a show: classical and contemporary music and dance are staged here from October to June; details are available from the ticket booth or on ☎372-0925.

Further along the street, at no. 73 W, four forbidding Doric columns mark the entrance to the **Dade County Courthouse**. Built in 1926 on the site of an earlier courthouse – where public hangings used to take place – for fifty years this was Miami's tallest building, its night-time lights showing off a distinctive stepped pyramid peak and beaming out a warning to wrong-doers all over the city.

The Metro-Dade Cultural Center

Little inside the courthouse is worth passing the security check for (the juiciest cases are tried in the New Courthouse; see "North of Flagler Street"). Instead, you should cross SW First Avenue towards the giant, air-raid shelter-like building of the **Metro-Dade Cultural Center**, entered via a ramp off Flagler Street. This was an ambitious attempt by renowned architect Philip Johnson to create a postmodern Mediterranean-style piazza, a congenial gathering place where Miami could display its cultural side. The theory almost worked: superb art shows, historical collections and a major library frame the courtyard, but Johnson forgot the power of the south Florida sun. Rather than pausing to rest and gossip, most people scamper across the open space towards the nearest shade.

Facing the piazza, the **Historical Museum of Southern Florida** (Mon–Wed, Fri & Sat 10am–5pm, Thurs 10am–9pm, Sun noon–5pm; $4; ☎375-1492) offers a comprehensive look at the multifaceted past of southern Florida. The section on the indigenous Seminole people has a strong collection of photographs and artifacts that reveal much about the native Americans' lifestyle (the Creek Indians began arriving in what was then Spanish-ruled Florida during the eighteenth century, fleeing persecution further north). Another fine display covers the trials and tribulations of early Miami settlers, enabling you to put faces to names such as Tuttle and Brickell that crop up as street, park or bridge titles all over the city. Also well chronicled are the fluctuating fortunes of Miami Beach: from its early days as a celebrities' vacation spot – with amusing photos of Twenties Hollywood greats – through to the recent renovation of the Art Deco strip. Recent history is also covered, with considerable space devoted to the arrival of Cuban refugees and immigrants.

A few yards from the historical museum, the **Miami Art Museum** (Tues, Wed, & Fri 10am–5pm, Thurs 10am–9pm, Sat & Sun noon–5pm; $5; free Thurs 6–9pm) showcases outstanding international traveling exhibitions, with a particular strength in Latin American works. Directly opposite is the **Main Public Library** (Mon–Sat 9am–6pm, Thurs 9am–9pm, Sun 1–5pm; closed Sun in summer), which, besides the usual lending sections, has temporary exhibitions on art and literary themes as well as a massive collection of Florida magazines and books.

Adjoining the Cultural Center, the **Metro-Dade Center** (also called Government Center) chiefly comprises county government offices, but useful bus and train timetables can be gathered from the **Transit Service Center** (daily 7am–6pm; ☎770-3131) by the Metrorail entrance at the eastern side of the building.

North of Flagler Street

The tempo drops and storefronts become less brash as you head **north of Flagler Street**. A busy Hispanic procession passes in and out of the 1925 Catholic **Gesú Church**, 118 NE Second Street, whose Mediterranean Revival exterior and stylishly decorated innards make a pleasing splash, but otherwise there's nothing else to slow you down until you reach the Neoclassical **US Federal Courthouse**, 300 NE First Avenue (Mon–Fri 8.30am–5pm), a few minutes' walk away.

Finished in 1931, the building first functioned as a post office; Miami's then negligible crime rate required just one room on the second floor for judicial purposes. The room did acquire a monumental **mural**, however: *Law Guides Florida's Progress*, by Denman Fink (the designer behind much of Coral Gables, see p.74), a 25-foot-long depiction of Florida's evolution from swampy backwoods to modern state; if the courtroom's locked, see if the security guard will grant you a peek. In 1985, fresco artist David Novros was commissioned to decorate the building's medieval-style inner **courtyard**, to which his bold, colorful daubs make a lively addition.

By the late Sixties, Miami's crime levels became too much for the old courthouse to handle, and the building of the $22 million **New Courthouse** was started next door (main entrance on North Miami Ave; Mon–Fri 8.30am–5pm). A gruesome creation of concrete and glass, the major advantage of the new courthouse – other than size – is that jurors can pass in and out unobserved: "Getting them out without getting them dead," as one judge commented.

Around Downtown

A few polite parks and shopping precincts lie within easy walking distance, but you'll need a car or a bus to make much progress **around downtown Miami**. To the north lies Little Haiti, one of the most strongly defined ethnic areas in the city, bordering a desolate, poverty-stricken district that you'd be well advised to avoid. In total contrast, if you go south, an extraordinary line of swanky modern banks and spectacular apartments show off Miami's freshly found affluence. To the west, the area between downtown Miami and Little Havana (see p.71) is filled with several kilometers of uninspiring houses.

North of Downtown

The Eighties saw the destruction of some decaying but much-loved buildings beside **Biscayne Boulevard** (part of Hwy-1) to make way for the **Bayside Marketplace**, 401 N Biscayne Boulevard (Mon–Sat 10am–10pm, Sun 11am–9pm; restaurants and bars stay open later), a large, pink shopping mall providing pleasant waterfront views from its terraces. Enlivened by street musicians and some choice international food stands, the place is less hideous than might be expected, but is clearly aimed at tourists. A number of pleasure trips around the bay begin here (see "Bus, boat and helicopter tours" and "Water taxis" pp.59-60) – and, in case you've ever wondered, it was just to the south, on the yacht-filled marina of Bayfront Park of the Americas, that *Miami Vice*'s Sonny Crockett moored his floating home.

To the north of the Bayside Marketplace, endless lines of container trucks turning into Port Boulevard attest to the importance of the **Port of Miami** – now one of the world's biggest cargo and cruise ship terminals. Just beyond, the perpetual flame of the John Kennedy Memorial Torch of Friendship symbolizes good relations between the US and its southern neighbors, and guards the entrance to **Bicentennial Park**, filled with markers to various US-approved Central American luminaries.

Between Bicentennial Park and Bayside Marketplace is the site of the future home of the Miami Heat basketball team. The **American Airlines Arena** is scheduled to open in December 1999, with restaurants and shops linked to Bayside by a pedestrian bridge.

Across Biscayne Boulevard, the **Freedom Tower**, originally home to the now defunct *Miami News*, earned its current name by housing the Cuban Refugee Center, which began operations in 1962. Most of those who left Cuba on the "freedom flights"* got their first taste of US bureaucracy here. The 1925 building, modeled on a Spanish bell tower, has been closed for some years due to restoration – its Mediterranean features are more impressive from a distance, anyway – and there are no plans at present to re-open it in any form.

Beyond the Freedom Tower, there's little more to see within walking distance, and you're on the fringe of some of the city's most impoverished – and dangerous – neighborhoods. You might venture a few blocks further to the **City of Miami Cemetery**, on the corner of North Miami Avenue and NE Eighteenth Street, though this should only be undertaken with a **walking tour**; $15 (☎375-1625 for details). There are historical stories aplenty here, but the graves are littered with used syringes, anything valuable has been stolen, and the family vaults of early Miami bigwigs have had their doors torn off by the homeless seeking shelter.

Continuing North: Little Haiti and the Police Museum

About 170,000 **Haitians** live in Miami, forming one of the city's major ethnic groups – albeit it far smaller than the Cuban population. Roughly a third of them live in what's become known as **LITTLE HAITI**, a two-hundred-block area that centers on NE Second Avenue, north of 42nd Street (buses #9 or #10 from the downtown area). Aside from hearing Haitian Creole on the streets (almost all Miami's Haitians speak English as a third language after Creole and French), you'll notice the colorful shops, offices and restaurants. For a taste of the culture, visit the **Caribbean Marketplace**, 5927 NE Second Avenue (Tues–Sun 9am–8pm), a large, Haitian-style building containing stalls and small stores selling Haitian handicrafts, books, records and food such as goat-stew. Established in 1990 to encourage local entrepreneurs and create a commercial focal point for the community, the Marketplace has been largely unsuccessful, with much of the space unused. The **Haitian Refugee Center**, 32 NE 56th Avenue, will give you a greater insight into why Haitians remain one of the more oppressed immigrant groups in Miami, most scraping their living as taxi drivers or hotel maids, hindered by poor education and English-language skills, and by the often racist attitudes of Anglos, Cubans and black Americans alike.

Close to Little Haiti (buses #3, #16 or #95 from downtown Miami), the **American Police Hall of Fame & Museum**, 3801 Biscayne Boulevard (daily 10am–5.30pm; $6; ☎573-0070), occupies the former local FBI headquarters – a shrine to law and order ironically located near to Liberty City and Overtown, scene of some of Miami's most desperate living. You can easily while away a spare hour here; besides CIA baseball caps and the car from the film *Blade Runner*, the first floor is devoted to a somber memorial to slain police officers. Upstairs you'll find information on gangsters; a dope addict's kit; an arsenal of weapons found on highways; the chain gang leg-irons still used in Tennessee; and moments of humor, including a signed photo

---

* Between December 1965 and June 1972, ten empty planes a week left Miami to collect Cubans – over 250,000 in total – allowed to leave the island by Fidel Castro. While US propaganda hailed them as "freedom fighters," most of the arrivals were simply seeking the fruits of capitalism, and, as Castro astutely recognized, any that were seriously committed to overthrowing his regime would be far less troublesome outside Cuba.

of Keith Richards, a member of the museum's celebrity advisory board. Throughout, bad taste abounds; you can even have your photograph taken in the electric chair or gas chamber.

Liberty City and Overtown

In December 1979, after a prolonged sequence of unpunished assaults by white police officers on members of the African American community, a respected black professional, Arthur MacDuffie, was dragged off his motorbike in **LIBERTY CITY** and beaten to death by a group of white officers. Five months later, an all-white jury acquitted the accused, sparking off what became known as the "Liberty City Riot." On May 18, 1980, the night after the trial, the whole of Miami was ablaze, from Carol City in the far north to Homestead in the south. Reports of shooting, stone throwing, and whites being dragged from their cars and attacked or even burned alive, were rife. The violence began on Sunday, roadblocks sealed off African American districts until Wednesday, and a citywide curfew lasted until Friday. In the final tally, eighteen were dead (mostly African Americans killed by police and National Guardsmen), hundreds injured, and damage to property was estimated at over $200 million.

Incredibly, the "worst racial paroxysm in modern American history" (not the first nor probably the last violent expression of Miami's racial tensions) caused no harm to Miami's broader fortunes, coming just as the city was establishing itself as a hub of Latin American finance and on the brink of becoming fashionable through *Miami Vice*. Even Liberty City soon found a chic international fashion district (see "Shopping," p.113) springing up in the disused warehouses on its periphery – the western edge of Little Haiti. Nonetheless, Miami's African Americans have remained at the bottom of the city's social heap. From the earliest days, "Coloredtown," as **OVERTOWN** was previously known, was divided by train tracks from the white folks of downtown Miami, and by the Thirties – when its jazz clubs thrilled multiracial audiences – conditions were so bad and overcrowding so extreme that Liberty City was built in an adjoining area to ease the strain.

In recent decades, Miami's black-white relations have been complicated by the extraordinary scale of Hispanic immigration, which has caused the city's African Americans to miss out even on the menial jobs that elsewhere in the US are their traditional preserve. This unique form of political dispossession was borne out by an official snub delivered by the city's Cuban American mayor, Xavier Suarez, to the visit in June 1990 of the then ANC deputy leader, Nelson Mandela. This incident, which stemmed from Mandela's refusal to denounce Fidel Castro, stimulated a well-organized **African American boycott** of the city's lucrative tourist industry, causing African American professional organizations around the US to cancel conventions planned for Miami. Dubbed the "quiet riot," the boycott cost the city millions of dollars in lost revenue.

Needless to say, these areas (and certain parts of Coconut Grove, North Miami Beach and South Miami) are not only depressing but also dangerous, and your very presence may be seen as provocative, particularly if you're white. If you do unwittingly find yourself driving through the area, keep your windows closed, doors locked, be wary when stopping at lights, and do not leave your car.

If you've a serious interest in the African American contribution to Miami and Florida, head for the **Black Archives History and Research Foundation of South Florida**, at 5400 NW 22nd Avenue (Mon–Fri 9am–5pm; free; ☎636-2390), a resource center that also arranges guided tours for a minimum of ten people through black historical areas.

South of Downtown Miami

Fifteen minutes' walk south from Flagler Street, the **Miami River** marks the southern limit of downtown. If your crossing is delayed by the drawbridge being raised to allow a ship through, glance westwards to the concrete modernity of the *Hotel Inter-Continental*, at the river's mouth, built on the site where Henry Flagler's *Royal Palm Hotel* stood at the turn of the century. At the behest of Miami's biggest landowners, Flagler – a millionaire oil baron whose railroad opened up Florida's east coast and brought wealthy wintering socialites to his string of smart hotels – extended the rail line here from Palm Beach. His luxury hotel and subsequent dredging of Biscayne Bay to accommodate cruise ships did much to put Miami on the map.

One landowner, William Brickell, ran a trading post on the south side of the river, an area now dominated by **Brickell Avenue**. Beginning immediately across the SE Second Avenue bridge and running to Coconut Grove (see p.79), Brickell Avenue was *the* address in 1910s Miami, easily justifying its "millionaires' row" nickname. While the original grand homes have largely disappeared, money is still Brickell Avenue's most obvious asset: over the bridge begins a half-mile parade of **banks**, the largest group of international banks in the US, whose imposing forms are softened by forecourts filled with sculptures, fountains and palm trees. Far from being places to change a travelers' check, these institutions are bastions of international high finance. From the late Seventies, Miami emerged as a corporate banking center, cashing in on political instability in South and Central America by offering a secure home for Latin American money. Among it was a lot of dirty money that needed laundering: there's more than a grain of truth to the tales of dark-suited men depositing cash-filled suitcases.

The sudden rise of the Brickell banks was matched by new condominiums of breathtaking proportions but little architectural merit a few blocks further along. These astronomically priced abodes, featured in the opening sequence of *Miami Vice*, include in their pastel-shaded midst the most stunning modern building in Miami: the **Atlantis**, at no. 2025. First sketched on a napkin in a Cuban restaurant and finished in 1983, the *Atlantis* crowned several years of innovative construction by a small architectural firm called Arquitectonica, whose style – variously termed "beach blanket Bauhaus" and "ecstatic modernism" – fused postmodern thought with a strong sense of Miami's eclectic architectural heritage. The building's focal point is a gaping square hole through its middle where a palm tree, a jacuzzi and a red-painted spiral staircase tease the eye. You won't be allowed inside unless you know someone who lives there, which might be just as well: even its designers admit the interior doesn't live up to the exuberance of the exterior, and claim the building to be "architecture for 55mph" – in other words, seen to best effect from a passing car.

Little Havana

Unquestionably the largest ethnic group in Miami, the impact of **Cubans** on the city over the last four decades has been incalculable. Unlike most Hispanic immigrants to the US, who trade one form of poverty for another, Miami's first Cuban arrivals in the late Fifties had already tasted affluence. They rose quickly through the social strata and nowadays wield considerable clout in the running of the city.

The first Miami Cubans settled a few miles west of downtown Miami in what became known as **LITTLE HAVANA**. According to tourist brochures, the streets are filled with old men in *guayaberas* (billowing cotton shirts) playing dominoes, and exotic restaurants whose walls vibrate to the pulsating rhythms of the homeland. The reality is more subdued: Little Havana's parks, memorials, shops and food stands all reflect the Cuban experience – and as such shouldn't be missed – but the streets are quieter than those of downtown Miami (except during the Little Havana festival in early March – see "Festivals", p.110). Like their US peers, as soon as the early settlers acquired sufficient dollars, they gave up the tightly grouped, modest homes of Little Havana for fully fledged suburban living.

For all the powerful emotions stirred up by its politics, there's not an awful lot to see in Little Havana; the appeal of the place is almost all atmospheric. On the graffitied streets, the prevailing mood is one of a community carrying on its daily business, and while the sights, smells and sounds are distinctly Cuban, many of the people you'll pass – at least those under fifty – are less likely to be Cuban than Nicaraguan or Colombian: the latest immigrant groups in Miami to use Little Havana as a first base.

Only the neighborhood's main strip, SW Eighth Street, or **Calle Ocho** (a direct Spanish translation), offers more than houses: tiny cups of sweet Cuban coffee are sold from street-side counters, the odors of cigars being rolled and bread being baked waft across the sidewalk, shops sell *Santeria* (a Voodoo-like religion of African origin) ephemera beside six-foot-high models of Catholic saints, and you'll spot the only branch of *Dunkin' Donuts* to sell guava-filled doughnuts.

CUBANS IN MIAMI: SOME BACKGROUND

Proximity to the Caribbean island has long made Florida a place of refuge for Cuba's activists. From Jose Martí in the 1890s to Fidel Castro in the early Fifties, the country's radicals arrived to campaign and raise funds, and numerous deposed Cuban politicians have whiled away their exile in Florida. However, until comparatively recent times, New York, not Miami, was the center of Cuban émigré life in the United States.

During the mid-Fifties, when opposition to Cuba's Batista dictatorship – and the country's subservient role to the US – began to assert itself, a trickle of Cubans started arriving in the predominantly Jewish section of Miami called Riverside, moving into low-rent properties vacated as the extant community grew wealthier and moved out. The trickle became a flood when Fidel Castro took power, and as Cuban businesses sprang up on SW Eighth Street and Cubans began making their mark on Miami life, the area began to be known as **Little Havana**,

Those who left Cuba were not peasants but the affluent middle classes with most to lose under communism. Regarding themselves as the entrepreneurial sophisticates of the Caribbean, stories are plentiful of high-flying Cuban capitalists who arrived penniless in Little Havana, took menial jobs, and, over the course of two decades – aided by a formidable network of old ex-pats – toiled, wheeled and dealed their way steadily upwards to positions of power and influence (and not just locally – leading Miami Cubans also hold considerable sway over the US government's policy towards Cuba).

The second great Cuban influx into Miami was of a quite different social nature and racial composition: the **Mariel boatlift** brought 125,000 predominantly black islanders from the Cuban port of Mariel to Miami in May 1980. Unlike their worldly-wise predecessors, these arrivals were poor and uneducated, and a fifth were fresh from Cuban jails – incarcerated for criminal rather than political crimes. Bluntly put, Castro had called the bluff of the US administration and dumped his misfits on Miami. Only a few of them wound up in Little Havana: most "Marielitos" settled in Miami Beach's South Beach where they proceeded to terrorize the local community, thereby becoming a source of embarrassment to Miami's longer-established and determinedly respectable Cubans.

Along Calle Ocho

The most pertinent introduction to Little Havana is the **Brigade 2506 Memorial**, between Twelfth and Thirteenth avenues on Calle Ocho. Inscribed with the brigade crest, topped by the Cuban flag and ringed by sculptured bullets, this simple stone remembers those who died at the Bay of Pigs on April 17, 1961, during the attempt by a group of US-trained Cuban exiles to invade the island and wrest control from Castro.

Depending on who tells the story, the outcome was the result either of ill-conceived plans, or due to the US's lack of commitment to Cuba – to this day, sections of the Cuban community hate the then US president John Kennedy only slightly less than they hate Fidel Castro. Every anniversary, veterans clad in combat fatigues and carrying assault rifles gather here to make pledges of patriotism throughout the night.

A less emotionally charged gathering place is **Maximo Lopez Domino Park**, a few yards away on a corner of Fourteenth Avenue; access to its open-air tables is (quite illegally) restricted to men over 55, and this is one place where you really *will* see old men in *guayaberas* playing dominoes.

Besides discussing the fate of Cuba, the domino players might also be passing judgement on the **Latin Quarter** that's replacing a line of old buildings on the north side of Calle Ocho. Described by city planners as an attempt to "create a world renowned

Exile Politics

However much Miami Cubans have prospered in the US, for many the "liberation" of their country is rarely far from their minds. Some older Cubans – driven by a fanatical hatred of Fidel Castro and communism – still consider themselves to be in exile, though few would seriously think about giving up their comfortable lifestyles to return, whatever regime governs Cuba.

Within the complexities of Cuban exile politics, there's a major rift: one school of thought holds that the US sold Cuba out to the USSR, beginning when President Kennedy* withheld air support from the invading Brigade 2056 at the Bay of Pigs in 1961, and favors a violent overthrow of the communist regime with a return to the survival-of-the-fittest ethic of the old days. The more pragmatic line runs that the Cuban clock can't be turned back, and that the only way for exiled Cubans to be usefully involved is to face up to the present situation and use their economic muscle to bring about changes.

Fuelled by a mix of *machismo* and hero-worship of early Cuban independence fighters, passions run high and action – usually violent – has been prized more than words. In Miami, Cubans even *suspected* of advocating dialogue with Castro have been killed; one man had his legs blown off for suggesting violence on the streets was counterproductive, and the Cuban Museum of Arts and Culture was bombed for displaying the work of Castro-approved artists.

In 1995, however, there was a break in the violence, as the hostility between exile factions was directed instead towards President Clinton and his policies of returning all future refugees to Cuba; for the first time since Castro came to power, Cubans had lost their special status, and instead were treated as any other economic migrant seeking to enter the US illegally. When the exiled Cuban leadership is eventually able to return to Cuba, one might expect the violent feuding to resume with a vengeance as parties struggle for power in the post-Castro era.

* In 1978, the US government's House Select Committee on Assassinations listed a (still active) Miami-based Cuban "action group," Alpha 66, as having "the motivation, capability, and resources" to have assassinated President Kennedy, and various, if unsubstantiated, links to the alleged assassin, Lee Harvey Oswald.

showcase of Latin American culture," the development seems destined to be a Hispanicized version of Bayside Marketplace (see "Around Downtown Miami," p.68), with Spanish-style ceramics, plazas and fountains decorating pricey boutiques and eateries aimed at tourists. Most Cuban objections to the scheme are to do with the name, which doesn't, they claim, do justice to the Cuban influence in the area.

Further west, the peaceful greenery of **Woodlawn Cemetery**, between 32nd and 33rd avenues (daily sunset–dusk), belies the scheming and skullduggery that some of its occupants indulged in during their lifetimes. Two former Cuban heads of state are buried here: Gerardo Machado, ousted from office in 1933, is in the mausoleum, while one of the protagonists in his downfall, Carlos Prío Socarras, president from 1948 to 1952, lies just outside. Also interred in the mausoleum (marked only by his initials) is **Anastasio Somoza**, dictator of Nicaragua until overthrown by the Sandinistas in 1979, and later killed in Paraguay.

Around Calle Ocho

With nondescript, low-income housing to the north and modest Spanish Revival Twenties bungalows to the south, there's little to detain you around Calle Ocho. One exception is the **Cuban Museum of the Americas**, 1300 SW Twelfth Avenue (Tue–Fri 10am–3pm; for latest opening times phone ☎858-8006), established by Cuban exiles. Its exhibitions of contemporary work have to be carefully chosen to avoid inflaming local passions; the museum suffered a bomb attack in 1989 for displaying the works of artists living in Cuba, regarded as collaborators by extreme anti-Castro exiles. A permanent collection is in the process of being formed, but there is not yet space to display it.

You might also drop into the *La Esquina de Tejas* restaurant, 101 SW Twelfth Avenue, where you can mull over the signed photos of Ronald Reagan. It was in this otherwise ordinary Cuban eatery that the president, seeking re-election, took a well-publicized lunch in 1983 in an effort to harness the powerful Cuban vote in Miami. Four years later, George Bush called by for a swift *café Cubano* and a drawn-out photo-call. Aside from his right-wing domestic policies, Reagan gained immense popularity among Miami Cubans for his support of the Nicaraguan Contras, viewed as kindred spirits in the guerrilla struggle against communism (it's widely acknowledged that the Contras ran their anti-Sandinista operation from offices in Miami and trained for combat in the Everglades). The community's affection was demonstrated by the renaming of Twelfth Avenue as "Ronald Reagan Boulevard."

There's no point in actually going there (except for a sports event; see "Listings"), but from here you can see the rising hump of the 70,000-seat **Orange Bowl** stadium, about ten blocks north. This is home to the University of Miami's football team, the Hurricanes, but is best remembered by older Cubans as the place where, on a December night in 1962, John Kennedy took the Brigade 2056 flag and vainly promised to return it "in a free Havana."

Coral Gables

All of Miami's constituent cities are fast to assert their individuality, but none has a greater case than **CORAL GABLES**, south of Little Havana: twelve square miles of broad boulevards and leafy streets lined by elaborate Spanish- and Italian-style architecture, which make the much more famous Art Deco district (see p.90) seem decidedly uncouth.

Whereas Miami's other early property developers built cheap and fast in search of a quick buck, the creator of Coral Gables, a local man named **George Merrick**, was more of an aesthete than an entrepreneur. Taking Mediterranean Europe as his inspiration, Merrick raided street names from a Spanish dictionary – by coincidence, many

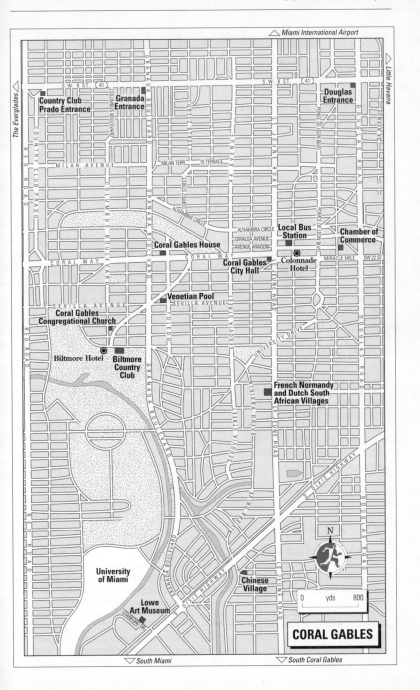

△ Miami International Airport

The Everglades ◁

▷ Little Havana

Country Club
Prado Entrance

Granada
Entrance

Douglas
Entrance

S.W. 8 ST. ④①

S.W. 8 ST. ④①

SW 8 TH ST

COUNTRY CLUB PRADO

GRANADA BOULEVARD

COLUMBUS BOULEVARD

CORTEZ STREET

44 AVENUE

LE JEUNE ROAD

PONCE DE LEON BLVD

DOUGLAS ROAD

MILAN AVENUE

MILAN TERR.

15 TERRACE

ALHAMBRA CIRCLE

Coral Gables House

ALHAMBRA CIRCLE
GIRALDA AVENUE
AVENUE ARAGON

Local Bus
Station

Chamber of
Commerce

CORAL WAY

CORAL WAY

Coral Gables
City Hall

Colonnade
Hotel

MIRACLE MILE

SW 22 ST

Venetian Pool

SEVILLA AVENUE

SEVILLA AVENUE

TOLEDO

SEGOVIA STREET

LE JEUNE ROAD

RED ROAD

Coral Gables
Congregational Church

Biltmore Hotel

Biltmore
Country
Club

UNIVERSITY DRIVE

RIVIERA DRIVE

SEGOVIA STREET

French Normandy
and Dutch South
African Villages

DOUGLAS ROAD

GRANADA BOULEVARD

S. DIXIE HIGHWAY

N

University
of Miami

RIVIERA DRIVE

DIXIE HIGHWAY

Chinese
Village

LE JEUNE ROAD

Lowe
Art Museum

STANFORD DR.

0   yds   800

CORAL GABLES

▽ South Miami

▽ South Coral Gables

CORAL GABLES: THE ENTRANCES

To make a strong first impression on visitors to Coral Gables, Merrick planned eight grand **entrances** on the main access roads, of which only four were completed before the bust. The three most impressive are to the north, along a two-and-a-half-mile stretch of SW Eighth Street.

The million-dollar **Douglas Entrance** (junction with Douglas Road) was the most ambitious, consisting of a gateway and tower with two expansive wings of shops, offices and artists' studios. During the Sixties it was almost bulldozed to make room for a super-market, but survived to become a well-scrubbed business area, still upholding Merrick's Mediterranean themes. Further west, the sixty-foot-high vine-covered **Granada Entrance** (junction with Granada Boulevard) is based on the entrance to the city of Granada in Spain. A better appetizer for Coral Gables is the **Country Club Prado Entrance** (junction with Country Club Prado), the expensive recreation of a formal Italian garden bordered by freestanding stucco-and-brick pillars topped by ornamental urns and lamps with wrought-iron brackets.

The "Villages"

Driving (or cycling) around the less busy parts of Coral Gables, you'll catch glimpses of several **"Villages,"** small pockets of residential architecture intended to add diversity to the area's Mediterranean looks. These include the brightly colored roofs and ornately carved balconies of the **Chinese Village**, on the "5100" block of Riviera Drive; the tim-ber-beamed town houses of the **French Normandy Village**, on the "400" block of Vizcaya Avenue, at Le Jeune Road; and, perhaps strangest of all, the twisting chimneys and scroll-work arches of the **Dutch South African Village**, also on the "400" block of Vizcaya Avenue.

of today's residents are wealthy, Spanish-speaking Cubans – and enlisted his artist uncle, Denman Fink, and architect Phineas Paist, to plan the plazas, fountains and care-fully aged stucco-fronted buildings.

Coral Gables land started selling overnight, with the five years following the first sale in 1921 bringing in $150 million, a third of which was channeled into the biggest adver-tising campaign ever known. The layout and buildings of Coral Gables quickly took shape, but the sudden end of Florida's property boom (see "History" in Contexts for the full account) wiped Merrick out. He ran a fishing camp in the Florida Keys until that was destroyed by a hurricane, and wound up as Miami's postmaster until his death in 1942.

Coral Gables, however, was built with longevity as well as beauty in mind. Despite successive economic crises, it never lost its good looks, and these days, boosted by a plethora of multinational companies in the renovated office buildings and by a very image-conscious resident population, it is still a lovely place to explore.

The Miracle Mile and around

The best way into Coral Gables is along SW 22nd Street, which on the other side of Douglas Road becomes the **Miracle Mile**, conceived by Merrick as the centerpiece of his business district and still the preferred shopping place of community-conscious locals. It continues to bear the imprint of Merrick's vision, even if the occasional spot of mundane Art Deco makes a bizarre addition to the more fanciful Mediterranean trimmings.

Dominated by department stores, Latin American travel agents and a staggering number of bridal shops, the Miracle Mile (actually only half a mile long) becomes increasingly expensive and exclusive as you head west. Notice the arcades and bal-conies along its course, and the spirals and peaks of the **Colonnade Building** (180 Aragon Avenue): now comprising a smart hotel (see "Accommodation" p.61) and shops, this was completed in 1926 – just a few months before the property crash – to accommodate George Merrick's land sales office.

Cut around the corner to collect info from the **Chamber of Commerce**, 50 Aragon Avenue (Mon–Fri 8.30am–5pm; ☎446-1657), and complete the Miracle Mile inside the grandly pillared **Coral Gables City Hall**, 405 Biltmore Way (Mon–Fri 8am–5pm), whose corridors are adorned with posters from the Twenties advertising the "City Beautiful" and with newspaper clippings bearing witness to the property mania of the time. There's also a case full of oddments from the *Biltmore Hotel* (see below), which fall some way short of encapsulating the moneyed elegance that characterized Merrick's spa resort. From the third floor landing you can view Denman Fink's impressive blue-and-gold mural of the four seasons, which decorates the interior of the bell tower.

About half a mile further west, at no. 907 on Coral Way – a typically peaceful and tree-lined Coral Gables residential street – George Merrick's childhood home, the **Coral Gables House** (Sun & Wed 1–4pm; $2), is now a museum charting his family's history. In 1899, when George was twelve, his family arrived here from New England to run a 160-acre fruit and vegetable farm – and, in the case of George's father, to deliver sermons at local Congregational churches. The farm was so successful that the house quickly grew from a wooden shack into a modestly elegant dwelling of coral rock and gabled windows (the inspiration behind the name of the city that later grew up around the family farm). The dual blows of the property crash and a citrus blight led to the gradual deterioration of the house, until restoration began in the Seventies. There's only enough inside to occupy half an hour, but it provides an interesting background on the founder of Coral Gables, who lived here until 1916.

Along De Soto Boulevard

There's no reason to continue along Coral Way, so backtrack instead to the junction with De Soto Boulevard, which curls southwards to three of Merrick's most notable achievements.

While his property-developing contemporaries left ugly scars across the city after digging up the local limestone, Merrick had the foresight – and the help of Denman Fink – to turn his biggest quarry into a sumptuous swimming pool. The **Venetian Pool**, 2701 De Soto Boulevard (June–Aug Mon–Fri 11am–7.30pm, Sat & Sun 10am–4.30pm; Sept–Oct, April–May Tue–Sun 11am–5.30pm; Nov–Mar Tue–Sun 10am–4.30pm; $5; ☎460-5356), an elaborate conglomeration of palm-studded paths, Venetian-style bridges and coral rock caves, was opened in 1924. Despite its ornamentation, the pool was never aimed at the social elite; admission was cheap and open to all, and even today's local residents get a special discount.

A few minutes' walk further south, on land donated by Merrick, stands the **Coral Gables Congregational Church**, 3010 De Soto Blvd (Mon–Fri 8am–4pm), a bright Spanish Revival flurry topped by a barrel-tiled roof and enhanced by Baroque features. The building's excellent acoustics make it a popular venue for jazz and classical **concerts**; ask for details at the church office, just inside the entrance.

Merrick's crowning achievement – aesthetically if not financially – was the **Biltmore Hotel**, 1200 Anastasia Avenue (☎445-1926), wrapping its broad wings around the southern end of De Soto Boulevard. The 26-story tower of the hotel can be seen across much of low-lying Miami: if it seems similar to the Freedom Tower (see "Around Downtown Miami," p.68), it's because they're both modeled on the Giralda bell tower of Seville Cathedral in Spain. The *Biltmore* was hawked as "the last word in the evolution of civilization," and everything about it was outrageous: 25-foot-high frescoed walls, vaulted ceilings, a wealth of imported marble and tile, immense fireplaces and custom-loomed rugs. To mark the opening in January 1926, VIP guests were brought in on chartered, long-distance trains, fed on pheasant and trout, and given the run of the casino. The following day they could fox-hunt, play polo or swim in the US's largest pool – whose first swimming instructor was Johnny Weissmuller, future Olympic champion and the original screen Tarzan.

Although high-profile celebrities such as Bing Crosby, Judy Garland and Ginger Rogers kept the *Biltmore* on their itineraries, the end of the Florida land boom and the start of the Depression meant that the hotel was never the success it might have been. In the Forties, many of the finer furnishings were lost when the hotel became a military hospital, and decades of decline followed. The future looked rosier in 1986, when $55 million was lavished on a restoration program, but the company involved went bust, and the great building remained closed. Only in 1993 did it finally re-open, after another multi-million dollar refit. Now, once again it is functioning as a hotel; you can step inside to admire the elaborate architecture, take afternoon tea for $15, or – best of all – join the free historical tours beginning at 1.30pm, 2.30pm and 3.30pm every Sunday in the lobby.

The neighboring **Biltmore Country Club**, also open to the public, has fared better. You can poke your head inside for a closer look at its painstakingly renovated beaux-arts features, but most people turn up to knock a ball along the lush fairways of the **Biltmore Golf Course**, which, in the glory days of the hotel, hosted the highest-paying golf tournament in the world.

South of the Biltmore: the Lowe Art Museum

One of the few parts of Coral Gables where Mediterranean architecture doesn't prevail is on the campus of the **University of Miami**, about two miles south of the *Biltmore*, whose dismal, box-like buildings have traditionally been filled by students with wealthy parents rather than healthy intellects. In recent years the university has undergone something of a renaissance and now attracts top faculties in many fields and a more academic student body.

The sole reason to visit the campus is the **Lowe Art Museum**, 1301 Stanford Drive (Tue, Wed, Fri, Sat 10am–5pm; Thurs 12–7pm; Sun noon–5pm; $5; ☎284-3535). Established in 1950, the Lowe underwent major renovation and extension work in 1995, and it now constitutes Miami's foremost art museum. The diverse permanent collection contains Renaissance and European Baroque art, Spanish "Old Masters," nineteenth-century European paintings, and a considerable number of contemporary American works. Non-Western art is also well represented, including varied pre-Columbian, African and East Asian collections, Guatemalan textiles, and one of the finest Native American art collections in the country. The Lowe also hosts some excellent national and international touring exhibitions; call ahead to find out what's on.

South Coral Gables

Just as the Venetian Pool was a clever disguise for a quarry, so Merrick turned the construction ditches that ringed the infant Coral Gables into a network of canals, calling them the "Miami Riviera" and floating gondolas along them. Although the idea never really took off, the placid waterways remain, running between the university campus and a secluded residential area on Biscayne Bay, just south of Coconut Grove (described below).

Dividing Coconut Grove and South Miami (see p.82), the **Matheson Hammock Park**, 9601 Old Cutler Road (6am–sunset; $3 parking fee), was a coconut plantation before becoming a public park in 1930. On the weekends, thousands decant here to picnic, use the marina and take a dip in the artificial lagoon, great for small children but with little to offer for adults; the rest of the sizeable park is much less crowded, and you can easily while away a few hours strolling around the wading pond – popular with people catching crabs – or along the winding trails above the mangrove swamps.

Virtually next door, the **Fairchild Tropical Garden**, 10901 Old Cutler Road (daily 9.30am–4.30pm; $8; ☎667-1651), turns the same rugged terrain into lawns, flowerbeds and gardens decorated by artificial lakes. A good way to begin exploring the 83-acre site – the largest tropical botanical gardens in the continental United States – is to hitch a ride on the free tram (departing hourly, on the hour, from inside the garden's entrance) for a forty-minute meander along the trails, with a live commentary on the various plants.

The tropical habitats reproduced here – some more successfully than others – range from desert to rainforest, though there's relatively little space devoted to fauna endemic to south Florida. As a research institution, Fairchild works with scientists all over the world to preserve the diversity of the tropical environment; many of the plant species here are extinct in their original environments, and efforts have been made to re-establish them in their places of origin.

Some two-thirds of Fairchild's plants were destroyed or badly damaged on August 24, 1992 by Hurricane Andrew. An area of the garden has been left untouched since then to show the effects of a hurricane and how plants respond to devastation. Following one of several rough trails through here will make the recovery of the rest of the garden seem that much more remarkable.

Food may not be brought into the gardens, but on weekends the **snack bar** is open. At other times you can use the picnic sites in neighboring Matheson Hammock Park (see p.78) or the café at Parrot Jungle (see p.83) a few minutes' drive away.

Coconut Grove

A stamping ground of down-at-heel artists, writers and lefties through the Sixties and Seventies, today's **COCONUT GROVE** is a glitterati hangout thanks to business-led revitalization. Art galleries, fashionable restaurants and towering bay-view apartments mark its central section – clear signs of a neighborhood whose fortunes are rising. But Coconut Grove, finely placed along the shores of Biscayne Bay, also retains much of value from its formative years. A century ago, a strange mix of Bahamian salvagers and New England intellectuals searching for spiritual fulfillment laid the foundations of a fiercely idiosyncratic community, separated from the fledgling city of Miami by a dense, jungle-like wedge of tropical foliage. The distance between Coconut Grove and the rest of Miami is still very much apparent: cleaner and richer than ever, but continuing to fan the flames of liberalism – and boasting the best batch of **drinking and music locales** outside of Miami Beach.

North Coconut Grove

In 1914, farm-machinery mogul James Deering followed his brother, Charles (of Deering Estate fame, see "South Miami"), to south Florida and blew $15 million on recreating a sixteenth-century Italian villa within the belt of vegetation between Miami and Coconut Grove. A thousand-strong workforce completed his **Villa Vizcaya**, 3251 South Miami Avenue (daily 9.30am–4.30pm; gardens open until 5pm; $10; ☎250-9133), in just two years. The lasting impression of the grandiose structure is that both Deering and his designer (the crazed Paul Chalfin, hell-bent on becoming an architectural legend) had more money than taste: Deering's madly eclectic art collection, and the concept that the villa should appear to have been inhabited for 400 years, resulted in a thunderous clash of Baroque, Renaissance, Rococo and Neoclassical fixtures and furnishings, and even the landscaped **gardens**, with their fountains and sculptures, aren't spared the pretensions. Nonetheless, Villa Vizcaya is one of Miami's more sought-out sights, with many diverting details – Chinese figures casting shadows across the tearoom, and a Georgian library, for instance – and one of the most visited. It's also a popular wedding reception venue, hence the brigades of beaming Cuban brides being photographed here. **Guided tours** leave frequently from the entrance loggia – dominated by a second-century marble statue of Bacchus – and provide solid background information, after which you're free to explore at leisure.

Straight across South Miami Drive from Villa Vizcaya, the **Museum of Science and Space Transit Planetarium**, 3280 S Miami Ave (daily 10am–6pm; last admission 5pm; $9; ☎854-4247), sets a different mood entirely. Its interactive exhibits provide a good two-hour family diversion, though a more forceful reason to visit is the collection of wildlife at the museum's rear. Vultures and owls are among a number of injured birds seeing out their days here, a variety of snakes can be viewed at disturbingly close quarters, and the resident tarantula is happy to be handled. The adjoining **planetarium** (☎854-2222; shows hourly on the hour) has the usual trips-around-the-cosmos shows, and hosts head-banging rock music laser shows (Fri & Sat nights 9pm; $6). Details are available by phone or from the ticket office inside the museum.

Where South Miami Drive becomes Bayshore Drive, close to Mercy Hospital, the road off to the left leads to the **Church of Ermita de la Curidad** (daily 9am–9pm), erected by Miami Cubans. A mural behind the altar traces the island's history, and the conical-shaped church is angled to allow worshippers to look out across the bay in the direction of Cuba.

Back on Bayshore Drive, for the next two miles or so you'll catch glimpses of lime-stone jutting through the greenery on the inland side. It was on this ridge, known as **Silver Bluff**, that several early settlers established their homes, later joined by the well-heeled notables of 1910s Miami; a few of their houses still stand, though none is open to the public. The area has remained a preserve of the rich, whose opulent abodes are shielded from prying eyes by carefully maintained trees.

Central Coconut Grove

The suggestion of major money around Silver Bluff yields to blatant statements of wealth once you draw closer to central Coconut Grove. Bayshore Drive continues between expensive, high-rise condos and jogger-filled, landscaped parks. Heading up Pan American Drive will take you to the **marina** on **Dinner Key**, a picnic spot for settlers at the turn of the century and now a mooring for lines of hundred-thousand-dollar yachts.

Next door, the **Coconut Grove Exhibition Center** is nowadays a popular venue for top-of-the-line car and interior furnishing shows. Its forerunner was the Dinner Key Auditorium, where in 1969 the rock legend **Jim Morrison**, singer with the Doors, dropped his leather pants to expose himself during the band's first – and last – Florida show; this caused Miami's police to clamp down on local rock clubs, and increased the band's notoriety a hundred-fold.

The gigantic Exhibition Center overshadows the more cheerful **Miami City Hall**, 3400 Pan American Drive (Mon–Fri 8am–5pm), the small and unlikely seat of local government. The blue-and-white-trimmed Art Deco building used to be an airline terminal: in the Thirties, passengers checked in here for the Pan American Airways seaplane service to Latin America, and the sight of the lumbering craft taking off used to draw thousands to the waterfront. In front of the City Hall a small plaque records the fact that Dinner Key was the place that veterans of the Bay of Pigs stepped ashore after their release from Cuba in 1962.

Walking from the City Hall across the Exhibition Center's parking lot brings you to the Havana Clipper restaurant, whose ground floor houses a mildly appealing historical collection (11.30am–midnight; free) of photos and old radio parts from the seaplane times (which lasted until improvements to Latin American runways made sea landings unnecessary).

Peacock Park, at the end of Bayshore Drive beside MacFarlane Road, was a notorious hippie haunt at the time of Morrison's misdemeanors in Coconut Grove. More recently it's been cleaned up to fit the area's present smart, sophisticated image, and now features tennis courts and some peculiar abstract rock sculptures. The **Chamber of Commerce**, 2820 MacFarlane Road (Mon–Fri 9am–5pm; ☎444-7270), on a corner of the park, has copious selections of free leaflets and maps of the area.

Along Main Highway

At the end of MacFarlane Road you hit **Main Highway** and Coconut Grove as most Miamians see it: several blocks of trendy cafés, galleries and boutiques. Though less enjoyable than Miami Beach's South Beach (see "Miami Beach," p.88), it's a fine place for a stroll, if only to watch the neighborhood's affluent fashion victims going through their paces. You can eat, drink and pose (for where to do all three, see "Eating" and "Drinking," p.97 and p.104) at **CocoWalk** – an enjoyable collection of open-air restaurants and bars, and yet more stylish shops – located between Main Highway and Virginia Street, at 3000 Grand Avenue. Or for a taste of sheer exclusivity, drop into **Streets of Mayfair** (Mon, Thurs & Fri 10am–9pm, Tues, Wed & Sat 10am-7pm, Sun noon–5.30pm), at the corner of MacFarlane Road and Grand Avenue, a designer shopping mall whose zigzagging walkways – decorated by fountains, copper sculptures, climbing vines and Romanesque doodles in concrete – wind around three floors of expense-account stores.

Heading south down Main Highway you'll come across the beige-and-white **Coconut Grove Playhouse**, at no. 3500. Opened in 1927 and still going strong on a mixed diet of Broadway blockbusters and alternative offerings, this is the best of the area's several examples of Mediterranean Revival architecture, but warrants only a passing glance as you move on to the most enduring historic site in Coconut Grove, at the end of a path right across Main Highway from the playhouse.

The tree-shaded track leads to a tranquil bayside garden and a century-old house known as the **Barnacle** (Fri–Sun, 9am–4pm; $1), built by "Commodore" Ralph Middelton Munroe: sailor, brilliant yacht-designer and a devotee of the Transcendalist Movement (advocating self-reliance, a love of nature and a simple lifestyle). The Barnacle was ingeniously put together in 1891 with local materials and tricks learned from nautical design. Raising the structure eight feet off the ground in 1908 improved air circulation and prevented flooding, a covered verandah enabled windows to be opened during rainstorms, and a skylight allowed air to be drawn through the house – all major innovations that alleviated some of the discomforts of living all year in the heat and humidity of south Florida. More inventive still, when Munroe needed more space for his family he simply jacked up the single-story structure and added a new floor underneath. Only with the guided tour (10am, 11.30am, 1pm & 2.30pm) can you see inside the house, where many original furnishings remain alongside some of Munroe's intriguing photos of pioneering Coconut Grovers. The grounds, however, you are free to explore on your own. The lawn extends to the shore of Biscayne Bay, while behind the house are the last remnants of the tropical hardwood hammock that extended throughout the Miami area.

Charles Avenue and Black Coconut Grove

The Bahamian settlers of the late 1800s, who later provided the labor that went into building Coconut Grove and nearby areas, mostly lived along what became **Charles Avenue** (off Main Highway, close to the playhouse), in small, simple wooden houses similar to the "conch houses" that fill Key West's Old Town (see "The Florida Keys").

You'll find a trio of these still standing on the "3200" block, though be warned that they are on the edge of **Black Coconut Grove** (not a name you'll find on maps, but one which everyone uses), a run-down area stretching westwards to the borders of Coral Gables. The fact that such a derelict district exists within half a mile of one of the city's most fashionably upmarket areas provides a stark reminder of Miami's racial divisions. Like all of Miami's black areas, white people should only approach with caution; and certainly not without a car.

South Coconut Grove

South of the playhouse, the outlook along Main Highway soon reverts to expansive older homes set back from the street. A couple of easily found minor sites are the only reasons to stop as you pass through towards South Miami. After half a mile, you'll spy the **Ransom Everglades School**, 3575 Main Highway, founded in 1903 for boarding pupils who split the school year between New York's Adirondack mountains and here. Oddly enough, the main schoolroom was a Chinese-style **pagoda** (Mon–Fri 9am–5pm; free), which still stands incongruously in the middle of what's now an upper-crust prep school. Inside the green-painted pine structure are a few amusing relics from the school's past.

A little further on, near the corner of Devon Road, the 1917 **Plymouth Congregational Church** (Mon–Fri 9am–4pm) has a striking, vine-covered, coral rock facade; remarkably, this finely crafted exterior was the work of just one man. Note, too, the 375-year-old main door, hand-carved in walnut, which looks none the worse for its journey from an early seventeenth-century monastery in the Spanish Pyrenees. If the church door beside the parking lot is locked, try the church office, on the other side of Devon Road.

South Miami

South of Coral Gables and Coconut Grove, monotonous middle-class suburbs consume almost all of **SOUTH MIAMI**, an expanse of cozy but dull family homes reaching to the edge of the Everglades, interrupted only by golf courses and a few contrived tourist attractions. Mini-malls, gas stations, cut-price waterbed outlets and bumper-to-bumper traffic are the star features of its primary thoroughfare, Hwy-1. You can't avoid this route entirely, but from South Coral Gables a better course is Old Cutler Road, which makes a pleasing meander from Coconut Grove through a thick belt of woodland (see also Matheson Hammock Park, p.78 and Fairchild Tropical Garden, p.79) between Biscayne Bay and the suburban sprawl. Cutting inland from Hwy-1 is unrewarding (and unthinkable without a car), since there are no stops of any major importance.

Along Old Cutler Road: the Deering Estate

Long before modern highways scythed through the city, **Old Cutler Road** was the sole road between Coconut Grove and Cutler, a small town that went into terminal decline in the 1910s after being bypassed by the new Flagler railroad. A wealthy industrialist and amateur botanist, Charles Deering (brother of James, the owner of Villa Vizcaya; see "Coconut Grove," above), was so taken with the natural beauty of the area that he purchased all of Cutler and, with one exception, razed its buildings to make way for the **Charles Deering Estate**, 16701 SW 72nd Avenue (☎235-1668), completed in 1922. Deering maintained the *Richmond Inn*, Cutler's only hotel, as his own living and dining quarters. Its pleasant wooden form now stands in marked contrast to the limestone mansion he erected alongside, whose interior – echoing halls, dusty chandeliers

VISITOR INFORMATION

While in this vicinity, you should take advantage of the excellent **Visitor Information Center** (daily 8am–6pm; ☎1-800/388-9669 or ☎245-9180), located on Hwy-1 close to the junction with Hwy-9336 (344th Street); it offers a wealth of information and is particularly strong on the Everglades.

and checker-board-tile floors – is Mediterranean in style but carries a Gothic spookiness. More impressive than the buildings are the three-hundred-acre **grounds**, where signs of human habitation dating back 10,000 years have been found amid the pine woods, mangrove forests and tropical hardwood hammocks.

The buildings were severely damaged or destroyed by Hurricane Andrew, and the estate has been closed while restoration takes place. At the time of this publication no foreseeable opening date has been mentioned. Phone ahead for more information.

Parrot Jungle, Metrozoo and the Gold Coast Railroad Museum

Parrot Jungle, 11000 SW 57th Avenue (9.30am–6pm; adults $11.67, children 3–12 $8.47; ☎666-7834), has parrots, parakeets and macaws of rainbow plumage swapping squawks as visitors wander along delightfully shaded pathways past their cages. The gardens are designed to protect both residents and visitors from the hot Florida sun and include hundreds of varieties of plants, waterfalls and a lake with Caribbean pink flamingos. Apart from birds, the park is home to numerous species of alligators and crocodiles, giant tortoises, chimpanzees and other primates. Even if you don't intend to enter Parrot Jungle, the *Parrot Café* (8am–5pm) offers views into the park and makes a useful stop if you're coming from the nearby Fairchild Tropical Garden (see p.79).

A more extensive display of wildlife – assuming you're not opposed to zoos in principle – is the **Metrozoo**, 12400 SW 152nd Street (daily 9.30am-5.30pm; 4pm last admission; adults $8, children $4; ☎251-0400), its once lush foliage only slowly recovering from the devastating effects of Hurricane Andrew. Even so, while psychological barriers such as moats and small hills are employed instead of cages, it's hard to imagine that many of the animals enjoy baking in the heat and humidity any more than their audience; both tend to spend their time here pursuing shade and a cool drink. If you do come, the snow-white Bengal tigers are the prize exhibit. Avoid visiting during the sweltering midday temperatures of summer, and when it rains – most of the zoo is outdoors.

Sharing the zoo's entrance, the **Gold Coast Railroad Museum** (Mon–Fri 10am–3pm, Sat & Sun 10am–5pm; adults $4, children under 12 free; ☎253-0063) houses a small but intriguing collection of old locomotives that can be clambered upon for closer inspection. Among them is the *Ferdinand Megellan*, a luxury Pullman car that was custom-built in 1928 for presidential use and features escape hatches and steel armor plating. Harry S. Truman traveled 21,000 miles in it on his 1948 re-election campaign, giving three hundred speeches from the rear platform.

Key Biscayne and around

A compact, immaculately manicured community five miles off the Miami shore, **KEY BISCAYNE** is a great place to live – if you can afford it. Seeking relaxation and creature comforts away from life in the fast lane, the moneyed of Miami fill the island's upmarket homes and condos: even Richard Nixon had his presidential winter house here, and singer Sting chose one of the luxury shorefront hotels for a recuperative pamper between tour dates. For visitors, Key Biscayne offers a couple of inviting beaches,

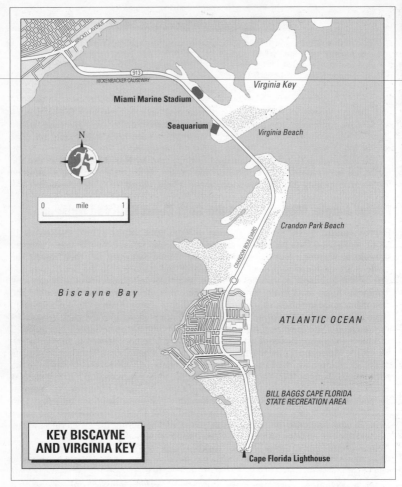

RICKENBACKER CAUSEWAY
Virginia Key
Miami Marine Stadium
Seaquarium
Virginia Beach

N

0   mile   1

Crandon Park Beach

Biscayne Bay

ATLANTIC OCEAN

BILL BAGGS CAPE FLORIDA
STATE RECREATION AREA

**KEY BISCAYNE
AND VIRGINIA KEY**

▲ **Cape Florida Lighthouse**

a third within a state park, and a fabulous cycling path running the full length, but bear in mind that much of the shade-producing vegetation was torn out by Hurricane Andrew and that it will take years before the newly planted trees develop. Cheap eats and lodgings are in predictably short supply.

Approaching Key Biscayne: Virginia Key and around

Without a private yacht, the only way onto Key Biscayne is via **Rickenbacker Causeway**, a four-mile-long continuation of SW 26th Road just south of downtown Miami; it soars high above Biscayne Bay, allowing shipping to glide underneath, and provides a breathtaking view of the Brickell Avenue skyline (see "Around Downtown Miami," p.68). Drivers have to pay a $1 toll; otherwise you can cross the causeway by bus (#B), bike or even on foot.

The first land you'll hit is the unexceptional and sparsely populated **VIRGINIA KEY**. The Miami Marine Stadium is the prominent building on the left, but this is now closed due to disrepair and underuse. A few yards beyond it is the beginning of a two-mile lane that winds through a cluster of Australian pines to **Virginia Beach** (daily 8am–sunset; cars $2). During the years of segregation, this was set aside for Miami's black community (chosen, cynics might presume, for its proximity to a large sewage works). Later, flocks of hippies became seriously laid-back around the secluded coves, which provide a private setting for (unofficial) nude sunbathing.

In contrast, on the right of the main road, the **Seaquarium** marine park (daily 9.30am–6pm; adults $19.95, children under 10 $14.95; parking costs extra; ☎361-5705) is a bustling place where you can while away three or four hours watching the usual roster of performing seals and dolphins – be sure not to miss Lolita, the 8000-pound star of the spectacular killer-whale show (daily, noon). The park's most important work – formulating breeding programs to preserve Florida's endangered sea life and serving as a halfway house for injured manatees and other sea creatures – goes on behind the scenes. Though the park is enjoyable – and the fact that it served as the backdrop for the *Flipper* TV series – remember that there are plenty more marine parks in Florida, such as Orlando's Sea World, and much more in Miami on which to spend your time and money.

Key Biscayne: Crandon Park Beach

Not content with living in one of the best natural settings in Miami, the people of Key Biscayne also possess one of the finest landscaped beaches in the city – **Crandon Park Beach** (8am–sunset; cars $3; ☎361-5421), a mile along Crandon Boulevard (the continuation of the main road from the causeway). Three miles of golden beach fringe the park, and you can wade out at knee-depth to a sandbar far from the shore. Filled by the sounds of boisterous kids and sizzling barbecues on weekends, at any other time the park is disturbed only by the occasional jogger or holidaymaker straying from the private beaches of the expensive hotels nearby. Relax beside the lapping ocean waters and keep a look out for manatees and dolphins, both known to swim by, but be sure to bring high factor sun screen and a beach umbrella as Hurricane Andrew tore out almost all of the palms immediately fronting the beach.

Residential Key Biscayne

Besides its very green, manicured looks, **residential Key Biscayne**, beginning with an abrupt wall of apartment buildings at the southern edge of Crandon Park Beach, has little to offer visitors. You'll need to pass through, however, on the way to the much more rewarding Bill Baggs Cape Florida Park (see below), and while doing so should make a loop along **Harbor Drive**, turning off along McIntire Drive. At no. 485 W stands the former home of ex-president Richard Nixon, who picked up his *Miami Herald* here one morning in 1972 to read of a break-in at the *Watergate Complex* in Washington; the seemingly insignificant event (only featured by the paper because two Miami Cubans were involved) led to Nixon's resignation two years later. On the same street, pick up information on the area at the **Chamber of Commerce**, 328 Crandon Blvd, Suite 217 (Mon–Fri 9am–5pm; ☎361-5207).

Key Biscayne: the southern tip

Crandon Boulevard terminates at the entrance to the 400-acre **Bill Baggs Cape Florida State Recreation Area** (daily 8am–sunset; cars $4, pedestrians and cyclists $1; ☎361-5811), which covers the southern extremity of Key Biscayne. Once thickly wooded, almost all the trees were destroyed in 1992 by Hurricane Andrew, but a massive planting program has taken place, including the introduction of native Floridian fauna. Until the trees mature, however, there's no shade from the often scorching sun, so take the usual precautions. An excellent swimming **beach** lines the Atlantic-facing side of the park, and a boardwalk cuts around the wind-bitten sand dunes towards the **Cape Florida lighthouse**, built in the 1820s. Only with the ranger-led **tour** (daily except Tues at 9am, 10.30am, 1pm, 2.30pm & 3.30pm; $1) can you climb through the 95-foot-high structure, which was attacked by Seminole Indians in 1836 and seized by Confederate soldiers to disrupt Union shipping during the Civil War. It remained in use until 1878, and now serves as a navigation beacon.

Stiltsville

Looking out from the park across the bay, you'll spy the grouping of fragile-looking houses known as **Stiltsville**. Held above water by stilts, these wooden dwellings were built and occupied by fishermen in the Forties and Fifties, and enraged the authorities by being outside the jurisdiction of tax collectors. Stiltsville's demise has been signaled by a recent law forbidding repair work on the ramshackle structures, whose state of disrepair was compounded by the destruction wrought by Hurricane Andrew; just one now has a full-time occupant, the others are occasionally used for parties.

Homestead and around

Suburbia yields to agriculture as you continue south along Hwy-1, where broad, fertile fields grow fruit and vegetables for the nation's northern states. Aside from offering as good a taste of Florida farmlife – the region produces the bulk of America's winter tomatoes – as you're likely to find so close to its major city, the district can be a money-saving stop (see "Accommodation") en route to the Florida Keys or the Everglades National Park.

Closer in mood to *The Waltons* than *Miami Vice*, **HOMESTEAD** is the agricultural area's main town, and the least galvanizing section of Miami. Krome Avenue, just west of Hwy-1, slices through the center, but besides a few restored 1910s-1930s buildings (such as the Old City Hall, no. 43 N), there's little to detain you other than the **Florida Pioneer Museum**, no. 826 (☎246-9531), where two yellow-painted train station buildings store photos and objects from Homestead's formative years – this end-of-the-line town was planned by Flagler's railroad engineers in 1904. To the rear, a 1926 caboose keeps moderately entertaining railroad mementos. The museum was badly damaged by Hurricane Andrew in 1992, so if you're thinking of visiting it, phone ahead to find out if it's open.

Around Homestead

Time is better spent **around Homestead** than actually in it, with plenty of diversions just a few minutes' drive from the town. You can also gather your own dinner in this area; keep an eye out for "**pick-your-own**" signs, where, for a few dollars, you can take to the fields and load up with peas, tomatoes and a variety of other crops.

The Coral Castle

The one essential stop is the **Coral Castle**, 28655 S Dixie Hwy (daily 9am–6pm; adults $7.75, children $5; ☎248-6344), whose bulky coral rock sculptures can be found about six miles northeast of Homestead, beside Hwy-1, at the junction with 286th Street. Remarkably, these fantastic creations, whose delicate finish belies their imposing size, are the work of just one man – the enigmatic **Edward Leedskalnin**. Jilted in 1913 by his sixteen-year-old fiancée in Latvia, Leedskalnin spent seven years working his way across Europe, Canada and the US before buying an acre of land just south of Homestead. Using a profound – and self-taught – knowledge of weights and balances, he somehow raised enormous hunks of coral rock from the ground, then used a work bench made from car running boards and handmade tools fashioned from scrap to refine the blocks into chairs, tables and beds; odd furniture that suggests the castle was intended as a love nest to woo back his errant sweetheart (last heard of in 1980, still in Latvia). Leedskalnin died here in 1951.

You can wander around the slabs, sit on the hard but surprisingly comfortable chairs, swivel a nine-ton gate with your pinkie, and admire the numerous coral representations of the moon and planets that reflected Leedskalnin's interest in astronomy and astrology; also on display is his twenty-foot-high telescope. But what you won't be able to do is explain how the sculptures were made. No one ever saw the secretive Leedskalnin at work, or knows how, alone, he could have loaded 1100 tons of rock onto the rail-mounted truck that brought the pieces here in 1936.

The Fruit and Spice Park, and Monkey Jungle

The subtle fragrances of the **Fruit and Spice Park**, 24801 SW 187th Avenue (daily 10am–5pm; $3.50; ☎247-5727), tickle your nostrils as soon as you enter. Rare exotica such as star fruit and the aptly named Panama candle tree are the highlights of a host of tropical peculiarities; on weekends the guided tour (1pm & 3pm; $1) will give you a good introduction to the secret lives of spices.

To the north of Homestead, at 14805 SW 216th Street, **Monkey Jungle** (daily 9.30am–5pm; 4pm last admission; adults $11.50, children 3–12 $6; ☎235-1611) is one of the few places of protection in the US for endangered primates. Covered walkways keep visitors in closer confinement than the monkeys, and lead through a steamy hammock where several hundred baboons, orang-utans, gorillas and chimps move through the vegetation. Despite a fair amount of freedom, the animals don't appear a terribly happy lot, possibly because of overcrowding. The monkeys spend most of their time scrounging food from visitors – take care not to get bitten or, just as unpleasant, relieved on by inmates angry if there are no treats on offer.

Biscayne National Park

If you're not going to the Florida Keys, make a point of visiting **Biscayne National Park** (daily 8am–sunset; ☎230-1144), at the end of Canal Drive (328th Street), east of Hwy-1. The bulk of the park lies beneath the clear ocean waters, where stunning formations of living coral provide a habitat for shoals of brightly colored fish and numerous other creatures too delicate to survive on their own. For a full description of the wondrous world of the living coral reef, see "John Pennecamp State Park," in "The Florida Keys".

The lazy way to view it is on the three-hour **glass-bottomed boat** trip (daily at 10am; adults $16.50, children under 12 $8.50; reservations ☎230-1100), but for a fuller encounter you should embark on a three-hour snorkel tour ($28 including all equipment). Gear can also be rented from the **visitor center** (Dec–April Mon–Fri 8am–5pm, Sat & Sun 9am–5.30pm; rest of the year Mon–Fri 10am–4pm, Sat & Sun 10am–6pm; ☎230-7275) near the entrance at **Convoy Point**. For tours and dives, phone at least a day ahead to make reservations.

Another option is to visit the park's **barrier islands**, seven miles out. A tour boat leaves for **Elliot Key** from Convoy Point at 1.30pm on Sundays between December and May. Once ashore, besides calling at the **visitor center** (Sat & Sun 10am–4pm) and contemplating the easy six-mile hiking trail along the island's forested spine, there's nothing to do on Elliot Key except sunbathe in solitude.

MIAMI BEACH

Three miles offshore from Miami, sheltering Biscayne Bay from the Atlantic Ocean, the long, slender arm of **Miami Beach** was an ailing fruit farm in the 1910s when its Quaker owner, John Collins, formed an unlikely partnership with a flashy entrepreneur called Carl Fisher. With Fisher's money, Biscayne Bay was dredged, and the muck raised from its murky bed provided the landfill that helped transform the island into the sculptured landscape of palm trees, hotels and tennis courts that – by and large – it is today.

In varying degrees, all twelve miles of Miami Beach are worth seeing – and its firm, crushed-coral-rock beach offers excellent sunbathing and swimming opportunities – though only **South Beach**, a fairly small area at the southern end, will hold your attention for long. Here, rows of tastefully restyled Thirties Art Deco buildings have become chic gathering places for the city's fashionable faces and the stamping ground of Miami's more creative and unconventional elements. It's no fluke that many of Florida's leading art galleries and nightclubs are found in this compact area. Heading north, **Central Miami Beach** was where Fifties screen stars had fun in the sun and helped cement Miami's international reputation as a glamorous vacation spot. Oddly enough, it's the monolithic hotels remaining from these times that give the area a modicum of appeal. Further on, **North Miami Beach**, despite splitting into several distinctive communities, has even less to kindle the imagination – a long way from the action and mostly overrun by package tourists – but makes a good back route if you're heading north from Miami towards Fort Lauderdale.

South Beach

Miami Beach's most exciting area is **SOUTH BEACH**, which occupies the southernmost three miles. Filled with pastel-colored Art Deco buildings, up-and-coming art galleries, modish diners and suntanned beach addicts, it attracts multinational swarms of photographers and film crews who zoom in on what has – thanks to the visuals of *Miami Vice* and the fashion photography of Bruce Weber (shooting nudes on the hotel roofs for the 1986 Calvin Klein *Obsession* campaign) – become the hottest high-style backdrop in the world.

Socially, South Beach is unsurpassed. By day, fine-bodied ravers soak up the rays on the beach, and by night the ten blocks of Ocean Drive are the heart and soul of the biggest party in Miami: chic terrace cafés spill across the wide sidewalk amid a procession of fashion models, tropical-shirted existentialists, wide-eyed tourists, tarot card readers and

---

APPROACHING MIAMI BEACH: THE CAUSEWAYS AND ISLANDS

The setting of countless *Miami Vice* car chases, the six **causeways** crossing Biscayne Bay between Miami and Miami Beach offer striking views of the city, especially at night when the lights of buildings downtown twinkle over the bay's dark waters. Some of the causeways also provide the only land access to the artificial residential islands that shelter the rich and famous from unwanted attention.

Best pickings are along **MacArthur Causeway**, running from just north of downtown Miami into Miami Beach's South Beach. A mile into it, **Watson Island Park** harbors the **Japanese Garden**, bequeathed to the city by a Japanese industrialist in 1961; pride of place goes to an eight-ton statue of Hotei – the Japanese god of prosperity. On subsequent islands are the former homes of gangster Al Capone (Palm Island), author Damon Runyon (Hibiscus Island), and actor Don Johnson (Star Island).

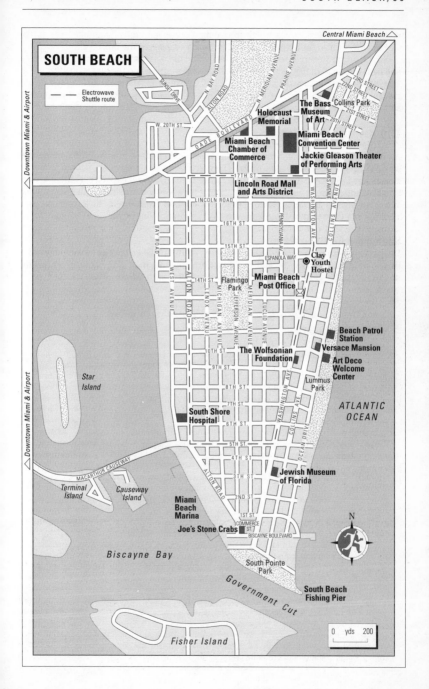

SOUTH BEACH

- - - Electrowave
Shuttle route

Central Miami Beach △

Downtown Miami & Airport

N BAY ROAD

SUNSET DRIVE

N MERIDIAN AVENUE

PRAIRIE AVENUE

23RD STREET

22ND STREET

21ST STREET

20TH STREET

Collins Park

The Bass
Museum
of Art

Holocaust
Memorial

Miami Beach
Convention Center

Miami Beach
Chamber of
Commerce

Jackie Gleason Theater
of Performing Arts

W. 20TH ST

ALTON ROAD

BOULEVARD

DADE

17TH ST

Lincoln Road Mall
and Arts District

JAMES AVENUE

LILENOX AVENUE

WASHINGTON AVE

COLLINS AVE

LINCOLN ROAD

16TH ST

BAY ROAD

PENNSYLVANIA AVE

15TH ST

ESPANOLA WAY

Clay
Youth
Hostel

WEST AVENUE

14TH ST

Flamingo
Park

Miami Beach
Post Office

ALTON ROAD

MICHIGAN AVENUE

JEFFERSON AVENUE

MERIDIAN AVENUE

EUCLID AVENUE

Star
Island

Downtown Miami & Airport

10TH ST

9TH ST

The Wolfsonian
Foundation

Beach Patrol
Station
Versace Mansion

Art Deco
Welcome
Center

WASHINGTON AVE

Lummus
Park

8TH ST

7TH ST

ATLANTIC
OCEAN

South Shore
Hospital

6TH ST

5TH ST

4TH ST

COLLINS AVE

OCEAN DRIVE

3TH ST

Jewish Museum
of Florida

ALTON ROAD

2ND ST

MACARTHUR CAUSEWAY

Terminal
Island

Causeway
Island

Miami
Beach
Marina

1ST ST

COMMERCE
ST

Joe's Stone Crabs

BISCAYNE BOULEVARD

N

Biscayne Bay

South Pointe
Park

South Beach
Fishing Pier

Government Cut

0   yds   200

Fisher Island

middle-aged trendies. Places worth frequenting are listed under "Nightlife," see p.105. Ocean Drive is also the scene of the Miami Beach cruise; see the box on p.91.

Not all South Beach is so sensuous. Just a few blocks from Ocean Drive, the streets still bear the scars of the area's poverty-stricken Seventies, and the arrival in 1980 of the "Marielitos," Fidel Castro's gift to the US of Cuban criminals and misfits (see "Little Havana," p.71), many of whom ended up here. Provided you stick to the main streets and exercise the usual caution, however, none of South Beach is unduly dangerous.

The Art Deco district

As much as the beach and the social life, it's the **Art Deco district**, containing the world's greatest concentration of Art Deco architecture, that brings people to South Beach. Art Deco here is a smorgasbord rather than a gourmet experience; there are no great buildings, just a great number of them – numbering in the hundreds between 5th and 23rd streets between Ocean Drive and Lennox Avenue – built during the late Thirties in a style that became known as "Miami Beach Art Deco."

Seeing the Art Deco district

Painstaking restoration notwithstanding, little of the Art Deco district looks today quite like it did in the Thirties. Nowhere is this more apparent than in the colors – "a palette of Post Modern cake-icing pastels now associated with *Miami Vice*," according to

---

ART DECO IN MIAMI BEACH

Art Deco's roots go back to the Paris of 1901, though in the US it only began to take hold as a building style in the Thirties. With it, the nation shook off the restraints of Classical Revivalism and the gloom of the Depression. Thrilling and new, Art Deco architecture embraced technology, borrowing streamlined contours from the aerodynamic designs of futuristic cars, trains and planes. It also incorporated playful and humorous themes, employing wacky ornamentation and vivid colors, as well as new materials such as aluminum, chrome and plastic. Often derided as vulgar, Art Deco nonetheless became a symbol of a country emerging from economic catastrophe to become the first modern superpower.

In the late Thirties, a small group of architects built prolifically – and fast – in Miami Beach. Employing the trademarks of Art Deco, they used local limestone and stucco to produce buildings that were cheap (and often cramped and uncomfortable) but instantly fashionable – defining the look of the nation's fun and sun mecca with a style soon dubbed "**Miami Beach Art Deco**" (sometimes called "**Tropical Deco**"). Recognizable Florida motifs, such as herons, pelicans, blooming flowers and blazing sunsets, decorated facades and porches. Nautical themes were prevalent, too: windows resembled portholes, balconies stretched out like luxury liner sundecks, and any ungainly bulges on roofs were disguised as ships' funnels. Many of the buildings were painted stark white, reflecting the force of the Florida sun with matching intensity.

It's a sobering thought that Miami Beach almost lost all of these significant structures, which fell into decline from the late Fifties and were sought after by property developers wishing to replace them with anonymous high-rise condos. In the mid-Seventies, the **Miami Beach Art Deco Preservation League** (Art Deco Welcome Center, 1001 Ocean Drive ☎531-3484) – whose first meeting drew just six people – was born with the aim of saving the buildings and raising awareness of their architectural and historical importance. The League's success has been dramatic – a major turning point was convincing the buck-hungry developers of the earning potential of such a unique area. The driving force of the movement, the late Barbara Capitman, failed in her attempt at a similar initiative in Opa-Locka, a socially blighted district in northwest Miami, nowadays better known for its crack dealers than its crazy, Arabesque architecture.

THE MIAMI BEACH CRUISE

A bumper-to-bumper procession of horn-honking, passenger-swapping autos along Ocean Drive between Fifth and Fourteenth streets, the **Miami Beach cruise** – part unofficial street party, part pick-up exercise – takes place on Fridays and Saturdays from around 7pm to 4am, and on Sunday afternoons from noon to 7pm. Join in if you dare!

disgruntled Florida architecture chronicler Hap Hatton – which appeared in 1980 when local designer Leonard Horowitz started adorning the buildings. Furthermore, the details of restoration reflect the tastes of the buildings' owners more than historical accuracy – but Miami Beach Art Deco of the 1990s is a sight to behold in its own right.

Examples of the Art Deco style are too numerous to list (or view) in full; just stroll around and keep your eyes open. For a more structured investigation, try taking the ninety-minute **walking tour** (Sat 10.30am, Thurs 6.30pm; $10) from the Art Deco Welcome Center, 1001 Ocean Drive, or the **bicycle tour** (Sun 10.30am; $10 including bike rental; reservations ☎672-2014) from Cycles on the Beach, 713 Fifth Street.

The district's contemporary look should be assessed from Ocean Drive, where a line of revamped hotels have exploited their design heritage; you can venture into the lobbies for a look, and many are worth visiting for their bars or restaurants (see "Eating" and "Nightlife"). Among them, the *Park Central*, no. 640, is a geometric *tour de force*, with octagonal windows, sharp vertical columns and a wrought-iron decorated stairway leading up to the mezzanine level, which displays monochrome photos of Miami Beach in the Twenties. Nearby, at no. 850, a corner of the *Waldorf Towers* is topped by an ornamental lighthouse. Just across the street in Lummus Park (the grassy patch that separates Ocean Drive from the beach), and more honestly redolent of the old days, stands the boat-shaped **Beach Patrol Station**, unmistakable for its vintage oversized date and temperature sign, and still the base of the local lifeguards.

Just ahead are two buildings at the center of the controversy currently raging through South Beach: should its Art Deco buildings be decorated only in officially approved pastel colors, or can they be allowed to evolve a particularly 1990s South Beach style and use much more vivid tones? The purple and orange frontage of the **Cardozo**, no. 1300, and the intense yellow exterior of the **Leslie**, no. 1244, were the recent work of Barbara Hulanicki, who founded London's scene-setting clothes store Biba in the 1960s. Hulanicki's exuberant tones have upset many South Beach purists, but seem set to be the look of South Beach to come.

Walk at least once after dark along the beach side of Ocean Drive. This frees you from the crowds and enables a clear view of the Art Deco hotels' **neon illuminations**, casting shimmering circles and lines of vivid blues, pinks and greens around the contours of the buildings.

Away from the image-conscious trappings of Ocean Drive, perhaps the district's most enduring relic, an example of the less ornate Depression Moderne style, is the **Miami Beach Post Office**, 1300 Washington Avenue (lobby Mon–Fri 6am–6pm, Sat 6am–4pm). Inside, streaming sunlight brightens the murals sweeping around a rotunda; there can be few more enjoyable places to buy a stamp.

South of Fifth Street: South Pointe Park and around

South of Fifth Street, a small and shabby area called **South Pointe** is being revamped by a major redevelopment project: more, it seems, to exploit the commercial potential of the location than to benefit the community. A marina and several restaurants have been added, and the luxury 26-story South Pointe Towers leaps skyward from South Pointe

Park (see below), dwarfing the stucco-fronted boxes in which most local people live. The best route through South Pointe is the mile-long shorefront boardwalk, beginning near the southern end of Lummus Park, and finishing by the 300-foot-long jetty lined with people fishing off **First Street Beach**, the only surfing beach in Miami and alive with tanned, athletic bodies even when the waves are calm. You can swim and snorkel here, too, but bear in mind that the big cruise ships frequently pass close by and stir up the current.

South Pointe Park

On its inland side, the boardwalk skirts **South Pointe Park** (daily 8am–sunset), whose handsome lawns and tree-shaded picnic tables offer a respite from the packed beaches. The park is a good place to be on Friday evenings when its open-air stage is the venue for enjoyable free **music events** (details are posted up around South Beach).

Seats on the southern edge of the park give you a view of **Government Cut**, a waterway first dredged by Henry Flagler at the turn of the century and now, substantially deepened, the route for large cruise ships beginning their journeys to the Bahamas and Caribbean. You might also witness an impounded drug-running vessel being towed along by the authorities. Don't be surprised, either, to hear the neighing of horses: Miami Beach's police horses are stabled on the eastern side of the park.

North along Washington Avenue

Running through South Beach parallel to Ocean Drive is **Washington Avenue**, much of it lined by small, Cuban-run supermarkets, trendy restaurants and boutiques, rundown retirement homes, and a string of nightclubs. Two of Miami Beach's museums are located here, while a third lies just to the west.

Ziff Jewish Museum of Florida

During the 1920s and 1930s, South Beach became an major destination for Jewish tourists escaping the harsh northeastern winters. In response, many of the hotels placed "Gentiles Only" notices at their reception desks, and the slogan "Always a view, never a Jew" appeared in many a hotel brochure. Despite this, by the 1940s South Beach had a largely Jewish population and, though today the center of the community has moved north along the Beach to around 40th and 50th streets, a considerable number of elderly Jews remain. The **Ziff Jewish Museum of Florida**, 301 Washington Avenue (Tues–Sun 10am–5pm; $4; ☎672-5044) bears testimony not only to Jewish life in Miami Beach, but in all of Florida. Housed in an elegant 1936-built Art Deco building, which served as an Orthodox synagogue for Miami Beach's first Jewish congregation, the museum documents Florida's Jewish heritage from the eighteenth century to the present day. Apart from its permanent collection, the museum hosts visiting exhibitions on Jews in Florida, the Caribbean and elsewhere.

Wolfsonian Foundation

Thousands of objects dedicated to design arts have been assembled by Mitchell Wolfson Jr at the **Wolfsonian Foundation**, 1001 Washington Avenue (Tues–Sat 11am–6pm, Sun 12–5pm; $5, free on Thurs from 6–9pm; ☎531-1001). Anyone with a passing interest in decorative, architectural or politics-inspired arts ought to be able to find something of interest in the galleries, which also provide a wonderfully cool haven from the shadeless avenue outside.

Española Way

Other than the Miami Beach post office (described above under "Seeing the Art Deco District"), nothing along Washington Avenue need delay you until you reach **Española**

Way, between 14th and 15th streets. While renowned for its Art Deco, Miami Beach also boasts several examples of the Mediterranean Revival architecture found across much of Miami; most of these are situated on this slender street overhung by narrow balconies and striped awnings.

Completed in 1925, Española Way was grandly envisaged as an "artists' colony," but only the rumba dance craze of the Thirties – said to have started here, stirred up by Cuban band leader Desi Arnaz* – came close to fitting the bill. Following South Beach's social climb in the Eighties, however, a group of browsable art galleries and art supply stores have revived the original concept; they now fill the first-floor rooms, while above them, small top-floor apartments are optimistically marketed as "artists' lofts."

Lincoln Road Mall and the Lincoln Road Arts District
A short walk further north, between 16th and 17th streets, the pedestrianized **Lincoln Road Mall** was considered the flashiest shopping precinct outside of New York during the Fifties, its jewelry and clothes stores earning it the label "Fifth Avenue of the South." Today, run-of-the-mill consumer durable stockists fill the section closest to Washington Avenue, and the focus of interest has shifted a few blocks west to the **Lincoln Road Arts District**, around Lenox Avenue. Here, among a number of art galleries breathing life into what were, a few years ago, fairly seedy offices and shops, the studios (viewing hours are displayed on their doors) and showrooms of **South Florida Art Center, Inc.**, 810 Lincoln Road, will tune you into the burgeoning South Beach arts scene. The area's increasingly cultured mood is reflected in the many restaurants and cafés along the mall (see "Eating"), and the area is a favorite place for evening strolls.

The Jackie Gleason Theater and the Miami Beach Convention Center
The first of two public buildings immediately north of Lincoln Road Mall, the 3000-seat **Jackie Gleason Theater of Performing Arts**, fronted by Pop artist Roy Lichtenstein's expressive *Mermaid* sculpture, stages Broadway shows and classical concerts. However, it is best known to middle-aged Americans as the home of wholesome entertainer Jackie Gleason's immensely popular TV show, *The Honeymooners*, which began in the Fifties and ran for twenty years.

On the far side of the theater, sunlight bounces off the white exterior of the massive **Miami Beach Convention Center**, which occupies a curious niche in US political history. At the Republican Convention held here in August 1968, Richard Nixon won the nomination that would take him to the White House. Nixon counted his votes oblivious to the fact that the first of Miami's Liberty City riots had just erupted (see "Around Downtown Miami").

The Holocaust Memorial
It's hard not to be moved by Kenneth Treister's **Holocaust Memorial**, 1933–1945 Meridian Avenue (9am–9pm), completed in 1990 and dedicated to Elie Wiesel. Depicting an arm tattooed with an Auschwitz number reaching towards the sky, with life-sized figures of emaciated, tormented people attempting to climb it, the deeply emotive sculpture rises from a lily pond in the center of a plaza, around which are graphic images recalling the Nazi genocide against the Jews.

---

*Arnaz (later to find wider fame as the husband of Lucille Ball) and his band often performed in the *Village Tavern*, inside the *Clay Hotel*, which is now the city's youth hostel; see "Accommodation."

The Bass Museum of Art

A little further north, within a sculpture-studded garden, is the fetching coral-rock building of the **Bass Museum of Art**, 2121 Park Avenue (Tues–Sat 10am–5pm, Sun 1–5pm, 2nd & 4th Weds 1–9pm; $5, Tues donations; ☎673-7530), whose major expansion, completed in 1995, was overseen by acclaimed Japanese architect Arata Isozaki. The museum's permanent collection – dominated by worthy European works mostly from the fifteenth to seventeenth centuries, with Rubens, Rembrandt and Dürer heading the cast – is a notch above anything you'll find elsewhere in the state. For anyone other than fine-art buffs, the contemporary visiting exhibitions offer greater stimulation.

Central Miami Beach

The energy of South Beach fades dramatically as you travel north of 23rd Street to **CENTRAL MIAMI BEACH**. Collins Avenue charts a five-mile course through the area, between Indian Creek – across which are the golf courses, country clubs and secluded palatial homes of Miami Beach's seriously rich – and the swanky hotels around which the Miami Beach high-life revolved during the glamorous Fifties. These often madly ostentatious establishments are the main attraction of Central Miami Beach; the strand itself is largely the preserve of families and older folk, and is backed by a long and lovely boardwalk that stretches over a mile from 21st Street.

Along Collins Avenue

The southern edge of Central Miami Beach is defined by the garbage-clogged **Collins Canal**, cut in the 1910s to speed the movement of farm produce through the mangrove trees that then lined Biscayne Bay. The canal is a dismal sight, but improves as it flows into the luxury yacht-lined **Indian Creek**, and along Collins Avenue you'll see the first of the sleek condos and hotels that characterize the area.

Unlike their small Art Deco counterparts in South Beach, the later **hotels** of Central Miami Beach are massive monuments to the Fifties. When big was beautiful, these state-of-the-art pleasure palaces drew the international jet set by offering much more than mere accommodation: a price that few could afford also bought access to exclusive bars, restaurants and lounges where film and TV stars cavorted to the envy of the rest of the US. Yet the good times were short-lived. As everyone tried to cash in, cheap imitations of the pace-setting hotels formed an ugly wall of concrete along Collins Avenue; quality sank, service deteriorated and the big names moved on. By the Seventies, many of the hotels looked like what they really were: monsters from another age. The Eighties saw Miami's social star re-emerge once again, and a revival got underway. Many of the polished-up hotels are now occupied by well-heeled Latin American tourists – along with gray-haired swingers from the US for whom Miami Beach never lost its cachet.

The Fontainebleau Hotel

Prior to Central Miami Beach becoming a celebrities' playground, the nation's rich and powerful built rambling shorefront mansions here. One of them, the winter home of tire-baron Harvey Firestone, was demolished in 1953 to make room for the **Fontainebleau Hotel**, 4441 Collins Avenue, a "dreamland of kitsch and consumerism" that defined the Miami Beach of the late Fifties and Sixties. Gossip-column perennials such as Joan Crawford, Joe DiMaggio, Lana Turner and Bing Crosby were *Fontainebleau* regulars, as was rebel crooner Frank Sinatra who, besides starting a scrambled-egg fight in the coffee shop, shot many scenes here as the private-eye hero of the Sixties film *Tony Rome*. Drop in for a look around the curving lobby overhung by weighty chandeliers, and venture through the tree-filled grounds to a swimming pool complete with rock grottoes and waterfalls.

If you can't face the bellhops lurking in the lobby, one feature you shouldn't miss is on an exterior wall: approaching from the south, Collins Avenue veers left just before the hotel, passing beneath Richard Haas' 13,000-square-foot *trompe l'oeil* mural. Unveiled in 1986, it creates the illusion of a great hole in the wall exposing the hotel directly behind – one of the biggest driving hazards in Miami.

More hotels and luxury homes

Truth be told, there's not much more to see in Central Miami Beach. For its place in local folklore, the *Fontainebleau* is easily the most tempting of the hotels, though you might snatch glances inside the *Shawnee*, no. 4343, and the *Castle Beach Club*, no. 5445, both Fifties survivors who've undergone stylized renovation, with marble floors, indoor fountains and etched glasswork. Meanwhile, the ultra-swish *Alexander*, no. 5225, has become a watering hole for Miami's present-day smart set.

Many of the rich people who live in Miami Beach have gracefully appointed homes up pine-tree-lined drives on the other side of Indian Creek. Cross the water on Arthur Godfrey Road and drive (or cycle) around the exclusive La Gorce Drive and Alton Road for an eyeful of what money can buy.

From further down Collins Avenue to North Miami Beach, hotels dominate the scene. In 1968, an unrestrained Norman Mailer wrote of the area: "Moorish castles shaped like waffle irons, shaped like the baffle plates on white plastic electric heaters, and cylinders like Waring blenders, buildings looking like giant op art and pop art paintings, and sweet wedding cakes, cottons of kitsch and piles of dirty cotton stucco. . ."

North Miami Beach and inland

Collins Avenue continues for seven uninspiring miles through **NORTH MIAMI BEACH**, enriched only by a few noteworthy beaches and parks. Confusingly, due to the machinations of early property speculators, the four small communities that make up this northern section of Miami Beach lack a collective appellation, and the area officially titled "North Miami Beach" is actually inland, across Biscayne Bay.

Surfside and Bal Harbour

Untouched for years as big-money developments loomed all around, the low-rise buildings of **Surfside** – the pleasant North Shore Park marks the community's southern limit – retain a rather appealing old-fashioned ambience, though the community is currently in the throes of gradual gentrification, and only the neighborhood's **beach**, between 91st and 95th streets, will make you want to stick around; incidentally, it's one of the few in Miami Beach to allow topless sunbathing.

Directly north, **Bal Harbour** – aspirations of "Olde Worlde" elegance reflected in its anglicized name – is similar in size to Surfside but entirely different in character: an upmarket area filled with the carefully guarded homes of some of the nation's wealthiest people. The exclusive Bal Harbour Shops, 9700 Collins Avenue, packed with outrageously expensive designer stores, sets the tone for the area. A better place to spend time, especially if you can lose your inhibitions easily, is **Haulover Beach Park**, just to the north, whose reputation as a nude beach doesn't overshadow the sprawling vegetation which backs onto more than a mile of pristine sand. There's also a great view of the Miami Beach skyline from the end of the pier.

Sunny Isles and Golden Beach

Beyond Haulover Park, **Sunny Isles** is as lifeless as they come: a place where European travel agencies dump unsuspecting package tourists and where, due to bargain basement prices, French Canadian tourists choose to return year after year, dominating the fast food restaurants and tacky souvenir shops along Collins Avenue. You'll quickly get a tan on Sunny Isles' sands, but everything around is geared to low-budget, package tourism and, if staying here without a car, you're likely to feel trapped. Of passing interest, however, are some architecturally excessive hotels erected during the Fifties: along Collins Avenue, watch out for the camels and sheiks guarding the *Sahara*, no. 18335; the crescent-moon-holding maidens of the *Blue Mist*, no. 19111; and the Moorish-Polynesian-Deco-Ultra-Bad-Kitsch style of the *Marco Polo*, no. 19200.

By the time you reach **Golden Beach**, the northernmost community of Miami Beach, much of the traffic pounding Collins Avenue has turned inland on the 192nd Street Causeway, and the anachronistic hotels have given way to quiet shorefront homes. Public beach access here is negligible, and unless you're intending to leave Miami altogether (Collins Avenue, as Hwy-A1A, continues north to Fort Lauderdale), there's a bigger draw to be found directly inland.

Inland: the Ancient Spanish Monastery

The Sunny Isles Causeway (163rd Street) leads across to "North Miami Beach," on the mainland. Despite its name, this area is a continuation of the depressed suburbs north of downtown Miami, and not a place to linger in unless you're visiting the **Ancient Spanish Monastery** (Mon–Sat 10am–5pm, Sun noon–5pm; $4). Publishing magnate William Randolph Hearst came across the twelfth-century monastery in Spain in 1925, bought it for $500,000, broke it into numbered pieces and shipped it to the US – only for it to be held by customs, who feared that it might carry foot-and-mouth disease. Photos in the monastery's entrance room show the 11,000 boxes that contained the monastery when it came ashore – and a docker standing over them, scratching his head.

The demands of tax officials left Hearst short of ready funds, and the monastery lingered in a New York warehouse until 1952, when the pieces were brought here and re-assembled as a tourist attraction. The job took a year and a half, done largely by trial and error thanks to incorrect repackaging of the pieces. Pacing the cloisters, as Cistercian monks did for 700 years, you can see the uneven form of the buttressed ceilings and rough, honey-colored walls. Now used as an Episcopal church, the monastery is a model of tranquility, its peacefulness enhanced by a lush garden setting.

If you're not driving, **getting to the monastery** is relatively easy with buses #E, #H and #V from Sunny Isles, #3 from downtown Miami, or services from the North Miami Beach Greyhound station, 16250 Biscayne Boulevard (☎945-0801). Each of these routes, though, leaves you with a nail-biting ten-minute walk through some very dodgy streets.

Continuing north: towards Fort Lauderdale

The coastal route, Hwy-A1A (Collins Avenue), and the mainland Hwy-1 (Biscayne Boulevard) both continue into Hollywood, at the southern edge of the Fort Lauderdale area, fully described in "The Southeast Coast." By **public transport** you can travel north with Broward County Transit (☎954/357-8400) buses from the vast Aventura shopping mall on the corner of Lehman Causeway (192nd Street) and Biscayne Boulevard.

PRACTICALITIES

Due perhaps to the cool night-time breeze that blows the humidity out of the subtropical heat, no one in Miami, it seems, can wait to get out and enjoy themselves. Entertainment listings are the most popular section of any newspaper, and the very thought of not devoting evenings and weekends to hedonistic pursuits would bring many locals out in a rash.

Social **drinking** usually serves as a curtain raiser on the night rather than an end in itself and is seldom allowed to impinge on **eating** time. Miamians think nothing of eating out three times a day seven days a week, and the range of food on offer spans most of the world and suits all budgets – discovering Cuban cuisine is one of the joys of the city. Don't be surprised if the place where you had dinner doubles as a **live music** spot: restaurant back rooms feature significantly on a small local live music network, where reggae shines strongly. The city's effervescent **club** scene is fun to explore, too – set around South Beach's Art Deco strip are some of the hippest nightspots in the whole country. Highbrow **arts** fans can choose between several orchestras, three respected dance groups and a diverse program of drama at several medium-sized theaters. And if these don't appeal, you can burn up excess energy cruising the **shops**, not the country's greatest totems of consumerism, but easily sufficient to slake a thirst for acquisition.

Miami is virtually impossible to **get around** at night without a car or taxi, though the bulk of the bars, live music spots and clubs are within walking distance of one another in South Beach. If you're staying in South Beach, you won't have to worry about parking or fret over the city's paucity of late-night buses; if you're not, you might use the "Electrowave Shuttle" to get there – and back – from downtown Miami (see p.59).

To find out **what's on**, read the listings in *New Times* (published on Thursdays), or in the Friday Weekend section of the *Miami Herald*.

Eating

With everything from the greasiest hotdog stand to the finest gourmet restaurant vying for business, **eating** in Miami is a buyer's market. All over the city, street stands, cafés and coffee shops offer decent, filling **breakfasts** and all-day **budget food** (a good feed for around $5), and many restaurants dish up huge **lunches** at remarkably low prices; $7–10 is about average. **Dinner** too can be good value, rarely costing more than $10–15, and you don't need to be rich to indulge in the occasional blowout; look out for **early-bird specials**, when some restaurants knock a few dollars off the price of a full evening meal simply to fill seats between 5 and 7pm. Be on the look-out, too, for the free food offered at **happy hours** (see "Drinking"), and the ample buffets that constitute Sunday **brunch** (see p.104).

Anywhere that serves breakfast is usually open at 6am or 7am, most restaurants do business between noon and midnight or 1am, some closing between lunch and dinner, and a few operate around the clock (see the box on p.100).

The big fast-food franchises and pizza chains are as plentiful here as elsewhere across the country, and "typical" **American** food, such as thick, juicy burgers and sizeable sandwiches, is easily found. Recent years have seen the development of a style of cooking termed as "**New Floridian**," which successfully combines nouvelle cuisine methods and presentation with Caribbean ingredients. Yet Miami is too cosmopolitan for a single food style to be dominant, and only **seafood**, every bit as plentiful and good as you would expect so close to fish-laden tropical waters, is a common feature among the city's plethora of cuisines drawn from every corner of the Americas – and beyond.

So common all over the city that it hardly seems an ethnic cuisine at all, **Cuban** food is what Miami does best. A sizeable lunch or dinner in one of the innumerable small, family-run Cuban diners (always pleased to show off their culinary skills to non-Spanish-speaking customers) will cost an absurdly low $4–7, a fraction of the prices charged by fancier Cuban restaurants – mostly in Little Havana and Coral Gables – now lauded by the nation's food critics thanks to the development of a lighter, more attractive "**Nuevo Cubano**" style of cooking. **Haitian** cooking is slowly gaining popularity in Miami, and the restaurants in Little Haiti, just north of downtown Miami, are just some of the places in which to sample it. **Argentinean**, **Jamaican**, **Nicaraguan** and **Peruvian** eateries bear witness to the city's strong Caribbean and Latin American elements, though aside from Cuban food, for sheer quality and value for money it's hard to better the many **Japanese** outlets, most north of downtown Miami and a few in South Miami – all much cheaper than their European counterparts – while in South Beach, sushi is the current rage. **Chinese** and **Thai** places are abundant, too, as are **Italian**. By contrast, **Indian** food is having a hard time taking root despite a couple of commendable restaurants in Coral Gables, and **Mexican** food is far less common than in most other parts of the US.

Downtown and around

Big Fish, 55 SW Miami Ave Rd (☎373-1770). Lively spot on the Miami River, with folding chairs, benches and picnic tables. Menu includes home-cooked fish sandwiches and fresh seafood chowder. Closed Sun; lunch only June-November.

Café del Sol, *Crowne Plaza Hotel*, 1601 Biscayne Blvd (☎374-0000). A safe introduction to the varied cuisines of Latin America and the Caribbean for those who don't want to venture into Little Havana. Moderate prices.

Cisco's Cafe, 5911 NW 36th St (☎871-2764). Ordinary Mexican food with extraordinary appetizers piled high on rainbow plates. Try the butter guacamole and homemade corn tortillas.

Dick Clark's American Bandstand Grill, at the Bayside Marketplace, 401 Biscayne Blvd (☎381-8800). Great collection of rock'n'roll memorabilia, from Fabian to the Beatles, to admire as you munch a charbroiled burger.

East Coast Fisheries, 360 W Flagler St (☎372-1300). The fish goes straight from the boats into the kitchen of this lively Miami River restaurant, but the cooking is plain and rather expensive.

Edelweiss, 2655 Biscayne Blvd (☎573-4421). Hearty German and Swiss food with traditional schnitzel, bratwurst and excellent strudel desserts.

Fishbone Grille, 650 S Miami Ave (☎530-1915). A busy but friendly restaurant serving the finest budget seafood in Miami. Located next to *Tobacco Road* (see "Drinking" and "Live Music") where many of the diners move on to.

Gourmet Diner, 13951 Biscayne Blvd (☎947-2255). Always a line for a winning Continental daily menu.

Hiro, 17516 Biscayne Blvd (☎948-3687). Miami's only late-night sushi bar, and where the city's sushi chefs hang out after work. Open until 4am.

Joe's Seafood Restaurant, 2771 NW 24th St (☎638-8602). The dockside setting improves the only-adequate seafood. Not to be confused with *Joe's Stone Crabs* (see "Miami Beach").

Rita's Italian Restaurant, 7232 Biscayne Blvd (☎757-9470). Family-run Italian diner with checkered tablecloths, hearty portions, good prices and an owner inclined to burst into song.

S & S Sandwich Shop, 1757 NE Second Ave (☎373-4291). Under the same ownership for nearly fifty years, proffering platefuls of meatloaf, turkey, stuffed cabbage, beef stew, shrimp Creole or pork chops for less than $6. Counter service only. Closed Sun.

Shagnasty's Saloon & Eatery, 638 S Miami Ave (☎381-8970). Restaurant section of *Tobacco Road* (see "Drinking" and "Live Music") offering hamburgers, fries and sandwiches, which are consumed by relaxing yuppies.

Las Tapas, at the Bayside Marketplace, 401 Biscayne Blvd (☎372-2737). Spanish bar and restaurant in Miami's zestiest shopping mall. Tapas served with sangria and a basket of bread.

Tark's Clam House, 13750 Biscayne Blvd (☎944-8275). Fast-and-fresh seafood: shrimp, Alaskan snow crab, stone crab claws, clams and oysters, all at low prices.

Little Havana

Ayestaran, 706 SW 27th Ave (☎649-4982). Long a favorite Cuban restaurant among those in the know, especially good value for its $5 daily specials.

El Bodegon de Castilla, 2499 SW Eighth St (☎649-0863). Iberian flavors embellish the local grouper, snapper and sole seafood dishes. A bit on the pricey side.

La Carreta, 3632 SW Eighth St (☎444-7501). The real sugar cane growing around the wagon wheel outside is a good sign: inside, home-style Cuban cooking is served at unbeatable prices.

Casa Juancho, 2436 SW Eighth St (☎642-2452). Pricey, but the tapas are good value at $6–8, and there's a convivial mood as strolling musicians serenade the wealthy Cuban clientele.

El Cid, 117 NW 42nd Ave (☎642-3144). A gargantuan Moorish-style castle where the staff dress as knaves and displays of freshly killed fowl greet you at the door. Lots of drinking, singing and eating, with affordable Spanish and Cuban delicacies.

Covadonga, 6480 SW Eighth St (☎261-2406). Cuban seafood specialties abound in this nautical-themed restaurant frequented by a local clientele.

La Esquina de Tejas, 101 SW Twelfth Ave (☎545-0337). Where Reagan and Bush both solicited the Hispanic vote. A dependable address for Cuban lunches and dinners.

Hy-Vong, 3458 SW Eighth St (☎446-3674). Tiny, dinner-only Vietnamese restaurant; a favorite of hip yuppies and Vietnam vets. No frills, slow service, but damn good food. Closed Mon.

Las Islas Canarias, 285 NW 27th Ave (☎649-0440). Tucked away inside a drab shopping mall. Piles of fine, unpretentious Cuban food at unbeatable prices.

Malaga, 740 SW Eighth St (☎858-4224). Inexpensive Spanish and Cuban cuisine, specializing in fresh fish dishes, served inside or in the courtyard.

El Padrinito, 3494 SW Eighth St (☎442-4510). Excellent Dominican entrees like grouper steak smothered in coconut sauce served in a homestyle setting.

La Palacio de los Jugos, 5721 W Flagler Ave (☎264-1503). A handful of tables at the back of a Cuban produce market, where the pork sandwiches and shellfish soup from the takeout stand are the tastiest for miles.

Versailles, 3555 SW Eighth St (☎444-0240). Chandeliers, mirrored walls, a great atmosphere and wonderful inexpensive Cuban food.

Coral Gables

Café Kolibri, 6901 Red Rd (☎665-2421). Bakery with gourmet, lowfat and vegan entrees. Also doubles as a restaurant with delicious Tuscan specialties.

Caffe Abbracci, 318 Aragon Ave (☎441-0700). Original dishes like pasta stuffed with pumpkin hold the attention of a fashionable crowd as they sip their vintage wine.

Canton, 2614 Ponce de Leon Blvd (☎448-3736). Hub of Eastern flavors of Cantonese, Mandarin and Szechuan, known for huge portions of honey garlic chicken. Good sushi bar as well.

Darbar, 276 Alhambra Circle (☎448-9691). Indian restaurant seeking to enlighten local tastebuds with a full selection of basics plus a few specialties. Closed Sun.

Doc Dammers' Bar & Grill, inside the *Colonnade Hotel*, 180 Aragon Ave (☎441-2600). Affordable eating in a spacious, old-style saloon; serving breakfast, lunch and dinner, and offering a happy hour in its piano bar. See the "Happy Hours" box on p.102.

Hofbrau Pub & Grill, 172 Giralda Ave (☎442-2730). Three daily specials, but come for the Wednesday night $7-all-you-can-eat fish fry. Closed Sun. See "Drinking."

House of India, 22 Merrick Way (☎444-2348). Quality catchall Indian food including some excellently priced lunch buffets.

24-HOUR EATS

The five below, all in South Beach, are places where you can get reasonably priced **food all night**. See the "Eating" listings for fuller details.

David's Coffee Shop, corner of Eleventh St and Collins Ave (☎534-8736).

Eleventh Street Diner, 1065 Washington Ave (☎534-6373). Fri and Sat only.

News Café, 800 Ocean Drive (☎538-6397).

Ted's Hideaway South, 124 Second St (no phone).

Wolfie's, 2038 Collins Ave (☎538-6626).

Mykonos, 1201 Coral Way (☎856-3140). Greek food in an unassuming atmosphere: spinakopita, lemon chicken soup, gyros, souvlaki and huge Greek salads.

Picnics at Allen's Drug Store, 4000 Red Rd (☎665-6964). Home-style cooking in an old-fashioned drugstore complete with a jukebox that blasts golden oldies.

Restaurant St Michel, in *Hotel Place St Michel*, 2135 Ponce de Leon Blvd (☎446-6572). Outstanding French and Mediterranean cuisine amid antiques and flowers. Not cheap, but very alluring.

Victor's Café, 2340 SW 32nd Ave (☎445-1313). Mambo musicians make for lively dining, but the Cuban food – while good – tends to be overpriced.

Wrapido, 2334 Ponce de Leon Blvd (☎443-1884). Pop in for a refreshing smoothie and a quick wrap sandwich in flavorful tortillas.

Yoko's, 4041 Ponce de Leon Blvd (☎444-6622). Intimate Japanese restaurant usually packed with students from the neighboring University of Miami.

Coconut Grove

Le Bouchon du Grove, 3430 Main Hwy (☎448-6060). Don't let the chi-chi name fool you. Here you'll find unpretentious French food, with fabulous Kir Royales and freshly prepared desserts at reasonable prices.

Café Med, 3015 Grand Ave (☎443-1770). Delicious Mediterranean cuisine in an excellent people-watching location. Get the Tropicale Carpaccio with hearts of palm, avocado and chunky parmesan shavings.

Café Tu Tu Tango, inside CocoWalk, 3015 Grand Ave (☎529-2222). A quirky and entertaining spot themed as an artist's garret; lengthy menu of good-quality food served in tapas-sized portions and at high speed.

Cheesecake Factory, inside CocoWalk, 3015 Grand Ave (☎447-9898). You'll need plenty of time to choose from the book-thick menu, which is an assortment of traditional American fare, innovative appetizers and 33 varieties of cheesecake.

Fuddruckers, 3444 Main Hwy (☎442-8164). A typical American joint with a touch of class – fancy wooden booths provide a nice background for your burgers and fries.

Greenstreet Café, 3110 Commodore Plaza (☎567-0662). Quaint sidewalk café with ecclectic assortment of foods ranging from Middle Eastern to Jamaican.

Grove Café, 3484 Main Hwy (☎445-0022). Succulent burgers to munch as you watch the Coconut Grove groovers swan by.

Hungry Sailor, 3064 Grand Ave (☎444-9359). Pseudo-British pub with moderately successful fish'n'chips and shepherd's pie, but does better with its conch chowder. See "Drinking" and "Live Music."

Mandarin Garden, 3268 Grand Ave (☎446-9999 or ☎442-1234). Very tasty, affordable Chinese food. The free parking is a big plus during traffic-jammed weekends.

Paulo Luigi's, 3324 Virginia St (☎445-9000). Favorite haunt of local NBA players who come for the deliciously inventive (and inexpensive) homestyle pasta and meat dishes.

Scotty's Landing, 3381 Pan American Drive (☎854-2626). Tasty seafood and fish'n'chips consumed at marina-side picnic tables in a simple setting.

Señor Frog's, 3480 Main Hwy (☎448-0999). Broad selection of reasonably priced Mexican food, but most people come to gulp down margaritas.

Taurus Steak House, 3540 Main Hwy (☎448-0633). A carnivore's heaven. Meat is the main dish in this creaking, old steakhouse that's been open for years.

Key Biscayne

Bayside Hut, 3501 Rickenbacker Causeway (☎361-0808). Atmospheric Tiki bar populated with stray cats and hungry boaters. Highlights include the fresh seafood and tasty seasoned french fries.

Beach House, 12 Crandon Blvd (☎361-1038). Gossipy locals' haunt serving three square meals a day.

The Sandbar, at *Silver Sands Motel & Villas*, 301 Ocean Drive (☎361-5441). Tucked-away seafood restaurant offering affordable lunch or dinner a pebble's throw from crashing ocean waves.

South Fork Grill & Bar, 3301 Rickenbacker Causeway (☎365-9391). Tex-Mex specialties in a gorgeous outdoor setting on the water. Try the frozen sangria.

Sundays on the Bay, 5420 Crandon Blvd (☎361-6777). Marina seafood eatery catering to the boats and beer set. Very casual. See "Live Music."

South Miami

Akashi, 5830 S Dixie Hwy (☎665-6261). Generous sushi boats and tender chicken teriyaki make this restaurant trip worthwhile.

Chifa Chinese Restaurant, 12590 N Kendall Drive (☎271-3823). In all probability the only restaurant in Florida specializing in Peruvian-Cantonese cuisine. Tasty deep-fried appetizers, run-of-the-mill main courses, plus a range of Chinese and Peruvian beers are served up at budget prices.

Fountain & Grill, at *Sunset Drugs*, 5640 Sunset Drive (☎667-1807). Large, clean and modern version of the traditional small-town diner. Noted for its grilled cheese sandwiches, burgers and meatloaf.

JJ's American Diner, 5850 Sunset Drive (☎665-5499) and 12000 N Kendall Drive (☎598-0307). Big burgers and sandwiches in a contemporary soda shop setting, complete with blaring rock'n'roll.

Old Cutler Inn, 7271 SW 168th St (☎238-1514). A neo-rustic country inn that's a neighborhood fave for its steaks, shrimps and delicious desserts.

Pars, 10827 SW 40th St (☎551-1099). Good Iranian food in a simple setting.

Sakura, 8225 SW 124th St (☎238-8462). Tiny, good-value sushi bar and restaurant that's always packed.

Shorty's Bar-B-Q, 9200 S Dixie Hwy (☎670-7732). Sit at a picnic table, tuck a napkin in your shirt and graze on barbecued ribs, chicken and corn on the cob – pausing only to gaze at the cowboy memorabilia on the walls.

Su Shin, SW 88th St, Kendall (☎271-3235). Great teriyakis, daily specials and sushi chefs with a sense of humor.

El Toro Taco, 1 S Krome Ave (☎245-8182). Excellent family-run Mexican restaurant. A gem in the center of Homestead that makes a good place to stop en route to the Keys.

Tropical Delite, 12344 SW 117th Ct (☎235-5111). Dirt-cheap Jamaican home cooking: jerk chicken and goat curry among the favorites.

Wagons West, 11311 S Dixie Hwy (☎238-9942). Maximum cholesterol breakfasts and other unhealthy fare are consumed in this always crowded, budget-priced shrine to cowboys and the Wild West; sit at wagon-shaped booths and admire the Western memorabilia on the walls.

South Beach and around

Las Americas, 450 Lincoln Rd Mall (☎673-0560). Inexpensive, no-frills Cuban food in a cafeteria-style atmosphere.

Casona De Carlitos, 2232 Collins Ave (☎534-7013). Hearty Argentinean food and live music, lots of Latin-style pasta and grilled red meat.

Chrysanthemum, 1256 Washington Ave (☎531-5656). Superb Peking and Szechwan cooking at moderate prices; a surprise in a city not known for quality Chinese food.

Cielito Lindo Mexican Restaurant, 1626 Pennsylvania Ave (☎673-0480). Low-cost Mexican food is served with a smile in this cozy restaurant, handily placed just off Lincoln Road.

Da Leo Trattoria, 819 Lincoln Rd (☎674-0354). A reliable Italian restaurant serving authentic fare at budget prices.

David's Coffee Shop, corner of Eleventh St and Collins Ave (☎534-8736). Low-priced Latin food served all day and night to a crowd that's sleazy but discerning. See "24-Hour Eats."

Eleventh Street Diner, 1065 Washington Ave (☎534-6373). All-American fare served around the clock on Fri and Sat; eat inside in cozy booths or outside on the terrace.

Joe's Stone Crabs, 227 Biscayne St (☎673-0365). Only open from October to May when Florida stone crabs are in season; expect long lines of people waiting to pay $20 for a succulent plateful.

Larios on the Beach, 820 Ocean Drive (☎532-9577). Best known for being owned by singer Gloria Estefan rather than for its sophisticated – and surprisingly affordable – "Nuevo Cubano" food served in a Latin nightclub atmosphere; when the live band strikes up, the diners dance.

Lucky Cheng's, 600 Lincoln Rd (☎672-1505). Moderate Chinese food served by waiters in drag.

Lulu's, 1053 Washington Ave (☎532-6147). Deep-south home cooking: fried chicken, greens, black-eyed peas and more, but you pay for the Elvis Presley memorabilia on the walls.

Maiko Japanese Restaurant, 1255 Washington Ave (☎531-6369). Highly imaginative sushi creations are what make this moderately-priced restaurant so popular.

Moe's Cantina, 616 Collins Ave (☎532-6637). A taste of the southwest in Miami, with good burritos and the best, sweet salsa this side of the Rio Grande.

News Café, 800 Ocean Drive (☎538-6397). Utterly fashionable sidewalk café with extensive breakfast, lunch and dinner menu and front-row seating for the South Beach promenade.

HAPPY HOURS

Almost every restaurant in Miami has a **happy hour**, usually on weekdays from 5 to 8pm, when drinks are cheap and come in tandem with a large pile of free food – varying from chicken wings and conch fritters to chips and popcorn. Watch for the signs outside or scan the numerous newspaper ads for the best deals – or try one of the following listings, which are consistently among the best in the city.

Smith & Wollensky's, 1 Washington Ave, Miami Beach (☎673-1708). Cut-price oysters, shrimp and drinks in Miami Beach's most congenial happy hour.

Coco Loco's, in the *Sheraton*, 495 Brickell Ave near downtown Miami (☎373-6000). No better place to finish off a day downtown; the drinks are high, but for a dollar you help yourself to a massive buffet.

Doc Dammers' Bar & Grill, inside the *Colonnade Hotel*, 180 Aragon Ave, Coral Gables (☎441-2600). Where the young(ish) and unattached of Coral Gables mingle after work to the strains of a pianist. See "Eating."

Monty's Raw Bar, 2550 S Bayshore Drive, Coconut Grove (☎858-1431). Cheap drinks wash down the seafood, and tropical music complements the bay view at Coconut Grove's best happy hour.

Shagnasty's Saloon & Eatery, 638 S Miami Ave, near downtown Miami (☎381-8970). The hip yuppie's happy hour hangout, with free appetizers and many discounted drinks.

Sloppy Joe's, 3131 Commodore Plaza, Coconut Grove (☎446-0002). Drink specials all night long in this young, hoppin' bar.

Norma's On the Beach, 646 Lincoln Rd (☎532-2809). Jamaican cooking at its most sophisticated, most tasty – and most expensive.

Pacific Time, 915 Lincoln Rd (☎534-5979). Modern American cooking with strong East Asian influences producing excellent results at moderate prices.

Palace Bar & Grill, 1200 Ocean Drive (☎531-9077). One of the few trendy places for breakfast, opening at 8am. Otherwise general, inexpensive fare including good burgers.

Puerto Sagua, 700 Collins Ave (☎673-1115). Where local Cubans meet gringos over espresso coffee, beans and rice. Cheap, filling breakfasts, lunches and dinners.

Rolo's, 1439 Alton Rd (☎535-2220). Bleach-blondes and tanned Latin surfers breakfast here before surf's up. Also serves Cuban- and American-style lunches and dinners, and stocks a formidable range of beers. See "Drinking."

The Strand, 671 Washington Ave (☎532-2340). A place to see and be seen in; offering nouvelle and regular American food for trendy regulars and slumming celebrities.

Sushi Hana, 1131 Washington Ave (☎532-1100). Large portions of beautifully presented Japanese food at unusually affordable prices.

Tantra, 1445 Pennsylvania Ave (☎672-4765). The sensual Indian flavors offered up here are no mistake – the restaurant's theme, enhanced by muted lighting and a beautiful waitstaff, is based on Tantric philosophies. Enjoy.

Tap Tap Haitian Restaurant, 819 Fifth St (☎672-2898). The tastiest and most attractively presented Haitian food in Miami, at very reasonable prices. Wander around the restaurant to admire the Haitian murals, and visit the upstairs gallery where exhibits on worthy Haitian themes are held.

Ted's Hideaway South, 124 Second St (no phone). Downbeat bar that proffers cheap fried chicken, steak and red beans and rice; see "Drinking."

Thai Toni, 890 Washington Ave (☎538-8424). Thai food at moderate prices in a fashionable hangout.

Wok & Roll, 1451 Collins Ave (☎672-0911). Trendy Japanese fare; try the giant dim sum plate. Deck seating facing Collins Ave makes for good evening people watching.

Wolfie's, 2038 Collins Ave (☎538-6626). Long-established deli drawing an entertaining mix of New York retirees and late-night clubbers – all served generous helpings by beehive-haired waitresses. Open 24 hours, and serving $1.99 "breakfast specials" throughout the day.

World Resources, 719 Lincoln Rd (☎535-8987). Excellent, inexpensive Thai food served in an informal sidewalk café setting. Live Asian, African and other music is played nightly.

Yuca, 501 Lincoln Rd (☎532-9822). Still the rave of food critics up and down the land, serving "Nuevo Cubano" cuisine in a gourmet-diner setting; great stuff, but expect to pay about $50 per person.

Northern Beaches and around

Al Amir, 12953 Biscayne Blvd (☎892-6500). Authentic Middle Eastern cuisine at good prices.

Bangkok Orchid, 5563 NW 72nd Ave (☎887-3000). Delicious Thai meals along a stretch lacking any other remotely exotic eateries.

Café Prima Pasta, 414 71st St (☎867-0106). One of the best Italian restaurants in Miami – and one of the least expensive. The place is tiny, so arrive early.

Chef Allen's, 19088 NE 29th Ave (☎935-2900). Outstanding "New Floridian" cuisine created by Allen Susser, widely rated as one of America's greatest chefs. Only dine here if money's not a problem.

Rainforest Café, 19575 Biscayne Blvd (☎792-8001). Theme restaurant complete with growling safari sounds, thunderstorms and tasty New World food.

Rascal House, 17190 Collins Ave (☎947-4581). Largest, loudest and most authentic New York deli in town; huge portions and cafeteria ambience.

BRUNCH

Sunday **brunch** in Miami is usually a more upmarket affair than its equivalent in New York or Los Angeles; high-quality buffet food is laid out in a stylish setting, and only occasionally accompanied by cheap drinks. Served from 11am to 2pm, brunch costs $5–30 depending on the quality of the food; again, check the newspapers for up-to-the-minute offers, or simply show up with a big appetite at one of the establishments listed below – all in Miami Beach unless stated.

Beach Villa Chinese Restaurant, at the *Beach Paradise Hotel*, 600 Ocean Drive (☎532-8065). Excellent dim sum brunch on Sat and Sun.

Colony Bistro, 736 Ocean Drive (☎673-6776). Gourmet brunch served in a small but stylish sidewalk cafe; great for people watching.

The Dining Galleries, at the *Fontainebleau Hotel*, 4441 Collins Ave (☎538-2000). Gargantuan buffet and doting service; also a sneaky way to glimpse the inside of this Fifties landmark hotel.

Grand Café, at the *Grand Bay Hotel*, 2669 S Bayshore Drive, Coconut Grove (☎858-9600). Fine food and lots of it in a very chic dining room – attracts the well-heeled glutton.

Il Ristorante, at the *Biltmore Hotel*, 1200 Anastasia Ave, Coral Gables (☎445-1926). Miami's most expensive brunch in the city's most historic hotel; overpriced but a worthwhile indulgence.

Sundays on the Bay, 5420 Biscayne Blvd, Key Biscayne (☎361-6777). The biggest and most enjoyable brunch in Miami; make a reservation to avoid waiting in line.

Drinking

Miami's **drinking** is more commonly done in restaurants, nightclubs and discos than in the seedy bars so beloved of American filmmakers. One or two dimly lit dives do capture the essence of the archetypal US bar, however, and a handful of Irish and British pubs stock imported ales. But boozing in restaurant lounges, back rooms of music spots or shorefront hotel bars is more in keeping with the spirit of the city. Most places where you can drink are open from 11am or noon until midnight or 2am, with the liveliest hours between 10pm and 1am. Among the following listings, some are suited to an early evening, pre-dinner tipple, while others – especially those in Coconut Grove and Miami Beach – make prime vantage points for watching the city's poseurs come and go. Prices are broadly similar, though the most pose-worthy places sometimes charge way above the average.

Downtown and around

Churchill's Hideaway, 5501 NE Second Ave (☎757-1807). A British enclave within Little Haiti, with soccer and rugby matches on video and UK beers on tap. See also "Live Music."

Tobacco Road, 626 S Miami Ave (☎374-1198). Crusty R&B venue (see "Live Music") that sees plenty of serious boozing in its downstairs bar.

Coral Gables

The Crown and Garter Pub, 270 Catalonia Ave (☎441-0204). Bar food staples plus Guinness, Bass and cider on tap contribute to making this a popular place for resident Brits and Anglophiles of all nationalities.

Duffy's Tavern, 2108 SW 57th Ave (☎264-6580). Pool tournaments and a large TV screen beaming sports events for the athletically minded drinker.

Hofbrau Pub & Grill, 172 Giralda Ave (☎442-2730). A fairly upmarket dining place with a mellow, tavern-like atmosphere.

John Martin's, 253 Miracle Mile (☎445-3777). Irish pub and restaurant with occasional folk singers and harpists accompanying a good batch of imported brews. See "Live Music."

Coconut Grove

Fat Tuesdays, inside CocoWalk, 3015 Grand Ave (☎441-2992). Part of a chain of bars famous for fruit-flavored frozen daiquiris, which you can imbibe while observing the milling crowds.

Hungry Sailor, 3064 Grand Ave (☎444-9359). A would-be British pub with overpriced Bass and Watneys on tap, though the atmosphere is made by the nightly live reggae; see "Live Music."

Monty's Bayshore Restaurant, 2550 S Bayshore Drive (☎858-1431). Drinkers often outnumber the diners (see "Eating"), drawn here by the gregarious mood and the views across the bay.

Taurus, 3540 Main Hwy (☎448-0633). Old Coconut Grove drinking institution, with a burger grill on weekends and a nostalgic Sixties-loving crowd.

Tavern in the Grove, 3416 Main Hwy (☎447-3884). Down-to-earth locals' haunt with bouncy jukebox and easy-going mood.

Virtual Café, 2911 Grand Ave (☎567-3070). Out-of-this-world theme bar complete with stomach-churning virtual reality games and a sinisterly-decorated interior resembling the Star Wars bar.

Key Biscayne

Bayside Hut, 3501 Rickenbacker Causeway (☎361-0808). Friendly beer-drinking crowd beside the bay. See "Eating" and "Live Music."

The Sandbar, at *Silver Sands Motel & Villas*, 301 Ocean Drive (☎361-5441). The poolside bar is a prime site for sipping cocktails as the ocean crashes close by.

South Beach

Banana Cabana, at the *Banana Bungalow Hostel*, 2360 Collins Ave (☎1-800-7-HOSTEL). Tiki bar setting by the pool, where all drinks start at a dirt-cheap $2.

Clevelander, 1020 Ocean Drive (☎531-3485). The ultimate poolside sports bar, with pool tables, sports-tuned TVs and partially clothed athletic physiques attacking the brews.

Club Deuce Bar & Grill, 222 Fourteenth St (☎531-6200). Raucous neighborhood bar open until 5am, with a CD jukebox, pool table and a clientele that includes cops, transvestites, artists and models.

Irish House, 1430 Alton Rd (☎534-5667). Old neighborhood bar with two well-used pool tables.

Marlin Hotel, 1200 Collins Ave (☎604-5000). Sleek and futuristic hotel bar smack in Art Deco central. You just might catch Arnold or Sly slink in for one of the dazzling martinis.

Rebar, 1121 Washington Ave (☎672-4788). The South Beach bar for the fashionably grungy.

Ted's Hideaway South, 124 Second St (no phone). Can beer for a dollar and special reductions on draft when it rains; serves basic bar food around the clock. See "Food" and "24-Hour Eats."

Nightlife

Miami's **nightlife** has taken a profound turn for the better since the days when leggy cabaret shows were the high point of the action. Right now, in every sense except the literal one, Miami is a very cool place to dance, drink and simply hang out in **clubs** rated by the cognoscenti as among the hippest in the world. The appeal of the trendiest clubs – few in number and secreted about Miami Beach's South Beach, shifting their name and changing site frequently – may fade once their novelty wears off and too many people come looking for them, but for the time being an air of excitement and vibrancy hangs over the scene and there are plenty of fresh ideas to excite the most jaded clubber. Read *New Times* for the latest raves – or, better still, quiz any likely-looking groover that you encounter around the cafés and bars of South Beach. If you don't give a fig for fashion and just want to dance your socks off, there are plenty of mainstream **discos** – no different from discos the world over – where you can do just that. More adventurously, track down one of the city's **salsa** or **merengue** (a slinky dance music from the Caribbean) clubs, hosted by Spanish-speaking DJs.

Not surprisingly, Fridays and Saturdays are the busiest, but there's a decent choice on any night and some of the mainstream discos boost their midweek crowds by offering cut-price drinks, free admission for women and bizarre asides such as aerobics shows and amateur strip contests. Most places open at 9pm, but don't even think of turning up before 11pm as they only hit a peak between midnight and 2am – although some continue until 7 or 8am and provide a free breakfast buffet for survivors. Usually there's a **cover charge** of $4–10 and a **minimum age** of 21 (it's normal for ID to be checked). Obviously you should dress with some sensitivity to the style of the club, but only by turning up in rags at the smartest door are you ever likely to be turned away on account of your clothes. All the following are in Miami Beach's South Beach unless stated otherwise. (For gay- and lesbian-oriented nightlife, see p.111.)

Clubs and discos

Amnesia, 136 Collins Ave (☎531-5535). Open-air glam club popular with the younger crowd.

Bash, 655 Washington Ave (☎538-2274). Many revelers get no further than the garden, though there's an intimate bar and a beckoning dance floor in this club co-owned by Madonna's ex Sean Penn and Simply Red's Mick Hucknall; no cover.

Chaos, 743 Washington Ave (☎674-7350). Serious celebrity spotting in this uber-hip dance club.

Groove Jet, 323 23rd St (☎532-20020). Very trendy, and becoming a place to be seen in. Dress up and arrive late.

Liquid, 1437-9 Washington Ave (☎532-9154). Local club gal, Ingrid Cassares, has the hottest club on the Beach. Stars galore congregate here – Madonna is a regular – for a wild rave-up and frequent fashion shows.

Living Room, 671 Washington Ave (☎532-2340) A wannabe model hangout with cushy couches you have to pay money to sit in. Small dance floor packs them in when they're not posing at the boomerang-shaped bar.

Mango's, 900 Ocean Drive (☎673-4422). Just follow the thumping bass to this outrageous oceanside club, where scantily-clad dancers prefer the bar top to the floors.

Red Square, 411 Washington Ave (☎672-9252). Russian-themed nightclub with an appropriately stocked vodka and caviar bar. Mind-numbing spotlights swirl around young dancers as they're caught up in this commie-crazed hotspot.

ShadowLounge, 1532 Washington Ave (☎531-9411). Surprisingly enormous interior for a South Beach club; it's most popular with a younger crowd and hosts weekly events and art exhibitions.

Warsaw Ballroom, 1450 Collins Ave (☎531-4555). The dingiest and busiest nightspot in town; Friday is exclusively gay (see "Gay and Lesbian Miami"), but Saturday is "straight night" and Wednesday is a riotous "strip night."

Zanzibar, 615 Washington Ave (☎538-6688). The safari-influenced theme nights here are as wild as the dancers, and the lines stretch around the block.

Salsa and merengue clubs

Bonfire Club, 1060 NE 79th St, Little Haiti (☎756-0200). Smooth and very danceable salsa sounds Wed–Sun; $2–5.

Club Tipico Dominicano, 1344 NW 36th St, Little Havana (☎634-7819). Top merengue DJ hosting the sessions Fri–Sun; $5.

Club Tropigala, 4441 Collins Ave, in the *Fontainbleau Hilton* (☎672-7469). Pulse to the rhythms of hot Latin sounds in the glamorous setting of the landmark *Fontainbleau Hotel*.

El Inferno, 981 SW Eighth St, Little Havana (☎856-5523). Popular local disco with Latin grooves Fri & Sat.

Live music

In a city that still goes crazy over the studio-based Latin-pop of local girl Gloria Estefan, you might not expect to find a **live music** scene at all in Miami. In fact, an impressive number of **locales** – many of them poky clubs or the back rooms of restaurants or hotels – host bands throughout the week. It's often a matter of quantity over quality, however. Be they glam, goth, indie or metal, the city's **rock bands** tend to be pale imitations of the better-known US and European groups who periodically add Miami to their tour schedules. **Jazz** fans fare slightly better, and there's a trustworthy **R&B** site plus a very minor **folk** scene. It's **reggae**, however, that's most worth seeking out; aside from acts flying in from Jamaica, the musicians among Miami's sizeable Jamaican population appear regularly at several small spots. There's a rare chance to hear live **Haitian** music in Miami, but for **country** sounds you'll have to leave the city altogether.

Other than for megastar performers (see below), to see a band you've heard of, expect to pay $6–15; for a local act, admission will be $2–5 or free. Most places open up at 8 or 9pm, with the main band onstage around 11pm or midnight.

The most comprehensive music **listings** are in *New Times*, but if you can't decide where to go on a Friday night, go along to South Pointe Park (see "Miami Beach"), where there's entertainment and usually a **free concert**; look for the posters strewn all over South Beach.

Miami also gets its share of **big performances**, with the venues listed below – none of which has much atmosphere – attracting top names in rock, soul, jazz, reggae and funk; tickets are $18–35 from a branch of Ticketmaster (outlets all over the city; phone ☎358-5885 for the nearest) or over the phone by credit card.

Rock, jazz and R&B

Cameo Theater, 1445 Washington Ave (☎673-9787). *The* spot for weird and wonderful lefty arty happenings, poetry readings and interesting bands. Cover varies.

Churchill's Hideaway, 5501 NE Second Ave, Little Haiti (☎757-1807). Good place to hear local hopeful rock and indie bands; $10–15. See "Drinking."

The Grind, 12573 Biscayne Blvd, N Miami (☎899-9979). College nights and indie rock with local eccentric bands.

Jazid, 1342 Washington Ave, Miami Beach (☎673-9372). Bordering on the club scene, this venue belts out smooth vocalists and hot tunes.

Les Deux Fontaines, 1230 Ocean Dr, Miami Beach (☎672-2579). Dixieland swing jazz; Thurs–Sun and Wed.

Mango's Tropical Café, 900 Ocean Drive (☎673-4422). It's hard to stand still when the Brazilian and Cuban bands who play on this terrace strike up. Usually no cover.

Scully's Tavern, 9809 Sunset Drive, South Miami (☎271-7404). Rock and blues bands playing for beer-drinking, pool-playing regulars; free.

Studio One 83, 2860 NW 183 St, Overtown (☎621-7295). Powerful rap, soul and reggae, but located in a dangerous area north of downtown Miami; $5–15.

BIG PERFORMANCE VENUES

James L. Knight Center, 400 SE Second Ave, downtown Miami (☎372-4633).

Pro Player Stadium, 2269 NW 199th St, 16 miles northwest of downtown Miami (☎623-6100).

Miami Arena, 721 NW First Ave, downtown Miami (☎374-5057).

Tobacco Road, 626 S Miami Ave, downtown Miami (☎374-1198). Earthy R&B from some of the country's finest exponents. See "Drinking." Free-$6.

Zeke's Road House, 625 Lincoln Rd, Miami Beach (☎532-0087). TV themed hangout highlighting the latest rock music.

Reggae

Bayside Hut, 3501 Rickenbacker Causeway, Key Biscayne (☎361-0808). Bayside reggae jams on Fri and Sat; free.

Hungry Sailor, 3064 Grand Ave, Coconut Grove (☎444-9359). Reggae bands fill the tiny corner stage of this pseudo English pub almost every night; free-$3. See "Eating" and "Drinking."

Sundays on the Bay, 5420 Crandon Blvd, Key Biscayne (☎361-6777). Unlikely but lively setting for live reggae Thurs-Sun; free. See "Eating."

Folk

JohnMartin's, 253 Miracle Mile, Coral Gables (☎445-3777). Spacious Irish bar (see "Drinking") and restaurant with Irish folk music several evenings a week; free.

Luna Star Café, 775 NE 125th St, N Miami (☎892-8522). Open mike nights and poetry readings.

World Resources, 719 Lincoln Rd, Miami Beach (☎673-5032). Belly dancing and percussion interpretations.

Haitian music

Tap Tap, 819 Fifth St, South Beach (☎672-2898). Best known for its excellent restaurant (see "Eating"), interesting gallery and regular live Haitian music – phone ahead for details.

Classical music, dance and opera

The Miami-based New World Symphony Orchestra, 541 Lincoln Rd (☎673-3331), gives concert experience to some of the finest graduate **classical** musicians in the US. Its season runs from October to April with most performances at the Lincoln Theater or the Gusman Center for the Performing Arts; tickets $10–30. For better-known names, look out for top-flight soloists guesting with the Miami Chamber Symphony (☎858-3500), usually at the Gusman Concert Hall; tickets $15–30.

The city's two major professional **dance** companies, the Miami City Ballet, 905 Lincoln Rd (☎532-7713) and the Ballet Theater of Miami (☎442-4840), appear at the Gusman Center for Performing Arts; tickets are $15–45, but the Miami City Ballet also holds cut-price, dress-rehearsal shows at the Colony Theater for under $10. A third group is the Ballet Flamenco La Rosa, 555 17th St (☎757-8475), whose frenetic Latin dance productions take place at the Colony Theater; tickets $10–20.

Opera is the poor relation of classical music and dance despite the efforts of the Greater Miami Opera, 1200 Coral Way (☎854-1643), which brings impressive names to varied programs at the Dade County Auditorium; tickets $10–60.

CENTERS FOR CLASSICAL MUSIC AND PERFORMING ARTS

Colony Theater, 1040 Lincoln Rd, Miami Beach (☎673-1026).

Dade County Auditorium, 2901 W Flagler St, downtown Miami (☎547-5414).

Gusman Center for the Performing Arts, 174 E Flagler St, downtown Miami (☎372-0925 or ☎374-8762).

Gusman Concert Hall, 1314 Miller Drive, University of Miami (☎284-2438 or ☎284-6477).

Jackie Gleason Center of the Performing Arts, 1700 Washington Ave, Miami Beach (☎673-7300).

Lincoln Theater, 541 Lincoln Rd, Miami Beach (☎673-3331).

Comedy

Whether it's the difficulty of finding jokes to span Miami's multicultural population, or simply its geographical distance from the stand-up comedy hotbeds of New York and Los Angeles, the city is very short of **comedy clubs**, although those it does have draw enthusiastic crowds and often comparatively big names. Admission will be $5–10; phone for show times.

Comedy clubs

Coconut's Comedy Club, at *Howard Johnson's Hotel*, 16500 NW Second Ave, North Miami (☎461-1161). Showcasing comic talent on the way up – or down. Thurs only.

Improv Comedy Club, inside *Streets of Mayfair*, 3399 Virginia St, Coconut Grove (☎441-8200). One of the nationwide chain of Improv comedy clubs and the best place in Miami for comedy, despite the rather formal atmosphere. Reservations required.

New Theater, 65 Almeira Ave (☎461-1161). Fri & Sat nights showcase the hilarious talents of the *Laughing Gas Comedy Improv Company.*

Theater

It may be small, but Miami's **theater** scene is of an encouragingly good standard. Winter is the busiest period, though something worth seeing crops up almost every week on the alternative circuit. If you're fluent in Spanish, make a point of visiting one of the city's **Spanish-language theaters**, whose programs are listed in the Friday *El Nuevo Herald* (a supplement of the *Miami Herald* newspaper): Bellas Artes, 1 Herald Plaza (☎350-2111) Teatro Martí, 420 SW Eighth Ave (☎545-7866) and Teatro Trail, 3717 SW Eighth St (☎448-0592), are three of the best; tickets are $12–15.

Major and alternative theaters

Coconut Grove Playhouse, 3500 Main Hwy, Coconut Grove (☎442-4000). Comfortable and well-established mainstream theater that bucks up its schedule with many interesting experimental efforts; $10–35.

New Theater, 65 Almeira Ave, Coral Gables (☎443-5909). Sitting neatly between mainstream and alternative, a nice place for a relaxing evening; $8–18.

Ring Theater, at the University of Miami, 1380 Miller Drive (☎284-3355). Assorted offerings year-round from the drama students of the University of Miami; $5–18.

Film

Except for the **Miami Film Festival** (details on ☎888-FILM), ten days and nights of new films from far and wide each February at the Gusman Center for Performing Arts, Miami is barren territory for film buffs. That said, at one point in American history, Florida might have rivalled Hollywood for film-capital-of-the-world rights (See "Contexts" for more information). Most **film theaters** are multiscreen affairs inside shopping malls showing first-run American features. Look at the "Weekend" section of the Friday *Miami Herald* for complete listings, or call the Movie Hotline (☎888-FILM). The main theater locations are Omni 6 AMC Theater (☎448-2088), in the Omni Mall at 1601 Biscayne Boulevard; Cinema 10, in the Miracle Center Mall, 3301 Coral Way; the 8-screen AMC in the CocoWalk, 3015 Grand Avenue; and Movies at the Falls, in the The Falls Mall, SW 136th St (☎255-2500); admission is $4–8.

MIAMI AND MIAMI BEACH FESTIVALS

The precise dates of the **festivals** listed below vary from year to year; check the details at any tourist information office or Chamber of Commerce.

January

Mid *Art Deco Weekend*: on Ocean Drive in the South Beach; talks and free events concerning the area's architecture (☎672-2014).

Taste of the Grove: pig out on food and free music in Coconut Grove's Peacock Park.

Late *Homestead Frontier Days*: home cooking and home-made arts and crafts at Harris Field in Homestead.

Key Biscayne Art Festival: enjoy music, arts and crafts and fresh seafood along Crandon Blvd.

February

Early *Miami Film Festival*: latest US and overseas films premiered in downtown Miami's Gusman Center for the Performing Arts (☎377-3456).

Mid *Coconut Grove Arts Festival*: hundreds of (mostly) talented unknowns display their works in Coconut Grove's Peacock Park and the nearby streets.

March

Early *Calle Ocho Festival*: massive festival of Cuban arts, crafts and cooking along the streets of Little Havana.

Carnival Miami: an offshoot of the Calle Ocho festival, with Hispanic-themed events across the city culminating in a parade at the Orange Bowl (☎644-8888).

Homestead Championship Rodeo: professional rodeo cowboys compete in steer wrestling, bull riding, calf roping and bareback riding competitions (☎372-9966).

Lipton International Players Championships: men and women compete in the world's largest tennis tournament held at the Crandon Park Tennis Center in Key Biscayne (☎446-2200).

April

Early *Miracle Mile Festival*: parades and floats along Miracle Mile singing the praises of Coral Gables.

Coconut Grove Seafood Festival: an excuse to eat loads of seafood in Coconut Grove's Peacock Park.

South Beach Film Festival: local and non-resident film directors debut short films at the Colony Theater, 1040 Lincoln Road.

May

The Great Sunrise Balloon Race & Festival: held at Homestead Air Force Base

For **arthouse**, **foreign-language** or fading monochrome **classic** films, find out what's playing at the Alliance Film/Video Coop., 924 Lincoln Rd (☎538-8242). Local **libraries** have screenings, as does the Bass Museum of Art, 2121 Park Ave (☎673-7530), on Tuesdays – newspaper listings carry details.

Gay and lesbian Miami

Miami's **gay** and **lesbian** communities are enjoying the city's boom times as much as anyone else, with a growing number of gay-owned businesses, bars and clubs opening up around the city. The scene, traditionally focusing on Coconut Grove, has recently gathered great momentum on South Beach. In either of these areas, most public places are friendly and welcoming towards gays and lesbians – though attitudes in other parts of Miami can sometimes be considerably less enlightened. The key source

June

Early *Goombay Festival*: a spirited bash in honor of Bahamian culture, in and around Coconut Grove's Peacock Park (☎372-9966).

Art in the Park: arty stalls and displays in the Charles Deering Estate in South Miami.

July

America's Birthday Bash: 4th of July: music, fireworks and a laser light show celebrate the occasion at Bayfront Park in downtown Miami (☎358-7550).

Tropical Agriculture Fiesta: enjoy fresh mangos along with offbeat fruits and other ethnic foods at the Fruit and Spice Park (☎247-5727).

August

First Sunday *Miami Reggae Festival*: celebration of Jamaican Independence Day with dozens of top Jamaican bands playing around the city.

September

Mid *Festival Miami*: three weeks of performing and visual arts events organized by the University of Miami, mostly taking place in Coral Gables (☎284-3941).

October

Hispanic Heritage Festival: lasts all month and features innumerable events linked to Latin American history and culture.

Early *Caribbean-American Carnival*: a joyous cavalcade of soca and calypso bands in Bicentennial Park.

Columbus Day Regatta: Florida's largest water sports event race commemorating Columbus's historic voyage (☎876-0818).

November

Mid *Miami Book Fair International*: a wealth of tomes from across the world spread across the campus of Miami-Dade Community College in downtown Miami (☎237-3258).

Harvest Festival: a celebration of southern Florida's agricultural traditions including homemade crafts, music and historical reenactments at the Dade County Fairgrounds in West Dade (☎375-1492).

December

26-1 Jan *Indian Arts Festival*: Native American artisans from all over the country gather at the Miccosukee Village to display their work.

30 *King Mango Strut*: a very alternative New Year's Eve celebration, with part-time cross-dressers and clowns parading through Coconut Grove.

31 *Orange Bowl Parade*: mainstream climax of the New Year bashes all over the city, with floats, marching bands and the crowning of the Orange Bowl Queen at the Orange Bowl stadium.

of info is the free *TWN* (*The Weekly News*), available from any of the places listed below and from many of the mixed bars and clubs around Coconut Grove and South Beach.

Resources

Gay Community Book/Video Store, 7545 Biscayne Blvd (☎754-6900). Copious books, magazines, newspapers and videos of gay and lesbian interest.

Gay and Lesbian Community Hotline, call ☎759-3661 for a recorded message which gives access – via touch-tone dialing – to more recorded info on gay bars and events, gay-supportive businesses, doctors and lawyers, and much more.

Clubs and discos

Cheers, 2492 SW 17th Ave, South Miami (☎857-0041). Cruisy, predominantly gay male bar with video room and pool tables under the stars; Monday is ladies' night, but women also drop in on the Friday disco.

Ozone, 6620 SW 57th Ave and Red Rd (☎667-2888). Features "Adorable Wednesdays," with two-for-one drinks all night. No cover.

Salvation, 1771 West Ave (☎673-6508). Giant warehouse converted into an anything-goes club with the shirtless and rippled partying to thumping techno beats.

Twist, 1057 Washington Ave (☎538-9478). More of a big, comfy bar than raging nightclub, though it boasts high energy techno on the small dance floor upstairs. Attracts a more upscale rather than beefcake clientele.

Warsaw Ballroom, 1450 Collins Ave, Miami Beach (☎1-800/9-WARSAW). While not exclusively gay (see "Nightlife"), this is the busiest and biggest gay disco in town.

Women's Miami

Though it lacks the extended networks of Los Angeles or New York, Miami is steadily becoming a better place for **women** seeking the support and solidarity of other women in business, artistic endeavors, or simply looking for a reliable and inexpensive source of medical care.

Women's organizations

Women's Caucus for Art Miami Chapter, 561 NW 32nd St (☎576-0041). Charitable organization striving to raise women's profile in the visual arts; membership open to men.

Women's Chamber of Commerce of Dade County, 7700 SW 88th St, suite 310 (☎446-6660). Promoting women-owned and women-run businesses throughout south Florida.

Health care and counseling centers

Eve Medical Center, 3900 NW 79th Ave (☎591-2288). Low-cost medical care and abortions in serene, supportive environment.

Miami Women's Healthcenter, at North Shore Medical Center, suite 301, 1100 NW 95th St (☎835-6165). Education, information, support and discussion groups, physician referrals, mammograms, seminars and workshops.

Planned Parenthood of Greater Miami, 656 NE 125th St, N Miami (☎895-7756). Economical health care for men and women; including birth control supplies, pregnancy testing, treatment of sexually transmitted diseases and counseling.

Women's Community Health Center, 12550 Biscayne Blvd, N Miami (☎895-1274). Health care for women.

Women's Resource & Counseling Center, 111 Majorca Ave, Coral Gables (☎448-8325). Friendly clinic providing individual, marriage, group and family counseling, psychotherapy and assertiveness training.

Shopping

Shopping for the sake of it isn't the big deal in Miami that it is in some American cities, though there's plenty of opportunity for eager consumers to exercise their credit cards. Bizarre as it may seem, Miami leads the field in **shopping mall** architecture, blowing millions of dollars on environments intended subtly to soften the hard commercialism of the stores which fill them – several malls are worthy of investigation for this reason alone. These days, old-style **department stores**, such as the dependable Macy's and Sears Roebuck & Co, generally show up inside the malls too, but Miami has one dignified survivor, Burdines, that stands alone.

The closer you get to the beach, the wackier Miami's **clothes** shops become – look out for zebra-print bikinis and Art Deco shirts. However, the best places for quality togs at discounted rates are the designer outlets of the **fashion district**, on Fifth Avenue between 25th and 29th streets, just north of downtown Miami; here you'll find classy outfits – most of Latin American origin – at slashed prices. With less finesse, there can be finds amid the discarded garb filling the city's **thrift stores**.

Unless you're existing on a shoestring budget – or are preparing a picnic – you won't need to shop for **food and drink** at all, although supermarkets like Publix and Winn-Dixie, usually open until 10pm, are plentiful – flip through the phone book to locate the nearest one. You can buy alcohol from supermarkets and, of course, from the many **liquor stores**, but if you're looking for quality grub or booze, only the largest of the supermarkets and a few specialist suppliers will oblige.

Gun shops have long outnumbered **bookshops** in Miami, but large discount chains like B. Dalton's and Waldenbooks have arrived, with branches in shopping malls, and there are also a few local outlets stocking quality reading material. Some of the city's record shops make good browsing territory, too, their contents spanning everything from doo-wop rarities to the smoothest salsa hits.

Malls and department stores

Aventura Mall, 19501 Biscayne Blvd, North Miami Beach (☎935-1110). One of the largest air-conditioned malls in the state, boasting virtually every major department store: Macy's, Sears, J C Penney. Pick up a map on entry or you'll never find your way out.

Bal Harbor Shops, 9700 Collins Ave, Miami Beach (☎866-0311). Don't come to buy but to watch designer-shopping in a temple of upmarket consumerism.

Bayside Marketplace, 401 N Biscayne Blvd, near downtown Miami (☎577-3344). Squarely aimed at tourists, but a good blend of diverse stores – selling everything from Art Deco ashtrays to bubblegum – beside the bay, with some excellent food stands.

Burdines, 22 E Flagler St, downtown Miami (☎577-2312). Run-of-the-mill clothes, furnishings and domestic appliances, but Miami's oldest department store – circa 1936 – is an entertaining place to cruise.

CocoWalk, 3015 Grand Ave, Coconut Grove (☎444-0777). In the heart of Coconut Grove, this complex has a relatively small range of stores, some good places to eat and a decent multiplex cinema.

Dadeland Mall, 7535 N Kendall Drive, South Miami (☎665-6226). More top-class department stores and specialty shops in a totally enclosed, air-conditioned environment conducive to passionate shopping.

The Falls, Hwy-1 and SW 136th St, South Miami (☎255-4570). Sit inside a gazebo and contemplate the waterfalls and the rainforest that prettify suburban Miami's classiest set of shops.

Florida Keys Factory Shops, 250 E Palm Drive, Florida City/Homestead (☎248-4727). Located where the Florida Turnpike meets Hwy-1 and conveniently located for people traveling to the Keys or Everglades. Dedicated shoppers will find huge savings on name brands.

Lincoln Road Mall, South Beach (☎673-7010). Not a shopping mall in the usual sense of the word, but, between Washington Ave and Alton Road, a pedestrian-only road lined with stores. Many are given over to art galleries, but there's also a whole range of trendy clothes stores and many excellent sidewalk cafés and restaurants.

Streets of Mayfair, 2911 Grand Ave, Coconut Grove (☎448-1700). The expensive stores take second place to the landscaped tropical foliage and the discreetly placed classical sculptures.

Clothes and thrift stores

Coral Gables Congregational Church Thrift Shop, 3010 De Soto Blvd, Coral Gables (☎445-1721). After viewing the church (see "Coral Gables"), drop into the interestingly stocked thrift store next door.

Details at the Beach, 2087 NW 2nd Ave (☎573-8903). Interesting clothing and furnishings in a store sure to delight interior designers.

Miami Twice, 6562 SW 40th St (☎666-0127). Department store specializing in vintage clothing, accessories and some furniture.

One Hand Clapping, 7165 SW 47th St, Miami Beach (☎661-6316). Amid a wondrous assortment of antique junk, there are hats, dresses and scarves to delight the time-warped flapper.

Food and drink

Epicure Market, 1656 Alton Rd, Miami Beach (☎672-1861). Tasty morsels for the gourmet palate and a mouthwatering array of hot foods for immediate consumption.

Estate Wines and Gourmet Foods, 92 Miracle Mile, Coral Gables (☎442-9915). Alongside the fine foods, an exquisite stock of wines chosen with the connoisseur in mind.

Perricone's Marketplace & Café, 15 SE 10th St, Downtown Miami (☎374-9693). Italian market with imported meats and cheeses, a homemade bakery, and a café on the premises.

Books

Books & Books, 296 Aragon Ave, Coral Gables (☎442-4408) and a small branch at 933 Lincoln Rd, Miami Beach (☎532-3222). Excellent stock of general titles but especially strong on Floridian art and design, travel and new fiction; also has author signings and talks: ☎444-POEM for the latest events.

Downtown Book Center, 247 SE First St, downtown Miami (☎377-9939). Large selection ranging from the latest blockbusters to esoteric and academic tomes.

Grove Antiquarian Books, 3318 Virginia St, Coconut Grove (☎444-5362). A relaxing oasis in the heart of lively Coconut Grove stocking quality used books and some valuable first editions covering all subjects.

The 9th Chakra, 817 Lincoln Rd (☎538-0671). Gifts for the soul, dreamcatchers and a plethora of reading materials ranging from simple meditation to reiki and spiritual instruction.

Records, CDs and tapes

Lily's Records, 1260 SW Eighth St, Little Havana (☎856-0536). Unsurpassed stock of salsa, merengue and other Latin sounds.

Spec's Music, 501 Collins Ave (☎534-3667). Mix of contemporary and hard-to-find music.

Revolution Records & CD's, 1620 Alton Rd (☎673-6464). Cuban records, as well as classic and modern rock.

Yesterday & Today Dance Music, 1614 Alton Rd, Miami Beach (☎534-8704). Dusty piles of blues, jazz, R&B and Sixties indie rarities.

Cuban curios

Ba-Balú!, 500 Española Way, South Beach (☎538-0679). Beach towels, coffee mugs and T-shirts sporting anti-Castro slogans or Cuban flags, CDs and tapes of Cuban music, *guayaberas* and cigars make original south Florida souvenirs.

Coral Way Antiques, 3127 SW 22nd St, Coral Gables (☎567-3131). Old postcards, books, military items and other Cuban "collectibles."

Listings

Airlines Air Canada, Airport Concourse G (☎1-800-776-3000); American Airlines, 150 Alhambra Plaza (☎1-800-433-7300); British Airways, 354 SE First St (☎1-800/247-9297); Continental, Airport Concourse "C" (☎1-800/525-0280); Delta, 201 Alhambra Circle (☎1-800/221-1212); Northwest Airlines/KLM, 150 Alhambra Plaza (☎1-800/225-2525); TWA, Airport Concourse "G" (☎1-800/221-2000); United, 178 Giralda Ave (☎1-800/241-6522); US Airways, 150 Alhambra Plaza (☎1-800/428-4322); Virgin Atlantic, 225 Alhambra Circle (☎1-800/862-8621).

Airport Miami International, six miles west of downtown Miami. (☎876-7000). Take local bus #7 from downtown Miami (an approximately half-hour journey), local bus #J from Miami Beach (around 40min), or a shuttle bus: Airporter (☎247-8874); Red Top (☎526-5764); Super Shuttle (☎871-2000). More details on p.55.

American Express main hotline ☎1/800-528-4800. Offices around the city: in downtown Miami, Suite 100, 330 Biscayne Blvd (☎358/7350); in Coral Gables, 32 Miracle Mile (☎446-3381); in Miami Beach, at Bal Harbor Shops, 9700 Collins Ave (☎865-5959).

Amtrak 8303 NW 37th Ave (☎1-800/872-7245).

Area Code ☎305.

Babysitting Central Sitting Agency: ☎856-0550.

Banks See "Money Exchange."

Bike rental See p.60

Boat rental Recreate the opening sequences from *Miami Vice* by skimming over Biscayne Bay in a motor boat. Equipped with 50hp engines, such vessels can be rented at hourly rates – from $45 for one hour – from Beach Boat Rentals, 2380 Collins Ave, Miami Beach (☎534-4307).

Coastguard ☎535-4313.

Consulates Canada, 200 S Biscayne Blvd, Ste. 1600 (☎579-1600); Denmark, PH 1D, 2655 Le Jeune Rd (☎446-0020); France, 1 Biscayne Tower, Ste. 1710 (☎372-9798); Germany, Suite 2200, 100 N Biscayne Blvd (☎358-0290); Netherlands, 800 Brickell Ave, Ste. 918 (☎789-6646); Norway, Suite 205, 1001 North American Way (☎358-4386); UK, Suite 2110, 1001 S Bayshore Drive (☎374-1522).

Crisis Hotline ☎358-4357.

Dentists To be referred to a dentist: ☎667-3647.

Doctor To find a physician: ☎324-8717.

Emergencies Dial ☎911 and ask for relevant emergency service.

Everglades daytrips In the absence of public transport, almost every tour operator in Miami runs half- or full-day trips ($20–35) to the Everglades, but these seldom involve more than a quick gape at an alligator and an air-boat ride – or even enter the Everglades National Park. Only All Florida Adventure Tours (☎1-800/33T-OUR3) operates ecology-centered tours ($80 for a day) to the park and surrounding areas; unfortunately, they rarely have places for individual travelers. The Everglades are comprehensively detailed in Chapter Six.

Gay & Lesbian community hotline ☎759-3661.

Hospitals with emergency rooms In Miami: Jackson Memorial Medical Center, 1611 NW Twelfth Ave (☎585-1111); Mercy Hospital, 3663 S Miami Ave (☎854-4400). In Miami Beach: Mt Sinai Medical Center, 4300 Alton Rd (☎674-2121); South Shore Hospital, 630 Alton Rd (☎672-2100).

Laundromats Check the *Yellow Pages* for the nearest; handiest for South Beach are: Wash Club of South Beach, 510 Washington Ave (☎534-4298) and Lolita's Laundromat, 405 15th St (☎538-8303).

Left Luggage At the airport, some Greyhound terminals (phone to be sure) and the Amtrak station.

Library The biggest is Miami-Dade County Public Library, 101 W Flagler St (Mon–Sat 9am–6pm, Thurs until 9pm; Oct–May also Sun 1–5pm; ☎375-2665) – see p.67.

Lost and found For something lost on Metro-Dade Transit, phone ☎375-3366 (Mon–Fri 8.30am–4.30pm). Otherwise call the police.

Money exchange Bring US dollar travelers checks or cash, but if you need to change money, facilities are available at the airport and the following: Barnett Bank, 701 Brickell Ave (with 42 branches elsewhere; call ☎350-7143 for the nearest); First Union National Bank, 200 S Biscayne Blvd

(☎599-2265); SunTrust Bank, 777 Brickell Ave (☎592-0800); NationsBank, 1 SE 3rd Ave (☎350-6350), and 1300 Brickell Ave (☎372-0800); Chequepoint, 865 Collins Ave (☎538-5348); Citibank International, 201 S Biscayne Blvd (☎347-1600).

Parking fines $18, increasing to $45 if not paid within thirty days (☎673-PARK).

Pharmacies Usually open from 8am or 9am until 9pm or midnight. 24-hour pharmacy branches of Eckerd at 1825 Miami Gardens Drive (☎932-5740); 1549 SW 107th Ave (☎220-0147); 2235 Collins Ave (☎673-9514); 200 Lincoln Rd (☎673-9502).

Police Non-emergency: ☎595-6263; emergency: ☎911.

Post offices In downtown Miami, 500 NW Second Ave; in Coral Gables, 251 Valencia Ave; in Coconut Grove, 3191 Grand Ave; in Homestead, 739 Washington Ave; in Key Biscayne, 59 Harbor Drive; in Miami Beach, 1300 Washington Ave and 445 W 40th St. All open Mon–Fri 8.30am–5pm, Sat 8.30am–12.30pm, or longer hours.

Rape hotline ☎549-7273.

Road conditions ☎470-5277.

Rollerblading Hugely popular in Miami, especially in South Beach. Rollertech, at 221 7th St, South Beach (☎538-8408), and Fritz Skates, at 726 Lincoln Rd (532-1954), both sell and rent out roller blades and safety gear, as well as offering lessons. Rental costs around $8 per hour, $24 per day, or $15 overnight (6.30pm–12 noon); to buy, prices range from $55 to $250.

Sports Miami Dolphins (☎620-2578), Florida's oldest pro football team, and the Florida Marlins (☎626-7400), the country's newest professional baseball team, play at Pro Player Stadium, 2269 NW 199th St, sixteen miles northwest of downtown Miami: box office open Mon–Fri 10am–6pm; most seats are $30 for football and around $10–15 for baseball. The football season is August through to December, and the baseball season April through to September. The Miami Heat basketball team plays NBA matches at the Miami Arena, 701 Arena Blvd, three miles north of downtown Miami: info on ☎577-HEAT; tickets $14–21. The basketball season is November through to April. Miami Freedom plays soccer at Milander Park in Hialeah, seven miles northwest of downtown Miami: info on ☎888-0838; tickets $9.50. Professional ice hockey is represented by the Florida Panthers (☎954/768-1900) who play at the Miami Arena between October and April. Miami University's football, basketball and baseball teams are all called the Miami Hurricanes: game and ticket (usually $5–13) info Mon–Fri 8am–6pm on ☎1-800/GO-CANES.

Thomas Cook In downtown Miami: 155 SE Third Ave (☎381-9525) and 80 Biscayne Blvd (☎379-8077); in Coral Gables: Suite 102, 901 Ponce de Leon Blvd (☎448-0269); in Miami Beach: at the *Fountainbleau*, 4441 Collins Ave (☎674-1907).

Ticketmaster Tickets for arts and sports events, payable by credit card: ☎358-5885.

Weather/surf information ☎324-8811 or 229-4522.

Western Union Offices all over the city; call ☎1-800/325-6000 to find the nearest.

travel details

Trains (AMTRAK 1/800-USA-RAIL)

Miami to: New York (3 daily; 26hr 25min–28hr 40min); Ocala (1 daily; 7hr 36min); Sebring (3 daily; 3hr 15min); St. Petersburg (1 daily; leaves 7.20pm to Orlando 5hr 33min, and buses depart Orlando for St. Petersburg at 1.05pm (2hr 40min) and 4.30pm (3hr 25min)); Tampa (1 daily; leaves at 5pm and takes 5hr 13min); Washington DC (3 daily; 22hr 20min–24hr 11min); Winter Haven (3 daily; 4hr).

Tri-Rail (5–15 daily)

Miami to: Boca Raton (1hr); Delray Beach (1hr 7min); Fort Lauderdale (31min); Hollywood (16min); West Palm Beach (1hr 34min).

Buses (GREYHOUND 1/800-231-2222)

Miami to: Daytona Beach (6 daily; 7hr 5min–7hr 55min); Ft. Lauderdale (25 daily; 55min); Ft. Myers (7 daily; 4hr–4hr 45min); Ft. Pierce (16 daily; 2hr 45min–4hr 5min); Jacksonville (13 daily; 7hr 5min–14hr-5min); Key West (3 daily; 4hr 40min); Orlando (12 daily; 5hr 29min–11hr 5min); Sarasota (5 daily; 6hr 5min–10hr); St. Petersburg (6 daily; 6hr 20min–10hr 14min); Tampa (9 daily; 6hr 55min–9hr 40min); West Palm Beach (15 daily; 1hr 40min–3hr 5min).

CHAPTER TWO

THE FLORIDA KEYS

F iction, films and folklore have given the **Florida Keys*** – a hundred-mile string of small islands running from the southeastern corner of the state to within ninety miles of Cuba – an image of sultry romance and glamorous intrigue that they don't always deserve. Throughout their length, and especially for the first sixty-odd miles, fishing, snorkeling and diving dominate – admittedly with great justification – and are ruthlessly hawked at every opportunity. The main attraction here is the **Florida Reef**, a great band of living coral just a few miles off the coast. Its range of color and dazzling array of ocean-life combine to create an exceptional sight. However, if you're not planning to indulge in watersports, you'll be hard pressed to find much else to fill your time. Here and there the islands' idiosyncratic history rears its head in the form of houses built by early Bahamian settlers and seedy waterside bars run by refugees from points north. And while there are some stunning natural areas and worthwhile ecology tours, the whole stretch is primarily a build-up to **Key West**, the real pearl on this island strand.

One of the better places to visit the reef is the **John Pennecamp State Park**, one of the few interesting features of **Key Largo**, the biggest but not the prettiest of the Keys. Like **Islamorada**, further south, Key Largo is rapidly being populated by suburban Miamians, moving here for the sailing and fishing but unable to survive without shopping malls. Islamorada is the best base for fishing, and also has some natural and historical points of note – as does the next major settlement, **Marathon**, which is at the center of the key chain and thus makes a useful short-term base. Thirty miles on, the **Lower Keys** get fewer visitors and less publicity than their neighbors. Don't dismiss them, though; in many ways these are the most unusual and appealing of the whole lot. Covered with dense forests, they are home to a tiny and endangered species of deer, and, at Looe Key, offer a tremendous departure point for trips to the Florida Reef.

Key West, the final dot of the North American continent before a thousand miles of ocean is the end of the road in every sense. Shot through with an intoxicating aura of abandonment, it's a small but immensely vibrant place. A unique laissez-faire atmosphere permeates the island, and it's nearly impossible to resist its allure. The only part of the Keys with a real sense of history, Key West was once – unbelievably – the richest town in the US and the largest settlement in Florida. There are old homes and museums to explore and plenty of bars in which to while away the hours.

Key West also has a couple of small **beaches**, something noticeably missing – due to the reef – elsewhere. But the meager sand and surf is easily made up for by the Keys' spectacular **sunsets**. As the nineteenth-century ornithologist John James Audubon once rhapsodized: "a blaze of refulgent glory streams portal of the West and the masses of vapour assume the semblance of mountains of molten gold."

The area code for all numbers in this chapter is ☎305.

---

* A variation on the word "cay," a key is a small island or bank composed of coral fragments. The Florida Keys are the largest grouping, but keys are common all along the state's southerly coastlines.

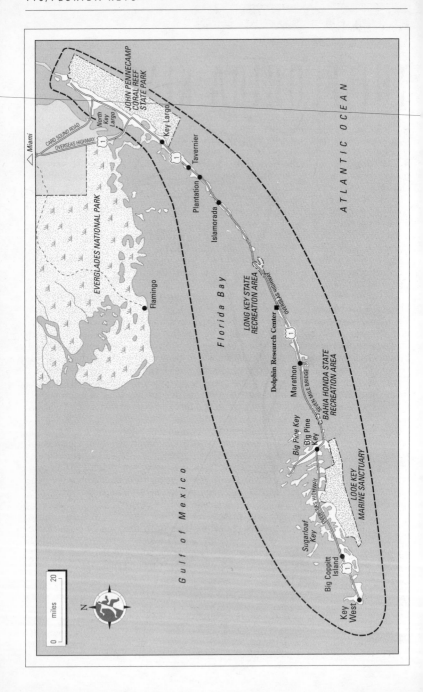

Practicalities

Traveling through the Keys could hardly be easier as there's just one route all the way through to Key West: the **Overseas Highway (Hwy-1)**. This is punctuated by **mile markers (MM)** – posts on which mileage is marked, starting with MM127, just south of Homestead (see "Miami & Miami Beach"), and finishing with MM0, in Key West. Almost all places of business use mile markers as an address, and throughout this chapter they are tagged with an "MM" (for example, "the *Holiday Inn*, at MM100"). Bear in mind that U-turns are not always possible on the Overseas Highway, so stay alert to avoid missing exits.

Traveling from Miami there are two options. Either take the **I-95** south to Hwy-1 or, for a shorter route, take the **Florida Turnpike Extension** toll route south and pick up Hwy-1 at Florida City. Most **motels** and **restaurants** are strung along the highway, often using the mile markers as addresses. **Public transport** is comprised of three daily Greyhound buses between Miami and Key West, which can be hailed down anywhere on the route (see "Travel details" at the end of the chapter), and a skeletal local bus service in Key West.

Accommodation is abundant but more expensive than on the mainland. During high season, November–April, budget for *at least* $50–85 a night, $35–55 the rest of the year. **Camping** is considerably less expensive and is well catered for throughout the Keys.

Note that throughout this chapter only the most basic **diving information** is given. Always take local advice before venturing into the water. (See "The Backcountry" on p.37 for information on outdoor safety).

ACCOMMODATION PRICE CODES

All **accommodation prices** in this book have been coded using the symbols below. Note that prices are for the least expensive double rooms in each establishment. For a full explanation see p.27 in Basics.

① up to $30	③ $45-60	⑤ $80-100	⑦ $130-180
② $30-45	④ $60-80	⑥ $100-130	⑧ $180+

North Key Largo

Assuming you're driving, the clever way to arrive in the Keys is with Card Sound Road (Hwy-905A; $1 toll), which branches off Hwy-1 a few miles south of Homestead. Doing so avoids the bulk of the tourist traffic and, after passing through the desolate southeastern section of the Everglades, gives soaring views of the mangrove-dotted waters of Florida Bay (where a long wait and a lot of luck might be rewarded with a glimpse of a rare American crocodile) – and a glimpse of the Keys as they all might have looked long ago before commercialism took hold.

The bulk of **North Key Largo**, where Hwy-905 touches ground, is free of development, and human habitation is marked only by the odd shack amid a rich endowment of trees. Despite elaborate plans to turn the area into a city called Port Bougainvillea, with high-rise blocks and a monorail (a terrifying prospect ended by sudden bankruptcy), much of the land here is now owned and protected by the state. Scare stories about drug smugglers and practitioners of the voodoo-like Santeria seem designed to ward off visitors, but in reality there's no more drug smuggling here than anywhere else in the Keys, and magic merchants come not to sacrifice innocent tourists but to gather weird and wonderful herbs for use in rituals. There's probably more danger from the exclusive Ocean Reef Club, whose golf course you'll spot after a few miles if you turn left where Hwy-905 splits; it's regarded by the FBI as the country's most

SWIMMING WITH DOLPHINS

Long before the Sixties TV show *Flipper* brought about a surge in their popularity, **dolphins** – marine mammals smaller than whales and differentiated from porpoises by their beak-like snout – were the subject of centuries of speculation and mythology. According to the wildest notion, dolphins once lived on land but became so disenchanted by the course of civilization at the time of Aristotle and Plato that they took to the sea, vowing to bide their time until humankind was ready to receive their wisdom. Whatever the truth, there's no disputing that dolphins are extremely intelligent, with brains similar in size to those of humans. They communicate in a **language** of clicks and whistles, and use a sonar technique called echolocation to detect food in dark waters and, perhaps, to create "sound pictures" for one another.

The world's dolphin population has been reduced by several factors, including the nets of tuna fishermen, but they are a common sight around the Florida Keys and are the star attraction of the state's many marine parks – though watching them perform somersaults in response to human commands gives just an inkling of their potential. By contrast, at the **Dolphin Research Center** (address below; Wed–Sun 9am–4pm, closed Mon & Tues) they are used in therapy programs for cancer-sufferers and mentally handicapped children; the exceptional patience and gentleness displayed by the dolphins (all of whom are free to swim out to sea whenever they want) in this work suggest that their sonar system may allow them to make an X-ray-like scan of a body to detect abnormalities and perhaps even to "see" emotions. Take a **tour** (Wed–Sun at 10am, 12.30pm, 2pm & 3.30pm; adults $7.50, under 13s $4.50) of the research center to become better informed on these remarkable – and still barely understood – mammals. The Dolphin Research Center is also one of three places in the Florida Keys where, by booking well ahead, you can **swim with dolphins** ($80 for around twenty minutes). Averaging seven feet long, dolphins look disconcertingly large at close quarters – and will lose interest in you long before you tire of their company – but if you do get the opportunity to join them, it's an unforgettable experience.

- In Key Largo: Dolphins Plus, MM100 (☎451-1993).
- In Islamorada: Theater of the Sea, MM84.5 (☎664-2431).
- In Marathon: Dolphin Research Center, MM59 (☎289-1121).

secure retreat for very important people – watch out for nervous, armed men in dark suits. If you want to explore North Key Largo at length, you'll have to eat and sleep in Key Largo or Tavernier (see below).

Further south, Hwy-905 merges with Hwy-1 near MM109. Known from here on as the **Overseas Highway**, Hwy-1 is the main – and only – road all the way to Key West.

John Pennecamp Coral Reef State Park

The one essential stop as you approach Key Largo is the **JOHN PENNECAMP CORAL REEF STATE PARK**, at MM102.5 (daily 8am–sunset; cars and drivers $3.75 plus 50¢ per passenger, pedestrians and cyclists $1.50). At its heart is a protected 78-square-mile section of living coral reef, part of the reef chain that runs from here to the Dry Tortugas, five miles off of Key West (see p.148).

Just a few decades ago, great sections of the reef were dynamited or hauled up by crane to be broken up and sold as souvenirs. These days, collecting Florida coral is illegal, and any samples displayed in tourist shops were most likely imported from the Philippines.

Despite the damage wrought by ecologically unsound tourism, experts still rate this as one of the most beautiful reef systems in the world. Whether you opt to visit the reef here – one of the better spots – or elsewhere in the Keys (such as Looe Key, see "The Lower Keys"), make sure you do visit it – the eulogistic descriptions you'll hear are rarely exaggerations.

Seeing the reef: practicalities

Since most of the park lies underwater, the best way to see it is with a **snorkeling tour** (9am, noon & 3pm; adults $24, under 16s $19) or, if you're qualified, a **guided scuba dive** (9.30am & 1.30pm; $37 excluding equipment; diver's certificate required). If you prefer to stay dry, a remarkable amount of the reef can be enjoyed on the two-and-a-half-hour **glass-bottomed boat tour** (9.15am, 12.15pm & 3pm; adults $13, under-12s $8.50). You can also rent a boat ranging from a single person kayak to a 22-foot power boat – canoes cost $8 per hour ($28 per half day), 12-foot sailboats $16 per hour ($48 for half a day) and power boats $25 or $35 per hour. Note that only during the summer are you likely to get a place on these tours or obtain a boat without booking ahead. To be sure, call ☎451-1621 to make a reservation, or drop into Sundiver Station, MM103 (☎451-2220). If there's no room, try one of the numerous local diving shops: American Diving Headquarters, MM106 (☎1-800/322-3483), and Captain Slate's Atlantis Dive Center, at MM106.5 (☎451-1325), are just two that operate their own trips out to the reef – and cover a larger area than park tours – at around the same rates.

At the reef

Only when you're **at the reef** does its role in providing a sheltered environment for a multitude of crazy-colored fish and exotic sea life become apparent. Even from the glass-bottomed boat you're virtually guaranteed to spot lobsters, angelfish, eels and wispy jellyfish shimmering through the current, shoals of minnows stalked by angry-faced barracudas – and many more less easily identified aquatic curiosities.

Despite looking like a big lump of rock, the **reef**, too, is a delicate living thing, composed of millions of minute coral polyps that extract calcium from the seawater and grow from one to sixteen feet every 1000 years. Coral takes many shapes and forms, resembling anything from staghorns to a bucket, and comes in a paint-box variety of colors due to the plants, *zooxanthellae*, living within the coral tissues. Sadly, it's far easier to spot signs of death rather than life on the reef: white patches show where a carelessly dropped anchor or a diver's hand have scraped away the protective mucus layer and left the coral susceptible to lethal disease.

This destruction got so bad at the horseshoe-shaped **Molasses Reef**, about seven miles out, that the authorities sank two obsolete Coast Guard cutters nearby to create an alternative attraction for divers. In as much as the destruction has slowed, this plan worked and today you'll enjoy some great snorkeling around the reef and the cutters. If you prefer diving and **wrecks**, head for **the Elbow**, a section of the reef a few miles northeast of Molasses, where a number of intriguing, barnacle-encrusted nineteenth-century specimens lie; like most of the keys' diveable wrecks, these were deliberately brought here to bolster tourism in the Seventies, which lessens their allure somewhat, and you definitely won't find any treasure.

By far the strangest thing at the reef is the *Christ of the Deep*, a nine-foot bronze statue of Christ intended as a memorial to perished sailors. The algae-coated creation, twenty feet down at Key Largo Dry Rocks, is a replica of Guido Galletti's *Christ of the Abyss*, similarly submerged off the coast of Genoa, Italy – and is surely the final word in Florida's long-time fixation with Mediterranean art and architecture. The glass-bottomed boat trip, by the way, doesn't visit the Elbow or the statue.

Back on land: the visitor center

Provided you visit the reef early, there'll be plenty of time left to enjoy the terrestrial portion of the park. The ecological displays at the **visitor center** (daily 8am–5pm) provide an inspiring introduction to the flora and fauna of the Keys and will give you a practical insight into the region's transitional zones: the vegetation changes dramatically within an elevation of a few feet. The park's tropical hardwood **hammock* trails** meander through red mangroves, pepper trees, and graceful franzipannes. Racoon, heron and fiddler crab tracks are everywhere, and hairy-legged, golden orb spiders dangle from many a branch. The park also boasts some fine man-made beaches (you won't find any more – man-made or not – until Key West), but note that the coral is very unforgiving to bare feet. Another option for exploring the park is to rent a **canoe** ($6 per hour; $30 per day) and glide around the mangrove-fringed inner waterways.

Key Largo

Thanks to the 1948 film in which Humphrey Bogart and Lauren Bacall grappled with Florida's best-known features – crime and hurricanes – almost everybody has heard of **KEY LARGO**. Yet the film's title was chosen for no other reason than it suggested somewhere warm and exotic, and the film, though set here, was almost entirely shot in Hollywood – hoodwinking countless millions into thinking that paradise was a town in the Florida Keys.

Recognizing a potential tourist bonanza, business people here soon changed the name of their community from Rock Harbor to Key Largo (a title that until then had applied to the whole island, derived from *Cayo Largo* – Long Island – the name given to it by early Spanish explorers), and tenuous links with Hollywood are maintained even today. The steam-powered boat that starred alongside Bogart in *The African Queen* is moored (when not on promotional tours) in the marina of the *Holiday Inn*, MM100, and the hotel's lobby displays a selection of stills of Bogart and co-star Katharine Hepburn acting their hearts out – in England and Africa.

Clinging to an image based more in movies than reality, Key Largo proper is really a jumble of filling stations, shopping plazas and fast-food outlets. There are one or two low-key attractions, and the offshore islands may persuade you to stay for a night or two. If you're in more of a hurry and are here in the early evening, at least make time to hop off the Overseas Highway to enjoy the sunset.

Information and accommodation

If you didn't stop at the well-stocked Visitor Information Center near Homestead (see "Miami & Miami Beach"), pull up at the new and highly informative **Florida Keys Visitor Center**, 106000 Overseas Highway, at MM106 (daily 9am–6pm; ☎1-800/822-1088). The colonial-style center has piles of brochures, money-saving vouchers and hotel booking information. Don't confuse the visitor center with the **Key Largo Tourist Center**, 103360 Overseas Highway (daily 9am–7pm; ☎453-0066; fax ☎453-9197), which promotes only the area's ritziest hotels.

In addition to beds, plenty of **motels** offer diving packages. Look for signs or try: *Economy Efficiency* (also known as *Ed & Ellen's*), 103365 Overseas Highway (☎451-4712; ②), which is basic but clean; *Largo Lodge*, 101740 Overseas Highway (☎451-0424; ⑤), offers comfortable apartments in a lovely garden setting right on the beach; and though not plush, *Seafarer*, MM97.6 (☎852-5349; ③) has spotless cottages and daily tours at 8.30am and 1.30pm to the local marine sanctuaries. Next door, prices go up at the *Kona Kai Resort* (MM98), 97802 Overseas Highway (☎852-7200; ⑦), but

---

*Cropping up all over Florida, **hammocks** are pockets of woodland able to flourish where the ground elevation rises a few feet above the surrounding wetlands. For a fuller explanation, see "Natural History" in Contexts.

the chalets are huge and stylish, a dozen strains of banana grow in the garden and the hotel has its own art gallery. Very costly but one-of-a-kind, *Jules' Undersea Lodge*, at 51 Shoreland Drive (☎1-800/858-7119 or ☎451-2353; ⑨), is a tiny "hotel" thirty feet below the ocean's surface. More theme park than place to stay, it is always booked well in advance. The two-bedroom accommodations are perfectly safe and are linked to land by an intercom system. The overnight, two-person luxury option ($1000) comes with all the amenities, including caviar and flowers. Just remember your diver's certificate – otherwise you'll have to take the hotel's three-hour crash course ($75) before you'll be allowed to unpack

Of the many **campgrounds** in and around Key Largo, the cleanest and cheapest is the *John Pennecamp Coral Reef State Park* (☎451-1202; see above). The *Key Largo Kampground*, MM101 (☎451-1431), is a reasonable alternative but has no grass pitches.

Around Key Largo

The tiny, uninhabited **islands** just off Key Largo make glorious forays, and there's no better way of exploring them than hiring a boat or catamaran. Signs abound for boat rentals, but the most reliable and user-friendly option is Wild Willie's Watersports, 103360 Overseas Highway (☎451-1633 or ☎453-4017), where owner Alan Gosney provides motorized catamarans for $35 or $80 per half day. Prices drop in summer, and with advance notice Gosney will even take you out personally. If you decide to go it alone, do heed his advice about the varying shades of shallow waters to avoid grounding your boat. If a glass-bottom boat tour is more up your alley, head to the *Holiday Inn* docks at MM100 (☎451-4655) where two-hour cruises at 10am, 1 and 4 pm cost $17.

A new and worthwhile attraction is **Dolphin Cove** (daily 8am–5pm; ☎451-4060), a five-acre marine environment research center just south of MM102. If you qualify (which means having a swimsuit, a towel and $100) you can indulge in a "dolphin encounter." Sessions are at 9am, 1pm & 3pm. If you can't afford a close encounter, $8 (under 16s $5) gets you in as a non-swimming observer. Dolphin Cove is also the departure point for Captain Sterling's Crocodile Tours (☎853-5161), one of the more knowledgeable in the area

The **Maritime Museum of the Florida Keys**, MM102 (10am–5pm, closed Thursdays; $5, under 13s $3), which occupies a fake castle whose sign advertises "Caribbean Ship Wreck Museum," is also worth a visit. The museum draws in visitors by playing up the Keys' reputation as a place where pirates buried treasure, and it does have an interesting, if small, collection of artifacts salvaged from shipwrecks.

Eating and drinking

Far enough south for fine Caribbean cuisine, but close enough to the Everglades for a taste of 'gator, this is a fine place to **eat**. The best breakfasts are found at *Ballyhoo's*, MM98 (☎852-0822), opposite the *Seafarer* hotel (see above). Opened twenty years ago by a couple of fishermen, it has pancakes, omelettes, croissants dipped in orange and egg and a wide selection of grills. *Ganim's Kountry Kitchen*, 99696 Overseas Highway (☎451-2895), has cheap breakfasts and lunches. Try the "Sealegs Supreme" salad of crab meat, tuna and fruit in honey mustard and the huge portions of sweet pies. *Frank Keys Café*, 100211 Overseas Highway (☎453-0310), in an attractive cottage hidden away in the trees off the highway, offers slightly more sophisticated – and considerably more expensive – seafood and other dishes. *Crack'd Conch*, MM105 (☎451-0732), specializing in conch dishes and fried alligator, is well known but a bit overrated. If you've got a hankering for 'gator, a better spot is *Snappers Raw Bar*, MM94 at Ocean View Boulevard

(☎852-5956). Enjoy the waterside, candlelit setting with an alligator starter, or swing by for the Sunday brunch (10am–2pm). *Mrs Mac's*, MM99 (☎451-3722), provides bowls of ferociously hot chilli and other home-cooked goodies, and *The Fish House*, MM102.4 (☎451-4665), is a must for all fish fiends.

Key Largo also has the Keys' biggest and cheapest **supermarket**, the Winn-Dixie (MM105), which is ideal for loading up on supplies for the journey ahead.

If you have no fear of bikers in leather jackets and tropical shorts, check out the *Caribbean Club*, MM104 (☎451-9970), for a lively **drink** (it also offers cheap jet-ski rentals during the day). For a mellower crowd, visit *Coconuts*, the bar at the *Marina del Mar Resort*, MM100 (☎451-4107). And if you'd like to relax with some good conch fritters and a beer, head up to *Alabama Jack's*, just north of the toll booth on the Card Sound Road (Hwy 905A). This former bordello is now something of an institution (for food).

Tavernier

Just ten miles south of Key Largo on the Overseas Highway is **TAVERNIER**, a small, homely town that was once the first stop on the Flagler railway (the Keys' first link to the mainland, see "South of Marathon"). There's not a whole lot here, but Tavernier's historic buildings and decent Cuban café (see "Practicalities" below) make it a worthy short stop.

Just before crossing into Tavernier, at MM93.6, is the **Florida Keys Wild Bird Rehabilitation Center** (daily 8.30am–5.30pm; free, but dependent on donations; ☎852-5339), an inspirational place where volunteers rescue and rehabilitate birds who have been orphaned or have met with other common catastrophes like colliding with cars or power lines. A wooden walkway is lined with huge enclosures, and signs detail the birds' histories.

Drop into **Harry Harris Park**, off the Overseas Highway along Burton Drive, on a weekend, and you could well find an impromptu party and free live music – locals sometimes drop by with instruments and station themselves on picnic tables for jam sessions.

Another reason to stop are the old buildings (a rarity in the Keys, outside of Key West) of the **historic district**, between MM91 and MM92. In addition to the plank walls and tin roofs of the turn-of-the-century Methodist Church (now functioning as a small visitor center) and post office, you'll see some of the Red Cross buildings erected after the 1935 Labor Day hurricane, which laid waste to a good chunk of the Keys. Built of foot-thick walls of concrete and steel, the new buildings were supposedly invincible to nature's fiercest poundings. Unfortunately, the use of seawater in the construction caused the walls to crumble, leaving only rusting steel frames. To find the historic center, turn down the side of the Tavernier Hotel, and then take the first right up Atlantic Circle Drive. More quaint than spectacular, it's the sort of place where the Waltons might have had a retreat.

Practicalities

Despite its dismal exterior, the *Sunshine Café*, at MM91.8 (no phone and no English spoken), is really a hidden gem. It serves top-notch Cuban coffee for $1 and trays of Cuban food like tamales (corn tortillas stuffed with pork and served with fried plantain) and the requisite black beans and rice. For really cheap, wholesome food, the *Sunshine Supermarket*, which is attached to the cafeteria, sells hot Cuban sandwiches and roasted pig. Next door, *The Copper Kettle* is a cozy place for candlelit dinners of honey Cajun shrimp and other regional delights. The restaurant is owned by the *Tavernier Hotel*, MM91.8 (852-4131; ④-⑤), a quaint, classic hotel painted gum pink that was originally built as an open air theater, but has been a hotel for the past 65 years.

Islamorada

Once over Tavernier Creek, you're at the start of a twenty-mile strip of islands: Plantation, Windley and Upper and Lower Matecumbe, which are collectively known as **ISLAMORADA**. More than any other section of the Keys, fishing is headline news here. Tales of monstrous tarpon and blue marlin captured off the coast are legendary, and there's no end to the smaller prey routinely hooked by total novices. (Even former president George Bush successfully cast a line or two in these waters.)

If you'd like to head out to sea, you'll be well provided for. There's no problem renting fishing boats, or, for much less, joining a fishing party boat from any of the local marinas. The biggest docks are at the Holiday Isle, 84001 Overseas Highway (☎1-800/327-7070), and Bud 'n' Mary's, MM80, which also sports a modest **Museum of Fishing** (Mon–Sat 10am–5pm; free).

There's notable **snorkeling** and **diving** in the area, too. Crocker and Alligator reefs, a few miles offshore, both have near vertical sides, whose cracks and crevices provide homes for a lively variety of crabs, shrimps and other small creatures that in turn attract bigger fish looking for a meal. Nearby, the wrecks of the *Eagle* and the *Cannabis Cruiser* provide a home for families of gargantuan amberjack and grouper. Get full snorkeling and diving details from the marinas (Holiday Isle or Bud 'n' Mary's) or any dive shop on the Overseas Highway.

Back on dry land, you might want to pass a couple of hours at the **Theater of the Sea**, MM84.5 (daily 9.30am–4pm; adults $14.95, under 13s $8.50; ☎664 2431), but only if the price doesn't deter you and you're not planning to visit any of the other marine parks in Florida, which are better. Sea lions, dolphins and a half-dozen tanks full of assorted fish and crustaceans are introduced by a knowledgeable staff, and, if you reserve ahead, you can swim with the dolphins ($95; see p.120).

For non-fishing folk, there's little in Islamorada to warrant an extended stay. The **Chamber of Commerce**, at MM82 (Mon–Fri 9am–5pm; ☎664-9767 fax ☎664-4289), is packed with general information and details on the latest cut-rate accommodation deals (see below). Half a mile further south, an Art Deco **monument** marks the grave of the 1935 Labor Day hurricane's 425 victims, killed when a tidal wave hit their evacuation train. The unkempt state of the stone is perhaps an indication of modern Keys dwellers' nonchalant attitude to the threat of a repeat disaster.

Islamorada's state parks

Indian Key, **Lignumvitae Key** and **Long Key** – three state parks at the southern end of Islamorada – offer a broader perspective of the area than just fishing and diving. The **guided tours** to Indian Key and Lignumvitae Key are particularly enchanting, and

---

THE BACKCOUNTRY

If you've access to a boat or sufficient money (around $200 a day) to rent one with a guide, Islamorada makes a good base for exploring the fish-laden waters and bird-filled skies of the **backcountry**. This is the term for the countless small, uninhabited islands that fill Florida Bay, beginning about eighteen miles west and constituting the edge of the Everglades National Park – more fully described in "The West Coast". Ask at any Islamorada marina for more details.

reveal a near-forgotten chapter of the Florida Keys' history and a virgin forest respectively. The Indian Key tour (Thurs–Mon 8.30am to 12.30pm) departs from Robbie's Marina, MM77.5 (☎664-4196; $15; children $10), as does the Lignumvitae Tour (9.30am–12.30pm plus an evening cruise one hour before sunset; $15). Alternatively, a tour of both Keys runs from Papa Joe's Marina, MM80, (daily for two or more people at 8.30am; $24; children $14; ☎664 5005).

Indian Key

You'd never guess from the highway that **Indian Key**, one of many small, mangrove-skirted islands off Lower Matecumbe Key, was once a busy trading center, given short-lived prosperity – and notoriety – by a nineteenth-century New Yorker called Jacob Houseman. After stealing one of his father's ships, Houseman sailed to Key West looking for a piece of the lucrative wrecking (or salvaging) business. Mistrusted by the close-knit Key West community, he bought Indian Key in 1831 as a base for his own wrecking operation. In the first year, Houseman made $30,000 and furnished the eleven-acre island with streets, a store, warehouses, a hotel and a permanent population of around fifty. However, the income was not entirely honest: Houseman was known to lead donkeys with lanterns along the shore to lure ships towards dangerous reefs, and he eventually lost his wrecking license for "salvaging" from an anchored vessel.

In 1838, Indian Key was sold to physician-botanist Henry Perrine, who had been cultivating tropical plants here with an eye to their commercial potential. A Seminole attack in 1840 burnt every building to the ground and ended the island's habitation, but Perrine's plants survived and today form a swath of flowing foliage that includes sisal, coffee, tea and mango plants. Besides allowing ample opportunity to gaze at the flora, the two-hour **tour** takes you around the one-time streets, up the observation tower and past Houseman's grave – his body was brought here after he died working on a wreck off Key West.

Lignumvitae Key

By the time you finish the three-hour **tour of Lignumvitae Key** you'll know a strangler fig from a gumbo limbo and will instantly be able to recognize many more of the hundred or so species of tropical trees in this two-hundred-acre hammock. A further treat are the sizeable spiders, such as the Golden Orb, whose silvery web regularly spans the pathway. The trail through the forest was laid out by a wealthy early Miamian, W. J. Matheson, whose 1919 limestone **house** is the island's only sign of habitation and shows the deprivations of early island living – even for the well-off. The house actually blew away in the 1935 hurricane, but was found and brought back.

Long Key State Recreation Area

Many of the tree species found on Lignumvitae can be spotted at **Long Key State Recreation Area**, MM67.5 (daily 8am–sunset; cars $3.75 plus $1 per passenger; pedestrians and cyclists $1.50). There's a nature trail that takes you along the beach and on a boardwalk over a mangrove-lined lagoon. Or, better still, you can rent a canoe ($4 per hour) and follow the simple **canoe trail** through the tidal lagoons in the company of mildly curious wading birds. **Camping** in the park costs $25.75. For further details call ☎664-4815.

Practicalities

You're unlikely to find **accommodation** in Islamorada for under $70 a night, although price wars among the bigger hotels can reveal occasional finds. The popular *Holiday Isle Beach Resort*, 84001 Overseas Highway, MM84 (☎1-800/327-7070; ⑤), is a psychedelic trip: vivid citrus-colored plastics and tiki huts fill this vacation village. The atmosphere is young and friendly and the hotel itself is very comfortable. Otherwise, the best bets are *Drop Anchor*, MM85 (☎664/4863; ④–⑥), *Key Lantern*, MM82 (☎664-4572; ③), and the *Islamorada Inn Motel*, MM87.8 (☎852-9376; ④–⑤). For information on other establishments, check with the Visitor Center (address above). If you have a tent, use either Long Key State Recreation Area (see above) or the RV-dominated *KOA* **campground** on Fiesta Key, MM70 (☎664-4922).

Provided you avoid the obvious tourist traps, you can **eat** well and fairly cheaply. Best of all is the excellent-value fare at *Islamorada Fish Company*, MM81 (☎664-9271), whose fresh seafood is exported all over the world. Despite a constant full-house (try and get here before 6pm), the staff is particularly friendly. *Manny & Isa's*, MM81.5 (☎664-5019), serves high-quality, low-cost Cuban food; *Whale Harbor*, MM84 (☎664-4959), lives up to its name, proffering massive seafood buffets to devil-may-care gluttons; the ramshackle but justifiably pricey *Green Turtle Inn*, MM81 (☎664-9031; closed Mon), has glorious chowders; and the *Hungry Tarpon*, at MM77.5 Lower Matecumbe Key (☎664-0535), serves superb fish from local recipes in a converted 1940s bait shop. For more elegant surroundings, try *Grove Park Café* at MM 81.7, whose European/Caribbean menu offers main courses that start around $8.

When it comes to **nightlife**, many people get no further than the huge tiki bar at *Holiday Isle* (address above), which always throbs on weekends to the sound of insipid rock bands. Alternatively, investigate the nightly drink specials at *Lor-e-lei's*, MM82 (☎664-4656), where nightly sunset celebrations reel in the crowds. For raunchy blues and boozing, visit the much less touristy *Woody's*, MM82 (☎664-4335), which picks up steam after 11pm.

The Middle Keys: Marathon and around

The Long Key Bridge (alongside the old Long Key Viaduct, see "South of Marathon," below) points south from Long Key and leads to the **Middle Keys**. The largest of these islands, which stretch from Duck Key to Bahia Honda Key, is Key Vaca – once a shantytown of railway workers'– which holds the area's major settlement, **MARATHON**. On first sight this is a town as commercialized and uninspiring as Key Largo, but it does have some worthwhile features, hidden just off the Overseas Highway.

If you didn't get your fill of tropical trees at Lignumvitae Key (see "Islamorada" above), turn right onto 55th Street at MM50.5 (opposite the K-Mart), which leads to 63 steamy acres of subtropical forest at **Crane Point Hammock** (Mon–Sat 9am–5pm, Sun noon–5pm; $7.50). A free booklet gives details of the trees you'll find along the one-mile **nature trail**, and you'll also pass one of the last examples of Bahamian architecture in the US: a house built in 1903 by Bahamian immigrants.

The hammock's excellent **Museum of Natural History of the Florida Keys** gives a thought-provoking rundown of the area's history – starting with the Caloosa Indians (who had a settlement on this site until they were wiped out by disease brought by European settlers in the 1700s) and continuing with the story of early Bahamian and American settlers. Not to be missed is the motley collection of artifacts near the museum shop, including a raft made of inner tubes that carried four Cuban refugees across ninety miles of ocean in the early 1990s.

A large section of the museum features interactive displays designed to introduce kids to the wonders of the keys' subtropical ecosystems, including the hardwood hammocks and reefs. Much the same ground is covered at the adjoining **Florida Keys Children's Museum**, which houses a tropical aquarium, a terrarium and an artificial saltwater lagoon where you can feed the fish. The hammock's resident mosquitoes are a painful nuisance, so consider investing in the bug sprays sold at the pharmacy directly across the highway.

SNORKELING, DIVING, FISHING AND SAILING

The choice locale for the pursuits of **snorkeling** and **scuba diving** is around **Sombrero Reef**, marked by a 142-foot-high nineteenth-century lighthouse, whose nooks and crannies provide a safe haven for thousands of darting, brightly colored tropical fish. The best time to go out is early evening when the reef is most active, since the majority of its creatures are nocturnal. The pick of local dive shops is Hall's Dive Center (☎1-800/331-4255), in the grounds of *Faro Blanco Marina Resort*, MM48.5. Five-day Basic Open Water Scuba Certificate courses ($385) are offered to novice divers, and night diving, wreck diving and Instructor's Certificate courses are available to the experienced. Once certified, you can rent equipment ($55) and join a dive trip (9am, 1pm, 5.30pm; $40).

Around Marathon, **spearfishing** is permitted a mile offshore (there's a three-mile limit elsewhere), and the town hosts four major **fishing tournaments** each year: in early May (for tarpon); late May (dolphin, the fish not the mammal); early October (bonefish); and early November (sailfish). Precise dates are available from the **Visitor Center** (see "Practicalities" below), 3330 Overseas Highway (Mon–Fri 9am–5pm; ☎1-800/842-9580). You may fancy your chances, but entering costs several hundred dollars and only the very top anglers participate. Just being around during a tournament, however, will give you an insight into the Big Time Fishing mentality, and if you feel inspired to put to sea yourself, wander along one of the marinas and ask about chartering a boat. Boats take out up to six people and charge between $400 and $850 for a full day's fishing (7am–4pm), including bait and equipment. If you can't get a group together, join one of the countless group boats for about $40 per person for a full day's fishing – remember, though, that it's easier to catch fish with fewer people aboard.

Although most of the boats at the local marinas are large power vessels designed for anglers, Marathon is also a major **sailboat** base, offering vessels for charter – with or without a captain – as well as sailing courses. A reliable source of both is A–B–Sea Charter (☎289-0373), at the Faro Blanco Marina Resort, MM48.5.

For a closer look at the Keys' natural life, take the waterborne **ecology tour** (selected days only, 10am & 2pm; $15; ☎743-7000) from the marina of the $200-a-night *Hawks Cay Resort* on Duck Key, reached by way of a causeway at MM61. Led by a radically minded local naturalist, the two-hour trip to an uninhabited island will furnish you with a wealth of information on the make-up of the Keys and the creatures who live in them.

If you have more sedate activities in mind, Marathon has a couple of small beaches. **Sombrero Beach**, along Sombrero Beach Road (off the Overseas Highway near MM50), is a slender strip of sand with good swimming waters and shaded picnic tables. Four miles north, the beach at **Key Colony Beach**, a man-made island dredged into existence during the Fifties for the building of pricey homes, is prettier and quieter.

Just east of Marathon is the **Dolphin Research Center**, MM59 at Grassy Key (Wed–Sun, 9am–4pm). For $95 you can learn about and swim with dolphins in an "encounter program," but you must book well in advance. Less expensive, but also less fun is the center's escorted walk (10am & 11am and 12.30pm, 2pm, and 2.30pm; $9.50).

Practicalities

For one-stop information on the surrounding area and accommodations, head to the **Visitor Center** at MM53.5, 12222 Overseas Highway (☎743-5417; fax ☎289-0183).

If relaxation is a priority, spend a night or two at one of Marathon's well-equipped **resorts**, such as *Faro Blanco Marine Resort*, 1996 Overseas Highway (☎1-800-759-3276; ④–⑦), whose small cottages and houseboats offer beautiful views of the mangroves. Similar accommodation is available at *Sombrero*, 19 Sombrero Boulevard (☎1-800/433-8660; ⑤–⑦), or *Banana Bay*, 4590 Overseas Highway (☎1-800/488-6636; ⑤–⑦). The least costly of the plentiful supply of cheaper **motels** are *Sea Dell*, 5000 Overseas Highway (☎1-800/648-3854; ③), and *Seaward*, 8700 Overseas Highway (☎743-5711; ③–④). *Flamingo Inn*, MM59 at Grassy Key (☎289-1478), has very comfortable beds, big clean rooms, a pool and good deals; ④). The only **campground** permitting tents (others are designed for motor homes and trailers only) is *Knights Key Park*, MM47 (☎743-9954).

Despite the commercial conformity of Marathon's main drag, there are several fine and friendly places to **eat**. Locals flock to *The Seven Mile Grill*, 1240 Overseas Highway (☎743-4481), just east of the Seven Mile Bridge (see below), for fine conch chowders and shrimp steamed in beer. *Castaway*, a hidden gem down 15th Street. at MM48 (☎743-6247), serves wonderful and cheap seafood and scrumptious honey-drenched buns. More upscale is *Crocodiles On The Water* (☎743-9018), just across from *Castaway* and part of the classy *Faro Blanco Marine Resort*. Cuban fish and oyster dishes are specialties, and desserts include frozen turtle pie, which just means praline ice cream served in a breezy, friendly atmosphere. If you're "seafooded out," *Crocogator's* makes a good retreat for true carnivores, though the owner sometimes has an attitude and the tables are cramped together. Good Cuban fare is found at *Don Pedro Restaurant*, MM53 (☎743-5247); *Herbie's*, 6350 Overseas Highway, MM50.5 (☎743-6373), is justly busy on account of its inexpensive seafood; *Porky's Too BBQ*, MM48 (☎743-6637), provides platefuls of beef and chicken; and quality Italian dishes can be enjoyed in the simple setting of the *Village Café*, at the gulf-side Village Plaza, 5800 Overseas Highway (☎743-9090).

Marathon goes to sleep early; the only place with a suspicion of **nightlife** is the tiki bar of *Shuckers Restaurant*, 725 11th Street (☎743-8686), which is also a prime vantage point for sipping a drink as the sun goes down.

South of Marathon: the Seven Mile Bridge

In 1905, Henry Flagler, whose railway opened up Florida's East Coast, undertook to extend its tracks to Key West. The Overseas Railroad, as it became known (though many called it "Flagler's folly"), was a monumental task that took seven years to complete and was marred by the appalling treatment of workers.

Bridging the Middle Keys gave Flagler's engineers some of their biggest headaches. North of Marathon, the two-mile-long Long Key Viaduct, a still-elegant structure of nearly two hundred individually cast arches, was Flagler's personal favorite and was widely pictured in advertising campaigns. Yet a greater technical accomplishment was the **Seven Mile Bridge** to the south, linking Marathon to the Lower Keys. At one point, every US-flagged freighter on the Atlantic was hired to bring in materials – including special cement from Germany – while floating cranes, dredges and scores of other craft set about a job that eventually cost the lives of 700 laborers. When the trains eventually started rolling (doddering over the bridges at 15mph), passengers were treated to an incredible panorama: a broad sweep of sea and sky, sometimes streaked by luscious red sunsets or darkened by storm clouds.

The Flagler bridges were strong enough to withstand everything that the Keys' volatile weather could throw at them, except for the calamitous 1935 Labor Day hurricane, which tore up the railway. The bridges were subsequently adapted to accommodate a road: the original Overseas Highway. Tales of hair-raising bridge crossings (the road was only 22 feet wide), endless tailbacks as the drawbridges jammed – and the roadside parties that ensued – are part of Keys folklore. The later bridges, such as the $45-million new **Seven Mile Bridge** between Key Vaca and Bahia Honda Key that opened in the early Eighties, certainly improved traffic flow but also ended the mystique of traveling the old road – and its walls are just high enough to hide the fabulous view.

The old bridges, intact but for the mid-sectional cuts to allow shipping to pass, now make extraordinarily long fishing piers and jogging strips. A section of the former

Seven Mile Bridge also provides the only land access to **Pigeon Key**, which served as a railway work camp from 1908 to 1935, and until recently was used by the University of Miami for marine science classes. Its seven original wooden buildings have been restored, and a new **railway museum** (tours $5; ☎289-0025) helps visitors understand the hardships routinely suffered by the workers. Cars are not permitted access to Pigeon Key, which contributes to the serene atmosphere of the place. A shuttle bus leaves hourly (9am–4pm; $4) from the Pigeon Key Visitor's Center at MM48.

The Lower Keys

Starkly different to their northerly neighbors, the **LOWER KEYS** are quiet, heavily wooded and predominantly residential. Aligned north–south and built on a limestone rather than a coral base, these islands have a flora and fauna that's very much their own, a lot of it tucked miles away from the Overseas Highway. Most visitors speed through the area on the way to Key West, just forty miles further, but the area's lack of rampant tourism and easily found seclusion make this a good place to linger for a day or two. The main settlement is **Big Pine Key**, where the **Lower Keys Chamber of Commerce**, at MM31 (Mon–Fri 9am–5pm, Sat 9am–3pm, ☎1-800/872-3722), is packed with information on the area.

Bahia Honda State Recreation Area

While not officially part of the Lower Keys, the first place of consequence you'll hit after crossing the Seven Mile Bridge is the 300-acre **Bahia Honda State Recreation Area** (daily 8am–sunset; cars with one person $2.50, two people $5 and then 50c for each additional person; pedestrians and cyclists $1.50; ☎872-2353), one of the Keys' prettiest spots. The northeasterly section of the park rings a lagoon with a natural **beach** and inviting, two-tone ocean waters.

While here, you should ramble on the **nature trail**, which loops from the shoreline through a hammock of silver palms, geiger and yellow satinwood trees, passing rare plants such as dwarf morning glory and spiny catesbaea. Keep a look out for white-crowned pigeons, great white herons, roseate spoonbills and giant ospreys (whose bulky nests are plentiful throughout the Lower Keys, often atop telegraph poles). Nature programs start at 11am and you can ask about special **walks** such as the Flagler Story Walk, though it's all pleasant enough without a guide.

The waters at the park's southern end are good for swimming (beware, though, that currents here can be very swift), as well as for snorkelling, diving and especially wind-surfing – rent equipment from the Bahia Honda marina's dive shop. You'll also notice the two-story **Flagler Bridge**. The unusually deep waters here (Bahia Honda is Spanish for "deep bay") made this the toughest of the old railway bridges to construct, and widening it for the road proved impossible: the solution was to put the highway on a higher tier. It's actually far safer than it looks and there's a fine view from the top of the bridge over the Bahia Honda channel towards the forest-coated Lower Keys.

Facilities in the park include a campground and cabins, a snack bar, and a dive shop offering reef snorkel trips, scuba trips and boat rental.

Big Pine Key and around

The eponymous trees on **Big Pine Key** are less of a draw than its **Key deer**, delight-fully tame creatures that enjoy the freedom of the island; don't feed them (it's illegal), and be cautious when driving – signs alongside the road state the number of road-kills to date during the year. The deer, no bigger than large dogs, arrived long ago when the

Keys were still joined to the mainland; they provided food for sailors and Key West residents for many years, but hunting and the destruction of their natural habitat led to near extinction by the late Forties. The **National Key Deer Refuge** was set up here in 1954 to safeguard the animals – one refuge manager went so far as to burn the cars and sink the boats of poachers – and their population has now stabilized between 250 and 300.

Pick up factual information on the deer from the **refuge headquarters** (Mon–Fri 8am–5pm; ☎872-2239), at the western end of Watson Boulevard, off Key Deer Boulevard. To see them, drive along Key Deer Boulevard or turn east onto No Name Key. You should spot a few; they often amuse themselves in domestic gardens. Your chances are best in the cooler temperatures of early morning or late afternoon.

Also on Key Deer Boulevard, the **Blue Hole** is a freshwater lake with a healthy population of soft-shelled turtles and at least one alligator, who now and then emerges from the cool depths to sun itself – parts of the lakeside path may be closed if he's staked out a patch for the day. Should the 'gator get your adrenalin pumping, take a calming stroll along the short **nature trail**, a quarter of a mile further south along Key Deer Boulevard.

Moving on: the rest of the Lower Keys

An even more peaceful atmosphere prevails on the Lower Keys south of Big Pine Key, despite the efforts of property developers. The **Torch Keys**, so-named for their forests of torchwood – used for kindling by early settlers – can be swiftly bypassed on the way to **Ramrod Key**, where Looe Key Marine Sanctuary is a terrific place for viewing the coral reef.

Perhaps the most expensive thing you'll see anywhere in the Keys, if not in all of Florida, is the balloon-like "aerostat" hovering over **Cudjoe Key**. With a budget of $16 million, it was used by the US government to beam TV images of American-style freedom – baseball, sitcoms, soap operas – to Cuba. Called TV Martí, the station was named after the late-nineteenth-century Cuban independence fighter, José Martí. In July 1993 the Clinton administration decided to end the broadcasts, and the aerostat's future is uncertain.

Looe Key Marine Sanctuary

Keen underwater explorers should home in on **Looe Key Marine Sanctuary**, clearly signposted from the Overseas Highway on Ramrod Key. Named after *HMS Looe*, a British frigate that sank here in 1744, this five-square-mile area of protected reef is in every part the equal of the John Pennecamp Coral Reef State Park (see above). The crystal-clear waters and reef formations create an unforgettable spectacle; rays, octopus and a multitude of gaily colored fish flit between tall coral pillars, big brain coral, complex tangles of elk and staghorn coral, and soft corals like purple seafans and sea whips.

The **sanctuary office** (Mon–Fri 8am–5pm; ☎872-4039) can provide free maps and information. You can only visit the reef itself on a trip organized by one of the many diving shops throughout the keys; the nearest is the neighboring Looe Key Dive Center (☎1-800-942-5397).

Perky's Bat Tower

On Sugarloaf Key, fifteen miles from Ramrod Key, the 35-foot **Perky's Bat Tower** stands as testimony to one man's misguided belief in the benefits of bats. A get-rich-quick book of the Twenties, *Bats, Mosquitoes and Dollars*, led Richter C. Perky, a property speculator who had recently purchased the island, into thinking bats would be the solution to the Keys' mosquito problem. With much hullabaloo, he erected this brown cypress lath tower and dutifully sent away for the costly "bat bait," which he was told would lure an army of bats to the tower. It didn't work: no bat ever showed up, the mosquitoes stayed healthy, and Perky went bust soon after. The background story is far more interesting than the actual tower, but if the tale tickles your fancy, you can view it from the bumpy road just beyond the sprawling *Sugarloaf Lodge*, at MM17.

Practicalities

For what they offer, **motels** in the Lower Keys are expensive. *Looe Key Reef Resort*, MM27.5 (☎872-2215; ④–⑤), is ideal for visiting the marine sanctuary, or there's *Parmer's Place*, MM28.5 (☎872-2157; ④–⑥). For a real splurge, stay at the idyllic *Little Palm Island*, MM28.5, Little Torch Key (☎872-2524; ⑧), whose thatched cottages are set in lush gardens a few feet from the beach. **Campgrounds** are plentiful; try the Bahia Honda State Recreation Area's *Big Pine Key Fishing Lodge*, MM33 (☎872-2351), *Seahorse*, MM31 (☎872-2443), and *Sugar Loaf Key KOA*, MM20 (☎745-3549). Three **bed and breakfast inns** on Big Pine Key make cozy alternatives, but book early: *Deer Run*, 1985 Long Beach Drive, MM33 (☎872-2015; ④–⑥); *Barnacle*, 1557 Long Beach Drive, MM33 (☎872-3298; or ☎1-800/465-9100; ⑥); and *Casa Grande*, 1619 Long Beach Drive, MM33 (☎872-2878; ⑤).

The best place to **eat** in the Lower Keys is *Mangrove Mama's*, at MM20 on Sugarloaf Key (☎745-3030; closed Sept), for its rustic atmosphere, great seafood and home-baked bread. A real locals' joint is *Big Pine Coffee Shop,* MM30 (☎872-2790). Sit at formica tables and gorge on crab salads and steamed shrimp by the half pound. Otherwise, on Big Pine Key, try *Island Jim's*, MM31.3 (☎872-2017), for good fare from breakfast through to dinner, or grab a sandwich at *Dip N'Deli*, MM31 at the *Big Pine Motel* (☎872-3030).

Nightlife is not a strong card; when locals want to live it up they go to Key West. Take a shot at the *No Name Pub*, at the eastern end of Watson Boulevard on Big Pine Key (☎872-9115), for varied beers and occasional live bands; the *Looe Key Reef Resort* (see above) for weekend drinking; or, if desperate, the lounge of the *Cedar Inn*, MM31 (☎872-4031).

Key West

Much closer to Cuba than mainland Florida, **KEY WEST** can often seem very far removed from the rest of the US. Famed for their tolerant attitudes and laid-back lifestyles, its 30,000 islanders seem adrift in a great expanse of sea and sky. Despite the million tourists who arrive each year, the place resonates with an anarchic and individual spirit that hits you the instant you arrive. Locals (known as *conchs* – after the giant sea snails eaten by early settlers – if they're long-term residents of Key West, or *freshwater conchs* if they're more recent arrivals) ride bicycles, shoot the breeze on street corners and smile at complete strangers.

Yet as wild as it may at first appear, Key West today is far from being the misfits' mecca that it was just a decade or so ago. Much of the sleaziness has been gradually brushed away through a steady process of restoration and revitalization – it takes a lot of money to buy a house here now – paving the way for a sizeable vacation industry that at times seems to revolve around party boats and heavy drinking. Not that Key West is near to losing its special identity; it's still nonconformist, and don't dare suggest otherwise. The liberal attitudes have attracted a large influx of gay people, estimated at one in five of the population, who take an essential role in running the place and sink thousands of dollars into its future.

The sense of isolation from the mainland – much stronger here than on the other Keys – and the camaraderie of the locals are best appreciated by adjusting to the mellow pace and joining in. Amble the side streets, make meals last for hours, and pause regularly for refreshment in the numerous bars. Key West's knack for tourism can be gaudy, but depending on what you want, it's quite simple to bypass the commercial traps and discover an island as unique for its present-day society as for its remarkable past.

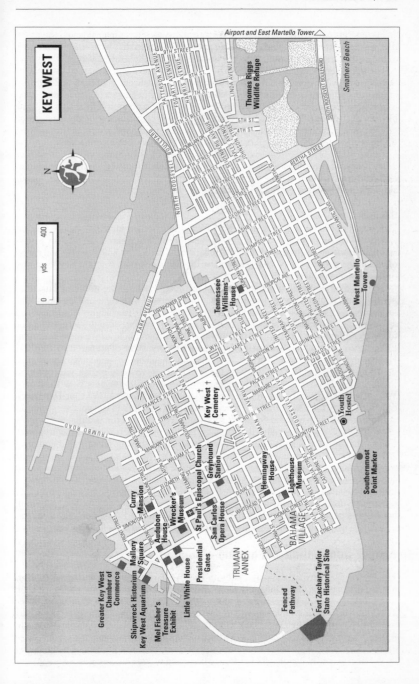

KEY WEST

Airport and East Martello Tower △

N

yds
0   400

Thomas Riggs
Wildlife Refuge

Smathers Beach

9TH STREET
9TH STREET
5TH ST
7TH ST
PETERSON AVENUE
FOGARTY AVENUE
HARRIS AVENUE
LINDA AVENUE
5TH ST
4TH ST
BERTHA STREET

BRIYANT BOULEVARD
NORTH ROOSEVELT BOULEVARD
SOUTH ROOSEVELT BOULEVARD
ATLANTIC BLVD

MACDONALD DRIVE
3RD STREET
2ND STREET
1ST STREET
GEORGE STREET
ASHBY STREET
THOMPSON STREET
LEON STREET
DRIVE
STREET
JOHNSON STREET
STAPLES AVENUE

PARK AVENUE

West Martello
Tower

CASA MARINA CT

EISENHOWER STREET

Tennessee
Williams'
House

TROPICAL AVE

ALBERT ST
TRUMAN ST
PINE STREET
NEWTON ST
ZANE STREET
WHITE STREET
VARELA STREET
UNITED STREET
SEMINARY STREET
SOUTH STREET
WASHINGTON STREET
JOHNSON STREET
PHISTER STREET
GRINNELL STREET
REYNOLDS STREET

WATSON ST

FRANCES STREET
GRINNELL STREET
PACKER STREET
MARGARET ST

Key West
Cemetery

SIMONTON STREET
MARGARET STREET
ELIZABETH ST
WILLIAM ST
ANGELA STREET
DUVAL STREET
FLEMING STREET
SOUTHARD STREET
EATON ST

ROYAL STREET
TRUMAN AVENUE
ROOSEVELT

CATHERINE STREET
SIMONTON STREET

SEMINOLE AVE

Youth
Hostel

TRUMBO ROAD

Curry
Mansion

Wrecker's
Museum

St Paul's Episcopal Church

Greyhound
Station

Hemingway
House

Lighthouse
Museum

Southernmost
Point Marker

Audubon
House

San Carlos
Opera House

Presidential
Gates

BAHAMA
VILLAGE

WHITEHEAD STREET
THOMAS STREET
EMMA STREET
PETRONIA STREET
ANGELA ST
OLIVIA STREET
CAROLINE ST
FRONT STREET
AMELIA STREET
VIRGINIA STREET
FORT STREET

Greater Key West
Chamber of
Commerce

Shipwreck Historium
Key West Aquarium

Mel Fisher's
Treasure
Exhibit

Mallory
Square

Little White House

TRUMAN
ANNEX

Fenced
Pathway

Fort Zachary Taylor
State Historical Site

The secret to discovering Key West's magical qualities is simple: sidestep the areas that, until recently, made up the so-called core of the island, but have since fallen prey to the tourist tribes who come to buy T-shirts and drink themselves silly.

The tourist epicenter is on **Duval Street**, whose northern end is marked by Mallory Square, a historic landmark that is now home to a brash chain of bars that entirely ignores the whimsical, freethinking spirit of the island. But just a few steps east of here is the **historic section**, a network of streets teeming with rich foliage and brilliant blooms draped over curious architecture. This area boasts many of the best guest houses, many eateries and wacky galleries; not to mention the streets themselves, which are peopled with characters straight out of the wildest of imaginations.

To the west of Duval Street, just off Whitehead Street, is **Bahama village**, an area of dusty lanes where cockerels wander and birds screech into the night. This unique enclave from yesteryear boasts some of the best hidden restaurants on the island, although developers are already speculating on the area's future.

Some history

Piracy was the main activity around Key West – first settled in 1822 – before Florida joined the US and the navy established a base here. This cleared the way for a substantial **wrecking industry**. Millions of dollars were earned by lifting people and cargo off shipwrecks along the Florida reef, and by the mid-nineteenth century, Key West was the wealthiest city in the US.

The building of reef lighthouses sounded the death knell for the wrecking business, but Key West continued to prosper. Many **Cubans** arrived with cigar-making skills, and migrant **Greeks** established a lucrative sponge enterprise (the highly absorbent sea sponges, formed from the skeletons of tiny marine creatures, were the forerunners of today's synthetic sponges). Industrial unrest and a sponge blight drove these businesses north to Tampa and Tarpon Springs, and left Key West ill-prepared to face the **Depression**. By the early Thirties, its remaining inhabitants – die-hard conchs who defied the suggestion that they move to the mainland – were living on fish and coconuts. In July, 1934 they finally declared bankruptcy, and under Roosevelt's New Deal, Key West was tidied up and readied for tourism. Unfortunately, the 1935 Labor Day hurricane blew away the Flagler railway – Key West's only land link to the outside world.

It was an injection of naval dollars during World War II – and the fact that the island's geographical location was an ideal vantage point from which to survey communist Cuba – that eventually saved Key West and provided the backbone for its economy.

Tourists started arriving in force during the Eighties, just as a taste for independence was rising among the locals. In April, 1982, US border patrols in relentless pursuit of drugs and illegal aliens began stopping all traffic leaving the keys. Locals promptly proclaimed the town to be the capital of the "**Conch Republic**." Partly an excuse for a booze-up, this declaration (followed immediately by surrender and a request for aid) made a humorous but serious political point: the community – already separated geographically from the mainland – would always strive to maintain a social separation as well.

Arrival, information and getting around

The Overseas Highway, the only road into Key West, runs through the bland eastern section of the island to the infinitely more interesting Old Town. On the way you'll pass the information-packed **Welcome Center** (daily 9am–7.30pm, Sun 9am–6pm; ☎296-4444) on North Roosevelt Boulevard. If you don't feel like stopping here, press on and use the **Greater Key West Chamber of Commerce**, 402 Wall Street (daily 8.30am–5pm; ☎294-2587), for free tourist pamphlets and discount vouchers. Four miles east of town is the **Key West International Airport** (☎296-5439), whose name belies its services – it only handles flights from Miami and other Florida cities. There are no

KEY WEST FESTIVALS

January–April *Old Island Days.* Tours, talks, concerts, flower shows and art festivals celebrating Key West's history.

April *Conch Shell Blowing Contest.* Ear-numbing music played on the shells of the creatures from which Key Westers take their nickname.

Late April *Conch Republic Celebration.* A party in Mallory Square with a symbolic raising of the Conch Republic flag, commemorating the declaration of the Keys' independence from the US in 1982 (see "Some history").

July *Hemingway Days.* Literary seminars, writers' workshops, daft trivia competitons, arm-wrestling and look-a-like contests to commemorate Ernest Hemingway, Key West's best-known ex-resident.

Late October *Fantasy Fest.* A gay-dominated version of Mardi Gras, with outrageous costumes paraded throughout the night along Duval Street.

Get **precise dates** on all of these from the Chamber of Commerce or Welcome Center (addresses above).

---

buses from the airport to town, and a taxi costs around $8. A novel means of getting from Miami into Key West is Chalk's International Airlines **seaplane** service (☎1-800-424-2557; about $190 round trip), which runs daily to Key West Harbor and includes a free water taxi transfer to Mallory Square.

For **getting around** the narrow, pedestrian-busy streets of the Old Town, you're far better off walking than driving. If street signs appear curiously absent, you'll find them painted vertically on the base of each junction lamp-post, though many are peeling off. If you're planning to venture further afield, **rent a bike** ($7–10 per day) or moped ($25–30 per day) from one of Adventure Scooter & Bicycle Rentals two locations: 708 and 925 Duval Street, or try the youth hostel (see "Accommodation"). Remarkably, there is a **bus service** (☎292-8164) on Key West: two routes, one clockwise and the other counterclockwise, loop around the tiny island roughly every fifteen minutes between 7am and 9am, and 2.30pm and 5.30pm.

The oft-plugged, ninety-minute **guided tours** of the island's main sights are a fair option, but only if you're really pushed for time and won't be able to explore on your own. The *Conch Tour Train* (Mallory Square; every 20–30min 9am–4pm; $12) or the *Old Town Trolley* (board at any of the marked stops around the Old Town; every 30min 9am–4.30pm; $14) dole out loud-speakered information, but the tours don't really foster an appreciation of the island's atmosphere.

A number of easily found **free publications** list current events: *Solares Hill* (monthly) is the most informative, but look out also for *Island Life* (weekly), *The Conch Republic* (monthly), and the gay-oriented gossip sheet *What's Happening* (weekly).

Accommodation

Unless you're traveling with children or in a group, choosing one of the excellent guest house/bed-and-breakfasts is far more fun than staying in a hotel – most hotels are either stationed on the bland road that leads to the island, or are over-hyped and priced to match.

Accommodation costs in Key West are always high – particularly from November to April when the simplest motel room will be in excess of $90 per night. Prices drop considerably at other times, but expect to pay at least $70 wherever you stay. Genuine **budget options** are limited to pitching a tent or renting a basic cottage at *Jabour's Trailor Court*, 223 Elizabeth Street (☎294-5723) or *Boyd's Campground* (☎294-1465). The *Key West Hostel*, 718 South Street (☎296-5719; members $17, non-members $20), has small dorms and good rates. Very cheap meals are served here, and the taxi ride between the hostel and the Greyhound station is around $5.

Wherever you stay, a reservation is essential from November to April, and would be a sensible precaution for weekend stays at any other time. If you arrive in October during **Fantasy Fest**, a hugely popular gay and lesbian Mardi Gras, expect a hike in room cost – if you can get one at all.

Many of the restored villas operating as guesthouses in the historic district are gay and lesbian run, and while most welcome all adults, few accept young children. A handful (listed below) are exclusively gay male, while only one is for lesbians only.

Guesthouses

Angelina Guest House, 302 Angela St (☎294-4480). Well-priced rooms in a restored former bordello with a great wrap-around veranda. Right in Bahama Village. ④.

Blue Parrot Inn, 916 Elizabeth St (☎1-800/231-BIRD; fax ☎296-5697). The friendly owners of this beautiful house (built in 1884) in the heart of the historic district serve excellent breakfasts in a lush, courtyard garden. No children. ⑥.

Caribbean House, 226, Petronia St (☎800-543-4518; fax ☎296-9840). In the middle of Bahama Village this plain house has simple rooms at good rates and is centrally located. ④–⑤.

Crocodile & Mermaid, 729, Truman Ave (☎294-1894 or ☎1-800/773-1894; fax ☎295-9925). A gem of a house with stunning interior decor. Fabulous gardens, a pool, and wine served each evening make for a deeply relaxing stay. No children under 16. ⑥–⑧.

Curry Mansion Inn, 511 Caroline St (☎1-800/253-3466 or ☎294-5349; fax ☎294-4093). Pricey but worth it for a night in this landmark Victorian home (see below). Enjoy the antiques, superb breakfasts, complimentary cocktail parties and use of the pool and showers all day after check-out. ⑥–⑧.

Duval House, 815 Duval St (☎294-1666; fax ☎292-1701). The lower-priced rooms are excellent value, and a bit more gets you a four-poster bed and a balcony overlooking the grounds. One of the few places with ample parking. ⑤–⑦.

Eden House, 1015 Fleming St (☎1-800/533-KEYS; fax ☎294-1221). One of Key West's most relaxing hideaways. Peaceful rooms surround the pool where Goldie Hawn filmed *Criss Cross* in 1990. There's a quiet area of hammocks under a giant tree, and the shady *Martin's Cafe* (see "Eating" below) is just a palm frond away. Big reductions off season. ⑦.

Island City House, 411 William St (☎1-800/634-8230). This grand mansion, built in the 1880s for a Charleston merchant family, offers studios and one- or two-bedroom apartments overlooking the pool and tropical gardens. ⑦–⑧.

Key Lime Village, 727 Truman Ave (☎294-6222 or ☎1-800/201-6222). Choose from the tiny cottages or the motel-style rooms in the nineteenth-century house. Lots of lovely trees and a pool make up for the lack of space. ⑥.

La Terraza de Marti, 1125 Duval St (☎296-6706). Better known locally as "La-Te-Da," this pastel-interior house is at the center of gay social life. The tree-studded complex includes several bars, discos and the classy *Godfrey's* restaurant (see "Nightlife"). While very popular with gays, the clientele is mixed. Prices drop by half out of season. ⑥–⑦.

Marquesa Hotel, 600 Fleming St (☎292-1919 or ☎1-800/869-4631; fax ☎294-2121). A grand guesthouse (built in 1884) with a formal clientele. The restaurant borders on pompous. Pop in to view the old photographs of Key West's yesteryear.

Simonton Court, 320 Simonton St (☎1-800/944-2687; fax ☎293-8446). Renovated from an old cigar factory, the main house has a wide selection of rooms, and well-equipped cottages dot this historic compound. No children. ⑤–⑦.

Tropical Inn, 812 Duval St (☎294-9977). Large, airy rooms in a charming restored "conch" house at the center of the action. Most of the rooms sleep three, and the more expensive ones have balconies. Ask about the neighboring cottages with hot tubs and kitchens. ④–⑤.

Wicker House, 913 Duval St (☎296-2475 or ☎1-800/880-4275). One of the least expensive guesthouses on Key West. Comprised of four restored "conch" houses. The cheaper rooms lack TVs and air-conditioning (but have ceiling fans). There is a communal jacuzzi, a pool and fine breakfasts are served in the garden. ④–⑤.

Exclusively gay guesthouses

Attitudes, 410 Fleming St (☎1-800/459-6212; fax ☎292-9030). Formerly known as *Colors*, this beautifully restored nineteenth-century house has huge, lovely rooms, and a hallway covered with tobacco-leaf-dyed papier mache. ⑤–⑦.

Big Ruby's, 409 Appelrouth Lane (☎296-2323 or ☎1-800/477-7829; fax ☎296-0281). Delightful, peaceful yet vibrant and social. There's lots of extras, like splendid Sunday brunches, free drinks, design-conscious rooms and the friendliest of staffs. Book in advance. The $300 a night penthouse suite is exceptional, and the whole place will soon be expanded.

Curry House, 806 Fleming St (☎294-6777 or ☎1-800/633-7439; fax ☎294-5322). The oldest all-male gay guesthouse in the area. Clean, well-liked and comfortable.

Lighthouse Court, 902 Whitehead St (☎294-9588). A very social address in the shadow of the lighthouse just opposite Hemingway's house. It's not cheap and service can vary, but it's hugely popular with the "in" crowd.

New Orleans House, 724 Duval St (☎294-8719 or ☎1-800/648-3780; fax ☎294-9298). Huge, very clean rooms with full kitchens are a highlight at this centrally located, if not too cozy, new guesthouse. The facade overlooks Duval St, so ask for a room at the back if you want to sleep before 3am. Huge discounts out of season. ⑥.

Pilot House, 414 Simonton St (☎294-8719; fax ☎294-9298). Sharing the same owners as *New Orleans House* (above), this guesthouse has contemporary suites in a classic, though over-renovated, Victorian house. The house was once owned by Joseph Otto, a prominent Prussian surgeon, who happens to have the maddest grave in Key West cemetery (see below). Great pools, breakfasts and a peaceful, convenient location.

Rainbow House, 525 United St (☎292-1450 or ☎1-800/749-6696). The lone lesbian-only guest house on the island, this attractive former cigar factory serves breakfast and has a pool and hot tub.

Hotels and motels

Atlantic Shores Resort, 510 South St (☎296-2491 or ☎1-800/526-3559). Open to all, this Art Deco resort is hugely in vogue with the gay crowd for its Sunday "tea-dances" (see "Gay life" below). Both men and women enjoy the clothing-optional sundecks overlooking the ocean. ④–⑧.

La Concha Holiday Inn, 430 Duval St (☎1-800/745-2191 or ☎296-2991; fax ☎294-3283). Now a link in the *Holiday Inn* chain, this colorful hotel first opened in 1925 and has been refurbished to retain some of its Twenties style. A big plus for most guests is the large swimming pool. ⑤–⑦.

Hampton Inn, 2801 N Roosevelt Blvd (☎1-800/426-7866). A branch of a reliable (and usually low-cost) hotel chain, with spacious rooms, a bar and a jacuzzi; rates, however, are far higher than most *Hampton Inns*. ⑦.

Sea Shell Motel, 718 South St (☎296-5719). If the adjoining youth hostel is full or doesn't appeal, this offers standard motel rooms at the lowest rates in the neighborhood. ④.

Southern Cross, 326 Duval St (☎1-800/533-4891). Key West's oldest hotel offers no-frills rooms; get one at the rear if you want to avoid the night-time hubbub along Duval Street. ⑤.

Southernmost Motel, 1319 Duval St (☎1-800/354-4455). The rooms at the US's most southerly motel are decked out in tropical shades; its pool-side tiki bar is the ideal place to meet other guests before taking the ten-minute walk to the heart of Key West. ⑤.

Tilton Hilton, 511 Angela St (☎294-8697). The fact that this is Key West's cheapest hotel is its best and only virtue. The rooms are very basic; be sure to look before paying. ③.

The Old Town

The square mile of the **Old Town** contains a good portion of what you'll want to see and is certainly the best place for imbibing Key West's finest feature: its atmosphere. Tourists are plentiful around the main streets, but the relaxed, casually hedonistic mood affects everyone, no matter if you've been here twenty years or twenty minutes. All of the Old Town can be seen on foot in a couple of days, though you should allow at least three – dashing about isn't the way to enjoy the place.

Along Duval Street

Anyone who saw Key West two decades ago would now barely recognize the main promenade, **Duval Street**, which cuts a mile-long swathe right through the Old Town, making it easy to regain bearings after exploring the side streets. Teetering precariously on the safe side of seedy for many years, much of the street has been transformed into a well-manicured strip of boutiques; beachwear and Israeli T-shirt shops cater to the vacationing middle-aged of Middle America. Yet its colorful "local characters" and round-the-clock action mean that Duval Street is still an interesting place to hang out.

Other than shops and bars, few places on Duval Street provide a break from tramping the pavement. One, however, is the **Wrecker's Museum** (daily 10am–4pm; $4; ☎294-9502), at no. 322, in one of the oldest houses in Key West. This gives some background to the industry on which Key West's earliest good times were based: salvaging cargo from foundering vessels. In the days before radio and radar, wrecking crews simply put out in bad weather and sailed as close as they dared to the menacing reefs, hoping to spot a grounded craft. Judging by the choice furniture that fills the museum, Captain Watlington, the wrecker who lived here during the 1830s, did pretty well. On the top floor modern cartoons recount several Key West folk tales, including the sea dunking of a preacher who dwelled too long on the evils of drinking.

Swarms of children wander through **Ripley's Believe It Or Not Odditorium** (daily 9am–11pm; $9.95, age 4–12 $6.95), a museum of trivia crammed with fanciful facts and figures about a myriad of unrelated subjects. A hologram of founder Robert Ripley bleats out the "believe it or not" mantra throughout the museum, provoking yawns from anyone over-ten.

A few blocks on, **St Paul's Episcopal Church**, at no. 401, is worth entering briefly for its rich stained-glass windows. If overwhelmed by piety, you might scoot around the corner for a look at the **Old Stone Methodist Church**, 600 Eaton Street. The oldest church in Key West, it was built in 1877 and is shaded by a giant Spanish laurel tree in its front yard.

The San Carlos Opera House and the southernmost point

At 516 Duval Street, the **San Carlos Opera House** (daily 9am–5pm; $3) has played a leading role in Cuban exile life since it opened (on a different site) as the San Carlos Institute in 1871. Financed by a $100,000 grant from the Cuban government, the present building dates from 1924. The soil on its grounds is from Cuba's six provinces, and a cornerstone was taken from the tomb of legendary Cuban independence campaigner José Martí. Following the break in diplomatic ties between the US and Cuba in 1961, the building fell on hard times – and was briefly used as a cinema, much to the annoyance of local Cubans – until it was revived by a million-dollar restoration project. Now, besides staging opera in its acoustically excellent auditorium and maintaining a well-stocked research library (including, most notably, the records of the Cuban Consulate from 1886–1961), it has a first-rate permanent exhibition on the history of Cubans in the US and, in particular, Key West.

You'll know when you get near the southern end of Duval Street because, whether it's a house, motel, filling station or restaurant, everything advertises itself as being "the Southernmost" of its kind. In case you're interested, the true **southernmost point** in Key West, and consequently in the continental US, is to be found at the intersection of Whitehead and South streets.

Mallory Square and around

In the early 1800s, thousands of dollars worth of marine salvage was landed at the piers, stored in the warehouses and sold at the auction houses on **Mallory Square**, just west of the northern end of Duval Street. The square's present-day commerce, however, is based on tourism, and little remains from the old days. By day, the square is a plain souvenir market selling overpriced ice cream, trinkets and T-shirts. But at night it is transformed for the **sunset celebration**. Jugglers, fire-eaters and assorted loose-screw types create a merry backdrop to the sinking of the sun. The celebration, which began in the Sixties as a hippie excuse for a smoke-in, is lively and fun, though it too is succumbing to commercialization.

Key West Aquarium and Mel Fisher's Treasure Exhibit

More entertaining than the square during the day is the small gathering of sea life inside the adjacent **Key West Aquarium**, 1 Whitehead Street (daily 10am–7pm; adults $8, under 15s $4), where ugly creatures such as porcupine fish and longspine squirrel fish leer from behind glass, and sharks (the smaller kinds such as lemon, blacktip and bonnethead) are known to jump out of their open tanks during the half-hour **guided tours** (11am, 1pm, 3pm and 4.30pm). If you intend to eat conch, a rubbery crustacean sold as fritter or chowder all over Key West, do so before examining the live ones here – they're not the world's most aesthetically pleasing creatures.

In the wild, the aquarium's fish might make their homes around the remains of sunken galleons that plied the trade route between Spain and its New World colonies during the sixteenth and seventeenth centuries. In **Mel Fisher's Treasure Exhibit**, 200 Greene Street (daily 9.30am–5pm; adults $6.50, age 13–18 $4), you'll get a good look at skilfully crafted decorative pieces, a highly impressive emerald cross, a liftable gold bar, plus countless vases and daggers alongside the obligatory cannon, all salvaged from two seventeenth-century wrecks. As engrossing as the collection is, it's really a celebration of an all-American rags-to-riches story. Now the high priest of Florida's many treasure seekers, Fisher was running a surf shop in California before he arrived in the Sunshine State armed with ancient Spanish sea charts. In 1985, after years of searching, he discovered the *Nuestra Señora de Atocha* and *Santa Margarita*, both sunk during a hurricane in 1622, forty miles southeast of Key West – they yielded a haul said to be worth millions of dollars. Among matters you won't find mentioned at the exhibit is the raging dispute between Fisher and the state and federal governments over who owns what, and the ecological upsets that uncontrolled treasure-seeking has wrought upon the Keys.

At Greene and Front streets, the imposing, Romanesque **Customs House** (☎296-3913) was built in 1891 and used as a post office, customs office and federal court house. Long derelict, the building is being gradually renovated for use as a local history museum – call ahead for details on exhibits and opening hours.

Just a block up Wall Street from Mallory Square (in front of the waterfront Playhouse Theater) is the recently opened **Historic Sculpture Garden** (open all the time; ☎294-4192), a bizarre, pretend graveyard full of sculpted heads of the men and women who have influenced Key West. It looks more like a waxwork chamber of horrors than an austere tribute, but the information plates disclose the interesting origins of the island's road names and the whole experience makes for a fun history lesson. The grounds are paved with engraved bricks, and, for $60, you can help preserve the area and know that thousands of tourists are trampling on – and maybe even reading – your name.

The Truman Annex and Fort Zachary Taylor

The old naval storehouse that contains the Fisher trove was once part of the **Truman Annex** (daily 8am–6pm; free), a decommissioned section of a naval base established in 1822 to keep a lid on piracy around what had just become US territory. Some of the buildings subsequently erected on the base, which spans a hundred acres between Whitehead Street and the sea, were – and still are – among Key West's most distinctive. For example, the dreamy Romanesque-revival-style Customs House (across Front Street from the Mel Fisher Treasure Exhibit).

The most famous among them, however, is the comparatively plain **Little White House** (daily 9am–5pm; adults $7.50, under 13s $3.75), by the junction of Caroline and Front streets. This house earned its name by being the favorite holiday spot of President Harry S. Truman (after whom the Annex was named), who first visited in 1946 and allegedly spent his vacations playing poker, cruising Key West for doughnuts, and swimming. Primitive plumbing meant that no one in the house was allowed to flush the toilet during his visits. The house is now a **museum** that chronicles the Truman years with an immense array of memorabilia.

In 1986, the Annex passed into the hands of a young property developer who purchased it for $17.25 million. The developer made a lot of fast friends by throwing open the weighty **Presidential Gates** on Caroline Street (which had previously parted only for heads of state) and encouraging the public to walk or cycle around the complex. If you feel so inclined, get the free **walking guide** from the well-marked sales office and embark on a building-by-building tour – the buildings' interiors, unfortunately, are closed to the public.

The Annex also provides access, along a fenced pathway through the operating naval base, to the less interesting **Fort Zachary Taylor State Historical Site** (daily 8am–sunset; cars $3.25 plus $1 per person, pedestrians and cyclists $1.50), built in 1845 and later used in the blockade of Confederate shipping during the Civil War. Over ensuing decades, the fort simply disappeared under sand and weeds. Excavation work has gradually revealed much of historical worth, though it's hard to comprehend the full importance without joining the 45-minute **guided tour** (daily at noon & 2pm). Most locals pass by the fort on the way to the best **beach** in Key West – a place yet to be discovered by tourists, just a few yards beyond.

Along Whitehead Street

A block west of crowded Duval Street, **Whitehead Street** is much quieter, has a range of tourable sights and, with its mix of rich and poor homes, reveals a more down-to-earth side of Key West.

At the junction of Whitehead and Wall St is the **Shipwreck Historium** (☎292-8990; daily shows start at 9.45am and run every 30 minutes until 4.45pm; $8). Enthusiastic guides attempt in vain to cajole audience participation as they recount the history of wrecking in Key West before letting visitors loose on the museum. The collection boasts some fine cargo from the Isaac Allerton, which sank in 1856 and remained untraced until 1985. Better still is the panoramic view from the top of the reconstructed viewing tower.

On the corner with Greene Street, the **Audubon House and Tropical Gardens** (daily 9.30am–5pm; $7.50, age 6–12 $3.50) was the first of Key West's elegant Victorian properties to get a thorough renovation – its success encouraged a host of others to follow suit and sent housing prices soaring. The name is taken from a man who actually had nothing to do with the place: famed ornithologist John James Audubon spent a few weeks in Key West in 1832, scrambling around the mangrove swamps (now protected as the Thomas Riggs Wildlife Refuge, see p.143), looking for the bird life he later portrayed in his highly regarded *Birds of America* portfolio. Yet Audubon's link to this house goes no further than the lithographs that decorate the walls and staircase. Original Audubon prints, hand-colored under his instruction, are for sale here at a few hundred to a few thousand dollars.

The man who owned the property was a wrecker named John Geiger. In addition to twelve children of their own, Geiger and his wife took in many others from shipwrecks and broken marriages. Self-guided **tours** through the house require the visitor to wear a personal stereo system, which broadcasts the ghostly voices of Mrs Geiger and the children chatting at you about how life was back in their day.

The Hemingway House

It may be the biggest tourist draw in Key West, but to the chagrin of Ernest Hemingway fans, guided tours of the **Hemingway House**, 907 Whitehead Street (daily 9am–5pm; adults $6.50, children $4), deal more in fantasy than fact. Although Hemingway owned this large, vaguely Moorish-style house for thirty years, he lived in it for barely ten, and the authenticity of the furnishings – a motley bunch of tables, chairs and beds much gloated over by the guide – is hotly disputed by Hemingway's former secretary.

Already established as the nation's foremost hard-drinking, hunting- and fishing-obsessed writer, Hemingway bought the house in 1931, not with his own money but with an $8000 gift from the rich uncle of his then wife, Pauline. Originally one of the grander Key West homes, built for a wealthy nineteenth-century merchant, the dwelling was seriously run down by the time the Hemingways arrived. It soon acquired such luxuries as an inside bathroom and a swimming pool, and was filled with an entourage of servants and housekeepers.

Hemingway produced some of his most acclaimed work in the deer-head-dominated study, located in an outhouse, which Hemingway entered by way of a homemade rope bridge. Here he penned the short stories *The Short Happy Life of Francis Macomber* and *The Snows of Kilimanjaro*; the novels *For Whom the Bell Tolls* and *To Have and Have Not*, which describes Key West life during the Depression.

Among the highlights of the tour are pictures of the author's four wives and a lovely sculpture of a cat by Picasso. Hemingway's studio is a spartan affair, with a quarry-tiled floor and deer heads that look onto his old Royal typewriter. In the garden, a water trough for the cats is supposedly a urinal from *Sloppy Joe's* (see "Nightlife"), where the big man downed many a pint. When Hemingway divorced Pauline in 1940, he boxed up his manuscripts and moved them to a back room at *Sloppy Joe's* before heading off to a house in Cuba with his new wife, journalist Martha Gellhorn.

To see inside the house (and the study) you have to join the half-hour **guided tour** (ten daily), but afterwards you're free to roam at leisure and play with some of the fifty-odd cats. The story that these are descendants from a feline family that lived here in Hemingway's day is yet another dubious claim: the large colony of inbred cats once described by Hemingway was at his home in Cuba.

The Lighthouse Museum and the Bahama Village

From the Hemingway House, you'll easily catch sight of the **Lighthouse Museum**, 938 Whitehead Street (daily 9.30am–5pm; adults $6, under 12s $2), simply because it *is* an 86-foot lighthouse – one of Florida's first, raised in 1847, and still functioning. There's a tiny collection of lighthouse junk and drawings at ground level, and it's possible (if tedious) to climb to the top of the tower, though the views of Key West are actually better from the top-floor bar of the *La Concha* hotel (see "Accommodation"). Most of the pictures taken here are not of the lighthouse but of the massive Chinese banyan tree at the base. But you can ogle the lighthouse's huge lens (installed in 1858): a twelve-foot high, headache-inducing honeycomb of glass.

The narrow streets around the lighthouse and to the west of Whitehead Street constitute **Bahama Village**, an engaging area refreshingly devoid of tourists and glossy restoration jobs. Most of the squat, slightly shabby homes – some of them once small cigar factories – are occupied by people of Bahamian and Afro-Cuban descent. Not only does this area have some of the best and most authentic eateries around, but it also holds onto the mythic Key West atmosphere waning elsewhere on the island. Sadly, the little tour trains are now running close by, and property developers have plans to bring Bahama Village up to speed with touristy areas to the east. For now, though, the place is still relatively untouched: locals still dress up on Sundays and file into the unusual, flaking churches, and the village teems with energy day and night. A more modern attraction here is the **community swimming pool** at the corner of Catherine and Thomas Streets, an Olympic size pool with fantastic ocean views.

Caroline and Greene streets, the dockside area and Key West Cemetery

At the northern end of Duval Street turn right onto **Caroline** or **Greene Street**, and you'll come across numerous examples of late-1800s "**conch houses**," built in a mix-and-match style that fused elements of Victorian, Colonial and Tropical architecture. The houses were raised on coral slabs, and rounded off with playful "gingerbread" wood trimming. Erected quickly and cheaply, conch houses were seldom painted, but many here are bright and colorful, evincing their recent transformation from ordinary dwellings to hundred-thousand-dollar winter homes.

In strong contrast to the tiny conch houses, the grand three-story **Curry Mansion**, 511 Caroline Street (daily 10am–5pm; adults $5, under 12s $1) – now a guesthouse (see above) – was once the abode of William Curry, Florida's first millionaire. Inside, amid a riot of Tiffany glass and sensational bird's-eye maple panelling, is a heady stash of strange and stylish fittings that include an antique Chinese toilet bowl and a lamp designed by Frank Lloyd Wright.

What sets this museum apart is that it is also the present-day home of Al and Edith Amsterdam. The owners for the past 25 years, the Amsterdams are personable hosts when not at their similar mansion in upstate New York. Much of the memorabilia and photographs are from their own younger days, including a Westley Richards gun belonging to Hemingway and given to Mrs Amsterdam by one of the author's wives. Exploring this sensational house is made all the more pleasurable by the Amsterdams' friendly, open-door policy. Clamber up into the attic and you'll be rewarded with a fairy-tale assortment of antique furniture, including a crazy, sequin-covered bed. Climbing even higher to the beautiful **Widows Walk** (a walkway around the roof top where sailors' wives looked for signs of their husbands' return), affords terrific views over the town. Other highlights of the house include the still-used 1940 Doverlift elevator and the 18th-century furnishings of the music room.

A delightful hour or two can be spent at the charming **Heritage House Museum,** 410 Caroline Street (daily 10am–5pm; tours $6, under 12s free; ☎296-3573). This double-veranda, Colonial-style home has been in the same family for seven generations, and the present owner, Jean Porter, lives in an annexe. Jean's mother, Jessie Porter, who died in 1979, was the great-granddaughter of William Curry (see above), and Miss Jessie, as she was known, was at the hub of Key West's efforts to preserve the historic section of town. Among the luminaries she counted as friends were Taleulah Bankhead, who visited with Tennessee Williams, Gloria Swanson and Thornton Wilder; their photographs are mounted in the hallway. Robert Frost also came and lived in a cottage in the garden. While you can wander about the garden, the cottage itself is out of bounds.

Other highlights include an enticing music room where you can play the 1865 French piano, a library of rare books, and a dining room twinkling with crystal and colorful dining chairs taken from a Spanish shipwreck. Outside, recordings of Robert Frost reading his poetry are played in the lush gardens upon request.

The dockside area

Between Williams and Margaret streets, the **dockside area** has been spruced up into a shopping and eating strip called **Land's End Village**, with a couple of enjoyable bars (see "Nightlife"). One with more than drinking to offer is *Turtle Kraals*, in business as a turtle cannery until the Seventies, when harvesting turtles became illegal. There are tanks of touchable sea life inside the restaurant and, just along the short pier, a grim gathering of the gory machines used to slice and mince green turtles – captured off the Nicaraguan coast – into a delicacy known as "Granday's Fine Green Turtle Soup". Apart from pleasure cruisers and shrimping boats along the docks, you might catch a fleeting glimpse of a naval hydrofoil – vessels of unbelievable speed employed on anti-drug-running missions from their base a mile or so along the coast.

Key West Cemetery

Leaving the waterfront and heading inland along Margaret Street for five blocks will take you to the **Key West Cemetery** (daily sunrise–6pm; free), which dates back to 1847, and whose residents are buried in vaults above ground (a high water table and solid coral rock prevents the traditional six-feet-under interment). Despite the lack of celebrity stiffs, the many witty inscriptions ("I told you I was sick") suggest that the island's relaxed attitude toward life also extends to death. Most visitors wander about self-guided, but a far better plan is to call local historian and preservationist **Sharon Wells** (☎294-8380). Her informative tour includes the grave of an E. Lariz, whose stone reads "devoted fan of singer Julio Iglesias," and the resting place of Thomas Romer, a Bahamian born in 1789. He died 108 years later and was "a good citizen for 65 of them." Look out also for the fenced grave of Dr Joseph Otto. Included on the plot is the grave of his pet deer, Elphina, and three of his Yorkshire terriers, one of which is described as being "a challenge to love."

A fifteen-minute walk from the cemetery, at 1431 Duncan Street, is the modest clapboard **house** kept by **Tennessee Williams**. Unlike his more flamboyant counterparts, Williams – Key West's longest-residing literary notable, made famous by his steamy evocations of Deep South life in plays such as *A Streetcar Named Desire* and *Cat on a Hot Tin Roof* – kept a low profile during his 34 years here (he arrived in 1941 and died in 1985).

The rest of Key West

There's not much more to Key West beyond its compact Old Town. Most of the **eastern section** of the island – encircled by the North and South sections of Roosevelt Boulevard – is residential, but Key West's longest beach is located here, and there are several minor points of botanical, natural and historical interest.

At the southern end of White Street, **West Martello Tower** is one of two Civil War lookout points complementing Fort Zachary Taylor (see p.140). In complete variance to the original military purpose, it's now filled by the intoxicating colors and smells of a **tropical garden** (Wed–Sun 9.30am–3.30pm; free). Though it makes a nice outdoor break, a more worthwhile target is the Tower's sister fort, East Martello (see below).

From the tower, Atlantic Avenue quickly intersects with South Roosevelt Boulevard, which skirts on one side the lengthy but slender **Smathers Beach** – the weekend parade ground of Key West's most toned physiques and a haunt of windsurfers and parasailors – and on the other side, the forlorn salt ponds of the **Thomas Riggs Wildlife Refuge**. From a platform raised above the refuge's mangrove entanglements, you should spot a variety of wading birds prowling the grass beds for crab and shrimp. Save for the roar of planes in and out of the nearby airport, the refuge is a quiet and tranquil place; to gain admission you have to phone the Audubon House (☎294-2116) to learn the combination of the locked gate.

Half a mile further, just beyond the airport, the **East Martello Museum and Gallery** (daily 9.30am–5.30pm; adults $3, under 13s $1) is the second of the two Civil War lookout posts. The solid, vaulted casements now store a fascinating assemblage on local history, plus the wild junk-sculptures of legendary Key Largo scrap dealer Stanley

Papio, and the Key West scenes created in wood by a Cuban-primitive artist called Mario Sanchez. There are also displays on local writers, and memorabilia from films shot in Key West; the island's old houses and dependable climate have made it a popular location – in recent years, the final scenes of Sydney Pollack's *Havana* were shot here.

Eating

While there are some excellent places to thrill the palate – and despite the abundant **restaurants** and **snack stands** along the main streets – it's difficult to eat cheaply in Key West. There's no shortage of chic venues for fine French, Italian and Asian cuisine, but if you want really good, inexpensive food and don't want to resort to fast food chains, visit any of the **Cuban sandwich shops**, which also do filling, tasty meals at a fraction of the price of a main-street pizza. Explore streets off the beaten path and understand that the less a place is hyped, the better the quality will normally be. Most menus, not surprisingly, feature fresh **seafood**, and you should sample **conch fritters** – a Key West specialty – at least once.

Cafés

Blue Heaven Bake Shop, 309 Petronia St (☎296-0867). The ownership is about to switch hands, but if they keep to the same formula, this will remain the funkiest cafe on the island, with superb muffins, sweet pies, gateaux and breads. A taste of Sixties hedonism in Bahama Village.

Camille's, 703 Duval St (☎296-4811). Laid-back lunches and dinners, but renowned for its locally acclaimed breakfasts, splendid atmosphere and luscious, casual food. Try a brunch of shrimp cakes, blueberry pancakes or French toast with mango coconut cream sauce for $6. You'll keep returning.

Conch Shop, 308 Petronia St, next to *Johnson's Grocery* (☎294 4140). Basic formica tables and a staff sweating over bubbling oil makes this down-to-earth eatery (serving "soul & sea food" since 1953) appear kind of gritty. Be brave – the fritters, served with potato salad and iced tea or jungle punch are excellent and very well priced.

Croissants des France, 816 Duval St (☎294-2624). Once known for its freshly-baked cream cakes and pastries, this still-popular address is now hit or miss.

Dalton's, 802 Duval St (☎293-0550). An excellent coffee house that serves caffeine every which way imaginable. There's a limited selection of cakes, and the benches are perfectly positioned for people watching.

Dennis Pharmacy, 1229 Simonton St (☎294-1890). A real drugstore dining experience with superb café con leche and Cuban sandwiches. The service is no frills, but there's plenty of local gossip to overhear while you sip. Only open until 5pm.

Dining In The Raw, 800 Olivia St (☎295-2600). There isn't much room to sit, but the exquisite vegetarian (mostly vegan) dishes can be prepared for take-out. Desserts are to die for and include a couscous banana cake, raw sweet potato pie and cranberry iced tea to wash it all down. You can call ahead to place take-out orders.

Five Brothers Grocery, intersection of South and and Grinnel Streets (☎296-5205). Expect long lines at this age-old grocery store, perfect for strong Cuban coffee and cheap Cuban sandwiches. This is *the* neighborhood find – locals love it.

Johnson's Grocery, 800 Thomas St in Bahama Village (☎294-8680). This grocery has legendary ice cold beer and the freshest sandwiches in town. Their small cafe also does great breakfasts and lunches. Closed Sunday.

Sandy's Cafe, 1026 White St (☎295-0159). A deliciously dingy shack serving terrific, cheap Cuban sandwiches. Try the Cuban-mix sandwich, $3.25.

Restaurants

A&B Lobster House, 700 Front St (☎294-2536). Overlooking the town's harbor, there could hardly be a more scenic setting for indulging in fresh seafood or sampling the offerings of the raw bar.

Alice's On Duval, 114 Duval St (☎292-4888). This place has great conch fritters and an eclectic menu that ranges from passionfruit salad to rack of lamb. Let someone else order the meat loaf, though.

Antonia's, 615 Duval St (☎294-6565). Excellent northern-Italian cuisine served in a formal though friendly environment; dinner only – expensive but worth it.

Around the World, 627 Duval St (☎296-2115). Dishes drawn from every corner of the globe; if nothing appeals, tuck into the sizeable salads and sample the extensive selection of wines and beers.

Blue Heaven Cafe, corner of Thomas and Petronia Streets (☎296-0867). Sit in this dirt yard in Bahama Village, watch the roosters wander from table to table, and enjoy the superb, freshly-cooked local dishes. A must.

BO's Fish Wagon, 801 Caroline St (☎294-9272). The over-the-counter fish'n'chips and conch fritters claim to be the cheapest in town.

Cafe des Artistes, 1007 Simonton St (☎294-7100). Pricey but fine tropical-French cuisine, using the freshest local seafood, lobster and steak.

Cafe Marquesa, 600 Fleming St (☎292-1244). Attractive small café offering an imaginative new American-style vegetarian-based menu at moderate prices.

Crab Shack, 908 Caroline St (☎294-7192). The crabs on the menu come from as far afield as Maryland and Alaska – which is odd considering they're so plentiful locally. The prices and food are both average.

Dim-Sum, 613 Duval St (☎294-6230). Thai, Indonesian and Burmese specialities are the core of an exotic Asian menu; don't expect dinner to be less than $20.

Duffy's Steak & Lobster House, 1007 Simonton St (☎296-4900). Usually packed. As the name suggests, there's an immense selection of steak and lobster dishes, all at very appealing prices.

El Siboney, 900 Catherine St (☎296-4184). Inexpensive traditional Cuban dishes and a casual atmosphere.

Jose's Cantina, 800 White St (☎296-4366). Excellent Cuban fare. Try the dolphin (fish, not mammal) with rice and plantains for $12. A well-liked, local restaurant with outdated decor, but good service.

Mangoes, 700 Duval St (☎292-4606). Eat indoors or outdoors under huge umbrellas; high quality seafood and steaks served in sumptuous sauces, and a variety of vegetarian dishes created with a Caribbean slant. Excellent service.

Seven Fish Restaurant, 632 Olivia St (☎296-2777). Not cheap, but not hyped for the tourist market either. The food, primarily fish, is excellent and very fresh.

Siam House, 829 Simonton St (☎292-0302). Authentic Thai cuisine served with care in a near-authentic Thai setting. Great food, friendly staff and very reasonable prices.

South Beach Seafood & Raw Bar, 1405 Duval St (☎294-2727). Seafood selections in a casual, ocean-front setting; large portions of chicken, beef and ribs are also on offer. Also a good bet for breakfast.

Yo Sake, 722 Duval St (☎294-2288). Choose from an extensive range of traditional Japanese dishes, sample the sushi bar, or choose one of the daily specials – usually excellent values.

Nightlife

The carefully cultivated "anything-goes" nature of Key West is exemplified by the **bars** that make up the bulk of the island's **nightlife**. Gregarious, rough-and-ready affairs, often open until 4am and offering a cocktail of yarn-spinning locals, revved-up tourists and (often) live country, folk or rock music, the mainstream bars are grouped around the northern end of Duval Street, no more than a few minutes' stagger apart. Much of Key West's best nightlife, though, revolves around its eateries, and the best are far from Mallory Square's well-beaten path.

Bars and live music venues

Bull & Whistle Bar, 224 Duval St (no phone). Loud and rowdy, this bar features the best of local musicians each night. Check the list on the door to see whose playing – or just turn up to drink.

Captain Tony's Saloon, 428 Greene St (☎294-1838). This rustic saloon was the original *Sloppy Joe's* (see below), a noted hangout of Ernest Hemingway – he met his third wife, Martha Gellhorn, here. Live music of various kinds every night.

Full Moon Saloon, 1200 Simonton St (☎294-9090). Another laid-back bar which offers live music – be it blues, jazz, reggae or rap. Thurs–Sat until 4am.

Green Parrot Bar, 601 Whitehead St (☎294-6133). A Key West landmark since 1890, this bar draws local characters to its pool tables, dart board and pinball machine, and offers live music on weekends.

Havana Docks, at the *Pier House Hotel*, 1 Duval St (☎296-4600). An upscale bar offering unparalleled patio views of the sunset and the lilting strains of a tropical island band. Inside, there's more live music – usually jazz or Latin – Wed–Sat.

Hog's Breath Saloon, 400 Front St. Very popular as a result of endless hype, this is a place to drink yourself silly and then buy a T-shirt to prove it.

Louie's, junction of Vernon and Waddell streets. Far from Duval Street, this is a classy and sophisticated hangout. Head for the outdoor bar ("The Afterdeck"). Open until 2am.

Margaritaville, 500 Duval St (☎292-1435). Owner Jimmy Buffett – a Florida legend for his rock ballads extolling a laid-back life in the sun – occasionally pops up to join the live bands that play here nightly.

Rumrunners, 200 Duval St. A multi-bar joint with reggae music until all hours. Cheap and tasty food.

Schooner Wharf, at the marina end of William St. A big dark dance floor, unusual music styles and lots of cocktail fill this laid-back bar.

Sloppy Joe's, 201 Duval St (☎294-5717). Despite the memorabilia on the walls and the hordes of tourists, this bar – with live music nightly – is not the one made famous by Ernest Hemingway's patronage. For the real thing, see *Captain Tony's Saloon*, above.

Turtle Kraals, Lands End Village, end of Margaret St (☎294-2640). A locals' hangout, offering mellow music from a guitar-and-vocal duo on Friday and Saturday nights.

Two Friends, 512 Front St (☎296-3124). A small, friendly bar with live jazz every night but Monday.

Viva Zapata, 903 Duval St (☎296-3138). You might start your evening at the happy hour in this lively Mexican restaurant, popular with locals as a drinking spot and for its complimentary nachos.

Gay life - bars and venues

Gay life in Key West is always vibrant and attracts frolicking hordes from North America and Europe. The party atmosphere is laid-back, sometimes outrageous, and there's an exceptional level of integration between the straight and gay communities. Unlike other Florida gay centers like South Beach, Key West does a fine job at keeping the catwalk strutting at bay (though it's always lurking at pool sides in the sun).

The tragedy of AIDS has hit Key West hard since the mid 1980s. Many of those stricken have come to soak up the temperate climate and the very-evident camaraderie of the locals. A somber but important trip to the ocean at the end of White Street reveals a striking AIDS memorial, where blocks of black granite are engraved with a roll call of those who have been struck down.

Just about all the gay bars – all within Duval Street's 800 block – are male-oriented, though welcoming to women.

Atlantic Shores Beach Club, 511 South St (☎296-2491). Due to its wild tea-dance extravaganzas, this is now *the* place to go every Sunday. The masses – both men and women – bronze in the sun, and about 30% of them are nude. If you're not staying at the attached hotel (see "Accommodation" above), there's a $3 fee for a lounger and towel. Perfect for sunset watching.

Bourbon St. Pub, 724 Duval St (☎296-1992). A friendly, busy bar with a huge cocktail bar where bare-but-for-G-string model boys dance till their pouches are full of dollar bills.

Divas, 711 Duval Street Popular for dancing and its regular drag shows, this is becoming a mainstay on the circuit.

Donnie's Club, 422 Appelrouth Lane, opposite Big Ruby's Guesthouse (see "Accommodation" above) (☎294-2655). A small, neighborhood bar where the guest-house staff come for a quiet drink and to shoot pool.

Eight-O-One Bar, 801 Duval St (☎294-4737). Known for its zany drag shows boasting Margo, "the oldest drag queen on earth," in its upstairs bar. The downstairs bar is more of a pick-up joint.

Epoch, 623 Duval St (☎296-8521). On the site of the fabled Copa, which burned down in 1995, this techno-loud bar has sophisticated lighting and a big dance floor.

La-Te-Da, 1125 Duval St (☎294-8435). The various bars and discos of this hotel complex have long been a favorite haunt of locals and visitors. Very friendly and more casually upscale than its neighbors.

One Saloon of Key West, 1 Appelrouth Lane (☎296-8118). A small, dark former leather bar now full of youngish men watching blue videos, which are a secondary attraction to the real flesh strutting on the bars.

Listings

Airport Four miles east of the Old Town, on South Roosevelt Blvd (☎296-5439). No public transport link to the Old Town; a taxi will cost $8–9. American Airlines, Delta and USAir fly into Key West, with flights mainly serving as feeders to their Miami services.

Bike rental From Adventure Scooter & Bicycle Rentals, at 708 and 925 Duval St and the *Youth Hostel*, 718 South St (☎296-5719).

Bookstores Best of all is the Key West Island Bookstore, 513 Fleming St (daily 10am–6pm), packed with the works of Key West authors and Keys-related literature, and with an excellent selection of rare and second-hand books. Blue Heron at 1014 Truman Ave (☎ 296-3508, Mon–Sat 9am–9pm, Sun if owners feel like it), is very knowledgeable and friendly. Specializing in gay studies and the works of local authors, it also has a good general stock. Flaming Maggies, 830 Fleming St (10am–6pm daily), stocks gay and lesbian interest books and also serves excellent coffee. Bargain Books, 1028 Truman Avenue (☎294-7446), has a massive stock of second-hand books and a huge wooden box with novels at 25c.

Buses Local information ☎292-8164.

Car rental Only worth it if you're heading off to see the other Keys. All companies are based at the airport: Alamo (☎294-6675); Dollar (☎296-9921); Hertz (☎294-1039); Thrifty (☎296-6514).

Cigars Key West used to be a major producer of cigars. Now they can only be purchased at La Tabaqueria in the lobby of the *Southern Cross Hotel* at 326 Duval St; on Fri, Sat & Sun you can see them being rolled.

Dive shops Diving and snorkeling trips and equipment rental can be arranged all over Key West. Try Captain Corner's, Zero Duval St (☎296-8865), or Reef Raiders, 109 Duval St (☎294-3635). (See also "Reef trips" and "Ecology tours"; below.)

Ecology tours Dan McConnell, based at Mosquito Coast Island Outfitters, 1107 Duval St (☎294-7178), runs six-hour kayak tours of back country mangroves ($48.15 per person) filled with facts on the ecology and history of the Keys; there's also an opportunity to snorkel in this unique environment. To explore the reef by boat, join the informative half- or full-day tours aboard the 65-foot schooner *Reef Chief* (phone ☎292-1345 for details).

Greyhound 615 1/2 Duval St (☎296-9072); to find it, turn right by the fire station off Simonton Street.

Hospitals 24-hour casualty department at Lower Florida Keys Health System, 5900 Junior College Rd, Stock Island (☎294-5531).

Late food shops Owls, 712 Caroline St, daily until 11pm; Sunbeam Market, 500 White Street, never closes.

Library 700 Fleming Ave; book sale on the first Saturday of each winter month.

Newsagents L. Valladares & Son, 1200 Duval St, stocks British and Irish newspapers and a vast selection of magazines from the US and elsewhere.

Post office 400 Whitehead St (Mon 8.30am–5pm, Tues–Fri 9.30am–5pm, Sat 9.30am–noon; ☎294-2257; zip code 33040).

Reef trips The glass-bottomed *Fireball* makes 6–7 trips a day from the northern tip of Duval St to the Florida Reef; $17.12 for 2 hours (☎296-6293). For snorkeling and diving, see "Dive shops," above.

Supermarket Fausto's Food Palace, 522 Fleming St (Mon–Sat 8am–8pm, Sun 8am–6pm).

Taxi Unlikely to be necessary except to get to the airport (see above); try Five (☎296-6666) or Friendly Cab (☎292-0000).

Watersports Jet-skiing, water-skiing and parasailing are all possible, in the right conditions, using outlets set up alongside Smathers Beach. For more details phone Sunset Watersports (☎296-5545) or Watersports on the Atlantic (☎294-2696).

Beyond Key West: the Dry Tortugas

Seventy miles west of Key West in the Gulf of Mexico is a small group of islands that the sixteenth-century Spaniard Ponce de León named the **Dry Tortugas** for the large numbers of turtles he found there (the "dry" was added later to warn mariners of the islands' lack of fresh water). Comprising Garden Key and its neighboring reef islands, the entire area has been designated a wildlife sanctuary to protect the nesting grounds of the snooty tern – a black-bodied, white-hooded bird that's unusual among terns for choosing to lay its eggs in scrubby vegetation and bushes. From early January, these and a number of other winged rarities show up on Bush Key, and they are easily spied with binoculars from Fort Jefferson on Green Key (see below).

Fort Jefferson

Green Key is the last place you'd expect to find the US's largest nineteenth-century coastal fortification, but **Fort Jefferson** (daily during daylight hours), which rises mirage-like in the distance as you approach, is exactly that. Started in 1846 and intended to protect US interests on the Gulf, the fort was never completed, despite thirty years of building work. Instead it served as a prison, until intense heat, lack of fresh water, outbreaks of disease and savage weather made the fort as unpopular with its guards as its inmates; in 1874, after a hurricane and the latest yellow fever outbreak, it was abandoned.

Following the signposted **walk** around the fort and viewing the odds and ends in the small **museum** won't take more than an hour – and spare time should be allocated to **swimming and snorkeling**: get a free map of the best locations from the park ranger's office, by the entrance.

You can **get to the fort** by air in half an hour with *Key West Seaplane* from Sunset Marina, 5603 Junior College Road, Stock Island ($139 half-day, $239 full day; ☎294-6978;) – a beautiful trip that takes you low over the turquoise water. Less expensive and more relaxed is the Tortugas high-speed **ferry**, *Yankee Freedom*, which leaves from the Key West Sea Port on Mon, Wed and Sat at 8am ($85, under 15s $50; ☎2947009 or ☎1-800/634-0939). After four to five leisurely hours at the fort, the ferry returns at 7pm. Avid bird-watchers can **camp** at Fort Jefferson for up to twenty days, though given its lack of amenities you have to come well prepared with your own supplies of water and food; only in an emergency can you count on help from park ranger. A round-trip ferry ticket including tent camping costs $94.

travel details

Buses

Three **Greyhound** buses a day run between Miami and Key West. Scheduled stops are listed below though the bus can be waved down anywhere on the route – stand by the side of the Overseas Highway and jump about like a maniac when you see the bus coming.

Scheduled stops are in North Key Largo (Central Plaza, 103200 Overseas Highway; ☎451-6280); Islamorada (*Burger King*, MM82; ☎852-4266); Marathon (6363 Overseas Highway; ☎743-3488); Big Pine Key (MM30.2; ☎872-4022); and Key West (615 1/2 Duval St; ☎296-9072).

From Miami to Big Pine Key (3hr 50min); Islamorada (2hr 20min); Key West (4hr 30min); Marathon (3hr 20min); North Key Largo (1hr 55min).

Ferries

A **ferry service** operated by Key West Excursions Friendship 1V (☎800/650-5397) will take you from Key West across to the mainland of Florida's Gulf of Mexico (see "West Coast" chapter). The ferry leaves from the A & B Marina on Front Street, and is a good way of getting to Florida's west coast without zigzagging back across the Keys and through the Everglades. Destinations alternate from year to year between Marco Island (departure Tues–Thurs at 6pm, arriving at 10pm), and Fort Myers (running Fri–Mon only at 6pm). Ticket prices are $75 one way, $95 for a same-day round trip, and $115 if returning on another day. Ferries do not take cars, and car hire is possible only from Fort Myers.

Planes

A more sensible option is to fly on an **island hopper**. Cape Air, (☎800/352-0714) flies to Naples from Key West daily at 9.30am, 12.30pm, 2.45pm, 5pm and 7pm. The flight takes just 45 minutes, and costs $91 one way, $157 round trip. The views from the eight-seater plane are sensational.

CHAPTER THREE

THE SOUTHEAST COAST

S tretching from Miami's northern fringe along almost half the state's Atlantic shoreline, the 130-mile **Southeast Coast** is the sun-soaked Florida of popular imagination, with bodies bronzing on palm-dotted beaches as warm ocean waves lap idly against silky-soft sands. Darkening this vision of paradise, however, is the fact that roughly half the region is the fastest-growing residential area in the state, leaving many of the once pristine and spectacular ocean strips walled by unappealing high-rises. While you can drop your beach towel without a worry just about anywhere, don't spend all your time on the Southeast Coast cultivating a tan. Take the time to explore some of the towns and seek out the undeveloped, protected sections, where you'll experience the Florida coastline as nature intended it.

The first fifty-odd miles of the Southeast Coast – **the Gold Coast** – are deep within the sway of Miami, comprising back-to-back conurbations often with little to tell them apart. That said, the first and largest, **Fort Lauderdale**, is certainly distinctive: the reputation for rowdy beach parties – stemming from its years as a student Spring Break destination – is well out of date; the town has cultivated a cleaner cut, sophisticated image of late, aided by an excellent art museum and an ambitious downtown improvement project. Further north, diminutive **Boca Raton** also has a style of its own: Mediterranean Revival architecture has been its hallmark since the Twenties, and it possesses some of the Gold Coast's finest beaches. Unconventional architect Addison Mizner shaped Boca Raton, but is best remembered for his work in **Palm Beach**: inhabited almost exclusively by multi-millionaires, yet accessible even to the most impecunious daytripper.

North of Palm Beach, the population thins and natural Florida asserts itself forcefully throughout the **Treasure Coast**. Here, rarely crowded beaches flank long, pine-coated barrier islands such as **Jupiter Island** and **Hutchinson Island**, whose miles of untainted shoreline are quiet enough for sea turtles to come ashore and lay their eggs.

By car, the scenic route along the Southeast Coast is **Hwy-A1A**, which sticks wherever possible to the ocean side of the **Intercoastal Waterway**. Beloved of Florida's boat owners, this stretch was formed when the rivers dividing the mainland from the barrier islands were joined and deepened during World War II to reduce the threat of submarine attack. When necessary, Hwy-A1A turns inland and links with the much less picturesque **Hwy-1**. The speediest road in the region, **I-95**, runs about ten miles west of the coastline, splitting the residential sprawl from the wide-open Everglades, and is only worthwhile if you're in a hurry.

ACCOMMODATION PRICE CODES

All **accommodation prices** in this book have been coded using the symbols below. Note that prices are for the least expensive double rooms in each establishment. For a full explanation see p.27 in Basics.

① up to $30	③ $45-60	⑤ $80-100	⑦ $130-180
② $30-45	④ $60-80	⑥ $100-130	⑧ $180+

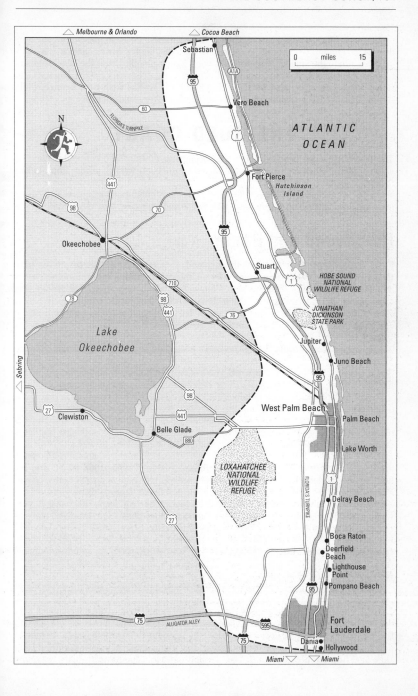

Although most **buses** keep to Hwy-1, the Southeast Coast is good news for non-drivers. Frequent Greyhound connections link the bigger towns, and a few daily services run to the smaller communities. Local buses, plentiful from the edge of Miami to West Palm Beach, are nonexistent in the more rural Treasure Coast. Along the Gold Coast, there's the additional option of the dirt-cheap Tri-Rail rush hour service, while Amtrak has two daily **trains** running as far north as West Palm Beach.

THE GOLD COAST

The widely admired beaches and towns occupying the fifty-mile commuter corridor north of Miami make the **Gold Coast** – named for the booty washed ashore from sunken Spanish galleons – one of the most heavily populated and tourist-besieged parts of the state. The sands sparkle, the nightlife rocks, and many communities have an assertively individualistic flavor – but if you're seeking peace and seclusion, look elsewhere.

Hollywood and Dania

From Miami Beach, Hwy-A1A runs through undistinguished Hallandale before reaching **HOLLYWOOD** – founded and named by a Californian – with a generous beach and a more cheerful persona than the better-known and much larger Fort Lauderdale, ten miles north. Allocate an hour to the pedestrian-only **Broadwalk**, parallel to Hwy-A1A (known here as Ocean Drive), whose snack bars and skateboarders enliven a casual amble, and the **Art and Culture Center of Hollywood**, 1650 Harrison Street (Tues–Sat 10am–4pm, Sun 1–4pm; $3), which exhibits works by emergent Florida artists.

Modestly priced **motels** line Hollywood's oceanside streets. For good value try the *Stardust Motel*, 915 N Ocean Drive (☎1-800/354-1718; ②), or the *Dolphin*, 342 Pierce Street (☎1-800/922-4498; ③). As usual, you'll save a few dollars by staying inland, where the *Shell Motel*, 1201 S Federal Highway (☎923-8085; ②), has the best rates.

It was in Hollywood, incidentally, that rap group **2 Live Crew** was arrested for obscenity in June 1990; the group was acquitted, but not before the case became an anti-censorship *cause celebre* across the country. On the whole, though, Hollywood's nightlife has little at music's cutting edge, but still plenty to enjoy: solid jazz and R&B are the staple fare of *Club M*, 2037 Hollywood Blvd (☎925-8396); as well as the mellow *O'Hara's Jazz Pub*, 1903 Hollywood Blvd (☎925-2555). Raunchy rock-and-roll prevails at the *J&S Restaurant and Lounge,* 5701 Johnson Street (☎966-6196), on Fri and Sat nights; blues and food are on offer, for dinner only, at the small and rather pricey *Sushi Blues Café*, 1836 S Young Circle (☎929-9560); and if you fancy a drink right on the beach, accompanied by music and Jamaican food, make for *Sugar Reef*, 600 N Surf Road (☎922-1119; closed on Tues in summer). Another cheap, and intimate, place to eat (but without music) is *Try My Thai*, 2003 Harrison Street (☎926-5585). You may also want to try *Eighty-Eight's Café Society*, 1716 Harrison Street (☎925-1775) for quick, cheap food; *Dave & Busters*, 13000 Oakwood Blvd (☎923-5505) for good economical American fare; or the awesome decor but pricier food at *Revolution 2029*, 2029 Harrison Street (☎920-4748).

Ocean Drive continues north into **DANIA**, whose prime asset isn't the grouping of pseudo-English antique shops along Hwy-1 but the pine trees and sands of the **John U Lloyd Beach State Recreational Area**, 6503 N Ocean Drive (daily 8am–sunset; cars $4, pedestrians and cyclists $1). Situated on a peninsula jutting across the entrance to the shipping terminal of Port Everglades, the park provides an enjoyable, 45-minute nature trail around its mangrove, seagrape and guava trees. If you're around during June and July (Wed & Fri 9pm), you can find out about loggerhead turtle watching;

The area code for Hollywood, Dania and Fort Lauderdale is ☎954.

trips include a twenty-minute slide presentation and a visit to a nest if one is available, but try to book a month or so in advance as they are immensely popular – and take plenty of insect repellent. Check with a park ranger (☎923-2833) for details on this and other scheduled activities.

With more time to spare, visit the **Graves Museum of Archaeology and Natural History**, 481 S Federal Highway (Tues–Sat 10am–4pm, Thurs until 8pm, Sun 1–4pm; $5), which will persuade any doubters that Florida was inhabited long before *Miami Vice*. In a large and diverse collection, including much from Africa and Egypt, copious Tequesta Indian artifacts unearthed locally mark an excellent pre-Columbian section.

Towards Fort Lauderdale: by boat, car or bus

To continue north without a car you can use BCT's **local bus** #1 (which you can catch at any BCT stop on Hwy-1), or the pricier Greyhound, 1707 Tyler Street in Hollywood (☎922-8228). Alternatively, if you're not weighed down by luggage, call the Water Taxi (☎467-6677) to ferry you from the recreational area to any dockable part of Fort Lauderdale – see "Fort Lauderdale" for more details.

Fort Lauderdale

A thinly populated riverside trading camp at the turn of the century, **FORT LAUDERDALE** came to be known as "the Venice of America" when its mangrove swamps were fashioned into slender canals during the Twenties. From the Thirties, inter-collegiate swimming contests drew the nation's youth here; a fact seized upon by the 1960 teen-exploitation film, *Where The Boys Are*, which instantly made Fort Lauderdale the US's number one Spring Break venue. Hundreds of thousands of students congregated around the seven miles of sand for a six-week pre-exam frenzy of underage drinking and lascivious excess, earning the place a global reputation for rambunctious beach life. By the late Seventies, the students were also bringing six weeks of traffic chaos, and proving a deterrent to regular tourists. Fighting back, the local authorities began a negative advertising campaign across the country's campuses, and enacted strict laws to restrict boozing and wild behavior around the beach.

Subsequently, the students turned their attentions to Daytona Beach (see "The Northeast Coast"), allowing Fort Lauderdale to emerge as an affluent business, historical and cultural center dominated by a mix of wealthy retirees and affluent yuppies keen to play down the beach-party tag and play up the town's settler-period history. It's not an unpleasant place at all (with a flourishing gay scene, see "Gay Fort Lauderdale" below), despite being a long way from the social inferno you might have been led to expect.

PROFESSIONAL SPORTS VENUES

Sports enthusiasts will find the Greater Fort Lauderdale area a hub of professional activity: you can catch the spring training (in March) of baseball's Baltimore Orioles and, during the regular season, watch the Florida Marlins. August sees the pre-season training of NFL's Miami Dolphins in nearby Davie, and it's not far to Miami to see the Miami Heat play professional basketball. Also, the recent addition of the Sunrise Civic Center provides a home for the newly created hockey team, the Florida Panthers.

Arrival, transport and information

Known as Federal Highway, Hwy-1 ploughs through the center of **downtown Fort Lauderdale**, three miles inland from the coast. Just south of downtown, **Hwy-A1A** veers oceanwards off Hwy-1 along SW Seventeenth Street and runs through **beachside Fort Lauderdale**. All the long-distance public transport terminals are in or near downtown: the Greyhound **bus station** is at 515 NE Third Street (☎764-6551), while the **train** and Tri-Rail station is two miles west at 200 SW 21st Terrace (Amtrak ☎1-800/872-7245; Tri-Rail ☎1-800-TRI-RAIL), linked to the center by regular buses #9, #10, #22, and #81.

The handiest service offered by the thorough **local bus** network (BCT ☎357-8400) is the #11, which runs twice hourly along Las Olas Boulevard between downtown Fort Lauderdale and the beach; **timetables** are available from Governmental Center, at the corner of Andrews Avenue and Broward Boulevard, or from the bus terminal directly opposite. There is also a free **Downtown Trolley** service, comprising two routes that run every ten minutes: the Courthouse (on SE Sixth Street) and BCT terminal loop (Mon–Fri 7.30am–5.30pm); and the lunchtime express, which travels the length of Las Olas Boulevard (Mon–Fri 11.30am–2.30pm). For a flat fare of $1, you can catch the **Wave Line Trolley** (half hourly 10.15am–10pm; ☎429-3100), which runs along the beach strip – Hwy-A1A between NE 41st Street and 17th Street Causeway.

More expensive than buses – but more fun – are **water taxis** (daily 10am–midnight; ☎467-6677), a series of small boats that will pick up and deliver you almost anywhere along Fort Lauderdale's many miles of waterfront. Though these taxis are without a doubt the best way to see the city, be aware that they can often run late, and you must be sure to call well in advance of midnight in order to assure a ride home (if you're eating out, ask your server to arrange a pick-up after your meal). An all-day pass, allowing unlimited usage, costs $15 (single tickets are $7).

If you'd rather have a structured **water tour** of the city, there are numerous tour operators in the area. The *Jungle Queen* (☎462-5596) offers dinner cruises and riverboat tours of Millionaire's Row, the Venetian Isles and the New River Jungles; the *Cyclone* (☎467-7433) is more amusement than sightseeing as it glides down the Intercoastal then hits warp speed as you pass Port Everglades – warning: you will get wet. *SunCruz* Casinos (☎929-3800) has day and evening gaming tours aboard a luxury casino yacht.

The **Convention and Visitors Bureau**, 1850 Eller Drive, Suite 303 (Mon–Fri 8.30am–5pm; ☎765-4466), has relocated to a remote area in the Port Everglades area, which is nearly impossible to find without a car. You're better off picking up a copy of the free *CityLink* magazine (available throughout the city) to find out what's going on. Also available is a free **entertainment and attractions hotline** (☎527-5600), staffed by operators fluent in five languages.

Accommodation

A handy free booklet, *Superior Small Lodgings Guide,* is available from the Convention and Visitors Bureau (see above), and lists reasonably priced **accommodation** that is inspected annually. Options for staying in downtown Fort Lauderdale are relatively limited, but the scores of **motels** clustered between the Intercoastal Waterway and the ocean can be exceptionally good value. If money is tight, the sufficient *International House Hostel*, 3811 N Ocean Blvd (☎568-1615; a) has free parking and beds for $12, though few private rooms (buses #11, #62, and #72 run close). The closest **campground** is *Easterlin*, corner of 1000 NW 38th Street and 10th Avenue, Oakland Park (☎ 938-0610; $1 per person), three miles north of downtown and reached by bus #14.

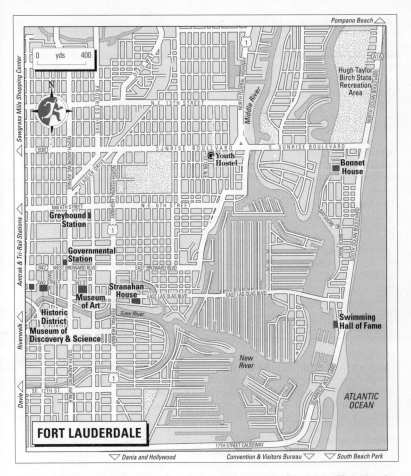

Banyan Marina Apartments, 111 Isle of Venice (☎1-800/524-4431). The attractive setting of these apartments, on a waterway a short drive from the beach and close to Las Olas Boulevard, explains the higher price. ④.

Bermudian Waterfront, 315 N Birch Rd (☎467-0467). North of the center but handy for the sea. As well as the regular economically priced rooms there are some 1- and 2-bedded suites with fully equipped kitchens. ①–⑦.

La Casa Del Mar, 3003 Granada Blvd (☎467-2037). Though this attractive B&B caters mainly to a gay clientele, all are welcome to enjoy wine and cheese afternoons by the pool, and the water taxi can pick you up from a block away. Ask for the "Judy Garland" room where the actual munchkins slept during a film festival.

Ocean Hacienda Inn, 1924 N Atlantic Blvd (☎1-800/562-8467). A great oceanfront hotel with a tropical garden, heated pool facing the ocean and surprisingly inexpensive rooms. ③.

Pillars Waterfront Inn, 111 N Birch Rd (☎1-800/800-7666). Quiet, relaxing motel with a pool; not far from the ocean. ③.

Riverside Hotel, 620 E Las Olas Blvd (☎1-800/325-3280). Elegant, comfortable, well-placed but over-priced downtown option. ④.

Royal Saxon Apartments, 551 Breakers Ave (☎566-7424). Fresh flowers and fruit in every room, and a ten-minute walk to restaurants and shopping. One of the best economical finds in Fort Lauderdale. ②.
Shell Motel at the Ocean, 3030 Bayshore Drive (☎463-1723). This cheerful motel is well-equipped and a stone's throw from the beach. ④.

Downtown Fort Lauderdale

Tall, anonymous, glass-fronted buildings make an uninspiring first impression, but **downtown Fort Lauderdale** has an outstanding modern art museum and a number of restored older buildings to usefully occupy several hours. Because of a multi-million-dollar effort to prettify the district, parks and promenades are linked by the pedestrian-only, one-and-a-half-mile **Riverwalk** along the north bank of the New River, which terminates at the state-of-the-art Museum of Discovery and Science.

The Museum of Art
In a postmodern structure shaped like a slice of pie, the **Museum of Art**, 1 E Las Olas Boulevard (Tues 11am–9pm, Wed–Sat 10am–5pm, Sun noon–5pm, $5; guided tours Tues, Thurs & Fri 1.30pm, free; ☎525-5500) provides ample space and light for the best art collection in the state, with an emphasis on modern painting and sculpture. The strongest exhibits are drawn from the museum's vast hoard of works under the banner of **CoBrA**, a movement beginning in 1948 with a group of artists from Copenhagen, Brussels and Amsterdam (hence the acronym), and typified by bright expressionistic canvases combining playful innocence with deep emotional power. Important names to look for include Asger Jorn, Carl Henning-Pedersen and Karel Appel, though many later adherents of the genre also produced formidable works – there are plenty of them here to admire.

The Historic District and the Stranahan House
The modern buildings of downtown Fort Lauderdale do little to suggest the community's past. For a quick look at some that do, walk a few blocks west from the Art Museum to the **historic district**, at the center of which is the **Historical Society**, on Riverwalk at 219 SW Second Avenue (Tues–Fri 10am–4pm, though times may vary; $2; ☎463-4431). Here you can pick up details on self-guided walking tours past (and sometimes inside) three of the oldest buildings in Fort Lauderdale, located nearby and in the process of being spruced up for the public: the 1907 **King-Cromartie House**, whose many then-futuristic fixtures include the first indoor bathroom in Fort Lauderdale; the three-story **New River Inn** (1905), which was the first hotel here; and the **Philomen Bryan House** (1905), once the home of the Bryan family, who constructed many other buildings in this area. To give perspective on the old buildings and the town's past in general, the Historical Society mounts informative temporary displays and stocks plenty of historical books and takeaway pamphlets.

A few minutes' walk east stands a more complete reminder of early Fort Lauderdale life: the carefully restored **Stranahan House** (audio tours available Wed, Fri & Sat 10am–4pm continuously, closed July & Aug; $5) behind the Hyde Park Market on Las Olas Boulevard. Erected in 1901, with high ceilings, narrow windows and wide verandas, the building is a fine example of the Florida frontier style, and served as the home and trading post of a turn-of-the-century settler, Frank Stranahan. A recording, hokey-sounding at times, tells the prosperous story of Stranahan, a dealer in otter pelts, egret plumes and alligator hides, which he purchased from Seminole Indians trading along the river. Ironically, Stranahan, financially devastated by the late-Twenties Florida property crash, later drowned himself in the same waterway.

The Museum of Discovery and Science

Directly west from the historic district, and marking the end of the Riverwalk, the gleaming **Museum of Discovery and Science** (Mon–Sat 10am–5pm, Sun 12–6pm; $6) is among the newest and best of Florida's growing number of child-oriented science museums. However, childless adults shouldn't think twice about coming (though they should aim to avoid weekends and school holidays, when the place is packed) because the exhibits present the basics of science in numerous ingenious and entertaining ways. You can even pretend to be an astronaut, rising in an air-powered chair to re-align an orbiting satellite, or making a simulated trip to the moon. The museum also contains a towering 3D IMAX film theater (daily shows – check admission booth for times; $9 or else buy a $12.50 combination ticket for both museum and IMAX; ☎467-6637).

The Broward Center for the Performing Arts

Continuing west from the Museum of Discovery and Science is the **Broward Center for the Performing Arts**, 201 SW Fifth Avenue (ticket info ☎462-0222), a pleasant, modern, waterfront building that houses Broadway shows and more offbeat productions in its intimate Amaturo Theater.

Around Las Olas Boulevard and the beach

Downtown Fort Lauderdale is linked to the beach by **Las Olas Boulevard** – at the cutting edge of fashion, art, food (from restaurants to sidewalk cafés) – and then by **the Isles**, well-tended canal-side land where residents park their cars on one side of their mega-buck properties and moor their luxury yachts on the other. Once across the arching intercoastal waterway bridge, about two miles on, you're within sight of the ocean and the mood changes appreciably: where Las Olas Boulevard ends, **beach-side Fort Lauderdale** begins – T-shirt, sunscreen and swim-wear shops are suddenly everywhere.

Along the seafront, **Ocean Boulevard** bore the brunt of Spring Break partying until the clean-up of the Eighties (see above). The whole area has benefited from a multi-million-dollar facelift, and now only a few beachfront bars bear any trace of the carousing of the past, though the sands, flanked by graciously aging coconut palms and an attractive new promenade, are by no means deserted or dull; joggers, rollerbladers and cyclists create a stereotypical beach scene, and a fair number of whooping students still turn up here each spring.

Since the bulk of Fort Lauderdale's accommodation is here, you'll have no difficulty exploring the beach, the bars, and a few other items of interest in either direction along the main strip.

South along Ocean Boulevard

A short way south of the Las Olas Boulevard junction, the **International Swimming Hall of Fame**, 501 Seabreeze Boulevard (Mon–Sat 9am–7pm, Sun 11am–4pm; $3), salutes aquatic sports with a collection even dedicated non-swimmers will enjoy. The two floors are stuffed with medals, trophies and yellowing press cuttings pertaining to the musclebound heroes and heroines of swimming, diving and many more obscure watery activities.

For a few hours of solitude, thread through the residential streets a mile further south to the placid **South Beach Park**, a restful spot at the tip of Fort Lauderdale's coastline.

North along Ocean Boulevard

As if the city needed anymore shopping malls, the lackluster commercial complex called **BeachPlace** sits just north of the Las Olas Blvd junction. Here you'll find three

---

SAWGRASS MILLS

Consumerism enters a new dimension twelve miles west of Fort Lauderdale at 12801 W Sunrise Boulevard, where **Sawgrass Mills** (Mon–Sat 10am–9.30pm, Sun 11am–8pm), a gathering of over 270 designer-name stores selling wares at less than retail prices, draws South Florida shoppers and bargain-hunting tourists by the thousands. Take buses #22, #36 or #72.

Even if you don't intend to buy anything, simply exploring this tropically-themed, mile-long mall – where the Big Names include Saks Fifth Avenue, Levis and Last Call at Neiman Marcus – can be mind-boggling.

---

levels of predictable shops (*Banana Republic*, *Gap*, *Speedo*, etc.) with a smattering of bars and restaurants, including *Howl at the Moon*, *Sloppy Joe's,* and the garish-orange *Hooters*. The good thing about BeachPlace is that you can hop up from the sand to grab a bite to eat, buy souvenir paraphernalia, or go to the restroom. Otherwise it's just another hyped-up mall with a spectacular waterfront location.

Further north, in the midst of the high-rise hotels and apartment blocks that now dominate the beachside area, Fort Lauderdale's pre-condo landscape can be viewed in the jungle-like 35-acre grounds of **Bonnet House**, 900 N Birch Road (mandatory tours Wed–Fri 10.15am, 11.30am, 12.15pm, 1.30pm; Sat & Sun 12.30pm, 1.15pm, 1.45pm, 2.30pm; $9; ☎563-5393), a few minutes' walk off Ocean Boulevard. Turn up fifteen minutes before your chosen tour time to assure a spot. The house and its surroundings – including a swan-filled pond and resident monkeys – were designed by Chicago muralist Frank Clay Bartlett and completed in 1921. The tours of the vaguely plantation-style abode highlight Bartlett's eccentric passion for art and architecture – and for collecting ornamental animals, dozens of which fill virtually all of the thirty rooms.

Another green pocket is nearby: beside Sunrise Boulevard, the tall Australian pines of the **Hugh Taylor Birch State Recreation Area** (daily 8am–sunset; cars $3.25, pedestrians and cyclists $1) form a shady backdrop for canoeing on the park's mangrove-fringed freshwater lagoon – a good way to perk yourself up after a morning spent prostrate on the beach.

Eating

Fort Lauderdale has many affordable, enjoyable **places to eat**, featuring everything from exotic Asian creations to homemade conch chowder. Restaurants are grouped in different sections of the town, however, and traveling between them can be difficult without a car. Note that if you take the Water Taxi (advisable, especially if you'll be drinking; see p.154), make sure to tell your server when your meal is over so they can arrange for the taxi to pick you up.

Café Europa, 726 E Las Olas Blvd (☎763-6600). Funky café, always packed, with a mouth-watering display of desserts, unusual pizza toppings and a wall full of city-skyline images that make travelers a little less homesick.

Casablanca Café, intersection of Alhambra and Ocean Blvd, opposite the beach (☎764-3500). An American piano bar in a Moroccan setting with a good, eclectic menu. Expect large portions.

Coconuts, 429 Seabreeze Blvd, directly on the Intercoastal (☎467-6788). Best place to watch the sunset in Ft Lauderdale, serving giant portions of prime rib, award-winning bay scallops and delicious coconut bread.

Ernie's BBQ Lounge, 1843 S Federal Hwy (☎523-8636). The scruffy but likeable *Ernie's*, south of downtown, is a local legend for its glorious conch chowder (add sherry to taste).

The Floridian, 1410 E Las Olas Blvd (☎463-4041). Downtown coffee shop with a cozy diner style, where many go for the mammoth breakfasts. Lunch and dinner aren't too shabby either, and make sure to grab a Tootsie Roll from the giant fishbowl on your way out.

Franco & Vinny's Mexican Cantina, 2870 E Sunrise Blvd (☎565-3839). Mexican favorites at giveaway prices near the beach.

Japanese Village, 716 E Las Olas Blvd (☎763-8163). Good Japanese food in a central location.

Lester's Diner, 250 State Rd 84 (☎525-5641). Cheap food first thing in the morning, with the added bonus of coffee served in a 32-ounce cup: a hefty kickstart.

Mangos, 904 E Las Olas Blvd (☎523-5001). Good pants-stuffing portions and a breezy outside dining area, perfect for listening to the roaring live music inside and for people watching along Las Olas Blvd.

Mistral, 201 S Atlantic Blvd (☎463-4900). Huge plates of sun-drenched, Mediterranean cuisine at the beachfront.

Shooters Waterfront Café, 3033 NE 32nd Ave (☎566-2855). Popular beach-area restaurant drawing large crowds for its generous portions of seafood, burgers and salads.

Southport Raw Bar, 1536 Cordova Rd (☎525-CLAM). Boisterous local bar offering succulent crustaceans and well-prepared fish dishes.

Sukhothai, at *Gateway Plaza*, 1930 E Sunrise Blvd (☎764-0148). Tasty, moderately spiced Thai dishes.

Drinking, live music and nightlife

Some of the restaurants above, particularly *Shooters* and the *Southport Raw Bar*, are also notable **drinking** spots. Other promising libation locations near the beach are the *Parrot Lounge*, 911 Sunrise Lane (☎563-1493), an easy-going bar specializing in over-sized pitchers of beer; at *Kim's Alley Bar,* 1920 E Sunrise Blvd in Gateway Plaza (☎763-7886), a 22-foot long, African mahogany bar dominates this popular watering hole; and *Elbo Room*, 241 S Atlantic Boulevard (☎463-4615), once a Spring Break favorite, is now an ideal place for an evening drink as the ocean breeze ruffles your hair. For those looking for pubs, crawl from the local favorite *Shakespeare's Pub & Grille*, 1015 NE 26th Street (☎563-7833), to the *Tudor Inn*, 5782 Power Lane (☎491-3697).

Live music is never far away. To find out who's playing where, call the free Entertainment Hotline (☎527-5600), pick up the free *CityLink* magazine from streetside newsstands, or consult the "Showtime" segment of the Friday edition of the local *Sun-Sentinel* newspaper. Reliable venues include *Bierbrunnen*, 425 S Ocean Boulevard (☎462-1008), for a variety of musical styles, German beer and bratwurst; *O'Hara's Pub*, 722 E Las Olas Boulevard (☎524-1764), a stylish jazz venue; *Cheers*, 941 E Cypress Creek Rd (☎771-6337), which brings the house down with rock-n-roll until 4am; the *Poor House*, 110 SW 3rd Ave (☎522-5145), which offers smoky blues and the occasional swing band; and *Desperado's Nightclub*, 2520 S Miami Rd (☎463-BULL), a joint for tush-pushin' country lovers, complete with a mechanical bull in the corner.

Fort. Lauderdale's vibrant **dance scene** has a **club** for every music taste. Among the favorites are *The Chili Pepper*, 200 W Broward Blvd (☎525-5996), playing a mix of techno and rock, or *Cafe Iguana*, 17 S Atlantic Blvd (☎763-7222). If, however, you're seeking the drunken hedonism of Spring Break, you might prefer the regular drink specials and bikini contests at the *Baja Beach Club*, 3200 N Federal Highway (☎561-2432).

Gay Fort Lauderdale

Fort Lauderdale has been one of **gay** America's favorite holiday haunts for years. The scene has quieted down considerably over recent years, but there's still plenty going on. For more information, call the Gay and Lesbian Community Center (☎563-9500); or pick up free copies of *Scoop* and *Hot Spots* magazines, located throughout the area.

Accommodation

Fort Lauderdale has a couple of comfortable **guesthouses** aimed at gay men: *Midnight Sea*, 3016 Alhambra Street (☎463-4827; ④), *The Palms on Las Olas*, 1760 E Las Olas

Boulevard (☎1-800/550-7656; ⑤), and *Royal Palms Resort*, 2901 Terramar Street (☎-564-6444). Of the **mixed** motels, try *La Casa Del Mar* (see "Accommodation" above), or the *Oasis*, 1200 S Miami Road (☎523-3043; ③), whose inland location keeps its prices down.

Bars and clubs

Gay bars and clubs in Fort Lauderdale fall in and out of fashion; read the statewide free weekly newspaper, *TWN*, or the free *CityLink* magazine for the latest in-spots. Usually among the pacesetters are: *Cathode Ray*, 1105 E Las Olas Boulevard (☎462-8611), a video bar that steadily warms up as the evening wears on; *The Copa*, 2800 S Federal Highway (☎463-1507), a long-running dance club that draws all ages; and *The Hideaway*, 2022 NE 18th Street (☎566-8622), a bar hot on the pick-up scene. For **eating** as well as drinking, try *Legends Café*, 1560 NE Fourth Avenue (☎467-2233), a BYO restaurant/bar that fills up quickly (it's best to make a reservation); and *Chardees*, 2209 Wilton Drive (☎563-1800), which has a lively piano bar and a fabulous Sunday brunch.

Inland from Fort Lauderdale

Away from its beach and downtown area, Fort Lauderdale is dismal suburbia all the way to the Everglades. Most people only pass through to reach "Alligator Alley" – the familiar name for **I-75**, which speeds arrow-straight towards Florida's West Coast a hundred miles distant (see "The West Coast").

An exception to the prevailing factories, housing estates and freeway interchanges is **DAVIE**, twenty miles from the coast on Griffin Road (take bus #9 from downtown), surrounded by citrus groves, sugar cane and dairy pastures. Davie's 40,000 inhabitants are besotted with the Old West: jeans, plaid shirts and Stetsons are the order of the day, and there's even a hitching post (for tethering horses) outside the *McDonald's*. Davie's cowboy origins go back to the 1910s settlers who came here to herd cattle and work the fertile black soil. If you're charmed by the attire, stock up in Grifs Western, 6211 SW 45th Street (☎587-9000), a leading purveyor of boots, hats and saddles; otherwise simply turn up for the **rodeo**, held most Saturdays at 8pm at the Davie 5 Star Rodeo, Davie Arena (☎384-7075). A smaller rodeo takes place most Wednesday evenings.

Like its counterparts elsewhere in the state, the **Native Village** at the Seminole Reservation (daily 9am–4pm; $5 for a self-guided tour; $8 for a guided tour; $10 for guided tour with alligator wrestling show; ☎961-4519), a mile south of Davie on Hwy-441, is a depressing place – flogging plastic tomahawks and staging alligator-wrestling shows for tourists. There is some sensitivity to be found, however, in the paintings by Guy LaBree, a local white man who spent time on Seminole reservations during his childhood and whose work is intended to pass legends and history on to younger Seminole generations. More predictably, it's the bingo hall across the road from the village that attracts most white people: laws against high-stakes bingo don't apply to Indian reservations, and you can win $100,000 or more here. You can buy your fill of tax-free cigarettes, too.

A more entertaining attraction on the Seminole Reservation is **Billie Swamp Safari**, (daily 8.30am–6.30pm; ☎1-800/949-6101). Resembling an inflated army jeep, hydroplane buggy tours take visitors cruising high above the Everglades where alligators, egrets and American buffalo are sure to be seen. You can also experience a traditional overnight camp-out in a native-style *chickee* (an open-sided, palm-thatched hut) and listen to ancient Seminole tales.

Twelve miles northeast of Davie at Coconut Creek, **Butterfly World**, 3600 W Sample Road (Mon–Sat 9am–5pm, Sun 1–5pm, last admission 4pm; $10.95; ☎977-4400), stocks, as its name suggests, a massive collection of butterflies. Many are hatched here from larvae – which you'll see in the laboratory – and flap out their short lives around nectar-producing plants inside several aviaries. Exhibits include the colorful Hummingbird

Habitat and the fragrant Rose Garden. Spotting Ecuadorian metalmarks, Malay sulpurs and their equally exotic peers, will keep amateur lepidopterists amused for hours.

North of Fort Lauderdale

With a car, stay on Hwy-A1A **north from Fort Lauderdale**: it's a far superior route to Hwy-1 and passes through several sedate beachside communities. One of these, **LAUDERDALE-BY-THE-SEA**, lies around four miles up the coast, and is one of the best places to don scuba diving gear and explore the reefs.

There are two pleasant **B&Bs** here: *Blue Seas Courtyard*, 4525 El Mar Drive (☎772-3336; ②); and, if you're feeling extravagant, *A Little Inn by the Sea*, 4546 El Mar Drive (☎1-800/492-0311; ⑤), whose luxurious linens and gourmet breakfasts justify the higher price. You'll soon search out the best **eateries**, among them the *Aruba Beach Café*, 1 E Commercial Blvd (☎776-0001), where you can tickle your tastebuds with Caribbean and New World cuisine.

Bus #11 runs this way as far as Atlantic Avenue in **POMPANO BEACH** and drops you off in Pompano Square, two miles on from Lauderdale-By-The-Sea. This is one of the larger beach towns, with a moderately good ocean strip. If you're independently mobile you should press on unless you have a penchant for greyhound harness racing. The Pompano Harness Track, 1800 SW Third St (☎972-2000), is Florida's only such arena and features racing from November to early April.

Three miles further, Hwy-A1A crosses the Hillsboro Inlet, whose 1907 lighthouse gives its name to the posh canal-side community of **LIGHTHOUSE POINT**. There's nothing to detain you here except *Cap's Place*, 2765 NE 28th Court (☎941-0418), which can only be reached from the inland side of the Intercoastal Waterway; follow directions from NE 24th Street. The food – fresh seafood at affordable prices – is one attraction, but the fact that the restaurant doubled as an illegal gambling den during the Prohibition era is another: Franklin D. Roosevelt, Winston Churchill and the Duke of Windsor, remembered by fading photos, are just three of those who have relaxed in the company of owner Cap Knight, a one-time rum-runner whose family presides over the restaurant.

More offbeat history is attached to **DEERFIELD BEACH**, four miles on. As Hwy-A1A twists to the right, you'll catch a glimpse of the triangular **Deerfield Island Park** in the Intercoastal Waterway. During the Thirties, the island was almost purchased by Al Capone, who, along with his gangster colleagues, frequented the *Riverview Restaurant*'s casino, underneath the Hillsboro Boulevard Causeway at 1741 Riverview Road. Capone's property bid was thwarted by his arrest for tax evasion, and the island, untarnished by development, is occupied today by raccoons and armadillos. Its two **walking trails** are reachable only with the free ferry from the *Riverview* on Wednesday and Saturday mornings; call ☎360-1320 for times.

Boca Raton and around

Directly north of Deerfield Beach, Hwy-A1A and Hwy-1 both enter Palm Beach County, the latter becoming the Stars-and-Stripes-decorated **Blue Memorial Highway**: "a tribute to the armed forces that have served the United States of America," confirming the conservatism of the region. You can practically smell the money crossing into the county's southernmost town, **BOCA RATON** (literally "the mouth of the rat"), where smartly-dressed valets park your car at supermarkets, and golf-mad retirees and executives from numerous hi-tech industries – most famously computer giant IBM – hibernate year round. More noticeably, Boca Raton has an abundance of Mediterranean Revival architecture, a style prevalent here since the Twenties and kept alive by strict building codes. The town's new structures have to incorporate arched entranceways, fake bell towers and red-tiled roofs whenever possible. Other than the architecture, best seen in downtown Boca Raton around Hwy-1, the town has some under-recognized beaches and parks.

Downtown Boca Raton

The origins of Boca Raton's Spanish-flavored architecture, which you see all over the **downtown** area, go back to **Addison Mizner**, the "Aladdin of architects" (a title earned because of the almost magical flare in his designs, which were influenced by the Moorish styles of southern Spain), who furnished the fantasies of Palm Beach's fabulously wealthy (see p.168) through the Twenties. Unable to give reign to his megalomaniacal desires elsewhere, Mizner swept into Boca Raton on the tide of the Florida property boom, bought 1600 acres of land and began selling plots of a future community "beyond realness in its ideality." Envisaging gondola-filled canals, a luxury hotel and a great cathedral dedicated to his mother, Mizner's plan was nipped in the bud by the economic crash, and he went back to Palm Beach with his tail between his legs.

The few buildings that Mizner did manage to complete left an indelible mark on Boca Raton. His million-dollar *Cloister Inn* grew into the present **Boca Raton Resort and Club**, a pink palace of marble columns, sculptured fountains and carefully aged wood (the centuries-old effect accomplished by the hobnailed boots of Mizner's workmen) that still claims the 160-foot-wide Camino Real – carrying traffic between Hwy-A1A and downtown Boca Raton – as its private driveway. With $200-a-night rooms, the resort is an upper-crust gathering place best viewed on the **guided tours** (Dec–April Tues 1.30pm; $5; ☎395-6766) run by the Boca Raton Historical Society; call to check times and book ahead.

For its part, the Historical Society resides in a more accessible Mizner work: the dome-topped **Old Town Hall**, 71 N Federal Highway (Mon–Fri 10am–4pm), built in 1927. The society's library, detailing the Mizner times and the rest of Boca Raton's past, is worthy of scrutiny; turn left along the corridor as you enter the building. Nearby, the **old railroad depot**, at the junction of Dixie Highway and SE Eighth Street, is another seminal Mizner-era building but without much allure: the depot (the Count de Hoernle Pavilion) is only opened for wedding receptions and meetings, and a couple of post-Mizner streamlined locomotives stand outside.

The well-heeled of Boca Raton can pay homage to Mizner at **Mizner Park**, off Hwy-1 between Palmetto Park Road and Glades Road, not a park at all, but one of several stylish, open-air shopping malls that have improved downtown Boca Raton in recent years. Decorated by palm trees and waterfalls, and packed with haute couture stores and several affordable places to eat (see "Practicalities," p.164), Mizner Park contains an open amphitheater for concerts, and is also home to the new and grandly titled **International Museum of Cartoon Art**, 201 Plaza Real (Tues–Sat 10am–6pm, Sun noon–6pm; adults $6, students $4; ☎391-2200).

To escape the Mizner influence altogether, go to the beaches (see below) or turn west onto Palmetto Park Road for the **Singing Pines Children Museum**, 498 Crawford Boulevard (Tues–Sat noon–4pm; $1; ☎368-6875). Housed in a driftwood cracker cottage – the simple abode of early Florida farmers (see Contexts) – the museum stocks entertaining remnants from the pioneer days alongside exhibitions aimed at kids. A mile further, the **Museum of Art**, 801 W Palmetto Park Road (Tues, Thurs, Fri 10am–4pm, Sat & Sun noon–4pm, closed Wed; suggested donation $3; ☎392-2500), has benefitted from generous patrons and inspired curatorship to become one of

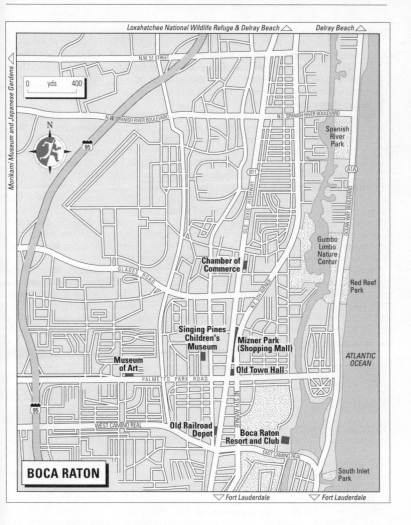

Florida's finest small art museums. Besides its temporary exhibitions on leading Florida artists, the museum has a permanent collection that includes the Mayers Collection of drawings by modern masters – Degas, Matisse, Picasso and Seurat are among those represented – and a formidable trove of African art.

Sports fanatics will revel in the **Sports Immortals Museum**, 6830 N Federal Hwy (Mon–Sat 10am–6pm, open on Sun during the summer only; $5; ☎997-2575), which houses an overwhelming assortment of sporting mementos, from Muhammad Ali's championship belt to the deadly baseball that killed Ray Chapman in 1920.

The area code for Boca Raton and Delray Beach is ☎561.

Beachside Boca Raton

An air of secrecy hangs over Boca Raton's four **beaches**: all are open to the public but, walled-in by tall rows of Australian pine, it is unlikely that you'll stumble across them by accident. They tend, therefore, to be the preserve of select Floridians rather than long-distance travelers (for more detailed information contact the Palm Beach County Parks and Recreation; ☎966-6600).

The southernmost patch, **South Inlet Park**, is the smallest and quietest of the quartet, often deserted in midweek save for a few people fishing along its short jetty. To reach it, watch for a track turning sharply right off Hwy-A1A, just beyond the Boca Raton Inlet. **South Beach Park**, a mile north, is a surfers' favorite, though the actual beach is a fairly tiny area of coarse sand. **Red Reef Park**, a mile further, is far better for sunbathing and swimming – activities that should be combined with a walk around the **Gumbo Limbo Nature Center** (Mon–Sat 9am–4pm, Sun noon–4pm; donations accepted; ☎338-1473), directly across Hwy-A1A, whose wide boardwalks take you through a tropical hardwood hammock and a mangrove forest beside the Intercoastal waterway. Keep your eyes peeled for ospreys, brown pelicans and the occasional manatee lurking in the warm waters. Between May and July you can join the center's night-time tours to watch sea turtles. These can be extremely popular, however, so you'd be well advised to book as far in advance as possible.

Boca Raton's most explorable beachside area, however, is **Spanish River Park** (daily 8am–sunset; cars $8 weekdays, $10 weekends & holidays, pedestrians and cyclists free), a mile north of Red Reef Park on Hwy-A1A. Here you'll find fifty acres of lush vegetation, most of which is only penetrable on secluded trails through shady thickets. Aim for the forty-foot observation tower for a view across the park and much of Boca Raton. The adjacent beach is a slender but serviceable strip, linked to the park by several nifty tunnels beneath Hwy-A1A.

Boca Raton is also a good place from which to visit **Loxahatchee National Wildlife Refuge** (see p.172). It's located about ten miles north of here, just off Hwy-441 and two miles south of Boynton Beach Boulevard/Route 804.

Practicalities

There are no Greyhound **bus terminals** in Boca Raton; the nearest are in Pompano Beach (☎954/946-7067) and Delray Beach, 402 SE Sixth Ave (☎272-6447). The Tri-Rail station is near the Embassy Suites, off Yamato Road and I-95 (☎1-800/TRI-RAIL), and their shuttle buses connect with the town center. The Palm Tran bus #91 (☎233-4BUS) operates from Monday to Saturday and runs from Mizner Park through downtown to the Sandalfoot Shopping Center; $1 one way.

The **Chamber of Commerce**, 1800 N Dixie Highway (Mon–Thurs 8.30am–5pm, Fri 8.30am–4pm; ☎395-4433), supplies the usual info, but don't expect a long list of budget diners and motels – nothing comes cheap in these parts. The cheapest **motels** near the beaches are *Shore Edge*, 425 N Ocean Boulevard (☎395-4491; ④), and *Ocean Lodge*, 531 N Ocean Boulevard (☎395-7772; ④), which also has kitchen units. During the low season you'll save money by sleeping inland at the *Paramount Hotel*, 2901 N Federal Highway (☎395-6850; ② in low season, but ⑤ in high season).

As for a **place to eat**, *Prezzo*, 7820 Glades Rd #175 (☎451-2800), tucked away inside the Arvida Parkway Center, features succulent homemade pastas and wood-oven pizza specialties. For a good-value breakfast, head for *Tom Sawyer's*, 1759 NW Second Avenue (☎368-4634), where you'll get monstrous helpings. At Mizner Park, the *Bavarian Colony Deli*, 435 Plaza Real (☎393-3989), *Mozzarella's American Café*, 351 Plaza Real (☎750-3580), and *Ruby Tuesday's*, 409 Plaza Real (☎392-5705), are all worth trying. *Max's Grille*, 404 Plaza Real (☎368-0080), is slightly upscale with a unique blend of American food that reflects various ethnic delicacies. There's more choice a mile or two further north on the N Federal Highway: standard American fare at the *Boca Diner*, no. 2801 (☎750-6744); barbecued ribs and steaks at *Tom's Place*, no. 7251 (☎997-0920); tasty sea fare at *The Seafood Connection*, no. 6998 (☎997-5562); and traditional English food at the English-run eatery *The Ugly Duckling*, no. 5903 (☎997-5929).

Inland from Boca Raton: The Morikami Museum and Japanese Gardens

South Florida is probably the last place you'd expect to find a formal Japanese garden complete with Shinto shrine, teahouse and a museum recording the history of the Yamoto, but ten miles northwest of Boca Raton at the **Morikami Museum and Japanese Gardens**, 4000 Morikami Park Road (Tues–Sun 10am–5pm; $4.25; ☎495-0233), you'll find all three. These are reminders of a group of Japanese settlers who came here intending to grow tea and rice and farm silkworms, but finished up selling pineapples until a blight killed off the crop in 1908.

Artifacts and photographs within the Morikami's older set of buildings remember the colony. Across the beautifully landscaped grounds, the newer portion of the museum stages themed exhibitions drawn from an enormous archive of Japanese objects and art, and has user-friendly computers ready to impart information about various aspects of Japan and Japanese life. A traditional **teahouse**, assembled here by a Florida-based Japanese craftsman, is periodically used for tea ceremonies.

Also in the area is the chance to see the Everglades from an **airboat**. Head for **Loxahatchee Everglades Tours**, West End Lox Road, due west of Boca Raton off State Road 7/Route 441 (daily 9am–5pm; ☎1-800/683-5873).

North towards Palm Beach

Most of the shoulder-to-shoulder towns **north of Boca Raton** have a nice patch of beach, and a couple are putting their modest histories on display, but none should be considered lengthy stops. If you're reliant on public transport, you can take the local CoTran **bus #1S**, which runs every hour through towns between Boca Raton and West Palm Beach.

Delray Beach

Five miles north of Boca Raton, **DELRAY BEACH** justifies a half-day visit: its powdery-sanded municipal **beach**, at the foot of Atlantic Avenue, is rightly popular, and is one of the few in Florida to afford a view of the Gulf Stream – a cobalt blue streak about five miles offshore.

Nipping a short way **inland** along Atlantic Avenue, you'll find more to pass the time. On the corner with Swinton Avenue, an imposing schoolhouse dating from 1913 forms part of **Old School Square** (Tues–Sat 11am–4pm, Sun 1–4pm; free; ☎243-7922), a group of buildings restored and converted into a cultural center. The spacious ground floor of the former school hosts temporary art exhibitions, though a peek upstairs reveals several one-time classrooms still furnished with desks and black-painted walls used to avoid the exorbitant cost of slate blackboards. Within sight, just across NE First Street, the **Cason Cottage** (Tues–Fri 10am–3pm; free), erected in 1920 for Dr John Cason, member of an illustrious local family, warrants a look for its simple woodframe design based on pioneer-era Florida architecture.

Delray Beach makes a sensible **lunch** stop. At the municipal beach, *Boston's on the Beach*, 40 S Ocean Boulevard (☎278-3364), serves incredibly fresh seafood. Among cheap beachside **accommodation**, the *Bermuda Inn*, 64 S Ocean Boulevard (☎276-5288; ⑤), and *Wright By the Sea*, 1901 S Ocean Boulevard (☎278-3355; ⑤–⑧) are your best bets.

Lake Worth

If you're pressing on by car, a more inspiring option than Hwy-1 is Hwy-A1A, which charts a picturesque course along twenty-odd miles of slender barrier islands, ocean views on one side and the Intercoastal waterway – plied by luxury yachts and lined with opulent homes – on the other. Whichever route you take, make a quick stop at **LAKE WORTH** (not to be confused with the actual lake of the same name that divides Palm Beach from West Palm Beach), ten miles north of Delray Beach, for the entertaining clutter of the **Historical Museum**, in the Utilities Department Buildings at 414 Lake Avenue (Tues–Fri 10am–2pm; free). Plant-filled bathtubs, artistically arranged rusting tools and picks aplenty from bygone decades are all infectiously doted over by the museum's curator.

Otherwise, there's nothing to hinder progress to Palm Beach (with Hwy-A1A) or West Palm Beach (with Hwy-1) just a few miles north.

Palm Beach

A small island town of palatial homes, pampered gardens and streets so clean you could eat your dinner off them, **PALM BEACH** has been synonymous for nearly a century with the kind of lifestyle only limitless loot can buy. A bastion of conspicuous wealth, whose pomposity – banning clothes lines, for example – knows no bounds, Palm Beach is, for all its faults, irrefutably unique.

The nation's upper crust began wintering here in the 1890s, after Standard Oil magnate Henry Flagler brought his East Coast railway south from St Augustine and built two luxury hotels on this then-secluded, palm-filled island. Throughout the Twenties, Addison Mizner began a vogue for Mediterranean architecture, covering the place with arcades, courtyards and plazas – and the first million-dollar homes. Since then, corporate tycoons, sports aces, jet-setting aristocrats, rock stars and CIA directors have flocked here, eager to become part of the Palm Beach elite and enjoy its aloofness from mainland – and mainstream – life.

Summer is very quiet and easily the least costly time to stay here. The pace hots up between November and May, with the winter months a whirl of elegant balls, fund-raising dinners and charity galas – local residents give more to tax-deductible causes in a year than most people earn in a lifetime. Winter also brings the polo season – watching a chukka or two is the one time Palm Beach denizens show themselves in the less particular environs of West Palm Beach (on the mainland), where the games are held.

Even by walking – much the best way to view the moneyed isle – you'll get the measure of Palm Beach in a day. Either drive in along Hwy-A1A from the south, or use one of the two bridges over Lake Worth from West Palm Beach, the nearest bus and train stop.

The waters off the beach also merit investigation; artificial reefs were created here in the 1960s to protect the coastline by preventing erosion of the natural reef. These are now a spectacular draw for divers; contact the Palm Beach County Convention and Visitors Bureau (see p.171) for further information.

Approaching Palm Beach: the south of the island

Near-neighbors like to think otherwise, but Palm Beach as a byword for wealth, extravagance and exclusivity begins about five miles north of the town of Lake Worth on Hwy-A1A, by the junction with Southern Boulevard (Hwy-98). Here, the **Palm Beach Bath and Tennis Club** is the first of the community's strictly members-only watering holes; its arched windows give sweeping ocean views – passers-by see just the

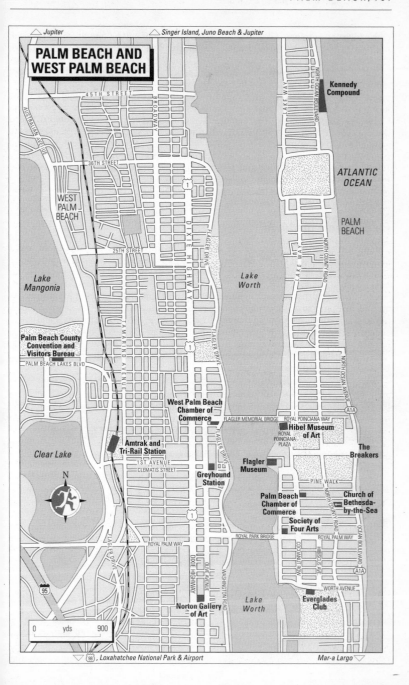

△ Jupiter   △ Singer Island, Juno Beach & Jupiter

PALM BEACH AND WEST PALM BEACH

Kennedy Compound

45TH STREET

BROADWAY

36TH STREET

WEST PALM BEACH

AUSTRALIAN AVE

ATLANTIC OCEAN

PALM BEACH

DIXIE HIGHWAY

FLAGLER DRIVE

LAKE WAY

NORTH OCEAN BOULEVARD

25TH STREET

Lake Mangonia

Lake Worth

TAMARIND AVENUE

NORTH COUNTY ROAD

Palm Beach County Convention and Visitors Bureau

PALM BEACH LAKES BLVD

West Palm Beach Chamber of Commerce

FLAGLER MEMORIAL BRIDGE   ROYAL POINCIANA WAY

A1A

Hibel Museum of Art

ROYAL POINCIANA PLAZA

The Breakers

Clear Lake

Amtrak and Tri-Rail Station

1ST AVENUE
CLEMATIS STREET

Greyhound Station

FLAGLER DRIVE

Flagler Museum

PINE WALK

Palm Beach Chamber of Commerce

Church of Bethesda-by-the-Sea

NORTH COUNTY ROAD

OCEAN BOULEVARD

N

Society of Four Arts

ROYAL PARK BRIDGE

ROYAL PALM WAY

DIXIE HIGHWAY

OLIVE AVENUE

WASHINGTON ROAD

COCOANUT ROW

HIBISCUS AVE

A1A

95

Lake Worth

WORTH AVENUE

Norton Gallery of Art

Everglades Club

FLAGLER DRIVE

| 0 | yds | 900 |

▽ 98, Loxahatchee National Park & Airport   Mar-a-Largo ▽

club's guarded entrance. Likewise, for the next couple of miles along this busy two-lane highway (a bad place to cycle or walk, or even stop your car) the high-class homes are shielded from prying eyes by walls of hedges.

You should have no trouble, however, spotting the red-roofed Italianate tower topping **Mar-a-Largo**. Finished in 1926, this was the $8-million winter abode of breakfast cereal heiress Marjorie Merriweather-Post, queen of Palm Beach high society for nearly forty years. On Merriweather-Post's death in 1973, Mar-a-Largo's 118 rooms and eighteen-acre grounds were bequeathed to the US government – who couldn't afford the upkeep. Instead, "Florida's most sybaritic private residence" was sold to property tycoon Donald Trump.

Further on, close to the Via La Selva turning, a sprawling property once owned by John Lennon and Yoko Ono can just be glimpsed. Hardly a place to enhance the ex-Beatle's anti-establishment credentials, it earlier belonged to turn-of-the-century multi-millionaire Cornelius Vanderbilt. Half a mile north, Hwy-A1A becomes Ocean Boulevard as it enters the town of Palm Beach.

Palm Beach: the town

The main residential section of Palm Beach – **the town** – is where you should spend most of your time, and **Worth Avenue**, cruised by classic cars and filled with designer stores and high-class art galleries, is a good place to start your stroll, even if you can only afford to window shop.

Other than expense-account acquisition, the most appealing aspect of the street is its architecture: stucco walls, crafted Romanesque facades, and narrow passageways leading to small courtyards where miniature bridges cross non-existent canals and spiral staircases climb to higher levels. On the top floor of one of the courtyard buildings, Via Mizner, situated on the corner with Hibiscus Avenue, sits the former *pied-a-terre* of the man responsible for the Mediterranean look replicated all over Palm Beach – the flamboyant architect **Addison Mizner**.

After heading up to Worth Avenue's western end to gawk at the vessels moored on Lake Worth – rows of ocean-going yachts with more living space than most people's homes – you should explore the rest of the town along Cocoanut Row or County Road.

PALM BEACH'S ARCHITECT: ADDISON MIZNER

A former miner and prizefighter, **Addison Mizner** was an unemployed architect when he arrived in Palm Beach in 1918 to recuperate following the recurrence of a childhood leg injury. Inspired by the medieval buildings he'd seen around the Mediterranean, Mizner, financed by the heir to the Singer sewing machine fortune, built the **Everglades Club**, at 356 Worth Avenue. Described by Mizner as "a little bit of Seville and the Alhambra, a dash of Madeira and Algiers," the Everglades Club was the first public building in Florida in the Mediterranean Revival style, and fast became the island's most prestigious social club.

The success of the club, and the house he subsequently built for society bigwig Eva Stotesbury, won Mizner commissions all over Palm Beach as the wintering wealthy decided to swap suites at one of Henry Flagler's hotels for a "million-dollar cottage" of their own.

Brilliant and unorthodox, Mizner's loggias and U-shaped interiors made the most of Florida's pleasant winter temperatures, while his twisting staircases to nowhere became legendary. Pursuing a medieval look, Mizner used untrained workmen to lay roof tiles crookedly, sprayed condensed milk onto walls to create an impression of centuries-old grime, and fired shotgun pellets into wood to imitate worm holes. By the mid-Twenties, Mizner had created the Palm Beach Style – which Florida architecture buff Hap Hattan called "the Old World for the new rich." Mizner later fashioned much of Boca Raton (see p.161).

Along Cocoanut Row

Four blocks north from its junction with Worth Avenue, **Cocoanut Row** crosses Royal Palm Way close to the stuccoed buildings of the **Society of the Four Arts** (Mon–Sat 10am–5pm, Sun 2–5pm; suggested donation $3; ☎655-7227). Between early December and mid-April this holds art shows and lectures of an impressive standard, and its **library** (May–Oct Mon–Fri 10am–5pm; Nov–April Mon–Fri 10am–5pm, Sat 9am–1pm) is worth a browse.

Half a mile further along Cocoanut Row you'll notice the white Doric columns fronting **Whitehall**, also known as the Henry Flagler Museum (Tues–Sat 10am–5pm, Sun noon–5pm; last tour leaves between 3.15pm and 3.30pm; $7; ☎655-2833). The most overtly ostentatious home on the island, Whitehall was a $4-million wedding present from Henry Flagler to his third wife, Mary Lily Kenan, whom he married (after controversially persuading the Florida legislature to amend its divorce laws) in 1901. Like many of Florida's first luxury homes, Whitehall's interior design was created by pillaging the great buildings of Europe: among the 73 rooms are an Italian library, a French salon, a Swiss billiard room, a hallway modeled on the Vatican's St Peter's and a Louis XV ballroom. All are richly stuffed with ornamentation but – other than mutual decadence – lack any esthetic cohesion. Flagler was in his seventies when Whitehall was built, 37 years older than his bride and not enamoured of the banquets and balls she continually hosted. He often sloped off to bed using a concealed stairway, perhaps to ponder plans to extend his railway to Key West – a display on the project fills his former office. From the 110-foot hallway, informative but not compulsory 45-minute **free guided tours** depart continuously and will leave you giddy with the tales – and the sights – of the earliest Palm Beach excesses. Don't miss the authentic railroad car, outside the exit to the gift shop, and the spectacular views of West Palm Beach from Flagler's enormous backyard.

Whitehall was built beside Flagler's first Palm Beach resort, the *Royal Poinciana Hotel*: a six-story, Colonial-style structure of 2000 rooms, which became the world's largest wooden building on completion in 1894. Other than a small plaque marking the spot, only the remains of a grand ballroom are left of the hotel, whose hundred-acre grounds spread to what's now Royal Poinciana Way. Here, on the corner with Cocoanut Row, you'll find Royal Poinciana Plaza, a soulless grouping of estate agents' and art dealers' offices, and also the **Hibel Museum of Art**, 150 Royal Poinciana Plaza (Tues–Sat 10am–5pm, Sun 1–5pm; Nov–Apr open Mon 10am–5pm; free; ☎833-6870). Forget Warhol and Rothko, the most commercially successful artist in the US is **Edna Hibel**, a septuagenarian resident of Singer Island (just north of Palm Beach, see p.173), whose works fill this deep-carpeted gallery. Inspired by "love," Hibel has been churning out coy, sentimental portraits, usually of serene Asian and Mexican women, since the late Thirties, often working seven days a week to meet demand. Pay a visit, though, if only to admire the unflappable devotion of the guides, and to figure out why Hibel originals change hands for $50,000.

Along County Road

In terms of things to see, **County Road** is the poor relation of Cocoanut Row – to which it runs parallel – but is still worth a stroll. Along it, two blocks north of Worth Avenue, Mizner's Mediterranean Revival themes are displayed in Palm Beach's very tidy local administration offices and bank buildings. By contrast, the 1926 **Church of Bethesda-by-the-Sea**, a fifteen-minute walk further, is a handsome imitation-Gothic pile replacing the island's first church (see "The North of the Island"): the large stained-glass windows depict Christianity around the world, but ignore them and walk instead through the echoing cloisters to the **Cluett Memorial Gardens** (daily 9am–5pm; free), a peaceful spot in which to take a stone pew and tuck into a picnic lunch.

The **area code** for Palm Beach is ☎561.

A little further north, County Road is straddled by the golf course of **The Breakers** hotel, erected in 1926 and the last of Palm Beach's swanky resorts. Inside, the lobby is filled with tapestries, chandeliers, huge fireplaces and painted ceilings; at 3pm on Wednesdays there's a **free guided tour** of the premises.

The north of the island

The limited points of interest beyond Royal Poinciana Way are best viewed from the three-mile **Lake Trail**, a bicycle and pedestrian path skirting the edge of Lake Worth, almost to the northern limit of the island. A bicycle is the ideal mode of transport here: rent one from Palm Beach Bicycle Trail Shop, 223 Sunrise Avenue (☎659-4583), for $18 a half day.

Most locals use the trail as a jogging strip, and certainly there's little other than exercise and fine views across the lake to make it worthwhile. Keep an eye out, though, for "Duck's Nest," the oldest remaining home in Palm Beach, built in 1891, and the original **Church of Bethesda-by-the-Sea**, dating from 1889. Serving a congregation of early homesteaders across a 125-mile stretch of coast, all of whom had to get here by boat, the shingled church is now a private house, but easily spotted by the clockface hanging from its short tower.

The lake trail expires a few minutes' pedal south of the Lake Worth Inlet, a narrow cut separating Palm Beach from the high-rise-dominated Singer Island. To get to the inlet – for a sight of the neighboring island and a modest feeling of achievement – weave on through the short residential streets.

For variation, cycle back to central Palm Beach along Ocean Drive (take care as there's no marked cycle path), which passes the two-acre former **Kennedy Compound**, at 1095 N Ocean Boulevard, bought by Joe Kennedy – father of John, Robert and Edward – in 1933. The Kennedys never fully integrated into ultra-conservative Palm Beach life; feeling unwelcome at the Everglades Club, Joe upset the establishment by joining the rival Palm Beach Country Club – and it's said that few Palm Beach tears were shed in 1963 when John (then President) was assassinated. It was on this estate that the most recent scandal to rock Palm Beach occurred: the arrest in April 1991 of William Kennedy Smith, nephew of Senator Edward Kennedy, on charges of sexual battery (Florida's legal term for rape), of which he was acquitted.

Practicalities

In a town that often fights shy of tourists, the **Chamber of Commerce**, 45 Cocoanut Row (Mon–Fri 9am–4.30pm in winter, 10am–4.30pm in summer; ☎655-3282) is a welcome provider of free maps and reliable **information**.

You'll need plenty of money to **stay** in Palm Beach: comfort and elegance are the key words, and prices can vary so greatly depending on the time of year that we've noted both high and low season prices below. *Palm Beach Historic Inn*, 365 S County Road (☎832-4009; ④–⑥), is a bed-and-breakfast spot with the best rates in town, but you'll need to book early. Otherwise, to save money come between May and December, when the lowest prices on the island are found at *The Chesterfield*, 363 Cocoanut Row (☎1-800/CHESTR-1; ④–⑧); the *Colony*, 155 Hammon Avenue (☎1-800/521-5525; ⑤–⑧); the *Heart of Palm Beach*, 160 Royal Palm Way (☎1-800/523-5377; ⑥–⑧); and *The Plaza Inn*, 215 Brazilian Avenue (☎1-800/233-2632; ④–⑥). Obviously, it's far cheaper to stay outside Palm Beach and visit by day – easily done from West Palm Beach even without a car; see below.

Encouragingly, you can **eat** relatively cheaply. *TooJay's*, 312 Royal Poinciana Plaza (☎659-7232), is a top-notch bakery and deli open from breakfast onwards, where you can choose from a wide selection of food, including scrumptious omelets for less than $6; *Green's Pharmacy*, 151 N County Road (☎832-4443), has a steady supply of diner fare for breakfast and lunch; and *Hamburger Heaven*, 314 S County Road (☎655-5277), dispenses delicious ground-beef burgers. More expensive options include *Testa's*, 221 Royal Poinciana Way (☎832-0992), which serves exquisite seafood and pasta at between $10 and $15 a throw; and *Charley's Crab*, 456 S Ocean Boulevard (☎659-1500), overlooking the dunes, serves up a mean shrimp cocktail among other scrumptious seafood. If money is no object (you'll spend at least $50 a head) and you're dressed to kill, make for the super-elegant French restaurant *Café L'Europe*, 331 S County Road (☎655-4020). Alternatively, the Publix supermarket at 265 Sunset Avenue is a useful port of call if the above are closed or you just want picnic fare.

Thrift stores

Amazingly high-class threads, some of it discarded after only a single use, turn up in Palm Beach's **thrift stores**, though the prices are above normal thrift-store levels. Worth perusing are The Church Mouse, 374 S County Road (☎659-2154; open Oct–May only); Goodwill Embassy Boutique, 210 Sunset Avenue (☎832-8199); Thrift Inc, 231 S County Road (☎655-0520; closed Sept), Hab Center Boutique & Consignment, 212 Sunset Avenue (☎655-7825), or Deja Vu, 219 Royal Poinciana Way (☎833-6624). Be warned though that many shops in Palm Beach close for the summer or operate on reduced hours – call before you go.

West Palm Beach and around

Founded to house the workforce of Flagler's Palm Beach resorts, **WEST PALM BEACH** has long been in the shadow of its glamorous neighbor across the lake. Only during the last two decades has the town gained some life of its own, with smart new office buildings, a scenic lakeside footpath – and less seemly industrial growth sprouting up on its western edge. Above all, West Palm Beach holds the promise of accommodation and food at a lower price than in Palm Beach, and is the closest you'll get to the island using public transport – CoTran buses from Boca Raton and Greyhound services stop here (details below), leaving a few minutes' walk to Palm Beach over one of the Lake Worth bridges.

Information, public transport and accommodation

The **Chamber of Commerce**, 401 N Flagler Drive, at the corner of Fourth Street (Mon–Fri 8.30am–5pm; ☎833-3711), has stacks of free leaflets, and can answer questions on the whole Palm Beach county area. The **Tourist Information Center** on Indiantown Road (directly between the I-95 and Florida Turnpike interchange) is difficult to get to without a car, but you'll get a more comprehensive selection of literature and a chance to glimpse their resident alligator in the backyard swamp. The West Palm Beach **train** (☎1-800/872-7245), Tri-Rail (☎1-800/TRI RAIL), and Greyhound (☎833-8534) stations are all located at 201 S Tamarind Avenue, and linked by regular shuttle buses to the downtown area. Most local CoTran **bus** (☎233-1111) routes converge at Quadrille Road.

Most budget chain **motel** prices in West Palm Beach are inflated. The best deals are to be found at *Queens Lodge*, 3712 Broadway (☎842-1108; ②); *Parkview Motor Lodge*, 4710 S Dixie Highway (☎1-800/523-8978; ④); *Mt Vernon Motor Lodge*, 310 Belvedere Road (☎1-800/545-1520; ②); or *Knights Inn*, 2200 45th Street (☎1-800/843-5644; ④). For a real treat that doesn't bust your wallet try the charming *Hibiscus House*, 501 30th

Street, just off Flagler Street (☎863-5633; ④). Loaded with kitsch alongside beautiful antiques – including a baby grand piano – it has balconies in practically every room and a delightful pool where homemade breakfasts are served. The owner is a virtual encyclopedia of Palm Beach, and is more than happy to impart his knowledge.

Downtown West Palm Beach

Other than basic needs, one of the few reasons to linger here is the classy collections of the **Norton Museum of Art**, 1451 S Olive Avenue (Tues–Sat 10am–5pm, Sun 1–5pm; $5 donation suggested; ☎832-5194), a mile south of the downtown area. Together with some distinctive European paintings and drawings by Gauguin, Klee, Picasso and others, the gallery boasts a solid grouping of twentieth-century American works: Mark Tobey's study of stifling urban motion, *The Street*, and Stuart Davis' *New York Mural* impress most. Among a sparkling roomful of Far Eastern pieces are seventh-century sculpted Buddhas, absorbingly complex amber carvings and a collection of 1500-500 BC tomb jades.

In the late Fifties the boom of shopping malls in Palm Beach practically shut down the small boutiques and cafés on **Clematis Street**, turning it into another bland area of downtown West Palm Beach. Today, thanks to a major renovation project, Clematis Street is once again home to a diverse mix of restaurants, shops, galleries and an exciting schedule of cultural activities. Daytime lunch concerts, the Thursday evening "Clematis by Night" events and a continual parade of food and arts-and-crafts vendors has brought the area to life. The second Tuesday of the month heralds "Clematis Backstage," which can range from concerts to holiday celebrations in the spacious outdoor Meyer Amphitheater, and on Saturday mornings the street turns green with a farmer's market. Colorfully landscaped, Clematis Street stretches from the Intercoastal waterway to the heart of downtown, culminating with the interactive **fountain** in Centennial Square, which shoots jets of water into the air amidst dripping and squealing adults and children.

Eating, drinking and nightlife

The majority of good places to **eat** congregate on Clematis Street. Try *Bimini Bay Café*, at no.104 (☎833-9554), a casual, tropically decorated restaurant with spectacular views of the Intercoastal; *My Martini Grille*, at no.225 (☎832-8333), serves American grill specialties and a variety of designer martinis; *Daddy O's*, at no.313 (☎833-1444), is the only venue to feature duelling rock-n-roll pianos, whose musicians play any request, from Rod Stewart to the *Barney* theme song; *Dax*, at no.300 (☎833-0449), cools you down with frozen cocktails and its second-floor, deckside view; and dinner at *Zazu City Grille*, at no.313 (☎832-1919), generally leads to dancing in the industrial-themed bar. For something on the lighter side, go to *Robinson's Pastry Shop*, at no.215 (☎833-4259), which sells wonderful freshly-baked snacks and sandwiches during the day, or try the *Respectable Street Café*, at no.518 (☎832-9999) – also good for an evening **drink** and **live music**.

Away from Clematis Street, try *Margarita Y Amigas*, 2030 Palm Beach Lakes Boulevard (☎684-7788), for spicy Mexican food; and for food with a side order of laughs, visit *The Comedy Corner*, 2000 S Dixie Highway (☎833-1812; closed June 28–July 6), which has a bar and stand-up comics ($10 admission).

Inland from West Palm Beach

If you have a car, West Palm Beach makes a good access point for the **Loxahatchee National Wildlife Refuge**, 10119 Lee Road in Boynton Beach (daily 6am–7.30pm; cars $3.25, pedestrians and cyclists $1; visitor center open Wed–Sun; ☎734-8303). Travel west along Hwy-80 for about five miles, then turn south along Hwy-441, and the well-signposted main entrance is twelve miles ahead. The 200 square miles of sawgrass marshes – the northerly extension of the Everglades (see p.322) – are only marginally penetrable on two easy **walking trails** from the **visitor center**. One meanders through a cypress hammock, and the other is a boardwalk that leads over the marshes to an observation tower. On either, you'll probably see a few snakes and alligators and get a firm impression of what undeveloped inland Florida is all about – and how incredibly flat it is. It's also possible to go on guided canoe trails, airboat rides, bird walks and "night prowls." Call ☎732-3684 for more information.

African and Asian wildlife is the star attraction of **Lion Country Safari** (daily 9.30am–5.30pm; last vehicles admitted 4.30pm; $14.95; ☎793-1084), on Southern Boulevard W (18 miles west of I-95 and before the junction of Hwy-98 and 441). Lions, elephants, giraffes, chimpanzees, zebras and ostriches are among the creatures roaming a 500-acre plot where human visitors are confined to their cars. It's awkward to reach and expensive to visit, but if you can't leave Florida without photographing a flamingo, Lion Country Safari could well be for you.

Venturing **further inland** to the Lake Okeechobee area (described in "Central Florida"), Hwy-80 from West Palm Beach runs the forty miles to the lakeside town of Belle Glade, a route traversed by CoTran bus #10 – but not a good place to be without independent transport.

THE TREASURE COAST

West Palm Beach marks the northern limit of Miami's hinterland and the end of the Southeast Coast's heavily touristed sections. Aside from some small and uninspiring towns, the next eighty miles – dubbed the **Treasure Coast** simply to distinguish it from the Gold Coast – missed out entirely on the expansion seen to the south and to the north, leaving wide open spaces and some magnificent swathes of quiet beach that attract Florida's nature lovers and a small band of well-informed tan-seekers.

Singer Island and Juno Beach

North out of West Palm Beach, Hwy-A1A swings back to the coast at **SINGER ISLAND**, a familiar name to anyone who's read Charles Willeford's novel *Sideswipe*: the author's Miami homicide cop, Hoke Moseley, holes up here for a few weeks before boredom drives him back south. The beaches are perfectly adequate but the place lacks life and is predominantly residential, with little budget-range accommodation, apart from *The Sands Hotel Resort*, 2401 Beach Court (☎842-2602; ③). Nearby, on Hwy-A1A, is the **John D. MacArthur Beach State Park** (daily 8am–sunset; visitor center open Wed–Sun 9am–5pm; cars $3.25, pedestrians and cyclists $1; ☎624-6950), one of the few beach state parks with worthwhile nature trails and swimming areas.

The next few miles are mostly golf courses and planned retirement communities, but one good stop is **JUNO BEACH**, where Hwy-A1A follows a high coastal bluff and, with luck, you'll find one of the unmarked paths down to the uncrowded sands.

Alternatively, keep going until you reach the beachside **Loggerhead Park**, also the site of the **Marine Life Center** (Tues–Sat 10am–3pm; free), intended for kids but allowing adults to brush up on their knowledge of marine life in general and sea turtles in particular – there's a turtle hatchery here and displays on their life cycles. The only time turtles give up the security of the ocean is between June and July, when they steal ashore to lay eggs under cover of darkness. This is one of several places along the Treasure Coast where expeditions are led to watch them; get the details at the museum or at ☎627-8280. Reservations are essential and taken from May on.

Jupiter and Jupiter Island

Splitting into several anodyne districts around the wide mouth of the Tequesta River, **JUPITER**, about six miles north of Juno Beach, was a rum-runners' haven during the time of Prohibition; these days it's better known as the home town of Florida's favorite son, actor Burt Reynolds. Most symbols of "Burt-ness" have gone under, such as his restaurant Backstage and the Jupiter Theater, and rumor has it that he's trying to get rid of his ranch. However, if anyone is on a serious Burt pilgrimage, take a walk through Burt Reynolds Park, beside Hwy-1 near the town center, to get to the **Florida History Center and Museum**, 805 N Hwy 1 (Tues–Fri 10am–4pm, Sat & Sun 1–4pm; $4; ☎747-6639), which describes pioneer life on and around the Tequesta River long before Burt's time. To gain more insight into how the pioneers lived, you can walk through an original home located on the grounds (Wed & Sun 1pm–4pm; $2). And, if you happen to be here on Oct 8, join in the rib-eatin', chilli-cookin', beer-swillin', foot-stompin' country dance and hoe-down at the **Burt Reynolds Ranch**, two miles south of town at 16133 Jupiter Farms Road (☎747-5390).

The only other thing in Jupiter to merit consideration is the redbrick **lighthouse** (☎747-8380), a nineteenth-century beacon on the north bank of the Jupiter inlet, with a small **museum** in the Jupiter Lighthouse Park (Sun–Wed 10am–4pm, $5; free Sun afternoons; last tour 3.15pm; ☎746-3101). The lighthouse can be seen from Beach Road, the route Hwy-A1A takes back to the coast after looping through the town. This route skirts the **Jupiter Inlet Colony** – a rich person's billet whose roads are guarded by photo-electric beams, enabling police to check any suspicious traffic cruising the dead-end streets – before heading north along Jupiter Island. If you're feeling peckish, a great, albeit pricey, place (order from the appetizer menu – portions are just as big) for **seafood** is *Charley's Crab*, 1000 N Hwy-1 (☎744-4710), back at the Jupiter inlet.

Jupiter Island

Two miles into **Jupiter Island** on Hwy-A1A, pull up at the **Blowing Rocks Preserve** (daily 9am–5pm; suggested donation $3), where a limestone outcrop covers much of the beach and powerful incoming tides are known to drive through the rocks' hollows, emerging as gusts of spray further on. At low tide, it's sometimes possible to walk around the outcrop and peer into the rock's sea-drilled cavities. A new education center (for all ages) includes an exhibit center, butterfly garden and boardwalk.

Seven miles further north, the shell-strewn Hobe Sound Beach marks the edge of **Hobe Sound National Wildlife Refuge**, which occupies the remainder of the island. Having achieved spectacular success as a nesting ground for sea turtles during the summer (turtle walks available in June and July; call ☎546-2067), the refuge is also rich in birdsong, with tweeting scrub jays among its tuneful inhabitants. To find out more about the flora and fauna, visit the small **interpretive center** (Mon–Fri 9–11am & 1–3pm; ☎546-2067), on the mainland where Hwy-A1A meets Hwy-1.

The northern end of Jupiter Island comprises **St Lucie Inlet State Preserve** (daily 8am–sunset; cars $3.25, pedestrians and cyclists $1; ☎744-7603), whose 928 acres include mangrove-lined creeks and over two miles of beach. It's occasionally possible to see manatees feeding in the grass beds north of the dock, and the boardwalk is interesting primarily for the skunk-like aroma emitted by the aptly named Shite-Stopper, a tropical tree.

Inland: the Jonathan Dickinson State Park

Two miles south of the Hobe Sound interpretive center on Hwy-1, the **Jonathan Dickinson State Park** (daily 8am–sunset; cars $3.25, pedestrians and cyclists $1; ☎546-2771) preserves a natural landscape quite different from what you'll see at the coast. Step up to the observation platform atop **Hobe Mountain**, an 86-foot-high sand dune, and survey the pines, palmetto (a stumpy, tropical palm fan) flatlands and the mangrove-flanked course of the winding Loxahatchee River. The intrepid can obtain hiking maps from the entrance office and set off along the nine-mile **Kitchen Creek trail**, which starts from the park's entrance and finishes in a cypress hammock at some basic campgrounds; beware that campground space must be booked in advance (☎546-2771). Cabins, at $50 a night, are also available; phone ahead at ☎1-800/746-1466.

Anyone less adventurous should rent a canoe from the people who rent out the cabins (see above) and paddle along the Loxahatchee River – don't be put off by the preponderance of alligators – to the **Trapper Nelson interpretive center**, named after a Quaker washed ashore near here in 1697. Another way to get there is by taking the two-hour cruise aboard the **Loxahatchee Queen II** (four daily Wed–Sun, 9am–3pm; $10; reservations ☎746-1466).

Stuart and Hutchinson Island

Another long barrier island lies immediately north of Jupiter Island. To reach it (with either Hwy-1 or Hwy-A1A), you'll first pass through **STUART**, a neat and tidy, but rather boring, town on the south bank of the St Lucie River. Stuart has a number of century-old wooden buildings proudly preserved on and around Flagler Avenue – pick up a **free walking guide** from the **Chamber of Commerce**, 1650 S Kanner Highway (Mon–Fri 9am–5pm; ☎287-1088) – and a Greyhound station at 757 SE Monterey Road (☎287-7777), but not much else to keep you engaged. There is a **bike rental** outlet, however, Pedal Power, 1211 SE Port St Lucie Boulevard (☎335-1310), which you'll need (if you don't have a car) to make the four-mile trip along Hwy-A1A, over the Intercoastal waterway and to Hutchinson Island (though the cycle path only begins at Jensen Beach – see below). For a bite to **eat** in downtown Stuart, try the *Riverwalk Café*, 201 SW St Lucie Avenue (☎221-1511) or *The Flagler Grill*, 47 SW Flagler Avenue (☎221-9517; open in summer only on Thur, Fri and Sat).

Hutchinson Island

Largely hidden behind thickly grouped Australian pines, several beautiful beaches line the twenty-mile-long **Hutchinson Island**, located to the east of Stuart along Hwy A1A (also known as Ocean Blvd). Keep your eyes peeled for the public access points. It would be hard, however, to miss **Stuart Beach**: facing Hwy-A1A it is a low-key stretch of brown sand where tourists are heavily outnumbered by locals – a fine venue for a few hours of ray absorption.

Close by, at 825 NE Ocean Boulevard, the **Elliott Museum** (daily 11am–4pm; $4; ☎225-1961) exhibits a sizeable hotchpotch of mechanical objects and ornaments, few of which seem to have much to do with inventor Sterling Elliott, whom the place is intended to commemorate. A talented inventor active during the 1870s, Elliott's creations displayed here include an automatic knot-tier and the first addressing machine, while his quadricycle – a four-wheeled bicycle – solved many of the technical problems that hindered the development of the car. It's hard, therefore, to fathom why much of the museum is given over to reconstructed turn-of-the-century shops, Victorian fashion accessories and a hangar full of vintage cars. A new addition to this mish-mash is autographed memorabilia of members of the Baseball Hall of Fame.

A mile south at 301 SE MacArthur Boulevard, **Gilbert's Bar House of Refuge** (Tues–Sun 11am–4pm; $2; ☎225-1875) is a better stop: a convincingly restored refuge for wrecked sailors that was one of five erected along Florida's east coast during the 1870s. Furnished in spartan Victorian style, the rooms of the refuge are best understood with the **free guided tour** (starting when you're ready, every day except

The area code for the parts of the Treasure Coast mentioned in this chapter is ☎561.

Saturday). There's more evidence of the refuge's importance in the entrance area – lifeboat equipment, ship's logs and a modern weather station – along with reminders of the building's more recent function as a sea turtle hatchery.

Pushing on, roughly halfway along the island, **JENSEN BEACH** has the only road to the mainland between Stuart and Fort Pierce, as well as a small but pleasant beach. Move on if you feel like eating because the pickings are pretty slim here. For accommodation try the *Dolphin Motor Lodge*, 2211 NE Dixie Highway (☎334-1313; ③). Jensen Beach also marks the start of a **cycle path**, which continues – passing one of Florida's two nuclear power stations (which has a visitor center with interactive exhibits; for opening times call ☎468-4111 or 466-1600; free admission) – to the Fort Pierce Inlet, which divides Hutchinson Island in two. To reach the northern half (known as North Hutchinson Island), you'll need to pass through the area's biggest town, Fort Pierce.

Fort Pierce

A number of rustic motels, bars and restaurants grouped along Hwy-A1A beside a more than adequate beach make the first taste of **FORT PIERCE** a favorable one. The bulk of the town (looped through by Hwy-A1A) lies two miles away across the Intercoastal waterway, where tourism plays second fiddle to processing and transporting the produce of Florida's citrus farms. The convivial coastal section makes an amenable base for island exploration, but the mainland town has only a few features likely to detain you for long. Scuba diving off the coast is, however, an entirely different prospect, giving you a chance to explore reefs and wrecks dating back to Spanish galleons; see "Practicalities," p.178 for details.

The Historical Museum

Beside Hwy-A1A, close to the Intercoastal waterway bridge at 414 Seaway Drive, the **St Lucie County Historical Museum** (Tues–Sat 10am–4pm, Sun noon–4pm; $2; ☎462-1795) keeps a cogent assembly of relics. Among them are a full-sized Seminole Indian *chickee* (a hand-carved canoe) and a solid account of the Seminole Wars, including the 1835 fort from which Fort Pierce took its name, and a re-creation of P.P. Cobb's general store, the hub of the turn-of-the-century town. Outside the museum, **Gardner House**, a 1907 "cracker" cottage can be given a once-over. Note the tall ceilings and many windows allowing the muggy Florida air to circulate in the days before air conditioning. The museum also contains an exhibition gallery and a fully restored 1919 fire engine.

Downtown Fort Pierce and around

Entering **downtown Fort Pierce**, your gaze is held by a sewage treatment works and the towers of a cement factory, which provide a stark contrast to Hutchinson Island's raging vegetation. If you've time, however, Hwy-A1A quickly escapes oceanwards to North Hutchinson Island. Don't bother with the downtown area but make an excursion a few miles north along Hwy-1. From mid-Nov to early April you may catch sight of manatees in the Indian River Lagoon. A viewing area is located at Moore's Creek at the marina, where Avenue C and North Indian River Drive meet.

The Capron Trail Monument and Indian River Drive
A couple of miles north of downtown Fort Pierce, Hwy-1 crosses St Lucie Boulevard, and a left turn along here leads to a memorial (by the junction with 25th Street)

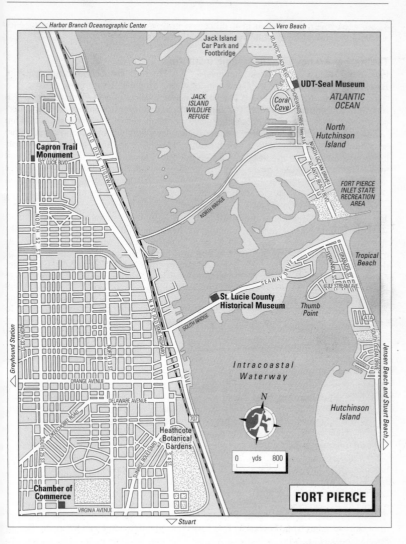

recalling the nineteenth-century soldiers who inched their way from here towards Fort Brooke – the site of present-day Tampa. Their machetes hacked out the **Capron Trail**, one of the first east-west cross-Florida routes. Driving back, stay on St Lucie Boulevard as it crosses Hwy-1 and turn left along **Indian River Drive**, where gracious, rambling wooden homes dating from the early 1900s line the Intercoastal Waterway.

The Heathcote Botanical Gardens

At 210 Savannah Road, off Hwy-1 and north of Jefferson Plaza, the **Heathcote Botanical Gardens** (Tues–Sat, 9am–5pm. Also open Sun 1–5pm, Nov–April only;

$2.50; ☎464-4672), are an oasis in an otherwise gray setting, and provide a relaxing and surprisingly cool place to while away a couple of hours.

The Harbor Branch Oceanographic Institution

Five miles north of St Lucie Boulevard, the **Harbor Branch Oceanographic Institution,** 5600 N Hwy 1 (90-min guided tours Mon–Sat 10am, noon & 2pm; $5; ☎465-2400 ext. 328 or ☎1-800/333-4264) is a phenomenally well-equipped deep-sea research and education center. The highly informative tours depart from the visitor center and cover such highlights as full-scale models of research submersibles and an "Aquaculture" exhibit featuring interactive displays and videos to show you how seafood can be specially cultured for human consumption and thus help to satisfy our increasing demand on the seas. You'll also get the chance to eat in the research center's canteen: a good feed for $5 – try the meatloaf and, of course, the seafood.

Practicalities

The Fort Pierce Greyhound **bus station** (☎461-3299) is six miles from downtown at 7005 Okeechobee Road, near the junction of Hwy-70 and the Florida Turnpike; a **cab** (try Grey Taxi Service, ☎461-7200) from here to the beach will cost around $12. A group of ordinary but inexpensive **lodging and eating** options are available close to the station. For rooms, try *Days Inn*, 6651 Darter Court off I-95 (☎466-4066; ④), the *Hampton Inn*, 2831 Reynolds Drive (☎460-9855; ③), or *Econo Lodge*, 7050 Okeechobee Road (☎465-8600; ③). Family-style food is available at the *Piccadilly Cafeteria*, 4194 Okeechobee Road, Orange Blossom Mall (☎466-8234), and seafood at *The Galley Grille*, 927 N US Hwy-1 (☎468-2081).

Otherwise, sleeping (with the exception of camping) and dining are best done close to the beach, two miles east of downtown Fort Pierce. Most **motels** are geared up for stays of several nights and many rooms include cooking facilities. Try the well-equipped *Days Inn*, 1920 Seaway Drive (☎461-8737; ⑤), or the more basic *Dockside Harborlight Resort*, 1160 Seaway Drive (☎1-800/286-1745; ③). There are further choices along Seaway Drive and the northern part of Ocean Drive; ask on the spot for the best deals. For **camping**, head inland and seven miles south of downtown Fort Pierce along Route 707 to *Savannah's* (☎464-7855), a sizeable square of reclaimed marshland beside the Intercoastal waterway where you can pitch a tent for $10. To explore this unspoiled landscape, take one of the nature trails or hire a canoe.

Food options in Fort Pierce include the unpretentious and inexpensive *Captain's Galley*, 825 N Indian River Drive (☎466-8495), whose traditional breakfasts and solid lunches and dinners have earned it a four-star recommendation from the *Miami Herald*; and the more refined *Mangrove Matties*, 1640 Seaway Drive (☎466-1044), which specializes in tasty steaks and seafood.

You can get general **information** from the **Chamber of Commerce**, 2200 Virginia Avenue (Mon–Fri 8.30am–5pm; ☎595-9999). There are various diving packages on offer, among them Dixie Divers, 1717 S Hwy 1 (☎461-4488) and Deep Six Dive, 2323 S Hwy-1 (☎465-4114), who both charge $20 for a 24-hour package.

Port St Lucie

Adjacent to and merging with southern Fort Pierce lies **PORT ST LUCIE**. The chief attraction here is the St Lucie County Sport Complex, at 527 NW Peacock Loop (☎340-1721), where the New York Mets baseball team complete their spring training. It's also the home of the St Lucie Mets, a minor league baseball team, whose season opens in April. At the close of the ninth inning you can rest your head in the nearby *Best Western*, 7900 S Hwy-1, Port St Lucie (☎878-7600; ⑤).

North Hutchinson Island

Covering 340 acres at the southern tip of **North Hutchinson Island** is the **Fort Pierce Inlet State Recreation Area** (daily 8am–sunset; cars $3.25, pedestrians and cyclists $1; ☎468-3985), at 905 Shorewinds Drive, off Hwy-A1A. Its location, overlooking the Fort Pierce Inlet and the community's beach, makes this a scenic setting for a picnic, as well as a launch site for local surfers. A mile north, on Hwy-A1A, a footbridge from the parking lot of the **Jack Island Wildlife Refuge** (same times and fees as above) leads onto the mile-long Marsh Rabbit Run, a boardwalk trail cutting through a thick mangrove swamp to an observation tower on the edge of the Indian River. Among bird life to watch out for are great blue herons and ospreys.

Concern for the environment is not something shared by the **UDT-SEAL Museum** (☎595-5845; Tues–Sat 10am–4pm, Sun noon–4pm; $2), at 3300 N Hwy-A1A between the recreation area and the wildlife refuge, dedicated to the US Navy's frogman demolition teams who've been exploding sea-mines and beach defenses since the Normandy landings. During World War II, the UDTs (Underwater Demolition Teams) trained on Hutchinson Island – like most of Florida's barrier islands, it was off-limits to civilians at the time. The more elite SEALs (Sea Air Land), the US equivalent of Britain's SAS, came into being during the Sixties. The museum covers the technicalities of establishing beachheads, though jingoism is predictably apparent – anyone who can't keep doubts over US foreign policy to themselves should steer clear.

Vero Beach and around

For the next fourteen miles, Australian pines mar Hwy-A1A's ocean view until North Hutchinson Island imperceptibly becomes **Orchid Island** and you reach **VERO BEACH**, the area's sole community of substance and one with a pronounced upmarket image. It makes an enjoyable hideaway, however, with a fine group of beaches around Ocean Drive, parallel to Hwy-A1A. There's little to tempt you from the sands, but it's worth taking the trouble to view the *Driftwood Resort*, 3150 Ocean Drive (☎231-0550), a Thirties hotel, now time-share apartments, erected from a jumble of driftwood, flea-market finds and pieces of Palm Beach mansions demolished to avoid taxes.

Vero Beach practicalities

Three miles from the coast, **inland Vero Beach** has a Greyhound terminal at the Texaco filling station, 1995 Hwy-1 (☎562-6588), and a **Chamber of Commerce** at 1216 21st Street (Mon–Fri 9am–5pm; ☎567-3491). At the beach, exceptions to pricey **accommodation** are the *Riviera Inn*, 1605 S Ocean Drive (☎234-4112; ④), and *Sea Spray Gardens*, 965 E Causeway Boulevard (☎231-5210; ②, self catering only), both with great deals off-season. Cost-effective **eateries** are the *Beachside Restaurant*, opposite the *Driftwood Resort*, at 3125 Ocean Drive (☎234-4477), *Nino's Café*, 1006 Easter Lily Lane (☎231-9311), and *Tangos,* 925 Bougainvillea Lane (231-1550; between Ocean Drive and Cardinal Drive).

North of Vero Beach: Sebastian Inlet

Tiny beachside communities dot the rest of the island, but you'll find most activity – and campgrounds ($17 Dec–Apr, $15 May–Nov) – around the **Sebastian Inlet State Recreation Area**, 9700 S Hwy-A1A (open 24 hours; cars $3.25, pedestrians and cyclists $1; ☎407/984-4852), sixteen miles north of Vero Beach. Roaring ocean breakers lure surfers here, particularly over Easter when contests are held, and anglers cram the jetties for the East Coast's finest fishing. Without a board or a rod, you can amuse yourself by keeping an eye out for the endangered bird life making sorties from nearby Pelican Island, the oldest wildlife refuge in the country and off-limits to humans. For a bit of dolphin and manatee watching, the *Inlet Explorer* (located inside Inlet Marina; $15 adults, $10 children under 12 ☎407/724-5424 or 1-800/952-1126) offers two-hour tours of the Indian River Lagoon. Alternatively, head a couple of miles south of the inlet to the **McLarty Treasure Museum**, at 13180 N Hwy-A1A (daily 10am–4.30pm; $1; ☎589-2147), where you can view treasure salvaged from an eighteenth-century Spanish fleet that was stricken by a hurricane.

Beyond Sebastian you reach the outskirts of the **Space Coast**, which is covered in "The Northeast Coast".

travel details

Trains

Hollywood to: Boca Raton (14 daily; 39min); Delray Beach (51 min); Fort Lauderdale (15min); West Palm Beach (1hr 16min).

Buses

Fort Lauderdale to: Delray Beach (2 daily; 1hr 10min); Fort Pierce (12 daily; 2hr 50min); Stuart (4 daily; 3hr 15min); Vero Beach (5 daily; 3hr 55min); West Palm Beach (14 daily; 2hr).

Hollywood to: Fort Lauderdale (11 daily; 10–30min); Orlando (8 daily; 5–6hr).

West Palm Beach to: Belle Glade (1 daily; 55min); Fort Pierce (7 daily; 1hr); Stuart (4 daily; 45min); Tampa (5 daily; 7–8 1/2hr); Vero Beach (4 daily; 2hr 30min).

AMANDA HALL

Lifeguard station, Miami Beach

F. & M. HALL

Ocean Drive, South Beach, Miami

NEIL SETCHFIELD

NEIL SETCHFIELD

Art Deco detail, South Beach, Miami

South Beach, Miami

NEIL SETCHFIELD

Playing dominoes, Little Havana, Miami

F. & M. HALL

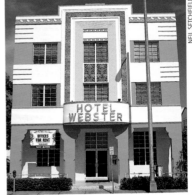

NEIL SETCHFIELD

Cardozo Hotel, Ocean Drive, Miami

Hotel Webster, South Beach, Miami

Starlite Hotel, South Beach, Miami

Wave Wall Promenade, Fort Lauderdale

Musclebound hunks, South Beach, Miami

J. ACHESON, AXIOM

Roadside sign, Key West

P. WHALLEY, TRAVEL INK

Pelicans, Key West

CHAPTER FOUR

THE NORTHEAST COAST

Substantially free of commercial exploitation, with washed-up sharks' teeth sometimes more plentiful than people on its beaches, the 190 miles of Florida's **Northeast Coast** are tailor-made for leisurely exploration. You'll often feel like doing nothing more strenuous than settling down beside the ocean, but throughout the region evidence of the forces that have shaped Florida – from ancient Native American settlements to the launch-site of the Space Shuttle – is easy to find and worth exploring. When planning your trip, remember that the Northeast Coast's tourist **seasons** are the reverse of those of the Southeast Coast: the crowded time here is the summer, when accommodation is more expensive and harder to come by than during the winter months.

Besides sharing a shoreline, the towns of the Northeast Coast have surprisingly little in common. Those making up the **Space Coast**, the southernmost area, primarily service the hordes passing through to visit the new and improved **Kennedy Space Center**, birthplace and still the launching pad of the nation's space exploits. Its public image is unrelentingly positive, but the Space Center is definitely worth a visit, as is the wildlife refuge that surrounds it. Every March and April, a different kind of blasting-off has traditionally occurred seventy miles north of the Space Coast at **Daytona Beach**, a small town with a big strand, which, until a recent bout of soul searching, happily hosted drunken legions of college kids indulging in the legendary excesses of the Spring Break holiday. Although the local authorities are discouraging the event, teenage carousing can still be found around this time; the rest of the year, Daytona is a mellower place to hang out.

Along the northerly section of the coast, the plentiful evidence of Florida's early European landings is nowhere better displayed than in comprehensively restored **St Augustine**, where sixteenth-century Spaniards established North America's earliest foreign settlement. In addition to the attractions of the town itself, there's the surrounding coast, part of a divine strand stretching to the **Jacksonville Beaches**, twenty miles north, where lying in the sun and tuning into the sprightly local nightlife will decadently waste a few days. Just inland, the city of **Jacksonville**, struggling to shrug off its grey and industrial image, merits only a cursory investigation as you strike out towards the state's northeastern extremity. Here, overlooking the coast of Georgia, slender **Amelia Island** is fringed by gorgeous silver sands, has a quirky Victorian-era main town, and is under the beady eye of dollar-crazed developers – arrive before they do.

ACCOMMODATION PRICES

All the accommodation listed in this book has been categorized into one of eight price bands, as set out below. The rates quoted represent the cheapest available double or twin room in high season – except for category ①, which indicates per-person rates for a dorm bed, and the categories given for units, cabins and vans, which represent the daily charge for the whole unit.

① Under $18	② $19–30	③ $31–45	④ $46–60
⑤ $61–74	⑥ $75–94	⑦ $95–124	⑧ $125 upwards

For more accommodation details, see p.27 in Basics.

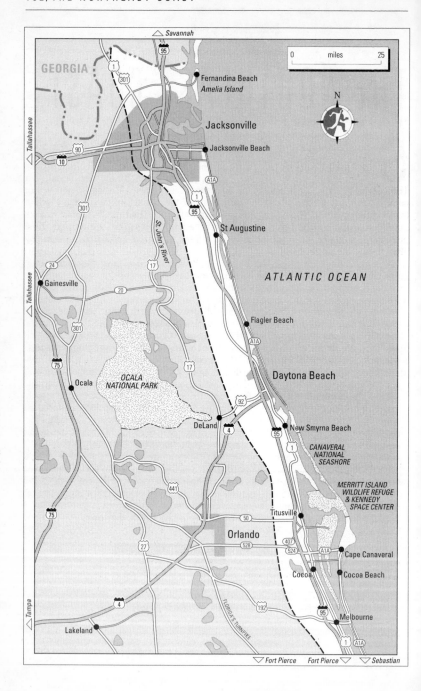

> The area code for Cocoa Beach and the Space Coast is ☎407.

The **road network** is very much a continuation of the Southeast Coast's system: **Hwy-A1A** hugs the coastline, while **Hwy-1** charts a less appealing course on the mainland and is a lot slower than **I-95**, which divides the coastal area from the eastern edge of Central Florida. Greyhound **buses** are frequent along Hwy-1 between the main towns, though the only **local bus services** are in Daytona Beach and Jacksonville. Forget the **train** – only Jacksonville has a station.

The Space Coast

The barrier islands that dominate the Treasure Coast (see "The Southeast Coast") continue north into the so-called **SPACE COAST**, the base of the country's space industry and site of the Kennedy Space Center, which occupies a flat, marshy island bulging into the Atlantic just fifty miles east of Orlando. Many of the visitors who flock here are surprised to find that the land from which the Space Shuttle leaves earth is also a sizeable wildlife refuge framed by several miles of rough coastline. Except for the beach-oriented communities on the ocean, the towns of the Space Coast are of little interest other than for low-cost overnight stops or meal breaks.

The Kennedy Space Center

Justifiably the biggest attraction in the area, the **Kennedy Space Center** is the nucleus of the US space program: it's here that space vehicles are developed, tested and blasted into orbit. The first launches actually took place across the water at the US Air Force base on Cape Canaveral (renamed Cape Kennedy in 1963 and changed back to the original in 1973), from which unmanned satellites still lift off. After the space program was expanded in 1964 and the Saturn V rockets proved too large to launch from there, the focus of activity was moved here to Merritt Island, positioned between Cape Canaveral and the mainland and directly north of Cocoa Beach.

The Space Center is well worth a visit for its solid documentation of US achievements, revealing how closely success in space is tied to the nation's sense of well-being.

THE KENNEDY SPACE CENTER: PRACTICAL INFO AND TIPS

The only **public entry roads** into the Kennedy Space Center are Hwy-405 from Titusville, and Route 3 off Hwy-A1A between Cocoa Beach and Cocoa: on either approach, follow signs for the Kennedy Space Center **Visitor Complex** (daily 9am–dusk; free), which has recently undergone a massive revamping and contains a museum, a life-size Space Shuttle Explorer replica, the Spaceport Theater, exhibit halls, the Astronaut Memorial, the Rocket Garden and an IMAX film theater.

Arrive early to avoid the crowds, which are thinnest on weekends and during May and September. To take the bus tour or to see one of the three IMAX films, you should **buy tickets** from the ticket pavilion as soon as you arrive (Bus tour $14 adults, $10 children; IMAX $7.50 adults, $5.50 children; combination ticket $19 adults, $15 children).

To **see a launch** from the Space Center, phone ☎407/867-4636 for recorded schedule information or ☎407/452-2121 ext. 260 to arrange a $10 pass (tickets must be purchased five days in advance and in person at the Visitor Complex). For **launch dates** and times, call ☎1-800-KSC-INFO. Note, however, that you'll get almost as good a view of a launch from anywhere within a forty-mile radius of the Space Center.

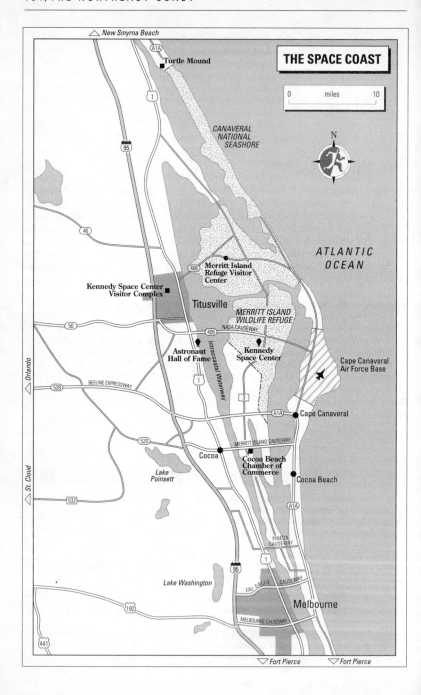

THE SPACE COAST

0 miles 10

New Smyrna Beach

Turtle Mound

CANAVERAL
NATIONAL
SEASHORE

N

ATLANTIC
OCEAN

Merritt Island
Refuge Visitor
Center

Kennedy Space Center
Visitor Complex

Titusville

MERRITT ISLAND
WILDLIFE REFUGE

NASA CAUSEWAY

Astronaut
Hall of Fame

Kennedy
Space Center

Cape Canaveral
Air Force Base

Orlando

BEELINE EXPRESSWAY

Intracoastal Waterway

Cape Canaveral

MERRITT ISLAND CAUSEWAY

St. Cloud

Cocoa

Cocoa Beach
Chamber of
Commerce

Cocoa Beach

Lake
Poinsett

PINEDA
CAUSEWAY

Lake Washington

EAU GALLIE CAUSEWAY

Melbourne

MELBOURNE CAUSEWAY

Fort Pierce   Fort Pierce

The Kennedy Space Center Visitor Complex

Everything at the **KSC Visitor Complex** is within easy walking distance of the parking lot, as is the departure point for the bus tour (see below). The **museum** will keep anyone with the faintest interest in space exploration entertained for a good hour. Except for any mention of the Challenger or other disasters, everything you might expect to see is here: actual mission capsules, space suits, lunar modules, a full-sized walk-through mock-up of the Space Shuttle, and an interactive exhibit on the 1997 Pathfinder mission to Mars, where scientists discovered life in the form of bacteria embedded in rocks. The rockets standing outside the museum in the **Rocket Garden** are deceptively simple in appearance and far daintier than the gigantic Saturn V (only seen out on the bus tour, see below) that launched the Apollo missions.

Next door to the museum, the **Galaxy Theater** shows three IMAX films, using 70mm film projected onto a five-story screen. Using dramatic shots from an orbiting space shuttle, *The Dream is Alive* (37 min) captures the sensations of space flight as well as the daily business of living in space; *Mission to Mir* (40 min) brings together the two Cold War rivals as the US and Russia demonstrate friendship aboard the Russian Space Station Mir; *L5:First City in Space* (35 min) is a 3-D film that highlights a future space settlement using real NASA footage and data, and depicts plans for the international space station, which is being created by thirteen countries and can be seen on the bus tour.

As far as **eating** goes, there are four canteens and various snack trolleys scattered around the Visitor Complex that provide standard pizza and hot-dog fare at astronomical

---

AMERICANS IN SPACE

The growth of the Space Coast started with the **"Space Race,"** which followed President John F. Kennedy's declaration in May 1961 to "achieve the goal, before the decade is out, of landing a man on the moon and returning him safely to Earth." This statement came in the chill of the Cold War, when the USSR – which had just put the first man into space following their launch of the first artificial satellite in 1957 – appeared scientifically ahead of the US, a fact which dented American pride and provided great propaganda for the Soviets.

Money and manpower were pumped into **NASA** (National Aeronautics and Space Administration), and the communities around Cape Canaveral expanded with a heady influx of scientists and would-be astronauts. The much-hyped Mercury program helped restore prestige, and the later Apollo moonshots captured the imagination of the world. The moon landing by Apollo 11 in July 1969 not only turned the dreams of science fiction writers into reality, but also meant for the first time – and in the most spectacular way possible – the US had overtaken the USSR.

During the Seventies, as the incredible expense of the space program became apparent and seemed out of all proportion to its benefits, pressure grew for NASA to become more cost-effective. The country entered a period of economic recession and NASA's funding was drastically slashed; unemployment – unthinkable in the buoyant Sixties – threatened many on the Space Coast.

After the internationally funded Skylab space station program, NASA's solution to the problem of wasteful one-use rockets was the reusable **Space Shuttle**, first launched in April 1981, able to deploy commercial payloads and carry out repairs to orbiting satellites. The Shuttle's success silenced many critics, but the Challenger disaster of January 1986 – when the entire crew perished during take-off – not only sent a deep sense of loss around the country but highlighted the complacency and corner-cutting that had crept into the space program after many accident-free years.

More recently, despite numerous satisfactory missions, technical problems and the exercising of stringent safety procedures have caused serious delays to the Space Shuttle program, illustrating what a colossal accomplishment the manned moon landings actually were. Of equal significance may well be the manned space station in orbit around the earth, planned for completion in the year 2000.

prices (excuse the pun). Though convenient for snacks and drinks (you can eat futuristic ice cream in solid-pellet form called "space dots"), you're better off packing a cooler and eating in the aptly named "Lunch Pad."

The Kennedy Space Center Tour

The **bus tour** (continuous departures 9.30am–5pm daily; $14, children $10) around the rest of the Merrit Island complex provides dramatic insight into the colossal grandeur of the space program. After zooming through the main gate and passing countless gators on the side of the road, the 52-story **Vehicle Assembly Building** (where the shuttles, like Apollo and Skylab before them, are put together and fitted with payloads) looms ahead. Unfortunately, access is prohibited, but if a door is open you'll catch a glimpse inside one of the world's largest structures. Equivalent in volume to three-and-one-half Empire State Buildings, the VAB is the first stop for the "crawlerway" – the huge tracks along which space shuttles are wheeled to the launch pad.

With luck, a space shuttle will be in place for take-off when the bus takes a loop around the **launch pad** – no different in reality from what you've seen on TV, and no more interesting than any other large pile of scaffolding if a shuttle isn't present (obviously, when a countdown is underway there are no bus tours; see the box on p.183 for launch-watching tips). Recently added to the tour is a peek at preparations for the **International Space Station** (ISS), a joint project between sixteen nations that will produce the first permanently-inhabitable space station. Visitors can see the facility where NASA is processing the space station's components and soak up informative tidbits like the fact that it will take 38 space flights and five years to haul the entirety of the space station into orbit.

Besides a nose-to-nozzle inspection of a Saturn V rocket, the most impressive part of the rest of the bus tour is a simulated Apollo countdown and take-off, watched from behind the blinking screens of a realistically mocked-up control room.

Air Force Space Museum

If you've not had your fill of space travel at the KSC Visitor Complex, a further attraction in the area is the **Air Force Space Museum** (Mon–Fri 10am–2pm, Sat & Sun 10am–4pm; free), situated a mile inside the gate of Cape Canaveral (on launch pad 26A), and a testament to NASA's skill at making money out of its old hardware. The museum consists of a large expanse of land rather akin to the Rocket Garden at the KSC Visitor Complex (see above), and two buildings containing exhibits and information on rocket development, some of which proves fascinating: one example is the fact that all the extraordinary developments of the space program stem from V2 rockets, which were originally fired by Nazi Germany against Britain in the closing years of the Second World War, and were subsequently launched into orbit by America in 1950.

For yet another angle on space travel, visit the **Astronaut Hall of Fame** (see Titusville, p.190), just down the road from the Kennedy Space Center.

Merritt Island National Wildlife Refuge

NASA shares its land with the **Merritt Island National Wildlife Refuge** (daily sunrise–sunset; free), entered via Route 402 from Titusville. Here you'll find alligators, armadillos, racoons, bobcats and one of Florida's greatest concentrations of bird life living alongside some of the world's most advanced technology.

Even if you're only coming for a day at the Space Center, it would be a shame to pass up such a spectacular place – though it has to be said that Merritt Island, on first glance, looks anything but spectacular, comprising acres of estuaries and brackish marshes interspersed by occasional hammocks of oak and palm, and pine flatwoods where a few bald eagles construct nests ten feet in circumference. Winter is the **best time to visit**, when the island's skies are alive with thousands of migratory birds from the frozen north, and when mosquitoes are absent. At any other period, and especially in summer, the island's Mosquito Lagoon is worthy of its name; bring ample insect repellent.

Seeing the refuge

Seven miles east of Titusville on Route 406, the six-mile **Black Point Wildlife Drive** gives a solid introduction to the basics of the island's ecosystem. At the entrance you can pick up the highly informative free leaflet, which describes specific stops along the route. From one you'll spot a couple of bald eagle nests, while another by the mudflats provides a good vantage point for watching a wide variety of wading and shore birds swooping on their dinner.

Be sure to do some walking within the refuge, too. Off the wildlife drive, the five-mile **Cruickshank trail** weaves around the edge of the Indian River. If the whole length is too strenuous for you, there's an observation tower just a few minutes' walk from the carpark. For a more varied landscape, drive a few miles further east along Route 402 – branching from Route 406 just south of the wildlife drive – passing the **visitor center** (Mon–Fri 8am–4.30pm, Sat 9am–5pm; closed Sun April–Oct; ☎861-0667), and tackle the half-mile **Oak Hammock trail** or the two-mile **Palm Hammock trail**, both accessible from the same carpark.

The Canaveral National Seashore

A slender, 25-mile-long beach dividing Merritt Island's Mosquito Lagoon from the Atlantic Ocean, the **Canaveral National Seashore** (winter 6am–6pm, summer 6am–8pm; free) begins at **Playalinda Beach** on Route 402, seven miles east of the refuge's visitor center. The National Seashore's entire length is top-notch beachcombing and surfing territory, and also suitable for swimming. Except when rough seas and high tides submerge it completely, you should take a wind-bitten ramble along the palmetto-lined path to wild **Klondike Beach**, north of Playalinda Beach, often coated with intriguing shells and marked in summer by the tracks left by sea turtles crawling ashore at night to lay eggs.

At the northern tip of the National Seashore, on **Apollo Beach** (only accessible by road from New Smyrna Beach, eight miles north of Apollo, see "Heading North: New Smyrna Beach," below), is the easily sighted **Turtle Mound**. This thirty-five-foot heap of oyster shells provided a home for Timucua Indians over several generations and was marked on maps by Florida's first Spanish explorers, being visible several miles out to sea. Take a few minutes to walk to the top of the mound, which offers a view over Merritt Island.

Cocoa Beach

A few miles south of the Kennedy Space Center, **COCOA BEACH** comprises just a ten-mile strip of shore and a few residential streets off Atlantic Avenue (Hwy-A1A). As well as being unquestionably the best base from which to see the Space Coast, it's also a favored haunt of surfers, who are attracted here by some of the biggest waves in Florida. Major (and minor) surfing contests are held here during April and May, and throughout the year the place has a perky, youthful feel. There's also a big volleyball contingent here, setting and spiking on four permanent courts. On weekends there's often free music around the pier and beachside parks, and to get an idea of the community's prime concerns you need only take a walk around the original Ron Jon Surf Shop, 4151 N Atlantic Avenue (☎799-8820), and its two branches a stone's throw away (the Water Sports Store and the Outpost Discount Store). All are open 24 hours a day and packed with surfboards (rental per day is $10 for a foam board; $20 for fibreglass), bicycles ($3 per hour or $40 per week), kites and extrovert beach attire.

Information and transport

The Cocoa Beach **Chamber of Commerce** is located on Merritt Island at 400 Fortenberry Road (Mon–Fri 9am–5pm; ☎459-2200), though there is also a limited information desk at the Ron Jon Surf Shop. A local **bus** service (*SCAT*; ☎633-1878) runs regularly to and from Cape Canaveral through Cocoa Beach (#9), and #6 runs from downtown Cocoa to Cocoa Beach; both routes cost $1 one way. The *Cocoa Beach Shuttle* (☎784-3831) runs to and from Orlando airport for $18 one way; call to be collected from any hotel on Hwy-A1A. To get around the beach area, rent a **bike** from the Ron Jon Surf Shop (details above). The nearest Greyhound station is on the mainland in Cocoa at 302 Main Street (☎636-6531).

Accommodation

Accommodation bargains are rare in Cocoa Beach. You can expect prices to be highest during February, July and August – and during space shuttle launches. The lowest rates for motels are with *Fawlty Towers*, 100 E Cocoa Beach Causeway (☎784-3870; ②); *Motel 6*, 3701 N Atlantic Avenue (☎783-3103; ③); *Best Western Ocean Inn*, 5500 N Atlantic Avenue (☎784-2550; ④); and, for bed and breakfast, *Luna Sea*, 3185 N Atlantic Avenue (☎1-800/586-2732; ②). For a longer stay, try the *Econo Lodge Cape Colony* resort, 1275 N Atlantic Avenue (☎1-800/795-2252; ⑤), which is an especially good value for several people sharing. To relax in style, stay at *Sea Esta Beachside Villas*, 686 S Atlantic Avenue (☎1-800/872-9444; ⑥), whose price includes home-cooked breakfasts and supper. The most tent-friendly **campground** is *Jetty Park*, 400 Jetty Drive (☎783-7111; $14.85), five miles north at Cape Canaveral.

Eating and nightlife

Many inland restaurants strive to undercut each other, resulting in some good **eating** deals if you have your own transportation; see "Inland" below for suggestions, and scan free magazines (found in motels and at the Chamber of Commerce) such as *Restaurant Dining Out* for money-saving coupons. Close to the beach, the options are fewer. For simple basics go to *Roberto's Little Havana*, 26 N Orlando Avenue (☎784-1868); and for great oysters and a $5 lunch buffet, head for *Rusty's Raw Bar*, 2 S Atlantic Avenue (☎783-2401). Good dinner options are *The Pier Restaurant*, on the pier (☎783-7549), which has a quality (and somewhat expensive) menu especially strong on seafood; and the cheaper *Old Fish House*, 249 W Cocoa Beach Causeway (☎799-9190).

Nightlife is most enjoyable if you start early at one of the beachside **happy hours**: try *Marlins' Good Time Grill*, also part of the pier complex (☎783-7549), or *Desperados*, 301 N Atlantic Avenue (☎784-3363). As the evening draws on, the *Pig and Whistle*, 801 N Atlantic Avenue (☎799-0724), offering TV soccer and overpriced bitter, is a refuge for homesick Brits; and *Coconuts*, 2 Minuteman Causeway (☎784-1422), has drinking and **live music** on the beach.

Inland: Palm Bay, Melbourne, Cocoa and Titusville

The chief attractions of the Space Coast's sleepy **inland towns**, strung along Hwy-1, are cheaper accommodation and food than at the beaches, plus areas of historical interest that provide relief from the usual tourist drag.

Palm Bay

The southernmost town is **PALM BAY**, thirty miles north of Vero Beach (see p.179). Despite boasting a higher population than any of its neighbors, it's the least geared to tourism, being largely a commuter-belt town for Space Coast employees. There's little to detain you here apart from the small **Turkey Creek Sanctuary**, 1502 Port

Malabar Boulevard (daily 7am–sunset; free), whose short boardwalk trail winds through three distinct (and simulated) native habitats – hardwood hammock, sand and pine scrub, and wet hardwood forest – that support endangered species of flora and fauna.

Melbourne

Just a few miles north of Palm Bay lies the pretty but dull town of **MELBOURNE**. The collections at its **Brevard Museum of Art and Science**, 1463 Highland Avenue (Tues–Sat 10am–5pm, Sun 1–5pm; $5; ☎242-0737), won't hold you here very long, but Melbourne's **restaurants** might: go to *Shooter's*, 707 S Harbour City Boulevard (☎725-4600), for good sandwiches and a great view of the Indian River; *Mac's Diner*, 2925 Kingston Lane (☎254-8818), for a buffet feed on weekdays or a breakfast buffet on weekends; *Durango Steakhouse*, 6767 N Wickham Rd (☎259-2934), serves up juicy southwest-style steaks; *Stacey's Buffet*, 1439 S Babcock St. (☎725-6436), boasts filling down-home cookin'; *New England Eatery*, 5670 Hwy A1A (723-6080) has fresh seafood at cheap prices; and *Conchy Joe's*, 1477 Pineapple Avenue (☎253-3131), has seafood and live reggae in the evenings. After eating, stroll along **Crane Creek**, a stretch of water between the Hwy-1 road bridge and the railway bridge, which is a **manatee** viewing area. A shoreline boardwalk, lined with oak trees and sabal palms, provides an attractive spot from which to glimpse these shy, endangered creatures.

If you're **staying** overnight, try the *Holiday Inn*, 420 S Harbor City Boulevard (☎723-5320; ②–③), or *Melbourne Harbor Suites*, 1207 E New Haven Avenue (☎1-800/242-4251; ④), on the harbor – a short walk from Crane Creek. When it's time to move on, catch a Greyhound **bus** at 460 S US 1 (☎723-4323).

Cocoa

In **COCOA**, thirty miles north of Melbourne and eight miles inland from Cocoa Beach, the cobblestoned pavements and turn-of-the-century buildings of **Old Cocoa Village** fill several small blocks south of King Street (Hwy-520) and make for a relaxing stroll. Among the twee antique shops and boutiques, seek out the *Porcher House*, 434 Delannoy Avenue (Mon–Fri 9am–5pm; free; ☎639-3500), a grand Neoclassical abode of 1916 vintage.

For a greater insight into the town's origins, head a few miles west to the **Brevard Museum of History and Natural Science**, 2201 Michigan Avenue (Mon–Sat 10am–4pm; $4; ☎632-1830), whose displays recount Cocoa's birth as a trading post when the first settlers arrived in the 1840s by steamboat and mule. There's also a respectable display on Florida wildlife and some informative leaflets that are particularly useful if you're planning to visit the Merritt Island National Wildlife Refuge (see p.186).

It's worth making a quick stop at the **Astronaut Memorial Hall and Planetarium**, 1519 Clearlake Road (Tue, Fri, Sat 6.30–9.30pm; $7; ☎634-3732), not for its run-of-the-mill science exhibits but for the **Space Shuttle Park** (free) beside the parking lot. Among the various bits of space hardware is – incredibly – an Apollo command module, its cobweb-covered interior strewn with bare wires and plugs – a bizarre fate for something that once represented the forefront of space science.

If you're **staying** in Cocoa, there are some small and uninviting motels lining Cocoa Boulevard. The best option is the *Econo Lodge* at no. 3220 N (☎632-4561; ③). For **eating**, try *Norman's Food and Spirits*, 3 Forrest Avenue (☎632-8782), which offers great lunch specials and entertaining karaoke in the evenings; alternatively, *Café Margaux*, 220 Brevard Avenue (☎639-8343), is a stylish spot for a pasta lunch.

To get to **Cocoa Beach** without your own car, a taxi ride (☎723-1234) will cost $15–20. The Greyhound **bus** station is at 302 Main Street (☎636-6531).

Titusville

If you don't visit the Kennedy Space Center, you'll at least get a great view of the towering Vehicle Assembly Building from **TITUSVILLE**, twenty miles north of Cocoa. If you find you have time on your hands here, visit the **Valiant Air Command Museum**, 6600 Tico Road (daily 10am–6pm; $6; ☎268-1941), a celebration of slightly more pedestrian flying machines than those at the Kennedy Space Center. Originally formed to commemorate the US Airforce's involvement in preventing Japan's invasion of mainland China in 1941, the museum today exhibits lovingly restored planes, with examples from all wars since that date. The best way to see them is in March, when the VAC holds an air show and most of these war veterans take to the skies.

Apart from this, all that's commendable about Titusville is ease of access to the Kennedy Space Center (via Hwy-405) and the Merritt Island National Wildlife Refuge (via Hwy-402). On the way to either place, visit the **Astronaut Hall of Fame** (daily 9am–6pm; $13.95, children $9.95; ☎269-6100), one of Florida's most entertaining interactive museums. Simulation rides allow visitors to experience stomach-churning g-forces, weightlessness and 360-degree spins. There's also a mock Space Shuttle and tours of **SpaceCamp USA**, where young wannabe astronauts spend several weeks spinning about in contraptions designed to simulate the extreme g-forces of space travel.

For **food**, search out the seafood and steaks at *Janet's Café Orleans*, 605 Hopkins Avenue (☎269-6020), or the seafood of *Dixie Crossroads*, 1475 Garden Street (☎268-5000). Inexpensive **motels** are plentiful along Washington Avenue (Hwy-1): *South Wind*, no. 1540 S (☎267-3681; ③), and *Siesta*, no. 2006 (☎267-1455; ③), are just two. Otherwise, try the *Best Western Space Shuttle Inn*, 3455 Cheney Highway (☎269-9100; ④), which also offers eco-tourism packages for exploring the unique flora and fauna of the area. For moving on, the Greyhound **bus** station is at 212 S Washington Avenue (☎267-8760).

Heading north: New Smyrna Beach

After the virgin vistas of the Canaveral National Seashore, the tall beachside hotels of **NEW SMYRNA BEACH**, thirty miles north of Titusville on Hwy-1, create the impression of a likeable low-key beach community, where the sea – protected from dangerous currents by offshore rock ledges – is perfect for **swimming**. To reach the beach (or the northern section of the Canaveral National Seashore, see p.187), you have to pass through the inland section of the town, before swinging east on Hwy-A1A.

The town itself has an unusual **history**. A wealthy Scottish physician, Andrew Turnbull, bought land here in the mid-1700s and set about creating a Mediterranean colony, recruiting Greeks, Italians and Minorcans to work for seven years on his plantation in return for fifty acres of land each. The colony didn't last: bad treatment, language barriers, disease and financial disasters hastened its demise, and many of the settlers moved north to St Augustine (see p.198).

The immigrants worked hard, however (by most accounts, they had little choice), laying irrigation canals, building a sugar mill and commencing work on what was to be a palatial abode for Turnbull. Close to Hwy-1, the **ruins** of the mill (at the junction of Canal Street and Mission Road) and his unfinished house (at Riverside Drive and Julia Street) are substantial enough to merit a look, and the nearby **Visitor Center and Chamber of Commerce**, 115 Canal Street (Mon–Fri 9am–5pm, Sat 9am–12pm; ☎1-800/541-9621), has a handy historical leaflet, as well as the usual local information.

Greyhound **buses** will drop you here at Steils Gas Station, 600 Canal Street (☎428-8211); if you want to stay over, the two cheapest **motels** are on Hwy-1 (locally called

> The area code for Daytona Beach and New Smyrna Beach is ☎904

Dixie Freeway): *Smyrna Motel*, no. 1050 N (☎428-2495; ②), which has an eagle's nest on its property, and *Shangri-La*, no. 805 N (☎428-8361; ①).

Continuing north from New Smyrna Beach, Hwy-A1A joins with Hwy-1 for ten miles before splitting off oceanwards near Ponce Inlet, five miles south of mainland Daytona Beach.

Daytona Beach

The consummate Florida beach town, with rows of airbrushed-T-shirt shops, amusement arcades and wall-to-wall motels, **DAYTONA BEACH** owes its existence to twenty miles of light brown sand where the only pressure is to relax and enjoy yourself. The downtown area was threatened during the summer of 1998 by wild fires that plagued much of the state. The fires got close enough to warrant the evacuation of the town's population, but the flames were thankfully stopped before they could attack downtown. The damage done, however, is obvious in Daytona's western suburbs.

For decades, Daytona Beach was invaded by half-a-million college kids going through the **Spring Break** ritual of underage drinking and libido liberation. The town controversially decided to end its love affair with the nation's students and emulated Fort Lauderdale (see "The Southeast Coast") in cultivating a more refined image – an attempt that has been only partially successful. **MTV** still makes the beach its summer haunt, inviting the scantily clad to cavort about as the station's "VJs" announce the current top videos.

Today this small, medium-paced, down-to-earth resort, with just a day's worth of sights beyond its famous sands, is the center of three major annual events: the world-famous **Daytona 500** stock-car meeting, held at the Daytona International Speedway; **Bike Week**, when thousands of leather-clad motorcyclists converge for races at the Speedway; and the relatively new **Biketoberfest**, which is much the same idea (see box on p.196 for more info on all three events).

Even before the students and bikers, the beach was a favorite with pioneering auto enthusiasts such as Louis Chevrolet, Ransom Olds and Henry Ford, who came here during the early 1900s to race their prototype vehicles beside the ocean. The land speed record was regularly smashed, five times by millionaire British speedster Malcolm Campbell who, in 1935, roared along at 276mph. As a legacy of these times, Daytona Beach is one of the few Florida towns where **driving on the beach** is permitted: pay $5 at any beach entrance, stick to the marked track, observe the 10mph speed limit, park at right-angles to the ocean – and beware of high tide.

Arrival and getting around

As Ridgewood Avenue, **Hwy-1** steams through **mainland Daytona Beach**, passing the Greyhound station, at no. 138 S (☎255-7076). By car, you should keep to **Hwy-A1A** (known as Atlantic Avenue), which enters the beachside area – filling a narrow sliver of land between the ocean and the Halifax River (part of the intracoastal waterway) a mile from the mainland.

Local buses (Votran ☎761-7700) connect the beaches with the mainland and the Greater Daytona Beach area, though there is no night or Sunday service (buses run until 6pm daily). The bus terminal is at the junction of US-1 and Bethune Boulevard in mainland Daytona Beach. At the beach, **trolleys** run until midnight along the central part of Atlantic Avenue from January to August only. A **taxi** between the mainland and the beach will cost around $10; cab companies include AAA Metro Taxi (☎253-2522) and Yellow Cab (☎255-5555).

BUSES BETWEEN DAYTONA BEACH AND ORLANDO AIRPORT

If you're enjoying yourself at the beach but have to fly home from Orlando, you can take advantage of the **Daytona-Orlando Transit Service** (DOTS ☎1-800/231-1965), whose shuttle buses run every ninety minutes (4.30am–9.30pm) from the corner of Nova Road and 11th Street to Orlando airport. On request, the buses also make stops in Deland and Sanford. The one-way fare is $26 ($46 round-trip). Call ahead for details and reservations.

Don't leave mainland Daytona Beach without calling at the **Convention and Visitors Bureau** in the Chamber of Commerce building at 126 E Orange Avenue (Mon–Fri 9am–5pm; ☎1-800/854-1234), for a wealth of free information.

The beach and around

Without a doubt, the best thing about Daytona Beach *is* the **beach**: a seemingly limitless affair – 500 feet wide at low tide and, lengthways, fading dreamily into the heat haze. Although it lives up to its racy reputation during the student mate-seeking season of Spring Break, at other times of the year there's little to do other than develop your tan, take the occasional ocean dip or observe one of the many pro volleyball tournaments that set up camp during the summer. Even the **pier**, at the end of Main Street, isn't up to much; you can loiter in one of two characterless bars, enjoy panoramic views of the town from the Space Needle ($2); take the *Sky Ride*, a cable-car-like conveyance that ferries you slowly from one end of the pier to the other over the heads of patient anglers; or try the *Sky Coaster Ride*, a 60mph amusement arcade affair.

Nearby, Main Street and Seabreeze Boulevard have better **bars and cafes** (see "Eating" and "Nightlife"), but for more diverse pursuits – such as rambling around sand dunes, climbing an old lighthouse or discovering Daytona Beach's history – you need to head twelve miles south to Ponce Inlet, three miles north to Ormond Beach or cross the Halifax River to the mainland.

South to Ponce Inlet

Travelling south along Atlantic Avenue (buses #17A or #17B; only the former goes all the way to Ponce Inlet), small motels and fast-food dives give way to the towering beachside condos of affluent Daytona Beach shores. As you approach **Ponce Inlet**, four miles ahead, the outlook changes again, this time to single-story beach homes and large sand dunes.

Here, at the end of Peninsula Drive – parallel to Atlantic Avenue – the 175-foot-high **Ponce Inlet Lighthouse** (daily 10am–9pm; $4) illuminated the treacherous coast, giving seaborne access to New Smyrna Beach (see p.190) from the late 1800s until 1970. Stupendous views make climbing the structure worthwhile, and the outbuildings hold engaging artifacts from its early days as well as mildly interesting displays on US lighthouses in general. Several **nature trails** scratch a path through the surrounding scrub-covered dunes to a (usually) deserted **beach**; pick up a map from the **ranger station** at the end of Riverside Drive. Once you've trekked up an appetite, drop into the eccentric *Lighthouse Landing* (see "Eating"), beside the lighthouse, whose cheap seafood is brought ashore at the adjoining marina.

North to Ormond Beach

In 1890, planning to bring his East Coast railway south from St Augustine, oil baron Henry Flagler bought the local hotel, built a beachside golf course and helped give **ORMOND BEACH**, three miles north of Main Street (buses #1A or #1B; the latter

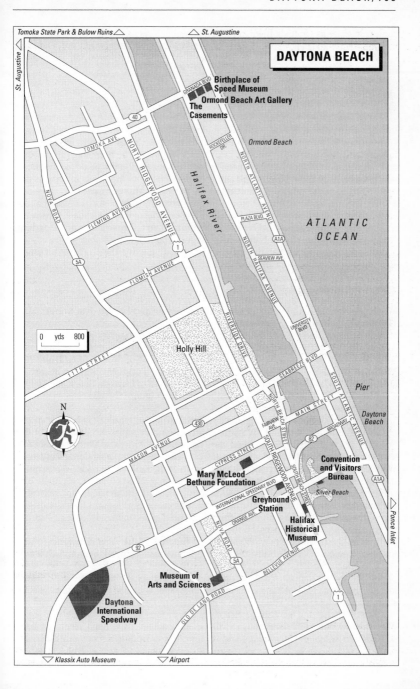

DAYTONA BEACH

Tomoka State Park & Bulow Ruins △

△ St. Augustine

St. Augustine

GRANADA BLVD

Birthplace of Speed Museum

Ormond Beach Art Gallery

The Casements

TOMOKA AVE

ROCKAFELLER DR.

Ormond Beach

NOVA ROAD

NORTH RIDGEWOOD AVENUE

FLEMING AVENUE

Halifax River

NORTH ATLANTIC AVENUE

PLAZA BLVD

ATLANTIC OCEAN

A1A

NORTH HALIFAX AVENUE

SEAVIEW AVE.

FLOMISH AVENUE

RIVERSIDE DRIVE

UNIVERSITY BLVD

0   yds   800

11TH STREET

Holly Hill

SEABREEZE BLVD

SOUTH ATLANTIC AVENUE

Pier

N

NORTH BEACH STREET

FAIRVIEW AVE.

MAIN STREET

BROADWAY

Daytona Beach

MASON AVENUE

CYPRESS STREET

SOUTH RIDGEWOOD AVENUE

SOUTH BEACH STREET

Convention and Visitors Bureau

Mary McLeod Bethune Foundation

INTERNATIONAL SPEEDWAY BLVD

Greyhound Station

Silver Beach

A1A

ORANGE AVE.

Halifax Historical Museum

NOVA ROAD

5A

BELLEVUE AVENUE

Museum of Arts and Sciences

Daytona International Speedway

OLD DE LAND ROAD

1

△ Ponce Inlet

▽ Klassix Auto Museum

▽ Airport

runs only as far as Granada Blvd), a refined tone that it retains to this day. Millionaires like John D Rockefeller wintered here, and the car-happy fraternity of Ford, Olds and Chevrolet used Flagler's garage to fine-tune their autos before powering them along the beach.

Facing the Halifax River at the end of Granada Boulevard, Flagler's **Ormond Hotel** stood until 1993, when it was demolished to much public mourning. The **Casements** (Mon–Fri 10am–2.30pm, Sat 10–11am; free), however, a three-story villa on the other side of Granada Boulevard, which was bought by Rockefeller in 1918, is in fine fettle (all the original furniture, though, was sold, and what remains was donated by neighbors). **Guided tours** of the house (which, oddly enough, now holds displays of Hungarian folklore and Boy Scouts of America bric-a-brac) run every thirty minutes from 10am and tell you more than you'll ever need to know about Rockefeller and his time here, which was mostly spent playing golf and pressing dimes into the hands of passers-by.

Also on Granada Boulevard, the **Birthplace of Speed Museum**, no. 160 (Tues–Sun 1–5pm; $1), makes a convenient stop, though it contains only pictorial records of the early Daytona Beach speed merchants and a few replicas of their machines. Nearby, at no. 78, the Polynesian-style **Ormond Memorial Art Museum and Gardens** (Mon–Fri 10am–4pm, Sat & Sun noon–4pm; free) puts on reasonable temporary art shows – if they don't appeal, the gallery's jungle-like **gardens**, with shady pathways winding past fishponds to a gazebo, just might.

The mainland

When you're tired of the sands or nursing your sunburn, cross the river to **mainland Daytona Beach**, where several waterside parks and walkways contribute to a relaxing change of scene, and four museums will keep you out of the sun for a few hours.

Near the best of the parks, on Beach Street, a few turn-of-the-century dwellings have been tidied up and turned into office space. At no. 252 S is the **Halifax Historical Museum** (Tues–Sat 10am–4pm; $3, free on Sat), which captures, with an absorbing stock of objects, models and photos, the frenzied growth of Daytona Beach and Halifax County. Amid the fine stash of historical fall-out, don't ignore the immense wall paintings of long-gone local landscapes.

One former Daytona Beach resident referred to in the museum is better remembered by the **Mary McLeod Bethune Foundation**, a couple of miles north at 640 Second Avenue. Born in 1875 to freed slave parents, Mary McLeod Bethune was a lifelong campaigner for racial and sexual equality, founding the National Council of Negro Women and serving as a presidential advisor. In 1904, against the odds, she founded the state's first black girls' school here – with savings of $1.50 and five pupils. The white-framed **house** (Mon–Fri 9am–4pm; free), where Bethune lived from 1914 until her death in 1955, contains scores of awards and citations alongside furnishings and personal effects, and sits within the campus of the large community college that has grown up around the original school.

If you're keen on prehistory, stop off at the **Museum of the Arts & Sciences**, 1040 Museum Boulevard (Tues–Fri 9am–4pm, Sat & Sun noon–5pm; $4, free on Sat), a mile south of International Speedway Boulevard (buses #6 and #7 pass close by), to scrutinize bones and fossils dug up from the numerous archeological sites in the area. These include the ferocious-looking, reassembled remains of a million-year-old giant ground sloth (thirteen feet long). There is also a **Planetarium** for which the staff will try to sell you a combo ticket, but it is only worth it if you fancy a long nap under a virtual star-scape. The other sections of the constantly expanding museum are intriguingly diverse: a stash of American paintings, furnishings and decorative arts from the seventeenth century onwards illuminates early Anglo-American tastes. A major African collection displays domestic and ceremonial objects from thirty of the continent's cultures, including pieces donated –strangely enough – by obscure television stars like Dirk Benedict (A-Team) and Linda Evans (Dynasty). Finally, Cuban paintings spanning two centuries (donated by Cuba's former dictator, Batista, who spent many years of exile in a comfortable Daytona Beach house) provide a glimpse of the island nation's important artistic movements.

Daytona International Speedway

About three miles west along International Speedway Boulevard (bus #9A & #9B) stands an ungainly configuration of concrete and steel that has done much to promote Daytona Beach's name around the world: the **Daytona International Speedway**, home of the Daytona 500 stock-car meeting and a few other less famous races. When high speeds made racing on Daytona's sands unsafe, the solution was this 150,000-capacity temple to high-performance thrills and spills, which opened in 1959.

If you can't catch a race, **Daytona USA** (daily 9am–7pm, $12 to enter, $6 for speedway tours, or $16 for a combo ticket; ☎947-6800), located next to the speedway, is the next best thing. Though it doesn't quite capture the excitement of a race, the guided **trolley tour** (every 30min daily 9.30am–5pm, except on race days) gives visitors a chance to see the sheer size of the place and the remarkable gradient of the curves, which help make this the fastest racetrack in the world – 200mph is not uncommon.

Inside, Daytona USA's interactive exhibits put you in the driver's seat: show the spectators how fast you can jack a race car off the ground during a sixteen-second pit stop. Feel the engines revving in your chest as you watch the thunderous Daytona 500 wide-screen movie, or call a race as it happens at the interactive commentator booth. Other exhibits showcase the history of NASCAR* (National Association of Stock Car Auto Racing) and the evolution of the race car.

Klassix Auto Museum

A mile west of the Speedway, the **Klassix Auto Museum**, at 2909 International Speedway Boulevard (daily 9am–6pm; $7.50), displays pristine examples of every Corvette design from 1953 to the present day, in historically accurate settings. The museum also houses various other collector and "muscle" cars, as well as vintage motorcycles, all engagingly offset by a 1938 Woody Wagon that boasts a top speed of 50mph. Catch bus #9A or #9B to get there.

North to Tomoka State Park and the Bulow Ruins

At the meeting point of the Halifax and Tomoka rivers, just off Hwy-1 six miles north of International Speedway Boulevard (bus #1B, then a mile's walk), the attractive Tomoka State Park (daily 8am–sunset; cars $3.25, cyclists and pedestrians $1; ☎676-4050) comprises several hundred acres of marshes and tidal creeks, bordered by magnolias and moss-draped oaks. It's ripe for exploration by canoe ($3 per hour or $15 per day) or by foot on the many paths.

A 1972 addition to the park, the tiny **Fred Dana Marsh Museum** (9.30am–4.30pm; admission included in park entrance fee) details the life and work of the man who, in the 1910s, was the first artist in the US to create large-scale murals depicting "the drama and significance of men at work." In the 1920s, Marsh also designed a then (and in some ways still) futuristic home for himself and his wife in Ormond Beach. The house is located just north of Granada Boulevard on Hwy-A1A, though admission is not allowed. Within the park itself, don't miss Marsh's immense sculpture, *The Legend of Tomokie*.

Take full advantage of the park by camping overnight (see "Accommodation"), which leaves time to visit the **Bulow Plantation Ruins** (daily 9am–5pm; free) – scant

---

*For the ultimate NASCAR racing experience, see p.243 for information on the **Richard Petty Driving Experience**, where you can do it yourself – for a price.

and heavily-vegetated remains of an eighteenth-century plantation destroyed by Seminole Indians (five miles north of the park off of Route 201).

Accommodation

From mid-May to November, scores of small **motels** on Atlantic Avenue slash their rates to $20–30 for a double – cheaper for two people sharing than staying at the youth hostel (see below). These rates go up by $10–15 from December to February, and soar to $60 during March and April (though the demise of Spring Break may serve to stabilize prices between December and mid-May). Pick up the free *Superior Small Lodging Guide* from the Convention and Visitors Bureau for helpful hints on where to stay.

The choice is almost limitless, but the best of the pick is the roomy, beachfront *Tropical Manor Motel*, no. 2237 S (☎1/800-253-4920; ②). Movie-themed rooms greet visitors at *Travellers Inn*, no. 735 N (☎253-3501; ②); and the following will give you a comfortable stay and a good rate: *Ocean Hut*, no. 1110 N (☎258-0482; ②); *Robin Hood*, no.1150 N (☎252-8228; ②); *Cove*, no. 1306 N (☎1-800/828-3251; ②); *Cypress Cove Motel*, no. 3245 S (☎761-1660; ②); and *Seascape Motel*, no. 3321 S (☎767-1372; ②).

Prices rise steadily as you move north along Atlantic Avenue towards Ormond Beach, but the *Econo Lodge-on-the-Beach*, 295 S Atlantic Avenue (☎1-800/847-8811; ③), the *Driftwood Beach Motel*, 657 S Atlantic Avenue (☎677-1331; ②), and the *Atlantic Waves Motel*, 1925 S Atlantic Avenue (☎1/800-881-2786; ②), all accommodate limited budgets.

Bed and breakfast in Daytona Beach means turning your back on the ocean and heading inland. The choices are the homely *Coquina Inn*, 544 S Palmetto Avenue (☎254-4969; ③), the jacuzzi-equipped *Live Oak Inn*, 444-448 S Beach Street (☎252-4667; ⑤–⑥), and *The Villa*, 801 N Peninsula Drive (☎248-2020; ④–⑤).

The youth hostel and camping

The *Streamline* **Youth Hostel**, 140 S Atlantic Avenue (☎258-6937), has received mixed reviews from travelers ranging from OK to horrible. And since it charges $25, you may feel more secure in one of the plethora of motels in the same price range. The nearest **campgrounds** are less than ideally placed: *Nova Family Campground*, 1190 Herbert Street (☎767-0095), ten miles south of mainland Daytona Beach (bus #17A & #17B or #7; $16 to pitch a tent); and *Tomoka State Park* (☎676-4050), seven miles north of mainland Daytona Beach (bus #1B stops a mile down the road; $8-16 to pitch a tent with rates highest in February).

DAYTONA SPEED WEEKS

The Daytona Speedway hosts several major race meetings each year, starting in early February with the **Rolex 24**: a 24-hour race for GT prototype sports cars. A week or so later begin the qualifying races leading up to the biggest event of the year, the **Daytona 500** stock-car race in mid-February. Tickets (see below) for this are as common as Florida snow, but many of the same drivers compete in the **Pepsi 400**, held on the first Saturday in July, for which tickets are much easier to get. As well as cars, the track is also used for motorcycle races: **Bike Week**, in late February and early March, sees a variety of high-powered clashes; **Biketoberfest**, held the third week in October, is highlighted by AMA championship racing; and the **Daytona Pro-Am** races at the end of October include numerous sprints and a three-hour endurance test.

Tickets (the cheapest are $20–25 for cars, $10–15 for bikes) for the bigger events sell out well in advance, and it's also advisable to book accommodation for those times at least six months ahead. For **information** and ticket details: ☎904/253-RACE.

Eating

Major appetites can be satisfied for modest outlay at several buffet **restaurants**: *Shoney's*, 2558 N Atlantic Avenue (☎673-4288), is open for breakfast, lunch and dinner; and *Checkers*, 219 S Atlantic Avenue (☎239-0010), has buffet breakfasts and an all-you-can-eat dinner session.

Seafood is the major lure in these parts, and two inexpensive restaurants that won't disappoint are: the *Clocktower Restaurant*, inside the *Adams Mark Resort* at 100 N Atlantic Avenue (☎254-8200), and *Shells*, 200 S Atlantic Avenue (☎258-0007). Other culinary favorites include the *St Regis Restaurant and Patio Bar*, 509 Seabreeze Blvd (☎252-8743); the strong Mexican flavors of the *Rio Bravo Cantina*, 1735 International Speedway Blvd (☎255-6500); and great burgers at *McK's Tavern*, 218 S Beach St (☎238-3321). Slightly pricier but with greater choices for lunch or dinner is *Julian's*, 88 S Atlantic Avenue (☎677-6767), a dimly lit mock-Tahitian lounge with a good menu. Also worth trying are the *Lighthouse Landing*, beside the Ponce Inlet lighthouse (☎761-9271), which is strong on fresh seafood, as is *Down the Hatch*, 4894 Front Street, Ponce Inlet (☎761-4831), with a waterfront location and outdoor raw oyster bar. *Aunt Catfish's*, 4009 Halifax Drive, a few miles south of Daytona Beach in Port Orange (☎767-4768), has mighty portions of ribs and seafood prepared to traditional Southern recipes. If you have a sudden desire for Japanese food, head for *Sapporo*, 3340 S Atlantic Avenue (☎756-0480).

Nightlife

Even without the Spring Break invasion of party-crazed students, it seems likely that Daytona Beach will retain its reputation as one of the best spots on Florida's east coast for making merry when the sun goes down. The nucleus of the beachside **nightlife** is *HoJo's Party Complex*, 600 N Atlantic Avenue (☎255-4471; $3–10), with bars, discos, live rock and reggae and ceaseless wet T-shirt competitions. There's more rabble-rousing, accompanied by dazzling light shows, at *Razzles*, 611 Seabreeze Boulevard (☎257-6236). *Ocean Deck*, 127 S Ocean Avenue (☎253-5224), boasts live music; and *Kokomos on the Beach* and *Waves*, both at 100 N Atlantic Avenue inside the Adams Mark Daytona Beach Resort (☎254-8200), have been known to offer a good time. Danceable **nightclubs** with a less collegiate crowd are the *Checkers Café*, (see above), and *Coliseum*, 176 N Beach Street (☎258-1500).

Simply for a **drink**, the *Boot Hill Saloon*, across from the cemetery at 310 Main Street (☎258-9506), can be enjoyable, but if you find its biker clientele threatening, alternatives are *The Oyster Pub*, 555 Seabreeze Boulevard (☎255-6348), where the beer is helped down by dirt-cheap oysters and a loud jukebox, and *The Spot*, a sports bar and part of the *Coliseum* complex (see above). For **live music**, look to the jazz notes of *Café Bravo Coffee Bar*, corner of Beach and Bay streets (☎252-7747); *Rockin' Ranch* in the Ellinor Village shopping center, 801 S Nova Road (☎673-0904); the swaggering two-step line dancing of *Billy Bob's Race Country USA*, 2801 S Ridgewood Avenue (☎756-0448); or the *Clocktower Lounge* in the Adams Mark Daytona Beach Resort (see above), an elegant piano bar with an ocean view.

North of Daytona Beach

Assuming you don't want to cut twenty miles inland along I-4 or Hwy-92 to DeLand and the Orlando area (see "Central Florida"), keep on Hwy-A1A **northwards** along the coast towards St Augustine – as usual, Greyhound buses take the less interesting Hwy-1.

The first community you'll encounter is **FLAGLER BEACH**, fourteen miles from Daytona Beach, comprising a few houses and shops, a pier and a very tempting beach. Nearby, at the **Flagler Beach State Recreation Area** (daily 8am–sunset; cars $3.25, cyclists and pedestrians $1), a good cross-section of coastal bird life can be spotted, particularly at low tide when freshly exposed sands provide a feast for swift beaks.

Further on, soon after passing the blazing blooms of **Washington Oaks State Gardens** (daily 8am–sunset; cars $3.25, pedestrians and cyclists $1), you can't miss the streamlined architecture of **Marineland** (daily 9am–5.30pm; $14.95; ☎1/800-824-4218), Florida's original sea-creature theme park. The state's biggest tourist draw when it opened in 1938, its status has been severely undermined by subsequent imitations such as the far superior Sea World (see "Central Florida"). Established as marine studios for underwater research and photography, the park's highlights include sharks, performing porpoises and a 3-D film depicting an undersea adventure, but none of these justifies the high admission fee.

Hwy-A1A crosses a narrow inlet three miles beyond Marineland onto **Anastasia Island**, close to the Spanish-built seventeenth-century **Fort Matanzas** on Rattlesnake Island. Never conquered, partly due to the sixteen-foot-thick walls and the surrounding moat, the fort is accessible only by **ferry** (departures every 15min daily except Tuesday, 9am–4.30pm; free), but it's of minor appeal in comparison to history-packed St Augustine.

A better stop might be the **St Augustine Alligator Farm** (daily 9am–6pm; $11.95), a few miles further north along Hwy-A1A. Visitors are greeted by shrieks from a vividly colored toucan and can take a walk through a wildlife-infested swamp. Time your visit to coincide with the "alligator show" (4 shows daily; call ☎904/824-3337 for exact times), when a keeper drags an alligator around by its tail to demonstrate how the creature expresses anger: it bellows loudly, arches its back and displays a gaping jaw. It's heart-stopping stuff – not least when the handler, sitting on the creature's back, puts his fingers between the gator's teeth.

Once past the Alligator Farm, you're well within reach of St Augustine, whose old center is just across Matanzas Bay, three miles ahead.

St Augustine

With the size and even some of the looks of a small Mediterranean town, there are few places in Florida as immediately engaging as **ST AUGUSTINE**, the oldest permanent settlement in the US and one with much from its early days still intact. St Augustine's eminently strollable narrow streets are lined by carefully renovated buildings whose architecture carries evidence of Florida's European heritage and the power struggles that led up to statehood. There's plenty here to fill a day or two, and for variation you can visit two alluring lengths of beach located just across the small bay on which the town stands.

Ponce de Leon, the Spaniard who gave Florida its name, touched ground here on *Pascua Florida* (Easter Sunday) in 1513, but it wasn't until Pedro Menendez de Aviles put ashore on St Augustine's Day in 1565 that settlement began, with the intention of subduing the Huguenots based to the north at Fort Caroline (see "The Jacksonville beaches," p.205). Repeated battles with the British began when Sir Francis Drake's ships razed St Augustine in 1586, but Spanish control was only relinquished when Florida was ceded to Britain in 1763, by which time the town was established as an important social and administrative center – soon to become the capital of East Florida.

The area code for St Augustine and Jacksonville is ☎904.

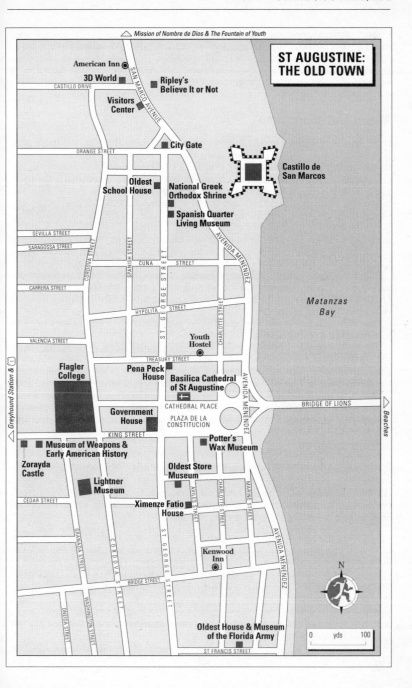

△ *Mission of Nombre de Dios & The Fountain of Youth*

**ST AUGUSTINE:
THE OLD TOWN**

American Inn ●

3D World ■

CASTILLO DRIVE

Ripley's
Believe It or Not

SAN MARCO AVENUE

Visitors
Center ■

City Gate ■

ORANGE STREET

Castillo de
San Marcos

Oldest
School House ■

National Greek
Orthodox Shrine ◄

Spanish Quarter
Living Museum ■

SEVILLA STREET

SARAGOSSA STREET

CORDOVA STREET

SPANISH STREET

CUNA STREET

ST GEORGE STREET

AVENIDA MENENDEZ

CARRERA STREET

HYPOLITA STREET

CHARLOTTE STREET

*Matanzas
Bay*

VALENCIA STREET

Youth
Hostel ◉

TREASURY STREET

Flagler
College

Pena Peck
House ■

Basilica Cathedral
of St Augustine ✚

AVENIDA MENENDEZ

BRIDGE OF LIONS

▷ *Beaches*

◁ *Greyhound Station &* ☺

CATHEDRAL PLACE

Government
House ■

PLAZA DE LA
CONSTITUCION

KING STREET

Museum of Weapons &
Early American History

Potter's
Wax Museum ■

Zorayda
Castle ■

Lightner
Museum ■

Oldest Store
Museum ■

CEDAR STREET

Ximenze Fatio
House ■

AVILES STREET

CHARLOTTE STREET

MARINE STREET

GRANADA STREET

WASHINGTON STREET

CORDOVA STREET

ST GEORGE STREET

Kenwood
Inn ◉

AVENIDA MENENDEZ

ONEIDA STREET

BRIDGE STREET

N

Oldest House & Museum
of the Florida Army ■

ST FRANCIS STREET

0   yds   100

Spain regained possession twenty years later, and kept it until 1821, when Florida joined the US. Subsequently, Tallahassee became the capital of a unified Florida, and St Augustine's fortunes waned. A railway and a posh hotel stimulated a turn-of-the-century tourist boom, but otherwise expansion bypassed St Augustine – which inadvertently made possible the restoration program that started in the Thirties. This has turned the otherwise quiet, residential community into a magnificent historical showcase.

Arrival and information

From Anastasia Island, **Hwy-A1A** crosses over Mantanzas Bay into the heart of St Augustine; **Hwy-1** passes a mile west along Ponce de Leon Boulevard. The Greyhound **bus** will drop you at 100 Malaga Street (☎829-6401), a fifteen-minute walk from the center.

St Augustine has no public transport system, but this poses no problem in the town, which is best seen **on foot**. There are two **sightseeing trains**, the *St Augustine Sightseeing Train* (red-and-blue) and the *St Augustine Historical Train* (green-and-white), distinguishable only by their colors. Both make approximately twenty stops during an hour-long narrated circuit of the main landmarks; you can hop on and off whenever you like. **Tickets** can be purchased from virtually any bed-and-breakfast or motel, but the primary purchase point is the Visitor's Center on San Marco Avenue (daily 8am–5pm; $12).

After a few hours of hard exploration, **harbor cruises**, leaving five or six times a day from the City Yacht Pier, near the foot of King Street, make a relaxing break; the 75-minute guided trip around the bay costs $8.50 – paying to ride the sightseeing train will earn you a discount on the cruise.

After delving into the town's historical value, getting to the beaches means a two-mile hike or calling a **taxi** (☎824-8161).

The **visitor center**, 10 Castillo Drive (Mon–Thur 8am–7.30pm, Fri & Sat 8am–9pm; ☎825-1000), offers the usual tourist brochures and discount coupons. It also has a free film on the history of the town, recommendations on a variety of historical guided tours (including those of *Tour St Augustine*, who offer well-organized and informative walking tours, as well as tailored itineraries ☎471-9010), and information on the numerous local festivals which range from torch-lit processions (third Sat in June) to chowder tastings (last weekend in Oct) and a Menorcan Fiesta (second weekend in September).

Accommodation

St Augustine attracts plenty of visitors, most of whom make short stays between May and October, when costs are $10–20 above the winter rates. The Old Town (see below) has many restored inns offering **bed and breakfast**: *Carriage Way*, 70 Cuna Street (☎829-2467; ③), *Cordova House*, 16 Cordova Street (☎825-0770; ④), and *Kenwood Inn*, 38 Marine Street (☎824-2116; ④), are the best priced.

To cut costs considerably, use the excellently situated *St Augustine Hostel*, 32 Treasury Street (check-in times 8am–10am and 5pm–10pm; $12; ☎808-1999), which has a giant kitchen and common room stuffed with local guidebooks. The owners, amazingly, only speak French, so communication could be a bit stunted.

Alternatively, try the cheap **motels** that ring the Old Town. Least expensive is the *American Inn*, 42 San Marco Avenue (☎829-2292; ③); further along the same road is *Equinox*, no. 306 (☎829-8569; ③). Across the bay from the Old Town but well within striking distance, you'll find the waterside *Anchorage Motor Inn*, 1 Dolphin Drive (☎829-9041; ③), *Royal Inn*, 420 Anastasia Boulevard (☎824-2831; ②), and the *Rodeway Inn*, 107 Anastasia Boulevard (☎826-1700; ④).

Costs are usually higher **at the beaches**, but the laid-back *Vilano Beach Motel*, 50 Vilano Beach Road (☎829-2651; ③), is a great base for enjoying the North Beach; to the south, the busier St Augustine Beach has more family-oriented weekly rented apartments than motels, though the small *Sea Shore*, 480 Hwy-A1A (☎471-3101; ②), and *Seaway*, 481 Hwy-A1A (☎471-3466; ③), are reliable.

The best place to **camp** is the *Anastasia State Recreation Area* (☎461-2033), four miles south, off Hwy-A1A (see "The Beaches," p.204), where you can pitch a tent for $17.

The Old Town

St Augustine's historic area – or **Old Town** – along St George Street and south of the central plaza, contains well-tended evidence of the town's Spanish period. Equally worth a look are the lavish structures along King Street, just west of the plaza, remaining from the turn-of-the-century resort times. Although St Augustine is small, there's a lot to see: an early start, around 9am, will give you a lead on the tourist crowds, and you should ideally allow for three days to fully explore the town.

The castle

Given the fine state of the **Castillo de San Marcos** (daily 8.45am–4.45pm; $4), on the northern edge of the Old Town beside the bay, it's difficult to believe that the fortress was started in the late 1600s. Its longevity is due to the design: a diamond-shaped rampart at each corner maximized firepower, and fourteen-foot-thick coquina (a type of soft limestone found on Anastasia Island) walls reduced vulnerability to attack – as British troops found when they waged a fruitless fifty-day siege in 1702. Time schedules for the free twenty-minute **talks** on the fort and local history are indicated in the courtyard.

Inside, there's not a lot to admire beyond a small museum and echoing rooms – some of them with military and social exhibits – but venturing along the 35-foot-high ramparts gives an unobstructed view over the low-lying city and its waterborne approaches, which the castle protected so successfully. Look for the eerie graffiti on the walls, scrawled by prisoners in the 1600s.

Along St George Street

Leaving the castle, the little eighteenth-century **City Gate** marks the entrance to **St George Street**, once the main thoroughfare and now a tourist-trampled pedestrianized strip – but home to plenty of genuine history. At no. 14, the **Oldest Wooden School House** (daily 9am-5pm in winter; 9am-8pm in summer; $2; ☎824-0192) still has its original eighteenth-century red cedar and cypress walls and tabby floor (a mix of crushed oyster shells and lime, common at the time). These architectural points are the main interest: the building was put into use as a school some years later, thereby inadvertently becoming, as the staff are quick to point out, the oldest wooden schoolhouse in the US. Pupils and teacher are now unconvincingly portrayed by speaking wax models.

Further along, at no. 41, an unassuming doorway leads into the petite **National Greek Orthodox Shrine** (daily 9am–5pm; free), where tapes of Byzantine choirs echo through the halls, and icons and candles stand alongside hard-hitting accounts relating the experiences of Greek immigrants to the US – some of whom settled in St Augustine from New Smyrna Beach (see p.190) in 1777.

More directly relevant to the town, and taking up a fair-sized plot at the corner of St George and Cuna streets, the **Spanish Quarter Living Museum** (9am–6pm Sun–Thur, until 9pm Fri & Sat; $6; ☎825-6830) includes eight reconstructed homes and workshops. Volunteers disguised as Spanish settlers go about their daily tasks at spinning wheels, anvils and foot-driven wood lathes. The museum should be visited either early in the day or during an off-peak period; lines of camera-wielding tourists and rowdy school groups substantially lessen the effect. The main entrance is through the Triay House, on N St George Street.

For a more intimate look at local life during a slightly later period, head for the **Pena Peck House**, at no. 143 (Mon–Sat 10am–4.30pm, Sun 12.30–4.30pm; $2; ☎829-5064). Thought originally to have been the Spanish treasury, by the time the British took over in 1763 this was the home of a physician and his gregarious spouse, who turned the place into a high society rendezvous. The Pecks' furnishings and paintings, plus the enthusiastic spiel of the guide, make for an enjoyable tour.

The Plaza

In the sixteenth century, the Spanish king decreed that all colonial towns had to be built around a central plaza, and St Augustine was no exception: St George Street runs into **Plaza de la Constitucion**, a marketplace dating from 1598, nowadays attracting shade-seekers and the occasional wino. On the north side of the plaza, the **Basilica Cathedral of St Augustine** (daily 7am–5pm; donation requested) adds a touch of grandeur, though it's largely a Sixties remodeling of the late eighteenth-century original, with murals by Hugo Ohlms depicting life in St Augustine. Periodic **guided tours** (times are sometimes pinned to the door) revel in the painstaking details of the rebuilding and the undistinguished stained-glass windows. Slightly more worthwhile, the ground floor of **Government House** (9am–7pm Mon–Thur, 9am–9pm Fri & Sat; $3; ☎825-5033), on the west side of the plaza, contains small displays of objects from the city's various renovation projects and archeological digs. In contrast, on the south side of the square, seeking shelter from a thunderstorm might be the sole justification for entering **Potter's Wax Museum** (summer daily 9am–9pm; winter 9am–5pm; $5), populated by effigies of people you may have heard of but probably won't recognize.

South of the Plaza

Tourist numbers lessen as you cross south of the plaza into a web of quiet, narrow streets with as much antiquity as St George Street. At 4 Artillery Lane, the **Oldest Store Museum** (Mon–Sat 9am–5pm, Sun noon–5pm; $5) does an excellent job of recreating an 1880s general store, filled to the rafters with the produce of the time: curious foods and drinks, fiery medicinal potions and oversized consumer essentials such as apple peelers, cigar moulders and wooden washing machines.

Close by, at 20 Aviles Street, the **Ximenez Fatio House** (Mon–Thurs 11am–4pm, Sun 1–4pm; free; ☎829-3575) was built in 1797 for a Spanish merchant and proved popular with the travelers who predated the town's first tourist boom, drawn by the airy balconies added to the original structure. Although the upper floor is a bit rickety, a walk around is safe and quick in the company of a guide who points out illuminating details. At 3 Aviles Street you can spend an interesting fifteen minutes in the small **Spanish Military Hospital** (9am–7pm Sun–Thur, 9am–9pm Fri & Sat; $2), built in 1791 and demonstrating the spartan care wounded soldiers could expect.

More substantial history is unfurled a ten-minute walk away at the **Oldest House**, 14 St Francis Street (daily 9am–5pm; $5; last admission 4.30pm; ☎824-2872), occupied from the early 1700s (and, indeed, the oldest house in the town) by the family of an artillery hand at the castle. The second floor was grafted on during the British period, a fact evinced by the bone china crockery belonging to the incumbent, one Mary Peavitt, whose disastrous marriage to a hopeless gambler provided the basis for a popular historical novel, *Maria*, by Eugenia Price (the gift shop has copies). A smaller room shows the pine-stripped "sidecar" style made popular by the arrival of Flagler's railway: it copies the decor of a train carriage.

Entered through the back garden of the house, the less than riveting **Museum of the Florida Army** (entry included with admission to the Oldest House; same hours) gives an inkling, mainly with old uniforms, of the numerous conflicts that have divided Florida over the years. Anybody you might see striding by in modern military garb probably belongs to the Florida National Guard, whose headquarters are across the street.

West of the Plaza: along King Street

A walk west from the plaza along **King Street** bridges the gap between early St Augustine and its turn-of-the-century tourist boom. You'll soon notice, at the junction with Cordova Street, the flowing spires, arches and red-tiled roof of **Flagler College**. Now utilized by liberal arts students, a hundred years ago it was – as the *Ponce de Leon Hotel* – an exclusive winter retreat of the nation's rich and mighty. The hotel was an early attempt by entrepreneur Henry Flagler to exploit Florida's climate and coast, but as he developed properties further south and extended his railway, the *Ponce de Leon* fell from favor – not helped by a couple of freezing winters. There are free guided tours in the summer. You can **walk around** the campus and the ground floor of the main building (daily 10am–3pm) to admire the Tiffany stained glass and the painstakingly restored painted ceiling in the dining room.

In competition with Flagler, the eccentric Bostonian architect Franklin W. Smith – seemingly obsessed with poured concrete and Moorish design (see the Zorayda Castle, below) – built a rival hotel of matching extravagance directly opposite the *Ponce de Leon*. He eventually sold it to Flagler, who named it the *Alcazar*. Fronted by a courtyard of palm trees and fountains, the building now holds the **Lightner Museum** (daily 9am–5pm; last admission 4.30pm; $6), where you could easily pass an hour poring over the Victorian cut glass, Tiffany lamps, antique music boxes and more. Much of it was acquired by publishing ace Otto C. Lightner from once-wealthy estates hard hit by the Depression.

A rather incongruous sight in St Augustine is Franklin W. Smith's (see above) recreation of the Alhambra. The architect was so impressed by the Moorish architecture he'd seen in Spain that he built a copy of a wing of the thirteenth-century palace here, at a tenth of the original size. In 1913, forty years after the **Zorayda Castle**, 83 King Street (daily 9am-5pm; $5; ☎824-3097), was finished, a well-heeled Egyptian consul purchased it to store his ankle-deep carpets and treasures from all points east: a 2300-year-old Sacred Cat Rug, said to put a curse on anyone who stands on it (which is perhaps why it hangs on the wall), and a divinely detailed gaming table inlaid with sandalwood and mother-of-pearl, are just two. As a giant folly stuffed with gems, the Zorayda Castle has much charm; only the 25c test-your-sex-appeal machine by the exit shatters the mood.

Just across the Zorayda's parking lot, a shack contains the **Museum of Weapons and Early American History** (daily 9.30am–5pm; $4). Reading the small collection of Civil War diaries gives an interesting personal view of the struggle, but this one-room cache will mainly appeal to survivalist types, with plenty of tools to shoot, stab and batter foes to death.

North of the Old Town: San Marco Avenue and around

Leading away from the tightly grouped streets of the Old Town, the traffic-bearing **San Marco Avenue**, beginning on the other side of the city gate from St George Street, passes the sites of the first Spanish landings and settlements and some remains of the Timucua Indians who greeted them. A couple of other potential stops are of much less relevance to the town but can be good for a laugh.

People either love or loathe them, but if you've never been inside one of the country's several **Ripley's Believe It or Not** collections, you shouldn't pass up the chance. This one, at 19 San Marco Avenue (daily 9am–10pm; $8.95; ☎824-1606), isn't the best but contains a riveting collection of oddities gathered by Ripley as he travelled around the world in the Twenties and Thirties. Whether it's a grandfather clock made from clothes pegs, the Lord's Prayer printed on the head of a pin or a toothpick model of the Eiffel Tower, each object seems stranger than the last, and it can be hard to tear yourself away.

Directly across the street from Ripley's is **3-D World**, 28 San Marco Avenue (daily 10am–10pm; $9 for all three shows), which shows three films ranging from the calming waters of "Blue Magic," where scores of colorful fish dart past your eyes, to action adventure films where a frenetic motion simulator pitches you headfirst into the "Castle of Doom" and then on to the "Curse of King Tut" – ill-advised for those susceptible to motion sickness.

Half a mile further along San Marco Avenue, don't be discouraged by the dull, modern church that now stands in the grounds of **Mission of Nombre de Dios** (summer daily 7am–8pm; rest of the year 8am–6pm; $4 donation requested). This sixteenth-century mission was one of many established by Spanish settlers in order to convert Native Americans to Christianity, simultaneously exploiting their labor and seeking to earn their support in possible confrontations with rival colonial powers.

A pathway leads to a 208-foot-tall stainless steel cross, glinting in the sun beside the river on the spot where Menendez landed in 1565. Soon after, Father Francisco Lopez de Mendoza Grajales celebrated the first Mass in North America, recording that "a large number of Indians watched the proceedings and imitated all they saw," which was a bit unfortunate since the arrival of the Spanish signalled the beginning of the end for the Indians. A side-path takes a mildly interesting course around the rest of the squirrel-patrolled lawns, passing a few relics of the mission, on the way to a small, ivy-covered re-creation of the original chapel.

In addition to the prospect of finding gold and silver, it's said that Ponce de Leon was drawn to Florida by a belief that the fabled life-preserving "fountain of youth" was located here. Rather tenuously, this fact is celebrated at a mineral spring touted as **The Fountain of Youth** (daily 9am–5pm; $4.75) in a park at the end of Williams Street (off San Marco Avenue), very near the point where he landed in 1513, and about half a mile north of the old mission site; it's unlikely, however, you'll live forever after drinking the fresh water handed to you as you enter the springhouse. The expansive acres of the park have far more significance as an archeological site. Besides remains of the Spanish settlement, many Timucua Indian relics have been unearthed, and you'll also come across some of the wiry plants that were the base of the "Black Drink," a thick, highly potent concoction used by the Timucuans to help them achieve mystical states.

The beaches

If you've reached St Augustine with Hwy-A1A you'll need no introduction to the fine **beaches** that lie just a couple of miles from the Old Town. Few other people do either, especially on weekends when the bronzers, beachcombers and water-sports fanatics descend in droves. A fine view of St Augustine and up and down the beaches is afforded by the **Lighthouse Museum**, 81 Lighthouse Avenue (daily 9am–6pm; $2.50 for the museum only, $5 if you want to climb to the top; ☎829-0745), which tells the story of keepers and the lights they tended.

Across the bay on Anastasia Island, **St Augustine Beach** is family terrain, but here you'll also find the **Anastasia State Recreation Area** (daily 8am–sunset; cars $3.25, cyclists and pedestrians $1), offering a thousand protected acres of dunes, marshes, scrub and a wind-beaten group of live oaks, linked by nature walks – though most people come here to catch a fish dinner from the lagoon. In the other direction (take May Street, off San Marco Avenue), **Vilano Beach** pulls a younger crowd and marks the beginning of a dazzling strand continuing for twenty undeveloped miles all the way to Jacksonville Beach (see below).

Eating

The tourist throng on and around St George Street makes eating in the old town an often pricey affair, particularly for dinner. However, early in the day you could try *Cuzzin's Sandwich Shoppe*, 124 St George Street (☎829-8697), for coffee or **breakfast**; or follow your nose to *The Bunnery*, 35 Hypolita Street (☎829-6166), for economical breakfasts, lunches and specialties that include sloppy cinnamon rolls, pecan sticky buns and brownies. Also good for lunch are the heavenly salad combinations and home-brewed ales at the *Monk's Vineyard*, 56 St George Street (☎829-2329); the tasty soups and salads at *Scarlett O'Hara's*, 70 Hypolita Street (☎824-6535); and the excellent burgers at *The Oasis*, 4000 Ocean Trace Road (also Hwy-A1A), with access from the beach (☎471-3424) – try the "Gonzo Burger," served with three kinds of cheese and piles of extras.

Most of the above are closed for **dinner** (though *Scarlett O'Hara's* does excellent fried crayfish suppers), and an evening meal for under $15 in the Old Town takes some finding. *O.C. Whites*, 118 Avenida Menendez (☎824-0808), may oblige; otherwise head across the bay. *Matanzas Bay Cafe*, 8805 Hwy A1A South (☎461-6824) has a great waterfront location. The *Gypsy Cab Company*, 828 Anastasia Blvd (☎824-8244), provides Greek, Italian and Cajun food in an Art Deco setting.

Nightlife

Try to exhaust yourself during the day because St Augustine has limited **nightlife**. In the Old Town, have a **drink** at the tavern-like *White Lion*, 20 Cuna Street (☎829-2388); during the 5–7pm happy hours at *Scarlett O'Hara's* (see "Eating"); or by the millwheel of the *Milltop*, 19 1/2 St George Street (☎829-2329), which has a great open-air view of the Castillo and the harbor. You could also linger over a cocktail overlooking the ocean from the deck bar of *Panama Hatties*, 361 S Beach Boulevard (☎471-2255); or try a vintage port and a fat cigar at *Stogie's Coffee House*, 36 Charlotte Street (☎826-4008), where locals come to gossip and listen to eccentric local bands.

If drinking is not on your agenda, then consider indulging in "A Ghostly Experience," a more historical than scary guided **walking tour** of haunted and spook-filled sites; tours start at 8pm in front of the Milltop bar. (For tickets call ☎471-9010; $6.)

The Jacksonville beaches

However good the beaches around St Augustine may be, they're just the start of an unblemished coastal strip running northwards for twenty miles alongside Hwy-A1A, with nothing but the ocean on one side, and the swamps and marshes of the Talamato River (the local section of the intracoastal waterway) on the other. The scene begins to change when you near the sculptured golf courses and half-million-dollar homes of **PONTE VEDRA BEACH** – one of the most exclusive communities in northeast Florida. Despite laws to the contrary, there is only one public access point to the beach in Ponte Vedra (off Ponte Vedra Boulevard, which splits from Hwy-A1A near Mickler Landing) but it's worth finding. The crowd-free sands are prime beachcombing terrain – retreating tides often leave sharks' teeth among the more common ocean debris.

Four miles on, the much less snooty **JACKSONVILLE BEACH** is an affable beachside community whose residents relax here and commute to work in the city of Jacksonville, twelve miles inland. The damage inflicted by a hurricane in 1976 perhaps

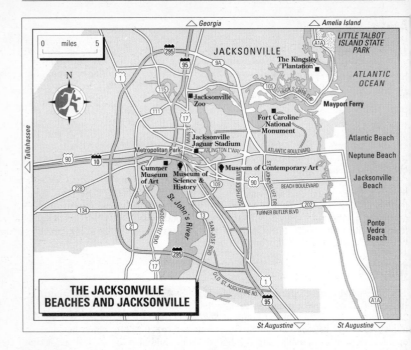

THE JACKSONVILLE
BEACHES AND JACKSONVILLE

accounts for the uncluttered feel. As it is, the place is inexplicably neglected by tourists outside of the summer months. The **pier** is the center of activity, and a fried-fish sandwich from its snack bar is the right accompaniment for observing novice surfers grappling with modest-sized breakers. If you start itching for some action of your own, you could do worse than visit **Adventure Landing**, 1944 Beach Boulevard (daily 10am till late; ☎249-1044). Getting in is free, but you pay for the attractions that most strike your fancy: highlights include a water park ($16.95), a go-kart race track ($4.50), a game of laser-tag with pirates in the dark ($5), and baseball batting cages ($1), where you can indulge fantasies of being Babe Ruth. A combo ticket for all attractions goes for $34.95, and the "Nightflash" evening reduced-rate ticket will get you in for $10 from 4–8pm Mon–Fri.

Once you cross Seagate Avenue, just under two miles north of the pier, Jacksonville Beach merges with the more commercialized **NEPTUNE BEACH**, which in turn blurs (at Atlantic Boulevard) with the identical-looking **ATLANTIC BEACH**. These last two places are the best to visit for eating and socializing in this area. Just north of Atlantic Beach, downbeat **MAYPORT** is dominated by its naval station, berth to some of the biggest aircraft carriers in the US Navy. It's best seen through a car window on the way to the Mayport ferry, crossing the St John's River, and the barrier islands beyond (see "Towards Amelia Island," p.211).

In contrast to the naval station is the **Kathryn Hanna Park**, 500 Wonderwood Drive (50c; ☎249-2316), just south of Mayport. Besides its mile and a half of unblemished beachfront, the park boasts 450 acres of woodland surrounding a large lake, around which wind ten miles of enjoyable biking and hiking trails. There's also a campground here (see "Sleeping, eating and nightlife," p.207).

Around the beaches

Only two things are likely to drag you away from the beaches. The **American Lighthouse Museum**, 1011 N Third Street (Tues–Sat 11am–4pm; free), has a moderately interesting collection of paintings, drawings, photos, plans and models of lighthouses and ships. Further away, a few miles inland on Girvin Road (off Atlantic Boulevard), the **Fort Caroline National Monument** (daily 9am–5pm; free; ☎641-7155) offers a more historical interlude: a small museum details the significance of the restored Huguenot fort here, which stimulated the first Spanish settlement in Florida (see "St Augustine," p.198). Another reason to come is the great view from the fort across the mile-wide St John's River and its ocean-going freighters.

Sleeping, eating and nightlife

Along the coast there'll be plenty of bargains in winter, but during the summer be ready to spend $40–55 for a basic **motel** room, and book ahead. *Sea Horse Oceanfront Inn*, 120 Atlantic Boulevard, Neptune Beach (☎246-2175; ③), *Surfside*, 1236 N First Street, Jacksonville Beach (☎246-1583; ②), and *Golden Sands*, 127 S First Avenue, Jacksonville Beach (☎249-4374; ①–②), have the lowest rates. If you don't mind staying six miles inland, save a few dollars by using the *Scottish Inn*, 2300 Phillips Highway (☎1-800/251-1962; ①), near the junction of I-95 and Hwy-90. Of the more expensive options, try the *Sea Turtle Inn*, 1 Ocean Boulevard, Atlantic Beach (☎1-800/874-6000; ⑤). With a tent, you can **camp** at the Kathryn Hanna Park (see p.206) for $10.

For **eating**, S Third Street at Jacksonville Beach offers two basic, cheap and reliable options: *Beach Hut Cafe*, at no. 1281 (☎249-3516; lunch only), and *Ellen's Kitchen*, at no. 1824 (☎246-1572). Slightly more costly are the fancy variations on deli staples at the *Sun Dog Diner*, 207 S Atlantic Boulevard, Neptune Beach (☎241-8221).

Nightlife on the beach is strong. For the hedonism of wet-T-shirt contests, head for *H2O*, 2500 Beach Boulevard (☎249-6992), inland from Jacksonville Beach on the intracoastal waterway. For a different, slightly more sedate atmosphere, try *The Fly's Tie Irish Pub*, 177 E Sailfish Drive, Atlantic Beach (☎246-4293), and enjoy the live Irish music and beer.

Jacksonville

With long-established lumber and coffee industries, and the deep St John's River making it a major transit point for seaborne cargo, **JACKSONVILLE** has long been suspicious of anything liable to upset its hard-working traditions; pleasure-seeking visitors are expected to stick to the beaches, twelve miles east, and even the US film industry was scared off in the 1910s when it came here seeking a base, settling instead in California. Lately, with a growing white-collar sector easing the blight of years of heavy industry, there have been efforts to heighten Jacksonville's appeal by creating parks and riverside boardwalks, but the sheer size of the city – at 841 square miles, the largest in the US – dilutes its character and makes it an impossible nut to crack without a vehicle. For all that, Jacksonville is not an unwelcoming place, and will sufficiently consume a day – even if you spend most of it strolling the riverside downtown.

Information and transportation

In downtown Jacksonville, the **Convention and Visitors Bureau**, 201 E Adams St (Mon–Fri 8am–5pm; ☎798-9148), has plenty of tourist leaflets and discount vouchers (there's also an affiliated information booth in the Jacksonville Landing mall), and is an easy walk from the Greyhound **bus** station at 10 N Pearl Street (☎356-9976). Some Greyhound services also stop in the gray surburbia of South and West Jacksonville – don't get off at either. The **train** station is an awkward six miles northwest of downtown at 3570 Clifford Lane (☎1-800/872-7245), from which a **taxi** (☎645-5466) downtown will cost around $8. The **local bus** service (☎630-3100) is geared to ferrying locals to and from work, bypassing many useful places and closing down early.

By **bus**, the journey between the **beaches** and downtown Jacksonville takes around fifty minutes with bus #BS 1 (along Atlantic Boulevard), #BS 2 (along Beach Boulevard) or #BS 3 (from Mayport). There's also the *Beaches Flyer*, a quicker rush-hour service along Beach Boulevard.

Accommodation

The city's far-flung layout means that the cheapest **accommodation** is represented by the motels around the perimeter, bothersome to get to without a car. The best prices are at the **chain hotels** near the airport, nine miles north of downtown Jacksonville: *Days Inn*, 1181 Airport Road (☎741-4000; ②), *Holiday Inn*, 14670 Duval Road (☎741-4404); ③), *Red Roof Inn*, 14701 Airport Entrance Road (☎741-4488; ②–③), *Super 8 Motel*, 10901 Harts Road (☎751-3888; ②), and *ValuLodge*, 1351 Airport Road (☎741-0094; ①). Downtown, beds are suitable primarily for expense-account holders: the *Parkview Inn*, 901 N Main Street (☎355-3744; ③), is the cheapest. Scenically sited on the south bank of the river, the *Radisson*, 1515 Prudential Drive (☎396-5100; ⑤), might be worth a flutter. Another cozy option is **bed and breakfast** at *The House on Cherry Street*, 1844 Cherry Street (☎384-1999; ④), about three miles south of downtown.

Downtown Jacksonville

Leaning on local businesses to divert some of their profits into area improvement schemes, an enlightened city administration has helped make **downtown Jacksonville** much less the forbidding forest of corporate high-rises that it initially looks. For an overview of downtown Jacksonville, take the **Skyway monorail** (Mon–Fri 6.30am–7.30pm; 25c; ☎630-3181) from the Convention Center to Hemming Park, a ten-minute journey at eye-level to the high-rise offices. Another way to get to grips with this sprawling city is to gain a bird's-eye view of it by hitching a ride on a hot-air balloon; Outdoor Adventures, 1625 Emerson Street (☎393-9030; see p.210), can take you up for $225 round-trip. Otherwise, take a wander along the banks of St John's River, which snakes through the city center, dividing downtown Jacksonville in two.

The north bank

Within four blocks of Bay Street on the **north bank** of the river, you'll find the few structures that survived the 1901 fire – which claimed much of early Jacksonville – as well as some of the more distinctive buildings from subsequent decades. These are best examined with the aid of the free *Downtown Walking* leaflet from the Convention and Visitors Bureau (see "Practicalities" below). One noteworthy building is the heavily restored **Florida Theater**, 128 E Forsyth Street, which opened in 1927 and became a center of controversy thirty years later when Elvis Presley's pelvic thrusts shocked the city's burghers. Another is the **Morocco Temple**, 219 N Newnan Street, built by Henry John Kluthco. This classically minded architect arrived to rebuild Jacksonville after the 1901 fire but later converted to Frank Lloyd Wright-inspired Modernism and erected this sphinx-decorated masterpiece in 1912.

The south bank

To cross to the **south bank** of the river, take the *River Taxi* ($2 one way; $3 round-trip) from the dock beside the gleaming Jacksonville Landing shopping mall, between Water Street and the river. You'll be dropped next to a mile-long pathway called the Riverwalk, west along which is the **Jacksonville Historical Center** (Mon–Sat 10am–5pm, Sun noon–5pm; free; ☎398-4301), a brief but interesting "walk-through" account of the city's origins and growth. Further on you'll come to the oversized **Friendship Fountain**, best seen at night when colored lights illuminate its gushing jets. Finally, the **Museum of Science and History**, 1025 Museum Circle (Mon–Fri 10am–5pm, Sat 10am–6pm, Sun 1–6pm; $6; ☎396-7062) has educational hands-on exhibits primarily aimed at kids, plus a planetarium offering hi-tech trips around the cosmos.

Nearby in San Marco on Atlantic Boulevard, dwarfed by neighboring office towers, the tiny **St Paul's Episcopal Church** is a hundred-year-old example of the "Carpenter Gothic" building style. Don't bother going inside – the church is now used for secular purposes – but read the plaque outside recalling naturalist William Bartram, who passed this way in the 1750s and briefly described "Cow-ford," as Jacksonville was then known, in his journal; see "Books" in Contexts.

Beyond downtown

With a car, it's easy to zip between the likely points of call scattered about this nebulous city, but it's much harder – and frankly not worth the effort – to do the same thing by bus. A good scrutiny of the art collections will take up an afternoon, but if you feel like being outside, make for Metropolitan Park, the extensive acreage of the zoo, or the thrills at Adventure Landing (see p.206).

The Museum of Contemporary Art and Cummer Museum

In this city of commerce and industry, you might not expect much from the **Jacksonville Museum of Contemporary Art** (Tues, Wed & Fri 10am–4pm, Thurs 10am–10pm, Sat & Sun 1–5pm; $3; ☎398-8336), which you'll find at 4160 Boulevard Center Drive, three miles from downtown Jacksonville and half a mile from the #BH 2 bus stop (from the downtown area, use the weekdays-only "Riverside Shuttle" bus). However, the sizeable stock of ancient Chinese and Korean porcelain turns many knowledgeable heads, and the smaller selection of pre-Columbian objects shouldn't be missed. The museum's main purpose, though, is to provide support and studios for local artists; the workspaces are often open to the public; further details are available at the reception desk.

There's more art across the city, just south of the Fuller Warren river bridge (I-95), in the **Cummer Museum of Art and Gardens**, 829 Riverside Drive (Tues–Fri 10am–4pm, Sat noon–5pm, Sun 2–5pm; $5), on the former estate of the wealthy Cummer family. The spacious rooms and sculpture-lined corridors contain works by prominent European masters from the thirteenth to nineteenth centuries, but American art is the strongest feature: Edmund Greacen's smokey cityscape *Brooklyn Bridge East River* and Martin Heade's *St John's River* are particularly evocative. Afterwards, take a stroll through the flower-packed formal English and Italianate **gardens**, which roll down to the river's edge, providing an apt view of Jacksonville's steely industrial character.

The Jaguar Stadium and Metropolitan Park

In 1994 Jacksonville was awarded one of the new National Football League franchises, much to the delight of the town, and what was once the Gator Bowl (home of college football) is now the stamping ground of the Jaguars. From all over Jacksonville

---

OUTDOOR ADVENTURES

If you're interested in exploring out-of-the-way areas in this region, **Outdoor Adventures**, 1625 Emerson Street, Jacksonville (☎393-9030), run a series of reasonably priced canoeing, kayaking, cycling and walking trips throughout an extensive area, ranging from as far afield as the Okefenokee Swamp and Suwanee River down to the Talbot Islands and the rivers and parks around Jacksonville.

---

you can see the floodlights of the 73,000-seat **Jacksonville Jaguar Stadium**, still the scene of the Florida-Georgia college football clash each November (an excuse for 48 hours of city-wide drinking and partying; tickets for the actual match are notoriously hard to get) in addition to the equally exciting Jaguars' home games. Outside of match days, the main reason to visit is the neighbouring **Metropolitan Park**, a plot of riverside greenery that provides a venue for enjoyable free events most weekends plus some big free rock concerts during spring and fall. In midweek it's often deserted and makes a fine spot for a quiet riverside picnic. The "Northside Connector" **bus** stops close by.

Jacksonville Zoo

Previously a depressing place with restrictive cages and poorly utilized space, **Jacksonville Zoo**, on Hecksher Drive, just off I-95 north of downtown Jacksonville (daily 9am–5pm; $6.50), is fast developing into one of the best around, giving its inmates plenty of space to prowl, pose and strut. A justifiable source of pride are the white rhinos, seldom bred in captivity, who live in the eleven-acre "African veldt." However, much of the zoo is under endless development, leaving serious gaps between animal displays and relegating the experience to a pricey nature hike. **Bus** #NS 10 stops outside – but only on weekends.

Anheuser Busch Brewery

After trekking about the US's largest city, you'll inevitably have worked up a thirst, and the **Anheuser Busch Brewery**, 111 Busch Drive (Mon–Sat 10am–4pm; free; ☎751-8118), purveyor of Budweiser, would like to quench it for you. After taking the free tour, which follows the Germanic roots of America's most popular beer, including informative exhibits like a mural on the evolution of beer-can openers, visitors indulge in the main attraction: free beer.

Eating

On downtown Jacksonville's north bank, *Akel's Deli*, 130 N Hogan Street (☎356-5628), offers **snacks** and quick **lunches**. Eating in the Jacksonville Landing mall is slightly pricier, though tempting: *The Mill Bakery* is a health-conscious Brew pub, with huge muffins; *Fat Tuesday* (☎353-1229) offers spicy Cajun lunches; and *Harry's Oyster Bar* (☎353-4927) has a generous seafood menu. On the south bank, *The Loop*, 4000-21 St John's Avenue (☎384-7301), has good-priced general menus, though the healthy lunches concocted by the *Filling Station*, 1004 Hendricks Avenue (☎398-3663), are more adventurous. For high-quality liquid refreshment, seafood and steaks, call at the *River City Brewing Co.*, 835 Museum Circle (☎398-2299), where you can sample homebrewed beer while listening to **live music**. The pick of the city's many stylish **dinner** restaurants is the *Wine Cellar*, 1314 Prudential Drive (☎398-8989), where a well-prepared fish or meat meal costs upwards of $15.

Nightlife

Nightlife in Jacksonville is a pale shadow of the rave-ups at the beach (see "The Jacksonville beaches" p.205), but check out the *Milk Bar*, 128 W Adams Street (☎356-MILK) – likely to have anything you could want, from house and reggae sounds to live punk bands and 25¢-beer nights; and *Havana-Jax*, 2578 Atlantic Blvd (☎399-0609), which has live rock groups and the occasional Latin band to spice up the Cuban-American cuisine.

Towards Amelia Island

Around thirty miles from Jacksonville are the barrier islands that mark Florida's north-east corner, of which **Amelia Island** is particularly appealing. To reach the islands, Hwy-105 will take you from Jacksonville along the north side of the St John's River, but a better route is Hwy-A1A from the Jacksonville beaches, which crosses the river with the tiny **Mayport ferry** (roughly every 30min 6.20am–10pm; cars $2.50, cyclists and pedestrians 50c). During this short voyage, pelicans swoop overhead to feed off the nearby shrimping boats.

The Kingsley Plantation

Near the ferry's landing point, Hwy-A1A combines with Hwy-105. Continuing north on Hwy-A1A, you'll soon cross onto Fort George Island and, before long, encounter the entrance to the **Huguenot Memorial Park** (daily 6am–sunset; 50¢ per person) on the east side of the road. Here there's a **campground** (☎251-3335), where you can pitch a tent for $5, and the **Natural State Bird Sanctuary**. Hwy-A1A continues past the endless, tree-lined driveway of the **Kingsley Plantation** (daily 9am–5pm; free; ranger talks Mon–Fri 1pm, Sat & Sun 1pm & 3pm), centerpiece of which is the elegant riverside house bought in 1817 by a Scotsman called Zephaniah Kingsley. The house and its 3000 acres were acquired with the proceeds of slavery, of which Kingsley was an advocate and dealer, amassing a fortune through the import and export of Africans. A pragmatic man, he was interested in the rights of freed slaves and wrote a treatise on the virtues of a patriarchal slave system more in keeping with the Spanish approach than the extremely brutal methods of the United States; he simply believed that well-fed, happier and freer (though not free) slaves made better workers. Nonetheless, the restored plantation reveals much about the plight of the forced arrivals and about Kingsley's remarkable wife: a Senegalese woman who ran the plantation and lived in extravagant style – perhaps compensating for her years as Kingsley's servant.

The Talbot Islands

One mile further on from the Kingsley Plantation, Hwy-A1A runs through **Little Talbot Island State Park** (daily 8am–sunset; cars $3.25, cyclists and pedestrians $1), which consumes almost the whole of a thickly forested 3000-acre barrier island inhabited by 194 species of birdlife. The park has two tree-shaded, ocean-facing picnic areas and a superb four-mile **hiking trail**, which winds through a pristine landscape of oak and magnolia trees, wind-beaten sand dunes and a chunk of the park's five-mile-long beach. **Canoes** can be hired for $4 an hour ($15 a day) and **bikes** for $2 an hour ($10 a day). If you're smitten by the natural charms and want to save the bother of finding accommodation on Amelia Island (see below), use the **campground** (☎251-2321) on the western side of the park beside Myrtle Creek ($14).

Alternatively carry on across the creek, onto tiny Long Island and over onto **Big Talbot Island**, which has two points of interest. Firstly, **Bluffs Scenic Shoreline** (signposted off the road), where the bluffs have eroded, depositing entire trees on the beach, some of them still standing upright with all their roots intact. Secondly, the **Black Rock Trail**, a one-and-a-half-mile hike through woods onto the Atlantic coast, to rocks once made from peat. Back on Hwy-A1A, the road continues to Amelia Island.

Amelia Island

Most first-time visitors to Florida would be hard pushed to locate **AMELIA ISLAND**, at the state's northeastern extremity, which perhaps explains why this finger of land, thirteen miles long and never more than two across, is so peaceful and only modestly commercialized despite the unbroken silver swathe of Atlantic beach gracing its eastern edge. Matching the sands for appeal, Fernandina Beach, the island's sole town, was a haunt of pirates before transforming itself into an outpost of Victorian high society – a fact proven by its immaculately restored old center.

Some parts of the island are being swallowed by upmarket resorts (much of the southern half is taken up by the *Amelia Island Plantation*, a golf and tennis resort with private walking and biking trails, expensive restaurants and $200-a-night rooms), but it's still worth coming here – provided you have a car. In Fernandina, at least, they still concern themselves more with the size of the shrimp catch than with pandering to tourists.

Fernandina Beach

Hwy-A1A runs right into the effortlessly walkable town of **FERNANDINA BEACH**, whose Victorian heyday is apparent in the restored buildings lining the short main drag, Centre Street. The English spelling reflects bygone political to-ing and fro-ing: the Spanish named the town but the British named the streets. Beside the marina, at the western end of Centre Street and adjacent to a vintage train carriage, you'll spot the useful **visitor center** (Tues–Fri 9am–5pm, Sat 10am–2pm, Mon 10am–5pm; ☎261-3248), where you can pick up a booklet produced by the Museum of History, highlighting driving and walking tours, as well as points of historical interest.

Remarkably, given the present-day calm, President James Monroe described Fernandina as a "festering fleshpot" after the 1807 US embargo on foreign shipping caused the Spanish-owned town to become a hotbed of smuggling and other illicit

---

AMELIA ISLAND HISTORY: THE EIGHT FLAGS

Amelia Island is the only place in the US to have been under the rule of **eight flags**. Following settlement by Huguenots in 1562, the Spanish arrived and founded a mission here. This was destroyed in 1702 by the British, who returned forty years later to govern the island (naming it in honor of King George II's daughter). The ensuing Spanish administration was interrupted by the US-backed "Patriots of Amelia Island," who ruled for a day during 1812; the Green Cross of the Florida Republic flew briefly in 1817; and, oddest of all, the Mexican rebel flag appeared over Amelia Island the same year. US rule has been disturbed only by Confederate occupancy during 1861.

These shifts reflect the ebb and flow of allegiances between the great sea-trading powers, as well as the island's geographically desirable location: for many years offering harbor to ocean-going vessels outside US control but within spitting distance of the American border.

activities as ways were sought to circumvent the ban. The acquisition of Florida by the US in 1821 did not diminish Fernandina's importance – this time as a key rail terminal for freight moving between the Atlantic and the Gulf of Mexico.

The Museum of History - and walking around Centre Street

The obvious place to gain insights into the town is the **Museum of History**, 233 S Third Street (Mon–Fri 11am–3pm; donation suggested) – once the county jail – whose scattering of memorabilia is backed up by photographs and maps. The 45-minute **guided tour** (Mon–Sat at 11am & 2pm; recommended donation of $2.50) of the museum is excellent, as are the longer **historical walks** (Thurs & Fri at 3pm from the visitor center; suspended June-Aug, except by appointment; $5) which feature many of the old buildings on and around Centre Street.

Even if you miss the tours, **walking around** on your own is far from dull. Centre Street and the immediate area are alive with Victorian-era turrets, twirls and towers, plus many notable later buildings. Among them, the **St Peter's Episcopal Church**, on the corner with Eighth Street, was completed in 1884 by New York architect Robert S. Schuyer, whose name is linked to many local structures and who never used the same style twice. The Gothic used for the church is a long way from the heavy-handed Italianate of the **Fairbanks House**, also by Shuyer, situated at the corner of Seventh and Cedar streets. This was commissioned by a newspaper editor as a surprise for his wife, who hated it and refused to step over the threshold. Today it has been transformed into a sumptuous bed-and-breakfast (☎1/800-261-4838; ⑥), ask for the top-floor honeymoon suite with private turret.

The beach

Well-suited to swimming and busy with beach sports, the most active of the island's **beaches** is at the eastern end of Fernandina's Atlantic Avenue, a mile from the town center. If you don't mind a long hike with sand between your toes, you can walk along the beach to Fort Clinch State Park, three miles north (see below). In the fall, you might be lucky enough to spot **whales** in the waters off Amelia Island. The "right whale," an endangered species, moves into inland waterways to calve.

North to Fort Clinch State Park

After Florida came under US control, a fort was built on Amelia's northern tip, three miles from Fernandina, to protect seaborne access to Georgia. The fort now forms part of **Fort Clinch State Park** (daily 8am–sunset; cars $3.25, pedestrians and cyclists $1), and provides a home for a gang of Civil War enthusiasts pretending that they're Union soldiers of 1864, the only time the fort saw action. Entrance to the fort itself costs $1, and the most atmospheric way to see it is with the soldier-guided **candle-lit tour** (most Fridays and Saturdays during summer; $2; reservations essential: ☎277-7274). With the pseudo Civil War garrison moaning about their work and meager rations, the tour may sound like a ham job, but in fact it is a convincing, informative – and quite spooky – hour's worth.

The rest of the park can hardly be overlooked: by road, you have to go through three miles of it before reaching the fort, passing an animal reserve (from which overgrown alligators often emerge, so if you do fancy a spot of hiking, stick to the marked 30- and 45-minute **nature trails**) and a turn-off for the stunning 2.5-mile long **beach**, where legions of crab-catchers cast their baskets off a long fishing jetty. From both jetty and fort there's an immaculate view of Cumberland Island (only accessible by ferry from St Mary's, on the Georgia mainland, or by canoe or kayak on organized trips run by Outdoor Adventures ☎393-9030, see p.210), a Georgian nature reserve famed for its wild horses – if you're lucky, a few will be galloping over the island's sands. You might also catch a glimpse of a nuclear-powered submarine gliding towards Cumberland Sound and the massive Kings Bay naval base. **Camping** in the park is available for $17.

Accommodation

Cheapest for **accommodation** are the four motels along Fletcher Avenue, a few miles south of Fernandina: *D. J.'s*, no. 3199 (☎261-5711; ④), the *Seaside Inn*, no. 1998 (☎261-0954; ④), *Ocean View*, no. 2801 Atlantic Ave (☎261-0193; ④), and *Beachside*, no. 3172 (☎261-4236; ④). Should these be full, the next-best budget bet is *Shoney's Inn*, 2707 Sadler Road (☎277-2300; ④).

With a bit more cash, savor Fernandina's historic atmosphere by staying in one of the town's antique-filled **bed-and-breakfast inns**: the *Bailey House*, 28 S Seventh Street (☎261-5390 or ☎1/800-251-5390; ④), *1735 House*, 584 S Fletcher Avenue (☎261-4148 or ☎1/800-872-8531; ④), and the *Florida House Inn*, 22 S Third Street (☎261-3300 or ☎1/800-258-3301; ④). Booking far in advance might secure you a room in the $196-a-night *Lighthouse*, 748 Fletcher Avenue (☎261-5878), which really *is* a small lighthouse, with space for four people.

Eating and nightlife

For its size, the island has an exceptionally good number of places to **eat**, the bulk of them on and around Fernandina's Centre Street. *The Marina*, 101 Centre Street (☎261-5310), is one of the island's oldest restaurants, with a seafood-based menu and a convivial atmosphere. It's renowned for "Fernandina Fantail Fried Shrimp" and as a **breakfast** hot spot, serving fried fish, eggs and cheese grits. Chinese food can be inexpensively sampled from the **lunchtime** buffet at the *Bamboo House*, 614 Centre Street (☎261-0508; closed Sun); and an all-you-can eat lunch is also offered at *Cousin's Pizza & Pasta*, 927 S 14th Street (☎277-4611). An atmospheric, traditional 1950s-style diner, *Maggie's*, 18 N Second Street, (☎261-9976), dishes up lunch buffets on weekdays and Sundays.

A touch more expensive, *Brett's Waterway Cafe*, at the Fernandina Harbor Marina at the end of Centre Street (☎261-2660), has generous American meals and great views; and *D.J.'s*, 3199 S Fletcher Avenue (☎261-5711), delivers tasty seafood beside the ocean. For a slap-up gourmet **dinner**, try the classy *Beech Street Grill*, corner of Eighth and Beech streets (☎277-3662).

You'll also find a limited menu of plain and simple dishes at the *Palace Saloon*, 117 Centre Street (☎261-6320), though you might prefer to save your visit to what's claimed to be the oldest **bar** in Florida – built in 1878, with a forty-foot hand-carved mahogany bar – for a night-time drink, not least because few other places warrant an after-dark investigation. This was the last tavern in the country to close after Prohibition began, taking two years to deplete its supply of spirits. If you're feeling brave, try a "Pirate's Punch": lemon, lime, orange and pineapple with a gin-and-rum kick.

travel details

Trains (AMTRAK ☎1-800/872-7245)

Jacksonville to: Miami (3 daily; 9–10hr); Orlando (2 daily; 3hr 15min); Pensacola (runs once a day on Tue, Thur, Fri; 8hr 50min); Tallahassee (same as Pensacola train; 3hr 15min); Tampa (1 daily; 4hr 51min).

Buses (GREYHOUND ☎1-800/231-2222)

Cocoa to: Daytona Beach (4 daily; 1hr 45min); Jacksonville (5 daily; 4–5hr); Melbourne (5 daily; 30min); New Smyrna Beach (4 daily; 1hr 15min); Titusville (4 daily; 30min).

Daytona Beach to: Jacksonville (9 daily; 1hr 40min–2hr 45min); Orlando (6 daily; 1hr 5min–1hr 40min); St Augustine (6 daily; 1hr).

Jacksonville to: Miami (15 daily; 7hr–14hr 55min); Orlando (10 daily; 2hr 30min–4hr); St Petersburg (8 daily; 6hr 25min–7hr 50min); Tallahassee (5 daily; 2hr 40min–3hr 50min); Tampa (11 daily; 5hr 20min–6hr 44min).

St Augustine to: Jacksonville (5 daily; 55min)

CHAPTER FIVE

CENTRAL FLORIDA

M ost of the broad and fertile expanse of **Central Florida**, stretching between the east and west coasts, was self-absorbed farming country when vacation-mania first struck the beachside strips; only as an afterthought to growing citrus and raising cattle were adventurous visitors ferried by steamboat along the region's rivers and across its gushing springs. Over the last two decades, this picture of tranquillity has been shattered: no section of the state has been affected by modern tourism more dramatically.

In the middle of the region, as contradictory as it may seem, the most visited part of Florida is also one of the ugliest: an ungodly clutter of freeway interchanges, motels, billboards and jumped-up tourist sights arching around the otherwise affable small city of **Orlando**. The blame for the vulgarity lies with Orlando's near-neighbor, **Walt Disney World**, which since the Seventies has sucked millions of people into the biggest and cleverest theme park complex ever created – sparking off a tourist-dollar chase of Gold Rush magnitude on its outskirts. The Disney parks are every bit as polished as their reputation suggests, but their surrounds are no advertisement for Florida, and it's a tragedy that many visitors see no more of the state than this aggressive commercialism.

The rest of Central Florida is markedly less brash. The slow-paced towns of **South Central Florida** make excellent low-cost bases for cruising the Orlando circuit – provided you're driving – and offer plenty of relaxed diversions in their lake-filled vicinity. Much the same can be said of **North Central Florida**, where tiny villages, far more prevalent than towns, hold the century-old homes of Florida's pioneer settlers. The biggest surprise here, however, is **Gainesville**, an outpost of learning and liberalism containing one of the state's two major universities – a welcome sight so deep in rural surrounds.

Since Walt Disney World redefined the geography of the region, **getting around** Central Florida by **car** has become generally easy and quick – but take time to leave the charmless freeways and journey down some of the multitude of minor routes linking the lesser towns and villages. Non-drivers will find that Orlando's **bus system** extends quite a bit beyond downtown; many of the smaller centers have good Greyhound **bus** connections; and some even see twice-daily **trains**. Car-less visitors wanting to get to the Disney parks are dependent on the local **shuttle buses** (see "Getting Around," p.219).

ACCOMMODATION PRICE CODES

All **accommodation prices** in this book have been coded using the symbols below. Note that prices are for the least expensive double rooms in each establishment. For a full explanation see p.27 in Basics.

① up to $30	③ $45-60	⑤ $80-100	⑦ $130-180
② $30-45	④ $60-80	⑥ $100-130	⑧ $180+

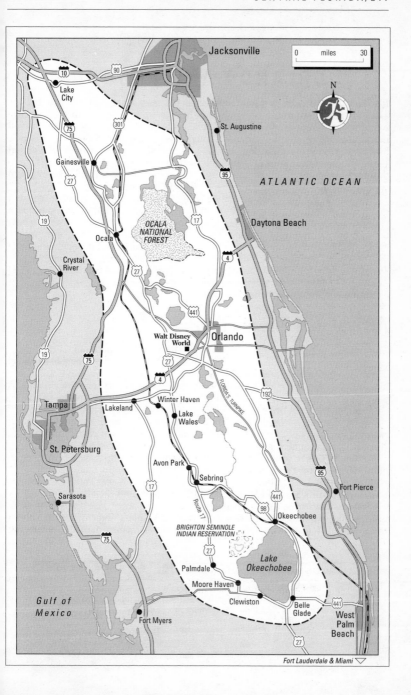

The area code for the Orlando area is ☎407.

ORLANDO AND AROUND

It's ironic that **Orlando**, an insubstantial city in the heart of peninsular Florida that was a quiet farming town just 25 years ago, now has more people passing through its environs than any other place in the state. Reminders of the old Florida are still easy to find in and immediately north of Orlando, though most people get no closer to Orlando's heart than a string of motels along Hwy-192, fifteen miles south of town. **International Drive** (five miles southwest of Orlando) – a long boulevard of convention hotels, heavily-themed shopping malls and schmaltzy restaurants – may be worth a drive-by just to see the buildings' extravagant, but utterly characterless, exteriors.

The reason for these apparent anomalies is, of course, **Walt Disney World**, a group of state-of-the-art theme parks southwest of Orlando pulling 35 million people a year to a previously featureless 43-square-mile plot of scrubland. It's possible to pass through the Orlando area and not visit Walt Disney World, but there's no way to escape its influence: even the road system was reshaped to accommodate the place and, whichever way you look, billboards tout more ways to spend your money. Amid a plethora of fly-by-night would-be tourist targets, only **Universal Studios Escape** and **SeaWorld Orlando** offer serious competition to the most finely realized concept in escapist entertainment anywhere on earth.

Arrival and information

The region's primary international **airport, Orlando International**, is nine miles south of downtown Orlando. Shuttle buses will carry you from the airport to any hotel or motel in the Orlando area for $10–15. If you're headed for downtown Orlando, use local bus #11, or #42 for International Drive (both buses depart from the airport's "A Side" concourse, every 60 minutes between 6am and 9pm). A taxi to downtown Orlando, International Drive or the motels on Hwy-192 will cost a little more than $25.

A second airport, **Orlando Sanford International**, is a small but growing facility twenty miles north of downtown Orlando that receives a lot of charter flights from Great Britain. From here, a taxi to downtown Orlando costs about $40.

Arriving by **bus** or **train**, you'll wind up in downtown Orlando at the Greyhound terminal, 555 N **John Young Parkway** (☎292-3422), or the **train station**, 1400 Slight Boulevard (☎843-7611). Other train stops in the area are in Winter Park (150 W Morse Boulevard; ☎645-5055) and Kissimmee (111 E Dakin Ave; ☎933-1170).

Giveaway magazines, strewn wherever you look, are packed with handy facts, but a better source of reliable **information** is the **Official Visitor Center**, 8723 International Drive, Suite 101 (daily 8am–8pm; ☎363-5872; *www.goflorida.com/orlando*), where you

---

ORLANDO AREA ORIENTATION: THE MAJOR ROADS

The major cross-Florida **roads** form a web-like mass of intersections in or around Orlando and Walt Disney World: **I-4** passes southwest–northeast through Walt Disney World and continues in elevated form through downtown Orlando; **Hwy-192** (the **Irlo Bronson Memorial Highway**) crosses I-4 in Walt Disney World and charts an east–west course fifteen miles south of Orlando; **Hwy-528** (the **Beeline Expressway**) stems from International Drive and heads for the east coast; and **Florida's Turnpike** cuts northwest–southeast, avoiding Walt Disney World and downtown Orlando altogether.

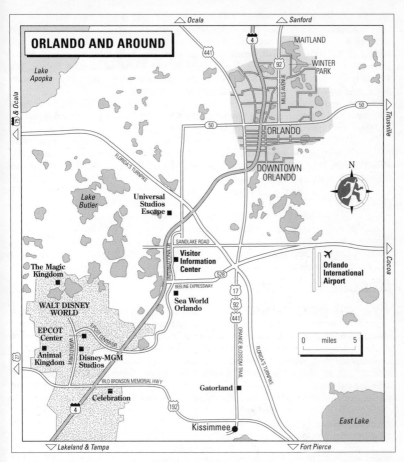

Map: ORLANDO AND AROUND. Labels include: Ocala, Sanford, MAITLAND, 441, 4, 92, WINTER PARK, MILLS AVENUE, Lake Apopka, 50, ORLANDO, Titusville, 75 & Ocala, FLORIDA'S TURNPIKE, DOWNTOWN ORLANDO, N, Lake Butler, Universal Studios Escape, Cocoa, SANDLAKE ROAD, Visitor Information Center, 528, Orlando International Airport, The Magic Kingdom, BEELINE EXPRESSWAY, 17, 92, 441, WALT DISNEY WORLD, Sea World Orlando, 0 miles 5, EPCOT Center, EPCOT CENTER DR, ORANGE BLOSSOM TRAIL, FLORIDA'S TURNPIKE, 27, Animal Kingdom, Disney-MGM Studios, IRLO BRONSON MEMORIAL HWY, Gatorland, Celebration, 4, 192, East Lake, Kissimmee, Lakeland & Tampa, Fort Pierce.

should pick up the free *Official Visitors Guide to Orlando*, plus any of hundreds of leaflets and discount coupons. If you're using the motels along Hwy-192, the equally well-stocked **Kissimmee-St Cloud CV**, 1925 Billbeck Blvd in Kissimmee (daily 8am–5pm; ☎1-800/327-9159 or ☎407/847-5000; *www.floridakiss.com*). The best entertainment guide to the area is the Friday "Calendar" section of the *Orlando Sentinel* newspaper.

Getting around

With most routes operating from 6.30am to 8pm on weekdays, 7.30am–6pm on Saturdays, and 8am–6pm on Sundays, **local bus lines** (☎841-8240) converge at the downtown Orlando terminal between Central and Pine streets. The system is known as the "Lynx," and bus-stop signs are cleverly marked with paw prints. You'll need **exact change** (85¢ and 10¢ for a transfer from one route to another) if you pay on board; you can also buy tickets from the terminal's information booth. A ten-ticket book sells for $8.50, including free transfers. The "Lynx" system makes 4000 stops in three counties, and the **most-used bus routes** are #1 to Loch Haven and Winter Park; #11 to the airport (a 45-min journey); and #8 to International Drive, where you can catch a shuttle bus (see below) to Walt Disney World and the area's other major tourist parks, or link with #42 to **Orlando International Airport** (an hour-long journey). Along International Drive, between SeaWorld Orlando and Universal Studios Escape, the **I-Ride** trolley service (☎354-5656) operates every fifteen minutes daily from 7am–midnight, costing 75¢ one way; children 12 and under ride free.

Orlando **taxis** are expensive: rates begin at $2.75 for the first mile plus $1.50 for each additional mile. For non-drivers, however, they're the only way to get around at night – try Town & Country (☎827-6350) or Yellow Cab (☎422-4561).

Cheaper than taxis are the **shuttle buses**, minivans or coaches run by private companies connecting the main accommodation areas such as International Drive and Hwy-192 with Walt Disney World, Sea World Orlando, Universal Studios Escape and the airports. You should phone at least a day ahead to be picked up, and confirm a time to come back. You pay the driver on board. *Mears Transportation Service* (☎839-1570) charges $10–13 for a round trip ride from downtown or International Drive to all the major attractions, and $15 one way to Orlando International Airport.

All the main **car rental** firms have offices at or close to Orlando International Airport. Competition is strong and rates can be high, so try to call in advance, as cars are scarce during busy seasons (the numbers are in "Getting around" in Basics).

Accommodation

Unless you're staying on Disney property and planning a Disney-only holiday, you'll need to be mobile wherever you stay in the far-flung Orlando area. Therefore, price should be more of a concern than location when looking for **accommodation**. If you're dependent on public transport, however, downtown Orlando is the best place to stay.

Genuinely budget-priced accommodation is offered only by the scores of cheap motels lined up **along Hwy-192** between Walt Disney World and Kissimmee; many offer special rates which can be yours simply by picking up a discount coupon at one of the information offices mentioned above. **International Drive**, dominated by pricey chain hotels, is where you're likely to end up if you come on a package trip – but bargains can be found during the slow winter periods. The hotels in the Lake Buena Vista area just outside Disney World are pricey, but they also offer excellent accessibility to the theme parks. Accommodation, though expensive, is also available within Disney World itself (see p.236 for details). **Campgrounds** are plentiful on and around Hwy-192 close to Kissimmee.

If you *do* have a car, an excellent option is to **rent a villa** from *Sunsplash Travel*, 125 Hilltop Street, Davenport, Florida 33837 (☎941/424-6193; from $560 a week). The three- to four-bedroom houses come with their own pools, garages, kitchens, washing machines and so on, and are located in an upscale residential area forty minutes from Orlando International airport, nine minutes from Walt Disney World and fifteen minutes from the nearest town, Haines City. Staff can provide discount tickets to Disney World and other attractions in the Orlando area, and will even supply a prospective itinerary for your stay. Book as far ahead as possible.

Downtown Orlando

Harley Hotel, 151 E Washington St (☎841-3220). A historic, now completely modernized hotel overlooking Lake Eola. ⑨.

The Veranda Bed & Breakfast Inn, 115 N Summerlin Ave (☎1-800/420-6822 or 849-0321). Charming nine-room bed-and-breakfast located in four historic buildings in Orlando's Thornton Park district. ⑨.

Winter Park

The Fortnightly Inn, 377 E Fairbanks Ave (☎645-4440). A night or two at this personable five-room bed-and-breakfast inn makes for a relaxing break from the rampant commercialism of the Orlando area. ⑤.

Langford Resort, 300 E New England Ave (☎644-3400). The price is right at this hotel with good facilities and service; the location – a leafy Winter Park side street – is great. ③.

Park Plaza, 307 Park Ave (☎647-1072). A Twenties hotel stuffed with wonderful wicker furniture and brass fittings; be sure to book early. Continental breakfast is included. ⑤.

International Drive and around

Days Inn Lakeside, 7335 Sand Lake Rd (☎351-1900). An enormous branch of the nationwide chain in a winning lakeside location, with a small beach and three pools. ②.

The Floridian, 7299 Republic Drive (☎1-800/445-7299 or ☎351-5009). A mid-sized hotel with an easy-going mood and nicely furnished rooms. ④.

Gateway Inn, 7050 Kirkman Rd (☎351-2000). Good-sized rooms, two pools and free shuttle buses to the major theme parks make this a good base for non-drivers concentrating on the big attractions. ③.

Heritage Inn, 9861 International Drive (☎1-800/447-1890). Plain rooms at modest rates, a pool and a breakfast buffet are reasons for staying in this somewhat kitsch shrine to Southern Victoriana; also has live jazz some evenings. ④.

The Peabody Orlando, 9801 International Drive (☎1-800/PEABODY). Twenty-seven stories of luxury rooms primarily aimed at delegates using the massive Orange County Convention Center across the street. If money's no object and you like in-room luxuries, access to a fitness center and floodlit tennis courts, this one's for you. Ducks parade through the lobby twice a day. ⑧.

Radisson Barcelo Hotel, 8444 International Drive (☎345-0505). Speed-swimming records have been set at the Olympic-sized pool here, though those looking for relaxation will find the spacious rooms and the location, directly opposite the restaurants of the Mercado Mediterranean Shopping Village (see "Eating," p..226), to be a winning combination. ⑤.

Red Roof Inn, 9922 Hawaiian Court (☎352-1507). Unelaborate but perfectly serviceable budget-range hotel with a pool and a coin-op laundromat. ③.

Westgate Lakes Family Resort, 10000 Turkey Lake Rd (☎352-8051). All rooms are suites with full cooking facilities, and the resort is spread across a ninety-acre lakeside site. ⑦.

Lake Buena Vista

Embassy Suites, 8100 Lake Ave (☎1-800/257-8483 or ☎239-1144). Two-room suites including free breakfast and in-room refrigerators and microwaves. ⑥.

Marriott Residence Inn, 8800 Meadow Creek Drive (☎1-800/244-4070 or ☎239-7700). A suite-style motel near Disney that accommodates large groups with multi-bedrooms and kitchenettes. Free breakfast and newspaper, and several swimming pools. Two other Marriott locations are at 7975 Canada Dr (☎1-800/227-3978 or ☎345-0117) and 4768 Hwy-192 (☎1-800/468-3027 or ☎396-2056). ⑦.

Perri House, 10417 Centurion Court (☎876-4830). An eight-room bed-and-breakfast hidden on four wooded acres just outside Disney off Sate Road 535. The rooms are clean and bright and the atmosphere is friendly (guests' first names and origins are written on a board in the breakfast room). Far from everything but Disney. ⑤.

Along Hwy-192

Best Western Kissimmee, 2261 E Hwy-192/E Irlo Bronson Memorial Hwy (☎1-800/944-0062). A good place to be with kids; there's a games room and play area, plus two pools. ③.

Casa Rosa, 4600 W Hwy-192, Kissimmee (☎1-800/432-0665). A generally quiet and relaxing motel with mood-enhancing Mediterranean-style architecture. ①.

Flamingo Inn, 801 E Hwy-192/E Vine St (☎1-800/780-7617). You can rely on this reasonably priced place being clean, tidy and well run; for in-room feasting, microwave ovens are available at no charge. ②.

Golden Link, 4914 W Hwy-192 (☎1-800/654-3957). A comparatively large motel, with heated pool, a self-service laundromat and rentable refrigerators. ②.

HIKING AND PICNICKING

Just north of Universal Studios Escape, off Hiawassee Road and near Conroy-Windermere Road, is **Turkey Lake Park** (adults $2, children $1), a quiet place to have lunch by a lake, take a short hike or let the kids run around a terrific playground. Fifteen miles west of downtown Orlando off Hwy 50 is the **West Orange Trail**, 4.6 miles of scenic, paved walkways that run from historic Winter Garden to the hills of Lake County. West Orange Trail Bikes and Blades Co. (☎877-0600) provides bike ($5) and skate ($6) rentals.

Holiday Inn Hotel & Suites, Main Gate East, 5678 Hwy-192 (☎1-800/FON-KIDS). The best hotel for kids, with a full childcare service. Drop them off at "Camp Holiday" and they'll never want to come back. ⑥.

Howard Johnson, 4647 W Hwy-192 (☎396-1340). Nice rooms with good amenities, including cable TV, a pool and a coin-op laundromat. ②.

Larson's Lodge Maingate, 6075 W Hwy-192 (☎1-800/327-9074). Another good place for kids. The rates might be a touch higher than others in the vicinity, but under-18s stay for free in their parents' room and facilities include a game room, a small playground and a jacuzzi. ⑤.

Thrift Lodge, 4624 W Hwy-192 (☎1-800-648-4148). Thrifty rooms with free coffee; kitchenettes are $10 extra. ②.

Villager Lodge, 4669 W Hwy-192 (☎396-1890). One of the bigger motels in the area, offering a pool, a coin-op laundromat and cable TV, as well as great-value special rates even in high season. ②.

Camping: Kissimmee

Numerous serviceable **campgrounds** stand beside Hwy-192, close to Kissimmee. Suited to tents ($23.95 with water and electric, $21.95 without) is the *KOA*, 4771 Hwy-192 (☎1-800/331-1453), which also has cabins for $32.95 and free shuttle buses to Walt Disney World. For a more peaceful setting, choose a site beside Lake Tohopekaliga, where the pace is leisurely and more fuss is made about fishing than visiting Mickey Mouse: pitch your tent at *Merry "D" RV Sanctuary*, 4261 Pleasant Hill Road (☎933-5837; $12), or Richardson's Fish Camp, 1550 Scotty's Road (☎846-6540; $15).

Orlando

Despite enormous expansion over the last decade, **ORLANDO** remains impressively free of the commercialism that surrounds it. Away from the small group of high-rise office buildings in downtown, the bulk of the city comprises smart residential areas enhanced by parks and lakes. Visiting the historical leftovers and art collections spread throughout the city could fill a day – and, for those who thought that the state begins and ends with theme parks, Orlando offers a taste of Florida living without the mouse-ear hats. Bus #1 from downtown Orlando links the city's key areas.

Downtown Orlando

Except to sample the artificial charms of *Church Street Station* (see "Nightlife," p.229), few visitors make their way into **Downtown Orlando**, which, despite the half-dozen corporate towers in its midst, is still redolent, in size and mood, of the tobacco-chewing cow-town that it used to be. Everything of consequence in the tiny downtown can be visited on foot within an hour.

Begin with a dawdle along **Orange Avenue**, which is mostly patrolled by lunch-seeking office workers. Pass the Egyptian-influenced, late-Twenties **First National**

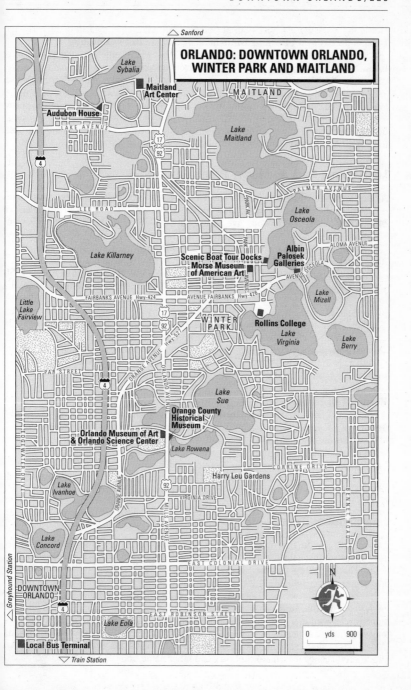

△ Sanford

ORLANDO: DOWNTOWN ORLANDO, WINTER PARK AND MAITLAND

Lake Sybalia

Maitland Art Center

MAITLAND

Audubon House

LAKE AVENUE

Lake Maitland

17
92

4

PALMER AVENUE

LEE ROAD

Lake Osceola

PARK AV.

Scenic Boat Tour Docks
Morse Museum of American Art

Lake Killarney

Albin Palosek Galleries

ALOMA AVENUE

AVENUE OSCEOLA

Little Lake Fairview

FAIRBANKS AVENUE Hwy 424

AVENUE FAIRBANKS Hwy 426

Lake Mizell

17
92

WINTER PARK

Rollins College

Lake Virginia

Lake Berry

PAR STREET

Hwy 527

ORANGE AVENUE

4

EDGEWATER DRIVE

Lake Sue

Orange County Historical Museum

Orlando Museum of Art & Orlando Science Center

Lake Rowena

CORRINE DRIVE

Lake Ivanhoe

92

ORANGE AVENUE

MILLS AVENUE

Harry Leu Gardens

VIRGINIA DRIVE

BENNETT ROAD

Lake Concord

EAST COLONIAL DRIVE

N

DOWNTOWN ORLANDO

4

△ Greyhound Station

EAST ROBINSON STREET

Lake Eola

0   yds   900

Local Bus Terminal

▽ Train Station

Bank on the corner of Church Street, and continue a few blocks north to the early-Art Deco of **McCrory's Five and Dime** building and the **Kress Building**.

Some of the wooden homes built by Orlando's first white settlers stand around **Lake Eola**, a ten-minute walk east of Orange Avenue. Many are undergoing expensive restoration as their owners strive to become bed-and-breakfast moguls. There's a good view of the houses from the oak-filled park that rings the placid lake, which is over-looked by elevated freeways. Linger here to contemplate the city's first hundred years – and the fact that Orlando's early black inhabitants didn't live in these leafy environs but were consigned to a much less picturesque district west of the railway line, parallel to Orange Avenue; still today, very much the wrong side of the tracks.

Loch Haven Park and Harry P. Leu Gardens

A large lawn squeezed between two small lakes, **Loch Haven Park**, three miles north of downtown Orlando, contains three buildings of varying interest. The **Orlando Museum of Art** 2416 N Mills Ave (Tues–Sat 9am–5pm, Sun noon–5pm; suggested donation $4) is likely to take up at least an hour: a permanent collection of pre-Columbian pieces backs up the usually excellent temporary exhibitions of modern American paintings culled from the finest collections in the world.

Across the park, the small **Orange County Historical Museum**, 812 E Rollins St (Mon–Sat 9am–5pm, Sun noon–5pm; $4), is more liable to jog the memories of elderly locals than excite out-of-towners. The artifacts, however, from photos to recreated hotel lobbies and grocers' shops, do an admirable job of reviving a time when, far from being a global tourist mecca, Orlando epitomized the American frontier town. Children will enjoy roaming around the nearby **Orlando Science Center**, 777 E Princeton St (Mon–Thurs 9am–5pm, Fri 9am–9pm, Sat noon–9pm, Sun noon–5pm; $8–14), a stunning, brand-new, $44-million complex where hands-on exhibits explain the funda-mentals of physics, biology, agriculture, astronomy and more to formative minds.

Harry P. Leu Gardens

A mile east of Loch Haven Park, **Harry P. Leu Gardens**, 1920 N Forest Avenue (daily 9am–5pm; $4, including a tour of Leu House), was purchased by a green-thumbed Orlando businessman in 1936 to show off plants collected from around the world. After seeing and sniffing the orchids, roses, azaleas and the largest camellia collection in the eastern US, take a trip around **Leu House** (guided tours only; daily 10am–3:30pm), a nineteenth-century farmhouse bought and lived in by Leu and his wife, now maintained in the simple but elegant style of their time and laced with family mementoes.

International Drive

Devoid of any of the charm one might find in downtown Orlando, **International Drive** (five miles southwest of Orlando and smack between Disney World, Universal Studios Escape and SeaWorld Orlando) is still worth a short visit for those interested in gawk-ing at big-budget tourism at its most obscenely creative. The strip boasts an F.A.O. Schwartz toy store, at no. 9101 (☎352-9900), whose location is marked by a 380-foot-high Raggedy Ann. Other wonders include a **Ripley's Believe It or Not Museum**, at no. 8201, housed in a dramatically lopsided building, and **Skull Kingdom**, a haunted mansion built to look like a castle with a skeleton facade emerging from the front wall. A Belz outlet shopping complex on International Drive's north end is good for heavily discounted Disney merchandise, Levi's and other name brands.

Winter Park

A couple of miles northeast of Loch Haven Park, **Winter Park** has been socially a cut above the rest of the city since it was launched in the 1880s as "a beautiful winter retreat for well-to-do people." For all its obvious money – a mix of new yuppie dollars and old wealth – Winter Park is a very likeable place, with a pervasive sense of community and a scent of California-style New Age affluence.

On Fairbanks Avenue, which brings traffic from Loch Haven into Winter Park, stand the hundred-year-old Mediterranean Revival buildings of **Rollins College**, the oldest college in the state and a tiny but highly regarded seat of liberal arts education. Other than neat landscaping, the campus has just one thing in its favor: the **Cornell Fine Arts Center** (Tues–Fri 10am–5pm, Sat & Sun 1–5pm; free), which offers a staid bundle of modest nineteenth-century European and American paintings, rather more interesting temporary shows, and an eccentric collection of old watch keys.

You'll find a more complete art collection a mile east of the college on Osceola Avenue, at the **Albin Palosek Galleries**, no. 633 (Sept–June Wed–Sat 10am–4pm, Sun 1pm–4pm; free): the former home of Czech-born sculptor Albin Palosek, who arrived penniless in the US in 1901 and spent most of his time over the next fifty years winning big-money commissions. The profits were eventually channeled into creating this house and studio, which contain more than two hundred of his technically accomplished, realist pieces.

Along Park Avenue: the Morse Museum and boat tours

Winter Park's upmarket status is compounded by its showcase street, **Park Avenue** (which meets Fairbanks Avenue close to Rollins): a row of top-of-the-line outfitters, jewellers and spick-and-span restaurants. Worth a special stop is the Scott Laurent Galleries, 348 N Park Ave (Mon–Fri 10am–6pm, Sun noon–5pm), a shop with an impressive collection of art, glass, ceramics and jewelry.

Should window-shopping lack appeal, drop into the **Charles Hosmer Morse Museum of American Art**, just off Park Avenue at 133 E Wolborne Avenue (Tues–Sat 9.30am–4pm, Sun 1–4pm; $3), which houses the collections of its namesake, one of Winter Park's founding fathers. The major exhibits are drawn from the output of Louis Comfort Tiffany – a legend for his innovative Art Nouveau lamps and windows that furnished high-society homes around the turn of the century. Great creativity and craftsmanship went into Tiffany's work: he molded glass while still soft, imbuing it with colored images of water lilies, leaves and even strutting peacocks. Tiffany's work is so stunning that the rest of the museum's possessions, including paintings by Norman Rockwell, seem to pale in comparison.

To discover why those who could afford to live anywhere choose Winter Park, take the **scenic boat tour** from the dock at 312 E Morse Boulevard (departures every hour daily 10am–4pm; $6). The hour-long voyage through wood-shrouded lakes and moss-draped canals is a picture-postcard view, usually reserved exclusively for the owners of the big-buck waterside homes.

Eatonville

Adjacent to Winter Park is the small town of **Eatonville**, the first incorporated African American municipality in the United States. The town was founded by three black men in 1875 so black Americans could "solve the great race problem by securing a home...in a negro city governed by negroes," according to a notice published in the local newspaper in 1889. Land was sold for $5–10 an acre, and renowned author Zora Neale Hurston, an Eatonville native, used the town as setting for novels such as *Their Eyes*

Were Watching God. The town is worth a stop to see the **Zora Neale Hurston National Museum of Fine Arts**, 227 E Kennedy Blvd (Mon–Fri 9am–4pm; free), which rotates exhibits of artists of African descent.

Maitland

The luscious sunsets over Lake Sybelia in **Maitland**, directly north of Winter Park, inspired a young artist named André Smith to buy six acres on its banks during the Thirties. With the financial assistance of Mary Bok (wealthy widow of Edward Bok; see "South Central Florida"), Smith established what is now the **Maitland Art Center**, 231 W Packwood Avenue (Mon–Fri 10am–4.30pm, Sat & Sun noon–4.30pm; free), a collection of stuccoed studios, offices and apartments decorated with Aztec-Mayan murals and grouped around garden courtyards. Smith invited other American artists to spend working winters here, but his abrasive personality scared many potential guests away. The colony continued in various forms until Smith's death in 1959, never becoming the esthetes' commune he hoped for. There are temporary exhibitions and a permanent collection, but it's the unique design of the place that demands a visit. While here, spare a thought for Smith's ghost, which, according to a number of local painters and sculptors who claim to have felt its presence, dispenses artistic guidance.

A few steps from the art center are the **Maitland Historical Museum** and the **Telephone Museum**, 221 W Packwood Avenue (Thurs–Sun noon–4pm; suggested donation $1). The front rooms of the combined museums house an ordinary collection of ageing photos and household objects, but the back room is filled with wonderful vintage telephones, commemorating the day in 1910 when a Maitland grocer installed telephones in the homes of his customers, enabling them to place orders from their armchairs.

The only other thing to make you dally in Maitland is the **Florida Audubon Society's Center for Birds of Prey**, 1101 Audubon Way (Tues–Sun 10am–4pm; suggested donation $5, $4 for children), the headquarters of the Florida Audubon Society, the state's oldest and largest conservation organization. The house is primarily an educational center and gift shop, but the adjacent rehabilitation facility is the largest in the Southeast, treating injured and orphaned birds such as ospreys, owls, hawks, eagles and falcons.

Eating: Orlando and around

Given the level of competition among restaurants to attract hungry tourists, **eating** in Orlando is never difficult and – if you escape the clutches of the theme parks – need not be expensive. In **downtown Orlando**, choices are comparatively limited, though the need to satisfy a regular clientele of lunch-breaking office workers keeps prices low. With a car, you might also investigate the local favorites scattered about downtown. Affluent **Winter Park** promises more variety, generally with higher standards and prices, though it does have a few serviceable low-cost diners.

Tourist-dominated **International Drive** offers a greater range, if less intimacy. The culinary hot-spots are the gourmet ethnic restaurants, but strict-budget travelers will relish the opportunity to eat massive amounts at one of several buffet restaurants – all for less than they might spend on a tip elsewhere. Buffet eating reaches its ultimate expression along **Hwy-192**, where virtually every buffet restaurant chain has at least one outlet, leaving the discerning glutton spoilt for choice.

Discount coupons in tourist magazines bring sizeable reductions at many restaurants, including "Show Restaurants," where $30 per head not only buys a multi-course feed and (usually) limitless beer, wine and soft drinks but also entertainment ranging from cavorting ninja warriors to medieval knights jousting on horseback.

Orlando

Bubbalou's Bodacious Bar-B-Q, 5818 Conroy Rd (☎295-1212). Down-home smoked meat sandwiches and platters at down-home prices, just north of Universal Studios Escape.

Coq au Vin, 4800 S Orange Ave (☎851-6980). The atmosphere in this French restaurant is so unpretentious, the service so down-to-earth and the prices so low that the top-notch cuisine is a delightful surprise.

Dexters of Thornton Park, 808 E Washington St (☎648-2777). Priced-right, trendy foods and an extensive beer menu, which attracts a young, urban clientele.

El Bohio Café, 5756 Dahlia Drive (☎282-1723). One of two local outlets (with *Vega's*, see below) for generous portions of well-priced Cuban food.

Jungle Jim's, inside Church Street Market, 55 W Church St (☎872-3111). Local branch of a fast-expanding chain where servers emerge from the jungle decor bearing enormous burgers, gigantic salads and Mexican-style dishes.

Lilia's Grilled Delights, 3150 S Orange Ave (☎851-9087). A fine selection of Filipino dishes, though quality can vary. If you're seriously hungry, go for the whole pig.

Numero Uno, 2499 S Orange Ave (☎841-3840). A small, good-value Cuban restaurant.

Le Provence, 50 E Pine St (☎843-1320). Well-presented but uninspired French cuisine, open for dinner only. Try the after-dinner cheese course.

Thai House, 2101 E Colonial Drive (☎828-0820). Tasty Thai food priced under $10.

Too-Jay's, 2624 E Colonial Drive (☎894-1718). Casual Jewish-style deli.

Vega's Café, 1835 E Colonial Drive (☎898-5196). Cuban diner with great-value lunches.

Vihn's, 1231 E Colonial Drive (☎894-5007). Hole-in-the-wall Vietnamese restaurant offering good food at giveaway prices for lunch and dinner.

White Wolf Café, 1829 N Orange Ave (☎895-5590). Down-to-earth café/antique store known for creative sandwiches and generous salads.

Winter Park

Brazilian Pavilion, 140 W Fairbanks Ave (☎740-7440). Sumptuous Brazilian creations; try the *peixe a Brasileria* (filet of snapper with tomatoes, scallions and coconut milk) or the *frango a Francesca* (chicken cutlet with fresh garlic and parsley).

The Briar Patch, 252 N Park Ave (☎628-8651). Well-prepared lunches and dinners. The salads are especially huge. Eat inside or on the terrace.

East India Market, 610 W Morse Blvd (☎647-7520). Gourmet pizzas and overambitious salads served at tables surrounded by flowers in an outdoor nursery.

The Hutch Coffee Shop, 109 E Lyman Ave (☎644-5948). A dependable, budget-priced coffee shop just off fashionable Park Ave.

La Venezia Cafe, 142 S Park Ave (☎647-7557). Elegant lunch place serving creative sandwiches and salads, and offering the most extensive coffee menu in town.

Maison des Crêpes, Hidden Garden Shops, 348 N Park Ave (☎647-4469). Some people come here solely for the feather-light crêpes, but the lunches and dinners are inventive and tasty.

Park Avenue Grill, 358 N Park Ave (☎647-4556). A fairly standard American menu but the window seats are an excellent vantage point for people-watching.

Power House, 111 E Lyman Ave (☎645-3616). Raise your energy levels with a vitamin-packed fruit juice; or sample one of the tasty soups.

Winnie's Oriental Garden, 1346 Orange Ave (☎629-2111). Applauded by locals as the best Chinese restaurant in town.

Winter Park Diner, 1700 W Fairbanks Ave (☎644-2343). In business longer than most people can remember, and still serving generous portions of classic diner food at prices to please.

International Drive and around

Bahama Breeze, 8849 International Drive (☎248-2499). Decent Caribbean food in an upbeat atmosphere.

Bergamo's, Mercado Mediterranean Shopping Village, 8445 International Drive (☎352-3805). Good-quality and slightly expensive pasta and seafood dishes. Dinner only.

Butcher Shop Steakhouse, Mercado Mediterranean Shopping Village, 8445 International Dr (☎363-9727). The biggest steaks and chops you've ever seen. Heaven for carnivores.

Café Tu Tu Tango, 8625 International Drive (☎248-2222). Fill up on creative appetizers at this lively hotspot.

Christini's Ristorante Italiano, 7600 Dr Phillips Blvd (☎345-8770). One of the truly excellent tables in Southwest Orlando. The food and service is so superb, it's worth the high prices.

Cricketers Arms, Mercado Mediterranean Shopping Village, 8445 International Drive (☎354-0686). Fish-and-chips, pies and pasties complement a range of imported ales and lagers at this inexpensive nook.

Italianni's, 8148 International Drive, Pointe Orlando (☎345-8884). Decent Italian food in a cavernous setting. The good make-your-own pizzas are a hit with kids.

Hard Rock Cafe, at Universal Studios Escape, 5800 S Kirkman Rd (☎351-7625). Orlando's outpost of the international chain known as much for their T-shirts and music memorabilia as for their groovy hamburgers.

Johnny Rockets, 9101 International Drive (☎903-0630). Good burgers and shakes in an old-fashioned diner setting.

José O'Day's, Mercado Mediterranean Shopping Village, 8445 International Drive (☎363-0613). Not the best Mexican food you'll ever taste, but portions are large and the atmosphere is enjoyable.

La Grille, 8445 International Drive(☎345-0883). Pricey but worthy contemporary French cuisine.

Ming Court, 9188 International Drive (☎351-9988). Chinese cuisine of an exceptionally high standard makes this a good spot on International Drive; less costly than you might expect.

Morrison's Cafeteria, 7440 International Drive (☎351-0051). Low-cost self-service eating; load your tray from an immense array of hot dishes, desserts and drinks.

Passage to India, 5532 International Drive (☎351-3456). Not-too-spicy Indian cuisine; *thali* is a house speciality, but the lunch time buffet offers the best value.

Ponderosa Steakhouse, 6362, 8510 & 14407 International Drive (☎352-9343; ☎354-1477; ☎238-2526). The biggest appetites will be fully satisfied here, where sizeable buffets – with plenty of options for non-meat eaters too – are laid out for breakfast, lunch and dinner.

Sizzler, 9142 International Drive (☎351-5369), 6308 International Drive (☎248-9711). Substantial breakfast buffet from 7am–11am; lunch or dinner brings ample steaks or seafood, plus an all-you-can-eat salad bar.

Western Steer, 6315 International Drive (☎363-0677). Breakfast, lunch and dinner buffets; the latter features five hot courses, as well as soups, salads, vegetables, fruit and ice cream, in limitless supply.

Lake Buena Vista

Bongo's Cuban Café, Downtown Disney's West Side, 1498 E Buena Vista Dr (☎828-0999). Gloria and Emilio Estefan's fair-but-fun Cuban cuisine. The decor is wildly fabulous and there are shows nightly.

California Grill, inside Disney's Contemporary Resort (☎WDW-DINE). Disney's culinary showpiece, with a menu from sushi to stews prepared in an open kitchen and served in a bustling dining room. One hundred wines available by the glass.

Crab House, 8496 Palm Parkway, in the Vista Center (☎239-1888). Lively seafood house specializing in many kinds of crab.

Flying Fish Café, at Disney's BoardWalk Inn (☎WDW-DINE). Excellent but pricey seafood in an energetic dining room. There's a notable sparkling wine menu.

House of Blues, Downtown Disney's West Side, 1490 E Buena Vista Dr (☎934-2583). Decent Creole- and Cajun-inspired food. Consider going during Sunday's popular Gospel brunch.

India Palace, in Vista Center, 8530 Palm Parkway (☎238-2322). Authentic Indian meals in a quiet setting. The lunch buffet is a good value.

Pebbles Restaurant, at Crossroads, 12551 SR535 (☎827-1111). Creative American cuisine with dishes priced within reach. Locals love it.

Planet Hollywood, Disney's Pleasure Island (☎827-7827). One of the world's top-grossing restaurants, serving burgers inside a giant globe.

Rainforest Café, Two locations: Downtown Disney's West Side and Disney's Animal Kingdom (☎827-8500 and ☎938-9100). Safari-themed restaurants with faux animals swinging through the trees and squealing. Walk through to see the creative decor then grab cheap eats elsewhere.

Tony Roma's Famous for Ribs, 12167 S Apopka-Vineland Rd (239-8040). It's all in the name: good smoked ribs.

Wolfgang Puck Café, Downtown Disney's West Side, 1482 E Buena Vista Dr (☎938-9653). Moderately priced, fabulously creative meals in a multi-level setting. The food in the upstairs dining room is more refined but far more expensive.

Wolfgang Puck Express, Two locations: Downtown Disney's West Side and Disney's Marketplace (☎938-9653 and ☎828-0107). Fast-food restaurant serving up the famed *Spago* chef's gourmet pizzas, as well as rotisserie chicken, good sandwiches and other all-American fare at affordable prices.

Along Hwy-192

Black-Eyed Pea, 5305 W Hwy-192 (☎397-1500). Large portions of Southern-style cooking – catfish, fried chicken and much more – served for lunch and dinner.

Cracker Barrel Old Country Store, 5400 W Hwy-192 (☎396-6521). Wholesome breakfasts and lunches in an Americana atmosphere, complete with country store.

Key W Kool's, 7225 W Hwy-192 (☎396-1166). For a break from buffets, sample the seafood and steaks served for lunch and dinner in this tropically themed restaurant; or show up for the two-dollar breakfast.

New Punjab, 3404 W Vine St/Hwy-192 (☎931-2449). The vegetarian dinner is excellent value.

Ponderosa Steakhouse, 5771 & 7598 Hwy-192 (☎397-2477 and ☎396-7721). A gigantic buffet offered all day. Three other branches on International Drive (see above).

Sizzler, 7602 W Hwy-192 (☎397-0997). Most substantial breakfast buffet in the vicinity; also on International Drive (see above).

Show restaurants

American Gladiators Orlando Live!, 5515 W Hwy-192 (☎390-0000). Live dinner-theater take-off of the ridiculous TV show.

Arabian Nights, 6225 W Hwy-192 (☎239-9223). Voted by Orlando locals as the best dinner-theater. Fifty-plus live horses help tell a comic version of the classic story.

Capone's Dinner & Show, 4740 Hwy-192 (☎397-2378). Give the secret password and enter this Prohibition-era speakeasy for a Twenties-style song-and-dance revue and an Italian-food buffet – both of mediocre quality.

Hoop De Doo Musical Revue, Disney's Fort Wilderness Resort (☎939-3463). Hokey but tons of fun cowboy-themed dinner theater. Reserve early.

King Henry's Feast, 8984 International Drive (☎351-5151). Knights duel and jesters amuse as a five-course meal is served and drinks are quaffed from tankards. Better than you'd think.

Mark Two Dinner Theater, 3376 Edgewater Dr (☎843-6275). Traveling Broadway shows play here as patrons partake of a five-entree buffet.

Medieval Times Dinner & Tournament, 4510 Hwy-192 (☎1-800/229-8300 or ☎239-8666). Knights joust on horseback as you feast inside this replica of an eleventh-century castle.

Sleuth's Mystery Dinner Theater, 7508 Republic Dr (☎363-1985). If you know red herring isn't a seafood dish, you're well on the way to solving the murder mystery played out in this Agatha-Christie-style set as you eat.

Wild Bill's Wild West Dinner Extravaganza, 5260 Hwy-192 (☎351-5151). Upbeat Western-themed dinner show in a mock log cabin featuring Native American Comanche dancers, knife throwers and more.

Nightlife

With the recent development of fun centers like the *Church Street Station* (see below), **nightlife** in Orlando is slowly gaining a grown-up reputation. Entertainment, like everything else, centers around Disney World, and with all the kiddies swarming through the area, the bar and club scene can be infantile. Still, Orlando hosts more business conventions than anywhere else on earth, and the average age of the night-time revelers has bucked considerably in a mature direction.

Downtown Orlando

Bonkers, 25 S Orange Ave (☎629-2665). An improvised comedy showcase open five nights a week.

Church Street Station, 129 W Church St (☎422-2434). Don't let the crowds who flock here nightly fool you into thinking this complex of bars, restaurants and an 1890s-style music hall, *Rosie O'Grady's*, merits the $17.95 admission fee. Once inside, you'll also have to pay handsomely for drinks.

Howl at the Moon Saloon, 55 W Church St (☎841-9118). It's hard to concentrate on your drink as dueling pianists whizz through a singalong selection of rock-and-roll classics and show tunes.

Sapphire Supper Club, 54 N Orange Ave (☎246-1419). High-quality traditional and contemporary jazz. See the "Calendar" pullout from the *Orlando Sentinel* for the line-up.

Zuma Beach, 46 N Orange Ave (☎648-8363). With a wide variety of music, from acid jazz to Latin American, you're sure to find something here to suit your taste.

Winter Park

Comedy Zone, at the *Holiday Inn*, 6515 International Dr (☎645-5233). A varying line-up of comics do shows at 8.30 and 10.30pm.

International Drive, Hwy-192 and around

Bennigan's, 6324 International Drive (☎351-4435). Sprawling sports bar with extended happy hours and 100 beers.

Crazy Horse Saloon, 7050 Kirkman Rd (☎363-0071). Rowdy country and bluegrass music; lots of drinking and high spirits.

Cricketers Arms, Mercado Mediterranean Shopping Village, 8445 International Drive (☎354-0686). English ales, European lagers and the latest soccer scores – and sometimes the matches themselves on giant TV screens.

Embassy, 5100 Adanson St (☎629-4779). High-tech disco complex which also includes a music club with national and local acts.

Fat Tuesday, 41 W Church St (☎843-6104). Just the place to initiate yourself into the joys of the frozen daiquiri, available in many different flavors. Most evenings there's also live music.

Sullivan's, 1108 S Orange Blossom Trail (☎843-2934). Live country music and line dancing; draws a friendly and enthusiastic crowd.

North of Orlando

Back-to-back residential areas dissolve into fields of fruit and vegetables **north of Orlando's** city limits. Around here, in slow-motion towns harking back to Florida's frontier days, farming still has the upper hand over tourism. Although it's easy to skim through on I-4, the older local roads connecting the major settlements have far more atmosphere.

Sanford and Mount Dora

A position on the south shore of Lake Monroe, fifteen miles north of Maitland on Hwy-92 (also known as Hwy-17), allows **SANFORD** to capitalize on riverboat cruises for a fair share of its tourist dollars. Cruises (from $35; ☎1-800/423-7401) embark from the marina on N Palmetto Avenue. For more of an insight into the modestly sized town – and the turn-of-the-century lawyer and diplomat who created it – dip inside the **Shelton Sanford Memorial Museum**, 520 E First Street (Tues–Fri 11am–4pm; free). Once called "Celery City" on account of its major agricultural crop, Sanford hasn't had a lot going for it since the boom years of the early 1900s, a period lovingly chronicled in the museum. For even more relics of the halcyon days, collect a self-guided tour map from the **Chamber of Commerce**, 400 E First Street (Mon–Fri 9am–5pm; ☎352/322-2212), and venture around 22 buildings of divergent classical architecture in the adjacent old downtown district, most of them now doing business as drugstores and insurance offices.

On the way back to Hwy-92 at Sanford's southwest corner, the **Seminole County Historical Museum**, 300 Bush Boulevard (Mon–Fri 9am–1pm, Sat & Sun 1–4pm; free), carries a multitude of objects from all over the county, including an intriguing selection of medicine bottles. You can also rummage around **Flea World** (Fri, Sat & Sun 8am–5pm; free), at the end of Bush Boulevard by the Hwy-92 junction – a large-scale attempt to sell items that nobody in their right mind would ever buy.

To see a Victorian-era Florida village at its most self-consciously quaint, take Route 46 west of Sanford for seventeen miles and feast your eyes on the picket fences, wrought-iron balconies and fancy wood-trimmed buildings that make up **MOUNT DORA**. The **Chamber of Commerce**, 341 Alexander Street (Mon–Fri 9am–5pm; ☎352/383-2165), has a free guide to the old houses and the inevitable antique shops that now occupy many of them. Of the shops that dot the hilly streets, visit The Jeweler Studio (☎352/383-1883) and Double Creek Pottery (☎352/735-5579). Also worth a stop is the tiny Old City Jail on Royellou Lane, where the cells police used to stash local drunkards years ago are on display.

Cassadaga

A village populated by spiritualists conjures up images of weirdos in forbidding mansions, but the few hundred residents of **CASSADAGA**, just east of I-4, ten miles north of Sanford, are disappointingly normal citizens in normal homes, offering to reach out and touch the spirit world for a very down-to-earth fee ($25 to $60 for a half-hour session). A group of northern spirit mediums bought this 35-acre site in 1875 and quickly caught the imagination of Florida's early settlers – for whom contacting the Other Side was a lot easier than communicating with the rest of the US.

Throughout the year, seminars and lectures cover topics ranging from UFO cover-ups to out-of-body traveling. For more details, visit the **Cassadaga Camp Bookstore** in the Andrew Jackson Davis Building, on the corner of Route 4139 and Stevens Street (Mon–Fri 9.30am–5.30pm, Sat 9.30am–6pm, Sun noon–6pm; ☎904/228-2880), which doubles as an information center and psychic bookshop.

DeLand and around

Intended to be the "Athens of Florida" when founded in 1876, **DELAND**, four miles north of Cassadaga, west off I-4, is really just a commonplace Central Florida town. It does, however, boast one of the state's oldest educational centers: the **Stetson University**, on Woodland Boulevard, whose red-brick facades have stood since the 1880s, partly funded by the profits of the cowboy hat of the university's title. Pick up a free tour map from the easily found DeLand Hall for a walk around the vintage buildings. Also on the campus, on the corner of Michigan and Amelia avenues, the **Gillespie Museum of Minerals** (summer Mon–Sat noon–4pm; free) displays Florida quartz, calcite and limestone, plus gemstones gathered from all over the world.

Assuming you're not rushing towards the east coast (Daytona Beach is twenty miles away on Hwy-92 or I-4; see "The Northeast Coast") or making haste for the Ocala National Forest, less than ten miles east on Route 44 (see "North Central Florida," p.257), **canoeing** provides a reason to hang around the DeLand area. Organized trips (around $15 a day for a nine-mile trip down the Little Wekiva River Run) are arranged at Katie's Wekiva River Landing (☎407/628-1482), five miles west of I-4 on Route 46. For general information, use DeLand's **Chamber of Commerce**, 336 N Woodland Boulevard (Mon–Fri 8.30am–5pm; ☎1-800/749-4350), which provides detailed pamphlets of walking and driving tours in the area. Around the corner is the **Henry A. DeLand House Museum**, 137 W. Michigan Ave (Tues–Sat noon–4pm) built in 1886 and recently refurbished in period style. Of particular note are a wood carving of The Lord's Prayer and antique kitchen appliances.

DeLeon Springs, Lake Woodruff National Wildlife Refuge and Barberville

At **DeLeon Springs State Recreation Area** (daily 8am–sunset; cars $3.25, pedestrians and cyclists $1), ten miles north of DeLand on Hwy-17, tourists coo over the thousands of gallons of water emerging from an underground spring. Outsider fascination at these labyrynths of underground water is an endless source of amusement for the residents of central and nothern Florida, for whom springs are a common sight. Everyone, however, agrees that DeLeon Springs is a pleasurable place. There's swimming, canoeing and picnicking in and beside the spring, and, when hungry, you can make your own pancakes in the *Old Spanish Sugar Mill Restaurant* (☎904/985-5644), a timbered diner beside the park, which opens at 9am on weekdays and at 8am on weekends, and stops serving at 4pm.

A few miles west, off Grand Ave, is the stunning **Lake Woodruff National Wildlife Refuge** (open sunrise to sunset; free), a 22,000-acre section of untouched wetlands that is home to 200 species of birds, including the endangered Southern Bald Eagle, 68 species of fish and more. A good bet for dinner in DeLeon Springs is *Karlin's Inn*, 4640 N Hwy-17, (Tues–Sat 5–9pm), a Continental restaurant with a Florida flair.

Seven miles further north on Hwy-17, the tiny crossroads community of **BARBERVILLE** celebrates rural Florida through its **Pioneer Settlement for the Creative Arts** (Mon–Fri 9am–4pm, Sat 9am–2pm; $2.50), a turn-of-the-century train station and general store. Here, an assembly of pottery wheels, looms, milling equipment and other tools are put to use during the informative 45-minute guided tour.

Blue Spring and Hontoon Island

The naturally warm waters at **Blue Spring State Park** (daily 8am–sunset; cars $3.25, pedestrians and cyclists $1), seven miles south of DeLand (on Hwy-17) in Orange City, attract **manatees** (the aquatic creatures loving known as "sea cows"). between mid-November and mid-March. These best-loved of Florida's endangered animals swim here from the cooler waters of the St Johns River – the colder it is there the more manatees you'll see here. Aside from staking out the manatees from several observation platforms (and watching a twenty-minute slide show describing their habits), there's also the chance to see **Thursby House**, a large frame dwelling built by pioneer settlers in 1872. **Accommodation** in the park includes a $16-a-night campground and $55-a-night cabins which sleep up to four people (☎904/775-3663).

Not far from Blue Spring is **Hontoon Island**, a striking dollop of wooded land set within very flat and swampy terrain. Without a private boat, Hontoon Island is reachable only with the sporadic **ferry**, which runs daily from 9am to an hour before sunset from a landing stage on Route 44 (the continuation of DeLand's New York Avenue). Unbelievably, the island once held a boatyard and cattle ranch, but today it's inhabited only by the hardy souls who decide to stay over in one of its six rustic **cabins** (reservations ☎904/736-5309; ②), or at one of its very basic **campgrounds**.

South of Orlando

Not much fills the rough acres directly **south of Orlando**, though Gatorland, one of the area's oldest and, in its way, most amusing destinations, sits on what's called the "Orange Blossom Trail" (known variously as Hwy-92, Hwy-17 and Hwy-441), which runs the sixteen miles between Orlando and Kissimmee.

Gatorland

An oversized alligator mouth serves as the entrance for **Gatorland**, 14501 S Orange Blossom Trail (daily 9am–sunset; $13.95; one child free per paying adult; otherwise children 9–12 $8.95 and children 3–9 $6.48), which has been giving visitors a close look at the state's most feared and least understood animal since the 1950s. Surprisingly lazy beasts, the residents of the park (actually a working farm, licensed to breed alligators for their hides and meat) only show signs of life at the organized feeding – the Gator Jumparoo show – when hunks of chicken are suspended from a wire and the largest alligators, using their powerful tail muscles, propel themselves out of the water to grab their dinner: a bizarre spectacle of heaving animals and ferociously snapping jaws. When you arrive, pick up a schedule for the three main shows: Gator Jumparoo, Gator Wrestling and Snakes of Florida. The latter features some of Florida's most deadly reptiles – coral snakes, pygmy rattlesnakes, cottonmouth moccasins and diamond-back rattlesnakes – none of which you'd enjoy meeting in the wild, but the show serves as a handy recognition exercise in case you do.

Kissimmee

A country-bumpkin counterpart to the modern vacation developments that ring it, **KISSIMMEE**, at the end of Orange Blossom Trail, has most of its fun during the Wednesday lunchtime cattle auctions at the **Livestock Market**, 805 E Donegan Avenue. The **motels** close to the town on Hwy-192 (see "Accommodation," p.220) make Kissimmee a cheap place to stay, and even without a car getting to the theme parks and elsewhere in the region is relatively simple: **trains** stop at 111 E Dakin Ave, Greyhound **buses** at 3501 W Vine St (☎847-3911), and there are frequent **shuttle bus** links to the major Orlando area attractions (see "Getting around," p.219).

In Kissimmee, take a walk around the fifty-foot obelisk called **Kissimmee Monument of States**, on Monument Avenue. Comprising garishly painted concrete blocks adorned with pieces of stone and fossil from various American states and 21 foreign countries, this monument was erected in 1943 to honor the former president of the local All-States Tourist Club.

A peaceful, rural back street is the setting for **Green Meadows Petting Farm**, 1368 S Poinciana Blvd (daily 9.30am–4pm; $13). Take a leisurely (sometimes painfully slow) two-hour tour of this old-fashioned petting zoo, where kids can milk a cow and ride a pony. The farm is a refreshing change of pace from the major parks. Another Kissimmee address to visit with animals is the fairly depressing **JungleLand Zoo**, 4580 Hwy-192 (daily 9am–6pm; $11.95, children 3-11 $6.95). Honestly, spend the extra money and go to Disney's Animal Kingdom. JungleLand's inhabitants have little more than a rubber ball for entertainment, and when the animals get riled up they rattle their cages, creating a tense, break-me-out-of-here atmosphere.

Celebration

Nestled between Kissimmee and Disney's theme parks is **CELEBRATION** (off Hwy-192 across from Watermania), a 4900-acre town created by Disney and officially opened in 1996. Disney did massive sociological research before settling on a design they believed would capture the American ideal of community: old-fashioned exteriors, homes close to the road so neighbors are more likely to interact and a congenial old-fashioned downtown area. World-famous architects were brought in to design major buildings: Phillip Johnson, Ritchie & Fiore designed the Town Hall; Michael Graves the post office; Cesar Pelli the cinema; and Robert A.M. Stern the health center. The first 350 home sites sold out before a single model was complete. Enthusiasts applaud Celebration's friendly small-town feeling, where new neighbors are greeted with home-baked brownies, town events are well-attended and children can walk care-free to

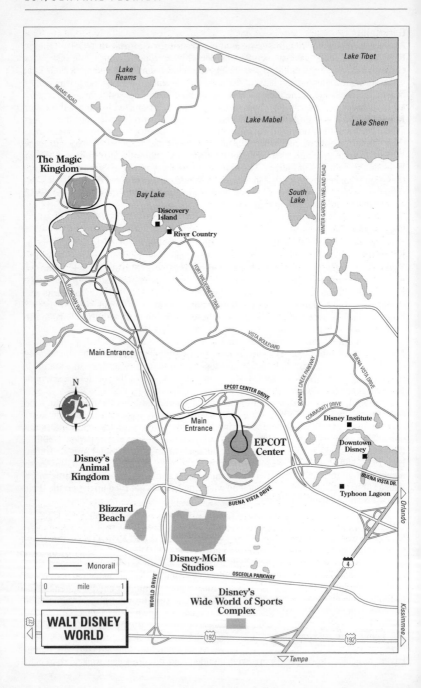

WALT DISNEY WORLD

school. Detractors use words like contrived and sterile, and point to stringent rules such as the insistence that all window treatments facing the outside must be white. The town, though, is worth a short visit – not only for the architecture and some of the best restaurants in the region, but to determine for yourself if this is the American Dream or a touch of Big Brother.

Walt Disney World

As significant as air conditioning in making the state what it is today, **WALT DISNEY WORLD** turned a wedge of Florida grazing land into one of the world's most lucrative vacation venues within ten years. Bringing growth and money to central Florida for the first time since the citrus boom a century ago, the immense and astutely planned empire (and Walt Disney World really *is* an empire) also pushed the state's media profile through the roof: from being a down-at-heel and slightly seedy mixture of cheap motels, retirement homes and clapped-out alligator zoos, Florida suddenly became a showcase of modern international tourism and in doing so, some would claim, sold its soul for a fast buck.

Whatever your attitude to theme parks, there's no denying that Walt Disney World is the pacesetter: it goes way beyond Walt Disney's original "theme park" – Disneyland, which opened in Los Angeles in 1955 – delivering escapism at its most technologically advanced and psychologically brilliant in a multitude of ingenious guises across an area twice the size of Manhattan. In a crime-free environment where wholesome all-American values hold sway and the concept of good clean fun finds its ultimate expression, Walt Disney World often makes the real world – and all its problems – seem like a distant memory.

SOME DISNEY HISTORY

When brilliant illustrator and animator Walt Disney devised the world's first theme park, California's **Disneyland** – which brought to life his cartoon characters, Mickey Mouse, Donald Duck, Goofy and the rest – he left himself with no control over the hotels and restaurants that quickly engulfed it, preventing growth and raking off profits Disney felt were rightly his. Determined that this wouldn't happen again, the Disney corporation secretly began to buy up 27,500 acres of central Florida farmland, and by the late Sixties had acquired – for a comparatively paltry $6 million – a site a hundred times bigger than Disneyland. With the promise of a jobs bonanza for Florida, the state legislature gave the corporation – thinly disguised as the Reedy Creek Improvement District – the rights of any major municipality: empowering it to lay roads, enact building codes, and enforce the law with its own security force.

Walt Disney World's first park, the **Magic Kingdom**, opened in 1971; predictably based on Disneyland, it was an equally predictable success. The far more ambitious **EPCOT Center**, unveiled in 1982, represented the first major break from cartoon-based escapism. Millions visited, but the rose-tinted look at the future received a mixed response. Partly due to this, and some cockeyed management decisions, the Disney empire (Disney himself died in 1966) faced bankruptcy by the mid-Eighties.

Since then, clever marketing has brought the corporation back from the abyss, and it now steers a tight and competitive business ship, always looking to increase Walt Disney World's 100,000 daily visitors and stay ahead of its rivals. Disney-MGM Studios, for example, aims to put a dent in Universal Studios Escape's trade (see p.245), while Pleasure Island's nightclubs, *Planet Hollywood* and the new *Downtown Disney's West Side* are clearly intended to compete with downtown Orlando's *Church Street Station* (see p.229). It may trade in fantasy, but where money matters, the Disney corporation's nose is firmly in the real world.

Here, litter is picked up within seconds of being dropped, subtle mind-games soften the pain of standing in line, the special effects are the best money can buy, and employees grin merrily as snotty-nosed kids puke down their legs. It's not cheap, forward planning is essential, and there are times when you'll feel like a cog in a vast machine – but Walt Disney World unfailingly, and with ruthless efficiency, always delivers what it promises.

Costs may come as a shock, especially to families (children under three are admitted free of charge, but note that little is designed specifically for their entertainment), but the admission fee allows unlimited access to all the shows and rides in a particular park – and you'll need *at least* a day per park to go on everything in each of the **four** main ones. Restaurants and snack bars – each as clinically themed as the parks – are plentiful but pricey. No alcohol is served in the Magic Kingdom.

Accommodation

If you want to escape the all-pervasive influence and high prices of Walt Disney World for the night, refer to the accommodation listings under "Downtown Orlando" (p.220). If not, you'll be relieved to find a growing number of **hotels** on Disney property, most of which are, in fact, fully equipped resorts. Predictably, each follows a particular theme to the nth degree, and prices are much higher – sometimes more than $300 per night – than you'll pay elsewhere. *All-Star Resorts*, however, is specifically intended for the less affluent visitor, costing $69 or $79 a night.

Each resort occupies its own landscaped plot, usually encompassing several swimming pools and a beach beside an artificial lake, and has several restaurants and bars. The Disney resorts are located in several areas, and transport, be it by boat, bus or monorail, is complimentary between them and the main theme parks. Disney guests can also use theme park parking lots for free. Theme-park admission tickets are also available at each resort, saving you valuable time otherwise spent lining up at park ticket booths. The standard of service should be excellent; if it isn't, make a stiff complaint and you'll probably be treated like royalty through the remainder of your stay.

At quiet times, rooms may be available at short notice, but with Disney resorts pitching themselves to convention-goers as much as vacationers, you may turn up on spec to find that there is no space at all, even in 1000-room properties such as the *Contemporary Resort*. To be assured of a room, book as far ahead as possible – nine months is not unreasonable. **Reservations** can be made through the phone number: ☎**407/W DISNEY** (☎934-7639 from overseas).

Disney Village resort area
Disney's Old Key West Resort. Key-West style time-share homes available for rent when unoccupied. ⑧.

Dixie Landings Resort. A moderately-priced, Southern-themed hotel, with rooms in the "manor house" or in the "bayou cottages" set in the grounds. ⑥.

Port Orleans Resort. Gaze from your wrought-iron balcony across the mini New Orleans re-created in this resort's courtyard. ⑥.

The Villas at Disney Institute. An assortment of getaway options in a rustic setting, near the education-oriented Disney Institute. The townhouses look like rustic treehouses but have modern amenities. ⑧.

EPCOT resort area
All-Star Resorts. The most affordable and garish of Disney's resorts, divided into the *All-Star Music Resort,* which is decorated with giant-sized, brightly colored cowboy boots, guitar-shaped swimming pools and the like; and the *All-Star Sports Resort,* complete with huge Coca-Cola cups, American football helmets and so on. Each complex has its own pool and about 1500 rooms. ④.

Caribbean Beach Resort. Disney's first attempt at a "budget-priced" hotel still works rather well. Typical motel rooms at this plushly landscaped property are located in one of five lodges, each with its own pool. ⑥.

Coronado Springs Resort. Disney's largest property to date and one of its more affordable, this hotel has 2000 Southwestern-style rooms built around a faux-Mayan pyramid. The food court is good for family meals. ⑥

The Dolphin. Topped by the giant sculpture of a dolphin and decorated in dizzying pastel shades and reproduction artworks from the likes of Matisse and Warhol. ⑧.

The Swan. Intended as a partner to the *Dolphin*, from which it's separated by an artificial lake and beach, and likewise whimsically decorated and equipped with every conceivable luxury. ⑧.

Yacht and Beach Club Resorts. Turn-of-the-century New England is the cue for these twin hotels, complete with clapboard facades and miniature lighthouse. Amusements include all manner of waterborne activities and a croquet lawn. ⑧.

Boardwalk Inn. A complex on the scale of the Contemporary and Grand Floridian Beach Resorts (see "Magic Kingdom Area," below), with rooms in the "inn" or – better value for groups of four or five – in studios. ⑧.

Magic Kingdom area

Contemporary Resort. The Disney monorail runs right through the center of this hotel, which takes its exterior design from the futuristic fantasies of the Magic Kingdom's Tomorrowland but is disappointingly characterless inside. ⑧.

Fort Wilderness Campground. Here you can pitch your tent ($35), hook up your RV ($54) or rent a six-berth trailer (around $185) – a good deal for larger groups.

The Grand Floridian Beach Resort. Gabled roofs, verandas and crystal chandeliers are among the frivolous variations on early Florida resort architecture at this elegant and relaxing base. ⑧.

Polynesian Village Resort. An effective, if tacky, imitation of a Polynesian beach hotel; the concept is most effective if you spend your time on the lakeside beach under the shade of coconut palms. ⑧.

Wilderness Lodge. This magnificent, oversized replica of a frontier log cabin is furnished with massive totem poles, a wood-burning fire in the lobby, and Southern-style wooden rocking chairs. ⑦.

The main parks

Walt Disney World's four main theme parks are quite separate entities. The **Magic Kingdom** is the Disney park everyone imagines, where Mickey Mouse mingles with the crowds and the emphasis is on fantasy and fun – very much the park for kids. Recognizable for its giant, golfball-like geosphere, **Epcot Center** is Disney's attempted celebration of science and technology, coupled with a very Disneyfied trip around various countries and cultures: dull for young kids, it's a sprawling area that involves a lot of walking. **Disney-MGM Studios** suits almost everyone; its special effects are enjoyable even if you've never seen the movies they're based on, and the Backstage Tour, despite moments of tedium, at least visits *real* studios – reality being a rare commodity in Walt Disney World. Disney's newest theme park, the more relaxed **Disney's Animal Kingdom**, is part new-age zoo, part theme park, bringing an African/Asian flavor to the swamplands of Southwest Orlando.

Doing justice to all four parks will take at least five days – one should be set aside for rest – and you shouldn't tackle more than one on any single day. If you only have a day to spare, pick the park that appeals most and stick to it: day tickets are only valid for one location anyway.

Disney Information: ☎407/824-4321

When to visit

While Epcot Center in particular absorbs crowds easily, it's best to avoid the **busiest periods**: during school vacations in the summer, and over Thanksgiving, Christmas and Easter. The busiest days vary from park to park (though, on average, Sunday is the least crowded day), so plan your itinerary once you've arrived or contact Disney Information for help.

Provided you **arrive early** at the park (just before opening time is best), you'll easily get through the most popular rides before the mid-afternoon crush, when lines can become monstrously long. If you're staying at a Disney World resort, you may be offered early entrance to the parks (before opening time) to help beat the crowds. If you can't arrive early, don't show up until 5 or 6pm, which in some seasons still leaves time to do plenty before the place shuts up. Each park has regularly updated noticeboards showing the latest **waiting times** for each show and ride – at peak times often about an hour and a half for the most popular rides and up to forty minutes for others.

Opening times and tickets

The parks are **open** daily from 9am to midnight during the busy periods, and from 9am to 6pm or later the rest of the year, with extended hours on holidays. During peak seasons the *Orlando Sentinel* lists each park's hours on the front page. A one-day, one-park ticket costs $44.52 (children aged 3–9 $36.04; under 3s go free), is available from any park entrance, and allows entry to one park only.

For seeing multiple parks, spread your visits over four or five days using one of the **passes** that permit entry to all four parks and free use of the shuttle buses around the complex. **Four-day passes** cost $149 (children aged 3–9 $119); **five-day passes** cost $189 (children aged 3–9 $151); **six-day passes** cost $249 (children aged 3-9 $199). There's also a $270.30 **year-long pass** ($230.02 for children), strictly for fanatics. If you're staying at a Disney World resort, you are eligible for reductions on all these prices.

As obvious as it may sound, if you arrive by car be sure to follow the signs to the park you want to visit and use its **parking lot** (fee $5 a day, which covers you for all the Disney World parking lots). These are enormous, so be sure to make a note of exactly where you're parked. Parking lots and hotels are linked to the main attractions by a comprehensive **transport system** of buses and a monorail (free to guests of the Disney World resorts).

The Magic Kingdom

Anyone who's been to Disneyland in LA will recognize much of the **Magic Kingdom**. Like the original Disney theme park, it's divided into several themed sections, each with its own personality. Building facades, rides, gift shops, even the particular characters giving hugs contribute to the unique feel of each section. The areas are called **Adventureland, Tomorrowland, Fantasyland, Frontierland, Liberty Square** and **Mickey's Toontown Fair**. Some of the rides are identical to their Californian forebears, some are greatly expanded and improved – and a few are much worse. Like its older sibling, the only way to deal with the place is enthusiastically: jump in with both feet and go on every ride you can.

A warning: Don't promise the kids (or yourself) too much beforehand. Sometimes lines are so long that it may be better to pass up some attractions. Although wait times are usually posted, lines can be deceiving: Disney masterfully disguises their true length, and keeps you cool with shade, fans and air conditioning wherever possible.

The park

From the main gates, you'll step into Main Street USA, a bustling consortium of luring souvenir shops selling the ubiquitous mouse-ear hats and other Disney paraphernalia in old-fashioned, town-square stores. Don't spend too much time here, as you can buy most of the same items throughout the park and in Disney hotels.

At the end of Main Street you'll see **Cinderella's Castle**, a stunning pseudo-Rhineland palace that looks like it should be the most elaborate ride in the park. In fact, it's just a shell that conceals all the electronics and machinery that drive the whole extravaganza. You merely walk through a tunnel in its center, and use it as a reference point when you've lost your bearings.

If you arrive early, beat the queues by immediately heading for the popular thrills-and-spills rides, which tend to draw the biggest crowds. The most nerve-jangling of these is **Space Mountain**, in essence an ordinary rollercoaster, but one where total darkness makes every jump and jolt unexpected. The ride may last less than three minutes but many people breathe a sigh of relief once it's over. **Splash Mountain** (memorably satirized in an episode of *The Simpsons*) is another glorified attraction, employing water to great effect and culminating in a fifty-foot drop. Like most rides, you must be of adequate height to board Splash Mountain, so if you have a tot who's too tiny, there's a playground discreetly placed to the right of the ride. **Big Thunder Mountain Railroad** puts you aboard a runaway train, which hurtles through gold-rush California in about three minutes. There's also the kid-oriented **Barnstormer**, a milder attraction perfect for thrillseekers-in-training.

You don't have to be a rollercoaster junkie to enjoy the Magic Kingdom. Many of the best rides in the park rely on "AudioAnimatronic" characters – impressive vocal robots of Disney invention – for their appeal. The most up-to-date are seen in **ExtraTERRORestrial Alien Encounter**, which will appeal especially to those who are fans of the *Alien(s)* films. A wonderful visual treat is **Transportarium**, where you're taken on a trip through time by the archetypal mad professor (whose voice is provided by Robin Williams). A whole slew of realistic robots inhabit **Pirates of the Caribbean**, a boat-ride through a pirate-infested Caribbean island complete with drunken debauchery and general mayhem.

Elsewhere, the **Haunted Mansion** is worth the wait, as much for the duration of the ride – one of the longest in the park – as for the clever special effects: there's a sliding ceiling in the entrance room and macabre goings-on as your "doom buggy" passes through a spook-filled cemetery. The leisurely **Jungle Cruise** is narrated by a pun-loving guide who takes you through waterfalls and cannibal camps in Africa's most "dangerous" territory.

Fantasyland is the one place where The Magic Kingdom shows its age (the park opened in 1971), but it also caters to the imaginations of its youngest visitors, making it one of the most-visited corners of the park. **It's A Small World** is a slow, pleasant boat ride past multi-ethnic childlike robots who sing the theme song over and over and over again. **Mr Toad's Wild Ride**, **Peter Pan's Flight** and **Snow White's Adventures** are creaky low-tech amusements, still very popular with young kids, but which wouldn't be out of place in a fairground. The dated Mr Toad may soon be replaced by a Winnie the Pooh ride, but historical-minded fans are fighting the switch. Another long-term survivor is **The Enchanted Tiki Birds**, with hundreds of AudioAnimatronic tropical birds and Tiki-god statues singing and whistling their way through a program of South Seas musical favorites.

While in Fantasyland, head to the **Fantasyland Character Connection** area, set up to the left of the **Mad Tea Party**, where you can meet and greet Disney's myriad characters. Otherwise, visit **Mickey's Toontown Fair**, where you're guaranteed to see several, or stay for the character-saturated **parade** (daily 3pm). The best vantage point is from a bench in Frontierland. Hint: stake one out around 2pm, and relax with a picnic as you wait for the cheerful parade to pass by.

EPCOT Center

Even before the new Magic Kingdom opened, Walt Disney was developing plans for the **EPCOT Center** (Experimental Prototype Community of Tomorrow). This was conceived in 1966 as a real community that would experiment and work with the new ideas and materials of a technologically advancing US. The idea failed to shape up as Disney had envisaged: EPCOT didn't open its gates until 1982, when global recession and ecological concerns had put a damper on the infallibility of science. One drawback of this park is simply its immense size: twice as big as the Magic Kingdom and, ironically, given its futuristic themes, very sapping on mankind's oldest mode of transport – the feet.

The park

EPCOT's 180-foot-high **geosphere** (unlike a semi-circular geodesic *dome*, the geo*sphere* is completely round) provides information desks and souvenir shops and sits at the heart of the **Epcot East/West** section of the park, which keeps close to EPCOT's original concept of exploring the history and researching the future of agriculture, transport, energy and communications. Inside the geosphere is the **Spaceship Earth Ride**, a fifteen-minute look at communication beginning with a pre-Cro-Magnon time tunnel and ending with a blast into the future to explore cutting-edge technologies.

Epcot East/West divides into seven pavilions – each corporately sponsored, so don't expect to learn anything about alternative energy sources or global warming – and each has its own rides, films and interactive computer exhibits. The **Wonders of Life** pavilion has the best of the rides, including **Body Wars**, a brief but exciting flight-simulator trip through a human body. While here, be sure to catch the entertaining **Cranium Command**, in which an AudioAnimatronic character is detailed to control the brain of a 12-year-old all-American boy.

Concentrate on beating the queues that often stretch outside **Universe of Energy**, a somewhat dated celebration of the harnessing of the earth's energy. Its highlight is a ride through the dinosaur-roamed primeval forests where today's fossil fuels originated.

In the **Journey Into Imagination** pavilion, a 3D cinematic thrill called **Honey I Shrunk the Audience** keeps you on the edge of your seat with excellent special effects. By contrast, the two **Innoventions** pavilions promise insight into the latest technological advances, but are more like glorified amusement arcades full of corporate advertising. **The Living Seas**, the world's largest artificial saltwater environment, occupied by a multitude of dolphins, sharks and sea lions, has far more to offer – not least for the chance to climb inside a diving suit.

Arranged around a forty-acre lagoon, the **World Showcase** section of EPCOT attempts to mirror the history, architecture and culture of eleven different nations. Each is presumably chosen for the ease of replicating an instantly recognizable landmark – Mexico has a Mayan Pyramid, France an Eiffel Tower – or stereotypical scene, such as the UK's pub, Germany's Bavarian village, and Morocco's inevitable bazaar. The elaborate reconstructions show careful attention to detail; highlights include the Viking longboat ride through **Norway**, **Japan**'s cultural museum, and the *Wonders of China* film. The most crowded place, though, is usually **The American Adventure** inside a replica of Philadelphia's Liberty Hall, where AudioAnimatronic versions of Mark Twain and Benjamin Franklin give a somewhat sanitized account of two centuries of US history in under half an hour. It's worth staying on till late evening to see performance acts at many of the countries, where natives do a myriad of singing and dancing acts for passing crowds. At night, the lagoon also transforms into the spectacular sound and light show, **IllumiNations**, which starts half an hour before closing.

Disney-MGM Studios

When the Disney corporation began making films and TV shows for adults – most notably *Who Framed Roger Rabbit?* – they also began plotting the creation of a theme park geared as much for adults as kids. Buying the rights to the gem-filled Metro-Goldwyn-Mayer (MGM) œuvre of films and TV shows, Disney acquired a vast repertoire of instantly familiar images to mold into shows and rides. Opening in 1990, **Disney-MGM Studios** served to mute the opening of Florida's Universal Studios Escape (see p.245), and at the same time found an extra use for the real film studios based here – the people you'll see laboring over storyboards on the Backstage Tour aren't there for show: they are genuinely making films.

The park

The first of several highly sanitized imitations of Hollywood's famous streets and buildings – causing much amusement to anyone familiar with the seedy state of the originals – **Hollywood Boulevard** leads into the park, its length brightened with re-enactments of famous movie scenes, strolling film star lookalikes and the odd Muppet.

Avoid a long wait in the sun by arriving early and going straight to the half-hour **Backstage Studio Tour**. A narrated tram ride takes you through back lots, whisking you past the windows of animation studios and film production offices (where you might see costumes and props being created) to the climax: the exploding **Catastrophe Canyon**, an ingenious set that demonstrates special effects at disturbingly close range. The tour's interest level goes up and down, depending on the movies in production at the time, but you won't feel you've had your money's worth if you miss it. The same applies to two other attractions that were previously part of the Backstage Tour: **The Magic of Disney Animation**, a thirty-minute self-guided tour with a hilarious ten-minute instructional film, again featuring Robin Williams; and **Disney-MGM Studios Backlot Tour**, an entertaining special effects and production tour that reveals the secrets behind making movies. Along the same lines and not to be missed, **The Indiana Jones Epic Stunt Spectacular** recreates and explains many of the action-packed set pieces from the Spielberg films. The **Backstage Pass to "101 Dalmations"** is a low-key foray into how the recent remake of the film was done; seeing how they created realistic robotic puppies, though, is particularly interesting.

Sharp turns and collisions with asteroids make **Star Tours**, a flight-simulator trip to the Moon of Endor piloted by *Star Wars* characters R2D2 and C-3PO, one of the most physical rides in the park – passengers' seatbelts are carefully checked before lift-off. Scariest of the rides is **The Twilight Zone Tower of Terror**, a thirteen-story drop that's enough to put you off elevators for life. For laughs, go to **SuperStar Television**, which plucks volunteers from the crowd to read the news, appear in *The Lucy Show* or team up with *The Golden Girls*. Also good fun is **Jim Henson's MuppetVision 4D**, a three-dimensional film whose special effects put you right inside the Muppet Show.

Adding a welcome dimension to the park are two theater productions: **Beauty and the Beast**, and **The Hunchback of Notre Dame – A Musical Adventure**. Both are live performances of shortened versions of the Disney movies. The costumes, sets and talents make them worth a visit.

Inside a replica of Mann's Chinese Theater is **The Great Movie Ride**, which repays the (usually) long line with a ride that allows visitors to enter scenes from classic movies like *The Wizard of Oz* and *Casablanca*. This enjoyable, 22-minute voyage employs more than sixty audio-animatronic figures, which are surprisingly lifelike. Afterwards, consider refreshing at either the *Prime Time Café*, decorated with Fifties-era formica kitchen tables and other period pieces, or the *Sci-Fi Dine-In Theater*, where patrons are served in Fifties-style cars while watching science fiction trailers and cartoons.

Disney's Animal Kingdom

Disney's Animal Kingdom was opened in April 1998 as an animal-conservation park with Disney's patented over-the-top twist. The result is a 500-acre theme park divided into five major "lands": **Africa**, **Camp Minnie-Mickey**, **DinoLand USA**, **Safari Village** and **Asia**, the latter of which will open in early 1999. The Animal Kingdom is a true tribute not only to our world's wildlife but also to the versatility of concrete, which is colored, imprinted upon and formed into an endless variety of shapes to help create mock-authentic ambiences for each land.

The park

Upon entering, visitors find **The Oasis**, where they are greeted by flamingos and other interesting birds, reptiles and mammals. Just beyond is **Safari Village**, the center of which is **The Tree of Life**, a 145-foot-high imitation tree. Depictions of animals are cleverly woven into the trunk and branches, and there's an amusing 3-D movie about bugs shown inside.

Once within the park, visitors have four major stops. The best is **Kilimanjaro Safaris**, where "lorries" of tourists are driven past giraffes, zebras, elephants, lions, gazelle and rhinos, all passing their time in what feels like authentic African wildlands (local oak trees have been trimmed to look like African acacias). The park's only thrill ride is in DinoLand USA: **Countdown to Extinction**, a roller-coaster-style vehicle that makes small drops and short stops in the dark as dinosaurs pop out of nowhere and roar.

Disney's Animal Kingdom has two plays, both worth catching. Head to DinoLand USA for a live version of *The Jungle Book*, pumped up for the Nineties with elaborate costumes. Across the park at Camp Minnie-Mickey is the *Festival of the Lion King*, a participatory production of upbeat music with some nifty acrobatics, loosely based on its namesake film.

The remainder of the park requires no more than casual strolling, but all of its corners warrant exploration. The **Conservation Station** lets you observe as veterinarians treat animals, and there are small booths in which sounds of the jungle come alive. The **Flights of Wonder** bird show showcases vultures, owls and other unusual birds, the **Gorilla Falls Exploration Trail** is home to a troop of lowland gorillas, and classic Disney characters in appropriate attire sign autographs in **Camp Minnie-Mickey**.

The rest of Walt Disney World

Several **other Disney-devised amusements** exist to keep people on Disney property as long as possible and to offer therapeutic relaxation to those suffering theme-park burn-out.

Blizzard Beach

Near Disney-MGM Studios and All-Star Resorts (see "Walt Disney World Accommodation," p.236). At peak times daily 9am–8pm, at other times hours vary; adults $25.95, children aged 3–9 $20.50.

A bizarre but immensely popular water park, **Blizzard Beach** is a combination of sand and fake snow surrounding Melt Away Bay, which lies at the foot of a snow-covered "mountain," complete with ski lift and water slides. The quickest way down is via Summit Plummet, designed to look like a ski jump, but in fact a steep water slide 120-feet high. If you don't want to get involved, you can lounge around and soak up some rays, then cool off in one of the pools rippled by wave machines. Arrive early in summer to beat the inevitable crowds.

Discovery Island

In Bay Lake, near the Magic Kingdom. Daily 10am–5pm in low season, 10am–6pm or later in high season; adults $11.95, children aged 3–9 $6.50.

In **Discovery Island**, Disney plays God and attempts to recreate the world by creating a "natural" habitat for a gorgeous variety of bird life. Here you'll find strutting peacocks, gliding swans and a flamingo-filled lagoon reached by prettily landscaped trails. Despite the steep admission price (it makes economic sense to combine it with River Country, see below), if you're not seeing any real Florida wildlife in the real Florida wilds, you'll enjoy this a lot.

River Country

At the Fort Wilderness Campground (see "Walt Disney World accommodation," p.236). Daily 10am–5pm in low season, 10am–7pm in high season; adults $15.95, children aged 3–9 $12.50.

River Country, built around the **Ol' Swimming Hole**, is a rustic version of Typhoon Lagoon (see below), offering fewer and less exciting slides – and no wave machines. Yet it scores well with the high-speed, corkscrewing descents from **Whoop-'N-Holler Hollow**, and the enjoyable cruise on inner tubes down the **White Water Rapids**. With a small beach and a nature trail leading to a shady cypress hammock, River Country is more relaxing than Typhoon Lagoon and is a good place to unwind between touring the main parks.

Typhoon Lagoon

Just south of Pleasure Island (see "Nightlife: Downtown Disney," p.244). Daily 10am–5pm in low season, 9am–6pm or later in high season; adults $25.95, children aged 3–9 $20.50.

Typhoon Lagoon, busiest in the summer and on weekends (often reaching full capacity), consists of an imaginatively constructed "tropical island" around a two-and-a-half-acre lagoon, rippled every ninety seconds by artificial waves. Bodysurf the breakers, skim over them with a raft, or plunge into them from **Humunga Kowabunga**, a pair of speed-slides fifty feet up the "mountain" beside the lagoon. There are several smaller slides, too, and a saltwater **Shark Reef** where snorkelers fearful of the open seas can explore a "sunken ship" and be sniffed by real (but not dangerous) nurse and bonnethead sharks. When you're exhausted, take an inner tube (provided at the start point) and float around **Castaway Creek**, a half-hour meander through grottoes and caves, only interrupted by a sudden drenching from a tropical storm.

Unlike the major parks, you can bring **food** to Typhoon Lagoon, but no alcohol or glass containers.

Richard Petty Driving Experience

Walt Disney World Speedway (at the south end of the Magic Kingdom Parking Lot) ☎1-800/BE-PETTY). Feb–Sept daily 9am–5pm, limited times in October, November and December.

The **Richard Petty Driving Experience** offers race-car fanatics and wannabes two ways to fulfill their fantasy: they can take a three-lap stock car ride around a one-mile tri-oval track driven by an expert for $105.99, or, for $423.99, take a three-hour "Rookie Experience" course that enables them to drive eight laps themselves.

Every January, the speedway hosts the **Indy 200**, a 200-lap, 200-mile run that is one of a series of races leading up to the Indianapolis 500. For tickets call ☎1-800/822-INDY.

DISNEY CRUISE LINE

Port Canaveral. Shuttles from Walt Disney World ☎566-7000.

Disney recently introduced its first cruise ship, the *Disney Magic*, on which three- and four-day voyages can be booked along with land-based vacations. The elegant ship – the luxurious decor includes inlaid Italian woodwork – departs from Port Canaveral, an hour from the theme park, and sails to Nassau and then Disney's own Bahamian island, **Castaway Cay**. Live shows are different every night, and separate entertainment areas are provided for children, adults, and families. Cabins begin at $799 per person for three nights including airfare. A sister ship, the *Disney Wonder*, will set sail in 1999.

Disney's Wide World of Sports
Two miles east of Disney's Animal Kingdom on Osceola Parkway. Hours depend on daily events; adults $8, children 3–9 $6.75 ☎939-1500.

Professional and amateur sporting events are held daily at **Disney's Wide World of Sports** complex, a brand-spanking-new collection of stadiums set inside Mediterranean architecture. Included are a 7500-seat baseball stadium in which the Atlanta Braves do their spring training; a 30,000-square-foot, 5000-seat Fieldhouse used for everything from basketball to badminton; a series of interactive football-related games called the NFL Experience, where visitors can test passing, punting and kicking skills; and a themed *All-Star Café* restaurant. Stop at the retail shop for stuffed Disney characters in athletic uniforms.

Disney Institute
Buena Vista Drive, north of Downtown Disney ☎1-800-496-6337; www.disneyinstitute.com.

The Disney Institute is a combination resort, spa and educational facility, where guests (who don't have to stay there) can take short classes on subjects such as rock climbing, animation, photography, cooking, gardening and "Disney Behind the Scenes."

Nightlife: Downtown Disney

Around 9pm, each Walt Disney World park holds some kind of closing-time bash, usually involving fireworks and fountains. For more solid night-time entertainment, the corporation devised the six-acre **Pleasure Island**, exit 26B off I-4, and part of the revamped **Downtown Disney**, which also includes the **West Side** and **Marketplace**. On this remake of an abandoned island, pseudo-warehouses are the setting for a mixture of theme shops, bars and nightclubs. Admission to the island is free from 10am to 7pm; after 7pm a charge of $18.95 is levied, which allows you limitless entry into the bars and clubs. Anyone under 18 must be accompanied by a parent, and alcohol will only be served to those who are 21 or over. Take your ID and be prepared to pay high prices for food and drink.

The only shows taking place to a timetable are at the *Comedy Warehouse* – where a handful of comedians do a five-times-a-week improvisational act and are not afraid to send up Mickey Mouse. The *Pleasure Island Jazz Company* offers live bands, with taped music between shows, plus a limited menu and a wine list. *Mannequins Dance Palace* is a swish disco that doesn't get cracking until midnight; the less ostentatious *8Trax* spins exclusively Seventies music.

The most original – and most enjoyable – place on Pleasure Island is the **Adventurers Club**, loosely based on a 1930s gentlemen's club and furnished with a motley collection of face masks (some of which unexpectedly start speaking), deer heads and assorted flea-market furniture. Between scheduled shows, actors and actresses move surreptitiously (despite their period attire) among the throng and strike up loud and unusual conversations with unsuspecting audience members. New additions to Pleasure Island include the *Wildhorse Saloon*, a barbecue joint with live country music and line dancing, and the *BET SoundStage Club*, owned by Black Entertainment Television and catering to African Americans with rhythm-and-blues, soul and hip-hop music.

Back on the mainland, next to Pleasure Island and glowing with neon lights, sits *Planet Hollywood*. Housed in a sphere, it seats 400 people and is the biggest branch in the restaurant chain to date. The new **Downtown Disney's West Side** offers some interesting dining alternatives (see "Eating: Orlando and around" above). DisneyQuest, a five-story, high-tech pay-for-play arcade, is a bastion of virtual-reality games, including a canoe course where you paddle through a virtual-reality river; goofing up results in getting splashed with very real water. Cirque du Soleil has made Downtown Disney its permanent home, and they perform ten times a week in a 1600-seat theater – the shows are fascinating, but tickets are exorbitantly priced: $59.89, $46.85 for children. On the other side of Pleasure Island is **Marketplace**, a shopping emporium crammed with the world's largest Disney store, a Christmas shop and a Lego store, where kids can ogle massive lego creations of, among others, a dragon and a spaceship.

ORLANDO FLEXTICKET

In the hopes of prying tourists from Disney's clutches, competitors have teamed up to offer special multi-park passes. The **Orlando FlexTicket** offers unlimited admission for three days to Universal Studios Escape, SeaWorld Orlando and Wet'nWild (a water park) for $99.95 (adults), $82.95 (children 3–9). For $129.95 (adults) or $107.95 (children), you can also include Busch Gardens Tampa Bay (two hours away) in the deal, and that pass is good for four days.

Universal Studios Escape

Half a mile north of Exits 29 or 30B off I-4. Daily from 9am, with closing times varying by season. One-day studio pass $39.75 for adults, $32 for children aged 3–9; two-day studio pass $59.75 for adults, $49.75 for children.

Year-round fine weather, a varied cast of natural landscapes and none of the union rules restricting film-making in California have helped Florida gain the favor of the US film industry. All signs suggest that Florida will be the US moving-image capital of the next century, and the opening of **Universal Studios Escape** in June 1990 has only reinforced the prediction.

The sequel to the long-established and immensely popular Universal Studios tour in Los Angeles, Florida's Universal, like its competitor Disney-MGM, is a working studio, filling over 400 acres with the latest in TV and film production technology. The Florida branch has already turned out major features such as *Parenthood*, *Psycho IV*, kid-oriented Nickelodeon shows and a bunch of tedious sitcoms.

Universal has proved to be extremely popular, becoming the fifth most visited theme park in the US. Overall, the rides are more spectacular than those at Disney-MGM, with less emphasis on film nostalgia – but the park has a less homely feel, snippy service and only the very energetic will be able to take in the whole place inside a day. Plans are afoot to ensure you stay much longer: a multi-billion dollar investment is gradually going to expand the park to *twice* its current size, creating a second theme park, a number of hotels, a golf course, and so on.

The park

Street sets replicating New York, Los Angeles and San Francisco – look for the dirt and chewing gum painted onto the walls and pavements – create a striking backdrop to the park, which is arranged around a large lagoon: the scene of the **Dynamite Nights Stuntacular**, a daredevil extravaganza featuring pyrotechnic displays each night.

For sheer excitement, nothing in the park compares to **Back to the Future**, a bone-shaking flight-simulator time trip from 2015 to the Ice Age. Next best is **Twister**, a suffocating but gripping experience in which you stand beside an imitation tornado, complete with lightning, flying objects and lots of rain (cover all camera equipment). **Jaws** owes its success to anticipation of horror and classy special effects, but the ride is over all too quickly. The updated **Earthquake –The Big One** gives you a glimpse of what it's like to be caught on a subway train when an 8.3 Richter-scale quake hits. **Terminator 2 3-D** has some nifty special effects if you can bear the long wait. **Hercules & Xena, Wizards of the Screen**, is a comical look at how special effects are created. **A Day in the Park with Barney** is a must if you've got preschoolers along, as the purple dinosaur and his pals Baby Bop and B.J. get everyone singing, then return for photos.

Moving on, the six-ton version of King Kong in **Kongfrontation**, which attacks your cable car amid cracks of thunder and lightning high above New York's East River, is neither particularly memorable nor worth the lengthy wait. Similarly, **ET's Adventure** is a rather dull ride on pretend bicycles to ET's home planet, although ET speaking your name (which was recorded earlier by a computer) as you leave is a pleasing touch.

Obviously less fun for kids but often more enjoyable than the rides, are the attempts to demystify TV and film production techniques. **Alfred Hitchcock: The Art of Making Movies**, explores some of the outrageous camera angles and visual tricks employed by the film maker to send shivers down the spines of millions. Apart from some rather tame efforts to frighten, the tour includes intriguing glimpses of some of his better films, a few startling scenes from the 3D version of *Dial M for Murder*, and a group of actors playing out crucial scenes – including the shower scene from *Psycho* – using an unfortunate audience member.

At **The Funtastic World of Hanna-Barbera**, there's an excellent simulated cartoon chase from the creators of *The Flintstones* and *Yogi Bear*, which will have you shaking in your seat. Afterwards, using the interactive computers, you can create your own cartoon audio effects – bangs, whoops and crashes – to your heart's content.

Universal Studios Citywalk

Not to be outdone by Downtown Disney and Church Street Station, the **Universal Studios Citywalk** is looking to cash in on those lucrative evening dollars. Scheduled to open by year-end 1998, Universal's night-time extravaganza will feature a mix of restaurants, live music, dance clubs, theaters and shops. Right now the roster includes a *Hard Rock Café*; Jimmy Buffett's *Margaritaville Café*, where you can indulge in that

---

▸ ISLANDS OF ADVENTURE

Construction is well underway on Universal's second Florida theme park, the 110-acre **Islands of Adventure**, scheduled to open adjacent to the original park in 1999. Heavy on thrill rides, the park will be divided into five islands: **Suess Landing**, where visitors travel through eighteen pages of the author's whimsical books and then dine on green eggs and ham; **Toon Lagoon**, with attractions based on Dudley Do-Right, Popeye and other classic cartoon figures; **Marvel Super Hero Island**, with thrill rides based on Spider-Man, the Incredible Hulk and Dr Doom; **Jurassic Park**, featuring the world's longest water slide (it plunges 85 feet), a "live" dinosaur petting and more; and the **Lost Continent** home of a 125-foot roller coaster and a stunt show with fifty pyrotechnical effects.

"cheeseburger in paradise;" a twenty-screen, high-tech cineplex; Bob Marley–A Tribute to Freedom, a recreation of the musician's Jamaican home and garden; and a Thelonius Monk Institute of Jazz Education Academy.

SeaWorld Orlando

Sea Harbor Drive, near the intersection of I-4 and 27A, or I-4 and the Bee Line Expwy. Daily 9am–7pm in low season, longer hours in high season; adults $39.75, children aged 3–9 $32.95.

It may have as many souvenir shops as fish, but **SeaWorld Orlando** is the cream of Florida's sizeable crop of marine parks and as such shouldn't be missed. To see it all and get the best value for your money, you'll need to allocate a whole day and be certain to pick up the free map and show schedule at the entrance.

The big event is the **Shamu** show – twenty minutes of tricks performed by a playful killer whale. The nearby **Shamu's Happy Harbor** is a paradise for children, offering inner tubes, slides, remote control boats and even an area where they can catapult water balloons at each other for $3 a bucket. The **Wild Arctic** complex (complete with artificial snow and ice) brings you close to beluga whales, walruses and polar bears, while a simulated ride takes you on a stomach-churning helicopter flight through an arctic blizzard. Be sure to check out the launch pad viewing area (on your right as you exit through the gift shop) to gain an insight into the mechanics of simulated rides.

The **Key West** area invites visitors to interact with the animals: pet slimy stingrays at Stingray Lagoon or feed dolphins at Dolphin Cove. SeaWorld's first thrill ride, **Journey to Atlantis**, is part water slide, part roller coaster, and has a sixty-foot drop. You will get drenched – by the ride and by other tourists who pay for the privilege of spraying you. Inside the adjacent gift shop are two aquariums: a 25,000-gallon, underfoot aquarium filled with stingrays and another overhead (6000 gallons) with hammerhead sharks; odd-looking illuminated jellyfish are in tanks built into a nearby wall.

With substantially less razzmatazz, plenty of smaller tanks and displays around the park offer a wealth of information about the undersea world. Among the highlights, the **Penguin Encounter** attempts to re-create Antarctica with scores of the waddling birds scampering over a make-believe iceberg; the occupants of the **Dolphin Pool** assert their advanced intellect by flapping their fins and drenching passers-by; and **Terrors of the Deep** includes a walk through a glass-sided tunnel, offering the closest eye-contact you're ever likely to have with a shark. As you might expect, in a park devoted to ocean life, there is now a water adventure show called **The Intensity Games**, which involves daredevil water-skiing and diving. It is, however, genuinely spectacular and well worth waiting to see one of the three daily shows.

Finally, if you've never been lucky enough to see a manatee in the wild, don't leave SeaWorld Orlando without taking in **Manatees: the Last Generation?**, where you can see a few of the endangered creatures and learn about the threat faced by their species. For an extra $5 you can take a **To The Recue Tour**, a behind-the-scenes look at how SeaWorld Orlando rescues and rehabilitates manatees, sea turtles and other marine life. Adventure seekers might pay $150 for a two-hour **Dolphin Interaction Program**, a one-on-one lesson on feeding and training dolphins.

Other attractions around Orlando

The Orlando area's small-time entrepreneurs are nothing if not inventive. No end of tacky, short-lived would-be attractions spring up each year and a large number of them swiftly sink without trace. The list below represents the best – or just the longest-surviving – of the thousand-and-one little places to visit **around Orlando**. Several other highly worthwhile attractions in the Orlando area, including Gatorland, Cypress Gardens and Bok Tower Gardens, are detailed on pp.233 and 251.

Splendid China

3000 Splendid China Blvd. Daily from 9.30, with closing times varying by season; adults $26.99, children aged 5–12 $16.99.
The best of these attractions, this park features over sixty authentic replicas celebrating 5000 years of Chinese architecture and history. Painstakingly reconstructed miniatures (including the Great Wall, the Forbidden City, the Leshan Buddha, and the Terracotta Warriors among others), plus museum exhibits, a variety of shows and fascinating displays make this an intriguing place to spend the day. The best time to visit is towards evening when the park is beautifully illuminated. A food-and-gift area called Chinatown requires no admission and is a nice stop for dinner.

Flying Tigers Warbird Air Museum

231 N Hoagland Blvd, next to Kissimmee airport. Mon–Sat 9am–5.30pm, Sun 9am–5pm; adults $8; children aged 6–12 $6.
The main hangar contains battle-weary Tiger Moths, Mustangs and assorted bombers and biplanes in various states of repair – all being commercially restored.

Mystery Fun House/Starbase Omega

5767 Major Blvd. Sun–Thurs 10am–9pm, Fri & Sat 10am–10pm; Mystery Fun House $10.95; Starbase Omega $9.85, combo ticket $19.95.
The real mystery of Mystery Fun House – with its unprepossessing collection of distorting mirrors, moving floors and talking furniture – is why more people don't ask for their money back. The most fun you'll have here is in the high-tech laser game, Starbase Omega, where, equipped with a laser gun, you can pretend to be a star trooper to your heart's content.

Old Town

5770 W Irlo Bronson Memorial Hwy/Hwy 192, Kissimmee. Daily 10am–11pm. Free, rides $2 to $5.
Old-fashioned amusement rides and 75 interesting, if slightly tacky, shops. The go-kart track and ferris wheel are a hoot, as are the bumper cars and laser tag game.

Reptile World Serpentarium

E Irlo Bronson Memorial Hwy/Hwy 192, just east of St Cloud. Tues–Sun 9am–5.30pm; adults $4.55, children aged 6–17 $3.48, children aged 3–5 $2.41.
A research center for the production of snake venoms, which are sold to hospitals and similiar institutions who in turn produce anti-venoms. Visitors are introduced to a caged collection of poisonous and non-poisonous snakes from around the world, and are shown demonstrations of venom extraction at 11am, 2pm and 5pm.

Ripley's Believe It or Not!

8201 International Drive. Daily 9am–11pm; $9.95, children aged 4–12 $6.95.
A model of the world's tallest man, a chunk of the Berlin Wall and a Rolls-Royce built from a million matchsticks are among the innumerable oddities and curiosities packed into this seemingly lopsided building.

Skull Kingdom

5931 American Way (off International Drive). Mon–Thurs 11.30am–11pm, Sat & Sun 11am–midnight; $9.95.

A standard haunted house packaged in a nifty skull-faced castle. The scariest and most annoying part is having costumed pimple-faced teenagers yell in your face, "Do you have cooties?" Realistic-looking animatrionic characters being tortured add a nice touch. Too scary for ages 7 and under.

Terror on Church Street
135 S Orange Ave. Sun–Thurs 7pm–midnight, Fri & Sat 7pm–1am; $12.
The price may be high, but this combination of live actors, high-tech special effects and imaginative audiotracks, all intended to scare people out of their wits, sometimes works surprisingly well.

Wet'n'Wild
6200 International Drive. Daily 10am–5pm, longer hours in summer; adults $25.95, children aged 3–9 $20.95.
Water slides, chutes, rapids and wave machines – the perfect thing for a day when the thermometer soars.

WonderWorks
International Drive at Pointe Orlando, Orlando. Daily 10 am–10pm. Adults $12.95, children 3–12 $9.95.
A collection of high-tech interactive gizmos housed cleverly inside an upside-down creaking house. Check out "Old Sparky," Florida's electric chair, which smokes as the original did when it accidentally set a victim on fire. Also of interest: contraptions in which you experience earthquakes and hurricanes. Perfect for 13-year-old boys.

A World of Orchids
2501 Old Lake Wilson Rd, Kissimmee. Daily 9.30am–5.30pm. Adults $8.95, children under 15 free if accompanied by a paying adult.
An enthralling air-conditioned tropical rainforest garden that showcases thousands of rare, exotic and beautiful flowering orchids from around the world. Blooms all year round.

SOUTH CENTRAL FLORIDA

Trapped between the holiday haunts of Orlando and the beaches of the Tampa Bay area, the main towns of **South Central Florida** haven't been done any favors by decades of phosphate mining, which have left their surrounds pockmarked with craters. However, matters are gradually being improved. Many of the unsightly holes have been turned into lakes (joining a large number of natural ones), and the prospect of boating, waterskiing and fishing on them is attracting visitors from the grip of Orlando. More interestingly, several of the region's small towns were formerly big towns around the turn of the century, and are keen to flaunt their past histories – and near them can be found several refreshingly under-hyped attractions, which were bringing tourists into the state when Walt Disney was still in short trousers.

Lakeland and around

A logical place to begin touring the region, **LAKELAND**, fifty miles southwest of Orlando along I-4, plays the suburban big brother to its even more rural neighbors, providing sleeping quarters for Orlando and Tampa commuters, who emerge on weekends to stroll the edges of the town's numerous lakes or ride on them in hideous swan-shaped paddle-boats.

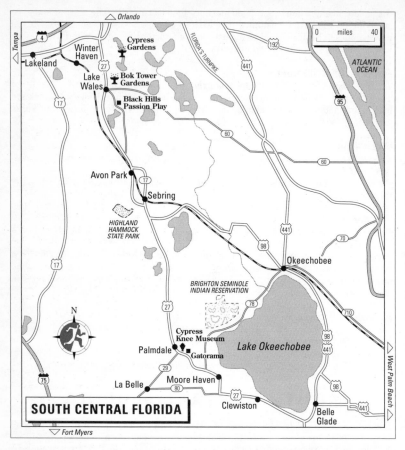

Aided by its busy railway terminal, Lakeland's fortunes rose in the Twenties, and a number of its more important buildings have been maintained as the **Munn Park Historic District** on and close to Main Street. Pay heed to the 1927 Polk Theater, 124 S Florida Avenue, and the restored balustrades, lampposts and gazebo-style bandstand on the promenade around Lake Mirror, at the east end of Main Street. A few minutes' walk from the town center, the generous size of the **Polk County Museum of Art**, 800 E Palmetto Street (Tues–Fri 9am–5pm, Sat 10am–5pm, Sun 1–5pm; free), suggests Lakeland is striving to heighten its cultural profile: the spacious temporary galleries air the latest innovative pieces by rising Florida-based artists.

A stronger draw, and something of a surprise in such a tucked-away community, is the largest single grouping of buildings by **Frank Lloyd Wright**, who redefined America's architectural thinking throughout the Twenties and Thirties. Maybe it was the rare chance to design an entire communal area that appealed to Wright – the fee he got for converting an eighty-acre orange grove into **Florida Southern College**, a mile southwest of Lakeland's center, certainly didn't; the financially strapped college paid on credit and got its students to provide the labor.

The area code for the parts of South Central Florida mentioned in this chapter is ☎941.

Much of the integrity of Wright's initial concept has been lost: buildings have been crudely adapted and used for purposes other than those for which they were intended, and newer structures have distorted the overall harmony. Even so, the campus is an inventive statement and easily negotiated using the free **maps** provided in boxes along its covered walkways. Interestingly, Wright's contempt for air conditioning caused him to erect thick masonry structures to shield the students from the Florida sun, and his desire to merge his work with the natural environment allowed for the creeping vegetation of the orange grove (now given way to lawns) to wrap around the buildings and provide further insulation.

Practicalities
Get a descriptive **walking tour map** of the Lakeland historic district from the **Chamber of Commerce**, 35 Lake Morton Drive (Mon–Fri 8.30am–5pm; ☎688-8551). For **eating**, the *Reececliff*, 940 S Florida Avenue (☎686-6661), a spartan diner in business since 1934, has ridiculously cheap breakfasts and lunches; *Harry's Seafood Bar & Grille*, 101 N Kentucky Ave (☎686-2228), provides a large menu of Cajun and Creole-inspired food in a fern-bar atmosphere; and *Silver Ring*, 106 Tennessee Avenue (☎687-3283), proffers sizeable Cuban sandwiches. Also worth sampling is the black bean soup at *Julio's*, 213 N Kentucky Avenue (☎686-1713).

Lakeland doesn't have any nightlife worth waiting around for, but if you're looking for **accommodation**, use the atmospheric *Lake Morton Bed & Breakfast*, 817 South Boulevard (☎688-6788; ③), or inexpensive motels such as *Knights Inn*, 740 E Main Street (☎688-5506; ②), or *Scottish Inn*, 244 N Florida Avenue (☎687-2530; ③).

Polk City: Fantasy of Flight

Ten miles north of Lakeland in **POLK CITY**, **Fantasy of Flight**, 1400 Broadway Blvd SE (☎984-3500) is trying to draw tourists with an interest in aviation. Part themed attraction and part private aircraft collection, Fantasy of Flight allows visitors to climb aboard a WWII B-17 Flying Fortress and pretend to drop bombs amidst the sounds of anti-aircraft fire. You can be closed into "flight simulators" to get a somewhat realistic flavor of mid-air combat, or you can fly 500 feet into the air in an "Ultralight" airplane or a helium-powered balloon. Perhaps most interesting is owner Kermit Weeks' collection of thirty-plus vintage planes, including the Lockheed Vega, which was the first plane ever flown around the globe.

Lake Alfred, Winter Haven and Cypress Gardens

The sole reason to visit **LAKE ALFRED**, fifteen miles east of Lakeland on Hwy-17 (also known as Hwy-92), is to rummage about inside the **junk and antique shops** lining Haines Boulevard. While bargains may be few, students of Americana are in for a treat as they sift through the vintage Coke signs, old kitchen tools, yellowing family albums and moth-eaten moose heads.

Like Lake Alfred, **WINTER HAVEN**, seven miles south, struggles to hold onto its passing traffic; the motels (see below) lining Cypress Gardens Boulevard exist for visitors to the long-popular **Cypress Gardens**, at the southeast corner of the town (summer daily 9.30am–5.30pm, winter 9.30am–9pm; $30.95 adults, $2.95 children 6–17, free children 5 and under; 1 child free with each paying adult). Gouged from a sixteen-acre swamp by dollar-a-day laborers during the Depression, Cypress Gardens makes a good place to unwind after the tumult of Walt Disney World, especially with kids. The relaxing ambience established by the neatly landscaped setting – a profusion of towering cypress trees and colorful plants arching around a lake – is enhanced by the Southern Belles: young ladies in hooped skirts who sit and fan themselves while being relentlessly photographed. Besides syncopated waterskiing on the lake and a small but worthwhile wildlife sanctuary, the gardens also boast the **Wings of Wonder** butterfly conservatory, a Victorian-style 5500-foot glass construction filled with rainforest plants and fifty species of free-flying butterflies (over a thousand in all), together with iguanas, turtles, doves and button quails. In the throes of an aggressive expansion brought on by new owners, Cypress Gardens has recently added a **Make 'Em Laugh Circus**: an eight-year-old named Christina does tremendous tricks with hula hoops, there's a Hot Nouveau ice skating show, live concerts (Big Band is a specialty), a magic show and other diversions to keep guests from leaving the park.

There are snack bars and restaurants inside Cypress Gardens (the barbecue sandwiches aren't bad), but it's cheaper to **eat** in the *International House of Pancakes* coffee shop, 1915 Cypress Gardens Boulevard (☎326-1772), purveyors of breakfasts, bounteous lunches and reasonable evening fare. The *Ranch House* is also a good spot for an **overnight stay** (for reservations call ☎1-800/366-5996; ②), as is *The Scottish Inn*, 1901 Cypress Gardens Boulevard (☎324-5998; ②).

Lake Wales and around

Fourteen miles southeast of Winter Haven on Hwy-27, **LAKE WALES** is a lackadaisical town with more of note on its fringes than in its center, though the **Lake Wales Depot Museum**, 325 S Scenic Highway (Mon–Fri 9am–5pm, Sat 10am–4pm; free), contains an entertaining collection of train parts, remnants from the turpentine industry on which the town was founded in the late 1800s, and a Warhol-like collection of crate labels from the citrus companies that prospered during the early 1900s.

At the museum, confirm directions to **Spook Hill**, an optical illusion that's been turned into a transparently bogus "legend," but one which would be a shame to miss (conveniently, it's on the way to Bok Tower Gardens, see below). By car, cross Central Avenue from the museum and turn right into North Avenue, following the one-way system. Just before meeting Hwy-17A, a sign indicates the spot to brake and put your vehicle into neutral: as you do so, the car appears to slide uphill. Looking back from the junction makes clear the difference in road gradients, which creates the effect.

Bok Tower Gardens

"A more striking example of the power of beauty could hardly be found, better proof that beauty exists could not be asked for," rejoiced landscape gardener William Lyman Phillips upon visiting **Bok Tower Gardens**, two miles north of Lake Wales on Hwy-17A (daily 8am–6pm; last admission 5pm; adults $4, children 5–12 $1), in 1956. As sentimental as it may sound, Phillips' comment was spot-on. Whether it's the effusive entanglements of ferns, oaks and palms, the bright patches of magnolias, azaleas and gardenias, or just the sheer novelty of a hill (this being the highest point in peninsular Florida), Bok Tower Gardens is one of the state's most lush and lovely places.

Not content with winning the Pulitzer Prize for his autobiography in 1920, Dutch-born office-boy turned author and publisher **Edward Bok** resolved to transform the pine-covered Iron Mountain (as this hump is named) into a "sanctuary for humans and birds," in gratitude to his adopted country for making his glittering career possible. President Coolidge, one of Bok's many famous friends, showed up to declare it open in 1929.

Marvellous though they are, these 128 acres would be just a glorified botanical garden were it not for the **Singing Tower** and the newly opened **mansion**. The tower, two hundred feet of marble and coquina, rises sheerly above the branches, poetically mirrored in a swan- and duck-filled lake. Originally intended to conceal the garden's water tanks, the tower carries finely sculptured impressions of Florida wildlife on its exterior and fills its interior with a 53-bell carillon: richly timbred chimes resound through the garden every half-hour. Only the 3pm recital is "live" (all the others are recordings), but you can discover more about its workings in the **visitor center**, which provides every detail imaginable about the garden and tower. Nearby is an old "cracker" cottage near the garden's entrance. ("Cracker" was the nickname given to the state's early cattle farmers.) The twenty-room Mediterranean-style mansion was renovated and opened in December 1995, its rooms decorated with 1920s furnishings. Guided tours last for one hour and cost $5.

A portion of the grounds has been left in its raw state, allowing wildlife to roam and be surreptitiously viewed through the glass front of a wooden hut. Visitors hack their way for twenty minutes along the **Pine Ridge trail**, through the pine trees, saw-edged grasses and wild flowers that once covered the entire hill.

Chalet Suzanne

In 1931, gourmet cook and world traveler Bertha Hinshaw, recently widowed and made penniless by the Depression, moved to an isolated site two miles north of Lake Wales, beside Hwy-17, to open a restaurant called **Chalet Suzanne**. Armed with self-devised recipes and tremendous powers of culinary invention – adding chicken livers to grilled grapefruit, for instance – Bertha created what's now among the most highly-rated meal stops in the country, and one that's still run by her family.

Aside from the food (a multi-course lunch costs upwards of $50, dinner costs upwards of $80; call for reservations ☎676-6011), the quirky architecture grabs the eye: drunkenly angled buildings painted in clashing pinks, greens and yellows, topped by twisting towers and turrets. Even if you're not dining or staying in one of the luxurious guest rooms (⑨), you're free to wander through the public rooms – whose furnishings are as loopy as the architecture, with decorative pieces picked up from Bertha's seven around-the-world trips.

The one sensible structure is the soup cannery, where "Romaine" soup – another of Bertha's creations – begins its journey to the nation's gourmet food shops. While here, don't be frightened by low-flying aircraft: a small runway beside the cannery is where corporate execs and freeloading food critics breeze in by private plane for a slap-up meal.

River Ranch

Twenty-five miles east of Lake Wales on S.R. 60 is **River Ranch**, 3200 River Ranch Rd (☎1-800/785-2102 or ☎941/692-1321), a Sixties-era, Western-themed resort and RV park. Shabby and dated, it's worth a stay for diversions such as an authentic Saturday night rodeo, line dancing in a Gold Rush-style saloon and a nightfall Swamp Buggy tour, where trained dogs ride along through the woods to help catch wild hogs. RV sites start at $25 a day, spacious guest rooms at $80.

Lake Kissimmee State Park

Nineteenth-century Floridian farming techniques may not seem the most inspiring subject in the world, but the 1876 Cow Camp section of **Lake Kissimmee State Park** (daily 8am–sunset; cars $3.25, pedestrians & cyclists $1), fifteen miles east of Lake Wales off Route 60, is an enjoyable and instructive re-creation of a pioneer-era cattle farm, complete with park rangers playing the parts of "crackers" and tending genuine cows and horses.

Elsewhere in the park, an observation point above Lake Kissimmee can be utilized for bird- and alligator-spotting.

South of Lake Wales: along Hwy-27

The section of Hwy-27 that runs **south from Lake Wales** is among Florida's least eventful roads: a four-lane snake through a landscape of gentle hills, lakes, citrus groves and sleepy communities dominated by retirees. Busy with farm trucks, the highway itself is far from peaceful, but provides an interesting backwoods course if you're making for either coast: smaller roads branch off towards Fort Myers, on the west coast, and, after Hwy-27 twists around the massive Lake Okeechobee, to the big centers of the southeast coast.

Avon Park, Sebring and around

Two miles south of Lake Wales on Hwy-27 stands the purpose-built amphitheater that stages the **Black Hills Passion Play**, a dramatic re-creation of the last week in the life of Christ. Seats for the five performances weekly between mid-February and mid-April cost $10 to $16 and are quickly snapped up. For more details, call ☎676-1495 or ☎1/800-622-8383.

Twenty miles further, **AVON PARK** acquired its name from an early English settler born in Stratford-upon-Avon; information on her and the community's general history is available at the **Avon Park Museum**, 3 N Museum Avenue (usually 10am–2pm; free). Once you've worn out the museum, leave Avon Park on Route 17, tracing a ten-mile path around a series of lakes to **SEBRING**, whose unusual semicircular street-plan was devised by its founder, George Sebring. He planted an oak tree here in 1912 to symbolize the sun, and declared that all the town's streets would radiate out from it. They still do, and Route 17 passes the small park now enclosing the great tree just prior to reconnecting with Hwy-27.

As quiet as can be for eleven months of the year, Sebring's tranquillity is shattered each March and September when tens of thousands of motor-racing fans pack its motels and restaurants, arriving for a twelve-hour endurance contest, the **12 Hours of Sebring**, held at a race track about ten miles east – if you're passing through around this time, plan accordingly.

Well away from the sound of revving engines, the orange grove and cypress swamp trails inside **Highlands Hammock State Park**, six miles west of Sebring on Route 634 (daily 8am–sunset; cars $3.25, pedestrians and cyclists $1), add up to a well-spent afternoon. Keep an eye out for the white-tailed deer, and time your visit to coincide with the informative ranger-guided **tram tour** (for times, call ☎386-6094).

Further homage is paid to cypress trees just beyond Palmdale, forty miles south of Sebring, at the **Cypress Knee Museum** (daily 8am–5pm; free), which stocks some of the most lifelike specimens of Cypress Knees – a lumpy growth on the tree which enables its submerged roots to breath. Close by, on Hwy-27, **Gatorama** (daily 8am–6pm; $6.95 adults, $3.50 children under 56 inches) is a working alligator farm, licensed to keep thousands of the toothy creatures for public viewing and for turning into handbags, boots and food – if you've already visited Orlando's Gatorland (see "South of Orlando," p.232), this is more of the same.

Moving on from here, Route 29, off Hwy-27 at Palmdale, runs west to La Belle, from which Hwy-80 continues thirty miles to Fort Myers (see "The West Coast"); Hwy-27 ploughs on around the southern edge of Lake Okeechobee.

Lake Okeechobee and around

Until recently, one of the best-kept secrets in Florida has been the outstanding natural beauty of **Lake Okeechobee**, the second-largest freshwater lake in the US. For many years the preserve of sugarcane, beef and dairy farmers, as well as fishermen in search of catfish or large-mouthed bass, the lake (whose name translates from Seminole Indian to mean "Big Water") has started to draw tourists. This is the result of both a state-wide push and the area's abundance of plants and **wildlife**. Birds feature strongly: over 120 varieties have been spotted, and this is one of the few places in the world where you can still sight a snail kite. Other inhabitants include bobcats, alligators, turtles, otters, snakes and, occasionally, manatees.

Home to Native Americans for centuries, the first farm settlers began arriving in the area in 1910, encouraged by the work carried out by wealthy Philadelphian Hamilton Disston, who, in the nineteenth century, started dredging canals and draining the land for agriculture. Next came the railroads, extending around three-quarters of the lake by the late 1920s and providing easy access to the rest of the state. Today the area is also served by three major **highways**, which join to encircle the lake and allow access to the towns dotted around its shores (see below). Staying a few days in one of these will allow you to explore Lake Okeechobee and its environs at your leisure.

Lake Okeechobee

Covering 730 square miles and averaging fourteen feet in depth, **Lake Okeechobee** is fed by several rivers, creeks and canals, and has always played an important role not only in the lives of communities close to its shores but also for the life-cycle of the Everglades. Since the completion of the dike, it has served as both a flood-control safety valve during the hurricane season and as a freshwater storage reservoir. Traditionally, the lake's waters have drained slowly south to nourish the Everglades after the summer rains, but the disruption caused by extensive "reclaiming" of land for farming is one of the hottest environmental issues in Florida.

Visiting the lake

The lake itself is best enjoyed **by boat** or by **walking/cycling trails** (there is a 110-mile trail that runs along the top of the Hoover Dike, which surrounds the lake). For more information on the trails, call the Florida Trail Association (☎1-800/343-1882), and to hire a bike, try Euler's Cycling Center, 50 Hwy-441 SE (☎357-0458). An exciting plan for the future is to connect the Okeechobee Scenic Trail with the Appalachian National Scenic Trail to create the longest in the US, joining Maine with Miami by the end of the century.

A sensitive and instructional way to learn about this habitat and its wildlife is a boat ride with **Swampland Tours**, based near the town of Okeechobee (see below) at the Kissimmee Bridge, 10375 Hwy-78 ($17.50 for two hours; tours depart daily 10am and 1pm, weather permitting; check times and book ahead ☎467-4411). The 22-mile tours into the 28,000-acre wildlife sanctuary are run by Barry "Chop" Légé in association with the Florida Audubon Society (see p.140), which owns the park. Barry's enthusiasm is infectious, and he will astonish you with his ability to spot all manner of creatures that you might otherwise miss; in any one trip, you're also likely to see at least 35 species of birds.

Okeechobee town

The largest lakeside community, **OKEECHOBEE** offers a base from which to explore and provides the most alternatives for accommodation, food and entertainment. The town was designed by the pervasive Henry M. Flagler (see "Palm Beach", p.166), whose grandiose plan demanded wide streets and wooden-framed buildings, some of which remain.

The town has a few places worthy of an hour or two visit, should the weather prevent you from more active pursuits: the **Historical Museum** (in the Historical Park; Thurs only 9am–1pm; free), the 1926 **County Court House**, a pretty example of Mediterranean Revival architecture, a style much favored by Flagler, and the **Freedman Raulerson House**, on Second Avenue, near the corner with Fourth Street. Details on these and other places of interest, as well as local events, can be found at the **Chamber of Commerce** at 55 S Parrott Avenue (Mon–Fri 9am–5pm; ☎763-6464).

If you're interested in **fishing**, still a primary activity in the area, go to Garrard Tackle Shop, 4259 Hwy-441 S (☎763-3416). They will supply all the gear and a guide to help ensure you catch something.

Practicalities

Although the town is easy to get to –Greyhound, 106 SW Third Street, ☎763-5328 and Amtrak ☎1-800/872-7245 both have depots – there is no local public transport system, and taxis stop running at 9pm. This means that if you don't have a car you'll be pretty much tied to the town in the evenings and may therefore want to limit your time to one or two nights. Of the places to **stay**, the quiet and unassuming *Wanta Linga Motel*, 3225 SE Hwy-441 (☎763-1020; ②) offers reasonably priced rooms. The *Days Inn*, 2200 SE Hwy-441 (☎1-800/874-3744; ④) offers standard, clean and comfortable accommodation, plus access to a fishing pier. The new *Holiday Inn Express*, 3975 S Hwy-441 (☎357-3529; ④) offers clean modern rooms, free breakfast and an outdoor pool. For **camping**, you'll find the largest *KOA* campground in **North America** just outside the town as you're heading towards the lake on Hwy-441 S (☎1-800/845-6846). A tent site costs $29.95, an RV site $32.95 and a one-room cabin (sleeping up to four) is $49.95. A nine-hole golf course is on the premises.

For **eating**, *Lightsey's Fish Co.*, Okee-Tantie Hwy-78 W (☎763-4276), serves a selection of fresh fish and homemade American fare at reasonable prices. Keep an eye out for their specials. *Old Habits*, 4865 SE Hwy-441 (☎763-9924), offers Southern-style food and hospitality. Alternatively, gorge yourself on the all-you-can-eat breakfast, lunch or dinner at *Pogey's*, SE Hwy-441 (☎763-7222), or on the steak and seafood at *Michael's Restaurant*, 1001 S Parrott Avenue (☎763-2069). The *Angus Restaurant*, 2054 Hwy-70 at junction 98 (☎763-2040), specializes in beef, for which the area is famous.

The west side of the lake

Leaving Hwy-27 just west of Moore Haven, Route 78 charts a 34-mile course along the **west side of the lake**, passing through Fisheating Creek and continuing into the tree-less expanse of Indian Prairie, part of the 35,000-acre **Brighton Seminole Indian Reservation**.

The Seminole Indians migrated here in the eighteenth century from Georgia and Alabama, replacing the already decimated original Native American population. After they, too, became the target of aggression, a small number managed to establish themselves here on the western side of the lake, where about 450 remain, as successful cattle farmers. Although they live in houses rather than traditional Seminole chickees, the residents here have remained faithful to long-held beliefs – handicrafts may be offered from the roadside, but you won't find any of the tacky souvenir shops common to reservations in more populous areas.

On this side of the lake, **accommodation** is limited to several well-equipped **campgrounds**, the best of which is *Twin Palms Resort* (☎946-0977), located thirteen miles from Moore Haven and 21 miles from the town of Okeechobee. This RV park offers self-contained cottages for $45 and tent sites for $12.50 per night.

Clewiston, Belle Glade and around

From Moore Haven, Hwy-27 is walled by many miles of sugar cane – half of all the sugar grown in the US, in fact – harvested between March and November by Jamaican

laborers who are flown in, housed in hostels and notoriously underpaid for their physically demanding and even dangerous work. Many in Florida, particularly the 43,000
locally employed in the sugar industry, seem content to turn a blind eye to the scan-
dalous treatment of the migrants. Their plight is not a subject wisely brought up in
CLEWISTON, fourteen miles from Moore Haven, which is dominated by the US Sugar
Corporation and, through the company's multi-million-dollar profits, is enjoying the
highest per capita income in the country. **BELLE GLADE**, a small town twenty miles
east, has the biggest sugar mill in the country and numerous trailer parks aimed largely at attracting fishermen. In its otherwise quiet history, one event stands out: the loss
of 2000 lives when the lake was whipped up by a hurricane in 1928. The Belle Glade
Chamber of Commerce is at 540 S Main Street (Mon–Fri 9am–5pm; ☎561/996-2745).

Acommodation is relatively plentiful, though squarely aimed at fishing folk – if
that's not your scene you may as well stay away. On Torrey Island, two miles west of
Belle Glade on Route 717, *The City of Belle Glade's Marina Campground* (☎561/996-
6322) has lots of campervan space and a tent area ($16.50 a night).

Moving on from here, Hwy-27 swings south from just ouside Belle Glade towards
Miami, eighty miles distant, while Hwy-441 cuts east forty miles to West Palm Beach.

NORTH CENTRAL FLORIDA

Millions of people each year hammer through **North Central Florida** towards
Orlando, almost all of them oblivious to the fact that a few miles east of the unrelentingly ordinary I-75 are the villages and small towns that typified Florida before the
arrival of interstate highways and made-to-measure vacations. The region has just two
appreciably-sized towns, one of which holds a major university, and a terrain that varies
from rough scrub to resplendent grassy acres lubricated by dozens of natural springs.
Giving this region a few days won't waste your time or break your budget: costs here
are extremely low.

Ocala and around

Known throughout the US for the champion runners bred and trained at the thor-
oughbred horse farms occupying its green and softly undulating surrounds, **OCALA**
itself is a town without much to shout about – though it makes an agreeable base for
seeing more of the immediate area. The **Chamber of Commerce**, 110 E Silver Springs
Boulevard (Mon–Fri 8.30am–5pm; ☎629-8051), can supply local facts, issue walking
maps of the town's mildly interesting historic districts and tell you which of the **horse
farms** are open for free self-guided tours.

The Garlits and Appleton museums

Ten miles from Ocala, Exit 67 off I-75, the **Don Garlits Museum of Drag Racing**
(daily 9am–5pm; $7.50 for the drag racing exhibit, $5 for the antique car exhibit)
parades dozens of low-slung drag-racing vehicles, including the "Swamp Rat" machines
that propelled local legend Don Garlits to 270mph over the drag tracks during the mid-
Fifties. Yellowing press cuttings and grainy films chart the rise of the sport, and a sub-
sidiary display of Chevys, Buicks and Fords – and the classic hits pumped out by a
Wurlitzer jukebox – evoke an *American Graffiti* atmosphere.

The area code for North Central Florida is ☎352.

An outstanding assembly of art and artifacts sits on the other side of Ocala, inside the **Appleton Museum of Art**, 4333 NE Silver Springs Boulevard (Tues–Sat 10am–4.30pm, Sun 1–5pm; $5 adults; under 17s free). Spanning the globe and five thousand years, the exhibits, collected by a wealthy Chicago industrialist, go together with remarkable cohesion, and there's barely a dull moment over two well-filled floors. Early Rembrandt etchings, a Rodin *Thinker* cast from the original mold and paintings by Jules Breton amid an exquisite stock of nineteenth-century French canvases are admirable enough, but the handicrafts are really special: look for the Turkish prayer rugs, the brightly colored Naxco ceramics, the wooden Tibetan saddle and the massed ranks of "Toggles" – Japanese *netsuke* figures carved from ivory.

Silver Springs

Approximately one mile east of Ocala on SR-40/Silver Springs Boulevard, **Silver Springs** (daily 9am–5.30pm, longer hours in summer; $29.95 adults, children $20.95) has been winning admirers since the late 1800s when Florida's first tourists came by steamboat to stare into the spring's deep, clear waters.

During the 1930s and 1940s, six of the original *Tarzan* films were shot here, starring Johnnie Weissmuller. Today, the park operates as a highly commercial enterprise: a menagerie of imported animals such as monkeys, giraffes and llamas, plus the inevitable petting zoo mar an otherwise attractive spot where you can happily while away the day. The admission fee, however, is high, especially considering the proliferation of springs all across central and northern Florida, some of them just a few miles east in the Ocala National Forest (see opposite). From a conservationist point of view, Wakulla Springs (near Tallahassee, see p.343) is a far better bet. However, if you do decide to visit Silver Springs, you'll get the most from the **Glass-Bottomed Boat Tour** (the best of three boat rides available), the **Jungle Cruise** and the **Jeep Safari**, all of which run regularly through the day. The **Big Gator Lagoon** attraction is fun during feeding time, when you get to throw hot dogs (three for $1) at the alligators and watch them jump for the food. **World of Bears** offers a glimpse of the creatures as well as an educational program about their lives at Silver Springs (a similar panther exhibit is scheduled to open in late 1998). If you feel like cooling off, or have kids in tow, buy a combo ticket, allowing entry to the adjacent **Wild Waters** (daily 10am–5pm), a typical water park with slides, wave pools, amusement arcades and so on.

HORSEBACK RIDING

A visit to this area isn't really complete without seeing one of its numerous **horse ranches**, but you'll need a car to reach them. If you want to go horseback riding rather than just looking around, try **Young's Paso Fino Ranch**, four miles along SR-326, off I-75, at no. 8075 NW (☎867-5305 or -5273; book ahead). One of the country's top ranches for breeding and training Paso Fino horses (the name means "fine gait" in Spanish), they offer instruction before taking you out on a trail ($25 for 1hr 30min, including instruction). The horses' easy disposition and exceptionally smooth gait make them an ideal choice for beginners as well as more advanced riders. If you're lucky, you'll meet Barbara Young, the owner, whose charm and enthusiasm know no bounds.

An ideal place to rest your saddle-sore butt after a hard day's horseback riding is the **Heritage Country Inn**, set in ranch country at 14343 W Hwy-40, off I-75 (☎489-0023). The $79 bed-and-breakfast is money well spent for the loving care and attention you'll receive. There are six unique bedrooms, ranging from the *Plantation Room* to the *English Thoroughbred Room*. A favorite among guests is the home-baked cinnamon bread.

Rainbow Springs State Park

A more natural setting for a walk and a swim is **Rainbow Springs State Park**, located about twenty miles west of Ocala and three miles north of Dunnellon, off Hwy-41 (daily 8am–sunset; $1 ☎489-5201). From 1890 until the 1960s, this park rivalled Silver Springs as a commercial venture, but has thankfully been allowed to return to its natural state. A popular haunt for locals, it's busy on weekends, with families picnicking on the grass and splashing around in the springs. At other times you can enjoy exploring woodland **trails** in peace and quiet, keeping an eye out for bobcats, raccoons, wild pigs, otters and a great variety of birdlife, then have a swim in the cool, crystal-clear waters. Phone ahead to take advantage of the **ranger-led walks**, **snorkelling** or **scuba diving**, which allow views of otherwise restricted areas. Inner-tube rentals are also available for a leisurely drift down the Blue Run River.

Practicalities

Motels line Silver Springs Boulevard between Ocala and Silver Springs: *Silver Springs Motel*, no. 4121 E (☎236-4243; ②); *Sun Plaza*, no. 5461 E (☎236-2343; ②); *Southland Motel*, no. 1260 E (☎351-0113; ③); and the *Holiday Inn–Ocala*, no. 3621 W (☎629-0381; ④), are all worth trying. For comparative luxury, try *Steinbrenners Ramada Inn*, 3810 NW Blitchton Road (☎732-3131; ④). The only local **campground** (aside from camping in the Ocala National Forest) to allow tents is the *KOA* (☎237-2138), five miles southwest of Ocala on Route 200. You can pitch a tent for $19.95 or rent a cabin for $34.95.

You'll seldom spend more than $5 for a filling **meal** in the town, with a wide selection of eateries along E Silver Springs Boulevard. For lunch or dinner, *Morrison's Cafeteria*, no. 1602 (☎622-7447), has a wide selection of homestyle foods served cafeteria style. *Sonny's*, no. 4102 (☎236-1012), specializes in barbecue, with $4.99 all-you-can-eat specials nightly. Slightly more expensive, *Richard's Place*, no. 316 (☎351-2233), does tasty things with vegetables; for something meaty and out of the ordinary, sample the large helpings of bratwurst and schnitzel at the *German Kitchen*, no. 5340 (☎236-3055). For a more refined experience, try lunch or tea in the pink dining room of *The Bistro at Victorian Gardens*, no. 917 (☎867-5980), a contemporary Italian restaurant.

Ocala National Forest

Translucent lakes, bubbling springs and a splendid 65-mile hiking trail bring weekend adventurers to the 400,000-acre **OCALA NATIONAL FOREST**, five miles east of Silver Springs on Route 40. Steer clear of the busy bits, and you'll find plenty to savor in seclusion. Alternatively, if you only have time for a quick look, take a spin along Route 19 (meeting Route 40, 22 miles into the forest), running north–south in the shade of overhanging hardwoods near the forest's eastern edge.

Juniper, Alexander and Salt springs

For swimming, canoeing (rent on the spot, for $16 per half-day), gentle hiking and lots of other people, especially on weekends and holidays, the forest has three warm-water springs that fit the bill; and each of them has a campground. The easiest to reach from Silver Springs is **Juniper Springs** (info: ☎625-2520), twenty miles ahead on Route 40, particularly suited to hassle-free canoeing with a seven-mile marked course. **Alexander Springs** (info: ☎669-7495), on Route 445 off SR-19 about ten miles southeast of Juniper Springs, has good canoeing, too, and its see-through waters are perfect for snorkeling and scuba-diving.

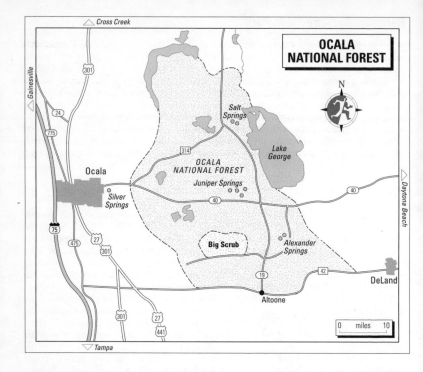

To the north of the forest, reachable with Route 314 or Route 19, the most developed site – it even has a gas station and laundromat – is **Salt Springs** (info: ☎685-2048 or -3070). Despite the name, the springs here pump up 52 million gallons of fresh water a day, and the steady 72°F temperature stimulates a semi-tropical landscape of vividly colored plants and palm trees. Swimming and canoeing are as good here as at the other two springs, but people come mainly for the **fishing**, casting off in anticipation of catfish, large-mouthed bass and speckled perch.

The Ocala hiking trail

The 67-mile **Ocala hiking trail** runs right through the forest, traversing many remote, swampy areas, and passing the three springs mentioned above. Very **basic campgrounds** appear at regular intervals (be warned that these are closed during the mid-November to early January hunting season). At the district rangers' offices (see the box opposite), pick up the excellent leaflet describing the trail, which is part of the Florida State Scenic Trail.

However keen you might be, you're unlikely to have the time or stamina to tackle the entire trail, though one exceptional area that merits the slog required to get to it is **Big Scrub**, an imposingly severe landscape with sand dunes – and sometimes wild deer – moving across its semi-arid acres. The biggest problem at Big Scrub is lack of shade from the scorching sun, and the fact that the nearest facilities of any kind are miles away – don't come unprepared. Big Scrub is in the southern part of the forest, seven miles along Forest Road 573, off Route 19, twelve miles north of Altoona.

OCALA NATIONAL FOREST INFORMATION

The Ocala **Chamber of Commerce**, 110 E Silver Springs Boulevard (daily 9am–5pm; ☎629-8051), has maps and general information, and visitor centers are located at three park entrances (daily 9am–5pm), offering details on every campground. The latest camping updates are available by phoning the camping areas at Juniper, Alexander and Salt springs (see p.259). For specialist hiking tips, call one of the district ranger offices – the northern and southern halves of the forest are administered respectively by the Lake George Ranger District, 17147 E Hwy-405, Silver Springs (☎625-2520), and the Seminole Ranger District, 40929 Route 19, Umatilla (☎669-3153).

North of Ocala

From the monotonous I-75, you'd never guess that the thirty or so miles of hilly, lakeside terrain just to the east contain some of the most distinctive and insular villages in the state. Beyond the bounds of public transport, they can be reached only by driving; head **north from Ocala** on Hwy-301.

Cross Creek and the Marjorie Kinnan Rawlings Home

Native Floridians often wax lyrical about Marjorie Kinnan Rawlings, author of *The Yearling*, the Pulitzer prize-winning tale of the coming of age of a Florida farmer's son, and *Cross Creek*, which describes the daily activities of country folk in **CROSS CREEK**, about twenty miles from Ocala on Route 325 (off Hwy-301). Leaving her husband in New York, Rawlings spent her most productive years writing and tending a citrus grove here during the 1930s – a time inaccurately re-created in Martin Ritt's 1983 film, *Cross Creek*.

The restored **Marjorie Kinnan Rawlings Home** (Thurs–Sun 10am–11am and 1pm–4pm; guided tours of up to ten people on the hour, with afternoon tours often fully booked; $3 adults, $2 children) gives an eye-opening insight into the toughness of the "cracker" lifestyle.

Micanopy, McIntosh and Paynes Prairie

Four miles north of Cross Creek, Route 346 branches off to meet Hwy-441 just outside **MICANOPY**. A voguish vacation destination during the late 1800s, Micanopy is making an effort to win back visitors by turning itself, and many of its century-old brick buildings, into antique and craft shops. They're OK for a quick browse, but if it's a weekend, you'd be much better traveling a few miles south along Hwy-441 to another village, **McINTOSH**, whose 400-strong population dresses up in Victorian costumes for the **1890 festival**, held every October, to escort visitors around the restored homes.

In contrast to such conviviality, the marshy landscapes of the **Paynes Prairie State Preserve** (daily 8am–sunset; cars $3.25, cyclists and pedestrians $1), filling a broad sweep of land (18,000 acres) between Micanopy and Gainesville, can't help but strike a note of foreboding. It's an eerie place in many ways, though one well stocked with wildlife: cranes, hawks, waterfowl, otters, turtles and various wading birds all make homes here, as do many alligators. During weekends from October to March, **ranger-led hikes** (reservations: ☎466-4100; free) uncover the fascinating natural history of the area – and some of the social history: habitations have been traced back to 10,000 BC.

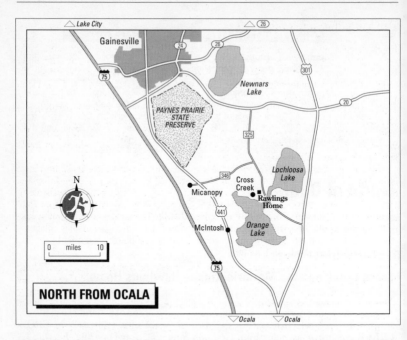

Without a guide, you can bone up on the background at the **visitor center** (daily 9am–5pm), four miles from Micanopy off Hwy-441, and peer into the moody wilderness from the nearby **observation tower**.

Gainesville and around

Without the University of Florida, **GAINESVILLE**, 35 miles north of Ocala, would be just another slow-paced rural community nodding off in the Florida heartland. As it is, the daintily sized place, once called Hogtown, is given a boost by its 40,000 students, who bring a lively, liberal spirit and account for the only decent **nightlife** in Central Florida outside Orlando. This, combined with a few low-key targets in and around the town, and plentiful cheap accommodation, make Gainesville a deserving base for a day or two.

Accommodation

Although Gainesville has rows of low-cost **motels** a couple of miles out of the center along SW 13th Street, be warned that these fill quickly when the Gators are playing at home. The closest tent-friendly **campground** is ten miles south at the Paynes Prairie State Preserve (see p.261; ☎466-3397).

Bambi, 2119 SW 13th St (☎1-800/34BAMBI). Slightly nearer to downtown than most of the inexpensive motels. ③.

Comfort Inn, 2435 SW 13th St (☎373-6500). One of the newer budget options. ③.

Econo Lodge, 2649 SW 13th St (☎373-7816). Reliable chain motel. ③.

Gainesville Lodge, 413 W University Ave (☎376-1224). The most convenient place to stay. Near downtown Gainesville and the campus. ③.

The town and university

Impressive sights are few in Gainesville's quiet center, where most of the people you'll see are office workers going to or from work or nipping out to lunch. At the junction of University Avenue and NE First Street you'll spot the **Clock Tower**, an undramatic relic culled from Gainesville's nineteenth-century courthouse. Inside are the clock workings and some photos from the old days. If these whet your historical appetite, explore northwards along Third Street, which reveals many of the showcase homes of turn-of-the-century Gainesville – Queen Anne, Colonial and various Revival styles dominate – and the palm-fronted **Thomas Center**, 306 NE Sixth Avenue (Mon–Fri 9am–5pm, Sat & Sun 1–4pm; free), once a plush hotel and restaurant, which now hosts small-scale art and historical exhibitions.

The old buildings are easily tracked down with the *Historic Gainesville* brochure issued by the **Visitors and Convention Bureau**, at 30 E University Avenue (Mon–Fri 8.30am–5pm; ☎374-5231). From the town center, it's an easy fifteen-minute walk along University Avenue to the university; though if you're feeling very lazy, take a **bus** (any number from #1 to #10) from beside the Clock Tower. The Greyhound station is centrally placed, at 516 SW Fourth Avenue (☎376-5252).

The University of Florida

Most of Gainesville's through-traffic passes half a mile west of the town center along 13th Street (part of Hwy-441), from which the **University of Florida (UF)** campus stretches three miles west from its main entrance by the junction with University Avenue. Call at the **information booth**, facing SW Second Street, for a free map, without which it's easy to get lost in the expansive grounds.

After it opened in 1906, the university's early alumni gave Florida's economy a leg-up by pioneering the state's fantastically successful citrus farms. These days, the curriculum is broader based and modern buildings dominate the campus, though the first you'll see are the red-brick "Collegiate Gothic" structures favored by US turn-of-the-century academic institutions. In the center of the campus, the 1953 **Century Tower** serves as a navigational aid and a time-keeping device – its electric bells issue a nerve-shattering carillon every hour.

Beyond the tower, the 83,000-seat **Florida Field/Ben Hill Griffin Stadium** – home of the Gators football team and a monument to the popularity of college sports in Florida – can hardly be missed, and neither can the adjacent **O'Connel Center**, an indoor sports venue, entering which is akin to walking into a giant balloon. Aside from staging evening volleyball and basketball games, and entertaining design buffs, the building offers only a cool, refreshing breather.

For a quick respite from the sun, the temporary shows in the **University Gallery** (Mon–Sat 9am–5pm, Sun 1–5pm; free), inside the Fine Arts Building, capture the best student art. Head back outdoors and walk about a mile west along Museum Road to the tidy **University Garden**, where a concealed footpath leads to **Lake Alice**, overlooked by a wooden observation platform gradually losing its battle against the surrounding vegetation. You could come here for a picnic, but the roar of insects, the constant scampering of lizards and the knowledge that alligators are plentiful, means keeping your guard up as you gaze over the sizeable lake.

At the corner of SW 34th St and Hull Rd is the **University of Florida Cultural Complex**, where the new **Florida Museum of Natural History** (Mon–Sat 10am–5pm, Sun 1–5pm; free) focuses on Florida's prehistory and wildlife. The **Harn Museum of Art** (Tues–Fri 11am–5pm, Sat 10am–5pm, Sun 1pm–5pm; free) hosts rotating contemporary exhibits. The nearby **Center for the Performing Arts**, 315 Hull Road (☎392-1900 or ☎392-2787 for ticket information), brings in traveling Broadway plays, symphonies, popular music, family entertainment and educational programs.

Eating

Gainesville is not a difficult place in which to find a good **meal**, with plenty of restaurants around the town center and the university.

Emiliano's Café, 7 SE First St (☎375-7381). Fresh-baked delights and substantial Costa Rican-style lunches.

Ernesto's Tex-Mex Café, 6 S Main St (☎376-0750). Reasonably priced standard American Mexican food.

Harry's Seafood Bar and Grill, 110 SE First St (☎372-1555). A sidewalk café serving New Orleans-style seafood, pasta, chicken, burgers and salads.

Wolfgang's Bistro, 11 SE First Ave (☎378-7850). A student favorite, offering food from all over the world.

Nightlife

The town's students keep a bright **nightlife** in motion, live rock music being especially easy to find. For **what's on** details, check the "Scene" section of Friday's *Gainesville Sun*, or the free *Moon* magazine, found in most bars and restaurants.

Hardback Café, 232 SE First St (☎372-6248). The best of the live music venues, attracting "alternative" acts on weekends and assorted painters and poets on other nights.

Lillian's Music Store, 112 SE First St (☎372-1010). Live bands or comedy and a 2–8pm happy hour.

Loungin, 6 E University Ave (☎377-8080). The hippest of Gainesville's clubs. Comics and acoustic acts early in the week, and house, acid, techno and classic disco grooves Thursday–Sunday.

Market Street Pub, 120 SW First St (☎377-2927). Brews its own beer and provides acoustic country and bluegrass music to help it down.

Around Gainesville

Three places close to Gainesville will help fill a day. Two of them are neighbors and served by local buses; the third can only be reached by car.

Kanapaha Botanical Gardens and the Fred Bear Museum

Flower fanciers shouldn't miss the 62-acre **Kanapaha Botanical Gardens** (Mon, Tues & Fri 9am–5pm, Wed, Sat & Sun 9am–sunset; $3 adults, $2 kids 6-13), five miles southwest of central Gainesville on Route 24, reachable with bus #1. More than most, the summer months are a riot of color and fragrances, although the design of the gardens means there's always something in bloom. Besides vines and bamboos, and special sections planted to attract butterflies and hummingbirds, the highlight is the herb garden, whose aromatic bed is raised to nose-level to encourage sniffing.

Across the road from the gardens, a signpost points to the **Fred Bear Museum** (daily 10am–6pm; $4 adults, $2.50 children), a mass of mounted, skinned and stuffed animals, and some (such as the elephant's ear table with hippo legs) turned into furniture. Many of the unfortunate creatures were caught and killed by Fred Bear himself, who runs the adjoining archery factory. Note: not a place for animal lovers.

The Devil's Millhopper

Of thousands of sinkholes in Florida, few are bigger or more spectacular than the **Devil's Millhopper**, set in a state geological site (daily 9am–sunset; cars $3.25, pedestrians and cyclists $1; free guided tour Sat 10am), seven miles northwest of Gainesville, off 53rd Avenue. Formed by the gradual erosion of limestone deposits and the collapse of the resultant cavern's ceiling, the lower reaches of this 120-foot-deep bowl-shaped dent have a temperature significantly cooler than the surface, allowing species of alpine plant and animal life to thrive. A winding boardwalk delivers you into the thickly vegetated depths.

North of Gainesville

Traveling **north of Gainesville** puts you in easy striking distance of the Panhandle to the west, and Jacksonville, the major city of the Northeast Coast. If you're uncertain of which way to turn, relax for a few hours at **Ichetucknee Springs** (daily 8am–sunset; cars $3.25, pedestrians and cyclists $1), the birthplace of the Ichetucknee River, whose chilled waters lend themselves to canoeing or inner-tube rafting along a six-mile course. **Canoes** can be rented outside the park for $20 a day, and there's an additional $4.25 charge per person to navigate the river. Weekdays, when beavers, otters and turtles sometimes share the river, are the best time to come; weekend crowds scare much of the wildlife away. The springs are 35 miles northwest of Gainesville, on Route 238, off I-75, and five-and-a-half miles north of Fort White.

There's no point in stopping in the unremarkable Lake City, thirteen miles north of the springs, nor in the Osceola National Forest, to the east of Lake City. This smallest of the state's three federally protected forests is mostly visited by hardened fishermen bound for its Ocean Pond, and you should aim instead for a couple of more fulfilling attractions in the near vicinity.

The Stephen Foster State Culture Center

Twelve miles north of Lake City, off Hwy-41, the **Stephen Foster State Culture Center** (daily 9am–sunset; cars $3.25, pedestrians and cyclists $1) offers a tribute to the man who composed Florida's state song, *Old Folks At Home*, immortalizing the waterway ("Way down upon the S'wanee river. . .") that flows by here on its 250-mile meander from Georgia's Okefenokee Swamp to the Gulf of Mexico. As it happens, Foster never actually saw the river but simply used "S'wanee" as a convenient Deep South-sounding rhyme. Besides exploring Florida's musical roots, the Center has a sentimental display about Foster, who penned a hatful of classic American folk songs including *Camptown Races*, *My Old Kentucky Home* and *Oh! Susanna* – instantly familiar melodies which ring out through the oak-filled park from a belltower – before dying in New York in 1863, aged 37.

The Olustee Battlefield Site

The **Olustee Battlefield Site**, thirteen miles west of Lake City beside Hwy-90 (Thurs–Mon 9am–5pm; free), is a sure sign you're approaching the Panhandle, a Confederate power base during the Civil War. The only major battle of the conflict in Florida took place here in February 1864, when 5000 Union troops pressing west from Jacksonville squared up to a similar-sized Confederate force. The five-hour battle, which left three hundred dead, nearly two thousand wounded and both sides claiming victory, is marked by a monument and a small interpretive center at the entrance (closed Tues & Wed), and by a trail around the respective troop positions. It's hard to imagine the carnage that took place in what is now – as it was then – a peaceful pine forest.

travel details

Trains

Orlando to: DeLand (2 daily; 58min); Jacksonville (2 daily; 3hr 12min); Kissimmee (7 daily; 18min); Lakeland (7 daily; 1hr 28min); Sanford (2 daily; 38min); Tampa (7 daily; 2hr 17min); Winter Park (2 daily; 15min).

Winter Haven to: Fort Lauderdale (2 daily; 3hr); Miami (2 daily; 4hr 2min); Sebring (2 daily; 38min); West Palm Beach (2 daily; 2hr 9min).

Buses

Clewiston to: Belle Glade (1 daily; 30min); West Palm Beach (1 daily; 1hr 35min).

Lakeland to: Avon Park (1 daily; 3hr 5min); Cypress Gardens (1 daily; 45min); Lake Wales (1 daily; 1hr 5min); Sebring (1 daily; 3hr 30min); West Palm Beach (1 daily; 5hr); Winter Haven (1 daily; 30min).

Orlando to: Daytona Beach (4–6 daily; 2hr 35min); DeLand (4–6 daily; 1hr); Fort Lauderdale (7 daily; 5hr 20min); Fort Pierce (7 daily; 2hr 25min); Gainesville (4 daily; 2hr 50min); Jacksonville (4–6 daily; 3hr 30min); Lakeland (5 daily; 1hr 35min); Kissimmee (2 daily; 40min); Miami (7 daily; 5hr 55min); Ocala (4 daily; 1hr 30min); Sanford (4–6 daily; 35min); Tallahassee (4 daily; 5hr 30min); Tampa (5 daily; 3hr 15min); West Palm Beach (7 daily; 4hr); Winter Haven (5 daily; 1hr 5min).

CHAPTER SIX

THE WEST COAST

I n the three hundred miles from the state's southern tip to the border of the Panhandle, Florida's **West Coast** embraces all the extremes. Buzzing, youthful towns neighbor placid fishing hamlets; mobbed holiday strips are just minutes from desolate swamplands. Surprises are plentiful: search for a snack bar and you'll stumble across a world-class art collection; doze off on an empty beach and you'll wake to find it packed with shell-collectors. The West Coast's one constant is its proximity to the Gulf of Mexico – and sunset views rivalled only by those of the Florida Keys.

The diverse and relatively highly populated **Tampa Bay area**, midway along the coast, is the obvious first stop if you're arriving from Central Florida. The West Coast's largest city, **Tampa** probably won't detain you long, though it has more to offer than its power-dressers and corporate towers initially suggest. **Ybor City**, for example, is Tampa's – and the entire coast's – hippest and most culturally eclectic quarter.

Directly across the bay, **St Petersburg** once took pride in being the archetypal Florida retirement community. Lately it has been recast in a younger mold, and is riding high on its acquisition of a major collection of works by surrealist artist Salvador Dalí. For the mass of visitors, though, the Tampa area begins and ends with the **St Petersburg beaches**, miles of sea, sun and sand fringed by uninspired vacation developments. The beaches are undiluted vacation territory, but are also a good base for exploring the Greek-dominated community of **Tarpon Springs**, just to the north.

The coast **north of Tampa** (known as the **Big Bend** for the way it curves toward the Panhandle) is consumed by dead-flat, beachless marshes, large chunks of which are wildlife refuges with little public access. No settlement here can boast a population of more than a few thousand, and many visitors bolt through on their way to the beach territories further south. The area, however, is one of Florida's hidden treasures. Scattered throughout is evidence of much busier and prosperous times, like the prehistoric sun-worshipping site at **Crystal River**. And **Cedar Key**, which was a thriving port over a century ago, is now the perfect tourist retreat. Locals here have preserved a laid-back way of life, and the community is a time-warped enclave of excellent eating and rewarding sights.

A string of barrier-island beaches runs the length of the Gulf **south of Tampa**. And while it may be the beaches that draw the crowds, the mainland towns that provide access to them have a lot in their favor, too. The first of any consequential size, **Sarasota** is the custodian of a fine-arts legacy passed down by John Ringling, the turn-of-the-century circus boss. Further south, Thomas Edison was one of a number of scientific pioneers who took a fancy to palm-studded **Fort Myers**, which neighbors **Sanibel** and **Captiva** – two atmospheric islands justifying a few days' relaxed discovery. As you pass

---

ACCOMMODATION PRICE CODES

All **accommodation prices** in this book have been coded using the symbols below. Note that prices are for the least expensive double rooms in each establishment. For a full explanation see p.27 in Basics.

① up to $30	③ $45-60	⑤ $80-100	⑦ $130-180
② $30-45	④ $60-80	⑥ $100-130	⑧ $180+

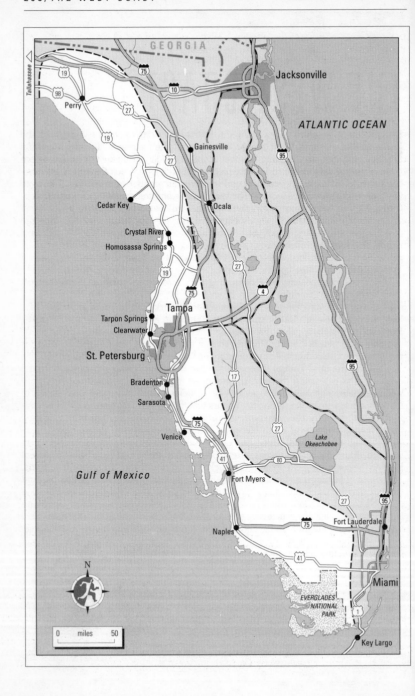

through, take the opportunity to strike inland: the southwest coast backs onto the **Everglades**, a vast expanse whose swamps and prairies are brimming with life. The window onto it all is **Everglades National Park**, which spreads east almost to the edge of Miami, and is explorable via simple walking trails, canoe, or by spending the night at backcountry campgrounds with only the alligators for company.

The West Coast is easy to **get around**. The region's **major roads** and I-4 from Central Florida all converge close to Tampa. From Tampa through the Big Bend, **Hwy-19** is the only route, served by two Greyhound **buses** daily in each direction. **Hwy-41** connects the main southwest coastal settlements, and is often known as the **Tamiami Trail**, a nickname incorporating Tampa and Miami, from its time as the only road link crossing the Everglades between the two cities. These days it's superseded for speed by the bland **I-75**. Greyhound services number five daily each way through the southwest coast, and a few towns are also connected by Amtrak buses from Tampa. The bigger centers have adequate **local bus service**, though the barrier islands and the Big Bend towns rarely have any public transport. Finally, travelers arriving from Key West can be delivered to Marco Island and Naples by ferry (see p.149).

THE TAMPA BAY AREA

The geographic and economic nerve center of the region, with a population almost on a par with that of Miami, the **Tampa Bay area** is easily the busiest and most congested part of the West Coast. But people do live here for reasons other than work. The wide waters of the bay provide a scenic backdrop for Tampa itself, which is a stimulating city. And the barrier-island beaches along the coast let the locals swap metropolitan bustle for luscious sunsets and miles of glistening sands. With sun, sand and sea, however, comes the inevitable span of chain restaurants and accommodations for the touring masses.

Tampa

TAMPA is a small city with an infectious, upbeat mood. You'll only need a day or two to explore it thoroughly, but you'll depart with a lasting impression of a city on the rise. The West Coast's undisputed business hub, it has been one of the major beneficiaries of the recent flood of people and money into Florida. Yet despite cultural and artistic offerings envied by many larger communities, and an international airport in its back yard, Tampa rarely gets more than a passing glance. Tourists speed through to Busch Gardens, a theme park on the city's outskirts, and the Gulf coast beaches half an hour's drive west – missing out totally on one of Florida's most youthful and energetic urban communities.

Tampa began as a small settlement beside Fort Brooke (a US Army base built to keep an eye on local Seminole Indians during the 1820s), and remained tiny, isolated and insignificant until the 1880s, when the railway arrived and the Hillsborough River – on which the city stands – was dredged to allow seagoing vessels to dock. Tampa became a booming port and simultaneously acquired a major tobacco industry as thousands of Cubans moved north from Key West to the new cigar factories of neighboring Ybor City. Although the Depression stalled the economic surge, the port remained one of the busiest in the country. And while the social problems that blight any US city are evident, Tampa continues to emerge as a forward-thinking, financially-secure community.

> The **area code** for the Tampa Bay and Ybor City areas is ☎813; St Petersburg, Clearwater, Gulfport and Tarpon Springs have a ☎727 area code.

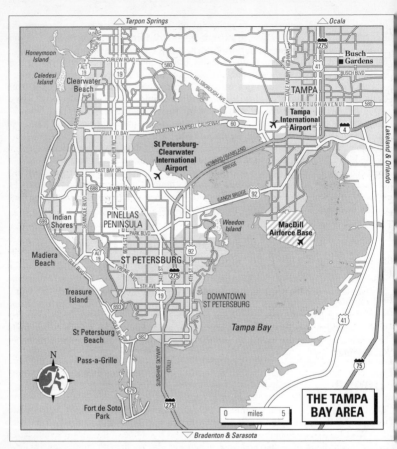

THE TAMPA
BAY AREA

Regardless of the deals being struck in its towering office blocks, which are surprisingly thoughtfully designed, **downtown Tampa** is quiet and compact. An art museum, a sensational Spanish revival cinema, and the *Tampa Bay Hotel* – one of the few reminders of times gone by – form the basis for a half-day ramble. What downtown may lack in atmosphere and history, is made up for three miles northeast in the **Ybor City** quarter, whose Latin American character originated with migrant cigar workers. It now boasts a plethora of historical markers to the heady days of the struggle for Cuban independence.

Uncharted territory for tourists, but well worth the detour if you have a car, is an area known locally as **Balichi Boulevard**. North of downtown on Nebraska Avenue, the area is named after a steak-stuffed sausage, and is a rather rundown part of town rich with Cuban restaurants, many of which have moved here to escape the quickly inflating rents of Ybor City.

If you have more time to spare, venture into **Hyde Park**, which contains the homes of Tampa's wealthiest early settlers. **Busch Gardens** and the **Museum of Science and Industry** are also worth a stop, or you could just amble into the wild – open country appears remarkably quickly just north of the busy city.

Arrival, information and getting around

The city's international **airport** (☎870-8700) is five miles northwest of downtown Tampa. Local bus #30 (see "City transport," below) is the least costly connection ($1.15), or use the around-the-clock Limo Inc vans (☎572-1111 or 1-800/282-6817), whose representatives have desks in the baggage claim area; book the day before you fly. They also cover St Petersburg, Clearwater and the beaches. The flat fare to any Busch Boulevard or coastal accommodation is $13 per person, or $22 for a round-trip ticket.

Taxis – the main firms are United (☎253-2424) and Yellow (☎253-0121) – are abundant but expensive. The fare to downtown Tampa or a Busch Boulevard motel costs $13–24; to St Petersburg or the St Petersburg Beaches, $30–45. All the major **car rental** companies have desks at the airport.

If you arrive **by car** from St Petersburg, the main route into Tampa is I-275, which traverses Old Tampa Bay and ends up in the west of downtown. From east or central Florida, you'll come in on the I-4, which intersects with I-75. Heed this: from I-75, it's essential to exit at Hwy 60 (signposted Kennedy Boulevard) for downtown Tampa. There are seven less convenient exits, and if you miss this one and end up in north Tampa, the city's fiendish one-way system will keep you in your car for hours.

Long-distance public transport terminates in downtown Tampa: Greyhound **buses** at 610 Polk Street (☎229-2174 or 1-800/231-2222), and **trains** at 601 N Nebraska Avenue (☎221-7600 or 1-800/872-7245).

Information

In downtown Tampa, collect vouchers, leaflets and general information at the **Visitors Information Center**, 400 North Tampa Street, Suite 1010 (Mon–Sat 9am–5pm; ☎1-800/44-TAMPA or 223-2752; fax 229-6616). In Ybor City, visit the **Ybor City Chamber of Commerce**, 1800 East Ninth Avenue (Mon–Fri 9am–5pm; ☎248-3712). Opposite Busch Gardens, the **Tampa Bay Visitor Information Center**, 3601 E Busch Boulevard (daily 10am–6pm; ☎985-3601) has local and state-wide information. For **nightlife** listings, try the Friday edition of the *Tampa Tribune*, the free *Weekly Planet*, or call the free Nightlife phone service at ☎854-8000.

Getting around

Although downtown Tampa and Ybor City are easily covered on foot, to travel between them – or to reach Busch Gardens or the Museum of Science and Industry – without a car, you'll need to use **local buses** (HARTline ☎254-4278), whose routes fan out from Marion Street in downtown Tampa. **Useful bus numbers** are the #8 to Ybor City; #5, #14 or #18 to Busch Gardens; #6 to the Museum of Science and Industry; and #30 to the airport. Only rush-hour commuter (express) buses run **between Tampa and the coast**: #100X to St Petersburg (for schedule information for this bus only, call ☎530-9911) and #200X to Clearwater. Alternatives are the numerous daily Greyhound buses or the twice-daily Amtrak bus. Another way to travel between downtown Tampa and Ybor City is on the **Tampa-Ybor Trolley** (☎254-4278), which runs Mon–Fri 9am–4pm, every twenty minutes; weekends and holidays 7.30am–5.30pm, every thirty minutes. The route takes you via Harbor Island and the Florida Aquarium (see p.273), and costs 50¢ one way.

Accommodation

Except for the area around Busch Gardens, Tampa is not generously supplied with low-cost **accommodation**. To save money, a good option is to sleep in St Petersburg or at the beaches, and treat the city as a day trip.

Within Tampa, the cheaper **motels** are all on E Busch Boulevard close to Busch Gardens: *Best Western Resort* at no. 820 (☎933-4011; ④–⑤), *Econo Lodge* no. 1701 (☎933-7681; ②–③), or *Howard Johnson's* no. 4139 (☎1-800/874-1768; ②–③) are the best of the bunch. Right by the Museum of Science and Industry, the *Days Inn at Busch Gardens*, 2520 N 50th Street (☎247-3300; ③–④), is another economical option. While Tampa itself does not have a youth hostel, nearby Clearwater has an excellent one ideal for exploring the entire area (see "Clearwater," below).

Any of the above makes a reasonable base for seeing the city by car. If you're dependent on buses, however, your choices are much more limited. You'll need to use one of the downtown business-traveler-orientated hotels such as the convenient *Riverside*, 200 N Ashley Drive (☎223-2222; ④–⑥), or, ten minutes' walk from downtown, the *Days Inn*, 2522 N Dale Mabry (☎1-800/448-4373; ③–⑤).

Other than the site at the Hillsborough River State Park (see "Around Tampa," p.276), the only local **campground** where tents are welcome is the *Camp Nebraska RV Park*, 10314 N Nebraska Avenue/Hwy-41 (☎971-3460), which lies a mile and a half north of Busch Gardens.

Downtown Tampa

Downtown Tampa's current prosperity is demonstrated by its upright office towers, especially at **Lykes Gaslight Square**, where massive, mirrored structures jut into the sky. But, aside from the riverside warehouses in various states of dilapidation around the northern end of pedestrian-friendly **Franklin Street** (once a pulsating main drag and still the best place to get your bearings), any hint of the city's past is largely left to text-bearing plaques, which detail everything from the passage of sixteenth-century explorer Hernando DeSoto to the site of Florida's first radio station. The single substantial relic of bygone days is the **Tampa Theater**, 711 Franklin Street (Mon–Sat 10.30am–5.30pm; ☎274-8981 or 274-8982), one of the few surviving "atmospheric theaters" erected by Mediterranean-mad designer John Eberson during the Twenties. When silent movies enthralled the masses, Eberson's movie houses heightened the escapist mood: ceilings became star-filled skies, balconies were chiselled into Moorish arches, gargoyles leered from stuccoed walls, and replica Greek and Roman statuary filled every nook and cranny.

Having fallen on hard times with the arrival of TV, the Tampa Theater is now enjoying a new lease on life as the home of the Tampa Theater Film Society, and boasts a full program of movies. Paying $5.75 for a ticket (see "Nightlife," p.279) is one way to gain access to the splendidly restored interior. Another is the guided tours ($2), which are highly entertaining but are held irregularly. In addition to the theater's magnificent lighting system that cultivates the feel of an open auditorium at night, a Wurlitzer organ rises from the orchestra pit fifteen minutes before each screening and serenades the crowd.

None of the contemporary buildings in downtown Tampa better reflects the city's striving for cultural recognition than the **Tampa Museum of Art**, on the banks of the Hillsborough River at 600 N Ashley Drive (Mon–Tues and Thurs–Sat 10am–5pm, Wed 10am–9pm, Sun 1–5pm; $5; free Wed 5–9pm; free guided tours on Wed and Sat at 1pm, Sun at 2pm). The highly regarded museum specializes in an incongruous mix of classical antiquities and twentieth-century American art. Selections from the permanent modern stock are cleverly blended with loaned pieces from the cream of recent US painting, photography and sculpture. A third gallery is devoted to major traveling exhibitions. The new sculpture gallery, which houses a collection of not-so-thrilling contemporary pieces, affords lovely views across the river to the Tampa Bay Hotel.

On the second Saturday of each month the museum also runs **guided walking tours** of downtown Tampa. Tours depart from the entrance of the museum at 10am. For more information call ☎274-8130.

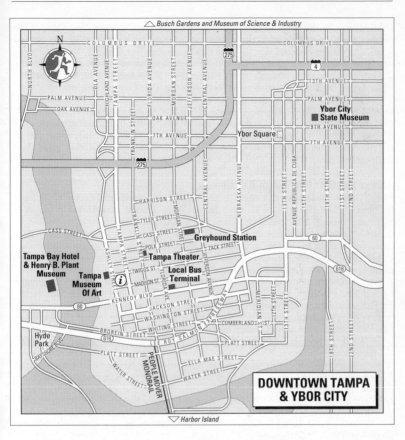

△ Busch Gardens and Museum of Science & Industry

DOWNTOWN TAMPA
& YBOR CITY

▽ Harbor Island

Continuing south, you'll feel like an insignificant speck at the feet of the city's tallest structures. For a better view of them – and their surroundings – take the short monorail ride (from the terminal on top of the Fort Brooke Parking Garage on Whiting Street; 50¢ each way) to **Harbor Island**, a large shopping mall on a small island dredged from the Hillsborough Bay. If strapped for time, walk through the concrete walkway of the Nations Bank Plaza and take the elevator to the 31st floor – the view is an exquisite vista of the whole city.

An attractive new addition to Tampa's dock area and the product of an $84 million budget, the **Florida Aquarium** (daily 9am–6pm; $13.95; audio wands an extra $2; parking $3) houses lavish displays of Florida's fresh- and salt-water habitats, ranging from springs and swamps to beaches and coral reefs. The permanent residents include an impressive variety of fish and other native creatures like otters, turtles, baby alligators and countless species of bird.

Far from the glamorous skyscrapers, the northeast section of the city has an unsafe reputation. Drug dealing is rife around the streets, and the area is permeated by a eerie sense of desolation. If you're heading to Ybor City on foot, this is the route; and though there isn't much reason to linger in this part of town, take a detour to **Oaklawn Cemetery**, which was set aside to bury the town's dead ("whites and slaves alike") in

1850. Along with the bones of one Florida governor and two Supreme Court judges, the picturesque graveyard guards the remains of soldiers from seven wars: the Second Seminole War, the Mexican War, the Billy Bowlegs Indian War, the Civil War, the Spanish American War and both World Wars. Hidden away at the far end of the cemetary, in the shadow of the faceless Morgan Street Penitentiary, is the tomb of the **Ybor family** – whose name lives on in Tampa's most exotic quarter, Ybor City (see below).

The only other attractions that might warrant a look-see here are two churches. Built in 1898, **Sacred Heart Catholic Church**, at 509 Florida Ave (☎229-1595), has a gleaming facade of mottled marble and a rich interior illuminated by stained glass. **St Paul African Methodist Church**, at 1100 Marion St just a few minutes' walk north, cannot match Sacred Heart's grandeur, but its red-brick, Victorian style and vivid stained glass are worth a visit.

Across the river: the Tampa Bay Hotel

From Harbor Island you can't miss the silver minarets, cupolas and domes of the main building of the University of Tampa – formerly the **Tampa Bay Hotel**. A fusion of Moorish, Turkish and Spanish building styles financed to the tune of $2 million by steamship and railway magnate **Henry B. Plant**, the structure is as bizarre a sight today as it was on its opening in 1891, when its 500 rooms looked out on a community of just 700 people. For a good look, walk across the river on Kennedy Boulevard and climb down the steps leading into Plant Park.

Plant had been buying up bankrupt railways since the Civil War and steadily inching his way into Florida to meet his steamships unloading at Tampa's harbor. Like Henry Flagler, whose tracks were forging a trail along Florida's east coast and whose upscale resorts in St Augustine (see "The Northeast Coast") were the talk of US socialites, Plant was wealthy enough to realize his fantasy of creating the world's most luxurious hotel. While the hotel boosted the prestige of the town, Plant's intention of "turning this sandheap into the Champs Elysées, the Hillsborough into the Seine" was never accomplished, and the hotel stayed open for less than ten years. Neglect (the hotel was only used during the winter months and left to fester during the scorching summer) and Plant's death in 1899, hastened its transformation from the last word in comfort to a pile of musty, crumbling plaster. The city authorities bought the place in 1905 and halted the rot, leasing the building to the fledgling Tampa University 23 years later.

In a wing of the main building, the **Henry B. Plant Museum**, 401 W Kennedy Boulevard (Tues–Sat 10am–4pm, Sun noon–4pm; suggested donation $3; ☎254-1891), has several rooms, including an original suite containing what's left of the hotel's furnishings: a gorgeous clutter of Venetian mirrors, elaborate candelabras, ankle-deep rugs, Wedgewood crockery and intricate teak cabinets – all the fruits of a half-million-dollar shopping expedition undertaken by Plant and his wife across Europe and Asia. Incredibly, when the hotel was closed up for five years, it was left unlocked, and many of the antiquities inevitably disappeared.

The hotel was Florida's first electric building, and low-wattage Edison carbon filters are used today to ensure the original, authentic gloom, which is perfect for taking in the richness of the Cuban mahogany doors. You can almost imagine guests calling room service for a grand piano (there were twelve). Note the re-assembled *Rathskellar*, a gentleman's social room previously in the hotel basement (now a student snack bar, see below), complete with German wine cooler and billiard tables. The final room reveals Mrs Plant's affection for over-sized ornamental swans.

A few strides from the museum, the former lobby is a popular rendezvous point for the university's three thousand students, who display their tans from the hotel's over-stuffed leather chairs surrounded by antique French statuary. You can roam around much of the building at will, but the details only fall into place on the free **guided tour**, which departs from the lobby (Sept–May Tues & Thurs at 1.30pm; call ☎253-3333 for more info). If you do miss the tour, make sure you see the evocative photographs of society life from the hotel's heyday in the long corridors. As for the furniture, though, there's precious little left – what human looters left behind, the termites finished off.

Hyde Park

If they don't ensconce themselves in a bay-view condo, Tampa's yuppies snap up the old wooden homes of **Hyde Park**, a mile southwest of downtown Tampa just off Bayshore Boulevard. Attracted by the glamour of the newly opened *Tampa Bay Hotel*, well-heeled arrivals in the 1890s duplicated the same architectural mold that defined the wealthier sections of turn-of-the-century American towns: a mishmash of Mediterranean, Gothic, Tudor and Colonial revival jobs, interspersed with Queen Anne cottages and prairie-style bungalows – rocking-chair-equipped porches being the sole unifying feature. Such complete blasts from the past are rare in Tampa and, provided you're driving (they don't justify a slog around on foot), the old homes are easy to appreciate on a twenty-minute drive on and around Swann and Magnolia avenues and Hyde Park and South boulevards. Even Tampans who prefer modern living quarters descend on Hyde Park to lay waste to their wages in the fashionable stores of **Olde Hyde Park Village**, beside Snow Avenue, where several classy restaurants offer affordable refreshment; see "Eating," p.278. "Tow Away Zone" signs pepper Hyde Park, so if you want to browse or lunch here, go to the free parking garage right in the village at the corner of Bristol Ave and S. Rome Ave.

Continuing south from Hyde Park, incidentally, brings you to the gates of **Mac Dill Air Force Base**. This, the nerve center of US operations during the 1991 Gulf War, was where the Queen of England knighted General "Stormin' Norman" Schwarzkopf later the same year.

Ybor City

In 1886, as soon as Henry Plant's ships (see above) ensured a regular supply of Havana tobacco into Tampa, cigar magnate Don Vincente Martinez Ybor cleared a patch of scrubland three miles northeast of present-day downtown Tampa and laid the foundations of **Ybor City**. Around 20,000 migrants – mostly Cubans drawn from the strife-ridden Key West cigar industry, joined by a smattering of Spaniards and Italians – settled here, creating an enclave of Latin American life and producing the top-class hand-rolled cigars that made Tampa the "Cigar Capital of the World" for forty years. Mass-production, the popularity of cigarettes and the Depression proved a fatal combination for skilled cigar makers. Ybor City lost its *joie de vivre*, and while the rest of Tampa expanded, its twenty tight-knit blocks of cobbled streets and red-brick buildings were engulfed by drab and dangerous low-rent neighborhoods.

Today, Ybor City is in the midst of a revival; it buzzes with tourists, and at night the atmosphere reaches carnival proportions, especially on weekends. It is trendy, culturally diverse and a terrific place to wander at will. Yet commercialism is taking hold fast. Shops still sell hand-rolled cigars, but, due to rising rents, the little hole-in-the-wall cafes that once doled out newly baked Cuban bread and fresh-brewed coffee have all but disappeared, and a new breed of stylish but essentially generic café-bars and restaurants is taking over. There are still some sensational, authentic places to savor Cuban cooking, but they are being forced further and further off the main drag.

Ybor City's Latin roots are instantly apparent, and explanatory background texts adorn many buildings. Soak up the atmosphere during the day, but don't expect the place to really get going until the evening, when the pulse is far quicker. The **Ybor City State Museum**, 1818 Ninth Avenue (Tues–Sat 9am–5pm; $2), offers just enough to help you grasp the main points of Ybor City's creation and its multi-ethnic make-up.

Enormous wall photographs show cigar rollers at work: thousands sat in long rows at bench-tables making 25¢ per cigar and cheering or heckling the *lector* (or reader) who recited the news from Spanish-language newspapers. Standing in the grounds, a cigar-worker's cottage, which you can enter, is more interesting than riveting, demonstrating the unelaborate turn-of-the-century domestic arrangements. The museum also organizes free **walking tours** around Ybor City, leaving Ybor Square from 10am–3pm every 30 minutes (call ☎247-6323 for more info).

The old Stemmenzy-Zago building, where cigar-rolling actually took place, is now called **Ybor Square**, 1901 13th Street at the corner of Eighth Avenue (Mon–Sat 10am–6pm, Sun noon–5.30pm). This cavernous structure – three stories supported by sturdy oak pillars – has been converted into a collection of tourist-aimed shops and restaurants, a depressingly commercialized market of fairy lights draped over T-shirt shops, and cafés without a local in sight.

Standing on the factory's iron steps in 1893, the famed Cuban poet and independence fighter José Martí spoke to thousands of Ybor City's Cubans, calling for pledges of money, machetes and manpower for the country's anti-Spanish, pro-independence struggles*. It's estimated that expatriate Cuban cigar workers contributed ten percent of their earnings, most of which was spent on the illicit purchase and shipment of arms to rebels in Cuba. A stone marker at the foot of the steps records the event and, across the street, the **José Martí Park** remembers Martí with a statue.

From the earliest days, each of Ybor City's ethnic communities ran its own social clubs, published newspapers and even organized a medical insurance scheme which led to the building of two hospitals. The hospitals still function today, as do several of the **social centers**. Stepping inside one of the centers (opening hours vary wildly) reveals patriotic paraphernalia and sometimes, in the basement, men-only dens of dominoes and drinking. If you can, visit *Centro Español*, at 1526 E Seventh Ave, *The Cuban Club*, 2010 Avenida Republica de Cuba N, or *Centro Asturiano*, 1913 N Nebraska Avenue, for a look at Ybor City life that most visitors miss. One Ybor City institution out-of-towners invariably do find is the *Columbia* restaurant, 2117 Seventh Avenue (see "Eating," p.278). Now filling a whole block, the *Columbia* opened in 1905 as a humble coffee stop for tobacco workers; inside, newspaper cuttings plaster the walls and recount the restaurant's lustrous past.

Around Tampa

The collar of suburbia around downtown Tampa contains few reasons to stop. Hereabouts, though, the city's least expensive motels cluster around the **Busch Gardens** theme park, which ranks among the state's top tourist attractions. While as enjoyable as any of its ilk, you might be inclined to skip the park and divide your attentions between the **Museum of Science and Industry** and (provided you're driving; it's unreachable by public transport) the 3000 pristine acres of the **Hillsborough River State Park**. On the way, don't be tempted by the Seminole Indian Village (5221 N Orient Road), part of a Seminole reservation where a token collection of native American arts and crafts is on sale to tourists, and high-stakes bingo is played.

---

*A few years after Martí's speech, Tampa became the embarkation point for the US's Cuban Expeditionary Forces. Thousands of US soldiers were housed in tents here waiting to join the Spanish-American War. On January 1, 1899, the Spanish pulled out of Cuba and Cuba acquired its independence.

Busch Gardens

Incredible as it may seem, most people are drawn to Tampa by a theme park re-creation of colonial-era Africa in the grounds of a brewery, at 3000 E Busch Boulevard (two miles east of I-275 or two miles west of I-75, exit 54, signposted Fowler Ave). In glossing over what was a period of imperial exploitation in the name of entertainment – not to mention the garden's subtitle, "The Dark Continent," which caused outrage within the local black community – **Busch Gardens** (daily 9am–6.30pm; longer hours in high season; adults $35.95, children $29.95; ☎987-5082) brazenly reshapes world history just as much as its arch rival, Walt Disney World. It costs a packet and is as tacky as hell, but if you do come you'll need to stick around all day to get your money's worth. Go on everything in the park (all the rides are included in the admission fee), and learn to love the kitsch without dwelling on its implications.

Traversable on foot or by pseudo-steam train, the 300-acre park divides into several areas. You'll first enter Morocco, where Moroccan crafts are sold at un-Moroccan prices, snake-charmers and belly dancers weave through the crowds, and the Mystick Sheiks Marching Band blast their trumpets into the ears of passers-by. Then comes the Myombe Reserve, where a collection of chimps and gorillas are kept in a tropical environment. Follow the signs to Nairobi and you'll find small gatherings of elephants, giant tortoises, alligators, crocodiles and monkeys in varying states of liveliness, and the animal hospital and children's zoo inhabited by cute, cuddly creatures that are happy to be stroked by kids. Directly ahead in Timbuktu, animals are less in evidence than amusement rides: a small roller-coaster and a children's fairground ride called "Sandstorm," neither of which is a patch on "Kumba" (see below). If the Ubanga-Banga bumper cars in the Congo don't hold lasting appeal, gird your loins for the swirling raft trip around the Congo River Rapids – which may encourage you to cross Stanleyville Falls on a roller-coaster, the best feature of neighboring Stanleyville. Whatever you do, don't miss the devastating "Kumba," the largest and fastest roller-coaster in the southeastern US. The biggest single section of the gardens, the Serengeti Plain, roamed by giraffes, buffalos, zebras, antelopes, black rhino and elephants, is the closest the place gets to showing anything genuinely African; see the beasts from the all-too-brief monorail ride. After all this, retire to the Hospitality House of the Anheuser-Busch Brewery, purveyors of Budweiser and owners of the park, where the beer is free but limited to two drinks (in a paper cup) per person.

The Museum of Science and Industry

Two miles northeast of Busch Gardens, at 4801 E Fowler Avenue, the **Museum of Science and Industry** (Sun–Thurs 9am–5pm, Fri–Sat 9am–7pm; ☎987-6100; $8) will entertain adults as much as kids. Intended to reveal the mysteries of the scientific world, the hands-on displays and machines are hard to resist and will easily fill half a day.

To get the most from your visit, study the program schedule carefully upon arrival: the main – and most interesting – features run at fixed times throughout the day. Plan your time around the Challenger Learning Center, an engrossing simulated space craft and mission control. The Gulf Coast Hurricane is a convincing demonstration that allows begoggled participants to feel the force of the strongest winds known. Energy Pinball, a massive walk-through pinball machine, lets you follow a ball along 700 feet of track. Finally, the Saunders Planetarium houses the unmissable MOSIMAX, Florida's first IMAX (or "maximum image") film theater in a dome, which shows films of outstanding visual and audio quality. The IMAX theater is $6 over and above the normal entry fee, but if you know you'll want to go, you can buy a combo ticket for $11 on your way in.

Hillsborough River State Park

Twelve miles north of Tampa on Hwy-301, shaded by live oaks, magnolias and sable palms, the **Hillsborough River State Park** (daily 8am–sunset; cars $3.25, pedestrians and cyclists $1; ☎987-6771) holds one of the state's rare instances of rapids – outside of a theme park – as the Hillsborough River tumbles over limestone outcrops before pursuing a more typical meandering course. Rambling the sizeable park's walking trails and canoeing the gentler sections of the river could fill a day nicely (and the park makes an enjoyable **camping** place; ☎986-1020; $14.50 to pitch a tent), but on a Saturday or Sunday you should devote part of the afternoon to the **Fort Foster Historic Site**, a reconstructed 1836 Seminole War fort that can only be seen with the **guided tour** (departures from the park entrance on Sat, Sun & major holidays only, 9–11am & 1–4pm; $1.75). Stemming from the US attempts to drive Florida's Seminole Indians out to reservations in the Midwest and make the state fit for the white man, the Seminole Wars raged throughout the nineteenth century and didn't end officially until 1937. Period-attired enthusiasts occupy the fort and recount historical details, not least the fact that more soldiers died from tropical diseases than in battle. Over the river, the occupants of the Seminole camp unfurl a somewhat different account of the conflict – both sides make for interesting listening.

Eating

Eating in Tampa means good quality and lots of choice – except in **downtown**, where street stands dispensing snacks to lunching office workers are the culinary norm. Some of the best and most interesting meals are served in Ybor City, whose Latin heritage and hip new reputation have made it a restaurant haven.

Downtown

Bern's Steak House, 1208 S. Howard Ave ☎251-2421. The best charcoal-broiled steaks you'll ever have. Dinner is costly (around $30), but it's unforgettable.

Café Pepé, 2006 W Kennedy Blvd ☎253-6501. This has been a Tampa landmark for years. Enjoy favorites like *filete salteado* and *paella*.

Gladstone's Grilled Chicken, 502 Tampa St ☎221-2988. You'll definitely be glad you tried the poultry here.

Manhattan Bagel Bar, 602 Franklin St ☎307-0555. Basic but a good choice for a quick bite before heading to the Tampa Theater (see above).

Ole Style Deli, 110 E Madison St ☎223-4282. A worthy address where businessmen devour $4 sandwiches. Service can be very slow, but breakfasts and salads are good.

Rathskellar. While in the vicinity of the *Tampa Bay Hotel* (see p.274), drop into this student-patronized eatery for a cheap, light meal.

Hyde Park

Café DeSoto, 504 E Kennedy Blvd ☎229-2566. The Cuban lunch specials are a steal. For example: a meal of roast chicken, black beans, rice and Cuban bread goes for $3.95.

CANOEING ON THE HILLSBOROUGH RIVER

To spend a half or whole day gliding past the alligators, turtles, wading birds and other creatures who call the Hillsborough River home, contact Canoe Escape, 9335 E Fowler Avenue (☎1-800/448-2672), who have devised a series of novice-friendly routes along the tea-colored river. Cost is $24 for two people for two hours, including instruction (extra person, $8), and you should make a reservation at least 72 hours in advance.

J. B. Winberie's, 1610 W Swann Ave ☎253-6500. Munch on health-conscious fish and salad dishes at one of the sidewalk tables and watch Hyde Parkers shop.

Jeff's Desserts, 815 S Rome Ave ☎ 259-9866. Known for its cakes, but also for inexpensive, hearty lunches.

Ybor City

Bernini, 1702 Seventh Ave ☎248-0099. An Italian joint serving up wood-fired pizza and pasta in the lovely old Bank of Ybor City (note the giant insect door handles).

Cafe Cohiba, 1430 E Seventh Ave ☎248-0357. Named after a renowned Cuban cigar, this is a chic place with even chicer prices. Original fare like baked brie with guava glaze is served to patrons willing to spend upwards of $35.

Castillo's, 1823 Seventh Ave ☎248-1306. One of the few places left to sample real Cuban sandwiches and invigorating Cuban coffee on Seventh Avenue.

Cephas, 1701 E 4th Ave ☎247-9022. A funky Jamaican restaurant run from the political-poster-decorated front room of Cephas Gilbert, who arrived in Ybor via Birmingham, England. He serves jerk chicken, curry goat chicken and fish while blasting music and regaling guests with his vivid life story.

The Columbia, 2117 E Seventh Ave ☎248-4961. Serving refined Spanish and Cuban food, this Tampa institution has become a fixture on the tourist circuit. Its eleven rooms hold nearly 2000 people, who are entertained six nights a week by flamenco dancers.

El Sol de Cuba, 3101 N Armenia Ave ☎872-9880. Unusual Chinese-Cuban ("Chino-Latino") cuisine served up in huge portions at bargain-basement prices.

Joffrey's Coffee House, Seventh Ave ☎248-5282. The delectable aromas of fruit, coffee and chocolate are always thick in the air.

Latam at the Centro, 1913 Nebraska Ave ☎223-7338. The best authentic Cuban restaurant around. Select from the luscious menu that includes lobster enchilada with fried plantains, and follow it up with a delectable "flan" (creme caramel) for dessert.

La Teresita Cafeteria, 3248 West Columbus Drive ☎879-4909. Cuban sandwiches go for $2, and dishes like *patas de cerdo* (pigs' feet) and *rabo encendido* (oxtail) are served with superb Cuban coffee. Locals chat and often break into fits of singing and guitar playing at the bar.

St Frances Cafe, 1811 North 16th St ☎247-6993. The owner, a secular Franciscan woman whose aim is to feed the hungry, serves gorgeous falafel, humus, homemade cheesecake and chocolate-butter-pecan shortbread – and you pay only what you feel you can afford.

Nightlife

Tampa **at night** has always been strong on drinking and live rock music; of late, the cultural profile has been improved by regular high-quality shows at the **Tampa Bay Permorming Arts Center** (☎222-1054), a state-of-the-art performance venue. For details on upcoming arts and cultural events, phone the Artsline at ☎229-ARTS; general nightlife listings are available for free on the Nightlife line ☎854-8000 (use your touch-tone phone to access details on comedy clubs, sports bars, local bands and more). For tickets to any major event, call Ticketmaster ☎287-8844.

Drinking

Many live music venues and nightclubs have tempting **drink** reductions, though the most cost-effective way to booze, as ever, is at the **happy hours** taking place all over the city – just watch for the signs. For later drinking, head to Ybor City's *Irish Pub*, 1721 E Seventh Avenue (☎248-2099), or the Gothic-inspired *Castle*, 2004 16th St at 9th Ave (☎247-7547). If you like to yell at TV sport shows after downing a few, sample the city's biggest **sports bars**: *Sidelines Sports Emporium*, 11425 N Dale Mabry Highway (☎960-2398), *Grand Slam* at the *Sheraton Grand Hotel* (☎286-4400), and *Baker's Billiards*, 1811 N Tampa Street (☎226-6541), which has fourteen full-sized pool tables.

Live music, nightclubs and the performing arts

Tampa's most dependable **live music** club is the blues- and reggae-dominated *Skipper's Smokehouse*, 910 Skipper Road (☎971-0666). In general, though, the sound that keeps Tampa jumping into the wee hours is no-nonsense hard rock: try *Killans Lounge*, 4235 W Waters Avenue (☎884-8965) and *Kasey's Cove*, 2025 E Fowler Avenue (☎977-2683). For big-name bands and mass crowds keep an eye on Tampa's **major venues**: the USF Sun Dome, 4202 S Fowler Avenue (☎974-3002), and Tampa Stadium, 4201 Dale Mabry Highway (☎872-7977). Another large and ultra-modern space is the Tampa Bay Performing Arts Center, 1010 N MacInnes Place (☎221-1045), where **opera**, **classical music** and **ballet** programs feature top US and international names. Ticket prices for big shows range from $10 to $45. The Ritz, 1503 E Seventh Avenue, in Ybor City (☎247-PLAY), has two stages and presents a mix of fringe and bigger-budget theatrical productions as well as live music.

Among Tampa's average **nightclubs**, the *Green Iguana*, 1708 East 7th Ave (☎248-9555), and *Hammerjax*, 901 N Franklin St (☎221-JAXX), are the best bets. Cover varies from nothing to $8. For a list of all things nightlife-related, pick up a copy of the *Weekly Planet* or the Friday edition of the *Tampa Tribune* (see "Information," p.271).

Film, comedy clubs and poetry readings

For a full list of **films** playing around the city, read the Friday edition of the *Tampa Tribune*. Foreign-language, classic or cult films crop up only at the Tampa Theater, 711 Franklin Street (see "Downtown Tampa,"p 272); pick up a schedule from the building itself or phone the 24-hour information line ☎223-8981; tickets are $5. Tampa has one notable **comedy club**, *Comedy Works*, 3447 W Kennedy Boulevard (☎875-9129), where the cover charge is $4–12. If it's Thursday, forsake the gags in favor of the **poetry readings** at the "Thirsty Ear Poetry Series" at the *Trolley Stop*, 1327 E Seventh Avenue (☎237-6302), a hangout for Tampa's coffee-drinking literary crowd.

Gay and lesbian Tampa

With the constant addition of more bars, clubs and resource centers, **gay and lesbian** life in Tampa is improving all the time. Get general information by calling The Line (☎586-4297), which produces the very informative What's Gay in Tampa Bay, or contact the Gay and Lesbian Community Center at 4265 Henderson Blvd (☎287-2687). The Florida-wide Encounter magazine, 1222 S Dale Mabry Hwy, is another good resource for information on Tampa's gay life. A good bookstore to try is Tomes & Treasures, 408 S. Howard Ave (☎251-9368).

Gay bars and clubs

The Pleasure Dome, 1430 E Seventh Avenue in Ybor City (☎247-2711), is one of the most popular **nightspots**. A mixed crowd drinks and dances on and about the two dance floors and three bars. Drag shows and Hi-NRG music abound, and don't be put off by the crumbling exterior. Other pulsating gay clubs include *Rascals*, 105 West Martin Luther King Blvd (☎237-8883), a dance club particularly packed on Thursdays. Also try *Mecca*, on the corner of Ninth Avenue and 16th Street in Ybor City – a stylish, pseudo-religious setting that welcomes men and women; there's a $6 cover or $10 for all you can drink on Thursdays. *Twenty Six-O-Six*, 2606 N Armenia Avenue (☎875-6993), is a very-leather, pick-up joint. *Angel's*, 4502 South Dale Mabry Hwy (☎831-9980) is friendly and unpretentious, and has nightly strippers. Close by is *Baxters*, 4010 South Dale Mabry Hwy (☎258-8830), which has live jazz. *The Cherokee Club*, 1320 E Ninth Avenue (☎247-9966), is primarily geared towards lesbians.

Listings

Airport Five miles northwest of downtown Tampa (☎870-8700); reach it with local bus #30, see "Arrival, information and transport." St Petersburg-Clearwater International Airport is the only other airport close by (☎535-7600).

Buses Greyhound bus lines ☎229 2174 or 1-800/231-2222. **Local bus information** ☎254-4278.

Car rental Thrifty Car Rental ☎289 4006; Avis, at Tampa Airport ☎396 3500; Budget ☎1-800/527-0700.

Dentists For referral: ☎886-9040.

Directory enquiries (local only) ☎411

Doctor For referral: ☎870-4444.

Hospital Tampa General ☎251 7000 on Davis Island. Emergency room ☎251-7100.

Left luggage At the Greyhound station, 610 Polk Street; the train station, 601 Nebraska Avenue; and at the airport.

Pharmacy Eckerd Drugs, 11613 N Nebraska Avenue (☎978-0775), is open around the clock.

Police Emergencies ☎911. To report something lost or stolen: ☎223-1515.

Post Office 5201 West Spruce Street or 925 North Florida Avenue. In Ybor City, 1900 East 12th Avenue.

Sports The city's professional football team, the Tampa Bay Buccaneers, plays at Tampa Stadium, 4201 Dale Mabry Highway (box office and information ☎870-2700); cheapest tickets are $15–35. Tampa's soccer team, the Rowdies (☎877-7800), play outdoor matches at Tampa Stadium and indoors at the Bayfront Center in St Petersburg, 400 First Street; tickets are $8–50.

Taxis ABC taxi ☎872-9294; Tampa Bay Cab ☎251-5555 or United Cab Co ☎253-2424.

Thomas Cook Nearest branch is in St Petersburg: Paragon Crossing, 11300 Fourth Street North ☎577-6556.

Ticketmaster Branches around the city: ☎287-8844.

Trains Amtrak ☎221-7601 or 1-800/872-7245.

Weather information ☎645 2323.

St Petersburg

Declared the healthiest place in the US in 1885, **ST PETERSBURG** is an instantly likeable place. Situated on the eastern edge of the Pinellas peninsula, it wasted no time in attracting the recuperating and the retired to its paradise of a climate – at one point putting five thousand green benches on its streets to take the weight off elderly backsides. By the early 1980s, few people under fifty lived in the town (which, incidentally, was named by a homesick Russian), and no one was surprised when it became the setting for the 1985 film *Cocoon*, in which a group of local geriatrics magically regain the vigor of their youth. Right now, St Petersburg seems to be emulating them. The average age of its residents has been almost halved, the revamped pier is a great place for open-air socializing, and – most remarkably of all – the town has acquired a major collection of works by the controversial surrealist artist **Salvador Dalí** – reason enough to be in St Petersburg, if only as a day's break from the beaches nine miles west on the Gulf coast (see "The St Petersburg beaches," below).

Arrival, information and accommodation

The main route **by car** into St Petersburg is I-275; don't get off before the "Downtown St Petersburg" exit or you'll face a barrage of traffic lights. The Greyhound **bus** station is centrally located at 180 Ninth Street N (☎1-800/231-2222). There are no trains between Tampa and St Petersburg, just a twice-daily Amtrak bus link (☎221-7600 or 1-800/872-7245). You can reach the St Petersburg beaches with **local buses** (PSTA; ☎530-9911),

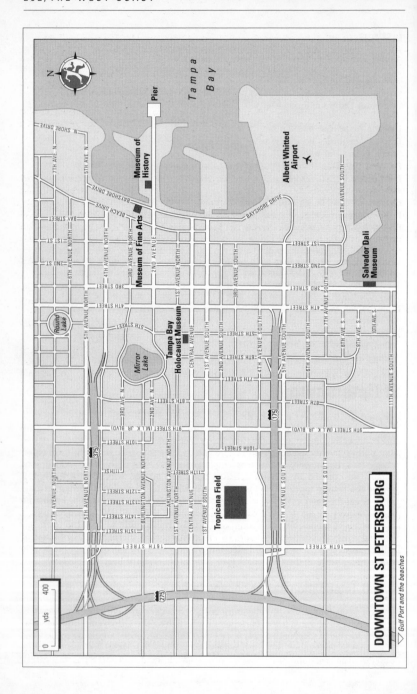

N

Tampa Bay

Pier

N. SHORE DRIVE

7TH AVE N

5TH AVE N

BAYSHORE DRIVE

Museum of
History

BAY STREET

1ST ST

BEACH DRIVE

Albert Whitted
Airport

8TH AVENUE SOUTH

6TH AVENUE NORTH

4TH AVENUE NORTH

3RD AVENUE NORTH

Museum of Fine Arts

2ND AVENUE

BAYSHORE DRIVE

2ND ST

3RD STREET

1ST AVENUE NORTH

1ST AVENUE SOUTH

3RD AVENUE SOUTH

1ST STREET

2ND STREET

3RD STREET

Salvador Dali
Museum

Round
Lake

5TH AVENUE NORTH

4TH STREET

1ST AVENUE SOUTH

1ST STREET

2ND STREET

4TH STREET

4TH AVENUE SOUTH

7TH AVE. S

8TH AVE. S

9TH AVE. S

10TH AVE. S.

Mirror
Lake

5TH STREET

Tampa Bay
Holocaust Museum

CENTRAL AVENUE

1ST AVENUE SOUTH

2ND AVENUE SOUTH

3RD STREET

4TH AVENUE SOUTH

5TH AVENUE SOUTH

6TH AVENUE SOUTH

11TH AVENUE SOUTH

3RD AVE N

2ND AVE N

8TH STREET

9TH STREET (M.L.K. JR BLVD)

7TH STREET

8TH STREET

I75

10TH STREET

2ND STREET

375

11TH STREET

12TH STREET

ARLINGTON AVENUE NORTH

BURLINGTON AVENUE NORTH

1ST AVENUE NORTH

CENTRAL AVENUE

10TH STREET

Tropicana Field

5TH AVENUE SOUTH

7TH AVENUE SOUTH

9TH STREET (M.L.K. JR BLVD)

7TH AVENUE NORTH

5TH AVENUE NORTH

11TH STREET

13TH STREET

14TH STREET

15TH STREET

16TH STREET

I275

16TH STREET

16TH STREET

0   yds   400

275

▷ *Gulf Port and the beaches*

DOWNTOWN ST PETERSBURG

though these are not always direct – see the "Buses between St Petersburg and the beaches" box on p.288. Most services arrive and depart from the Williams Park terminal, at the junction of First Avenue N and Third Street N, where an information booth gives route details.

Gather the usual tourist **information** and discount coupons from the **Chamber of Commerce**, 100 Second Avenue N (Mon–Fri 8am–5pm; ☎821-4715; fax 895-6326), and look out for the "Weekend" section of the *St Petersburg Times* for entertainment and nightlife listings. The ground floor of the pier – see below – also has a well-stocked tourist counter.

Accommodation

Sleeping in St Petersburg can be less costly than it is at the beaches. The *St Petersburg International Youth Hostel*, in the historic *McCarthy Hotel*, at 326 First Avenue N (☎822-4141), charges $15, and double rooms are also available from $32. Weekly rates are even better, and there's free coffee and a communal microwave. The *Randolph Hotel*, at 400 2nd Ave, has just been renovated and rooms are $95 a week – they're not available nightly. For details, call the *McCarthy Hotel* (above), who own this one too, just across the park.

The area is also rich in charismatic bed and breakfasts. Try *Orleans Bishop Bed & Breakfast*, 256 1st Ave North (☎894-4312; ④), a cosy building with ornate, cast-iron verandas and a choice of fine breakfasts; *Sunset Bay Inn*, 635 Bay St (☎896-6701; ④), is a charming house just north of the pier; or the beautiful *Bayboro House*, 1719 Beach Drive (☎823-4955; ⑤), south of town. Another sound option is the centrally located *Bay Gables*, 136 Fourth Ave NE, (☎822-8855; ⑤), which has a cheerful atmosphere and great breakfasts.

Motels are plentiful and can be easy on the pocket – around $39 year round. There are dozens along Fourth Street, but the closest to the center of town are *The Banyan Tree* at no. 610 N (☎822-7072; ①–②), *Landmark* at no. 1930 (☎895-1629; ①–②), and *Kentucky* at no. 4246 (☎526-7373; ①–②).

The town

However you reach downtown St Petersburg, the first thing you'll see at the western edge of town is **Tropicana Field** at 1, Stadium Drive. Formerly the Thunderdome, this huge building, shaped like a half-collapsed soufflé, opened in the spring of 1998 as home to the local major league baseball team, the **Tampa Bay Devil Rays**. Not surprisingly, locals take great pride in the team, though to justify the funds for the new stadium, St Petersburg had to neglect other causes – like homelessness. The controversy has resulted in local demonstrations decrying the city's decision to put baseball before welfare. Nonetheless, the stadium is a hit, and if you fancy reserving tickets for a game (the season is March to October) call the visitor line at ☎1-800/345-6710 or ☎825-3250.

If your preferences run more toward culture than sport, consider a self-guided **walking tour** around the town's historic buildings; pick up the *St Petersburg Preservation Program* brochure at the Chamber of Commerce (see above), and use the enclosed Central Business District map. Not all of the old buildings listed are much to look at, but be sure to walk along **Fourth Avenue**, passing the grandstands of the **Shuffleboard Club**, no. 536 N, the original home of this amazingly popular sport. And, directly across Fourth Avenue N, is the Mediterranean-revival facade of the **Coliseum Ballroom**, built in 1924 and still throbbing to big band sounds – see "Nightlife," p.286.

The pier and around

If the wide streets of downtown St Petersburg seem deserted, this is because everyone gravitates to the quarter-mile-long **pier** jutting from the end of Second Avenue N, a few minutes' walk east. Arts-and-crafts exhibitions often line the pier, and you'll find stacks of tourist information at the Chamber of Commerce desk (Mon–Sat 10am–8pm, Sun 11am–6pm; ☎821-6164), which is near the entrance to the inverted-pyramid-like building, whose five stories are packed with restaurants, shops, fast-food counters and an aquarium.

Opposite the entrance to the pier is the **Museum of History**, 335 Second Avenue NE (Mon–Sat 10am–5pm, Sun 1–5pm; $5; ☎894-1052). Modest displays recount St Petersburg's early twentieth-century heyday as a winter resort (which lasted until the wider and sandier Gulf coast beaches became accessible), and the inaugural flight of the world's first commercial airline, which took off from St Petersburg in 1914. There's documentation, too, on **Weedon Island**, five miles north of the town and once the base of a small film industry. Significant pottery finds were unearthed from Native American burial mounds here, until they were ransacked by looters in the 1960s. Now a state-protected wildlife refuge, the island is mostly used for fishing, but a multi-million dollar **Native American Cultural Center** brimming with artifacts is due to open here in 2000.

One block west of the pier, a group of Mediterranean Revival buildings houses the **Museum of Fine Arts**, at 255 Beach Drive NE, (Tues–Sat 10am–5pm, Sun 1–5pm; $6, $10 or more for special exhibitions; regular free guided tours; ☎896-2667). For years this has been one of the state's better art collections; now, however, given the giant strides made by other, newer museums and the new rival Dalí Museum (see below), it looks increasingly outmoded.

Inside, the works of seventeenth-century art are competent but not imposing, though Monet's *Houses of Parliament* and Daumier's amusing *Connoisseur of Prints* are two that shine. Also on display are pre-Columbian pieces, plus ceramics, glasswork and antiquities from Europe and Asia. More inspiring is the section on modern European art, featuring drawings by Kandinsky; and the American contemporary room displays some of Georgia O'Keeffe's flowers, as well as George Luks' *The Musician*.

A short walk south of the Museum of Fine Arts is the massive **Florida International Museum**, 100 Second Street N (daily during exhibition periods only, 9am–6pm; $13.95, students $5.95; ☎1-800/777-9882), which encompasses an entire block. The museum opened in 1995, with the first of its exhibitions, "Treasures of the Czars," containing works from the Moscow Kremlin museums. It's certainly worth investigating what's on here, as the exhibitions, which last for about a year at a time, are grand in scale and often sumptuous. *The Lost Cultures of the Incas and Aztecs* shows until mid-1999. To gain entry (and to ensure an easy flow of people around the museum), you must book ahead at the number given above.

The Dalí Museum and Great Explorations

Few places make a less likely depository for the biggest collection of works by maverick artist Salvador Dalí than St Petersburg, but this is exactly what's on show at the **Salvador Dalí Museum**, 1000 S Third Street (Mon–Sat 9.30am–5.30pm, Sun noon–5.30pm; $8; ☎822-6270), a mile and a half south of the pier. It stores more than a thousand Dalí works from the collection of a Cleveland industrialist who struck up a friendship with the artist in the Forties, bought stacks of his works and ran out of space to show them – until this purpose-built gallery opened in 1982.

Hook up with the **free tours**, which begin whenever a sufficient number of people are mustered. The tours trace a fact-filled path around the chronologically arranged paintings (some shown on rotation), from early experiments with Impressionism and Cubism to the soft watches of the seminal surrealist canvas *Persistence of Memory*, and on to works from Dalí's "Classic" period (1943), which grapple with the fundamentals of religion, science and history. Some – such as the overwhelming *Discovery of America by Christopher Columbus*, and the multiple double-images of the *Hallucinogenic Toreador* – are so big they have been hung in a specially deepened section of the gallery.

Dalí never visited the museum, though if he had it's easy to imagine him nipping across the street to explore the hands-on exhibits of **Great Explorations**, 1120 Fourth Street S, (Mon–Sat 10am–5pm, Sun noon–5pm; $5; ☎821-8885), which, like Tampa's much larger Museum of Science and Industry (see p.276), strives to make the rudiments of science accessible with inventive games. The technology of fun includes bubbles that can be climbed inside, an elaborate test-your-fitness display, and a chance to feel your way through a pitch-black tunnel.

Tampa Bay Holocaust Museum

St. Petersburg's newest museum is the emotionally wrenching **Tampa Bay Holocaust Museum** at 55 5th Street (Mon–Fri 10am–4pm, Sun noon–4pm, closed Saturday; $6; ☎392-4678), which chronicles the genocide of Europe's Jewish population with sensitive and intelligent clarity, and also sets in context the history of anti-Semitism, beginning with the first anti-Jewish legislation in Europe in 1215AD. Set in a striking white building with a black glass triangular entrance, the museum has both permanent and temporary exhibits.

The brainchild of local businessman and World War Two veteran Walter Loebenberg, who escaped Germany in 1939, the center successfully achieves its objective of projecting an understanding for future generations. Most dramatic is a massive, original boxcar – # 1130695-5 – that carried thousands of starving victims to their deaths – the only one of its kind in the States. Upstairs, the work of artists Judy Chicago and Donald Woodman explore with horrifying ease how Holocaust imagery can be superimposed on America in the 1990s. There are also some stunning sculptures on Jewish and secular themes – though for the best of these, head for the superb annual show at Temple Beth El (☎347-6136), which takes place during the last week of January.

The Sunken Gardens

If you've had your fill of culture, head for the **Sunken Gardens**, 1825 Fourth Street (daily 10am–5pm; $14), a mile north of the pier. Nearly seventy years ago, a water-filled sinkhole here was drained and planted with thousands of tropical plants and trees, which now form the shady and sweet-scented gardens. For a crash-course in exotic botany, scrutinize the texts along the pathway that descends gently through bougainvillaea, hibiscus and staghead ferns. Only the parrot shows, a new alligator

---

THE PINELLAS TRAIL

If you're looking for an intriguing alternative to the usual beach-hopping progress of tourists up or down the coast, take the **Pinellas Trail,** a 34-mile hiking/cycling track that runs between St Petersburg and Tarpon Springs. You can pick up a free, informative and highly portable guide to the trail at any of the Chambers of Commerce or visitor centers between these two destinations. The guide describes the route and picks out points of interest, providing easy-to-manage maps. Numerous exit and entry points encourage a leisurely approach, so allow yourself time to meander off the well-marked confines of the trail, and if you don't feel inclined to tackle its entirety, you can take a bus or drive to various pre-selected areas for day excursions. Despite some uglier sections through urban centers (tricky on a bike), the trail offers enjoyable scenery along its rural portions and a chance for contemplation away from tanning and water sports.

show and the depressingly small cages housing some of the resident animals dim an hour's unhurried pleasure. At the time of this writing, the gardens were being threatened with closure, so check with the Chamber of Commerce before you go (see "Arrival, information and accommodation," p. 281).

Eating

As the atmosphere in St Petersburg grows increasingly hipper, so does the choice of places to **eat.** Creative cuisines spiced with Cuban and Spanish accents are especially prevalent near the pier, and good food anywhere in town generally comes at a reasonable price.

Bensons, 244 1st Ave North (☎823-6065). It may be pricey, but *Bensons* has superb sandwiches, good salads and great coffee.

Cha Cha Coconuts, 800 2nd St, 5th floor (☎822-6655). Caribbean dishes accompanied by tall, frosty island drinks and live entertainment.

The Chattaway, 358 22nd Ave (☎823-1594). A one-time grocery store, gas station and trolley stop, *The Chattaway* is now a great American diner.

Columbia, 800 2nd St, 3rd floor (☎822-8000). High-quality Cuban and Spanish food for $10–15.

Gold Coffee Shop, 336 First Ave (☎822-4922). Inexpensive and simple, this is a good bet for an all-American breakfast.

Jeffs Desserts, 300 Central Ave (☎896-9866). Inexpensive spinach-and-feta pie, sandwiches and salads are just warm-ups before the relaxed, young crowd tackles the serious chocolates, pastries and cream creations for dessert.

La Tropicana Restaurant, 320 First Avenue NE (☎898-9902). The basic decor is made up for by the excellent Cuban sandwiches.

Mark Twain's Literary Café, 260 1st Ave N (☎821-6983). Moderately-priced salads and pasta dishes served in a stylish setting.

Ovo Cafe, 515 Central Ave (☎895-5515). A blast of pure chic, but if you keep to salads and drinks only, you can enjoy the minimalist, classic decor without smashing your budget.

Saint Petersburg Bagel Company, 249 Central Ave (☎398-5327). Good carry-out bagels and quick service.

Southern Garden Cafe, 199 N 9th St (☎896-2665). Delightfully downscale, this is a wacky place to chill out with lively music and lots of inexpensive Cajun and Creole main courses.

South Gate Restaurant, 29 3rd St North (☎823-7071). Family-style fare at a nice price. Try the blueberry waffles for breakfast or the lamb and beef gyros at dinner time.

Tamarind Tree, 537 Central Ave (☎898-2115). Vegetarian cuisine, and plenty of it for under $5.

Ted Peters' Famous Smoked Fish, 1350 Pasadena Avenue (☎381-7931). Indulge in hot smoked-fish dinners with all the trimmings. Expensive but worth it.

Nightlife

It's been said that if you fire a cannon down Central Avenue after 9pm on any night, you won't hit a soul. This may have been true in the past, but just enough bars and cafés have since opened to make it a bit more of a risk. If you're at the Pier, start the evening in *Alessi's* (☎894-1133), then go up to roof level to hear the free band playing at *Cha Cha Coconut's* (☎822-6655) – the cool ocean breeze and St Petersburg skyline make the lightweight rock sounds palatable. Elsewhere, a steady procession of **rock** bands appear at *Jannus Landing*, 19 Second Street North (☎896-1244), and *The Big Catch*, 9 NE First Street (☎821-6444). *Moe's Place*, 10056 Gandy Boulevard (☎579-1145), is a bizarre little shack stuck in the middle of an intersection. With the slogan "Anything goes at Moe's," it has long happy hours, a friendly restaurant and live music. Turn up with your own booze (there's no bar) at the *Coliseum Ballroom*, 535 Fourth Avenue

(☎892-5202), a **big band** venue for decades, which boasts one of the biggest dance floors in the US; weekend cover is $11, less during the week, and $4 for the tea dance (1-3.30pm). If you're a **jazz** fan, try *The Silver King Tavern*, 1114 Central Avenue (☎821-6470); **country-music** enthusiasts should head for *The Bull Pen Lounge*, 3510 34th Street N (☎526-3366).

There are a couple of friendly, dependable **gay bars** in town. *Golden Arrow*, 10604 Gandy Boulevard (☎577-7774), is at exit 15 off I275. So dark you have to grope your way to the bar, it's a neighborhood place that rarely sees a tourist. To the south of St Petersburg is the livelier *Sharp A's Lounge,* 4918 Gulfport Boulevard South (☎327-4897), just north of the Skyway Bridge.

Gulfport

Absent from tourist brochures and unseen by the thousands of visitors who hustle between downtown and the St Petersburg beaches, **GULFPORT** is a charming enclave of peaceful eateries, interesting art galleries and the single most charming place to stay (see below) in the area. It's also the only area of coast this side of Clearwater (see below) that hasn't been stuffed to the brim with vacation paraphernalia.

From downtown St Petersburg travel a few miles south on I-275 and get off on Gulfport Boulevard (exit 6), which serves as the central axis for the town. Much of Gulfport is an unpretentious and rather bland mix of weather-beaten houses, coin laundries and little grocery stores. Turn off Gulfport Boulevard onto Beach Boulevard, however, and you'll discover a stretch of antique shops and restaurants shaded by oak trees dripping with Spanish moss. At the end of the road is the **Gulfport Casino**, 5500 Shore Boulevard (☎893-1070), where **ballroom dancing** to a live orchestra has the locals strutting their stuff on Sundays, Tuesdays and Thursdays (country dancers have it their way on Wednesdays).

The *Sea Breeze Manor*, 5701 Shore Boulevard (☎343-4445 fax 343-4447; ⑤–⑧), a gloriously restored, seaside house with sumptuous beds, antique furnishings and home-baked breakfasts, makes a great alternative to staying in St Petersburg proper. There are lots of **eating** options round here, too. The stylish new Cuban eatery *Habana Café*, at 5402 Gulfport Boulevard (☎321-8855), serves shrimp of all sorts (Guantanamo Bay, Creole butterfly, ajillo), all for around $5. Try *Mansfields,* which faces the Casino at the end of Beach Boulevard, for grouper, clam, ribs and catfish; or *La Côte Basque*, at 3104 Beach Boulevard, which specializes in flounder and roast lamb.

The St Petersburg beaches

Framing the Gulf side of the Pinellas peninsula – a bulky thumb of land poking between Tampa Bay and the Gulf of Mexico – 35 miles of barrier islands form the **St Petersburg beaches**, a convenient name for one of Florida's busiest coastal strips. Each beach area has a name of its own, though you're likely to hear them branded "the Holiday Isles," or the "Pinellas County Suncoast." When the famed resorts of Miami Beach lost their allure during the Seventies, the St Petersburg beaches grew in popularity with Americans. More recently they've become a major destination for package-holidaying Europeans – English accents and the *Daily Mirror* are commonplace. The sands are broad and beautiful, the sea is warm and the sunsets are fabulous – but in no way is this Florida at its best. That said, staying here can be very cost-effective (especially during the summer); a few of the islands have been kept in their pre-tourism state and deserve exploration; and it's quite feasible to combine lazing on the beach with day trips to the more interesting inland areas.

BUSES BETWEEN ST PETERSBURG AND THE BEACHES

From the Williams Park terminal in St Petersburg, take PSTA bus #12, #29 or #35 to the Palms of Pasadena Hospital stop, just off Gulf Boulevard, where Bats buses (☎367-3086) cross the Corey Causeway **to St Petersburg Beach and Pass-a-Grille** (Mon–Sat 7.15am–5.50pm, Sun & holidays 7.45am–5.50pm). PSTA bus #3 from the Williams Park terminal runs to the junction of Central Avenue and Park Street, where the Treasure Island Transit (☎360-0811) continues **to Treasure Island**, plying Gulf Boulevard between 79th and 125th avenues (hourly Mon–Sat 8.15am–4.15pm except 12.15pm; $1 one way). There's a direct connection from Williams Park **to Madeira Beach and Indian Shores** with #71, and **to Clearwater** with #18 and #52, from where #80 continues **to Clearwater Beach**. PSTA bus fares cost $1.50 one way; transfers are free. For further transport details, see "Buses around Clearwater Beach," p.290.

Information

Several beach areas have **Chambers of Commerce** readily dispensing handy information: St Petersburg Beach, 6990 Gulf Boulevard (Mon–Fri 9am–5pm; ☎360-6957; fax 360-2233); Treasure Island, 152 108th Avenue (Mon–Fri 9am–5pm; ☎367-4529; fax 360-1853); Madeira Beach, 501 150th Avenue (Mon–Fri 9am–5pm; ☎391-7373; fax 391-4259). In Clearwater Beach, visit the booth at Pier 60, 1 Causeway Boulevard (Mon–Fri 9am–5pm; ☎462-6466). At any of the above, and in shops, restaurants and motels, look for **free magazines** such as the *St Petersburg Official Visitors Guide* and *See St Pete and Beaches*; if you want the latest nightlife listings, buy the Friday edition of the *St Petersburg Times*.

Accommodation

With the exception of camping, your choices are limited when seeking **somewhere to sleep** around the beaches. **Hotels** are plentiful but tend to be filled with package tourists and are pricier than motels. Two unusual but expensive options are the luxurious *Don Cesar*, 3400 Gulf Boulevard (☎360-1881; ④–⑥), described on p.289, or the fetchingly restored *Clearwater Beach Hotel*, 500 Mandalay Avenue (☎441-2425; ④–⑥).

Better values can be had at the **motels** that line mile after mile of Gulf Boulevard and the neighboring streets – typically $40–55 in winter, $10–15 less during the summer, though if you're staying long enough, many offer discounted weekly rates. Some can also offer **self catering** accommodation (basic amenities like a fridge and stove) for $5–10 above the basic room rate. Remember, too, that a room on the beach side of Gulf Boulevard costs $5–10 more than an identical room on the inland side.

Lack of competition causes prices in **Pass-a-Grille** to be around $10 higher than you might pay a few miles north, but the district makes an excellent base. Try the *Pass-a-Grille Beach Motel*, 709 Gulf Way (☎367-4726; ④), or, for a lengthy stay, opt for the cottages at *Gamble's Island's End Resort*, 1 Pass-a-Grille (☎360-5023; ⑤–⑥). For the best deals in **St Petersburg Beach**, check out *Blue Horizon*, 3145 Second Street W (☎360-3946; ④); *Carlton House*, 633 71st Avenue (☎367-4128; ④); *Florida Dolphin*, 6801 Sunset Way (☎360-7233; ④); *Gulf Tides Motel*, 600 68th Avenue (☎367-2979; ④); or the *Ritz*, 4237 Gulf Boulevard (☎360-7642; ④).

Further north on **Treasure Island**, try *Beach House*, 12100 Gulf Boulevard (☎360-1153; ④); *Green Gables*, 11160 Gulf Boulevard (☎360-0206; ③); *Jolly Roger*, 11525 Gulf Boulevard (☎360-5571; ④); or *Sunrise*, 9360 Gulf Boulevard (☎360-9210; ④). In **Madeira Beach**, choose from *Beach Plaza*, 14560 Gulf Boulevard (☎391-8996; ④); *Gulf Stream*, 13007 Gulf Boulevard (☎391-2002; ④); or *Skyline*, 13999 Gulf Boulevard (☎391-5817; ④).

In **Clearwater Beach**, you'll find west-coast Florida's only HI-affiliated youth hostel, 606 Bay Esplanada (☎443-1211), which is very welcoming; beds cost $15. Otherwise, the lowest rates are at *Bay Lawn*, 406 Hamden Drive (☎443-4529; ④); *Cyprus Motel Apts*, 609 Cyprus Avenue (☎442-3304; ④); *Gulf Beach*, 419 Coronado Drive (☎447-3236; ④), and *Olympia Motel*, 423 E Shore Drive (☎446-3384; ④).

Camping

There are no **campgrounds** along the main beach strip, though the nearest and nicest spot, at Fort de Soto Park (see p.290; ☎866-2662), is adjacent to sand and sea. The alternatives are inland: *St Petersburg KOA*, 5400 95th Street W (☎1-800/848-1094), five miles east of Madeira Beach; and *Clearwater/Tarpon Springs KOA*, 37061 Hwy-19 N (☎937-8412), six miles north of Clearwater. The latter is handier for Clearwater Beach and its surroundings – though neither site is much use without private transport (both charge $24.75 to pitch a tent).

The southern beaches

In twenty or so miles of heavily-touristed coast, just one section has the look and feel of a genuine community: the slender finger of **PASS-A-GRILLE**, at the very southern tip of the barrier island chain. One of the first beach communities on the West Coast, settled by fishermen in 1911, modern Pass-a-Grille comprises two miles of tidy houses, well-kept lawns, small shops and a cluster of bars and restaurants. On weekends, informed locals come to Pass-a-Grille's beach to enjoy one of the area's liveliest stretches of sand and the unobstructed views of the tiny islands that dot the entrance to Tampa Bay. There is no bus service to Pass-a-Grille; your best bet is to take a bus to St Petersburg Beach (see p.288) and then a cab, or rent a bike.

A mile and a half north of Pass-a-Grille, at St Petersburg Beach, you won't need a signpost to locate the **Don Cesar Hotel**, 3400 Gulf Boulevard (free guided tours Fri 11.30am; details on ☎360-1881), a grandiose pink castle with white-trimmed arched windows and vaguely Moorish turrets rising above Gulf Boulevard and filling seven beachside acres. Conceived by a Twenties property speculator, Thomas J Rowe, the *Don Cesar* opened in 1928, but its glamour was short-lived. The Depression forced Rowe to use part of the hotel as a warehouse, and later drove him to allow the uncouth New York Yankees baseball team to make it their spring training base. After decades as a military hospital and then as federal offices, the building received a $1-million face-lift during the Seventies, and regained its hotel function – a vacation base for anyone with upwards of $150 a night to spare. The present interior bears little resemblance to its original appearance, but you should stride past the marble columns and crystal chandeliers of the lobby into the lounge, where you can soak up the understated elegance from the depths of a sofa or, just outside, from the poolside – often in demand as a film set and used as a location for much of Robert Altman's satirical film *Health*.

Just beyond the *Don Cesar*, Pinellas County Bayway cuts inland and makes a good route to take to Fort de Soto Park (see below). Keeping to Gulf Boulevard brings you into the main section of **ST PETERSBURG BEACH**, uninspiring rows of hotels, motels and eating places grouped along Gulf Boulevard and continuing for several miles. A very short break in the monotony is provided by a batch of pseudo-English shops around Corey Avenue. Further north, **TREASURE ISLAND** is even less varied, culminating in an arching drawbridge that crosses over to **MADEIRA BEACH** and the wood-walled, tin-roofed shops, restaurants and bars of **John's Pass Village**, 12901 Gulf Boulevard. Linked by a creaking boardwalk, the shops and the local fishing and pleasure-cruising fleet moored close by are mildly entertaining if you're at a (very) loose end. Madeira Beach itself is another sleepy place – though if you can't make it to Pass-a-Grille (see above), the local beach justifies a weekend fling.

Four miles north of Madeira Beach, at **INDIAN SHORES**, the **Suncoast Seabird Sanctuary**, 18328 Gulf Boulevard (daily 9am–sunset; donations requested; free guided tours Tues 2pm), offers a break from bronzing. The sanctuary is a respected treatment center for sick birds: convalescing pelicans, herons, turkey vultures and many other winged creatures bearing the brunt of human incursions into their natural habitat.

Fort de Soto Park

If you have a car, you can soak up some of the history surrounding the St Petersburg beaches by heading across the Pinellas County Bayway, immediately north of the *Don Cesar*, then turning south along Route 679 to spend a day on the five islands comprising **Fort de Soto Park** (sunrise–sunset; free). The Spaniard credited with discovering Florida, Ponce de León, is thought to have anchored here in 1513, and again in 1521 when the islands' indigenous inhabitants inflicted on him what proved to be a fatal wound. Centuries later, the islands became a strategically important Union base during the Civil War, and in 1898 a fort was constructed to forestall attacks on Tampa during the Spanish-American War. The remains of the fort – which was never completed – can be explored on one of several **walking trails**, which wind through an impressively untamed, thickly vegetated landscape featuring Australian pines and oaks.

Three miles of swimmer-friendly **beaches** line the park, which in midweek possess an intoxicating air of isolation – a far cry from the busy beach strips. The best way to savour the area is by **camping**, see "Accommodation", p.288.

The northern beaches

Much of the **northern section** of **Sand Key**, the longest barrier island in the St Petersburg chain, is lined by stylish condos and time-share apartments – this is one of the wealthier portions of the coast. It ends with the pretty **Sand Key Park**, where tall palm trees frame a scintillating strip of sand. The classic beach vista is marred only by the nearby high-rises, which include the *Sheraton Sand Key Resort*; custom at this hotel was given a temporary boost by the calamitous liaison that took place here in 1987 between TV evangelist Jim Bakker and the model Jessica Hahn.

Sand Key Park occupies one bank of Clearwater Pass, across which a belt of sparkling white sands characterize **CLEARWATER BEACH**, yet another community devoted to the holiday industry. Motels fill its side streets and European package tourists are everywhere, but an endearing small-town ambience makes this a pleasant place to spend a couple of days. For information about accommodation, try the

---

BUSES AROUND CLEARWATERBEACH

Clearwater Beach is good news for travelers without cars. **Around the beach strip**, the free *Clearwater Beach Trolley* runs half-hourly during the day between Sand Key (from the *Sheraton Sand Key Resort*) and Clearwater Beach (along Gulfview Boulevard, Mandalay Avenue and Acacia Street). **To the mainland**, the cheapest option is the *Jolly Trolley*, which stops at various points along the beach and will take you to downtown Clearwater for 50¢. Alternatively, catch bus #80, which operates between Clearwater Beach and Clearwater's Park Street terminal (info: ☎530-9911). **Useful routes** from the terminal are: #80 to Honeymoon Island; #18 and #52 to St Petersburg; #66 to Tarpon Springs; and #200X (rush hours only) to Tampa. A much less frequent, mainland link is provided by two daily Amtrak buses, running from Tampa in lieu of trains; they stop in Clearwater at 657 Court Street, and at Clearwater Beach's Civic Center. The Greyhound station in Clearwater is at 2811 Gulf to Bay Boulevard (☎796-7315).

Chamber of Commerce, 100 Coronado Drive (Mon–Fri 9am–5pm; (☎447-7600; fax 443-7812). A crucial plus for non-drivers is the regular bus links between Clearwater Beach and the mainland town of **CLEARWATER** – reached by a two-mile causeway – where you'll find connections to St Petersburg and Tarpon Springs, and a Greyhound station (see box opposite). Clearwater has its own **information point** separate from that of Clearwater Beach at 1130 Cleveland St (Mon–Fri 8.30am–5pm; ☎461-0011; fax 449-2889).

Beyond its sands and two long piers, there's not much to do in Clearwater Beach: if the brine beckons, take the two-hour *Captain Memo* "pirate cruise" (leaving at 10am, 2pm, 4.30pm and, April–Sept only, 7pm; $28; ☎446-2587) from the marina just south of the causeway; or, more adventurously, make a day trip to the Caladesi or Honeymoon islands, a few miles north.

Listed on the national register of historic places and a short trip inland from the intracoastal waterway is the 1897 **Belleview Biltmore Resort Hotel**, 25 Belleview Boulevard, Clearwater (☎442-6171), a beautiful wooden construction in the grand tradition, sitting high on a bluff and consisting of 145 rooms. Originally owned by the railroad magnate Henry B. Plant, who entertained important shippers and celebrities here, the *Belleview* has been immaculately preserved and is well worth a look inside and out. To best appreciate the place, join one of the **historic tours** (daily 11am; $5, or $15 including lunch).

Honeymoon and Caladesi islands

In 1921, a hurricane ripped apart a five-mile-long island directly north of Clearwater Beach to create the aptly named Hurricane Pass and two islands, now protected state parks (both charging admission of $4 per car; $1 pedestrians and cyclists), which offer a chance to see the jungle-like terrain that covered the whole coast before the bulldozers arrived. Of the two, only **Honeymoon Island** can be reached by road; take Route 586 off Hwy-19 just north of Dunedin (or bus #80 from Clearwater). The condos that sprout from Honeymoon Island dent its natural impact, but a wild pocket at the end of the road is well worth exploring on the walking trail that runs around the edge of the entire island.

For a more authentic experience of untouched Florida make for **Caladesi Island**, just to the south. From a signposted landing stage beside Route 586 on Honeymoon Island, a **ferry** ($6 round-trip) crosses between the islands daily between 10am and 6pm (hours may vary, check at ☎734-5263). Once ashore at Caladesi's mangrove-fringed marina, boardwalks lead to a beach of unsurpassed tranquility: perfect for swimming, sunbathing and shell collecting. While here, though, summon up the strength to tackle the three-mile **nature trail**, which cuts inland through saw palmetto and slash pines to an observation tower. Be certain to bring food and drink to the island; without them, the poorly stocked snack bar at the marina is the sole source of sustenance.

Eating

It's easy to find a decent place to **eat** around the beaches. At 807 Gulf Way, the *Hurricane Restaurant* (☎360-9558; you can also pitch a tent here for $16.50) sports a well-priced menu of the freshest seafood; further north, the *Sea Horse*, 800 Pass-a-Grille (closed Tues; ☎360-1734), is strong on sandwiches; *Pep's Sea Grille*, 5895 Gulf Boulevard (☎367-3550), creates inspired combinations of pasta and seafood; *Debby's*, 7370 Gulf Boulevard (☎367-8700), serves substantial breakfasts and lunches at insubstantial prices; *46th South Beach*, 46 46th Avenue, St Pete's Beach (☎360-9414), offers nightly specials such as the "one-pound you-peel-em shrimp dinner" and Bloody Marys for just $1; and *O'Malley's Bar*, 7745 Blind Pass Way (☎360-2050), grills the thickest, juiciest burgers around. If you're feeling wealthy, and inordinately hungry, on a Sunday, show up in smart attire for the lunch-time **buffet** at the *Don Cesar*, 3400 Gulf Boulevard (☎360-1881), which starts at 10.30am and costs $28.95 per person.

In Clearwater Beach, *Alex*, 305 Coronado Drive (☎447-4560), and *Coca Cabana Motel*, 669 Mandalay Avenue (☎446-7775), are good for cheap breakfasts, as is the always-packed *IHOP (International House of Pancakes)* attached to the Quality Inn at 655 South Gulfview Blvd. *Frenchy's Shrimp and Oyster Café*, 41 Baymont Street (☎446-3607), cooks up grouper burgers and shrimp sandwiches; *Seafood & Sunsets*, 351 S Gulfview Boulevard (☎441-2548), provides inexpensive seafood, ideally consumed while watching the sun sink. Larger appetites should be sated by the **dinner buffets** for $11.95 spread out at the *Holiday Inn Sunspree,* 715 S Gulfview Boulevard (☎447-9566).

Nightlife

As you'd expect, most **nightlife** is aimed at tourists, though there are exceptions. Many hotel and restaurant bars have lengthy **happy hours** and lounges designed for watching the sunset while sipping a cocktail – look for the signs and ads in the free tourist magazines. For more cut-rate boozing, investigate *Jammins*, 470 Mandalay Avenue (☎441-2005), or the *Beach Bar*, 454 Mandalay Avenue (☎446-8866).

Bland pop bands are two-a-penny in the hotels. For better **live music**, aim for one of the following: the *Hurricane Restaurant*, 807 Gulf Way (☎360-9558), featuring some of the area's top **jazz** musicians; the *Harp and Thistle*, 650 Corey Avenue (☎360-4104), hosting Irish folksters most nights; *Bennigan's*, 4625 Gulf Boulevard (☎367-4521), for the **reggae** bands on Saturday nights. In Clearwater Beach, there's reggae of fluctuating standards at *Cha Cha Coconuts*, 1241 Gulf Boulevard (☎569-6040). **Country** music can be heard every night at *Joyland*, 11225 Hwy-19 S (☎573-1919).

North of Clearwater: Tarpon Springs

Greek sponge-divers driven out of Key West by protectionist locals during the early 1900s resettled in **TARPON SPRINGS**, ten miles north of Clearwater off Hwy-19 (use Alt 19 to arrive in the center and have a map on hand. If coming by bus, #19 and #66 run from the south). These early migrants began what has become a sizeable Greek community in a town previously the preserve of wealthy wintering northerners. Demand for sponges was unprecedented during World War II (among other attributes, sponges are excellent for mopping up blood), but later the industry was devastated by a marine blight and the development of synthetic sponges. The Greek presence in Tarpon Springs remains strong, however, and is most evident in January when 40,000 participate in the country's largest Greek Orthodox Epiphany celebration. Each year an even greater number of tourists traipse around the souvenir shops lining the old sponge docks, largely neglecting the rest of the small town which – from restored buildings to weeping icons – has much more to intrigue.

The town

Greek names appear on every shop front throughout Tarpon Springs, and although most of the shops lining the busy Alt 19 (called Pinellas Ave here) bill themselves as antique dealers, their displays gleam with newness. Don't stop here, but head towards the "docks" signs. On the right you'll see the strongest symbol in this Greek community: the resplendent Byzantine Revival **St Nicholas Orthodox Cathedral**, on the corner of Pinellas Avenue and Orange Street (daily 10am–4pm; free), partly funded by a

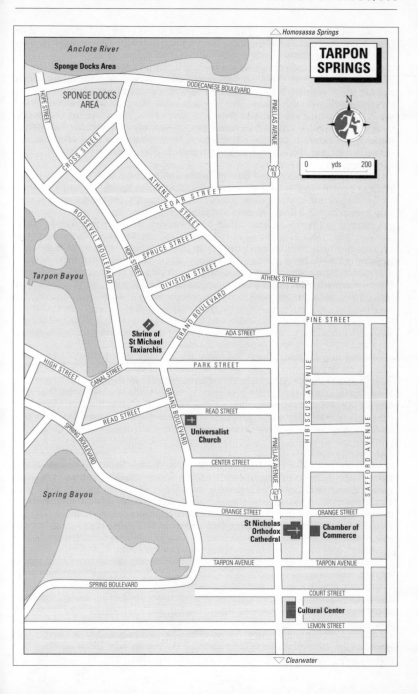

half-percent levy on local sponge sales and finished in 1943. The full significance of the cathedral's ornate interior is inevitably lost on those not of the faith, though the icons and slow-burning incense create an intensely spiritual atmosphere.

After leaving the cathedral, drop into the nearby **Tarpon Springs Cultural Center**, 101 S Pinellas Avenue (Mon–Fri 8am–5pm, Sat 10am–5pm; free except for special events), which regularly stages imaginative exhibitions about Tarpon Springs' past and present as well as art exhibitions. This Neo-classical building has served as the city hall since 1915, a period when Tarpon Avenue, a street away, was a bustling commercial strip. This is where butchers, bakers and grocers once plied their trades from stumpy masonry structures, many of which still stand. Several have now been converted into curio-filled antique shops, which make for a good half-hour's amble.

The Universalist Church and George Innes Junior Collection

Walking west along Tarpon Avenue takes you downhill to **Spring Bayou**, a crescent-shaped lake ringed by the opulent homes of Tarpon Springs' pre-sponge-era residents, who were primarily a mix of tycoons and artists.

Universalist Church, 57 Read St (Oct–May Tues–Sun, rest of the year daily 2–5pm; $1 donation; ☎937-4682), is known for its collection of whimsical paintings by the early-twentieth century landscapist George Innes Junior. To mark what would have been the 100th birthday of his late father (George Innes Senior, also a renowned artist), Innes painted a delicate rendition of the Spring Bayou, now the centerpiece of the church's collection. Innes spent much of his career mired in depression and mediocrity, but this singular work seemed to ignite a creative spark, and prompted the series of hauntingly beautiful paintings that dominate the church's walls today. The paintings all once hung in the Louvre, but after George Junior's death, his widow paid for their safe return. Helpful locals guide you through a tour of the pictures; of particular note are the murals Innes painted to stop up the church's windows, which were blown out by a hurricane in 1918.

Keeping to a religious theme and just a few minutes' walk from the Universalist Church, the simple wooden **Shrine of St Michael Taxiarchis**, at 113 Hope Street (always open), was erected by a local woman in gratitude for the unexplained recovery of her "terminally ill" son in 1939. Numerous instances of the blind regaining their sight and the crippled throwing away their walking sticks after visiting the shrine have been reported, all detailed in a free pamphlet. While here, study the icons closely for tear-tracks; several allegedly began crying – regarded as a bad omen – during 1989.

The sponge docks

Along Dodecanese Boulevard, on the banks of the Anclote River, the **sponge docks** are a disappointing conglomeration of one-time supply stores turned into gift shops touting cassettes of Greek "belly-dancing music" and, of course, sponges ($2–3 for a small specimen). A boat departs regularly throughout the day on a half-hour **sponge-diving trip** (St Nicholas Boat Line; 693 Dodecanese Bld; $5; ☎942-6425). The trip includes a cruise through the sponge docks, a talk on the history of sponge diving, and a demonstration of harvesting performed in a traditional brass-helmeted diving suit; these days only a few sponge boats still operate commercially.

You'll pay less, and learn more about the local community and sponge diving, among a group of shops at 510 Dodecanese Boulevard, whose **Spongerama Exhibition** (daily 10am–5pm; free) traces the roots and growth of Tarpon Springs' Greek settlers, and shows the primitive techniques still used in the industry. Be warned, though, that some of the exhibit models are showing signs of aging, and sponging terminology sounds much more raunchy than it really is – "nude sponging" and "thrusting hookers" are two themes explored in the displays. A shop sells alligator heads with their mouths held open, but the only real reason to hang around is the free **sponge diving shows**, which run roughly half hourly from 10am to 4.30pm just outside Spongerama.

One place to avoid is the **Noell's Ark Chimp Farm**, 4612 South Pinellas Ave (☎937-8683), which sells itself as a home for retired zoo and circus animals. It's actually a bunch of elderly apes and orangutans in sad concrete cells – making them look like inmates on death row. A better choice, particularly if you're with children and have had all you can stand of the shops at the docks, is a small **aquarium**, 850 Dodecanese Blvd (daily 10am–5pm; ☎938-5378), which has live coral sponges and daily shark feeding shows. For a really lazy and very pleasurable half day, you can take a **boat tour** to nearby **Anclote Key** with Island Wind Tours from 600 Dodecanese Blvd (☎934-0606). One hour is $5, half a day is $20.

Practicalities

Collect general **information** and a map guide to historical sites and points of interest in downtown from the **Chamber of Commerce**, 11 E Orange Street, opposite the cathedral (Mon–Fri 8.30am–5pm; ☎937-6109). On weekends, head for the **visitor center** at the *City Marina* (Tues–Sun 10.30am–4.30pm; ☎937-9165).

Tarpon Springs makes a sensible **overnight stop** if you're continuing north. A number of motels dot the junctions with Hwy-19, and the most central are *Sunbay Motel*, 57 W Tarpon Avenue (☎934-1001; ②); and the *Gulf Manor Motel*, 548 Whitcomb Boulevard (☎937-4207; ③), which is in a beautiful setting overlooking the Bayou.

For **eating**, check out *Pappas Restaurant*, 10 West Dodecanese Blvd (☎937-5101), whose large parking garage is a blessing in itself (there's aren't many places to leave your car in the center of town), and the large if rather pricey portions of classic seafood are very satisfying. For excellent syrupy pastries, or to stock up on homemade Greek breads, head to *Apollo Bakery* at the docks, and don't forget their chocolate baklava ($1.99). Cheap breakfasts can be found at *Bread and Butter Deli*, 1880 Pinellas Avenue (☎934-9003). In the Arcade at 210 Pinellas Avenue, the *Times Square Deli & Café* (☎934-4026) has sandwiches and snacks to eat in or take away. For a fuller sit-down meal, sample the inexpensive Greek dishes at *Costa's*, 510 Athens Street (☎938-6890), or *Plaka*, 769 Dodecanese Boulevard (☎934-4752).

THE BIG BEND

Popularly known as the **Big Bend** for the way it curves towards the Panhandle, Florida's **northwest coast** is an oddity: it has no beaches. Instead, thousands of mangrove islands form a fractured and almost unmappable shoreline, infrequently interrupted by snoozing villages, natural springs and – in one instance – an outstanding Native American ceremonial site. Sand-crazy visitors miss it all by barrelling towards the Tampa Bay beaches on Hwy-19, the region's only major road, leaving the Big Bend one of the few sections of coastal Florida undisturbed by mass tourism – and one of the most rewarding for inquisitive visitors who want more from the state than a tan.

Homosassa Springs and around

As you leave the Tampa Bay area on Hwy-19, the roadside clutter of filling stations and used-car lots recedes north of New Port Richey – an uninteresting place of condos and time-share properties – and gives way to a more soothing, if often monotonous, landscape of hardwood and pine forests along with uncharitable expanses of swamp. After sixty or so miles, watch out for the amusing dinosaur-shaped roof of Harold's Auto Center and, just ahead by the junction with Route 50, two theme parks. The first, **Weeki Wachee** (daily 9.30am–5.30pm in winter, longer hours in summer; $16.95, children

3–16, $12.95; ☎596-2062), offers a thoroughly kitsch underwater choreography routine performed by "mermaids" in one of the Big Bend's many natural springs, and a trip through a wildlife preserve (park grounds open 8am–sunset; free). Buying a combination ticket will allow you access to the adjacent **Buccaneer Bay water park**, where you can swim and play on the water slides to your heart's content.

Any thirst for animals and (real) sea life is better sated twenty miles north at **HOMOSASSA SPRINGS**, the first community of any size on Hwy-19. Here, at the **Homosassa Springs State Wildlife Park** (daily 9am–5.30pm; $7.95; ☎628-2311), squirrel-infested walking trails lead to a gushing spring, and an underwater observatory offers sightings of the numerous fish and manatees swimming through it. To get a feel for the town, go a couple of miles west along the oak-lined Route 490, passing the crumbling walls and rusting machinery of the **Yulee Sugar Mill**, originally owned by David Yulee. Florida's first Congressman and the financier of the 1860s Cedar Key to Fernandina Beach rail line (see "Cedar Key," p.297), Yulee extended a section south to Homosassa Springs; the closest the place has ever been to civilization. With the railway long gone, the tranquil town's old wooden houses are finding favor with young artists: drop into the Riverworks Gallery, 10844 W Yulee Drive, to see some of the better works.

Crystal River and around

Seven miles further along Hwy-19, **CRYSTAL RIVER** is among the region's larger communities – its population is a whopping four thousand. Many residents are retirees, fearful of the crime in Florida's urban areas and unable to afford the more southerly sections of the coast. You'd never guess it from the drab Hwy-19, but quite a few arrivals are also drawn here by the sedate beauty of the clear river from which the town takes its name. **Manatees** take a shine to it as well: they can be seen all year round here, but during the winter greater numbers are found in the numerous inlets of **Kings Bay**, a section of the river just west of Hwy-19. By snorkeling or scuba diving, you stand a fair chance of meeting one of these friendly, walrus-like creatures; **guided dives** are set up for around $25 an hour by dive shops in the vicinity. Check with the Chamber of Commerce (see below) for the best deals.

Crystal River's present dwellers are by no means the first to live by the waterway; it provided a source of food for Native Americans from at least 200 BC. To gain some insight on Indian culture, take State Park Road off Hwy-19 just north of the town to the **Crystal River State Archeological Site, 3400 North Museum Point** (daily 8am–sunset; cars $3.25, pedestrians and cyclists $1; ☎795-3817), where the temple, burial and shell midden mounds are still visible. Inside the **visitor center** (daily 9am–5pm), there's an enlightening assessment of finds from the 450 graves discovered here, indicating trade links with tribes far to the north. More fascinating, however, are the connections with the south: the site contains two *stele*, or ceremonial stones, much more commonly found in Mexico. The engravings – thought to be faces of sun deities – suggest that large-scale solar ceremonies were conducted here. The sense of the past and the serenity of the setting make the site a highly evocative educational experience. Don't pass it by.

Practicalities

Other than diving and visiting the archeological site, Crystal River doesn't have much to justify a long stop, though if you're traveling by Greyhound (the station is at 200 N

The area code for Homosassa Springs, Crystal River, Yankeetown and Cedar Key is ☎352.

Hwy-19; ☎795-4445), it's useful as an overnight stop. The cheapest **accommodation** is provided by *Days Inn*, just north of the town on Hwy-19 (☎795-2111; ②); more expensive but more relaxing is the *Plantation Inn*, on Route 44 (☎1-800/632-6662 or 795-4211; ⑤–⑧). If you're planning some diving and an overnight stay, check out the dive-and-accommodation packages offered by the *Best Western*, 614 NW Hwy-19 (☎795-3774; ③). The closest **campground** is *Sun Coast*, half a mile south on Hwy-19 (☎795-9049), where it costs $17 to pitch a tent. For **food**, use the basic but dependable *Crystal Paradise Restaurant*, 508 Citrus Avenue (☎563-2620). The **Chamber of Commerce**, 28 NW Hwy-19 (Mon–Thurs 8.30am–5pm, Fri 8.30am–4pm; ☎795-3149), can supply general facts on Crystal River and around.

Yankeetown and around

Ten miles north of Crystal River, Hwy-19 spans the **Florida barge canal**. Conceived in the 1820s to provide a cargo link between the Gulf and Atlantic coasts, work on the canal only started in the 1930s and – thanks largely to the efforts of conservationists – was abandoned in the 1970s with just six miles completed. The bridge offers a view of the Crystal River nuclear power station, the area's major employer and the reason why local telephone books carry instructions on how to survive a nuclear catastrophe.

Further on, taking any left turn off Hwy-19 will invariably lead to some tiny, eerily quiet community, where fishing on the local river is the only sign of life. One such place is **YANKEETOWN**, five miles west of Inglis on Route 40, reputedly named after some Yankee soldiers who moved here following the Civil War. To get the complete middle-of-nowhere effect, spend a night at the surprisingly glamorous *Izaak Walton Lodge*, at the corner of Riverside Drive and 63rd Street (☎447-2311; ③–⑤), an angler's billet since 1923 and still the fomenting place of local gossip. The lodge also has a fine **restaurant** (closed Mon), which serves beautifully cooked fish and meat in a romantic setting overlooking the moonlit river. With more time, it's worth asking at the lodge about their range of scenic boat tours, canoe trips and fishing excursions.

This area contains many parks and preserves, most with something to recommend them. Two of the largest are **Withlacoochee State Forest** (south of Route 44) and **Chassahowitzka National Wildlife Refuge** (west of Hwy-19). Further north, the protected wildlife habitats of the **Wacassassa State Preserve** cover the salt marshes and tidal creeks on the coastal side of Hwy-19 as you travel on from Yankeetown. A breeding ground for deer and turkey, and sometimes visited by black bear and Florida panthers, these swampy lands are intended to allow the state's indigenous creatures to replenish their numbers. Humans are not allowed free rein, though there are periodic ranger-guided **canoe trips** through the area; call for details ☎543-5567.

Cedar Key

Whatever you do on your way north, don't deny yourself a day or two at the splendidly isolated and charmingly scenic community of **CEDAR KEY**. To find it, turn left onto Route 24 at the hamlet of Otter Creek and drive for 24 miles until the road ends. In the 1860s, the railroad from Fernandina Beach (see "The Northeast Coast") ended its journey here, turning the community – which occupies one of several small islands – into a thriving port. When ships got bigger and moved on to deeper harbors, Cedar Key began cutting down its cypress, pine and cedar trees to fuel a pencil-producing industry. Inevitably, the trees were soon gone, and by the turn of the century Cedar Key was all but a ghost town. The few who stayed eked out a living from fishing and harvesting oysters, as many of the thousand-strong population still do.

Only during the last ten years have there been signs of a revival: many decaying, timber-framed warehouses have been turned into restaurants and shops, and more holiday homes are appearing. Given the town's remoteness, however (there's no public transport from other communities in the area), it's unlikely that Cedar Key will ever be deluged with visitors – the only remotely busy periods are during the seafood festival in October and the arts-and-crafts show during April – and the place remains a fascinating example of old Florida.

The island and around

With its rustic, ramshackle galleries, old wooden houses on Second Street, and the glittering reflections off the waters of Cedar Key's unspoilt bay, the island is perfect for exploring. The **Historical Society Museum**, on the corner of D and Second streets (Mon–Sat 11am–5pm, Sun 2–5pm; $1) reveals the fact that this, in fact, is not the original Cedar Key. The uninhabited island cloaked in foliage across the water bore the town's name until the end of the nineteenth century, when a hurricane tore every building to pieces. The devastated ruins of a bed-and-breakfast still sulk near the dock, and now serve as the adopted home of a troupe of pelicans. The birds' presence has helped make this Cedar Key's most popular postcard scene.

The museum also supplies various leaflets, including a 50¢ map of Cedar Key, and a **historic walking tour** guide for $2. For an enriching, take-home history book of the place, consider the $6.95 *A History of Cedar Key* which paints a vivid picture of local life from the Seminole Indian War to the island's boom-town era of sawmills and lumber yards. You can also pick it up at the Cedar Key Bookstore on Second Street, or peek for free at the *Island Hotel* (see below).

If you're staying for several days, take a boat trip out to the twelve islands within a five-mile radius of Cedar Key – set aside in 1929 by President Hoover as the **Cedar Keys National Wildlife Refuge**. *Island Hopper*, at the City Marina on Dock Street (☎543-5904), operates $10 cruises daily (11am, 1pm, 3pm & 5pm) on little crafts that wind their way through the refuge. The only place the *Island Hopper* stops at is the gorgeous island of **Atsena Otie Key**, the original Cedar Key. Since the 1896 hurricane, all that remains in terms of habitation is the old cemetery (the hurricane reportedly ripped bodies from the earth, flinging them into nearby trees). The *Hopper* stops for around thirty minutes, which allows just enough time to see the graveyard and collect shells at the shoreline.

Among the other outlying islands, **Seahorse Key** boasts a pretty lighthouse built in 1851. At 52 feet, it is the highest point of land on the Gulf Coast. Wanderers are welcome except between March and June when the island becomes a sanctuary for nesting birds.

For a more personalized tour of the area, consider the **kayak tours** run by Wild Florida Adventures (☎528-2741 or 1-888/247-5070), which explore much of The Big Bend as well as the lower Suwannee River. A half-day tour (4 hours) costs $45; full-day tours ($65) cover more of the **Lower Suwannee National Wildlife Refuge**, which fronts 26 miles of the Gulf of Mexico, and is an ideal place to see the nesting grounds of a multitude of birds, including white ibis, egret, blue herons, ospreys and brown pelicans.

Practicalities

The **Chamber of Commerce**, next door to the former city hall on Second Street (daily 10am–2pm; closed Thurs & Sat; ☎543-5600), has a cozy visitor's center with all the usual neighborhood information. There's an increasing amount of places offering **accommodation,** and the visitor's center has a useful color-picture guide detailing what's on offer. The character-soaked, 140-year-old *Island Hotel*, at the corner of Second and B streets (☎543-5111; ④), has sloping wooden floors, overhanging verandas and sepia murals dating from 1915. For huge, comfortable suites on the waterfront, head to the luxurious *Island Place* by the dock (☎543-5307; fax 543-9141; ⑤). For a standard room or a cottage with a kitchen, try the *Faraway Inn*, on the corner of Third and G streets (☎543-5330; ③–④); or *Pirates' Cove* half a mile from the center on Route 24 (☎543-5141; ②–④). **Tents** can be pitched at *Sunset Isle RV Park*, three miles away on Route 24 (☎543-5375; $12), or at the secluded and basic *Shell Mound Park*, five miles away on Route 326, off Route 347 (☎543-6153; $3.50–5).

Eating freshly caught seafood is a pleasurable way to while away a few hours in Cedar Key: oysters, smoked mullet and fried trout are among the local, rather expensive specialities. Three likely spots to sample the goods are close to each other along Dock Street (and too conspicuous to have street numbers): *The Captain's Table* (☎543-5441) serves sandwiches of flounder, oyster or crabcake for around $5. Lunches of fried shrimp, scallops or mullet go for $8, and dinner is bigger portions of the same for $14–20. The *Brown Pelican* has dinner specials at $9.95 and does devilled and soft claw crab, oysters, perch and flounder. Lunch is $8. Next door, the *Sunset Room Restaurant* (☎543-5428) has a big model manatee outside and boasts having the "highest view in Cedar Key" – a dubious claim considering the island is pancake-flat. For good, cheap food and a perfect place to sip your morning coffee on Dock Street, head to *Pat's Red Luck Café*. Another cheap alternative, away from the dock, is *Annie's Café*, on the corner of Hwy-24 and Sixth Street (☎543-6141), serving good, home-style breakfasts and lunches. For cheap, wholesome eats, try the plain-looking *Cook's Café* (☎543-5548) on 2nd St; the fresh fish special of grouper, mullet and shrimp is a bargain.

The island is made for walking, but renting a **bike** from the dock on Third Street (☎543-9143) is also an enjoyable option. If you're driving, the one thing you're sure to notice are the absurdly slow speed limits – sometimes down to fifteen miles per hour despite the absence of traffic. Don't be lulled into thinking the traffic police don't bother. They do.

North towards the Panhandle

Back on Hwy-19, there's a featureless ninety-mile slog to the next noticeable town, **PERRY**. The lumber industry for which the place is famous is celebrated in the **Forest Capitol State Museum**, one mile south of the town, at 204 Forest Park Drive (Thurs–Mon 9am–5pm; $1); exhibits include an 1860 furnished "cracker" home. Otherwise, nothing breaks the journey **north towards the Panhandle**, fifty miles distant. To reach Tallahassee, stick to Hwy-19 (from here also known as Hwy-27), or, for the Panhandle coast, branch west with Hwy-98. The Panhandle is fully detailed in Chapter Seven.

THE SOUTHWEST COAST

Flavoring the 150 miles of coast south of Tampa Bay are several individualistic towns with origins dating back to the early days of Florida's incorporation into the US. Residents here lead enviable lives away from big city hurly-burly, and until recently had an easy job preserving their seclusion. Nowadays, newer communities in the vicinity are beginning to expand at a colossal rate, and large-scale tourism is creeping steadily southwards. Nonetheless, the southwest coast is still one of Florida's most quietly absorbing sections: a fine balance of mainland sights and beaches beg for exploration, and the **Everglades National Park** at the region's southern-most border is the grand finale.

The area code for the section of the Florida coast south of Tampa Bay to Naples is ☎941.

South from Tampa Bay

Taking I-275 south from St Petersburg (a preferable route to the lacklustre I-75 or Hwy-41 from Tampa), you'll soar over Tampa Bay on the new **Sunshine Skyway Bridge**, high enough to allow ocean-going ships to pass beneath and for the outlines of land and sea to become blurred in the heat haze. It was built to replace the original Sunshine Skyway, which was rammed by a phosphate tanker during a storm in May 1980, causing the central span of the southbound section to collapse. With visibility down to a few feet, drivers on the bridge failed to spot the gap, and 35 people, including the occupants of a Greyhound bus, plunged 250 feet to their deaths; this tragedy was the worst of several fatal accidents on the Sunshine Skyway. The southern and northern sections have now been turned into fishing piers (access costs $3 per vehicle), while the central section, submerged in the waters at the mouth of Tampa Bay, creates an artificial reef. The new Sunshine Skyway Bridge is rife with tales of phantom hitch-hikers: they thumb rides across, only to vanish into thin air before reaching the other side. For the dollar toll, it beats anything at Walt Disney World.

Palmetto and the Gamble Plantation

Frequently dismissed in favor of Bradenton (see below), the little town of **PALMETTO**, five miles south of the Sunshine Skyway Bridge, makes for a pleasant foray, and is untouched by the commercialism of the bigger towns and beaches beyond. Perched on the northern shore of the Manatee River, Palmetto's prettiest section is Riverside Drive, an avenue of grand old mansions. The 1889 **J.A. Lamb House** at no. 1100, a stunning Queen Anne villa carved from heart pine with fairytale-like features in its twenty rooms, is probably the most impressive – though it's a private residence and not open to the public.

Next door, the *Five Oaks Inn*, at no. 1102 (☎723-1236), is a fine place to stay (rooms start at $75), and serves as a good base for visiting Bradenton and the beaches. Built in 1910, the Inn's interior has graceful arches, elegant silver and, if you stay, breakfast and cocktails served on a sweeping veranda.

If you have time to spare, veer east from Palmetto along Tenth Street (Hwy-301) to **ELLENTON**, a riverside settlement where the 1840s **Gamble Plantation**, 3708 Patten Avenue, is one of the oldest homes on Florida's west coast and the only slave-era plantation this far south. Composed of thick, tabby walls (a mixture of crushed shell and molasses) and girded on three sides by sturdy columns, the house belonged to a Confederate major, Robert Gamble, a failed Tallahassee cotton planter who ran a sugar plantation here before financial uncertainty caused by the impending Civil War forced him to leave.

In 1925, the mansion was designated the **Judah Benjamin Confederate Memorial** in remembrance of Confederate Secretary Benjamin, who took refuge here in 1865 after the fall of the Confederacy. With Union troops in hot pursuit, he hid here until friends found him a boat in which he sailed from Sarasota Bay to England, where he joined the English Bar and practiced law. A showcase of wealthy (and white) Old South living, the house – stuffed to the rafters with period fittings – can only be seen on the **guided tour** (Thurs–Mon 9.30am, 1pm and 3pm; $3; ☎723-4536), which, besides describing the building, its contents and owners, offers a very Confederate view of the Civil War.

Bradenton and around

A major producer of tomato and orange juice, **BRADENTON**, across the broad Manatee River from Palmetto, is a hard-working town whose center comprises several unlovely miles of office buildings along the river's south bank. While mainland Bradenton is far from exciting, **Anna Maria Island** (the northernmost point of a chain of barrier islands running from here to Fort Myers), and the **Bradenton beaches** eight miles west of downtown, make up for Bradenton proper's lack of charm. Travel along Route 789, known along Lido Key as Gulf of Mexico Drive, a much more picturesque (if slightly longer) route to Sarasota than the inland options.

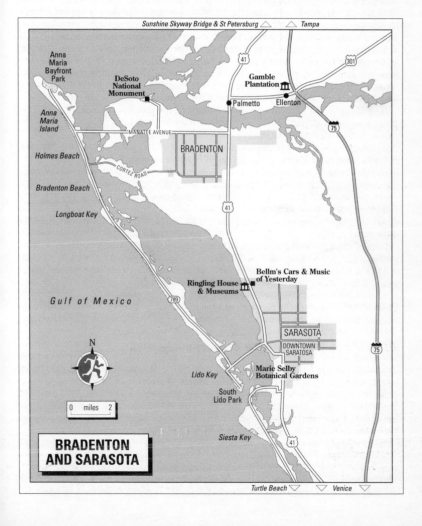

The town and around

In central Bradenton, the **South Florida History Museum and Bishop Planetarium**, 201 Tenth Street (Mon–Sat 10am–5pm, Sun noon–5pm; $7.50), takes a wide-ranging look at the region's past; its displays, dioramas and artifacts reflect every phase of habitation from Native American civilization onwards – including a re-creation of the sixteenth -century Spanish home of Hernando de Soto (see below). If you're around in April, the museum sponsors a month-long **Florida Heritage Festival**, which culminates with a ceremonial crowning of a local as the new Hernando de Soto. The most popular attraction here is not, however, the museum artifacts, but the **aquarium**, home to Snooty – at fifty years old, the oldest manatee born in captivity. The big news for Snooty in 1998 was Newton, a five-year-old orphaned male manatee who is not only a new friend, but the first creature – other than lettuce-chucking aquarium keepers – that Snooty has ever seen.

Manatees are endangered, but Florida law prohibits breeding them; resources, they say, are better spent on the care and rehabilitation of wild manatees who've suffered the brunt of ship's propellers or river poisoning. The closest relative of these great creatures is the elephant, and manatees share the same lackadaisical pace of their earth-bound cousins. Ten minutes of watching Snooty and Newton glide about is enough, but the aquarium is intelligently laid out to provide varying views of the creatures. The Snooty and Newton show is at 12.30pm, 2pm and 3.30pm, and is included in the entry price.

The **Bishop Planetarium** is open throughout the day, but try to go on Friday or Saturday nights at 9pm, when a remarkable rock-and-roll laser light show does dramatic things to the music of Pink Floyd, Jimi Hendrix, Pearl Jam and Led Zeppelin.

Further knowledge of turn-of-the-century settlers can be acquired at the **Manatee Village Historical Park**, on the corner of Manatee Avenue E and Fifteenth Street E (Mon–Fri 9am–4.30pm, Sun 1–4pm, July–Aug closed Sat & Sun; free), which has a courthouse, church, general store and "cracker" cottage dating from Florida's rough-and-ready frontier days.

Five miles **west of central Bradenton**, Manatee Avenue (the main route to the beaches) crosses 75th Street W, at the northern end of which is the **de Soto National Memorial** (daily 9am–5pm; free). This is believed to mark the spot where Spanish conquistador Hernando de Soto came ashore in 1539. The three-year de Soto expedition, hacking through Florida's dense subtropical terrain and wading through its swamps, led to the European discovery of the Mississippi River – and numerous pitched battles with Native Americans. An exhibition records the key points of de Soto's trek, and, from December to April, park rangers dressed as sixteenth-century Spaniards add informative pointers to the lifestyles of Florida's first adventurers. For more about the de Soto expedition, see "History" in Contexts.

Anna Maria Island and the Bradenton beaches

In contrast to central Bradenton's grayness, the ramshackle beach cottages, seaside snack stands and beachside bars on **Anna Maria Island**, onto which Manatee Avenue runs, are bright and convivial. From the end of Manatee Avenue, turn left along Gulf Drive for **Coquina Beach**, where the swimming is excellent and the weekend social life youthful and merry; with a quieter time in mind, take a right turn along Marina Drive for the calm **Anna Maria Bayfront Park**.

South of Anna Maria Island, **Longboat Key** is all about privacy: its pricey homes are shielded by rows of tall Australian pines, and while all the sands along this nineteen-mile-long island are public property, access points are few and far between, making the beach almost impossible to reach for non-residents. Not until you reach Lido Key, further south, are there more useable beaches – described on p.307 under "The Sarasota Beaches."

Practicalities

In central Bradenton, the **Chamber of Commerce**, 222 Tenth Street (Mon–Fri 9am–5pm; ☎748-3411 fax 745-1877), has the usual tourist information; better for beach facts is the **Anna Maria Island Chamber of Commerce**, 503 Manatee Avenue (Mon–Fri 9am–5pm; ☎778-1541).

Accommodation on a budget is not easy within walking distance of the beach: the best bet of the motels here is the *Silver Surf Motel*, 1301 Gulf Drive (☎1-800/441-7873 or 778-6626; ⑤), which has a heated pool, a private beach and big rooms that can accommodate three or four people; the neighboring *Queensgate*, 1101 Gulf Drive (☎778-7153; ⑤–⑥), is also a good option. More costly but cozier – and you'll need to book ahead – is the *Duncan House* bed and breakfast, 1703 Gulf Drive (☎778-6858; ⑤–⑥). The house, built in the 1880s, began its life in downtown Bradenton and was moved by barge in 1946 up the Manattee River. If beach prices are too high or there's no space (as often occurs between December and April), use one of the bland motels on the mainland-approach roads, such as *Baxter's*, 3225 14th Street (☎746-6448; ③), or *Hoosier Manor*, 1405 14th Street (☎748-7935; ③).

You should do your **eating** on Anna Maria Island (see "Beaches," above). One of the most popular local place for breakfast is *Gulf Drive Café*, 900 Gulf Drive. The average age of the clientele is pretty high – lots of poofed blue hair – but the Belgian waffles are divine. Top choices for fresh seafood lunches or dinners are *Rotten Ralph's*, 902 S Bay Boulevard (☎778-3953), *Beach House*, 200 Gulf Drive N (☎779-2222) and *The Sandbar*, 100 Spring Avenue (☎778-0444); the latter has decks on the beach. On Holmes Beach, try *Paradise Bagels*, 3210 East Bay Drive (☎779-1212), which boasts nineteen varieties of bagels, ten blends of cream cheese and great coffee.

Sarasota and around

Rising on a gentle hillside beside the blue waters of Sarasota Bay, bright, intriguing **SARA-SOTA** is both affluent and welcoming, a combination lacking in other west coast communities such as Naples (see below). Sarasota is also one of the state's leading cultural centers: home to numerous writers and artists, and the base of several respected performing-arts companies. This is a place where opera-and theater-goers in formal attire are happy to join hip students in coffee bars, and the tone of the town is intelligently upbeat.

Despite periodic conservative flappings (such as recent attempts to outlaw skimpy swimwear at the local beaches), the community is far less stuffy than its wealth might suggest. During the past couple of years, downtown Sarasota has seen a real injection of life – lots of new cafés, bars and eateries complement the excellent grouping of book-shops for which the place is known. A few miles north up the Tamiami Trail (Hwy 41), the **Ringling estate** – home of the late art-loving millionaire from whom modern Sarasota takes its cue – is a fine diversion. And the barrier-island **beaches**, a couple of miles away across the bay, are the lounger's paradise.

Arrival, transport and information

Whether arriving from north or south, **Hwy-41** (always referred to here as the Tamiami Trail) zips through Sarasota, passing the main causeway to the islands just west of downtown and skirting the Ringling estate in the north. I-75 runs parallel to the Tamiami, and while it's not as enticing, it's a lot quicker. Downtown Sarasota is an easy

The area code for the Sarasota area is ☎941

grid of streets mostly named after fruits, though Main Street contains most of the eating and nightlife venues.

Local **bus** routes (SCAT; information ☎316-1234, 4.30am–8.30pm, except Sun) radiate out from the downtown Sarasota terminal on Lemon Avenue, between First and Second streets. **Useful routes** are #2 or #10 to the Ringling estate; #4 to Lido Key; #18 to Longboat Key; and #11 to Siesta Key. The Amtrak bus from Tampa also pulls into the Lemon Avenue station, but all passengers arriving on Greyhound buses are dropped at 575 N Washington Boulevard (☎955-5735). If you're around for a week or more, a good way to explore the town and the islands is by **renting a bike** for around $20 per day from Sarasota Bicycle Center, 4048 Bee Ridge Road (☎377-4505); the Village Bike Shop, on Siesta Key at 5101 Ocean Boulevard (☎346-2111); or the Backyard Bike Shop, on Longboat Key at 5610 Gulf of Mexico Drive (☎383-5184). To see the islands cheaply and with the minimum of exertion, take the trolley for $2 (you can hop on and off as many times as you like), which runs three times a day (9.30am, 12.30pm & 3.30pm), starting at the *Best Western Siesta Beach Resort*. It takes you to all the islands, making plenty of stops along the way. (For schedule info call ☎346-3115.)

For **information** in Sarasota, call at the **Visitors and Convention Bureau**, 655 N Tamiami Trail (Mon–Sat 9am–5pm; ☎1-800/522-9799), or the **Chamber of Commerce**, 1819 Main Street (Mon–Fri 9am–5pm; ☎955-8187). On **Siesta Key**, you'll find a Chamber of Commerce at 5100 Ocean Boulevard (Mon–Fri 9am–5pm; ☎349-3800). Besides the customary discount coupons and leaflets, look for the free magazines, *Sarasota Visitors Guide* and *See*, and the Friday edition of the *Sarasota Herald Tribune*, whose pull-out section, "Ticket," has entertainment listings.

Accommodation

On the **mainland**, motels run the length of Hwy-41 between the Ringling estate and downtown Sarasota, typically charging $35–50. *Cadillac Motel*, at no. 4021 (☎355-7108; ③), is friendly, very clean and family run. *Flamingo Colony Motel*, at no. 4703 (☎355-5135; ③), has a pool and guest laundry. *Sunset Terrace*, at no. 4644 (☎355-8489; ③), is slightly more upscale and has a pool, family apartments, complimentary breakfast and shuttle service from the airport. The *Best Western Golden Host Resort*, no. 4675 (☎1-800/722-4895 or 355-5141; ④–⑤), is a good bet for reasonable off-season rates.

At the **beaches**, prices are higher. The best rates on Lido Key are the *Lido Vacation Rentals*, 528 S Polk Drive (☎388-1004 or 1-800/890-7991; ④), which has friendly service, access to an Olympic-sized pool and a fine location. Otherwise, be prepared to fork out a substantial sum for a night at the *Harley Sandcastle*, 1540 Benjamin Franklin Drive (☎388-2181; ⑤), or the *Half Moon Beach Club*, 2050 Benjamin Franklin Drive (☎388-3694; ⑥). In general, Siesta Key is even more expensive, with many places renting out fully equipped apartments for a week in preference to motel rooms by the night. Two on Midnight Pass Road that may be worth a try are *Surfrider Beach Apartments*, no. 6400 (☎349-2121; ⑤), and *Gulf Sun Apartments & Motel* no. 6722 (☎349-2442; ⑤). The only budget alternative is the *Gulf Beach Travel Trailer Park*, 8862 Midnight Pass Road (☎349-3839), though it consists almost exclusively of RV sites; if you can get a **tent** site, be prepared to pay upwards of $20.

Downtown Sarasota

Visitors who ogle the Ringling estate and nearby beaches without making a foray into downtown Sarasota, will miss one of the most enticing towns on the coast. Until recently, the area was dying on its feet, but with restored architectural oddities, excellent theater and some of the best art galleries in Florida, a very positive aura now permeates the town.

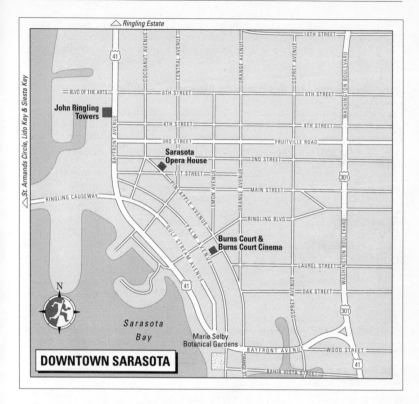

Anyone bemoaning the lack of decent **bookshops** in Florida should take heart: here you'll find the biggest and most varied selection in the state. The best-filled shelves are at the Main Bookshop, 1962 Main St, which abounds in used books, comics and records. The old easy chairs foster a relaxed atmosphere reminiscent of Key West. Other good bets are Charlie's News, 341 Main St, and Parkers, at no. 1488.

A block away from Main Street, take a moment to look at the **Sarasota Opera House**, at the corner of 1st Street and Pineapple Ave. Opened in 1926, this Mediterranean Revival style building hosted the Ziegfeld Follies and a young Elvis Presley (see "Nightlife"). Just a few blocks north, the decaying husk of the old **John Ringling Towers,** once a splendid hotel, awaits demolition. Rumor has it that a Ritz Carlton will be raised in its place. Just a few steps farther is the **Sarasota Visual Arts Center and Shapiro Sculpture Garden**, 707 N Tamiami Trail (Mon–Fri 10am–4pm, Sat & Sun 1–4pm; free; ☎941/365-2032), which has some splendid temporary exhibitions and quirky permanent sculptures.

For an excellent example of perfectly preserved Spanish-style architecture, and a delightful foray into an untouristed section of downtown, head south of Main Street a few blocks past the pretty Methodist Church to **Burns Court**, a hidden enclave of 1920s bungalows, each with Moorish details. Almost all the Spanish/Mediterranean buildings in town were built around 1926, just before the Depression, when the style was most in vogue. At the end of this lane stands the shocking-pink **Burns Court Cinema**, a splendid alternative picture house run by Sarasota Film Society. For tickets call ☎955-3456 or 955-9338; the box office is open noon–5pm and tickets sell for $5.50.

Further south, follow the curve of the bay for half a mile to the **Marie Selby Botanical Gardens,** 811 S Palm Avenue (daily 10am–5pm; $8), whose walled perimeter hides a small but startling gathering of growths inside. Time spent meandering along the fragrant pathways can't fail to improve your mood. There's always something in bloom.

Northern Sarasota: the Ringling Museum Complex

As you reach Sarasota from the north, don't fail to tour the house and art collections of **John Ringling,** a multi-millionaire who not only poured money into the fledgling community beginning in the 1910s, but also gave it a taste for fine arts that it's never lost. One of the owners of the fantastically successful Ringling Brothers Circus, which began touring the US during the 1890s, Ringling – an imposing figure over six feet tall and weighing nearly 280 pounds – ploughed the circus's profits into railways, oil and land. By the Twenties he had acquired a fortune estimated at $200 million.

Charmed by Sarasota and recognizing its investment potential, Ringling built the first causeway to the barrier islands and made the town his circus's winter base, saving a fortune in northern heating bills and generating tremendous publicity for the town in doing so. His greatest gift to Sarasota, however, was a Venetian Gothic mansion – a combination of European elegance and American-millionaire extravagance – and an incredible collection of European Baroque paintings, displayed in a purpose-built museum beside the house. Grief-stricken following the death of his wife in 1927, and losing much of his wealth through the Wall Street crash two years later, Ringling died in 1936, reputedly with just $300 to his name. The **Ringling Museum Complex** is two miles north of downtown Sarasota beside Hwy-41 at 5401 Bay Shore Road (daily 10am–5.30pm; $9, children under 12 free, free admission to the art museum on Sat). The buildings are linked by pathways over a 66-acre site, though all are easy to walk between and clearly signposted. To get here from downtown Sarasota, use **buses** #2 or #10.

The Ringling House: Ca′ d′Zan

Begin your exploration of the Ringling estate by walking through the gardens to the former Ringling residence, **Ca′ d′Zan** ("House of John," in Venetian dialect), an elaborate if ostentatious piece of work serenely situated beside the bay. It was the inappropriate setting for the 1998 film adaptation of *Great Expectations.* The multitude of attractive trees was a gift from Thomas Edison, who nurtured the young seeds at his Fort Myers Home. The most dramatic, a Chinese banyan, shades the circular *Banyan Cafe* (☎359-3183), where you can grab lunch for around $8.

Completed in 1925, reputedly at a cost of $1.5 million, the house was planned around an airy, two-story living room marked on one side by a fireplace of carved Italian marble and on the other by a $50,000 organ belonging to Ringling's musically-inclined wife. The other rooms are similarly filled with expensive items, but unlike their mansion-erecting contemporaries elsewhere in Florida, John and Mable Ringling knew the value of restraint: their spending power never exceeded their sense of style, and the house remains a triumph of taste and proportion – and an exceptionally pleasant place to walk around. Take the free **guided tour** departing regularly from the entrance, then roam on your own.

The Art Museum

The mix of inspiration and caution that underpinned Ringling's business deals also influenced his art purchases. On trips to Europe to scout for new circus talent, Ringling became obsessed with **Baroque art** – then wildly unfashionable – and over five years, largely led by his own sensibilities, he acquired more than five hundred Old Masters; a collection now regarded as one of the finest of its kind in the US. To display the paintings, many of them as epic in size as they were in content, Ringling selected a patch of

Ca' d'Zan's grounds and erected a spacious **museum** around a mock fifteenth-century Italian palazzo, decorated by his stockpile of high-quality replica Greek and Roman statuary. As with Ca' d'Zan, the very concept initially seems absurdly pretentious but, like the house, the idea works: the architecture matching the art with great aplomb. Here also, you should take the free **guided tour** departing regularly from the entrance, before wandering around at your leisure.

Five enormous paintings by **Rubens**, commissioned in 1625 by a Hapsburg archduchess, and the painter's subsequent *Portrait of Archduke Ferdinand*, are the undisputed highlights of the collection, though they shouldn't detract from the excellent canvases in succeeding rooms: a wealth of talent from Europe's leading schools of the mid-sixteenth to mid-eighteenth centuries. Watch out, in particular, for the finely composed and detailed *The Rest on the Flight to Egypt*, by Paolo Veronese, and the entertaining *Building of a Palace* from Piero de Cosimo. In contrast, recently acquired contemporary works include sculpture from Joel Shapiro and John Chamberlain, and paintings by Frank Stella and Philip Pearlstein.

The Circus Gallery

The Ringling fortune had its origins in the big top, and the **Circus Gallery** is worth a brief visit. The cuttings and memorabilia of famous dwarfs and freak-show performers are more intriguing than the standard-issue tiger cages and costumes. Among the most diverting tidbits is the account of Tom Thumb's wedding in New York, which actually took the Civil War off the front pages. Thumb (his real name was Charles Stratton) stopped growing at 35 inches. His wife, Lavinia, was three inches shorter. There's also a display on Chang and Eng, the mid-nineteenth century Siamese twins who came here from Siam in 1829 and during their 62 years joined at the ribs, married sisters in 1843, had 22 children and died within three hours of each other in 1874.

The Asolo Theater And Asolo Center For Performing Arts

Ringling brought an eighteenth-century, Italian-court playhouse from the castle of Asolo to the grounds of his estate. Its interior is fascinating, though only open for special events and conferences; inquire at the reception (☎355-7115) for a schedule.

The **Asolo Center for Performing Arts**, not to be confused with the Asolo Theater, is right next door and has a strong program of theatrical events throughout the year. The main stage was brought over from Dunfermline, Scotland, where it was built in 1903. While not as enticing as the off-limits Asolo Theater, the center has an elegant, gilded interior. Free tours (Wed–Sat 10am, 10.45 and 11.30am) go back stage. See "Nightlife" for performance details.

Bellm's Cars & Music of Yesterday

Only vintage car enthusiasts and devotees of old music boxes will derive any pleasure from **Bellm's Cars and Music of Yesterday**, across Hwy-41 from the entrance to the Ringling Estate (daily 9.30am–5.30pm; $8). Nearly 200 aged vehicles – a few Rolls-Royces among them – are gathered together with hurdy-gurdies, cylinder discs and an enormous Belgian pipe organ, combining to make an awful racket.

The Sarasota beaches

Increasingly the stamping ground of European package tourists spilling south from the St Petersburg beaches, the powdery white sands of the **Sarasota beaches** – fringing two barrier islands, which continue the chain beginning off Bradenton – haven't been spared the attentions of property developers either, losing much of their scenic appeal to towering condos. For all that, the Sarasota beaches are worth a day of anybody's time

– either to lie back and soak up the rays, or to seek out the few remaining isolated stretches. Both islands, **Lido Key** and **Siesta Key**, are accessible by car or bus from the mainland, though there's no link directly between them.

Lido Key

Financed by and named after Sarasota's circus-owning sugar daddy, the Ringling Causeway – take buses #4 or #18 – crosses the yacht-filled Sarasota Bay from the foot of Main Street to **Lido Key** and flows into **St Armands Circle**, a glorified roundabout ringed by upmarket shops and restaurants, and dotted with some of John Ringling's replica classical statuary – muscle-bound torsos surrealistically emerging from behind palm fronds. Other than staging entertaining arts-and-crafts events on weekends and offering a safe place to stroll after dark, St Armands Circle has little to occupy those without a limitless budget. After a look around – head to the north end of Lido Key beach, which is relatively condo-free, and then trek south along Benjamin Franklin Drive. This route passes more accessible beaches, fine in themselves though overrun by the holiday-making set. After two miles, you'll find the more attractive **South Lido Park** (daily 8am–sunset; free): a belt of dazzlingly bright sand beyond a large grassy park, with walking trails shaded by Australian pines. Busy with barbecues and tanned bodies on Saturday and Sunday, the park is a delightfully subdued spot for weekday rambles.

Away from the beaches, the only place of consequence on Lido Key is a mile north of St Armands Circle at City Island Park, just off John Ringling Parkway: the **Mote Marine Aquarium**, 1600 Ken Thompson Parkway (daily 10am–5pm; $7), the public offshoot of a marine laboratory studying the ecological problems threatening Florida's sea life. Some of the work – such as research into the mysterious "red tide," an unexplained algae that appears every few years, devastating sea life and causing sickness among people along the coast – is outlined, and there's a great assortment of live creatures, from seahorses to loggerhead turtles. The centerpiece of the 22 aquariums is a massive outdoor shark tank, where you can view several species up close through underwater windows.

Adjacent to the Mote Aquarium, you'll find **Pelican Man's Bird Sanctuary**, 1708 Ken Thompson Parkway (daily 10am–5pm; free, though donations are welcomed; ☎388-4444). Injured and sick migratory birds from all over the world, together with native Floridian species, are cared for here by over 200 volunteers. You'll come away furnished with facts about the various ways our feathered friends come to grief (usually at the hands of man) and how they are nursed back to health before being re-released into the wild.

Siesta Key

Far funkier and more laid-back than Lido or Longboat Key, **Siesta Key** (arrive via Siesta Drive off Hwy 41 about five miles south of downtown Sarasota) attracts a younger crowd and has less-manicured surroundings than other spots on the coast. The affluent, however, have not ignored Siesta Key – this is, after all, where Paul Simon has a condo. Beach-lovers should hit **Siesta Key Beach**, beside Ocean Beach Boulevard, a wide white strand that can – and often does – accommodate thousands of partying sun-worshippers. To escape the crowds, continue south past Crescent Beach, which meets a second road (Stickney Point Road) from the mainland, and follow Midnight Pass Road for six miles to **Turtle Beach**, a small body of sand that has the islands' only campground; see p.304.

Eating

Due to the increase in evening entertainment venues and the resurgence of a youthful downtown scene, Sarasota's restaurant and café culture has taken off. Exquisite restaurants with prices to match are popping up everywhere, but every taste and

LORETTA CHILCOAT

UNIVERSAL STUDIOS FLORIDA

Burt Reynolds Ranch, Jupiter

Arnie strikes back, Universal Studios Escape

MGM Studios, Orlando

Great Blue Herons, Sanibel Island

Fort Lauderdale beach

Southern Black Racer Coluber Constrictor

Air plant, the Everglades

Alligator, the Everglades

Corkscrew Swamp Sanctuary

Spring Break mania, Daytona Beach

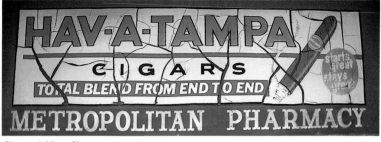
A. ENOCK, TRAVEL INK

Cigar ad, Ybor City

C. BRADLEY, AXIOM

Swamplands, Central Florida

budget is easily catered to. Keep in mind that the same food at posh St Armands Circle can cost twice as much as on Main Street, where most restaurant options are located.

Downtown

Bein & Joffrey's, 1345 and 1995 Main St (☎953-5282 and ☎906-9500 respectively). A coffee house, deli and bagel bakery with superb breakfasts, muffins and cakes.

The Bijou Cafe, 1287 First St ☎366-8111. Expensive lunch and dinner menus of sea food, fowl and meat served in surprisingly basic surroundings.

Broadway Pizza, 1044 Tamiami Trail North (☎953-4343). For over fifty years this has been a local institution for cheap, excellent pizza.

Burns Lane Café, 516 Burns Lane (☎955-1653). This recent arrival does a good job of luring visitors in with gourmet dishes of lamb, salmon, and crab cakes.

Café Kaldi, 1568 Main Street (☎366-2326). Terrific coffee house turned cyber café, where students sip an incredible range of coffees and wince as would-be musicians practise their art.

First Watch, 1395 Main Street (☎954-1395). There isn't much character to the joint, but the excellent American-style breakfast and lunch offerings assure there's always a line.

Il Panificio, 1703 Main St ☎366-5570. Italian deli and coffee shop with superb (and huge) home-made pizzas, sandwiches and strong espressos.

Main Bar Sandwich Shop, 1944 Main Street; no phone. Great sandwiches since 1958.

Nature's Way Café, 1572 Main Street (☎954-3131). A good vegetarian option known for its sandwiches, fresh-fruit salads and frozen yogurt.

Patrick's, 1400 Main Street (☎952-1170). A sports bar/restaurant serving steaks and chops ($12–17) and burgers ($6).

Tropical Thai Restaurant, 1420 Main Street (☎364-5775). Reasonably-priced lunches with especially good soups, shrimp dishes and local and imported beers.

Yoder's, 3434 Bahia Vista Street ☎955-7771. There are thriving Mennoanite and Amish communities in the Sarasota area and this restaurant has won awards for the homemade goodness of its old-fashion Amish cuisine. A local favorite. Two other Amish restaurants worth trying are: *Sugar & Spice*, 1850 Tamiami Trail ☎953-3340 and *Der Dutchman*, 3713 Bahia Vista Street ☎955-8007.

Yoshino, 417 Burns Court (☎366-8544). Good Japanese food served in what looks like a private home.

At the beaches

The Broken Egg, 210 Avenida Madera ☎346-2750. A favorite with locals looking for a filling, all-American breakfast or lunch.

Café L'Europe, 431 St Armands Circle ☎388-4415. Expensive, gourmet food and fine wines.

Cha Coconuts, 717 St Armands Circle ☎388-3300. A young crowd spills out of the very-busy, very-loud bar. The menu claims "Caribbean cuisine," but it's really just fish sandwiches and burgers.

The Old Salty Dog, 5023 Ocean Boulevard ☎349-0158. English-style fish-and-chips alongside regular seafood and hot dogs.

Turtles, 8875 Midnight Pass Road ☎346-2207. Outstanding seafood dinners for under $15.

Surfrider, 6400 Midnight Pass Road ☎346-1199. Another excellent option for reasonably-priced seafood.

Theater and Nightlife

Some of the state's top small theatrical groups are based in Sarasota: **drama** devotees should scan local newspapers for play listings or phone the theaters directly. For **opera** buffs, the Sarasota Opera House has been staging grand performances since the 1920s, and, though not known for his arias, Elvis Presley also performed here in his younger days. For information and tickets call ☎366-8450; the box office is open daily, 10am–4pm. The major repertory, the Asolo Theater Company, based at the **Asolo Center for the Performing Arts**, 5555 N Tamiami Trail (☎351-8000), has a strong program throughout the year (tickets $30, gallery seats $10, students $5). The other companies (tickets $10–30), however, tend to stick to a winter season: Theater Works, 1247 First Street (☎952-9170), in a big, blue building, has excellent comedy. In addition to its innovative shows, it is also the host of LOOSE (Light Opera of Sarasota), the town's newest cultural organization; visit the box office Mon–Fri 10am–3pm, and one hour before performances. Also check out the Florida Studio Theater, 1241 N Palm Avenue (daily 9am–9pm, Mon till 6pm; tickets $15–25; ☎366-9000); the Golden Apple Dinner Theater, 25 N Pineapple Avenue (☎366-5454; $29); and Players of Sarasota, 838 N Tamiami Trail (☎365-2494; $15.50).

Outside of theater, Sarasota's **nightlife** is finally enjoying an upsurge after enduring a long reputation for limpness. On weekend evenings, Main Street attracts both student types looking to chill and a more rough-and-ready, Dukes-of-Hazard crowd. Local bands jam outside the *Main Street Depot*, at the corner of Main St and Lemon Ave, while an inebriated hoard listens from plastic tables. The *Gator Club,* at 1490 Main St, is trying to challenge the *Main Street Depot* for loudest-bar honors. Set in a big, flaking warehouse, it has blues and reggae on Mondays, Motown on Sundays and house bands on Saturday nights (music generally starts at 9.30pm). If you follow their absurd dress code (no hats, no uncollared shirts and no bags – but jeans are fine), you can head upstairs to the best Scotch bar in town. For an older crowd hip to mellow jazz, try *Barbecue Heavan*, at 1435 Main Street (☎365-2555), which has blues and jazz every Thursday and Saturday night, 8pm till way late. On **Siesta Key**, the *Old Salty Dog,* 5023 Ocean Boulevard (☎349-0158), is a popular joint, as is *The Beach Club* (across the street), a local watering hole with nightly live music – mostly techno dance stuff for the 25–40 set. *Daiquiri Deck*, 5350 Ocean Blvd (☎349-8697), specializes in frozen daiquiris and is hugely popular as an after-beach venue. Elsewhere, there's more **live music** at: *The Brass Parrot*, 555 Palm Avenue (☎316-0338), mostly jazz and blues; and *The Lost Kangaroo Pub*, 427 12th Street W (☎747-8114), where "The Yellow Dog Jazz Band" appears regularly. For reggae, look in at *Cha Cha Coconuts*, 417 St Armands Circle (☎388-3300).

All mainstream **films** are shown at the striking (and popular) Hollywood 20 cinema, a remarkable structure done in pure Art Deco. Inside, a neon-lilac glow bathes the popcorn-devouring crowds.

Gay nightlife

The gay night scene revolves between a small range of friendly, lively bars. *Rowdy's,* 1330 Dr Martin Luther King Way (☎953-5945), has a chatty, mostly-local crowd, and getting there at 4pm on a Sunday means a free barbecue and great atmosphere. *Roosters,* 1256 Old Stickney Point Road (☎346-3000) is the liveliest of the bunch and is conveniently on route to the islands. *Bumpers*, on Ringling Boulevard, is a gay dance club on Thursday and Saturdays, and hosts a youngish crowd. Gay-interest **films** are most likely to appear at the Burns Court Cinema.

Inland from Sarasota: Myakka River State Park

Should your knowledge of Florida be limited to beaches and theme parks, broaden your horizons fourteen miles inland from Sarasota on Route 72. Here you'll find a great tract of rural Florida barely touched by humans, whose marshes, pinewoods and prairies form **Myakka River State Park,** 3715 Jaffa Drive (daily 8am–sunset; cars $3.25, pedestrians and cyclists $1, ☎365-0100). On arrival, drop into the **interpretive center** for insight into this fragile (and threatened) ecosystem. Begin exploring it by walking along the numerous paths or canoeing on the calm expanse of the Upper Myakka Lake. **Airboat rides** (four times a day; $7) seem at odds with the tranquil ethos of the place, and a little **trolley** offers rather quieter tours (1pm and 2.30pm; $7). If you're equipped for **hiking**, following the forty miles of trails through the park's

wilderness preserve is a better way to get close to the cotton-tailed rabbits, deer, turkey, bobcats and alligators who live in the park; before commencing, register at the entrance office and get maps and weather conditions – be ready for wet conditions during the summer storms. Other than the five basic campgrounds on the hiking trails ($12–15), park **accommodation** (details and reservations: ☎361-6511) comprises two well-equipped **campgrounds** and a few four-berth **log cabins** ($55 a night).

South from Sarasota: Venice and around

In the Fifties, the Ringling Circus moved its winter base twenty miles south from Sarasota to **VENICE**, a small town modelled on its European namesake: a place of broad avenues and Italianate architecture surrounded by water. However, it's the **beaches** that make the town. Used by a mix of sunbathers, water-sports enthusiasts and stooping beachcombers hunting for the fossilized sharks teeth commonly washed ashore, the best strands are along the Venice Inlet, a mile west of Hwy-41.

If you have your own transport, you can also explore the underexploited coastline around **Englewood beaches**, south of Venice on Route 775, pockmarked by small islands and creeks. Sooner or later, though, you'll have to rejoin Hwy-41, which, out of Venice, turns inland to chart an unremarkable fifty-mile course through retirement communities such as Punta Gorda and Port Charlotte, before reaching the far more appetizing Fort Myers (see below).

Practicalities

If you're arriving in Venice by Greyhound bus, you'll be dropped at 225 S Tamiami Trail (☎485-1001), from which your first port of call might be the **Chamber of Commerce**, 257 N Tamiami Trail (Mon–Fri 8.30am–5pm; Nov–March also Sat 9am–12pm; ☎488-2236), for local information. **Local buses** (SCAT; ☎316-1234) #13 and #16 (25¢ fare) link Venice with the beaches and surrounding areas.

Spending a night in this quiet community might seem an attractive proposition, though prices can be steep: of the motels, try the *Kon-Tiki*, 1487 Tamiami Trail (☎485-9696; ④), or the *Gulf Tide*, 708 Granada Avenue (☎484-9709; ⑤). More luxurious is the *Inn at the Beach Resort*, 101 The Esplanade (☎1-800/255-8471; ③). The *Venice Campground* is at 4085 E Venice Avenue (☎488-0850; $20), in an oak hammock by the river.

For **eating**, *James Place*, 117 W Venice Avenue (☎485-6742), provides great, cheap breakfasts and daily hot lunch specials in an Anglo-Irish setting; *The Crow's Nest*, 1968 Tarpon Center Drive (☎484-9551), is a marina pub with a waterfront view, serving fresh seafood, sandwiches and snacks.

Fort Myers

Though lacking the elan of Sarasota (fifty miles north) and the exclusivity of Naples (twenty miles south), **FORT MYERS** is one of the up-and-coming communities of the southwest coast. The town took its name from Abraham Myers, who helped establish a fort here in 1860 after the Seminole war. During the war, the town was activated as a base where cattle were rounded up to supply beef to Federal gunboats patrolling the gulf off Sanibel Island (see below). Fortunately, most of the town's late-twentieth-century growth occurred on the north side of the wide Caloosahatchee River, leaving the traditional center relatively unspoiled. The home and work place of inventor Thomas Edison, who lived in Fort Myers for many years, provides the strongest interest in a town that otherwise relies on its scenery. Its riverside setting and regimental lines of palm trees along the main thoroughfares are arresting enough to delay your progress towards the local beaches, fifteen miles south, or the islands of Sanibel and Captiva, a similar distance west.

Arrival and information

Fort Myers, like many south Florida towns, sprawls farther than you'd imagine. Hwy-41 here is known as Cleveland Avenue. Hwy-80 runs through downtown Fort Myers and curves into McGregor Boulevard to the west, where you'll find the Edison home. It's all made fairly confusing, though, by the fact that most tourist maps fail to refer to downtown and the wider city on the same map, and because most of the road signs are remarkably poor. To reach Edison's house, it may be simpler to rely on mass transit. There's only a mile between his home and downtown, and it's covered by **local buses** (☎277-5012) and a trolley service. To get from downtown Fort Myers to the beaches, take any bus to the Edison Mall, then use #50 to Summerlin Square, from where a trolley continues to Estero Island (otherwise known as Fort Myers Beach) and Lovers Key. Note that there's no local public transport on Sundays. The Greyhound station is at 2275 Cleveland Avenue (☎334-1011), just south of downtown Fort Myers. Stacks of **information** await you at the **Visitor and Convention Bureau**, 2180 W First Street (Mon–Fri 8am–5pm; ☎1-800/237-6444; fax 334 1106), and the **Chamber of Commerce**, Edwards Drive, (Mon–Fri 8am–5pm; ☎332-3624 fax 332-7276).

Accommodation

Accommodation costs in and around Fort Myers are low between May and mid-December, when 40–50 percent is lopped off the standard rates. For a motel **in downtown Fort Myers**, look along First Street: *Sea Chest*, no. 2571(☎332-1545; ②), which has a heated pool; *Ta Ki-Ki*, no. 2631 (☎334-2135; ③); and *Tides*, no. 2621 (☎334-1231; ③). For no frills but a comfortable and clean stay, try the *Towne House Motel*, 2568 First St, off Route 80 (☎334-3743; ③). There's cable TV and a pool, and the place tends to be popular with visiting baseball teams. For considerable luxury without pomp, and sharp reductions out of season, try the *Homewood Suites Hotel*, 5255 Big Pine Way (☎275-6000; ⑦).

At the beaches, seek a room along the motel-lined Estero Boulevard and be prepared to spend $100 in season ($70 otherwise). Midweek you may find cheaper deals at *Beacon*, no. 1240 (☎463-5264; ④); *Gulf*, no. 2700 (☎463-9247; ④); *Laughing Gull*, no. 2890 (☎463-1346; ④); *The Outrigger Beach Resort*, no. 6200 (☎463-3131; ⑤); or, a few miles inland, *Island*, 201 San Carlos Boulevard (☎463-2381; ③). Of the **campgrounds**, only *Red Coconut*, 3001 Estero Boulevard (☎463-7200), is right on the beach. Two others further inland are *Fort Myers Campground,* 16800 South Tamiami Trail (☎267-2141), and *San Carlos*, 18701 San Carlos Boulevard (☎466-3133).

Downtown Fort Myers

Once across the Caloosahatchee River, Hwy-41 hits **downtown Fort Myers**, which is picturesquely nestled on the river's edge. Aside from a few restored homes and storefronts around Main Street and Broadway, modern office buildings predominate. For thorough insight into the town's past, stop by the **Fort Myers Historical Museum**, 2300 Peck Street (Tues–Sat 10am–4pm; $2.50), whose exhibits include details on the exploits of Doctor Franklin Miles, a Fort Myers inhabitant who developed Alka Seltzer. The invention of the world's great hangover cure was overshadowed, however, by the deeds of Thomas Edison, comprehensively recalled a mile west of downtown Fort Myers on McGregor Boulevard – also the route to the Fort Myers beaches and the Sanibel Island causeway.

In 1885, six years after inventing the light bulb, workaholic **Thomas Edison** collapsed from exhaustion and was instructed by his doctor to find a warm working environment or face an early death. While on holiday in Florida, the 37-year-old Edison noted a patch of bamboo sprouting from the banks of the Caloosahatchee River and bought fourteen acres of it. Having cleared a section, he established what became the **Edison Winter**

Home, 2350 McGregor Boulevard (guided tours every 30min; Mon–Sat 9am–5pm, Sun noon–5pm; $10; an extra $2 allows you entry into the Ford Winter Home, see below), where he spent each winter until his death at the age of 84.

A liking for bamboo was no idle fancy: Edison was a keen horticulturist and often utilized the chemicals produced by plants and trees in his experiments. The **gardens** of the house, where the tours begin (get a ticket from the signposted office across McGregor Boulevard), are sensational and provided Edison with much raw material: a variety of tropical foliage, from the extraordinary African sausage tree to a profusion of wild orchids nurtured by the inventor, intoxicatingly scented by frangipani. By contrast, Edison's **house** is an anticlimax: a palm-cloaked wooden structure with an ordinary collection of period furnishings glimpsed only through the windows. A reason for the plainness of the abode may be that Edison spent most of his waking hours inside the **laboratory**, attempting to turn the latex-rich sap of *solidago Edisoni* (a giant strain of goldenrod weed which he developed) into rubber – anticipating the shortage caused by the outbreak of World War II. A mass of test tubes, files and tripods are scattered over the benches, unchanged since Edison's last experiment, performed just before his death in 1931.

Not until the tour reaches the **museum** does the full impact of Edison's achievements become apparent. A design for an improved ticker-tape machine provided him with the funds for the experiments which led to the creation of the phonograph in 1877, and financed research into passing electricity through a vacuum that resulted in the incandescent light bulb two years later. Scores of cylinder and disc phonographs with gaily painted horn-speakers, bulky vintage light bulbs, and innumerable spin-off gadgets, make up an engrossing collection; here, too, you'll see some of the ungainly cinema projectors derived from Edison's Kinetoscope – bringing the inventor a million dollars a year in patent royalties from 1907.

A close friend of Edison's since 1896, when the inventor had been one of the few people to speak admiringly of his ambitious car ideas, **Henry Ford** bought the house next door to Edison's in 1915, by which time he was established as the country's top automobile manufacturer. Unlike the Edison home, you can go inside the **Ford Winter Home** (tour hours as for Edison home; to view *this* house you must buy a combination ticket to the Edison House also, $10), though the interior, restored to the style of Ford's time but lacking the original fittings, hardly justifies the admission price: despite becoming the world's first billionaire, Ford lived with his wife in modest surroundings.

Before leaving the old homes, pause to admire the sprawling **banyan tree** outside the ticket office: grown from a seedling given to Edison by tire-king Harvey Firestone in 1925, it's now the largest tree in the state.

The Fort Myers beaches

Still being discovered by the holidaying multitudes, the **Fort Myers beaches**, fifteen miles south of downtown Fort Myers, are appreciably different in character from the West Coast's more commercialized beach strips, with a cheerful seaside mood that's worth getting acquainted with. Accommodation (see above) is plentiful on and around Estero Boulevard – reached by San Carlos Boulevard, off McGregor Boulevard – which runs the seven-mile length of **Estero Island**; the hubs of activity being the short fishing pier and the **Lynne Hall Memorial Park**, at the island's northern end.

Estero Island becomes quieter and increasingly residential as you press south. Estero Boulevard eventually swings over a slender causeway onto the barely developed **San Carlos Island**. A few miles ahead, at **Lovers Key** (daily 8am–5pm; $1.50), a footpath picks a trail over a couple of mangrove-fringed islands and several mullet-filled creeks. The domain of weekend fishing enthusiasts, it's a spectacularly secluded beach where occasional washed-up drink cans are the only signs of human existence – the perfect base for stress-free beachcombing and sunbathing. If you don't fancy the half-mile walk, a free trolley-bus will transport you between the park entrance and the beach.

Inland from Fort Myers: the Calusa Nature Center

Just as the beaches are kept in good condition, so is much of the eastern perimeter of the town, which is protected by a series of parks that make scenic spots for picnicking, canoeing and walking. For a more informative look at the local landscape, spend a couple of hours at the **Calusa Nature Center and Planetarium**, 3450 Ortiz Avenue (Mon–Sat 9am–5pm, Sun 11am–5pm; $3), and trek the boardwalk trails through cypress and pine woods. Cast an eye, too, around the aviary – where injured birds regain their strength before returning to the wild – and the indoor **museum**. Here, alongside general geological and wildlife exhibits, you'll find a caged specimen of each of the state's four varieties of poisonous snakes; the facial expressions of the mice, fed to each snake once a day, are not a sight for the faint-hearted.

For anyone interested in untamed Florida, but lacking the desire to traipse through the wild for days, **Babcock Wilderness Adventures**, 8000 State Road 31 at Punta Gorda (☎1-800/500-5583) is a must. Forty miles inland and northeast of Fort Myers (take exit 26 on I-75), the Babcock crew lead excellent narrated **tours** (Nov–April 9am–3pm, mornings only May–Oct, reservations essential; $17.95, children $9.95) in a covered swamp buggy. Their vast ranch (it's three times the size of Washington DC) was bought in 1914 by Edward Babcock and was adapted as a wildlife refuge by his son Fred. From open fields with wild pigs and bison to swamp areas where alligators carpet the pathway, the tour chugs through a wild, ever-changing terrain. Among the highlights – and there are plenty – is the **bald cypress swamp**, a primeval scene of stunning trees and blood-red bromeliads reflected in still, tea-colored water. Another is the gold Florida panthers, although they're not pure bred. Only around thirty true Florida panthers are left, and inbreeding has caused most of the young to be stillborn. You'll also be offered the opportunity to stroke the surprisingly dry, smooth belly of a baby alligator, and learn about how trade in the reptile's meat and skin is carried out – an odd juxtaposition at this essentially very caring establishment. More quirky is Babcock's resident three-horned cow Lulu, a popular sight from her birth in 1967 until her death in September 1997. Her head has now been mounted near the entrance – looking rather worse for wear.

One creature you won't find at Babcock's is a manatee. Fortunately, just one stop further north on I75, they're the center of attention at the recently-opened **Manatee Park** (free). Here, along the banks of the Orange River, large information boards explain how manatees are identified by their scar patterns, which are caused by collisions with boat propellers. The most-often-sighted – and, therefore, the most scarred – manatees are given names. Due to its proximity to the interstate and the Fort Myers Power Company, the park isn't too aesthetically pleasing. Still, the manatees seem to like it, and it represents your best chance of seeing these ten-foot sea cows, which can weigh more than 3000 pounds. Wander to the first inlet, where they congregate in the calm, shallow waters; they're easiest to spot in the early morning, but chances are you'll see at least a couple at any time of day.

Eating

Inexpensive breakfasts, snacks and lunches are easily found in **downtown Fort Myers**: try *Melanie's Restaurant*, 2158 McGregor Boulevard (☎334-3139), *Dolly's Bites and Delights*, 2235 First Street (☎332-1600), or pick up a fresh-baked goodie from *Mason's*, 1615 Hendry Street (☎334-4525). For a fuller lunch, head for the super-friendly *Oasis Restaurant*, 2222 McGregor Boulevard (☎334-1566), wedged into the Edison Ford Square Shopping Center. Despite the grim appearance and 1950s signs, try the *Farmers'*

Market Restaurant, 2736 Edison Avenue (☎334-1687), for good country cooking. A convivial place for an evening bite is *The French Connection Cafe*, 2282 1st St, serving French onion soup, crepes and excellent Reubens sandwich. More glamorous dining is to be had at the funky *Graveyard Rock 'n' Comedy Grill* (☎334-8833; see below), where entrees are $13-19. It gets mobbed, so be sure to reserve. **At the beaches**, the laid-back *Café du Monde*, 1740 Estero Boulevard (☎463-8088), produces tempting morsels from homemade recipes. *Top O' The Mast*, 1028 Estero Boulevard (☎463-9424), is a solid bet for seafood, and, if you have a massive appetite, go to *The Reef*, 2601 Estero Boulevard (☎463-4181), for all-you-can-eat nightly specials, ranging from catfish to frogs' legs.

Nightlife

Fort Myers may not be a nightlife haven, but great new cafés and bars are opening all the time. Head down to the junction of Hendry St and First streeets where impromptu **bands** play outside on Thursday nights (sometimes on weekends). Just steps away is *The Cigar Bar* (☎337-4662), the most laid-back, stylish bar in town, filled with leather Chesterfields, a black grand piano and the mounted heads of bison, oryx, and bears with cigars protruding from their lips. Everyone indulges in a huge range of bourbons and single malts and, unsurprisingly, smokes. An attached speciality cigar shop stocks everything from $1 cigarillos to pre-embargo Cuban cigars that cost $35 each.

One of the more unusual joints is *The Graveyard Rock 'n' Comedy* Grill, at 1528 Hendy St, the site of the old city mortuary, which has a huge bar shaped like a coffin and stand-up comedians doing their schtik while you dine (see above).

Peter's La Cuisine, 2224 Bay St (☎332-2228), is very costly for eating, but has opened a new floor which functions as an open-air night club. Below, a jazz bistro is cheaper and less formal than the ground-floor restaurant. For a relaxed drink and live guitar music on Saturday nights, *The Liquid Cafe,* at the corner of Hendry and First streets (☎461-0444), is a cool place with blue light and steel columns. It also has a good casual food menu. Another mellow place is *Opus Jazz Bistro*, 2278 1st Street, where tropical blues bands play every Thursday.

For **gay nightlife,** an unusual bar and club is *The Bottom Line*, 3090 Evans Ave (☎337-7292), a cavernous place isolated in a desolate stretch of downtown. For a drink in a friendly if gloomy, unlit pub, try *The Office*, at 3704 Grove St. It's in the Pizza Hut Plaza opposite the Red Lobster sign. More gregarious and inviting is *Apex*, at 4226 Fowler St. Apart from table-top dancers and drag acts, this is a very friendly locals' bar. There's a different theme every night.

Sanibel and Captiva islands

When the Lee County authorities (who control the whole Fort Myers area) decided to link **Sanibel Island**, the most southerly of an island grouping around the mouth of the Caloosahatchee River, by road to the mainland in 1963, Sanibel's thousand or so occupants fought tooth and nail against the scheme, but eventually lost. A decade later, they got their revenge by seceding from the county, becoming a self-governing "city" and passing strict land-use laws to prevent their island sinking beneath holiday homes and hotels.

Those who remember the old days insist that the island has gone to the dogs: motels and restaurants are more numerous than ever before, and visitors always outnumber the present 7000 residents. But Sanibel is a credit to those who run it: high-rises have been kept out, the beaches are superb, and sizeable areas are set aside as nature preserves. Other than the complete lack of public transport from the mainland, there's no excuse not to visit the twelve-mile-long, two-mile-wide island: arrive for a few hours and you could find yourself staying several days (though if you do, you'll need a fat wallet – living expenses are high here).

North of Sanibel, a road continues to **Captiva Island**, even less populated, its only concession to modern-day economics being an upmarket holiday resort at its northern tip, from which boat trips render some of the neighboring islands accessible.

Practicalities

To reach Sanibel and Captiva from mainland Fort Myers, take College Parkway west off of Hwy 41, turning almost immediately onto Summerlin Road. Summerlin winds its way to Sanibel Causeway, which links to the island. There's a $3 vehicle **toll** to get onto Sanibel.

Your first stop on Sanibel should be the **Visitor Center**, 1159 Causeway Boulevard (Mon–Sat 9am–7pm, Sun 10am–5pm; ☎472-1080; fax 472-1070), packed with essential **information** and numerous free publications. There is no longer any public transport, and no plans to restart the old trolley tours, so without a car, you'll have to rent a **bike**: Finnimore's Cycle Shop, 2353 Periwinkle Way (☎472-5577), and The Bike Rental Inc, 2330 Palm Ridge Road (☎472-2241), offer a good selection; bike rental is around $5 a day. You can also rent bikes and scooters from the Bike Rentals shop just before the toll booth (☎454 0097). There are no organized tours on the island, and a rather unsatisfactory alternative is buying a **self-guide tape** for $12.95 from the visitor center.

Accommodation on the islands is always more expensive than on the mainland, though rates are less between May and November. *Kona Kai*, 1539 Periwinkle Way (☎472-1001; ⑤), is among the least costly; if you'd rather be on the beach, use *West Wind Inn*, 3345 W Gulf Drive (☎472-1541; ⑦), or *Best Western*, 3287 W Gulf Drive (☎472-1700; ⑧). A good alternative to standard rooms are the wooden cottages, sleeping two to four, at *Seahorse*, 1223 Buttonwood Lane (☎472-4262; ④). Sanibel also has a **campground**, *Periwinkle Trailer Park*, 1119 Periwinkle Way (☎472-1433; $22 to pitch a tent).

For **eating**, the best coffee house is *The Bean Cafe,* at 2240 Periwinkle in Sanibel Square (☎395-1919), serving a huge range of goodies, including incredible cappuccino cheesecake. the *Lighthouse Café*, 362 Periwinkle Way (☎472-0303), serves good-value meals throughout the day; and *Cheeburger Cheeburger*, 2413 Periwinkle Way (☎472-6111), has a variety of burgers. For a more substantial lunch or dinner, you'll find a wide selection of seafood at *The Mucky Duck*, Andy Rosee Lane (closed Sun; ☎472-3434), and at *Pippins Bar & Grill* 1975 Periwinkle Way (☎395 2255). Alternatively, mouth-watering pasta and Cajun dishes are a specialty at the slightly more expensive *Jacaranda*, 1223 Periwinkle Way (☎472-1771).

Sanibel Island

People visit **Sanibel Island** for its beaches, and it is true that the island is blessed with long braids of beaches strewn with shells. Even paradises, however, have their problems. Cars move slowly through its main drag, and despite the lack of public transport, parking your car can be almost impossible. Signs prohibit parking wherever you look and the parking lots at the main beaches are clogged with vacationers lining up for a precious space. Fortunately, most people head to the first beaches they come to, and if you press on west and north, you'll be rewarded by far more pleasant spots, with fewer people and instant parking.

The first sight you'll come across on the island is the undramatic **Sanibel lighthouse** (erected in 1884), a relic most arrivals feel obliged to inspect (from the outside only) before spending a few hours on the presentable beach at its foot. After the beach, trace your way along Periwinkle Way and turn right into Dunlop Street, acknowledging the island's tiny city hall on the way to the **Island Historical Museum** (mid-Oct to mid-Aug Wed–Sat 10am–4pm, Dec–March open also Sunday, 1–4pm; $1). The museum is a century-old, pioneer settler's home with furnishings and photos of early Sanibel

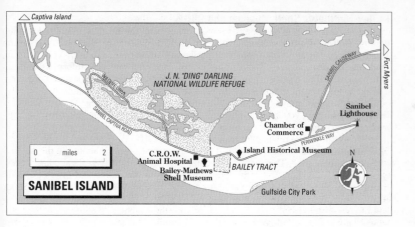

arrivals – those who weren't seafarers tried agriculture until the soils were ruined by saltwater blown up by hurricanes – and displays on the pre-European dwellers, the Calusa Indians, including a thousand-year-old skeleton.

Continuing along Periwinkle Way, Tarpon Bay Road cuts west to the coast, passing the rampant vegetation of the **Bailey Tract**, a jungle-like rectangle of untamed land in the midst of a residential area: poorly marked trails will take you deep among the alligators and the wildfowl – for the careful and courageous only. In either direction from the end of Tarpon Springs Road, resorts and tourists mark the beaches; turning left along Casa Ybel Road and Algiers Lane leads to the more promising **Gulfside City Park**, a slender sandy strip shaded by Australian pines and bordered by a narrow canal, with a nicely secluded picnic area. Before you leave, follow the bike path off Algiers Road for a few yards to a tiny **cemetery**, where a few wooden markers remember those who perished, some a hundred years ago, in their attempts to forge an existence on the then inhospitable island.

The J. N. "Ding" Darling National Wildlife Refuge

In contrast to the smooth beaches along the Gulf side of the island, the opposite edge comprises shallow bays and creeks, and a vibrant wildlife habitat under the protection of the **J N "Ding" Darling National Wildlife Refuge** (daily except Fri sunrise–sunset; cars $5, cyclists and pedestrians $1); the main entrance and **information center** are just off the Sanibel–Captiva Road. Alligators, brown pelicans and ospreys are usually easy to spy, but much of what you'll see at the refuge is determined by when you come: during the fall, migrating songbirds are plentiful, thousands of wintering ducks show up in subsequent months, and in spring, graceful roseate spoonbills sweep by just before sunset.

The five-mile **Wildlife Drive** requires slow speeds and plenty of stops if you're to see the well-camouflaged residents by car. If you're cycling, take heed of the wind direction before entering: you'll usually keep the wind at your back and not in your face by pedaling north to south. You'd do better, though, to plod the four miles of the **Indigo trail**, beginning just beyond the information center. There's a second, much shorter, foot route close to the north end of Wildlife Drive: the **Indian Shell trail**, which twists between mangrove and buttonwood, and passes a few lime trees (remaining from the efforts to cultivate the island) to a Native American **shell mound** – a hump in the ground, much less spectacular than you might hope.

Bailey-Matthews Shell Museum and CROW

Taking the local love of shells to its logical conclusion, the newly opened, non-profit-making **Bailey-Matthews Shell Museum**, at 3075 Sanibel-Captiva Road (Tues–Sun 10am–4.30pm; $5), is devoted entirely to molluscs from all over the world. A cornucopia of colors, shapes and sizes is spread before you in such a way as to inform as well as entertain, revealing the formation of shells, their diversity and uses, past and present. The museum's several rooms merit an hour or two of quiet contemplation.

Still on Sanibel-Captiva Road, near the entrance to the J. N. "Ding" Darling Wildlife Refuge (see above), you'll find a "hospital" for injured, orphaned and sick native wildlife from all over southwest Florida. Since most of the several thousand patients treated here each year are the result of human interference, **CROW** (Care and Rehabilitation of Wildlife Inc.) puts some of its energy into educating the public about the threats we often unwittingly pose. This ten-acre sanctuary, established thirty years ago and large-ly staffed by volunteers, recently opened its doors to the public and offers **guided tours** for small groups (Mon–Fri at 11am, Sun at 1pm; $3; book ahead on ☎472-3644). A short but enlightening talk on the dangers posed by carelessly discarded fishing lines and other detritus, is followed by a walk around the sanctuary's outdoor enclosures, which contain a multitude of mammals, birds, amphibians and reptiles until they are (hopefully) ready for release back into the wild. It all serves as a poignant reminder of man's impact on the environment, as well as the healing powers of nature.

Bowman's Beach

One of Sanibel's loveliest swathes of sand, **Bowman's Beach** lies to the north of the island; to reach it, watch for Bowman's Beach Road off the Sanibel–Captiva Road just prior to Blind Pass. Popular with the shell-hunting crowds, this is also an excellent spot for sunset-watching, and, in the more secluded sections, **naturists** perfect their all-over tans – though the visitor center will remind you it's forbidden by Florida State Law.

Captiva Island

Immediately north of Bowman's Beach, the Sanibel–Captiva Road crosses Blind Pass by bridge and reaches **Captiva Island**, markedly less developed than Sanibel and inhabited only by a few hundred people. If you're not going to call on one of them, the sole site of note is the tiny **Chapel-by-the-Sea**, at 11580 Chapin (down Wiles Drive). Mostly used for weddings, the chapel is unlikely to be open, and you should walk instead around the unusual **cemetery**, just opposite, where many of the island's origi-nal settlers are buried. With crashing waves a shell's throw away and the graves pro-tected from the sun by a roof of seagrape, it's a fitting final resting place for an islander. A few miles further, Captiva's northern tip is covered by the tennis courts, golf cours-es and Polynesian-style villas of the ultra-posh *South Sea Plantation*, where the cheap-est beds are $150 a night in season. There's no point in hanging around here, except for the **boat trips** to the neighboring islands.

SHELLING ON SANIBEL AND CAPTIVA ISLANDS

Something Sanibel and Captiva share are **shells**. Literally tons of them are washed ashore with each tide, and the popularity of shell collecting has led to the bent-over con-dition known as "Sanibel Stoop." The potential ecological upset of too many shells being taken away has led to laws forbidding the removal of any live shells (ie one with a crea-ture living inside), on pain of a $500 fine or a prison sentence. Novices and seasoned con-chologists alike will find plenty to occupy them on the beaches; to identify your find, use one of the shell charts drawn in most of the giveaway tourist magazines – or watch the experts at work during the **Sanibel Shell Festival** in early March.

BOAT TRIPS FROM CAPTIVA ISLAND

Several organized **boat trips** begin from the docks at the *South Sea Plantation*. The best of them is the lunch cruise, departing at 10.30am and returning at 3.30pm, allowing two hours ashore at either Cabbage Key (see above) or at a gourmet restaurant on Useppa Island; cost is $27.50. The price does not include food while ashore – there's no obligation to eat once you land, but taking your own food on the boat isn't allowed. Another option is the hour-long sightseeing cruise at 3.30pm for $16.50.

Whenever you sail, you're likely to see **dolphins**: many of them live in the warm waters around the islands, sometimes leaping above the water to turn somersaults for your benefit.

For further **details** and to make **reservations** for all sailings, call Laptiva Cruises (☎472 5300).

Beyond Captiva Island: Cabbage Key

Of a number of small islands just north of Captiva, **Cabbage Key** is the one to visit. Even if you arrive on the lunch cruise from Captiva (see the box below), skip the unexciting food in favor of prowling the footpaths and the small marina: there's a special beauty to the isolated setting and the views across Pine Island Sound. Do take a peep into the **restaurant**, though, to see the most expensive wallpaper in Florida: an estimated $25,000 worth of dollar bills, each one signed by the person who left it pinned up in observance of a Cabbage Key tradition. If you get the urge **to stay** longer, the inn has six simple rooms on offer at $65 and, more expensively, a few rustic cottages in the grounds; reserve at least a month in advance (☎283-2278).

South of Fort Myers

While Sanibel and Captiva islands easily warrant a few days of exploration, there's less to keep you occupied on the mainland on the seventy-mile journey **south from Fort Myers** towards the Everglades National Park. The towns you'll pass will carry less appeal than the nearby beaches, or the vistas of Florida's interior at the end of inland detours. Set aside a few hours, however, to examine one of the stranger footnotes to Florida's history: the oddball religious community of the Koreshans.

The Koreshan State Historic Site

Around the turn of the century, some of the nation's radicals and idealists began viewing Florida as the last earthly wilderness; a subtropical Garden of Eden where the wrongs of modern society could be righted. Much to the amusement of hard-living Florida farmers, some of them came south to experiment with utopian ways, though few braved the humidity and mosquitoes for long. One of the more significant arrivals was also the most bizarre: the **Koreshan Unity** community, which came from Chicago in 1894 to build the "New Jerusalem" on a site now preserved as the **Koreshan State Historic Site**, 22 miles from Fort Myers, just south of Estero beside Hwy-41 (daily 8am–sunset; cars $3.25, pedestrians and cyclists $1; ☎992-0311).

The flamboyant leader of the Koreshans*, **Cyrus Teed**, was an army surgeon when he underwent the "great illumination": an angel appearing and informing him that the Earth was concave, lining the inner edge of a hollow sphere, at the center

---

*There is no link between the Koreshans and David Koresh, leader of the religious cult who barricaded themselves into their Waco, Texas, headquarters and battled with federal troops before they and their compound were incinerated in April 1993.

of which was the rest of the universe. Subsequently, Teed changed his name to "Koresh" and gained a following among Chicago intellectuals who, like him, were disillusioned with established religions and were seeking a communal, anti-materialistic way of life. Among the tenets of the Koreshan creed were celibacy outside marriage, shared ownership of goods, and gender equality. The aesthetes who came to this desolate outpost, accessible only by boat along the alligator-infested Estero River, quickly learned new skills in farming and house building, and marked out thirty-foot-wide boulevards, which they believed would one day be the arteries of a city inhabited by ten million enlightened souls. In fact, at its peak in the three years from 1904, the community numbered just two hundred. After Teed's death in 1908, the Koreshans fizzled out, the last member – who arrived in 1940, fleeing Nazi Germany – dying in 1982.

The Koreshan library and museum

The Koreshan site will be a disappointment unless you first call at the **Koreshan library and museum**, 8661 Corkscrew Road (tours Mon–Fri at 1pm, 2pm, 3pm & 4pm; $1; four person minimum; details on ☎992-0311), for background on the Koreshans' beliefs, plus the chance to see numerous photos and portraits of Teed, some of his esoteric books, and copies of the still-published Koreshan newspaper, *The American Eagle*. Along the broad thoroughfares at the neighboring **site**, several of the Koreshans' buildings have been restored. Among them are Teed's home; the Planetary Court, meeting place of the seven women – each named after one of the seven known planets – who governed the community; and the Art Hall, where the community's cultural evenings were staged, where Koreshan celebrations (such as the solar festival in October and the lunar festival in April) still occur, and where the *rectilinator*, a device which "proved" the Koreshan theory of the concave Earth, can be seen.

Bonita Springs and the Corkscrew Swamp Sanctuary

A fast-growing residential community, **BONITA SPRINGS**, seven miles south of the Koreshan site, has negligible appeal besides providing access to **Bonita Beach**, along Bonita Beach Road, and the less impressive **Everglades Wonder Gardens**, on the corner of Terry Street and Hwy-41 (daily 9am–5pm; $8), keeping a multitude of the state's indigenous creatures in cramped confinement.

Make more of an effort and you'll get a better impression of natural Florida twenty miles **inland** on Route 846 (branching from Hwy-41 a few miles south of Bonita Springs) at the National Audubon Society's **Corkscrew Swamp Sanctuary**, 375, Sanctuary Road, Naples (May–Nov daily 8am–5pm; Dec–April 7am–5pm; $6.50; ☎657-3771), an enormous gathering of Spanish-moss-draped cypress trees rising through a dark and moody swamp landscape. Tempering the strange joy of the scene, though, is the knowledge that all of the much larger area presently safeguarded by the Big Cypress Swamp National Preserve (see "The Everglades," below) used to look like this; uncontrolled logging felled the five-hundred-year-old trees and severely reduced Florida's wood stork population, who nest a hundred feet up in the tree tops. The remaining wood stork colony is still the largest in the country, but is now faced with the threat of falling water levels.

The two-hour **guided tour** is excellent, especially with the help of the leaflet from the visitor center. A unique facet of this park, though, is found at the outset, on the way to the restrooms. Here an ingenious, though remarkably simple "living machine" aids water management in the park by recycling waste matter from the restrooms through a purely natural environment to produce purified water. Within a visually pleasing plant-filled glasshouse construction, the cycle relies on sunlight, bacteria, algae and snails to break down the waste, a process that is later continued by vegetation, such as alligator flag, arrowhead, and small insects and animals. The result is purified water that fulfils statuary hygiene standards. At the time of writing, plans were afoot to introduce butterflies into the "garden," eventually creating a colony, and it's mildly amusing to think that if you avail yourself of the facilities in Corkscrew Swamp, a part of you will remain here for some time to come, helping to preserve it.

Continuing south: Naples

There's a science-fiction sense of the unreal in **NAPLES**, where elderly men drive very slowly around silent streets in huge, gleaming cars. Everything feels cushioned in wealth. Hardly a soul walks, and the most action in town is the sprinklers that spray the obsessively-manicured lawns. You'll get the hang of the place on Fifth Avenue, where the boatyards have been turned into upscale clothes shops, art galleries and restaurants. The many miles of public **beaches** make the pervading social snobbishness more than bearable, and **Lowdermilk Park**, about two miles north of the pier, is the most gregarious of the local sands, especially on weekends.

There's very little of real historic interest, and to prove it, the low faceless building now housing **Fantozzi's Cafe** (see below) is billed a historic monument: the 1922-built cube has been everything to Naples, from its first town hall, to a courthouse, drugstore, movie theater, Presbyterian church, Catholic church, tap dance shop and zoo. Just a few steps on is **Palm Cottage**, at 137 12th Avenue, one of the few house left in Florida built of tabby mortar, which was made by burning seashells.

To ogle the fruits of Naples' money, head north up Hwy 41 to the *Ritz Carlton Hotel* (☎598-3300) at the end of Vanderbilt Beach Road. While you'd need $3500 for a night in the presidential suite, sweeping through the grand entrance for a coffee at the bar is an inexpensive way to appreciate the hotel's towering splendour. The building looks like a 1930s vision of classical decadence, but it actually appeared in the late 1980s.

Practicalities

For **information**, try the **Chamber of Commerce**, 895 5th Avenue S (daily 9am–5pm; ☎262-6141; fax 435-9910) or the **Golden Gate Visitor Center** at 3847 Tollgate Boulevard (daily 9am–5pm; ☎352-0508). They're not the most friendly of offices, but if you push hard enough, they'll supply you with local bus schedules. Greyhound buses stop in Naples at 2669 Davis Boulevard S (☎774-5660 or 1-800/231-2222 for schedules).

Accommodation, not surprisingly, isn't cheap. A good choice is *The Olde Naples Inn,* 801 3rd St (☎262-5194; ④–⑤), which isn't old at all: the rooms are large, there's a pool and breakfast is included. If you're looking to spend under $50 a night, try the *Flora-Sun-Motel*, 9483 Tamiami Trail North (☎597-5101; ②); *Gordy's Motel*, 11238 Tamiami Trail East (☎774-3707; ②); or the *Gulfshore Motel*, 2805 Shoreview Drive (☎774-1100; ②)

Contrary to almost everything else, **eating** in Naples does not have to cost a fortune. For a real blast of Cuban character, it's worth seeking out the *10th Street Cafeteria,* at 271 10th Street N (☎263-3632), a real, old-style Cuban café that serves excellent sandwiches, cheap cheeseburgers and powerful coffee. *Cafe Plantain*, 947 3rd Ave N, is a trek from the beaches, but serves good sandwiches, chorizopan, blackbean veggie burgers and plantains. More convenient to the so-called old town and beach is *Fantozzi's*, on the corner of Broad Ave and 3rd St South, a popular cafe serving frozen yogurts and gourmet sandwiches. *Flamingoes*, on Route 41 at the end of 5th Ave N, is a simple breakfast and lunch café with stylish chrome-filled Fifties decor. It's no-frills, but the service is friendlier than most. For a more typical Naples meal, the recently opened *Zoe's* at 101 5th Ave has a wide, eclectic menu with smoked Thai chicken, Gulf shrimp and lots of noodle dishes. You can order half portions to cut costs; main courses run from $7 to $25. Another elegant if rather pompous place is

Bistro 821, a little further up at 821 5th Ave. The appealing menu here includes lots of fresh salads and fish dishes.

Nightlife is a rather limited affair. *Zoe's* (above) is open until 10pm as a restaurant, but the bar and live music go on until late. Almost opposite, *McCabe's Irish Pub and Grill* is very popular with a younger crowd.

Marco Island

It's no great loss that the Greyhound buses don't go anywhere near **MARCO ISLAND** (directly south of Naples), where artificial bald eagle nests are among the techniques dreamed up by property developers to bring back the wildlife their high-rise condos have driven away. At the northern end of the island, the old village of Marco has some charm, and **Tigertail Beach Park**, at the end of a boardwalk from Hernando Drive, is a fine place to relax – though neither really makes the journey (seven miles along Route 951 off Hwy-41) worthwhile. The Everglades, within easy striking distance, are a far superior target.

Seventeen miles south of Naples on Hwy-41, the landscape becomes an unbroken swathe of forest. **Collier-Seminole State Park**, at 20200 E Tamiami Trail (8am–sunset; $3.25 per vehicle, $1 cyclists or pedestrians; ☎394-3397), is a tropical hammock filled with Florida royal palms and a six-and-a-half-mile walking trail; a hiking guide is available at the Park's main office. If you want to camp here (and it's not a bad base from which to explore the Everglades), there are two sites, one for tents, the other for RVs (enquire at the office at the above number).

The Everglades

> *Nothing anywhere else is like them: their vast glittering openness, wider than the enormous visible round of the horizon, the racing free saltness and sweetness of their massive winds, under the dazzling blue heights of space. They are unique also in the simplicity, the diversity, the related harmony of the forms of life they enclose. The miracle of the light pours over the green and brown expanse of sawgrass and of water, shining and slow-moving below, the grass and water that is the meaning and the central fact of the Everglades of Florida. It is a river of grass.*
> Marjory Stoneman Douglas, *The Everglades: River of Grass*

Whatever scenic excitement you might anticipate from one of the country's more celebrated natural areas, no mountains, canyons nor even signposts herald your arrival in the **Everglades**. From the straight and monotonous ninety-mile course of Hwy-41, the most dramatic sights are small pockets of trees poking above a completely flat sawgrass plain that stretches to the horizon. It looks dead and empty; you wonder what all the fuss is about. Yet these wide open spaces resonate with life, forming part of an immensely subtle and ever-changing ecosystem that has evolved through a unique combination of climate, vegetation and wildlife.

Originally encompassing everything south of Lake Okeechobee, throughout this century the Everglades' boundaries have steadily been pushed back by human demands for farmland, fresh water and urban development; only a comparatively small section around Florida's southeastern corner is under the federal protection of the **Everglades National Park**. It's here, where public access is designed to inflict minimum damage, that the vital links holding the Everglades together become apparent: the all-important cycle of wet and dry seasons; the ability of alligators to discover water and dig for it with their tails; and the tree islands providing sanctuaries for animals during the flood period. None of this can be comprehended from a car window, or with a half-hour ride through the sawgrass on an airboat: noisy, destructive contraptions touted all along Hwy-41 but banned inside the park.

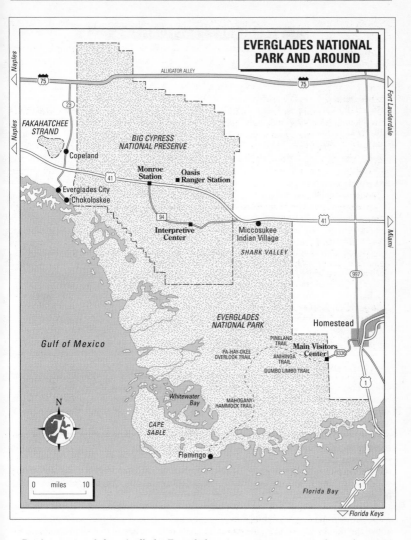

Don't expect to fathom it all: the Everglades are a constant source of surprise, even for the few hundred people who live in them. Use the visitor centers, read the free material, take the guided tours and, above all, explore slowly. It's then that the Everglades begin to reveal themselves, and you'll realize you're in the middle of one of the natural world's most remarkable ecosystems.

Some geology and natural history

Appearing as flat as a table-top, the oolitic limestone (once part of the seabed) on which the Everglades stand actually tilts very slightly – by a few inches over seventy miles – towards the southwest. For thousands of years, water from summer storms and the

EVERGLADES PRACTICALITIES

Orientation

A busy two-lane road, not the scenic drive you might expect, **Hwy-41** (the **Tamiami Trail**) runs east from Naples around the northern edge of the park, providing the only land access to the Everglades City, Shark Valley and Chekika (at the end of Richmond Drive, nine miles south of Hwy-41, on Route 997) park entrances, and to Fakahatchee Strand, the Big Cypress National Preserve and the Miccosukee Indian Village. To reach the Flamingo entrance, touch the edge of Miami and head south. **No public transport** of any kind runs along Hwy-41 or to any of the park entrances, though daytrips are available from Miami (see p.115). Between Naples and Fort Lauderdale, Greyhound buses use "Alligator Alley," the popular title for Route 84, twenty miles north of Hwy-41 and recently converted into a section of I-75.

When to visit

Though open all year, the park changes completely between its **wet** (summer) and **dry** (winter) seasons. The best time to visit is **winter** (Nov to April), when receding flood-waters cause wildlife, including migratory birds, to congregate around gator holes and sloughs (fresh water channels); ranger-led activities – such as guided walks, canoe trips and talks – are frequent; and the mosquitoes are bearable.

The picture is entirely different in **summer** (May to Oct), when afternoon storms flood the sawgrass prairies and pour through the sloughs, leaving only the hammocks visible above water. Around this time, mosquitoes become a severe annoyance, rendering the backcountry campgrounds almost uninhabitable; organized activities are substantially reduced; migratory birds have gone; and the park's wildlife spreads throughout the park due to a plentiful supply of food.

A clever compromise is a visit **between the seasons** (late April to early May or late Oct to early Nov), which avoids the worst of the mosquitoes and the winter tourist crowds, but at the same time reveals plenty of wildlife and the park's changing landscapes.

overflow of Lake Okeechobee has moved slowly through the Everglades towards the coast. The water replenishes the sawgrass, which grows on a thin layer of soil – or "marl" – formed by decaying vegetation on the limestone base, and gives birth to the algae at the foot of a complex food chain that sustains much larger creatures, most importantly alligators.

Alligators earn their "keepers of the Everglades" nickname during the dry winter season. After the summer floodwaters have reached the sea, drained through the bedrock or simply evaporated, the Everglades are barren except for the water accumulated in ponds or "gator holes" – created when an alligator senses water and clears the soil covering it with its tail. Besides nourishing the alligator, the pond provides a home for other wildlife until the summer rains return.

Sawgrass covers much of the Everglades, but where natural indentations in the limestone fill with marl, tree islands – or "hammocks" – appear, just high enough to stand above the flood waters and fertile enough to support a variety of trees and plants. Close to hammocks, often surrounding gator holes, you'll find wispy green-leafed willows. Smaller patches of vegetation, like small green humps, are called "bayheads." Pinewoods grow in the few places where the elevation exceeds seven feet; and in the deep depressions that hold water the longest, dwarf cypress trees flourish, their treetops forming a distinctive "cypress dome" when large numbers cover a extensive area.

Human habitation and exploitation

Before dying out through contact with Europeans, several Native American tribes lived hunter-gatherer existences in the Everglades; the shell mounds they built can still be seen in sections of the park. In the nineteenth century, Seminole Indians, who'd fled white

Entering the park and accommodation

Entering the park is free at Everglades City (though you can only see it by boat or canoe). At Shark Valley ($4), Flamingo ($5) and Chekika ($5) you **pay** per car; tickets are valid for seven days and can be used at all sites. Only Shark Valley closes for the night. With the exception of the wilderness waterway canoe trail between Everglades City and Flamingo, you can't travel from one section of the park into another.

Apart from the two organized campgrounds and a hotel at Flamingo, park **accommodation** is limited to backcountry campgrounds. In most cases these are raised wooden platforms with a roof and chemical toilet, accessible by boat or canoe; to stay, you need a permit, issued free from the relevant visitor center. One backcountry site at Flamingo, Pearl Bay, is accessible to **disabled visitors**.

Ten miles outside the park in Florida City, the *Everglades International Hostel*, 20 SW 2nd Ave (☎248-1122 or ☎1-800/372-3874), may be the best option for budget-minded travelers who want to maximize their time in the Everglades. Beds go for $10 a night, and the hostel is perfectly situated for continuing on to the Florida Keys or to Miami International Airport.

Practical tips

In the park, wear a hat, sunglasses and loose-fitting clothes with long sleeves and long trousers, and carry plenty of **insect repellent**. Besides the hazards of sunburn (there's very little shade) and mosquitoes, you need take no special measures for the walking trails, most of which are short trots along raised boardwalks.

Traveling and camping in the **backcountry** requires more caution. Most exploration is done by boat or canoe along marked trails, with basic campgrounds situated on the longer routes. Take a **compass, maps** (available from visitor centers) and ample provisions, including at least a **gallon of water** per person per day. Supplies should be carried in **hard containers**, as racoons can chew through soft ones. Be sure to leave a **detailed plan** of your journey and its expected duration with a park ranger. Finally, pay heed to the latest **weather forecast**, and note the tidal patterns if you're canoeing in a coastal area.

settlers in the north, also lived peaceably in the area (for more on them, see "Miccosukee Indian Village," p.326). By the late 1800s, a few white settlements – such as those at Everglades City and Flamingo – had sprung up, peopled by fugitives, outcasts and loners, who, unlike the Indians, looked to exploit the land rather than live in harmony with it.

As Florida's population grew, the damage caused by uncontrolled hunting, road building and draining the Everglades for farmland gave rise to a significant conservation lobby. In 1947, a section of the Everglades was declared a national park, but unrestrained commercial use of nearby areas continued to upset the Everglades' natural cycle; a problem acknowledged – if hardly alleviated – by the preservation in the Seventies of the Big Cypress Swamp, just north of the park.

As human understanding increases, so the severity of the problems faced by the Everglades becomes ever more apparent. The 1500 miles of canals built to divert the flow of water away from the Everglades and towards the state's expanding cities, the poisoning caused by agricultural chemicals from the farmlands around Lake Okeechobee, and the broader changes wrought by global warming, could yet turn Florida's greatest natural asset into a wasteland – with wider ecological implications that can only be guessed at.

Everglades City and around

Purchased and named in the Twenties by an advertising executive dreaming of a subtropical metropolis, **EVERGLADES CITY**, thirty miles from Naples and three miles south off Hwy-41 along Route 29, has a population of under five hundred living around a disproportionately large city hall. The Everglades **Chamber of Commerce**

Welcome Center (open daily 8.30am–5pm; ☎695-3941) is at the junction of Route 29 (sign posted Everglades City) and Hwy 41. Most who visit are solely intent on diminishing the stocks of fish living around the mangrove islands – the aptly titled **Ten Thousand Islands** – arranged like jigsaw-puzzle pieces around the coastline.

For a closer look at the mangroves that safeguard the Everglades from surge tides, ignore the ecologically dubious tours advertised along the roadside and take one of the park-sanctioned **boat trips**. Try either Everglades National Park Boat Tours (☎695-2591) or Majestic Everglades Excursions (☎695-2777). There are departures every 30 minutes 9am–5pm; the last trip departs at 4.30pm or 5pm depending on sunset time; tours last 90–105 minutes ($13) and leave from the dock on Chokoloskee, a blob of land – actually an Indian shell mound – marking the end of Route 29. The dockside **visitor center** (daily 8.30am–4.30pm in summer, 7.30am–5pm in winter; ☎941/695-3311) provides information on the cruises and the excellent ranger-led **canoe trips** (Sat 10am in winter). Anybody adequately skilled with the paddle, equipped with rough camping gear, and with a week to spare, should have a crack at the hundred-mile **wilderness waterway**, a marked trail through Whitewater Bay to Flamingo (see below), with numerous backcountry campgrounds en route.

Other than boat-accessed camping, there's no **accommodation** inside this section of the park. In Chokoloskee, though, you can rent an RV by the night for $45–60 at *Outdoor Resorts* (☎695-2881), or, back in Everglades City, get a simple cottage on the grounds of the *Everglades Rod & Gun Lodge*, 200 Riverside Drive (☎941/695-4211; ③). There's also basic motel rooms (and RV space) in the cheaper but shabby *Barron River Marina RV Park Motel and Villas* on Route 29 (②).

Big Cypress National Preserve

The completion of Hwy-41 in 1928 led to the destruction of thousands of towering bald cypress trees – whose durable wood is highly marketable – lining the roadside sloughs. By the Seventies, attempts to drain these acres and turn them into saleable residential plots had caused enough damage to the national park for the government to create the **Big Cypress National Preserve** – a massive chunk of protected land mostly on the northern side of Hwy-41. Sadly, neither the bald cypress trees nor the wood storks that once flourished here are present in anything like their previous numbers (a better place to observe both is the Corkscrew Swamp Sanctuary; see p.320). The only way to traverse the Big Cypress Swamp is on a very rugged 29-mile hiking trail, beginning twenty miles east on Hwy-41 at the **Oasis Visitor Center** (daily 8.30am–4pm; ☎941/695-4111).

While it's not actually part of the national preserve, be sure to visit the nearby **Fakahatchee Strand**, directly north of Everglades City on Route 29: a water-holding slough sustaining dwarf cypress trees (much smaller than the bald cypress; gray and spindly during the winter, draped with green needles in summer), a stately batch of royal palms, and masses of orchids and spiky-leafed air plants. If possible, see it on a **ranger-guided walk** (details on ☎941/695-4593).

If your car's suspension is dependable, turn right at Monroe Station, four miles west of the Oasis Ranger Station, onto Loop Road, a gravel road that's potholed in parts and prone to sudden flooding. This winds its way through cypress and pinewoods to Pinecrest, where an **interpretive center** makes sense of the varied terrains all around. The road rejoins Hwy-41 at Forty Mile Bend, just west of the Miccosukee Indian Village.

The Miccosukee Indian Village

Driven out of central Florida by white settlers, several hundred Seminole Indians retreated to the Everglades during the nineteenth century to avoid forced resettlement in the Midwest. They lived on hammocks in open-sided "chickees" built from cypress and cabbage palm, and traded, hunted and fished across the wetlands by canoe. Descendants of the Seminoles, and of a related tribe, the **Miccosukee** still live in the Everglades, though the coming of Hwy-41 – making the land accessible to the white man – brought another fundamental change in their lifestyle as they set about grabbing their share of the tourist dollars.

Four miles east of Forty Mile Bend, the **Miccosukee Indian Village** (daily 9am–5pm $7; ☎223-8380) symbolizes the tribe's uneasy compromise. In the souvenir shop, good quality traditional crafts and clothes stand side-by-side with blatant tat, and in the "village," men turn logs into canoes and women cook over open fires: despite the authentic roots, it's such a contrived affair that anyone with an ounce of sensitivity can't help but feel uneasy – the arrow-shooting gallery and the awful alligator-wrestling don't help. Since it's the only chance you're likely to get to discover anything of Native American life in the Everglades, it's hard to resist taking a look; though a plateful of traditional pumpkin bread from the *Miccosukee Restaurant* (☎305/223-8388), across the road, and a read of the *Seminole Tribune* newspaper, describing present-day concerns, might serve you better.

Shark Valley

In no other section of the park does the Everglades' "River of Grass" tag seem as appropriate as it does at **Shark Valley** (daily 8.30am–6pm; cars $4, pedestrians and cyclists $2), a mile east of the Miccosukee Indian Village. From here, dotted by hardwood hammocks and the smaller bayheads, the sawgrass plain stretches as far as the eye can see. It's here, too, that the damage wrought by humans on the natural cycle can sometimes be disturbingly clear. The thirst of Miami coupled with a period of drought can make Shark Valley resemble a stricken desert.

Seeing Shark Valley
Aside from a few simple walking trails close to the **visitor center** (winter daily 8.30am–5.15pm; reduced hours during the summer; ☎305/221-8455), you can see Shark Valley only from a fourteen-mile loop road. Too lengthy and lacking in shade to be covered comfortably on foot, and off-limits to cars, the loop is ideally covered by **bike** (rental; costs $3.25 an hour; return by 4pm). Alternatively, a highly informative two-hour **tram tour** (departures hourly from 9am in winter; at 9am, 11am, 1pm & 3pm in summer; $6; reservations necessary March–July ☎305/221-8455) will get you around and stop frequently to view wildlife, but won't allow you to linger in any particular place.

Set out as early as possible (the wildlife is most active in the cool of the morning), ride slowly and stay alert: otters, turtles and snakes are plentiful but not always easy to spot, and the abundant alligators often keep uncannily still. During September and October you'll come across female alligators tending their young; the brightly striped babies often sun themselves on the backs of their extremely protective mothers; watch them from a safe distance. More of the same creatures – and a good selection of bird life – can be seen from the **observation tower** overlooking a deep canal and marking the far point of the loop.

It may seem hard to believe but Shark Valley is only seventeen miles from the western fringes of Miami. To **see more of the park**, continue east on Hwy-41, turn south along Route 997, and head west for eleven miles along Route 9336 from Homestead to the park's main entrance.

Pine Island

Everglades City has the islands and Shark Valley has the sawgrass, but the **Pine Island** section of the park – the entire southerly portion, containing Cape Sable and Flamingo (see below) – holds virtually everything that makes the Everglades tick: spend a well-planned day or two here and you'll quickly grasp the fundamentals of its complex ecology. From the **park entrance** (always open; cars $5, pedestrians and cyclists $3), the road passes the **main visitor center** (daily 8am–5pm; ☎305/242-7700) and continues for 38 miles to the tiny coastal settlement of Flamingo, a one-time pioneer fishing colony now comprising a marina, hotel and campground. There's no compulsion to drive the whole way, and the short walking trails (none more than half a mile) along the route will keep you engaged for hours; sensibly, though, you should devote one day to walking and another to the canoe trails close to Flamingo.

Accommodation

There are well-equipped **campgrounds** at Long Pine Key, near the main visitor center, and Flamingo ($4 to pitch a tent; $8 to hook up your RV), as well as many backcountry sites (free) on the longer walking and canoe trails. Reservations are not accepted for any of the campgrounds: spare space at Flamingo (which invariably fills first) or Long Pine Key can be checked on the board just inside the park entrance. If there is space and the visitor center is closed, you can use the site but should pay at the visitor center before 10am the following day. For the backcountry sites, you will, of course, need a permit: these are issued free at the visitor centers. The only **rooms** within the park are at *Flamingo Lodge* (☎941/695-3101 or ☎305/253-2241; ⑨), including a continental breakfast) – you'll need to make a reservation months in advance if arriving between November and April.

Towards Flamingo: walking trails

A good place to gather information on the Everglades' various habitats is the Royal Palm **visitor center** (summer daily 8am–4.15pm, winter 8am–5pm; down the Royal Palm turn-off, a mile from the main park entrance). Apparently unimpressed by the multitudinous forms of nature and animal life throughout the Everglades, large numbers of park visitors simply want to see an alligator, and most are satisfied by walking the **Anhinga Trail**, a mile from the main visitor center. Turtles, marsh rabbits and the odd racoon are also likely to turn up on the route, but you should watch for the bizarre anhinga, a black-bodied bird resembling an elongated cormorant, which, after diving for fish, spends ages drying itself on rocks and tree branches with its white-tipped wings fully spread. Beat the crowds to the Anhinga Trail and then peruse the adjacent but very different **Gumbo Limbo Trail** (much of the vegetation along the trail was destroyed by Hurricane Andrew in 1992 and is now beginning to grow back), a hardwood hammock packed with exotic subtropical growths: strangler figs, gumbo limbos, royal palms, wild coffee and resurrection ferns. The latter appear dead during the dry season, but "resurrect" themselves in the summer rains to form a lush collar of green.

By comparison, the **Pinelands Trail**, a few miles further by the Long Pine Key campground, offers an undramatic ramble through a forest of slash pine, though the solitude comes as a welcome relief after the busier trails: the hammering of woodpeckers is often the loudest sound you'll hear. More bird life – including egrets, red-shouldered hawks and circling vultures – is viewable six miles ahead from the **Pa-hay-okee Overlook Trail**, which emerges from a stretch of dwarf cypress to face a great tract of sawgrass – a familiar sight if you've arrived from Shark Valley.

Although related to California's giant redwoods, the mahogany trees of the **Mahogany Hammock Trail**, eight miles from the overlook, are disappointingly small despite being the largest of the type in the country; a greater draw are the colorful snails and golden orb spiders lurking amongst their branches. The sight of the red mangrove trees – recognizable by their above-ground roots – rising from the sawgrass is a sure indication that you're approaching the coast.

Flamingo and around

A century ago, the only way to reach **FLAMINGO** was by boat, a fact that failed to deter a small bunch of settlers who came here to fish, hunt, smuggle and get paralytic on moonshine whisky. It didn't even have a name until the opening of a post office made one necessary: "The End of the World" was favored by those who knew the place, but "Flamingo" was eventually chosen due to an abundance of roseate spoonbills – pink-plumed birds, killed for their feathers – wrongly identified by locals. The completion of the road to Homestead in 1922 was expected to bring boom times to Flamingo, but as it turned out, most people seized on this as a chance to leave. None of the old buildings remain, and present-day Flamingo does a brisk trade servicing the needs of sports fishing fanatics. On land, the **visitor center** (summer daily 9am–5pm; winter 7.30am–5pm; ☎941/695-2945) and the marina of the *Flamingo Lodge* (see p.329), are the activity bases.

There are several walking trails within reach of Flamingo, but more promising are the numerous **canoe trails**. Rent a canoe ($25 a day) from the marina, and get maps and advice from the visitor center. Obviously, you should pick a canoe trail that suits your level of expertise; a likely one for novices (though not alone if you've no experience whatsoever) is the three-mile **Noble Hammock Trail**, passing through sawgrass and around mangroves, using a course pioneered by bootleg booze-makers. For polished paddlers, the hundred-mile **wilderness waterway** to Everglades City (see p.325), lined by plentiful backcountry campgrounds, is the trip you've been waiting for.

If you lack faith in your own abilities, take one of the **guided boat trips** from the marina. The most informative, the **Pelican Backcountry Cruise** (daily 12.30pm & 3.30pm; $12; reservations on ☎305/253-2241), makes a two-hour foray around the mangrove-enshrouded Whitewater Bay, offering good views of **Cape Sable**, a strip of deserted beach and rough prairie hovering uncertainly between land and sea. An alternative, and a must for birdwatchers, is the **Bald Eagle Florida Bay Sunset Cruise** (daily 7pm and sunset; $8.50), a ninety-minute tour of the marine feeding and nursery grounds.

travel details

Trains

Tampa to: Bradenton (2 daily; 1hr 10min); Clearwater (2 daily; 45min); Clearwater Beach (2 daily; 1hr); DeLand (2 daily; 3hr 14min); Jacksonville (2 daily; 5hr 28min); Kissimmee (2 daily; 1hr 36min); Lakeland (2 daily; 32min); Orlando (2 daily; 12hr 16min); Palatka (2 daily; 4hr 1min); Sanford (2 daily; 2hr 54min); Sarasota (2 daily; 1hr 40min); St Petersburg (2 daily; 30min); Treasure Island (2 daily; 1hr); Winter Park (2 daily; 2hr 31min).

St Petersburg to: Tampa (2 daily; 35min); Treasure Island (1 daily; 30min); Winter Haven (2 daily; 2hr 45min).

Buses

Tampa to: Avon Park (1 daily; 3hr 5min); Bradenton (5 daily; 1hr); Clearwater (6 daily; 30min); Crystal River (3 daily; 3hr 13min); Fort Lauderdale (5 daily; 7hr 5min); Fort Myers (5 daily; 2hr 5min); Lake Wales (1 daily; 1hr 55min); Lakeland (1 daily; 1hr); Miami (5 daily; 8hr 55min); Naples (5 daily; 4hr 5min); Orlando (7 daily; 1hr 30min); Sarasota (5 daily; 1hr 35min); Sebring (1 daily; 3hr 30min); St Petersburg (15 daily; 35min); Tallahassee (3 daily; 6hr 35min); Venice (5 daily; 2hr 10min); West Palm Beach (1 daily; 6hr); Winter Haven (1 daily; 1hr 30min).

St Petersburg to: Clearwater (11 daily; 30min); Tampa (11 daily; 35min–1hr).

CHAPTER SEVEN

THE PANHANDLE

B utting up against the southernmost borders of both Alabama and Georgia, Florida's long, narrow **Panhandle** has much more in common with the Deep South than with the rest of the state. Cosmopolitan sophisticates in Miami and Tampa have countless jokes lampooning the folksy lifestyles of the people here – undeniably more rural and down-to-earth than their counterparts around the rest of the state – but the Panhandle has more to offer than many give it credit for; certainly, you won't get a true picture of Florida without seeing at least some of it.

A century ago, the Panhandle actually *was* Florida. At the western edge, **Pensacola** was a busy port when Miami was still a swamp; fertile soils lured wealthy plantation owners south and helped establish **Tallahassee** as a high-society gathering-place and administrative center – a role which, as the state capital, it retains; and the great Panhandle forests fuelled a timber boom that brought new towns and unrivalled prosperity. But the decline of cotton, the felling of too many trees and the coming of the East Coast railway eventually left the Panhandle high and dry.

The region today divides neatly in two. Much of the **inland Panhandle** consists of small farming towns that see few visitors, despite their friendly rhythm, fine examples of Old South architecture, and their proximity to springs, sinkholes and the **Apalachicola National Forest** – perhaps the best place in Florida to disappear into the wilderness. The **coastal Panhandle**, on the other hand, is inundated with tourists, who flock in from the southern states and wreak havoc during the riotous student spring breaks. Much of the coastline is marked by rows of hotels and condos, but there are also protected areas that are home to some of the finest stretches of unspoilt sand anywhere in the state. The blinding white sands are almost pure quartz, washed down over millions of years from the Appalachian mountains, and they squeak when you walk on them. Not to be outshone, the Gulf waters here are two-tone: emerald green close to the shore and deep blue further out.

Provided you're driving, **getting around** presents few problems. Across the inland Panhandle, **I-10** carries the through traffic, and **Hwy-90** links the little places and many of the natural sights between Tallahassee and Pensacola. It's easy, too, to turn south off I-10 or Hwy-90 and get to the coast in under an hour. The main route along the coast is **Hwy-98**, with a number of smaller, scenic roads leading off it. Several daily Greyhound buses connect the bigger centers, but rural and coastal services are fewer, and some parts see no bus services at all. The Los Angeles–Jacksonville Amtrak service crosses the Panhandle, stopping once a day in each direction at Tallahassee and Pensacola.

ACCOMMODATION PRICE CODES

All **accommodation prices** in this book have been coded using the symbols below. Note that prices are for the least expensive double rooms in each establishment. For a full explanation see p.27 in Basics.

① up to $30	③ $45-60	⑤ $80-100	⑦ $130-180
② $30-45	④ $60-80	⑥ $100-130	⑧ $180+

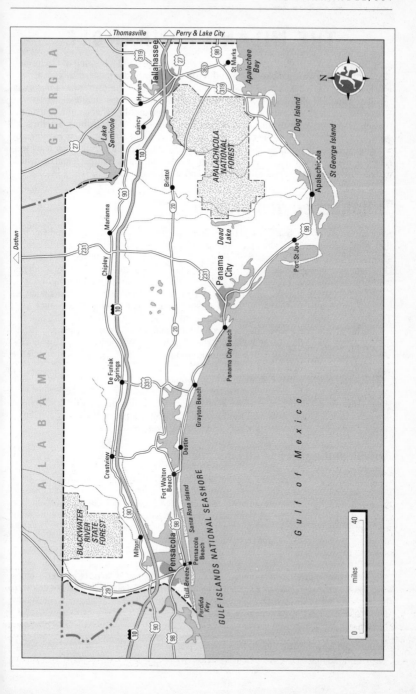

THE INLAND PANHANDLE

Vast tracts of oak and pine trees, dozens of winding rivers and a handful of moderately sized agricultural bases make much of the **inland Panhandle** powerfully evocative of Florida in the days before mass tourism took hold. Despite the presence of the sociable state capital, **Tallahassee**, it's the insular rural communities strung along Hwy-90 – between Tallahassee and the busy coastal city of **Pensacola** – that set the tone of the region. These small towns, including **Marianna**, **Chipley** and **De Funiak Springs**, all grew rich from the turn-of-the-century timber industry and now pull their earnings by working some of the richest soil in Florida. Due to some architectural gems, they warrant a look-see as you pass through to the area's compelling natural features, which include the state's only explorable caverns and two massive forests.

Tallahassee and around

State capital it may be, but **TALLAHASSEE** is a provincial city of oak trees and soft hills that won't take more than two days to explore in full. Around its small grid of central streets – where you'll find plentiful reminders of Florida's formative years – briefcase-clutching bureaucrats mingle with some of Tallahassee's 25,000 university students, who brighten the mood considerably and keep the city awake late into the night.

Though built on the site of an important prehistoric meeting-place and taking its name from Apalachee Indian ("*talwa*" meaning town; and "*ahassee*" meaning old), Tallahassee's **history** really begins with Florida's incorporation into the US and the search for an administrative base between the former regional capitals, Pensacola and St Augustine. Once this site was chosen, the local Native Americans – the Tamali tribe – were unceremoniously dispatched to make room for a trio of log cabins in which the first Florida government sat in 1823.

The scene of every major wrangle in Florida politics, and the home of an ever-expanding white-collar workforce handling the paperwork of the country's fourth fastest-growing state, Tallahassee's own fortunes have been hindered by the lightning-paced development of south Florida. Oddly distanced from most of the people it governs, the city remains a conservative place with a slow tempo – and a strong sense of the past.

Arrival, getting around and information

I-10 cuts across Tallahassee's northern perimeter; turning off along Monroe Street takes you past most of the budget accommodation and on into downtown Tallahassee, three miles distant. **Hwy-90** (known as Tennessee Street) and **Hwy-27** (Apalachee Parkway) are more central – arriving in or close to downtown. Coming by **bus** presents few problems: the Greyhound terminal is at 112 West Tennessee Street (☎222-4240 locally, or ☎1-800/231-2222 for reservations), within walking distance of downtown and opposite the local bus station. The Amtrak station is housed in a historic (1855) building at the intersection of Gaines Street and Railroad Avenue (☎224-2779), one block from Railroad Square in downtown Tallahassee. Tallahassee's **airport** is twelve miles southwest of the city (☎891-7800); frustratingly, no public transport services link it to the town. A **taxi** to the center will cost around $15 (try City Taxi, ☎562-4222, or Yellow Cab, ☎222-3070); some motels offer a free pick-up service.

The area code for Tallahassee and the rest of the Panhandle area covered in this chapter is ☎850

Getting around

Downtown Tallahassee can easily be seen **on foot; local buses** (TalTran ☎891-5200) need only be used to reach outlying destinations. Collect a **route map and timetable** from the **bus station** (officially known as "Transfer Plaza") at the corner of Tennessee and Duval streets. You can get a **free ride** into downtown Tallahassee from the bus station with the **Old Town Trolley**, which runs to the Civic Center (near the New Capitol Building) and back at ten-minute intervals on weekdays between 7am and 6pm; hop on at any of the "Trolley Stop" signs. The *Old Town Trolley Tour Guide* leaflet also gives a brief history of each of the eighteen stops and their surrounds. Despite the area's hills, there is plenty of good **cycling** terrain. Rent a bike from Tec's Pro Shop, 672 Gaines Street (☎681-6979; $18 per day), or St Mark's Trail Bikes and Blades, 4780 Woodville Hwy (☎656-0001; $4.50 per hour).

Information

The **Chamber of Commerce**, 100 N Duval Street (Mon–Fri 8.30am–5pm; ☎224-8116) has stacks of leaflets relating to the city and the surrounding area. For material covering Tallahassee, the rest of the Panhandle and much of the rest of the state, use the **Tallahassee Area Visitor Information Center** (Mon–Fri 8am–5pm, Sat & Sun 8.30am–4.30pm; ☎1-800/628-2866 or ☎413-9200) on the ground floor of the New Capitol Building – see "Downtown Tallahassee," below. While there, be sure to pick up the engaging *Walking Guide to Historic Downtown Tallahassee* booklet (free), a comprehensive guide to the buildings and history of the area.

Accommodation

Finding **accommodation** in Tallahassee is only problematic during two periods: the sixty-day sitting of the state legislature beginning with the first Tuesday in March – if you're arriving then, try to turn up on a Friday or Saturday when the power-brokers have gone home; and on fall weekends when the Seminoles (Florida State University's immensely well-supported football team) are playing at home. If you can't avoid these periods, book well ahead.

The cheapest **hotels** and **motels** are on N Monroe Street about three miles north of downtown: the very comfortable *La Quinta*, at no. 2905 (☎385-7172; ④) has much bigger and better rooms than the exterior suggests; and the *Econo Lodge*, no. 2681 (☎1-800/424-4777; ③), *Super 8*, no. 2702 (☎1-800/800-8000; ③), and the *Days Inn*, no. 2800 (☎1-800/325-2525; ③) are also trusty bets. Staying downtown is more expensive, except during the summer when there are $28-a-night rooms on the FSU campus inside *Osceola Hall*, 500 Chapel Drive (☎222-5010; ①). Failing that, you can splurge for the luxurious *Governors Inn*, 209 S Adams Street (☎1-800/342-7717; ⑦), or the more economical *Comfort Inn*, 1302 Apalachee Parkway (☎877-3141; ②).

There are no **campgrounds** within the city. The nearest that accept tents are beside Lake Talquin to the west, the closest being the *Tallahassee RV Center & Campground*, 6401 W Tennesee Street (Exit 28 off I-10; ☎575-0145; $16 to pitch a tent), or *Seminole Lodge-Sneads campground*, 2360 Legion Road (Exit 23 off I-10; ☎593-6886; office open 5am-6pm; $12.50 to pitch a tent). Alternatively, the nearest **RV-only** sites are *Tallahassee RV Park* (☎878-7641; $18–20), five miles east on Hwy-90, and *Bell's Campground* (☎576-7082; $18–20), five miles west on Hwy-90.

Downtown Tallahassee

The soul of Tallahassee is the mile-square downtown area, where the main targets – the two Capitol Buildings, the State Museum of History and the two universities – are within walking distance of Adams Street, a peaceful and partly pedestrianized main drag,

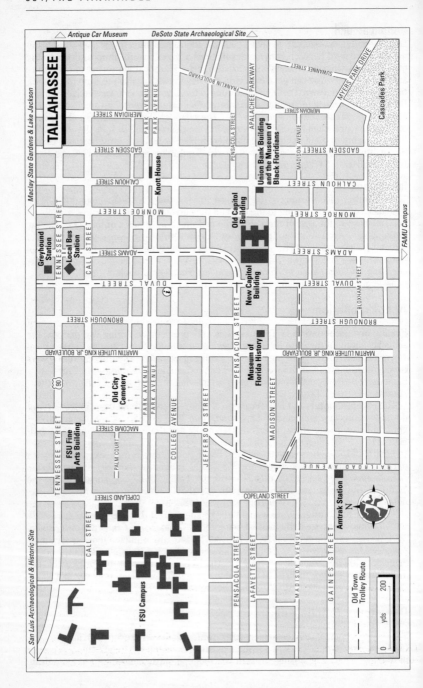

TALLAHASSEE

△ Antique Car Museum   DeSoto State Archaeological Site △

Maclay State Gardens & Lake Jackson

FRANKLIN BOULEVARD
APALACHEE PARKWAY
MYERS PARK DRIVE
SUWANNEE STREET

Cascades Park

PARK AVENUE
PARK AVENUE
MERIDIAN STREET
PENSACOLA STREET
MERIDIAN STREET
MADISON AVENUE
GADSDEN STREET
CALHOUN STREET
MONROE STREET
ADAMS STREET
DUVAL STREET
BLOXHAM STREET
BRONOUGH STREET

Knott House

Union Bank Building and the Museum of Black Floridians

Old Capitol Building

Greyhound Station
Local Bus Station

TENNESSEE STREET
CALL STREET
GADSDEN STREET
CALHOUN STREET
MONROE STREET
ADAMS STREET
DUVAL STREET
BRONOUGH STREET

New Capitol Building

FAMU Campus

Old City Cemetery

US 90

PARK AVENUE
PARK AVENUE
COLLEGE AVENUE
JEFFERSON STREET
MACOMB STREET
PALM COURT
TENNESSEE STREET
CALL STREET
COPELAND STREET

FSU Fine Arts Building

MARTIN LUTHER KING JR. BOULEVARD

Museum of Florida History

PENSACOLA STREET
MADISON STREET

COPELAND STREET

San Luis Archaeological & Historic Site

FSU Campus

MARTIN LUTHER KING JR. BOULEVARD

RAILROAD AVENUE

Amtrak Station

N

PENSACOLA STREET
LAFAYETTE STREET
MADISON AVENUE
GAINES STREET

Old Town Trolley Route

0   yds   200

whose restored Twenties storefronts more often than not conceal attorneys' offices. A unique and charming feature of downtown Tallahassee is the **canopy roads**, thoroughfares lined with oak trees, whose branches, heavy with Spanish moss, arch across the road. Next to the allure of these splendid tree corridors – the best examples being Miccossukee, Centerville, Old St Augustine, Meridian and Old Bainbridge roads – the **New Capitol Building**, at the junction of Apalachee Parkway and Monroe Street (Mon–Fri 8.30am–5pm; free; Visitor Information Center open in lobby Sat & Sun 8.30am–4.30pm, see "Information," above), is an eyesore. Vertical vents make the seat of Florida's legal system resemble a gigantic air-conditioning unit. The only way to escape the sight of the structure, unveiled to much outrage in 1977, is to go inside, where the 22nd-floor observation level provides an unobstructed view over Tallahassee and its environs; if you're visiting from mid-February to April, stop off at the fifth floor for a glance at the House of Representatives or the Senate in action. Should you feel the need to learn more about the building, join the free 45-minute **guided tours** (on the hour, Mon–Fri 9–11am & 1–4pm, Sat & Sun 9am–3pm); not particularly exciting but full of information.

Florida's growing army of bureaucrats made the New Capitol Building necessary. Previously, they'd been crammed into the ninety-year-old **Old Capitol Building** (Mon–Fri 9am–4.30pm, Sat 10am–4.30pm, Sun noon–4.30pm; free; main entrance facing Apalachee Parkway), which stands in the shadow of its replacement. Designed on a more human scale than its modern counterpart, with playful red and white awnings over its windows, it's hard to imagine that the Old Capitol's walls once echoed with the decisions that shaped modern Florida. Proof is provided, however, by the political history displays in the side rooms: absorbing exhibits lifting the lid on the state's juiciest scandals and controversies.

Along Apalachee Parkway from the Old Capitol's entrance is the nineteenth-century **Union Bank Building** (Tues–Fri 10am–1pm, Sat & Sun 1–4pm; free). The bank's past has been unsteady: going bust in the 1850s after giving farmers too much credit; reopening to administer the financial needs of emancipated slaves after the Civil War; and later serving variously as a shoe factory, a bakery and a cosmetics shop.

Museum of Black Floridians

Today, the Union Bank Building is home to the **Museum of Black Floridians** (Mon–Fri 9am–4pm; free; ☎561-2603), which chronicles the history and persecution of Florida's black community. The first black Floridians accompanied Spanish explorers to Florida in the sixteenth century, and many more came as runaways in the early nineteenth century, taking refuge among the Creek and Seminole Indians. The museum explores these stories and the many facets of black culture through documents and displays. Among the most intriguing are a collection of black piggy banks depicting derogatory images of African Americans, which were popular in white households from the turn of the century through to the 1960s. Another exhibit charts the rise of Madame C.J. Walker, the first black female millionaire whose line of beauty salons aimed to make African American women look more European. As well as tributes to black American entertainers such as Josephine Baker, the museum has some chilling Ku Klux Klan memorabilia, including an original Klan sword and a fairly recent application for membership, which proves the Klan is far from being ancient history: "Join the Junior Klan" leaflets were recently left at Tallahassee's prestigious Leon County High School, and in 1997, the Klan won permission to march through town, but was turned back by protesting students on Monroe Street.

The Capital Cultural Center

Tallahassee is one of only two US state capitals not to have a major art museum. The **Capital Cultural Center**, set to open in late 1998 at 350 Duval Street (one block from the State Capitol), will change all that. Art exhibits proposed for the grand opening include an homage to American still-life painting and selections on loan from New York's Metropolitan Museum of Art. For information on opening times and all planned exhibits, call ☎671-4888.

The Museum of Florida History

For a more rounded history – easily the fullest account of Florida's past anywhere in the state – visit the **Museum of Florida History**, 500 S Bronough Street (Mon–Fri 9am–4.30pm, Sat 10am–4.30pm, Sun noon–4.30pm; free). Detailed accounts of Paleo-Indian settlements and the significance of their burial and temple mounds – some of which have been found on the edge of Tallahassee (see "Around Tallahassee," below) – are valuable tools in comprehending Florida's prehistory. The imperialist crusades of the Spanish, both in Florida and across South and Central America, are also outlined through copious finds. Other than portraits of hard-faced Seminole chiefs, whose Native American tribes were driven south into Florida backcountry, there's disappointingly little on the nineteenth-century Seminole Wars – one of the sadder and bloodier skeletons in Florida's closet. There's plenty, though, on the turn-of-the-century railroads that made Florida a winter resort for wealthy northerners, and on the subsequent arrival of the "tin can tourists," whose nickname referred to the rickety Ford campervans (forerunners of the modern Recreational Vehicles) they drove to what was by then called "the Sunshine State" – an ironic epithet for a region that had endured centuries of strife, feuding and almost constant warfare.

Tallahassee's universities: FSU and FAMU

West from Adams Street, graffiti-coated fraternity and sorority houses along College Avenue line the approach to **Florida State University (FSU)**. This has long enjoyed a strong reputation for its humanities courses, taught from the late 1800s in the Collegiate Gothic classrooms you'll see as you enter the wrought-iron gates, but has recently switched emphasis to science and business, hence the newer, less characterful buildings on the far side of the campus. Shady oaks and palm trees make the grounds a pleasant place for a stroll, but there's little cause to linger. The student art of the **University Gallery and Museum** (Mon–Fri 9am–4pm; free), in the Fine Arts Building, might consume a few minutes, but you'd be better occupied rummaging around inside Bill's Bookstore, just across Call Street at 107 S Copeland Street (☎224-3178), whose large stock includes many student cast-offs at reduced prices.

The more interesting of Tallahassee's two universities, in spite of being financially much the poorer, is the **Florida Agriculture and Mechanical University (FAMU)**, about a mile south of the Capitol buildings. Florida's major black educational center since its founding in 1887, FAMU contains the **Black Archives Research Center and Museum** (Mon–Fri 9am–4pm; free), which is due to reopen in winter l998 after a renovation of the wooden, nineteenth-century Carnegie Library in which it's housed. While not as extensive as the Museum of Black Floridians (see above), the collection gives an illuminating insight into the situation of black people in Florida and the US, including letters and memorabilia of those who helped bring about change, including Martin Luther King and Booker T. Washington, and two Florida women who contributed to the rise of black awareness: educator and folklorist Mary McLeod Bethune (see "Daytona Beach" in "The Northeast Coast"), and author Zora Neale Hurston (see "Books" in Contexts).

The Knott House

Another important landmark in Florida's black history, and one of the city's best restored Victorian homes, is the **Knott House Museum**, 301 E Park Avenue (Wed–Fri 1–4pm, Sat 10am–4pm; free). It was built by a free black in 1843 and later became home to Florida's first black physician. Florida's slaves were officially emancipated in May

1865 by a proclamation read from the house's very steps. The house takes its name, however, from the Knotts, a white couple who bought it in 1928. State treasurer during a period of economic calamity (Florida had been devastated by two hurricanes as the country entered the Depression), William Knott became one of Florida's most respected and influential politicians until his retirement in 1941. His wife, Luella, meanwhile, devoted her energies to the temperance movement (partly through her efforts, alcohol was banned in Tallahassee for a fifty-year period) and to writing moralistic poems, many of which you'll see attached to the antiques and furnishings that fill this intriguing relic. The absence of intrusive ropes cordoning off the exhibits allows for an unusually intimate visit of the house and its history.

Old City Cemetery

A somewhat different perspective on Tallahassee's past is provided by a walking tour around the **Old City Cemetery**, between Macomb Street and M.L. King Jnr Boulevard (daily sunrise–sunset; free), which was established outside the city's original boundaries in 1829, and restored in 1991. Its layout, consisting of four quadrants, is striking as a testament to segregation, even in death: graves of Union soldiers lie in the southwest quarter, while those of Confederates are kept at a distance in the southeast portion; slaves and free Blacks were consigned to the western half of the ground, while whites occupied the eastern part. Among the names marked on gravestones, you'll find many of Tallahassee's former leading figures: their stories are told in an informative leaflet, *A Walking Tour of Old City Cemetery*, available at Tallahassee's Visitor Information Center (see "Information" above).

Eating

One of the few places to get **breakfast** in downtown Tallahassee is *Goodies*, 116 E College Avenue (☎681-3888), which also serves **lunch** (sandwich specials and big salads). Other lunch options are the stylish New York style *Andrew's Capital Grill & Bar*, 228 S Adams Street (☎222-3444), and *Andrew's Second Act*, at the same address – an elegant restaurant that also offers more expensive dinners. The *Uptown Café*, 111 E College Avenue (☎222-3253), provides reasonably priced sandwiches and salads at lunch time and bagels for breakfast.

For light, California-style eating, *Café Cabernet*, 1019 N Monroe Street (☎224-1175), has the biggest wine selection in town. Munch on gourmet sandwiches and sip coffee at the laid-back *Waterworks*, 104 1/2 S Munroe Street (☎224-1887), which turns into Tallahassee's best live-music joint at night (see below). A bit pricey but certainly original, *Kool Beanz Café*, 921 Thomasville Road (☎224-2466), offers starters like smoked rabbit and andouille gumbo and follows with entrees like spice-rum seared mahi with pineapple-blackbean salsa and plantain fries. Service is variable and be warned – the spice levels are set on hot.

Out of downtown Tallahassee, the best cheap option is the bland-looking *Shoney's*, at 2903 Monroe St, where you'll get as much soup, salads and fruit-related desserts as you can eat. *Mom and Dad's*, 4175 Apalachee Parkway (☎877-4518; closed Mon), has delicious and affordable homemade Italian food; and the *Wharf Seafood Restaurant*, 4141 Apalachee Parkway (☎656-2332), carries a great range of what its name suggests. There's more low-cost seafood – with a riotous atmosphere and live Fifties music – at *Barnacle Bill's*, 1830 N Monroe Street (☎385-8734). Another cheap and fun place for seafood, gumbo and British beer is *Paradise Grill*, 1406 N Meridian Road (☎224-2742). *The Mill*, 2329 Apalachee Parkway (☎656-2867), has burgers, salad buffets, sandwiches and exquisite pizzas to accompany its home-brewed beers. South of town, *Seven Hills*, at 3613 Woodville Hwy (☎656-6112), is a great little café serving specialty coffees, heavenly cheesecakes, quiche and cream cakes in a friendly kitchen-style setting.

Nightlife

Bolstered by its students, Tallahassee has a strong **nightlife**, with a leaning to social drinking and live rock music (see below). There's also **comedy** at the Comedy Zone, Ramada Inn North, 2900 N Monroe Street (☎386-1027), and a fair amount of **drama**, headed by the student productions at the University Theater on the FSU campus (☎644-6500), and the Tallahassee Little Theater, 1861 Thomasville Road (☎224-8474). Find out **what's on** from the "Limelights" section of the Friday *Tallahassee Democrat* newspaper; the *Florida Flambeau*, the FSU student paper containing listings and recommendations; or, for live music details, listen to radio station WFSU at 89.7 FM.

Bars

On nights leading up to Seminole football matches, *Doc's*, 1921 W Tennessee Street (☎224-5946), is packed with clean-cut collegiate sports fans. Other strongly collegiate hang-outs are *Po' Boys Creole Café*, 224 E College Avenue (☎224-5400) and 679 W Tennessee Street (☎681-9191), *Potbelly's*, 459 W College Avenue (☎224-2233), and *Poor Paul's Pourhouse*, 618 W Tennessee Street (☎222-2978). The jazz on Friday nights at *Late Night*, 809 Gay Street (☎224-2429), creates a groovy mood as students mingle in a sultry setting. Less student-dominated, *Calico Jack's*, 2745 Capitol Circle NE (☎385-6653), offers beer, oysters and stomping southern rock'n'roll records; *Halligan's*, 1700 Halstead Boulevard in Oak Lake Village (☎668-7665), is popular for its pool tables and chilled mugs of beer; and *Clyde's & Costello's*, 210 S Adams Street (☎224-2173), pulls a smart and very cliquey crowd, which grows a bit rowdy during Thursday's four-for-one drink offer.

Live music and clubs

Big name **live bands** appear at *The Moon*, 1020 E Lafayette Street (☎222-6666 for recorded info), or at the vast *Leon County Civic Center*, at the corner of Pensacola Street and Martin Luther King Jnr Boulevard (☎222-0400). For a taste of the past, try the *American Legion Hall*, 229 Lake Ella Drive (☎222-3382), which hosts a big-band dance night every Tuesday and old-fashioned country the rest of the week; *Andrew's Upstairs*, 228 S Adams Street (☎222-3444), hosts modern jazz combos; and there's rock and blues at the log-cabin-like *Bullwinkle's*, 620 W Tennessee Street (☎224-0651). The *Cow Haus*, 469 St Francis Street (☎425-2697), showcases known and unknown indie acts, as does *The Cab Stand*, 1019 N Munroe Street (☎224-0322), which also features blues. The *Paradise Grill*, 1406 Meridian Road (☎224-2742) is popular with the 25-plus age group and offers live bands Thurs–Sat.

Currently at the apex of the **nightclub** scene are *Late Night Library*, 809 Gaines Street (☎224-2429), a cool dance-music club catering to a college crowd, and *Top Flight Club*, 623 Osceola Street (☎425-2697), which offers live jazz and blues and is always good for a drink, dance or laugh. The funkiest joint in town is the *Waterworks*, 104½ S Monroe Street (☎224-1887), an intimate venue decorated with a fusion of Fifties chairs, African art, and brightly painted junk. You won't want to leave.

Tallahassee's **gay nightlife** is comprised of several bar/clubs, the most popular of which is *Brothers*, 926 West Thorpe Street (☎386-2399), a design-conscious venue with a friendly crowd that's almost exclusively gay on Sundays, Thursdays and Fridays. The rest of the week pulls in a mixed clientele. *Club Park* Ave, 115 Park Avenue (☎599-9143), is a bit more slick, and is gay-only on Saturday nights.

Listings

Art galleries Tallahassee has a credible arts scene: around Railroad Square, close to the junction of Springhill Road and Gaines Street, near the FSU campus, are some innovative galleries, and several local artists have open studios there. Other contemporary art showcases are Nomads, 508 W Gaines St; the La Moyne Gallery, 125 N Gadsden St, The 621 Gallery, 567 Industrial Drive, and Signature Gallery, 2779 NE Capital Circle.

Car rental Most companies have branches at the airport (see p.332), and at the following locations: Alamo, 1720 Capitol Circle (☎576-6134); Avis, 3300 Capitol Circle (☎331-1212); Budget, 1415 Capitol Circle (☎1-800/527-0700); Lucky's, 2539 W Tennessee St (☎575-0632); Thrifty Car Rental, 1385 Blountstown Hwy (☎576-RENT).

Dentist Dental Information Service: ☎1-800/282-9117.

Hospital Non-emergencies: Tallahassee Regional Medical Center, 1300 Miccosukee Road (☎681-1155).

Pharmacy Walgreens, in the Tallahassee Mall, 2415 N Monroe Street (☎385-7145), open Mon–Sat 10am–9pm, Sun 12.30–5.30pm.

Sports Tickets for FSU baseball (March–May) and football (Sept–Nov) matches are on sale at the stadiums two hours before the games begin: ☎644-1073 and ☎644-1830 respectively. For info on FAMU sports teams, all known as the Rattlers, call ☎599-3200. There's a full fixture list in the local telephone book.

Western Union The most convenient locations are Easy Mail West, Inc at 1717 Apalachee Parkway and 3491 Thomasville Road; Mail Boxes Etc at 1350 East Tennessee Street; and Winn Dixie, 813 North Monroe St. Call ☎1-800/325-6000 for other locations.

Around Tallahassee

Scattered around the fringes of Tallahassee, half a dozen diverse spots deserve brief visits: a remarkable antique car museum, prehistoric mounds, archaeological sites and lakeside gardens. All are easily accessible by car, though most are much harder to reach by bus.

The Antique Car Museum

The **Antique Car Museum**, 3550 Mahan Drive (Mon–Sat 10am–5pm, Sun noon–5pm; $7.50, children $5; ☎942-0137) is well worth the three-mile drive east along Tennessee Street, which changes to Mahan Drive en route. The museum's owner, DeVeo Moore, began his career modestly by shoeing horses. But through quiet determination, which inspires admiration or distaste depending on who you ask in Tallahassee, he is now one of the region's richest men. Selling just one of his businesses in early 1998 netted $37.5 million. The biggest crowd-puller in the collection is the gleaming 21-foot long Batmobile from the Tim Burton movie, bought for $500,000, and complete with Batman's suits and gloves and a flame-thrower attachment. The most valuable car is a $1.2 million 1931 Duesenberg Model J, but the most intriguing specimen is an 1860-built horse-drawn hearse believed to have carried Abraham Lincoln to his final resting place.

The consummate collector, Moore didn't limit his collecting to just automobiles. Among the eclectic exhibits are "anti-colic" baby bottles and whole rooms of scooters and cash registers. The museum is expanding almost exponentially, and plans are afoot to find a new location by the year 2000.

The San Luis and de Soto archaeological sites

Slowly being unearthed at the **San Luis Archaeological and Historic Site**, 2020 W Mission Road, about three miles west of downtown Tallahassee (bus #21), the village of San Luis de Talimali was a hub of the seventeenth-century Spanish mission system, second only to St Augustine. At its zenith in 1675 its population numbered 1400. Stop by the **visitor center** (Mon–Fri 9am–4.30pm, Sat 10am–4.30pm, Sun noon–4.30pm; free) for a general explanation and to see some of the finds – or join the hour-long free **guided tour** (Mon–Fri at noon, Sat at 11am & 3pm, Sun at 2pm) to appreciate the importance of the place. On some weekends, period-attired individuals re-enact village life; it sounds tacky but can be fun.

The **de Soto State Archaeological Site**, two miles east of downtown Tallahassee at the corner of Goodbody Lane and Lafayette Street, is where Spanish explorer Hernando de Soto is thought to have set up camp in 1539 and held the first Christmas celebration in North American history. The historical associations are more dramatic here than at the San Luis site, but there's much less tangible evidence of the past, and the site is in fact closed to the public except for special events. All there is to see is a few holes in the ground, and it's not at all an essential stop even when it's open. For more information on the de Soto expedition, which was the first European team to cross the Mississippi River, see "History" in Contexts.

Tallahassee Museum of History and Natural Science
Three miles southwest of the city, the **Tallahassee Museum of History and Natural Science** (Mon–Sat 9am–5pm, Sun 12.30–5pm; $6.50), off Lake Bradford Road (bus #15) at 3945 Museum Drive, is primarily aimed at kids, though it could fill an hour even if you don't have young minds to stimulate. The centerpiece is a working nineteenth-century-style farm, complete with cows and wandering roosters. Elsewhere, there's a short nature walk, a few cases of snakes and a couple of old buildings of moderate note: a 1937 Baptist Church and a vintage schoolhouse.

Maclay State Gardens
For a lazy half-day, journey four miles northeast of downtown Tallahassee to **Maclay State Gardens**, set in a lakeside park at 3540 Thomasville Road, north of I-10, Exit 30 (park: daily 8am–sunset, cars $3.25; garden: daily 9am–5pm, Jan–April $3, rest of year free; bus #16 stops close by). New York financier and amateur gardener Alfred B. Maclay bought this large piece of land in the Twenties and planted flowers and shrubs in order to create a blooming season from January to April. It worked: for four months each year the gardens are alive with the fragrances and fantastic colors of azaleas, camellias, pansies and other flowers, framed by dogwood and redbud trees and towered over by huge oaks and pines. Guided tours of the gardens are conducted on weekends around mid-March (call ☎487-4556 for details and times), but they're worth visiting at any time, if only to retire to the lakeside pavilion for a snooze as lizards and squirrels scurry around your feet.

The admission fee to the gardens also gets you into the **Maclay House** (open Jan–April only), filled with the Maclays' furniture and countless books on horticulture.

While you're here, take your time to explore **the rest of the park** and Lake Hall. A picnic area gives great views of the lake, as does the short **Lake Overstreet Trail**, which meanders through the wooded hillside overlooking it. There's also a swimming area close to the parking area nearest the park's entrance.

Lake Jackson and the Indian Mounds
Most boat-owning locals moor their vessels beside the sizeable **Lake Jackson**, five miles north of downtown Tallahassee. On an inlet known as Meginnis Arm is the **Lake Jackson Mounds State Archaeological Site**, off Hwy-27 at Crowder Road (daily 8am–sunset; free), where rich finds, such as copper breastplates and ritual figures, suggest that this eighty-acre site was once an important Native American ceremonial center. Other than large humps of soil and a sense of history, all that's here now are a few picnic tables and an undemanding nature trail over a small ravine. By car, follow the signs off Monroe Street; on foot, the site's a three-mile trek from the #1 bus stop.

North of Tallahassee

There's a wide range of roads that snake **north from Tallahassee**, and a surprising number of them offer low-key but enjoyable forays. The Georgia border is only twenty miles away, and the most direct route is the Thomasville Road (Route 319) to, unsurprisingly,

THOMASVILLE, a sleepy little town just across the Georgia border, and a one-time winter haven for wealthy Northerners who built magnificent plantations on the Florida side of the border. Five miles south of Thomasville, the **Pebble Hill Plantation** (Tues–Sat 10am–5pm, Sun 1–5pm, closed most of Sept; hour-long guided tour of house, with the last tour leaving at 4pm; $7, grounds only $3; ☎912-226-2344) remains from the time of cotton picking and slavery, and shows how comfortable things were for the wealthy whites who ran the show. Much of the original Pebble Hill burnt down in the Thirties, and what you see now is a fairly faithful rebuilding of the sumptuous main house, complete with the extensive fine art, antique, crystal and porcelain collections that belonged to the house's final owner, Elisabeth Ireland Poe, and was rescued from the fire. Note that babies and children aged six or under are not allowed in the house. Each April the house comes back to life as people throng to a spring plantation ball.

If you're feeling carnivorous, take Centerville Road north from Tallahassee (Route 151), which, after twelve miles, leads to **Bradley's Country Store** (Mon–Fri 9am–6pm, Sat 9am–5pm). For seventy years, Bradley's has been peddling Southern-style food, specializing in smoked sausages and unusual delicacies like country-milled grits, hogshead cheese and liver pudding.

Havana

Twelve miles northwest of Tallahassee along Monroe Street (Route 27) is tiny **HAVANA** (pronounced Hey-vannah). Once known for its tobacco plantations and vegetable-canning industry, the town (population 1900) was dead on its feet until it discovered that filling its pretty brick buildings with a rash of tourist-oriented antique shops could breathe new life into the community. Even with the influx of tourists, the place retains a cozy feel and makes for a worthwhile visit – as long as you're not expecting to pick up a bargain.

The main body of antique stores huddles around Second St, but a more diverting setting for shopping is the **Havana Cannery** on Ninth St (Wed–Sun 10am–6pm, Fri & Sat 10am–10pm; ☎539-3800), once a burgeoning fruit-canning business and now a maze of antique stores. After canning seven million pounds of fruit during World War II, the company lost out to larger rivals and shifted to honey-packing until shutting down in 1994.

The **McLauchlin House**, at the corner of Seventh Avenue and Second Street (Wed–Sat 10am–5.30pm, Sun noon–5pm; ☎539-0901) is as interesting for its former inhabitants as for its architecture. Nellie McLauchlin, who still lives nearby, was born in the house 97 years ago. She was married here 77 years ago, and her husband, Joe, died at the age of 103 in 1998. Now home to six more antique shops, the 150-year-old farmhouse is a gem to look at: there's a wrap-round porch, sloping floors and uneven doors. There's not much else to see in Havana, but if you hit town in early March, look for the **MusicFest**, a three-day jazz-and-blues event ($30; ☎353-3309).

Eating in Havana is never a problem. You're sure to come across the *Twin Willows Café*, 211 NW First Street, situated amongst a plethora of antique shops. The dill-chicken and Greek salads are very fresh but rather overpriced. For a better deal and more fun, try *Dolly's Expresso*, 206 NW First Street (☎539-6716). The owners are from Key West, and serve Cuban sandwiches, luscious desserts (try a wicked chocolate-cheese cannoli) and great coffee. At the Havana Cannery, *Shade* (☎539-8401; closed Mon & Tues) is a great choice for traditional southern dishes like black-eyed pea fritters with sour cream, fried green tomato sandwiches and cornmeal-fried catfish.

The best option for an overnight **stay** is *Historic Havana House*, 301 E Sixth Ave (☎539-5611; ⑤), a lovely bed-and-breakfast that doesn't allow smoking or children under eight.

South of Tallahassee

On weekends, many Tallahassee residents head south to the Panhandle's beaches (see "The Coastal Panhandle," p.349). If you're not eager to join them, make a slower trek **south** along Routes 363 or 61, tracking down a few isolated pockets of historical or geological significance; or take Hwy-319 and lose yourself in the biggest and best of Florida's forests.

One of the most enjoyable ways to explore is by **cycling or roller-blading** the 16-mile Tallahassee–St Marks Historic Railroad Trail, a flat and straight course through placid woodlands following the route of a long-abandoned railroad. Bikes and blades can be rented for four hours from Tec's Pro Bike Shop, 4780 Woodville Highway (☎656-0001; $16 and $15 respectively).

Leon Sinks Geological Area

Seven miles south of Tallahassee on Route 319 is the **Leon Sinks Geological Area** (8am–8pm; free), a fascinating karst (terrain that has been altered by rain and ground water dissolving underlying limestone bedrock). The area contains several prominent sinkholes, numerous depressions, a natural bridge and a disappearing stream, all of which give a unique glimpse of the area before man's interference. There are three manageable trails of between half a mile and three miles, described in a guide available from the ranger station at the entrance.

The Natural Bridge Battlefield Site and St Marks

Ten miles southeast of Tallahassee, a turn off Route 363 at Woodville leads to the **Natural Bridge Battlefield Site** (daily 8am–sunset; free) where, on March 4, 1865, a motley band of Confederates saw off a much larger group of Union soldiers, preventing Tallahassee from falling into Yankee hands. Not that it made much difference – the war ended a couple of months later – but the victory is celebrated by a monument and an annual re-enactment on or close to the anniversary: several hours of shouting, loud bangs and smoke.

Twelve miles south of Woodville, Route 363 expires at the hamlet of **ST MARKS**, where the **San Marcos de Apalache Historic Site** (Thurs–Mon 9am–5pm, free; museum $1) offers decent pickings for students of Florida history – this sixteenth-century Spanish-built fort was visited by early explorers such as Pánfilo de Narváez and Hernando de Soto, and two hundred years later became Andrew Jackson's headquarters when he waged war on the Seminole Indians. Round off a visit at one of the nearby fishcamp eating places, such as *Posey's* (no phone), on Old Fort Drive.

If you prefer wildlife to history, backtrack slightly along Route 363 and turn east along Hwy-98. Three miles on you'll find the main entrance to **St Marks National Wildlife Refuge** (daily sunrise–sunset; cars $3, pedestrians and cyclists $1), which spreads out over the boggy outflow of the St Marks River. Bald eagles and a few black bears reside in the refuge, though from the various roadside look-out points and observation towers you're more likely to spot otters, white-tailed deer, racoons and a wealth of bird life. A drive to the end of the road leads to the picturesque St Marks Lighthouse. Just inside the entrance, a **visitor center** doles out useful information (Mon–Fri 8am–4.15pm, Sat & Sun 10am–5pm).

Wakulla Springs

Fifteen miles south of Tallahassee, off Route 61 on Route 267, **Wakulla Springs State Park** (daily 8am–sunset; cars $3.25, pedestrians and cyclists $1), contains what is believed to be one of the biggest and deepest natural springs in the world, pumping up half a million gallons of crystal-clear pure water from the bowels of the earth every day – difficult to guess from the calm surface. The principal reason for visiting Wakulla Springs is to enjoy the barely touched scenery and to appreciate a part of Florida that is still intact after hundreds of years.

It's refreshing to **swim** in the cool waters, though it's somewhat disconcerting that the marked areas are just inches from those where swimming is prohibited due to alligators. To learn more about the spring, you should take the fifteen-minute narrated **glass-bottomed boat tour** ($4.50) and peer down to the swarms of fish hovering around the 180-foot-deep cavern through which the water comes. Join the forty-minute **river cruise** ($4.50) for glimpses of some of the park's other inhabitants: deer, turkeys, turtles, herons and egrets – and the inevitable alligators. If *déjà vu* strikes, it may be because a number of films have been shot here, including several of the early *Tarzan* movies and parts of *The Creature from the Black Lagoon*. To see the alligators and snakes at their most active, take the **moonlight cruise** at twilight ($4.50).

You shouldn't leave without strolling through the **Wakulla Lodge**, 550 Wakulla Park Drive (☎224-5950; ④), a hotel built beside the spring in 1937, which retains many of its original features: Moorish archways, stone fireplaces and fabulous hand-painted Toltec and Aztec designs on the lobby's wooden ceiling. Take the opportunity, also, to pay your respects to the stuffed carcass of "Old Joe," one of the oldest and largest alligators ever known, who died in the Fifties, measuring eleven feet long and supposedly aged 200; he's in a glass case by the reception desk. **Spending a night** here is actually comparatively cheap. The lodge and its surrounds have a relaxing ambience that can prove quite addictive. An added bonus is that once the daytrippers have departed, you'll have the springs and wildlife all to yourself.

Further south: the Apalachicola National Forest

With swamps, savannahs and springs dotted liberally about its half-million acres, the **Apalachicola National Forest** is the inland Panhandle at its natural best. Several roads enable you to drive through a good-sized chunk, and many undemanding spots offer a rest and a snack, but to see more of the forest than its picnic tables and litter bins you'll have to make an effort: leaving the periphery and delving into the pristine interior, exploring at a leisurely pace, following hiking trails, taking a canoe on one of the rivers, or simply spending a night under the stars at one of the basic campgrounds.

Practicalities

The northeast corner of the forest almost touches Tallahassee's airport, fanning out from there to the edge of the Apalachicola River, about 35 miles west. Most of the

---

APALACHICOLA NATIONAL FOREST INFORMATION

Always equip yourself with maps, a weather forecast and advice from a ranger's office before setting off on a hike or canoe trip through the forest (for more on how to travel in the backcountry safely, see Basics). The Ochlockonee River divides the forest into two administrative districts, and the following offices are responsible for the west and east sides of the forest respectively:

Apalachicola Ranger District, Hwy-20, near Bristol; ☎643-2282.
Wakulla Ranger District, Route 6, near Crawfordville; ☎926-3561.

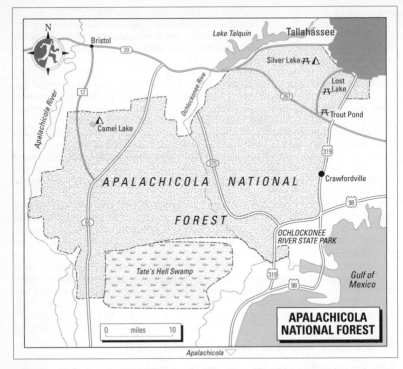

Apalachicola ▽

northern edge is bordered by Hwy-20, the eastern side by Hwy-319 and Hwy-98, and to the south lies the gruesome no-man's-land of Tate's Hell Swamp (see below).

The main **entrances** are off Hwy-20 and Hwy-319, and three minor roads, Routes 267, 375 and 65, form cross-forest links between the two highways. **Accommodation** is limited to camping. With the exception of Silver Lake (see below), all the sites are free with basic facilities – usually just toilets and drinking water. For more information, call ☎643-2282. The only place to **rent a canoe** near the forest is TNT Hideaway (☎925-6412), on Route 2 near Crawfordville, on Hwy-319.

One section of the forest, Trout Pond (open April–Oct only; $2 per car), on Route 373, is intended for **disabled visitors** and their guests, with a wheelchair-accessible lakeside nature trail and picnic area.

The edge of the forest: Lost Lake and Silver Lake

For a brief taste of what the forest can offer, make for **LOST LAKE**, seven miles from Tallahassee along Route 373, where there's little except a few picnic tables beside a small lake. The area's well-suited to a nibble and a waterside laze, and is less busy than the campervan-infested **SILVER LAKE**, nine miles east of the city, off Hwy-20. Swimming or camping at Silver Lake will cost you $2 and $5 respectively; anticipate the company of too many other people.

Deeper into the forest: hiking and canoeing

Several short, clearly marked **nature walks** lie within the forest, but the major **hiking trail**, strictly for ardent and well-equipped backpackers, is the thirty-mile

Apalachicola trail, which begins close to Crawfordville, on Hwy-319. This passes through the heart of the forest and includes a memorable (and sometimes difficult, depending on the weather conditions and water level) leg across an isolated swamp, the Bradwell Bay Wilderness. After this, the campground at Porter Lake, just to the west of the wilderness area, with its toilets and drinking water, seems the epitome of civilization.

The trail leads on to **Camel Lake**, whose campground has drinking water and toilets, and the less demanding nine-and-a-half-mile **Camel Lake Loop trail**. By vehicle, you can get directly to Camel Lake by turning off Hwy-20 at Bristol and continuing south for twelve miles, watching for the signposted turn-off on the left.

Although there are numerous put-in points along its four rivers, **canoeists** can paddle right into the forest from the western end of Lake Talquin (close to Hwy-20), and continue for a sixty-mile glide along the Ochlockonee River – the forest's major waterway – to the Ochlockonee River State Park, close to Hwy-319. Obviously, the length of trip means that to do it all you'll have to use the riverside **campgrounds** (info from the Supervisor's Office, National Forests Florida, 325 John Knox Road, Tallahassee). Those with drinking water are at Porter Lake, Whitehead Lake and Mack Landing; be warned that these are often concealed by dense foliage, so study your map carefully.

South of the forest: Tate's Hell Swamp

Driving through the forest on Route 65 or Route 67, or around it on Hwy-319 (which merges with Hwy-98 as it nears the coast), you'll eventually pass the large and forbidding area called **Tate's Hell Swamp**. According to legend, Tate was a farmer who pursued a panther into the swamp and was never seen again. It's a breeding ground for the deadly water moccasin snake, and gung-ho locals sometimes venture into the swamp hoping to catch a few snakes to sell to less reputable zoos; you're well advised to stay clear.

West of Tallahassee

To discover the social character of the inland Panhandle, take Hwy-90 **west from Tallahassee**: 180 miles of frequently tedious rural landscapes and time-locked farming towns that have been down on their luck since the demise of the timber industry fifty years ago. When it gets too much to bear, you can easily switch to the speedier I-10, or cut south to the coast. But the compensations are the endless supply of rustic eating places, low-cost accommodation, several appealing natural areas – and a chance to see a part of Florida that the travel brochures rarely reveal.

Quincy

Twenty miles west of Tallahassee on Hwy 90 is a sign that says "Welcome to Quincy City." With a fleeting glance at the surroundings – thick forest and not a building in sight – most tourists barrel on by without a second thought. Don't make this mistake. Underrated **QUINCY** is not only the capital of Gadsen County, but it was also one of the first towns to strike it rich because of Coca Cola. The Atlanta-based pharmacist who patented the fizzy drink sold company stock to friends in Quincy. They made a mint and built grandiose villas throughout the town at the beginning of the twentieth century. From the square on **Madison Street**, observe the immaculate **court house**, surrounded by topiary and a grand marble memorial to slain Confederate soldiers, erected by the "Ladies of Gadsden" in 1884. Just opposite, on East Jefferson St, the wall of Padgett's jewellery store is covered with the original Coke ad. Painted here in 1905, it espouses coke as "delicious and refreshing, five cents at fountains and bottles." Check in at the **Chamber of Commerce**, 221 N Madison Street (☎627-9231), for more **information** about the town.

Most of the central square is unremarkable, looking like a dowdy filmset from a B-grade cowboy movie. But if you walk to its north side, you'll see what Quincy was once all about: tobacco, the substance that made Quincy prosperous before the arrival of Coca Cola. **The Leaf Theater**, 118 East Washington Street (Mon–Fri 9.30am–1pm; ☎875-9444), is a 1930s tribute to the tobacco leaf – the theater's tiles and motifs are riddled with shade-leaf tobacco emblems. Near the theater is one of the best places to **eat**, the *Gadsden Carriage House Restaurant*, 104 E Washington St (☎875-4660), fabulous for its local fare and Celtic music nights.

Wealthy Quincy, with its bungalow homes of delicate trellises and sweeping verandas, begins on E Washington Street. The most exquisite mansions, though, are between Love and King streets. The finest of all also happens to be the only bed-and-breakfast in town: *McFarlin House*, 305 E King St (☎875-2526), an exquisite, turreted mansion whose sumptuous interior and 42-pillar porch were created for John McFarlin, Quincy's richest tobacco planter, in 1895.

Lake Seminole and the Three Rivers State Recreational Area

Fifty miles out of Tallahassee, within spitting distance of the Georgia border, Hwy-90 reaches Sneads, a small town dominated by the large **Lake Seminole**, created by a Fifties hydroelectric project. On the lake's Florida side (other banks are in Georgia and Alabama), spend an enjoyable few hours in the **Three Rivers State Recreational Area** (daily 8am–sunset; cars $3.25, pedestrians and cyclists $1), two miles from Sneads on Route 271. A mile-long **nature walk** from the park's **camping area** (☎482-9006) leads to a wooded, hilly section where squirrels and alligators are two-a-penny, and white-tailed deer and grey foxes lurk in the shrubbery. Primarily, though, the lake is popular for its massive and abundant catfish, bream and bass. To spend a night by the lake without camping, use the ten-room *Seminole Lodge* (☎593-6886; ③), at the end of Legion Road, just outside Sneads.

Marianna and the Florida Caverns State Park

Twenty-five miles further along Hwy-90, **MARIANNA** is one of the larger inland Panhandle settlements, despite having a four-figure population for whom the twice-monthly horse sale is the only source of excitement. There isn't much to commend the place, except that it tries to sell itself (rather unsuccessfully) as "The Belle of the Panhandle" and it has been the seat of Jackson County since 1829. The **Chamber of Commerce**, 2928 Jefferson Street (Mon–Fri 8am–5pm; ☎482-8061), however, will give you a walking-tour map of the town's elegant Old South homes (the Chamber of Commerce itself sits inside one).

If you want to **stay** in town, the delightful, if strange, *Hinson House* bed-and-breakfast, 4338 Lafayette Street (☎526-1500; ③–④), is a beautifully restored villa with authentic

---

CROSSING THE TIME ZONE

Crossing the Apalachicola River, which flows north–south across the Inland Panhandle, roughly 45 miles west of Tallahassee, takes you into the **Central Time Zone**, an hour behind Eastern Time and the rest of Florida. In the Coastal Panhandle, the time shift occurs about ten miles west of Port St Joe, on the boundary between Gulf and Bay counties.

furnishings and breakfasts served in a formal dining room. The owner has created a permanent sense of Christmas, with not only a year-round lit-up tree in the hallway, but twinkling lights on the stairs, windows patterned with fake frost and golden reindeer all over the fireplace.

For **eating**, your best bets are *Madison's*, 2881 Madison Street (☎256-4000), or the *Red Canyon Grill*, 3297 Caverns Road (☎482-4256), both of which serve up standard American diner fare. Otherwise, run-of-the-mill options include *Jim's Buffet & Grill*, 4473 Lafayette Street (☎526-3300) or *Captain D's Seafood Restaurant*, 4253 Lafayette Street (☎482-6230). A popular Mexican eatery is *Old Mexican Restaurant*, 4434 Lafayette Street (☎482-5552).

Florida Caverns State Park

The best thing about Marianna is its proximity to **Florida Caverns State Park** (daily 8am–sunset; cars $3.25, pedestrians and cyclists $1), three miles north on Route 167, where hourly **guided tours** (9am–5pm; $4) venture through 65-foot-deep caverns filled with strangely shaped calcite formations. The caves are not new discoveries; they were mentioned in Spanish accounts of the area and used by Seminole Indians to hide from Andrew Jackson's army in the early 1800s – an unnerving experience in the days before electric lights illuminated the booming rock chambers. Back in the sun, the park has a few other features to fill a day comfortably. From the **visitor center** (☎482-1228) by the caverns' entrance, a **nature trail** leads around the floodplain of the Chipola River, curiously dipping underground for several hundred feet as it flows through the park. At the **Blue Hole Spring**, at the end of the park road, you can swim, snorkel or scuba-dive – and sleep at its **campground** ($14).

Chipley and Falling Waters State Recreation Area

Continuing west, the next community of any size is **CHIPLEY**, 26 miles from Marianna. The town takes its name from William D. Chipley, who put a railroad across the Panhandle in the mid-1800s to improve the timber trade, and gave rise to little sawmill towns such as Chipley. The railroad is still here (restricted locally to freight), but the boom times are long gone. The town itself is, for the most part, unexciting, and the Neoclassical enormity of the **Washington County Court House** on Hwy 90 (also called Jackson Avenue) seems very out of place. The only other building of interest is the large and elegant **First United Methodist Church**, built in 1910 and set on hand-hewn log foundations. If you can find someone to let you in, the interior is most unexpected: towering over the vast, curved golden-oak pews is a huge pipe organ and semi-opaque stained glass that is especially radiant on a sunny day.

Chipley's historic district is on S Third Street, down the western side of the Court House. The houses here date from 1900 to 1920 and are not worth more than a cursory glance. More interesting, if only as a well preserved example of the inland-Panhandle's ubiquitous Main Streets, is the area just north of Hwy 90, a charming row of brick-faced old shops along the railroad tracks. **Antique shops** abound here, and Chipley's best are at the Historic Chipley Antique Mall, 1368 Railroad Avenue North (☎638-2535).

The Falling Waters State Recreation Area

Leave town along Route 77 and head for **Falling Waters State Recreation Area** (daily 8am–sunset; cars $3.25, pedestrians and cyclists $1), three miles south and the home of Florida's only **waterfall**. The so-called fall is in fact a 100-foot drop into a tube-like sinkhole topped by a viewing platform. A trail passes several other sinks (without waterfalls), and another leads to a decaying oil well – remaining from an unsuccessful attempt to strike black gold in 1919. The park has a **campground** (☎638-6130; $8), but for **accommodation** under a roof, head back to Chipley to the dull but cheap chalet rooms at *Budget Hotel*, 700 Hwy-90 (☎638-1850; ①–②), or *Chipley Motel*, 404 Hwy 90 (☎638-1322; ①–②). For **food**, try the *Chinese Garden Restaurant*, next to the *Chipley Motel* at 1320 Hwy 90 (☎638-3080). Local farmers pack into *Granny's Country Kitchen*, 1284 W Jackson Ave, open daily until 2pm for hearty breakfasts and lunch buffets.

De Funiak Springs

A real jewel of the inland Panhandle, **DE FUNIAK SPRINGS**, forty miles west of Chipley on Hwy 90, was founded as a fashionable stop on the newly completed Louisville-Nashville railroad in 1882. Drawn to the large, naturally circular lake, nineteenth-century socialites built fairy-tale villas to fringe the waters here, and three years later the Florida Chautauqua (pronounced chat-aqua) Alliance – a benevolent religious society espousing free culture and education for all – made the town its southern base. The Alliance was headquartered at the grandiose Hall of Brotherhood, which still stands on Circle Drive – an ideal cruising lane to view the splendid villas, painted in gingerbread-house style with white or wedding-cake blue trim. With the death of its founders and the coming of the Depression, the Alliance faded away, and in 1975 their 4000 seat auditorium was demolished by Hurricane Eloise. In recent years, there has been renewed interest in the Chautauqua ethos, however, and a **Chautauqua Assembly Revival** is now held here around the first week of March (call ☎892-4300 for details). In addition to workshops and craft activities, this is the only time you can view the interiors of the historic houses. If you miss that, the only building open to the public is the smallest, the **Walton-De Funiak Library**, 3 Circle Drive (Mon 9am–7pm, Tues & Fri 9am–6pm, Sat 9am–3pm; free), which has been lending books since 1886 and recently acquired a small stash of medieval European weaponry, donated by a local collector.

Another unlikely find is the **Chautauqua Vineyards**, on Hwy-331 just north of the junction with I-10, whose diverse wines may not be the world's finest but have picked a few awards in their ten years of existence (free tours and tastings, Mon–Sat 9am–5pm, Sun noon–5pm).

Stopping over in De Funiak Springs is a sound move if you're aiming for the more expensive coastal strip 25 miles south along Hwy-331. The *Days Inn*, 1325 S Freeport Road (☎892-6615; ②), has good rates but is closer to I-10 than the town. To stay in step with the town's historical mood, opt instead for *Hotel de Funiak*, 400 E Nelson Ave (☎892-4383; ④–⑤), a charming restored hotel in the old business district but still close to the lake. While in town, make sure to **eat lunch** amid the antiques at the delightful *Busy Bee Café*, 35 7th Street (☎892-6700). For **dinner**, the restaurant at *Hotel de Funiak* (above) serves classic food in a cozy atmosphere. For cheaper eats, you'll have to head back to I-10 for the usual array of *Waffle House*-style quick-stop restaurants.

The Blackwater River State Forest

Between the sluggish towns of Crestview and Milton, thirty miles west of De Funiak Springs, the creeks and slow-flowing rivers of **Blackwater River State Forest** are jammed each weekend with waterborne families enjoying what's officially dubbed "the canoe capital of Florida." In spite of the crowds, the forest is by no means overcommercialized, being big enough to absorb the influx and still offer peace, isolation and unruffled nature to anyone intrepid enough to hike through it. Alternatively, if you're not game for canoeing or hiking but just want a few hours' break, the **Blackwater River State Park** (daily 8am–sunset; cars $2, pedestrians and cyclists $1), within the forest four miles north of Harold off Hwy-90, has some easy walking trails.

From Milton, Hwy-90 and I-10 both offer a mildly scenic fifteen-mile drive over Escambia Bay to the hotels and freeways on the northern fringes of Pensacola, the city marking Florida's western extremity (see p.360).

Accommodation in the forest

With the exception of the restored 1800s "cracker" **cabins** at Tomahawk Landing (see below; ①–⑤, depending on the comfort level), forest accommodation is limited to **camping** ($8–10). There are fully equipped sites at the Krul Recreation Area (☎957-4201), near the junction of Forest Road 4 and Route 19, and at the Blackwater River State Park (see above; ☎623-2363). Free basic sites intended for hikers lie along the main trails.

Hiking and canoeing

Hardened **hikers** carrying overnight gear can tackle the 21-mile **Jackson Trail**, named after Andrew Jackson who led his invading army this way in 1818 seeking to wrest Florida from Spanish control. On the way, two very basic shelters have hand-pumps for water. The trail runs between Karick Lake, off Hwy-189, fourteen miles north of Hwy-90, and the Krul Recreation Area. The shorter **Sweetwater Trail** is a good substitute if your feet aren't up to the longer hike. An enjoyable four-and-a-half-mile walk, it leaves the Krul Recreation Area and crosses a swingbridge and the Bear Lake dam before joining the Jackson trail.

Canoeing in the forest is offered by Adventures Unlimited, at **Tomahawk Landing** on Coldwater Creek (☎623-6197 or 1-800/239-6864), twelve miles north of Milton on Hwy-87; here you can rent tubes, canoes and kayaks for around $8, $13 and $20 respectively per day. Two- and three-day trips, with overnight gear and food provided, can also be arranged for around $28 per person.

THE COASTAL PANHANDLE

Lacking the glamour and international renown of Florida's other beach strips, the **coastal Panhandle** is nonetheless no secret to residents of the Southern states, who descend upon the region by the thousands during the summer. Consequently, a few sections of the region's 180-mile-long coastline are nightmarishly overdeveloped: **Panama City Beach** revels in its "redneck Riviera" nickname, and smaller **Destin** and **Fort Walton Beach** are only marginally more refined. By contrast, little **Apalachicola**, and the **South Walton beaches**, both easily reached by car (they're inaccessible by bus) but out of the main tourist corridor, have much to recommend them: beautiful unspoilt sands, and off-shore islands where people are a rarer sight than wildlife.

Apalachicola and around

A few miles south of the Apalachicola National Forest (p.343), and the first substantial part of the coast you'll hit on Hwy-98 from central Florida, the **Apalachicola area** contains much of value. Mainland beaches may be few, but sand-seekers are compensated by the brilliant strands of three barrier islands, and the small fishing communities you'll pass through are untainted by the aggressive tourism that scars the coast fifty miles west.

Apalachicola

Now a tiny port with an income largely derived from harvesting oysters (nine out of every ten eaten in Florida are farmed here), **APALACHICOLA** once rode high on the cotton industry, which kept its dock busy and its populace affluent during the early

1800s. A number of stately columned buildings attest to former wealth; one, at 84 Market Street, is occupied by the **Chamber of Commerce** (Mon–Fri 9.30am–4pm, Sat 10am–3pm; ☎653-9419), where you can pick up a map to find the others along an enjoyable half-hour's stroll.

To reach Apalachicola, Hwy-98 crosses the four-mile Gorrie Memorial Bridge, which commemorates a man held in high regard by present-day Floridians. Arriving in the town in 1833, physician **John Gorrie** was seeking a way to keep malaria patients cool when he devised a machine to make ice (previously transported in large blocks from the north). Gorrie died before the idea took off and became the basis of modern refrigerators and air-conditioners. The **John Gorrie State Museum**, on the corner of Sixth Street and Avenue D (Thurs–Mon 9am–noon & 1–5pm; $1), remembers the man and his work, as well as the general history of Alpachicola. Only a replica of the cumbersome ice-making device stands here – the original is in the Smithsonian Institute in Washington DC.

Accommodation and eating

There isn't a lot to Apalachicola, but the town makes a good base for visiting the barrier islands (see below). The crusty *Rainbow Inn*, 123 Water Street (☎653-8139; ③), has the least expensive rooms, and **bed and breakfast** can be had at *Coombes House Inn*, 80 Sixth Street (☎653-9199; ③), and the *Gibson Inn*, 57 Market Street (☎653-2191; ④). The latter also offers murder-mystery weekends and a full lunch and dinner menu in their own somewhat-pricey restaurant. You'll find lower prices just outside town (one-and-a-half miles west) at the *Rancho Inn*, 240 Hwy-98 (☎653-9435; ②).

Good places to **eat** in town include the *Apalachicola Seafood Grill and Steakhouse*, 100 Market Street (☎653-9510), for a wide range of lunch and dinner specials; and the *Boss Oyster Bar*, 125 Water Street (☎653-8139), where you can tuck into fresh Apalachicola oysters. Adjacent to the *Rancho Inn* (see above), you'll find the *Red Top Café* (☎653-8612), which serves inexpensive, Southern cooking for lunch and dinner.

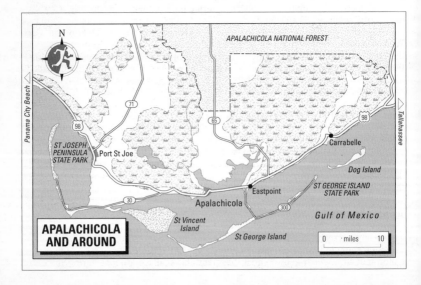

The barrier islands: St George, Dog and St Vincent

A few miles off the coast, framing the Apalachicola Bay and the broad, marshy outflow of the Apalachicola River, the three Apalachicola **barrier islands** are well-endowed with beaches and creatures – including thousands of birds who use them as rest stops during migration – and two of them hold what must qualify as the most isolated communities in Florida. It's worth seeing one of the islands if you have the chance: all three can be visited with Jeanni's Journeys (☎927-3259), which provides a variety of instructional guided canoe trips and hikes; but only the largest island, St George, is accessible by road – Route 1A, which leaves Hwy-98 at Eastpoint.

Twenty-seven miles of powdery white sands and wide ocean vistas are not the only reason to come to **St George Island**, where shady live oak hammocks and an abundance of osprey-inhabited pine trees add color to a day's lazy sunning. A few restaurants, beach shops, the eight-room *St George Inn* (☎927-2903; ④) and the *Buccaneer Inn* (☎927-2585; d) occupy the island's central section. The eastern sector is dominated by the racoon-infested **St George Island State Park** (daily 8am–sunset; cars $3.25, pedestrians and cyclists $1), where a three-mile **hiking trail** leads to a very basic **campground**, costing $4 (there's a better-equipped site at the start of the hike, costing $9; ☎927-2111).

A couple of miles east of St George, **Dog Island**, only accessible by boat (signs advertising crossings are all over the marina in Carrabelle, on Hwy-98), has a small permanent population living in little cottages nestled among Florida's tallest sand dunes. Several footpaths lead around the windswept isle, which won't take more than a few hours to cover. The only **accommodation** is the pricey bed-and-breakfast options at the *Pelican Inn* (☎1-800/451-5294); reservations are essential.

The freshwater lakes and saltwater swamps of **St Vincent Island**, almost within a shell's throw of St George's western end, form a protected refuge for loggerhead turtles, wild turkeys and bald eagles, among many other creatures. In November **guided trips** set out to see them (info: ☎653-8808); at any other time, you'll have to negotiate a boat ride from the mainland.

St Joseph Peninsula State Park and Port St Joe

For a final taste of virgin Florida coast before hitting heavily commercial Panama City Beach, take Route 30 – eighteen miles from Apalachicola, off Hwy-98 – to the **St Joseph Peninsula State Park** (daily 8am–sunset; cars $3.25, pedestrians and cyclists $1). A long finger of sand with a short **nature trail** at one end and a spectacular nine-mile **hiking route** at the other, the park has rough **camping** ($7) at its northern tip and better-equipped sites ($15) and **cabins** ($55; ☎227-1327) about halfway along near Eagle Harbor.

The peninsula wraps a protective arm around **PORT ST JOE** on the mainland, another dot-on-the-map fishing port that has seen better days. One such day came in 1838 when a constitution calling for statehood (which Florida didn't acquire until seven years later) and liberal reforms was drawn up here*, only to be deemed too radical by the legislators of the time. At the **Constitution Convention State Museum** (Mon–Sat 9am–noon & 1–5pm; $1), signposted from Hwy-98 as you enter the town, daft, battery-powered waxworks re-enact the deed. There's also more credible mementos of the town's colorful past, including an explanation of how the town's reputation for pirate pursuits earned it the title "wickedest city in the Southeast" during its early years.

---

*Strictly speaking, the constitution was drawn up in the town of St Joseph (later devastated by yellow fever, two hurricanes and a fire), whose site Port St Joe now occupies.

Panama City Beach

An orgy of motels, go-kart tracks, mini-golf courses and amusement parks, **PANAMA CITY BEACH** is entirely without pretensions, capitalizing as blatantly as possible on the appeal of its 27-mile beach. The place is entirely commercial, but with the shops, bars and restaurants all trying to undercut one another, there are some great bargains to be found – from air-brushed T-shirts and cut-price sunglasses to cheap buffet food. With everybody out to have a good time, there's some fine cruising to be done, too; not least during the Spring Break months of March and April when thousands of students from the Deep South states arrive to drink and dance themselves into oblivion. As vulgar and crass as it often is, Panama City Beach cries out to be seen. Come here once, if only as a voyeuristic daytrip – you may well be smitten enough by its tacky charm to stay longer.

Seasons greatly affect the mood. Throughout the lively **summer** (the so-called "100 Magic Days"), accommodation costs are high and advance bookings essential. In **winter**, prices drop and visitors are fewer; most are Canadians and – increasingly – northern Europeans, who have no problems sunbathing and swimming in the relatively cool (typically around 65°F) temperatures.

What Panama City Beach doesn't have is any **history** worth mentioning. It began as an offshoot of **Panama City**, a dull place of docks and paper mills eight miles away over the Hathaway Bridge (which Hwy-98 crosses). Today there's little love lost between the two communities; they have nothing in common besides a name.

Arrival, getting around and information

For a city that is essentially a very long beach, **getting your bearings** could hardly be simpler, even if there are only two real, if rather similar landmarks (City Pier to the west, County Pier to the east). Much of the piers were destroyed during Hurricane Opal in 1996, but restoration plans were quickly enforced and they're pretty much back to normal now. **Front Beach Road** (part of Hwy-98A, which starts at the foot of the Hathaway Bridge) is the main track, a two-lane highway, often called "the Strip," that's very much the place to cruise on weekends. The speedier, four-lane **Middle Beach Road** loops off Front Beach Road for a few blocks around County Pier from the

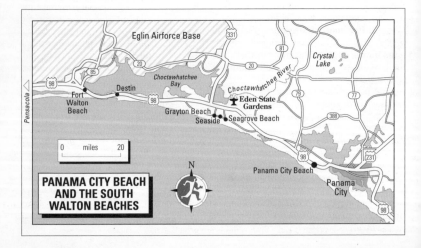

junction with **Thomas Drive** (which links the eastern extremity of the beach). If you don't want to see gaudy Panama City Beach at all, **Back Beach Road** (Hwy-98) will take you straight through its anonymous residential quarter.

Greyhound **buses** pick up and drop off at the Shell station, 17325 W Hwy 98, leaving a fifteen-minute walk to the nearest motels. Traveling by other bus lines, however, you may well end up in Panama City (917 Harrison Avenue; ☎785-7861), rather than Panama City Beach, and you'll need to use one of the four daily Greyhound services linking them.

Panama City Beach is incredibly bad for **walking**; **public transport** is non-existent and **taxis** are prohibitively expensive, even for a short journey. Without a car, rent a **bicycle** (around $12 per day) or a **scooter** (around $30 per day; driver's license necessary) from any of the myriad beach shops; try Beach Things, 13226 Front Beach Road (☎234-0520), Uncle Harvey's, 17280 Front Beach Road (☎235-9963), or California Cycle Rentals, 8906 Thomas Drive (☎230-8080).

For free news-sheets, magazines and discount coupons, drop into the **Visitors Information Center**, 12015 Front Beach Road (Mon–Sun 8am–5pm; ☎1-800722 3224).

Accommodation

Visitors to Panama City Beach outnumber residents, and though there are plenty of **places to stay**, these fill with amazing speed, especially on weekends. **Prices** are higher than you'll pay elsewhere in the Panhandle – $60–80 for a basic motel room in summer – so if you're counting the bucks, stay inland and drive to the beach. In winter prices drop by 30–40 percent, with monthly rentals being even cheaper. Camping is the only way to cut costs; sites are rarely more expensive than their equivalents elsewhere, though only a couple are good for tents.

Motels

As a very general rule, **motels** at the eastern end of the beach are smarter and slightly pricier than those in the center, and those at the western end are quiet and family-orientated. That said, you're unlikely to find much to complain about at any place that takes your fancy.

To the **east**, you could try *Bay Villa*, 4501 W Hwy-98 (☎785-8791; ③); *Lagoon*, 5915 N Lagoon Drive (☎235-1800; ③); or *Pana Roc*, 5507 Thomas Drive (☎234-2775; ③). In the **center** on Front Beach Road there's *Barney Gray* no. 10901 (☎234-2565; ③); *Beachside* no. 10710 (☎234-3997; ③); *Driftwood Lodge* no. 15811 (☎234-6601; ③); or *Siesta* no. 9113 (☎234-2510; ③). To the **west** on Front Beach Road, five worth recommending are *Blue Dolphin* no. 19919 (☎234-5895; ④); *Desert Palms* no. 17729 (☎234-2140; ③); *Impala* no. 17751 (☎234-6462; ③); *Sea Witch* no. 21905 (☎234-5722; ③); or *Sugar Sands Motel* no. 20723 (☎1-800/367-9221; ③).

Campgrounds

Several large and busy **campgrounds** cater mainly to RVs. The most central are *Miracle Strip RV Resort*, 10510 W Hwy 98 (☎234-3833; $20), and *Racoon River*, 12405 Middle Beach Road (☎234-0181; $18). For quieter confines that are better for **tents**, try *Magnolia Beach*, 7800 Magnolia Road (☎235-1581; $16), and the waterfront *St Andrews State Recreation Area*, 4415 Thomas Drive (☎233-5140; $9–20 with electricity). Also on Thomas Drive is *KOA* at no. 8800 (☎234-5731 $13–23).

Around the beach

Getting a tan, running yourself ragged at beach sports, and going wild at night are the main concerns in Panama City Beach – you'll be regarded as a very raw prawn indeed if you go around demanding history, art and culture.

If you remain dissatisfied, try go-karting (around $7 for ten minutes), visiting one of the amusement parks (usually $17 for an all-inclusive day ticket), going on a fishing trip (take your pick of the party boats on the Thomas Drive Marina, from around $30 a day), scuba-diving (several explorable shipwrecks litter the area; details from any of the numerous dive shops), a waverunner trip to Shell Island (see below; $69), parasailing ($35 for a ten-minute ride), bungee jumping ($18) or a four-mile helicopter ride (starting at $30 for two people). Otherwise, the following provide the only variation.

Gulf World Marine Park
15412 Front Beach Road. Daily 9am–7pm; $10.95 (☎234-5271).
A cramped marine park, which has performing sea lions and dolphins, shark-feeding sessions, and stingrays ripe for petting. Mildly more unusual is the "parrot show," featuring a roller-skating parrot and a high-wire-walking parakeet.

Museum of Man in the Sea
17314 W Hwy-98. Daily 9am–5pm; $5; ☎235-17314.
All you ever needed to know about diving is contained in this large collection that includes enormous eighteenth-century underwater helmets, bulky airpumps, bodysuits, deep-sea cutting devices, and torpedo-like propulsion vehicles. A separate display documents *Sealab*, the US Navy's underwater research vessel, the first of which was fitted out in Panama City and now stands outside the museum. This entertaining stop makes an ideal prelude to a day's snorkelling.

St Andrews State Recreation Area
4415 Thomas Drive. Daily 8am–sunset; cars $3.25, pedestrians and cyclists $1; ☎233-5140.
Get here early and you'll spot a variety of hopping, crawling and slithering wildlife by following one of the nature trails around the pine forest and salt marshes within the park. By noon the hordes have arrived to swim, fish and prepare picnics. If you're with kids, they'll enjoy splashing in the shallow lagoon sheltered by an artificial reef known as The Jetties, rated Florida's number one beach for beauty and cleanliness in 1995. Take advantage of the campground to enjoy the quietest times in this spot.

Shell Island
Half an hour by ferry from the Captain Anderson Marina, at the foot of Thomas Drive. Boat departures every 30mins from 10am–3pm; return ticket $8. Alternatively, five minutes from St Andrews State Recreation Area, departing every 30mins 9am–5pm in summer, and 10am–3pm in winter; $7.50.
This seven-mile strip of sand is a haven for shell collectors and sun worshippers alike. With little shade on the undeveloped island, dark glasses are essential; the glare off the sands can be blinding. There are numerous boat trips from Captain Anderson Marina, most of which include a brief stop at Shell Island. Prices vary wildly amongst tour operators, so shop around.

Zoo World
9008 Front Beach Road. Daily 9am–dusk; $8.95; ☎230-1243.
If you're not opposed to animals being incarcerated, you'll enjoy this small collection of lions, tigers, orang-utans and other creatures. Many of the inmates prefer to sleep through the midday heat, so try to time your visit for early morning or late afternoon.

Eating

With an emphasis on basic wholesome cooking, and lots of it, the cheapest places to **eat** are the **buffet** restaurants, charging $4–10 for all you can manage. Try *Bishop's Family Buffet*, 12628 Front Beach Road (☎234-6457), for substantial meals three times daily; the *Golden Anchor*, 11800 Front Beach Road (☎234-1481), for sizeable seafood lunches and dinners; or *Katman'du*, at the intersection of Hwy-79 and Front Beach Road (☎235-9866), offering cheap and tasty breakfasts and catfish to die for.

Wherever you can get a buffet it's also possible to order from the menu, but if that's your real intention you're better off having **lunch or dinner** at one of the places listed below.

Cajun Inn at the Edgewater Beach Resort Shopping Center (☎235-9987). Mouthwatering selection of Cajun and Creole American cuisine.

Hamilton's, 5711 N Lagoon Drive (☎234-1255). Blackened alligator nuggets stand out among the more regular dishes. Dinner only.

Mikato, 7724 Front Beach Rd (☎234-1388). Japanese food prepared by knife-throwing chefs.

Mike's Diner, 17554 Front Beach Rd (☎234-1942). Honest-to-goodness coffee shop that opens early, closes late and is great value throughout the day.

Ruthie T's, two blocks east of Joan Avenue on Thomas Drive (☎234-2111). Soul food with heart and a house special of blackened prime rib with attitude.

Shuckum's Oyster Pub & Seafood Grill, 15618 W Hwy-98 (☎235-3214). Cheap oysters in many styles, including fried in a sandwich.

Sweet Basil's, 11208 Front Beach Rd (☎234-2855). Classy Italian food combined with the freshest seafood.

The Treasure Ship, 3605 Thomas Drive (☎234-8881). A seafood restaurant built to resemble a wooden sailing ship, with pirates hopping around the tables.

Nightlife

Even if you only stay a few minutes, you should visit one of the two beachside **nightlife** fleshpots: *Club La Vela*, 8813 Thomas Drive (☎234-3866), or *Spinnaker*, 8795 Thomas Drive (☎234-7822) – both open 10am to 4am, with free entry. Each has dozens of bars, several discos, live bands and a predominantly under-25 clientele eagerly awaiting the weekend bikini and wet T-shirt contests, and thrice-weekly "hunk shows." Because competition between the two clubs is so intense, there'll often be free beer in the early evening. During the day, the action is by the clubs' open-air pools, where you're over-dressed if covering anything more than your genitalia.

Everywhere else is tranquil by comparison. Although they may also have live music, a number of **bars** are worth a call simply for a drink. Check out *Sharky's*, 15201 Front Beach Road (☎235-2420), a massive tiki bar right on the beach; *Schooner's*, 5121 Gulf Drive (☎234-9074), for its ocean-view beachside tables; or *Pineapple Willy's Beachside Restaurant & Beach Bar*, 9900 S Thomas Drive (☎235-0928), where you can munch barbecue ribs steeped in Jack Daniels to the sound of Sixties and Seventies classic rock bands.

West of Panama City Beach: the South Walton beaches

West of Panama City Beach, motels eventually give way to the more rugged and less developed **beaches of South Walton County**: fifty miles of some of Florida's best-kept coast. With a few exceptions, accommodation here is in resort complexes with sky-high rates, but it's a great area to spend a day. **Route-30A** (far superior to Hwy-98, which takes an inland route) is an eighteen-mile scenic route linking the region's small beach communities. For **general information** on the South Walton beaches and surrounding area, phone the South Walton Tourist Development Council: ☎1-800/822-6877, or visit their offices at the junction of Route 331 and Hwy-98, twenty miles west of Panama City Beach and ten miles east of San Destin.

Deer Lake Park and Seagrove Beach

DEER LAKE PARK, ten miles west of Panama City beach on Route-30A, is a dramatic stretch of creamy-white sand dunes on a coastline studded with smooth driftwood. The best beach of the South Walton bunch, it somehow goes almost without mention in the area's tourist brochures. The road signposted "Deer Lake Park" ends at a parking lot, and a five-minute walk through scrubland leads to the beach, a favorite hideout for nude sunbathing – officially, it's forbidden, but the rules are infrequently enforced.

A few miles west, **SEAGROVE BEACH** shares the same attractive shoreline as Deer Lake Park, and is also home to a particularly good **bakery**, the *Granola Girls Gourmet Bakery*, 4935 E Hwy-30 (☎231-2023; closed Mon), perfect for fresh muffins, bagels, filled croissants and granola. For more upmarket dining, try the stylish *Café Thirty A*, Hwy 30A, a rotisserie and bar serving mainly fish and meat dishes. More casual, *Sweet Dreams Café*, in the Seagrove Plaza, does brunch, lunch and great espressos. There's limited tent **camping** at Seagrove Beach's *RV Resort* (☎231-2826; $10). Whether you camp or not, the *RV Resort* is a good place to rent a **bike** ($10 a day with big reductions for weekly rentals), and they provide a useful free pickup and delivery service.

Seaside and Grayton Beach

An exception to the casual, unplanned appearance of most South Walton beach towns, **SEASIDE**, just west of Seagrove Beach, is an experiment in urban architecture, begun in 1981 by a rich, idealistic developer called Robert Davies. The theory is that Seaside's pseudo-Victorian cottages foster village-like neighborliness and instill a sense of community. In reality, they do nothing of the sort, and it's basically a wealthy and sterile resort these days. Still, as elitist and economically discriminating as this place is, there's no escaping the unique appeal of the streets; you won't see houses like this anywhere else, and though you'll never feel like you belong, it's worth half an hour of anyone's time. There's no shortage of expensive places to eat or stay here; if you have cash to spare look into *Josephine's French Country Inn*, 101 Seaside Ave (☎231-1940), where you can expect glamorous if prissy cooking. For luscious cakes and an earfull of Seaside's local gossip, head for *Modica*, 53 Central Square (☎231-1214), a fabulous gourmet grocery store.

Fortunately, the antidote to Seaside's sterility is just a few miles further along Route 30A at **GRAYTON**, whose secluded position (it's hemmed in by protected land) and ramshackle wooden dwellings have taken the fancy of a number of artists who now reside here. Some of their work is regularly on show at the beachside *Gallery at Grayton* (Tues–Sat 9.30am–5pm). Also worth a visit is the workshop of **Joe Elmore**, on S Hwy-331, two miles past the Chamber of Commerce at the junction of Hwy-331 and Hwy-98 (daily 8.30am–4.30pm; ☎267-3511). Elmore is a wood sculptor who works with a chainsaw; his remarkably detailed creations can be admired here – as can several of his chainsaws.

Many who come to Grayton skip straight through to the **Grayton Beach State Recreation Area** (daily 8am–sunset; cars $3.25, pedestrians and cyclists $1), just east of the village. The recreation area is walled by sand dunes and touches the banks of a large brackish lake, and a night at the park's **campground** ($14) leaves plenty of time for a slow exploration of the village and its natural surrounds. Route 30A rejoins Hwy-98 seven miles west of Grayton.

Blue Mountain Beach and Santa Rosa Beach

Just west of Grayton, relatively undiscovered **BLUE MOUNTAIN BEACH** is a welcome escape from the spring break crowds that zip past without a second glance. Don't make the same mistake; the quiet beach is an expanse of creamy white sand bordered by unpretentious vacation homes. There's a gourmet grocery store at *Blue Mountain Plaza*, though for delicious, health-conscious lunches, wander across the street to *For The Health of It,* no. 2217 on Scenic Route 30A, where lime-bean chowder and sesame pastas are served amid a huge selection of organic everything.

A mile further west is **SANTA ROSA BEACH**. Slightly more developed than Blue Mountain, Santa Rosa has one of the better places to **stay** in the region: *Highlands House Bed & Breakfast,* 4193 W Scenic 30A (☎267-0110; ④), an excellent, well-furnished lodging with panoramic views and a perfect beach-side setting, all for considerably less than the selection of characterless new hotels that dot the area. A couple of good – though not cheap – places to **eat** here are *Goatfeathers Seafood Market & Restaurant* (closed Wed), which has excellent seafood; and *D&K's Café* (☎267-0054; closed Sun–Tues), down a tiny track called Vicki Street and serving Cajun and Deep South dishes in a pretty red and green cottage.

Hidden up Satinwood Road, just opposite *Goatfeathers* (above), is *The S. House* (Tues–Sat 10am–4pm; ☎267-2194 or ☎267-2551), an **antique** shop dealing in a cache of vintage clothes, furniture and collectable oddities from the region. If you ask, the friendly owner will show you his orchid house, which is dripping with color just outside.

Inland: Eden State Gardens

Away from the coast road, only **Eden State Gardens** (Thurs–Mon 8am–sunset; free), reached by Route 395 from Seagrove Beach a mile east of Seaside, is worth a visit. The gardens, now disturbed only by the buzz of dragonflies, were once the base of the Wesley Lumber Company, which helped decimate Florida's forests during the turn-of-the-century timber boom. Impressed with the setting, the company's boss pinched some of the wood to build himself a grandiose two-story plantation-style home, the **Wesley House** (guided tours on the hour 9am–4pm Thurs–Mon; $1.50; ☎231-4214). After the death of the last Wesley, the house stood empty for ten years until Lois Maxon, a spinster with an interest in antiques, bought it in 1963 as a showcase for her collections. Movie buffs may recognize the interior as the setting for the film *Froggs.*

Destin and around

Heading west from Panama City, you'll encounter **DESTIN** and its newer, more resort-like cousin, San Destin. San Destin, six miles east of Destin, sprung up during the past decade and comprises a soulless complex of high-rise and high-security vacation resorts – even if you wanted to, you can't drive through without proving which place you're paying through the nose for. The real Destin, once a small fishing village and a cult name among anglers for the fat marlin and tuna lurking in an undersea canyon a few miles offshore, is a less pristine version of San Destin, featuring towering condos, which emerge through the heat haze as you approach on Hwy-98 and bear witness to two decades of unrestrained exploitation that have stripped away much of the town's character. Pick up tourist information at the **visitors center**, 1021 Hwy-98 (Mon–Fri 9am–5pm; ☎837-6241), signposted to your right as you arrive on Hwy-98.

Accommodation

You'll seldom find **accommodation** under $60 a night among the monolithic hotels in central Destin, so head four miles east to the **motels** along Route 2378, also known as Old Hwy-98 or Beach Road. The lowest rates are at *Sun'n'Sand* no. 4080 (☎837-6724; ④); *Crystal Beach Motel* no. 2931 E (☎837-4770; ④); and *Surf High* no. 3000 (☎837-2366; ⑦, but more reasonable prices in low season). For several people planning a **long stay**, *Surfside* no. 4701 (☎837-4700; ⑥) is a good option. Other reasonably priced alternatives include the *Hampton Inn*, 1625 Hwy-98 E (☎654-2677; ⑤), and *Silver Beach Motel & Cottages*, eight miles east of Fort Walton Beach (see below), 1050 Hwy-98 (☎837-6125; ③ for motel rooms).

Of the **campgrounds**, only two accept tents: *Destin RV Resort*, 3175 Cobia Street (☎837-6215; $18); and, in central Destin, *Destin Campground*, 209 Beach Drive (☎837-6511; $17).

The town and beach

Evidence of Destin's sudden expansion can be found amid the fading photos of bygone days in the **Old Destin Post Office Museum** (Mon & Wed 1.30–4.30pm; free), opposite the library on Stahlman Avenue; while the **Fishing Museum**, at 20009 Emerald Coast Parkway (Mon–Sat 11am–4pm; $2), with its mounted record-breaking catches, and thousands of pictures of landed fish with their grinning captors, is proof of Destin's high esteem among hook-and-line enthusiasts.

An escape from the condo overkill is provided by enticing white sands situated just east of Destin. The **beach** here is family territory, but it offers relaxation, excellent sea swimming and classic Gulf-coast sunsets. To reach it, take **Route 2378**, lined by unobtrusive motels and beach shops, which makes a coast-hugging loop off Hwy-98, starting about four miles from Destin.

While in the vicinity, resist any temptation to visit the **Museum of the Sea and Indian**, at 4801 Beach Drive (winter daily 9am–4pm summer 8am–6pm; $3.75), an entirely uninspiring place where you're loaned a cassette player and pointed to a dull batch of sea creatures, shells and Native American artifacts.

Eating and nightlife

On old Hwy-98, *The Back Porch,* at no. 1740 (☎837-2022) is Destin's oldest seafood and oyster house and one of the few places open late (until midnight). Otherwise, the 24-hour *Destin Diner*, 1083 Hwy-98 (☎654-5843), dishes up hearty and economical breakfasts, burgers and frothy milkshakes in surrounds of neon and chrome. Later in the day, there's a buffet at the *Seafood Factory*, 21 Hwy-98 (☎837-0999); and there's seafood and steaks prepared on a California open grill at *Sunset Bay Café*, 9300 Hwy-98 (☎267-7108). Along Route 2378 you can munch a fish sandwich or shrimp salad at *Captain Dave's* no. 3796 (☎837-2627), while gazing over the ocean. If you've never tried one, the *Krispy Kreme*, 795 Hwy 98, has the best melts-in-your-mouth selection of doughnuts (the original glazed – 40¢ each – are the best).

Destin's **nightlife** has little vigor: a few of the beachside bars and restaurants offer nightly drink specials – look for the signs – or you can drink to the accompaniment of undistinguished rock bands at the *Hog's Breath Saloon*, 1239 Siebert Street (☎244-2199); dance the night away at *Nightown*, 140 Palmetto Avenue (☎837-6448), two blocks east of the Destin Bridge (see below); or enjoy the floor shows accompanied by Fifties and Sixties music at *Yesterday's*, 1079 E Hwy-98 (☎837-1954), easy to spot with its classic Chevy and Thunderbird out front.

Okaloosa Island and Fort Walton Beach

Hwy-98 leaves Destin by rising over the **Destin Bridge**, giving towering views of the two-tone ocean and intensely white sands, before hitting the crazy golf courses and amusement parks of **Okaloosa Island**. The island's **beaches**, immediately west, are a better sight, kept in their raw state by their owner – the US Air Force – and making a lively weekend playground for local youths and high-spirited beachbums.

A mile west, the neon motel signs that greet arrivals to **FORT WALTON BEACH** offer no indication that this was the site of a major religious and social center during the Paleo-Indian period; so important were the finds made here that the place gave its name to the "Fort Walton Culture" (see "History," in Contexts for more). These days it's military culture that dominates, as the town is home to Eglin, the country's biggest Air Force base. Aside from a few crewcuts and topless bars, however, you'll see little evidence of the base close to Hwy-98, and much of Fort Walton Beach has a more downbeat and homely feel – and slightly lower prices – than Destin. The local **visitors center**, 1540 Hwy-98 E (Mon–Fri 8am–5pm; ☎1-800/322-3319), has abundant information on eating and accommodation.

Accommodation

The cheapest **motels** are along Miracle Strip Parkway (the local section of Hwy-98): *Super 8*, no. 333 SW; (☎244-4999; ③), *Travel Lodge* no. 209; (☎244-5137; ④), *Days Inn* no. 135; (☎1-800/325-2525; ④), or *Greenwood*, 1340 Hwy-98 (☎244-1141; ③). The nearest **campground** is the RV-only *Playground RV Park*, four miles north on Hwy-189 (☎862-3513); campers with **tents** should make for *Gulf Winds Park*, ten miles west on Hwy-98 (☎939-3593), or, slightly further on, *Navarre Beach Family Campground* (☎939-2188), just outside Navarre.

The Indian Temple Mound and Air Force Armament museums

If you were inspired by the sizeable temple mound standing incongruously beside the busy highway into Fort Walton Beach, then you might wish to inspect the small **Indian Temple Mound Museum** (Mon–Fri 11am–4pm Sat 9am–4pm; $2), at the junction of Hwy-98 and Route 85, which is crammed with elucidating relics.

For an insight into more contemporary culture, the **Air Force Armament Museum**, 100 Museum Drive, Eglin (daily 9.30am–4.30pm; free), six miles north of Fort Walton Beach on Route 85, has a large stock of what the local Air Force base is famous for: guns, missiles and bombs – and the planes that carry them. The first guided missiles were put together here in the Forties, and work on developing and testing (non-nuclear) airborne weaponry has continued unabated ever since.

Eating and nightlife

Mother Earth's Good Time Café, 512 Eglin Parkway (☎863-3092), uses nothing but fresh natural ingredients and country recipes; and *Thai Saree*, 163 Eglin Parkway (☎244-4600) serves excellent Thai food for lunch and dinner. The pricier *Royal Orchid*, 238 N Eglin Parkway (☎864-3344), dishes up great Indian dinners. Seafood buffets are offered at *Sam's Oyster House*, 1214 Siebert Drive (☎244-3474), but best of all are the high-quality steak and seafood dinners at the *Coach-N-Four*, 1313 Lewis Turner Boulevard (☎863-3443).

Fort Walton Beach **nightlife** amounts to little more than the usual **beachfront bars**, mostly on Okaloosa Island, with some good happy hours. The best are *Pandora's*, 1120

Santa Rosa Boulevard (☎244-8669), which draws tourists and locals to its nightly specials; and *Fudpucker's Beachside Bar & Grill*, 108 Santa Rosa Boulevard (☎243-3833), with live entertainment on "The Deck." A good **gay bar/club** (actually the only gay club between Panama City and Pensacola) is *Frankly Scarlet's*, 223 Hwy 98 (☎664-2966), a friendly, lively place equally welcoming to lesbians as to gay men.

West from Fort Walton

If you're driving, travel **west from Fort Walton** along Hwy-98 and branch off on Route 399 for sixty scenic miles along **Santa Rosa Island** to the Gulf Islands National Seashore, near Pensacola Beach (see "Pensacola and around" below). The parallel route, the continuation of Hwy-98, is much duller, but is the one the daily Greyhound **bus** takes from the station at 101 SE Perry Avenue (☎243-1940). A worthy stop for tasty food at rock-bottom prices is the friendly yet idiosyncratic *Hazel's Country Kitchen*, one mile west of the Navarre Bridge on Hwy-98 (☎939-3437).

Pensacola and around

Tucked away at the western end of the Panhandle, **PENSACOLA** is built on the northern bank of the broad Pensacola Bay, five miles inland from the nearest beaches. Although its prime features are a naval aviation school and some busy dockyards, Pensacola is also a historic center: occupied by the Spanish in 1559 – only a hurricane that destroyed the settlement prevented Pensacola from becoming the oldest city in the US – it repeatedly changed hands between the Spanish, French and British before becoming the place where Florida was officially ceded by Spain to the US in 1821. The city has retained enough evidence of its seesawing past to give substance to a short visit, but it also makes a good and economical base for exploring one of the prettiest and least spoilt parts of the coastal Panhandle; just cross the Bay Bridge to the coast, you'll find Pensacola Beach neighboring the wild, protected beaches of the Gulf Islands National Seashore.

Arrival, information and getting around

Unless you're arriving from the inland Panhandle on I-10 or Hwy-90, aim to take the scenic route to Pensacola, along Santa Rosa Island on **Route 399** (also known here as Via De Luna Drive). Doing this, you'll first strike Pensacola Beach, from which Pensacola Beach Road swings north, crossing the Santa Rosa peninsula and joining **Hwy-98** before crossing the three-mile-long Pensacola Bay Bridge into the city. At the foot of the bridge, on the city side, is the **visitor information center** (daily 8am–5pm; ☎1-800/874-1234; fax ☎434-7626), packed with the usual worthwhile handouts.

Unfortunately, the Greyhound **bus** station is far from central, being seven miles north of the city center at 505 W Burgess Road (☎476-4800); bus #10A links it to Pensacola proper. **Local buses** (for information call ☎595-3228, exit 611) serve the city but not the beach; the main terminal is at the junction of Gregory and Palafox streets. To get from the city to the beach without your own transport, take a **taxi** (Cross Town Taxi ☎456-8294, or Yellow ☎433-3333); the fare will be roughly $10–12.

Accommodation

The main approach roads from I-10, N Davis Boulevard and Pensacola Boulevard, are both lined with unmissable billboards advertising **budget chain hotels** for $30–50 a night. **Central** options are more limited: cheapest are the *Seville Inn*, 223 E Garden

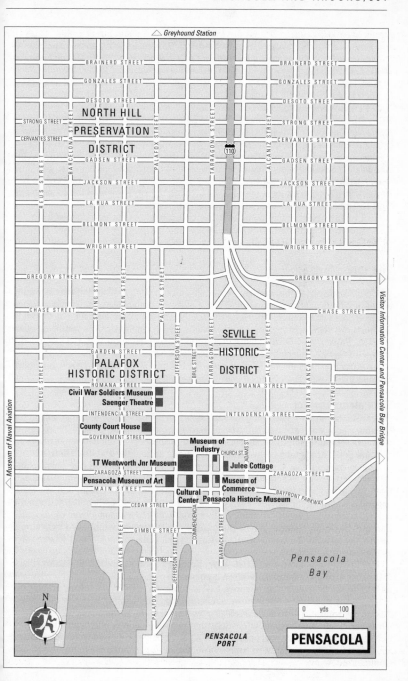

Street (☎1-800/277-7275; ②) and the *Civic Inn*, 200 N Palafox Street (☎432-3441; ②); and *Days Inn*, 710 N Palafox Street (☎438-4922; ③) is just slightly more expensive. A few miles west of the center is the *Mayfair Motel & RV Park*, 4540 Mobile Highway (☎455-8561; ②). Finally, for an excellent bed-and-breakfast, head to the charming *Noble Manor*, 110 W Strong St (☎434-9544; ⑤), which does special packages and has a great location in the North Hill District.

At **Pensacola Beach**, the lowest prices are at *Gulf Aire*, 21 Via De Luna Drive (☎932-2319; ③), and the *Sandpiper Inn*, 23 Via De Luna Drive (☎932-2516; ③). *The Hampton Inn*, 2 Via De Luna Drive (☎932-6800; ⑤) is extremely comfortable, with a continental breakfast included in the cost.

The closest **campground** is the *Fort Pickens Campground* (☎1-800/365-2267), on the Gulf Islands National Seashore, a few miles west of Pensacola Beach (see p.366). Two others are further out: *Big Lagoon*, ten miles southwest on Route 292A on Perdido Key (☎492-1595; $8); and *Circle G* (☎944-1096; $10), on the city's forested fringe, near Exit 2 off I-10, about twelve miles from the center.

On **Perdido Key**, accommodation other than camping is pricey: choose from *The Best Western*, 13585 Perdido Key Drive (☎492-2755; ⑤), and *Perdido Bay Golf Resort*, 1 Doug Ford Drive (☎492-1243; ⑤), both of which offer good deals during the off season.

The city

While not as lively as it once was, Pensacola still warrants exploration due to a number of buildings of architectural merit and a relaxing atmosphere. The city is grouped in three distinct, adjoining **districts**: the south-central Palafox District, North Hill in the northern section of the city, and the Seville District in Pensacola's southeast quarter. The Palafox and Seville districts are the most interesting historically, and the streets of Seville especially are flanked by house after house of interest. The only other attraction that might delay serious sunbathing at Pensacola Beach is a naval aviation museum.

The Palafox District

Pensacola was already a booming port at the turn of the century, and the opening of the Panama Canal was expected to further boost the city's fortunes. Sadly, the surge in wealth never came, but the optimism of the era is apparent in the delicate ornamentation and detail in the turn-of-the-century structures around the **Palafox District**.

Take a look first at the **County Court House**, at the junction of Palafox and Government streets, which, besides its legal function, has also seen service as a customs house, a post office and tax offices. Opposite, the slender form and vertically aligned windows of the **Seville Tower** exaggerate the height of what, in 1909, was the tallest building in Florida. A block further north, at 118 Palafox Place, the Spanish Baroque **Saenger Theater** is now the base of the Pensacola Symphony Orchestra; if the door is open, take the opportunity to have a peek at the interior – twice as evocative as the outside.

Also meriting a look, the **Civil War Soldiers Museum**, 108 S Palafox Place (Mon–Sat 10am–4.30pm; $4), houses a collection of uniforms, weaponry and many unsettling medical tools – all of which saw action in the Civil War – which graphically illustrate the conditions endured by soldiers during the conflict between the States. Ask at the entrance, which doubles as a well-stocked bookstore specializing in the Civil War, about the thirty-minute videos that puts the exhibits into context. Note the newspaper article on the wall behind the counter, which mentions Myrtle, a volunteer who occasionally works here and whose father and grandfather served in the Confederate Army.

North Hill

Between 1870 and 1930, Pensacola's professional classes took a shine to the **North Hill** area, just across Wright Street from the Palafox district, and commissioned elaborate homes in a plethora of fancy styles. Strewn across the tree-studded fifty-block area are pompous Neoclassical porches, cutesy Tudor-Revival cottages, low-slung California bungalows, and rounded towers belonging to fine Queen Anne homes. Private residences, none are open to the public, and the best way to see them is by driving around Palafox, Spring, Strong and Brainerd streets.

The clamor to build houses in this fashionable neighborhood led to the ruin of **Fort George**, which once barracked two thousand British troops here and fell to the Spanish at the Battle of Pensacola in 1781. Only an imitation cannon and a plaque at the corner of Palafox and LaRua streets commemorates the original location of the fort.

The Seville District: Historic Pensacola Village

As a commercial center, Pensacola kicked into gear in the late 1700s with a cosmopolitan mix of Native Americans, early settlers and seafaring traders gathering here to swap, sell and barter on the waterfront of the **Seville District**, about half a mile east of Palafox Street. Those who did well took up permanent residence, and many of their homes remain in fine states of repair, forming – together with several museums – the **Historic Pensacola Village** (Mon–Sat 10am–5pm; guided tours $6, children $2.50). Each ticket is valid for two days and allows access to all of the museums and former homes (and you should see them *all*, the effect of the whole is far greater than the sum of its parts) in an easily navigated four-block area. Start at the **Museum of Commerce**, next door to the visitor center on the corner of Zaragoza and Tarragona streets, an entertaining indoor re-creation of Palafox Street in its turn-of-the-century heyday, using many of the original storefronts and shop fittings. Much of the prosperity of Pensacola was based on the timber industry, a point celebrated by a noisy, working sawmill in the **Museum of Industry**, just across Zaragoza Street.

To catch up on earlier local history, cross Church Street to the sedate **Colonial Archaeology trail**, where bits of pottery and weapons suggest the lifestyles of the city's first Spanish inhabitants, and a marked path leads around the site of the British-era Government House, an outpost of the British empire which collapsed in the 1820s. Virtually next door, the 1809 **Julee Cottage** belonged to Julee Panton, a "freewoman of color" – a euphemism for being black and not a slave – who had her own land and business, and even her own slave. The building's exhibits record her life and deeds, and the achievements of later black people with Pensacola associations.

Other **restored homes** in the vicinity signify the mishmash of architectural styles, from Creole to Greek Revival, favored by wealthier Pensacolians in the late 1800s. Filled with period furnishings, they make for an enjoyable browse – despite the somewhat twee attendants who sit in them, dressed in period costume during the summer season.

If you have neither the energy nor inclination to visit all the museums and old homes of the Historic Village, head instead to the **Pensacola Historic Museum** (Mon–Sat 9am–4.30; $2), currently at 115 Zaragoza St, while restoration is completed on its usual home: the Old Christ Church at 405 S Adams Street, easily spotted by its sturdy masonry tower. Built in 1832, the church now keeps an imposing clutter, from fossils and Native American pottery to cut-glass ornaments owned by the well-to-do settlers of the early 1900s.

The **T. T. Wentworth Jnr Museum**, on Plaza Ferdinand (Mon–Sat 10am–4pm; $6; free admission with Historic Pensacola Village ticket) contains the random, garage-sale-like collections of Mr Wentworth, who intended to create a museum of oddities à la Ripley (see the "Ripley Museum," p.138), though thankfully his ambitious were thwarted. The existing ephemera are briefly diverting, though it's the yellow-brick Renaissance building (constructed as the city hall in 1907) itself that is the real attraction. The upstairs has been converted to a museum of the local history, which is comprehensive, but not overly exciting. It was in Plaza Ferdinand, incidentally, that Florida was officially accepted into the US – a statue to Andrew Jackson, the state's first governor, salutes the fact.

Museum of Art

Cleverly incorporated into the old jailhouse, Pensacola's **Museum of Art**, opposite the Cultural Center at 407 South Jefferson St (Tues–Fri 10am–5pm, Sat 10am–4pm; $2, free on Tuesdays), was built in 1906 on what was once the shoreline of Pensacola Bay (after ships started dumping their ballast stones, the shoreline was pushed out by half a mile). The art isn't of any particular distinction, but the building itself is worth exploring: old prison cells have been preserved as exhibition space, classrooms for children now occupy the former women's incarceration area and temporary exhibits fill the upstairs all-male cell block.

The Museum of Naval Aviation and Fort Barrancas

You don't have to be a military fanatic to enjoy the **Museum of Naval Aviation** (daily 9am–5pm; free; bus #14), inside the US naval base on Navy Boulevard, about eight miles southwest of central Pensacola, though having a good imagination will help: visitors can climb into many of the full-sized training cockpits and play with the controls.

The main purpose of the museum, however, is to collect and display US naval aircraft, from the first flimsy seaplane acquired in 1911 to the Phantoms and Hornets of more recent times. Among them are a couple of oddities: a small Vietnamese plane, which carried a Vietnamese family onto a US carrier during the fall of Saigon, and the Command Module from the first Skylab mission, whose crew were naval pilots. It's all rather impressive, and serves to underline Pensacola's role as the home base of US naval aviation. The base trains thousands of new pilots each year. Don't miss the seven-story tall IMAX movie screen, on which a pilot's-eye-view of flight makes for quite a visual sensation (IMAX tickets cost $4.50).

On the other side of the road lies the visitor center for **Fort Barrancas** (daily 9.30am–5pm; guided tours on Sat & Sun 2pm; cars $4, pedestrians and cyclists $2), part of the National Seashore area (see below). It's worth spending an hour or so at this well-preserved 1698 Spanish fort, whose design includes a fascinating system of connecting interior vaults.

Eating

Central Pensacola boasts a large number of restaurants and interesting cafés. Try *Van Gogh's Haus of Coffee & Art*, 610 East Wright Street, for its Seventies-inspired interior and light snacks. For cheap specialty sandwiches, head to the square on West Garden St, where, at no. 236, *Garden St Deli* (☎470-0305) serves excellent value-conscious meals at checkered-table-clothed tables. You'd never know it without asking, but as a young man, the owner began the city's biggest annual party (see "Memorial Day," below). *Elise's*, 11 S Palafox Street (☎432-5100), has inexpensive breakfasts and lunches, as does *EJ's*, 232 E Main Street (☎432-5886). *Hall's Catfish & Seafood*, 920 E Gregory Street (☎438-9019), has fish-laden dinner buffets; *McGuire's Irish Pub*, 600 E Gregory Street (☎433-6789), serves immense portions and draft porter in a lively atmosphere; the *Founaris Brothers Greek Restaurant*, 1015 N Ninth Avenue (☎432-0629), dishes up cheap and cheerful fare; and for a touch of class, the *1912 Restaurant* at the *Pensacola Grand Hotel*, 200 E Gregory Street (☎433-3336), offers high-quality, high-priced cuisine.

You'll find more choice at **Pensacola Beach**: *Sundae's*, at 37 Via De Luna Drive is a cheerful place serving good gourmet coffees and rich ice creams. At *The Great Brit*

Inn, at 49 Via De Luna (☎916-1288), you can get standard pub fare while gazing at the front ends of a Triumph TR6, a white MG and an old Jag that jut from the walls. *Butler's,* 27 Via De Luna Drive (☎932-6537), and *The Sundeck Sidewalk Café,* 12 Via De Luna Drive (☎932-0835), do well-priced breakfasts and lunches; while *Boy on a Dolphin,* 400 Pensacola Beach Boulevard (☎932-7954), and the pricier *Flounder's Chowder & Ale House,* 800 Quietwater Beach Road (☎932-2003), both offer hearty seafood dinners. The laid-back *Olliejava,* next door to the Hampton Inn on Via De Luna Drive, serves great breakfasts and dinner. Evening specialties include sautéed shrimp, burritos, chips and salsa, and great crawfish soup. Despite its basic diner decor, *Chan's Market Café & Bakery,* 16 Via de Luna (☎932-8454), serves exceptionally good seafood sandwiches and home-baked side orders of okra, corn fritters as well as great pancakes and cookies. Look to the end of the room for a remarkable 1880 photo of the Indian Chief Geronimo.

Nightlife

In **central Pensacola**, avoid the *Seville Quarter,* 130 E Government Street (☎434-6201), a tourist-orientated bar and disco decked out to reflect Pensacola's history, but too expensive and contrived to be fun. Better is *McGuire's Irish Pub,* 600 E Gregory Street (☎433-6789; see "Eating," above), which serves home-brewed ale.

At **Pensacola Beach** the most hyped place to drink is *Flounder's Chowder & Ale House* (see "Eating," above), which draws as many drinkers as diners and has live music about once a week; and *The Dock* (☎934-3314), beside the pier, which is packed every Friday and Saturday night. For a rum cocktail, drop into *Sandshaker Lounge,* 731 Pensacola Beach Boulevard (☎932-2211). The funkiest place to sip beer is *Olliejava* (see "Eating," above), where long-haired locals strum guitars and tell tales late into the night.

Gay nightlife

For a city with a conservative reputation, Pensacola has a lively **gay scene** and a wild gay Mardi Gras celebration that annually envelopes the city (see below). The best gay **coffee house** is *Cup N Saucer,* 7 East Gregory Street (☎435-9228), which serves the gooiest cheese-cake and cinnamon rolls to a mixed clientele. It's also the only after-hours coffeehouse in town. Next door is *Pride,* a store selling all the usual gay-oriented trinkets. For a friendly local pub, head to *The Round Up,* 706 East Gregory Street (☎433-8482), which has a pleasant covered veranda, but a strict ID policy – take official ID (like a passport) if you could be taken for under 30. The biggest club is *Riviera,* on Main Street, behind the Pensacola Cultural Center.

THE MEMORIAL DAY PARTY

Every year between the Friday and Monday of the last week of May, Pensacola is consumed by a gay and lesbian party, which began when a twenty-year-old local, Dickie Carr, threw a party at the *San Carlos Hotel* (recently demolished to build the courts of law). Dickie's father, who managed the hotel in the Seventies, said he would foot the bill for any of the five hundred rooms which weren't taken. They all were. The party took place on Memorial Day, and has become an annual event involving most of the town and drawing large numbers of outsiders. Despite a brief and quickly-squashed homophobic reaction for local businesses in 1985, the party gets bigger every year, pulling Americans from every state. If you're about, the party begins at Navarre beach on Friday morning and heads back into town at around 4pm, and repeats over the next two days.

Around Pensacola

On the other side of the bay from the city, the glistening quartz beaches of two **barrier islands** are ideal for sunbathing: Santa Rosa Island, running fifty miles from Fort Walton and containing Pensacola Beach; and Perdido Key, to the west of Santa Rosa. Also demanding investigation is the **Gulf Islands National Seashore**, a generic name for several parks, each with a specific point of interest (natural or historical), stretching 150 miles along the coast from here to Mississippi, and including, in this part, the Naval Live Oaks Reservation, the western section of Santa Rosa Island, Fort Barrancas, and the eastern section of Perdido Key.

Gulf Breeze and the Naval Live Oaks Reservation

En route to Santa Rosa Island, via the three-mile-long Pensacola Bridge, you'll pass through **GULF BREEZE**: a well-scrubbed, well-off community that's going all-out to attract homebuyers. Besides a few supermarkets, the only reason to give it more than a passing thought is the **Naval Live Oaks Reservation** (daily 8am–sunset; free), about two miles east along Hwy-98. In the 1820s, part of this live-oak forest was turned into a tree farm, intended to ensure a supply of shipbuilding material for years to come. Precise calculations were made as to how many trees would be needed for a particular ship, and the requisite number of acorns then planted – followed by a fifty-year wait. Problems were plentiful: the oak was too heavy for road transportation, wood rustlers cut down trees and sold them to foreign navies, and the final blow for the farm was the advent of iron-built ships.

The **visitor center** (daily 8.30am–4.30pm), near the entrance, has exhibits and explanatory texts on the intriguing forest, where fragments from Native American settlements from as far back as 1000 BC have been found. To escape the glare of the sun for an hour or so, take one of the short but shady **forest trails**, which include a two-mile section of what was, in the early 1800s, Florida's major roadway, linking Pensacola and St Augustine.

Pensacola Beach

From Gulf Breeze, another (shorter) bridge ($1 toll) leads across a narrow waterway to Santa Rosa Island and the epitome of a Gulf Coast strand, **PENSACOLA BEACH**. Featuring mile after mile of fine white sands, rental outlets for beach and water-sports equipment, a pier lined with fishermen, and beachside bars and snack stands, it's hard to beat for uncomplicated oceanside recreation. With its sprinkling of motels and hotels (see p.360) Pensacola Beach also makes an alternative – if pricier – base to mainland Pensacola.

Fort Pickens and Navarre Beach

From Pensacola Beach, it's just two and a half miles along the Fort Pickens Toll Road (9am–sunset; cars $6, pedestrians and cyclists $3) to the western end of Santa Rosa Island and the entrance to a part of the Gulf Islands National Seashore. Here, vibrant white sands are walled by a nine-mile stretch of high, rugged dunes, and the only reminder of civilization – other than the road – is a foliage-encircled campground. Hoofing over the dunes is strictly forbidden, but several tracks lead from the road to the beach, where you'll find plenty of space and seclusion – and sometimes even dolphins. To learn more about the dunes, and the curious ecology of the island, join one of the frequent **ranger-led walks**; for details call ☎934-2622, or read the bulletin boards situated around the park.

At the western tip of the island are the substantial remains of **Fort Pickens** (daily 9.30am–4pm; free), built by slaves in the early 1800s to protect Pensacola from seaborne attack. Plenty can be gleaned by walking around the fort's creepy passageways and rooms on your own: pick up the free tour leaflet at the visitor center. A small

museum explains the origins of the structure, details the flora and fauna of the national seashore area, and records the travails of the seventeen Apache Indians who were imprisoned here in 1886. Among their number was a chief, Goyahkla, better known as **Geronimo**, who served his sentence roaming the sands. The Apaches, whose tribal lands covered much of the southwestern US, were one of the last Native American tribes to surrender to the advancing White settlers, signing a peace treaty with the sympathetic General Crook in 1886. Soon after, the higher-ranking General Sheridan reneged on the terms of the surrender and incarcerated Geronimo and his fellows, leading Crook to resign from the army in protest.

Beside the fort, some crumbling concrete walls remain from seacoast batteries erected in the Forties, which, together with the pillboxes and observation posts that litter the area, are a reminder that the fort's defensive function lasted until the end of World War II, only becoming obsolete with the advent of guided missiles.

Heading back east along Route 399, the stretch of sand between Pensacola Beach and Navarre Beach is clean and pristine: there are no developments (the area is part of the National Heritage Coastline), and inspirational vistas are plenty. **NAVARRE BEACH** itself, unfortunately, is an explosion of unpleasant development, neither as pretty as Seaside nor as impersonally glamorous as San Destin. Yet just beyond where Route 399 curves north to cross the Pensacola Sound is one of the loveliest stretches of reef dunes and sand on the coast. Hurricane Opal did its best to raze the dunes to nothing in 1996, but impressive conservation work has restored much of the coast. Use the parking lot near the *Juana's Pagodas* tikki hut, a popular grill and bar. This is where those in the know access the beach; after about half a mile, a run of wooden stakes indicate the start of a vast **nude sunbathing** area.

Perdido Key

Another barrier island, to the west of Santa Rosa, **Perdido Key** offers more pristine beaches. Its eastern section, protected as part of the Gulf Islands National Seashore, provides five miles of island untouched by roads. A one-and-a-quarter-mile nature trail allows you to explore the area, and if you're smitten with the seclusion, stick around to swim or pitch your tent at one of the primitive campgrounds. Note that you need a permit to use the island's parking lot ($4 for up to seven days; arrange one by calling ☎492-1595, at the Big Lagoon State Recreation Area). The remainder of Perdido Key is much like Santa Rosa Island: a hotbed of sport, drinking and suntanning rituals.

travel details

TRAINS

Pensacola to: Jacksonsville (Mon, Wed, Fri; 4hr 30min); Tallahassee (Tues, Thurs, Fri, Sun; 4hr 15min).

Tallahassee to: Jacksonsville (Mon, Wed, Fri; 4hr 20min); Pensacola (Tues, Thurs, Fri, Sun; 4hr 15min).

BUSES

Panama City Beach to: Destin (2 daily; 50min); Fort Walton Beach (2 daily; 1hr 10min); Panama City (2 daily; 30min); Pensacola (2 daily; 2hr 15min).

Pensacola to: Destin (2 daily; 1hr 25min); Fort Walton Beach (2 daily; 1hr 5min); Mobile (8 daily; 1hr); New Orleans (6 daily; 4hr 15min); Panama City Beach (2 daily; 2hr 15min); Tallahassee (7 daily; 4hr 25min).

Tallahassee to: Chipley (2 daily; 2 hours); De Funiak Springs (2 daily; 3hr); Gainesville (6 daily; 2hr 30min); Jacksonsville (6 daily; 3hr); Marianna (6 daily; 1hr 15min); Miami (5 daily; 12 hr); New Orleans (7 daily; 9hr); Orlando (11 daily; 6hr 30min); Panama City Beach (2 daily; 2hr 20min); Pensacola (7 daily; 5hr); Tampa (7 daily; 6hr); Thomasville (4 daily; 1hr).

THE HISTORICAL FRAMEWORK

Contrary to popular belief, Florida's history goes back far beyond Walt Disney World and motel-lined beaches. For thousands of years, its aboriginal inhabitants lived in organized social groupings with contacts across a large section of the Americas. During the height of European colonization, it became a Spanish possession and, for a time, was under British control. Only in the nineteenth century did Florida become part of the US: the beginning of a period of unrestrained exploitation and expansion and the start of many of the problems with which the state continues to grapple today.

ORIGINS OF THE LAND

Over billions of years, rivers flowing through what's now **northern Florida** carried debris from the Appalachian mountains to the coast, and their deposits of fine-powdered rock formed the beaches and barrier islands of the Panhandle. Further south, the highest section of a seabed plateau – the **Florida peninsula** – altered in shape according to the world's ice covering. The exposed land sometimes measured twice its present size; during other periods, the coastline was far inland of its current position, with wave action carving out still-visible bluffs in the oolitic

limestone base. In the **present era**, beginning about 75 million years ago, rotting vegetation mixed with rainfall to form acid that burned holes in the limestone, and natural freshwater springs emerged; the underground water accumulated from heavy rains which preceded each Ice Age. Inland forests of live oak and pine became inhabited 20,000 years ago by mastodons, mammoths and saber-toothed tigers, thought to have traveled – over many generations – across the ice-covered Bering Strait from Siberia.

FIRST HUMAN HABITATION

Two theories exist regarding the origins of Florida's **first human inhabitants**. It's commonly believed that the earliest arrivals followed the same route as the animals from Siberia, crossing North America and arriving in northern Florida around 10,000 years ago. A minority of anthropologists takes the alternative view that the first Floridians were the result of migration by aboriginal peoples in South and Central America. Either way, the **Paleo** (or "Early") **Indians** in Florida lived hunter-gatherer existences – the spear tips they used are widely found across the central and northern parts of the state.

Around 5000 BC, social patterns changed: settlements became semi-permanent and diet switched from meat to shellfish, snails and mollusks, which were abundant along the rivers. Traveling was done by dugout canoe and, periodically, a community would move to a new site, probably to allow food supplies to replenish themselves. Discarded shells and other rubbish were piled onto the **midden mounds** still commonly seen in the state.

Though pottery began to appear around 2000 BC, not until 1000 BC was there a big change in lifestyle, as indicated by the discovery of **irrigation canals**, patches of land cleared for **cultivation**, and cooking utensils used to prepare grown food. From the time of the Christian era, the erection of **burial mounds** – elaborate tombs of prominent tribespeople, often with sacrificed kin and valuable objects also placed inside – became common. These suggest strong religious and trading links across an area stretching from Central America to the North American interior.

Spreading east from the Georgian coastal plain, the **Fort Walton Culture** became prevalent from around 200 AD. This divided society into a rigid caste system and people lived in villages planned around a central plaza. Throughout Florida at this time, approximately 100,000 inhabitants formed several distinct tribal groupings: most notably the **Timucua** across northern Florida, the **Calusa** around the southwest and Lake Okeechobee, the **Apalachee** in the Panhandle and the **Tequesta** along the southeast coast.

EUROPEAN SETTLEMENT

After Christopher Columbus located the "New World" in 1492, Europe's great sea powers were increasingly active around the Caribbean. One of them, Spain, had discovered and plundered the treasures of ancient civilizations in Central America, and all were eager to locate other riches across these and neighboring lands. The **first European sighting** of Florida is believed to have been made by John and Sebastian **Cabot** in 1498, when they set eyes on what is now called Cape Florida, on Key Biscayne in Miami.

In 1513, the **first European landing** was made by **Juan Ponce de León**, a Spaniard previously employed as governor of Puerto Rico (a Spanish possession) and who was eager to carve out a niche for himself in the expanding empire. While searching for Bimini, Ponce de León sighted land during *Pascua Florida*, the Spanish Easter "Festival of the Flowers," and named what he saw **La Florida** – or "Land of Flowers." After landing ashore somewhere between the mouth of the St John's River and present-day St Augustine, Ponce de León sailed on around the Florida Keys, naming them *Los Martires*, for their supposed resemblance to the bones of martyred men, and *Las Tortugas* (now the Dry Tortugas), named for the turtles he saw around them.

Sent to deal with troublesome natives in the Lower Antilles, it was eight years before Ponce de León returned to Florida, this time with a mandate from the Spanish king to **conquer and colonize** the territory. Landing on the southwest coast, probably somewhere between Tampa Bay and Fort Myers, Ponce de León met a hostile reception from the Calusa Indians and was forced to withdraw, eventually dying from an arrow wound received in the battle.

Rumors of gold hidden in Apalachee, in the north of the region, stimulated several Spanish incursions into Florida, all of which were driven back by the aggression of the indigenes and the ferocity of the terrain and climate. The most successful undertaking – even though it ended in death for its leader – was the **Hernando de Soto expedition**, a thousand-strong band of war-hardened knights and treasure seekers, which landed at Tampa Bay in May 1539. Recent excavations in Tallahassee have located the site of one of de Soto's camps, where the first Christmas celebration in North America is thought to have taken place before the expedition continued north, later making the first European crossing of the Mississippi River – for a long time marking Florida's western boundary.

Written accounts of the expeditions are a major source of information about the aboriginal life of that period, though anthropology was not a major concern of the Spanish, and the news that Florida did not harbor stunning riches caused interest to wane. Treasure-laden Spanish ships sailing off the Florida coast between the Americas and Europe proved attractive to pirate ships, however, many of them British and French vessels hoisting the Jolly Roger. The Spanish failure to colonize Florida made it a prime base for attacks on their vessels, and a small group of **French Huguenots** landed in 1562, building Fort Caroline on the St John's River.

The French presence forced the Spanish into a more determined effort at settlement. Already commissioned to explore the Atlantic coast of North America, **Pedro Menéndez de Avilés** was promised the lion's share of whatever profits could be made from Florida. Landing south of the French fort on August 28, 1562, the day of the Spanish Festival of San Augustín, Menéndez named the site **St Augustine** – founding what was to become the longest continuous site of European habitation on the continent. The French were quickly defeated, their leader **Jean Ribault** and his crew massacred after being driven ashore by a hurricane; the site of the killing is still known as *Matanzas*, or "Place of Slaughter."

THE FIRST SPANISH PERIOD (1585–1763)

Only the enthusiasm of Menéndez held Florida together during the early decades of Spanish rule. A few small and insecure settlements were established, usually around **missions** founded by Jesuits or Franciscans bent on Christianizing the Indians. It was a far from harmonious setup:

homesick Spanish soldiers frequently mutinied and fought with the Indians, who responded by burning St Augustine to the ground. Menéndez replaced St Augustine's wooden buildings with "tabby" (a cement-like mixture of seashells and limestone) structures with palm-thatched roofs, a style typical of early European Florida. While easily the largest settlement, even St Augustine was a lifeless outpost unless a ship happened to be in port. Despite sinking all his personal finances into the colony, Menéndez never lived to see Florida thrive, and he left in 1571, ordered by the king to help plan the Spanish Armada's attack on Britain.

Fifteen years later, as war raged between the European powers, St Augustine was razed by a naval bombardment led by **Francis Drake**, a sign that the **British** were beginning to establish their colonies along the Atlantic coast north of Florida. Aware that the Indians would hold the balance of power in future colonial power struggles, a string of Spanish missions were built along the Panhandle from 1606; besides seeking to earn the loyalty of the natives, these were intended to provide a defensive shield against attacks from the north. By the 1700s the British were making forays into Florida, ostensibly to capture Indians to sell as slaves. One by one, the missions were destroyed, and only the timely arrival of Spanish reinforcements prevented the fall of St Augustine to the British in 1740.

With the French in Louisiana, the British in Georgia and the Spanish clinging to Florida, the scene was set for a bloody confrontation for control of North America. Eventually, the **1763 Treaty of Paris**, concluding the Seven Years' War in Europe, settled the issue: the British had captured the crucial Spanish possession of Havana, and Spain willingly parted with Florida to get it back.

THE BRITISH PERIOD (1763–1783)

Despite their two centuries of occupation, the Spanish failed to make much impression on Florida. It was the British, already developing the colonies further north, who grafted a social infrastructure onto the region. They also divided Florida (then with only the northern section inhabited by whites) into separate colonies: **East Florida** governed from St Augustine, and **West Florida** governed from the growing Panhandle port of **Pensacola**.

By this time, aboriginal Floridians had largely died out through contact with European diseases, to which they had no immunity, and Florida's Indian population was becoming composed of disparate tribes arriving from the west, collectively known as the **Seminoles**. Like the Spanish, the British acknowledged the numerical importance of the Indians and sought good relations with them. In return for goods, the British took Indian land around ports and supply routes, but generally left the Seminoles undisturbed in the inland areas.

Despite attractive grants, few settlers arrived from Britain. Those with money to spare bought Florida land as an investment, never intending to develop or settle on it, and only large holdings – **plantations** growing corn, sugar, rice and other crops – were profitable. Charleston, to the north, dominated sea trade in the area, though St Augustine was still a modestly important settlement and the gathering place of passing British aristocrats and intellectuals. West Florida, on the other hand, was driven by political factionalism and often the scene of skirmishes with the Seminoles, who received worse treatment than their counterparts in the east.

Being a new and sparsely populated region, the discontent that fuelled the **American War of Independence** in the 1770s barely affected Florida, except for St Augustine, which served as a haven for British Royalists fleeing the war, many of whom moved on to the Bahamas or Jamaica. Pensacola, though, was attacked and briefly occupied in 1781 by the Spanish, who had been promised Florida in return for helping the American rebels defeat the British. As it turned out, diplomacy rather than gunfire signaled the end of British rule in Florida.

THE SECOND SPANISH PERIOD (1783–1821)

The **1783 Treaty of Paris**, with which Britain recognized American independence, not only returned Florida to Spain, but also gave it Louisiana and the prized port of New Orleans. Spanish holdings in North America were now larger than ever, but with Europe in turmoil and the Spanish colonies in Central America agitating for their own independence, the country was ill-equipped to capitalize on them. Moreover, the complexity of Florida's melting pot, comprising the British, smaller numbers of ethnically diverse European settlers, and the increasingly assertive Seminoles (now well established in fertile central Florida, and often joined by Africans escaping slavery further north), made it impossible for a declining colonial power to govern.

As fresh European migration slowed, Spain was forced to **sell land to US citizens**, who bought large tracts, confident that Florida would soon be under Washington's control. Indeed, in gaining Louisiana from France in 1800 (to whom it had been ceded by Spain), and moving the Georgia border south, it was clear the US had Florida in its sights. Fearful of losing the commercial toehold it still retained in Florida, and aligned with Spain through the Napoleonic wars, Britain landed troops at Pensacola in 1814. In response, a US general, **Andrew Jackson**, used the excuse of an Indian uprising in Alabama to march south, killing hundreds of Indians and pursuing them – unlawfully and without official sanction from Washington – into Pensacola, declaring no quarrel with the Spanish but insisting that the British depart. The British duly left, and Jackson and his men withdrew to Mobile (a Floridian town that became part of Alabama as the Americans inched the border eastwards), soon to participate in the Battle of New Orleans, which further strengthened the US position on the Florida border.

THE FIRST SEMINOLE WAR

Jackson's actions in 1814 had triggered the **First Seminole War**. As international tension heightened, Seminole raids (often as a result of baiting on the US side) were commonly used as excuses for US incursions into Florida. In 1818, Jackson finally received what he took to be presidential approval (the "Rhea Letter," thought to have been authorized by President Monroe) to march again into Florida on the pretext of subduing the Seminoles but with the actual intention of taking outright control.

While US public officials were uneasy with the dubious legality of these events, the American public was firmly on Jackson's side. The US government issued an ultimatum to Spain, demanding that either it police Florida effectively or relinquish its ownership. With little alternative, Spain formally **ceded Florida to the US** in 1819, in return for the US assuming the $5 million owed by the Spanish government to American settlers in land grants (a sum which was never repaid). Nonetheless, it took the threat of an invasion of Cuba for the Spanish king to ratify the treaty in 1821; at the same time Andrew Jackson was sworn in as Florida's first American governor.

TERRITORIAL FLORIDA

In territorial Florida it was soon evident that the East and West divisions were unworkable, and a site midway between St Augustine and Pensacola was selected as the new administrative center: **Tallahassee**. The Indians living on the fertile soils of the area were rudely dispatched towards the coast – an act of callousness that was to typify relations between the new settlers and the incumbent Native Americans for decades to come.

Under Spanish and British rule, the Seminoles, notwithstanding some feuding between themselves, lived peaceably on the productive lands of northern central Florida. These, however, were precisely the agriculturally rich areas that US settlers coveted. Under the **Treaty of Moultrie Creek** in 1823, most of the Seminole tribes signed a document agreeing to sell their present land and resettle in southwest Florida. Neither side was to honor this agreement: no time limit was imposed on the Seminole exodus, and those who did go found the new land to be unsuitable for farming. The US side, meanwhile, failed to provide promised resettlement funds.

Andrew Jackson spent only three months as territorial governor, though his influence on Florida continued from the White House when he became US president in 1829. In 1830 he approved the **Act of Indian Removal**, decreeing that all Native Americans in the eastern US should be transferred to reservations in the open areas of the Midwest. Two years later, James Gadsen, the newly appointed Indian commissioner, called a meeting of the Seminole tribes at Payne's Landing on the Oklawaha River, near Silver Springs, urging them to cede their land to the US and move west. Amid much acrimony, a few did sign the **Treaty of Payne's Landing**, which provided for their complete removal within three years.

THE SECOND SEMINOLE WAR (1821–1842)

A small number took what monies were offered and resettled in the west, but most Seminoles were determined to stay and the **Second**

Seminole War ensued, with the Indians repeatedly ambushing the US militiamen who had arrived to enforce the law, and ransacking the plantations of white settlers, many of whom fled and never returned. Trained for set-piece battles, the US troops were rarely able to deal effectively with the guerrilla tactics of the Seminoles. It was apparent that the Seminoles were unlikely to be defeated by conventional means and in October 1837, their leader, **Osceola**, was lured to St Augustine with the promise of a truce – only to be arrested and imprisoned, eventually to die in jail. This treachery failed to break the spirit of the Seminoles, though a few continued to give themselves up and leave for the west, while others were captured and sold into slavery.

It became the policy of the US to drive the Seminoles steadily south, away from the fertile lands of central Florida and **into the Everglades**. In the Everglades, the Seminoles linked up with the long-established "Spanish Indians" to raid the Cape Florida lighthouse and destroy the white colony on Indian Key in the Florida Keys. Even after bloodhounds were – controversially – used to track the Indians, it was clear that total US victory would never be achieved. With the Seminoles confined to the Everglades, the US formally **ended the conflict** in 1842, when the Seminoles agreed to stay where they were – an area earlier described by an army surveyor as "fit only for Indian habitation."

The six-year war crippled the Florida economy but stimulated the growth of a number of **new towns** around the army forts. Several of these, such as Fort Brooke (Tampa), Fort Lauderdale, Fort Myers and Fort Pierce, have survived into modern times.

STATEHOOD AND SECESSION (1842–1861)

The Second Seminole War forestalled the possibility of Florida **attaining statehood** – which would have entitled it to full representation in Washington and to appoint its own administrators. Influence in Florida at this time was split between two camps. On one side were the wealthy slave-owning plantation farmers, concentrated in the "cotton counties" of the central section of the Panhandle, who enjoyed all the traditions of the upper rung of Deep South society. They were eager to make sure that the balance of power in Washington did not shift towards the non-slave-owning "free" states, which would inevitably bring a call for the abolition of slavery. Opposing statehood were the smallholders scattered about the rest of the territory – many of whom were Northerners, already ideologically against slavery and fearing the imposition of federal taxes.

One compromise mooted was a return to a divided Florida, with the West becoming a state while the East remained a territory. Eventually, based on a narrowly agreed **constitution** drawn up in Port St Joseph on the Panhandle coast (on the site of present-day Port St Joe), Florida **became a state** on March 3, 1845. The arrival of statehood coincided with a period of material prosperity: the first railroads began spidering across the Panhandle and central Florida; an organized school system became established; and Florida's 60,000 population was doubled within twenty years.

Nationally, things were less bright. The issue of slavery was to be the catalyst that led the US into civil war, though it was only a part of a great cultural divide between the rural Southern states – to which Florida was linked more through geography than history – and the modern industrial states of the North. As federal pressure intensified for the abolition of slavery, Florida formally **seceded from the Union** on January 10, 1861, aligning itself with the breakaway Confederate States in the run-up to the Civil War.

THE CIVIL WAR (1861–1865)

Inevitably, the **Civil War** had a great effect on Florida, although most Floridians conscripted into the Confederate army fought far away from home, and rarely were there more than minor confrontations within the state. The relatively small number of Union sympathizers generally kept a low profile, concentrating on protecting their families. At the start of the war, most of Florida's **coastal forts** were occupied by Union troops as part of the blockade on Confederate shipping. Lacking the strength to mount effective attacks on the forts, those Confederate soldiers who remained in Florida based themselves in the interior and watched for Union troop movements, swiftly destroying whatever bridge, road or railroad lay in the invaders' path – in effect creating a stalemate, which endured throughout the conflict.

Away from the coast, Florida's primary contribution to the war effort was the **provision of food** – chiefly beef and pork reared on the central Florida farms – and the transportation of it across the Panhandle towards Confederate strongholds further west. Union attempts to cut the supply route gave rise to the only major battle fought in the state, the **Battle of Olustee**, just outside Live Oak, in February 1864: 10,000 participated in an engagement that left 300 dead and both sides claiming victory.

The most celebrated battle from a Floridian viewpoint, however, happened in March 1865 at **Natural Bridge**, when a youthful group of Confederates defeated the technically superior Union troops, preventing the fall of Tallahassee. As events transpired, it was a hollow victory; following the Confederate surrender, the war ended a few months later.

RECONSTRUCTION

Following the cessation of hostilities, Florida was caught in an uneasy hiatus. In the years after the war, the defeated states were subject to **Reconstruction**, a re-arrangement of their internal affairs determined by, at first, the president, and later by a much harder-line Congress intent on ensuring the southern states would never return to their old ways.

The Northern ideal of free-labor capitalism was an alien concept in the South, and there were enormous problems. Of paramount concern was the future of the **freed slaves**. With restrictions on their movements lifted, many emancipated slaves wandered the countryside, often unwittingly putting fear into all-white communities that had never before had a black face in their midst. Rubbing salt into the wounds, as far as the Southern whites were concerned, was the occupation of many towns by black Union troops. As a backlash, the white-supremacist **Ku Klux Klan** became active in Tennessee during 1866, and its race-hate, segregationist doctrine soon spread into Florida.

Against this background of uncertainty, Florida's **domestic politics** entered a period of unparalleled chicanery. Suddenly, not only were black men allowed to vote, but there were more black voters than white. The gullibility of the uneducated blacks and the power of their votes proved an irresistible combination to the unscrupulous and power-hungry. Double-dealing and vote-rigging were practiced by diverse factions united only in their desire to restore Florida's statehood and acquire even more power. Following a constitution written and approved in controversial circumstances, Florida was **re-admitted to the Union** on July 21, 1868.

Eventually, in Florida as in the other Southern states, an all-white, **conservative Democrat government** emerged. Despite emancipation and the hopes for integration outlined by the Civil Rights Act passed by Congress in 1875, blacks in Florida were still denied many of the rights reasonably regarded as basic. In fact, all that distanced the new administration from the one that led Florida into secession was awareness of the power of the federal government and the need to at least appear to take outside views into account. It was also true that many of the former slave-owners were now the employers of freed blacks, who remained very much under their white masters' control.

A NEW FLORIDA (1876–1914)

Florida's bonds with its neighboring states became increasingly tenuous in the years following Reconstruction. A fast-growing population began spreading south – part of a gradual diminishing of the importance of the Panhandle, where ties to the Deep South were strongest. Florida's identity became forged by a new **frontier spirit**. Besides smallholding farmers, loggers came to work the abundant forests, and a new breed of wealthy settler started putting down roots, among them Henry DeLand and Henry S. Sanford, who each bought large chunks of central Florida and founded the towns that still bear their names.

As northern speculators invested in Florida, they sought to publicize the region, and a host of articles extolling the virtues of the state's climate as a cure for all ills began to appear in the country's newspapers. These early efforts to promote **Florida as a tourist destination** brought the wintering rich along the new railroads to enjoy the sparkling rivers and springs, and naturalists arrived to explore the unique flora and fauna.

With a fortune made through his partnership in Standard Oil, **Henry Flagler** opened luxury resorts on Florida's northeast coast for his socialite friends, and gradually extended his Florida East Coast Railroad south, giving birth to communities such as **Palm Beach** and making the remote trading post of **Miami** an accessible, expanding town. Flagler's friendly rival, **Henry Plant**, connected *his* railroad to **Tampa**, turning a desolate hamlet into a thriving port city and a major base of cigar manufacturing. The **citrus industry** also revved into top gear: Florida's climate enabled oranges, grapefruits, lemons, and other citrus fruits to be grown during the winter and sold to an eager market in the cooler north. The **cattle farms** went from small to strong, Florida becoming a major supplier of beef to the rest of the US: cows were rounded up with a special wooden whip which made a gunshot-like sound when used — hence the nickname "**cracker**," which was applied to rural settlers.

One group that didn't benefit from the boom years was the blacks. Many were imprisoned for no reason, and found themselves on chaingangs building the new roads and railroads; punishments for refusing to work included severe floggings and hanging by the thumbs. Few whites paid any attention, and those who were in a position to stop the abuses were usually too busy getting rich. There was, however, the founding of **Eatonville**, just north of Orlando, which was the first town in Florida — and possibly the US — to be founded, governed and lived in by black people.

THE SPANISH-AMERICA WAR

By the 1890s, the US was a large and unified nation itching for a bigger role in the world. As the drive in **Cuba** for independence from Spain gathered momentum, an opportunity to participate in international affairs presented itself. Florida already had long links with Cuba — the capital, Havana, was just ninety miles from Key West, and several thousand Cuban migrants were employed in the Tampa cigar factories. During 1898, tens of thousands of US troops — the Cuban Expeditionary Force — arrived in the state, and the **Spanish-American War** was declared on April 25. As it turned out, the fighting was comparatively minor. Spain withdrew, and on January 1, 1899, Cuba attained independence (and the US a big say in its future). But the war was also the first of several major conflicts that were to prove beneficial to Florida. Many of the soldiers would return as settlers or tourists, and improved railroads and strengthened harbors at the commercially significant ports of Key West, Tampa and Pensacola did much to boost the economy.

THE BROWARD ERA

The early years of the 1900s were dominated by the progressive policies of **Napoleon Bonaparte Broward**, who was elected state governor in 1905. In a nutshell, Broward championed the small man against corporate interests, particularly the giant land-owning railroad companies. Among Broward's aims were an improved education system, a state-run commission to oversee new railroad construction, a tax on cars to finance road building, better salaries for teachers and the judiciary, a state-run life insurance scheme, and a ban on newspapers — few of which were well-disposed towards Broward — knowingly publishing untruths. Broward also enacted the first **conservation laws**, protecting fish, oysters, game and forests; but at the same time, in an attempt to create new land to rival the holdings of the rail barons, he conceived the drainage program that would cause untold damage to the Everglades.

By no means did all of Broward's policies become law, and he departed Tallahassee for a US Senate seat in 1910. Nonetheless, the forward-thinking plans of what became known as the **Broward Era** were continued through subsequent administrations — a process that went some way toward bringing a rough-and-ready frontier land into the twentieth century.

WORLD WAR I AND AFTER

World War I continued the tradition of the Spanish-American War by giving Florida an economic shot in the arm, as the military arrived to police the coastline and develop seawarfare projects. Despite the influx of money and the reforms of the Broward years, there was little happening to improve the lot of Florida's blacks. The Ku Klux Klan was revived in Tallahassee in 1915, and the public outcry that followed the beating to death of a young black on a chaingang was answered only by the introduction of the sweatbox as punishment for prisoners considered unruly.

Typically, most visitors to Florida at this time were more concerned with getting drunk than social justice. The coast so vigilantly protected from advancing Germans during the war was left wide open when **Prohibition** was introduced in 1919; the many secluded inlets became secure landing sites for spirits from the Caribbean. The illicit booze improved the atmosphere in the new resorts of **Miami Beach**, a picture-postcard piece of beach landscaping replacing what had been a barely habitable mangrove island just a few years before. Drink was not the only illegal pleasure pursued in the nightclubs: gambling and prostitution were also rife, and were soon to attract the attention of big-time **gangsters** such as Al Capone, initiating a climate of corruption that was to scar Florida politics for years.

The lightning-paced creation of Miami Beach was no isolated incident. Throughout Florida, and especially in the southeast, new communities appeared almost overnight. Self-proclaimed architectural genius **Addison Mizner** erected the "million dollar cottages" of Palm Beach and began fashioning **Boca Raton** with the same mock-Mediterranean excesses, on the premise: "get the big snob and the little snob will follow;" visionary **George Merrick** plotted the superlative **Coral Gables** – now absorbed by Miami – which became the nation's first pre-planned city and one of the few schemes of the time to age with dignity.

In the rush of prosperity that followed the war, it seemed everyone in America wanted a piece of Florida, and chartered trains brought in thousands of eager buyers. The spending frenzy soon meant that for every genuine offer there were a hundred bogus ones: many people unknowingly bought acres of empty swampland. The period was satirized by the Marx Brothers in their first film, *Cocoanuts*.

Although millions of dollars technically changed hands each week during the peak year of 1925, little hard cash actually moved. Most deals were paper transactions with buyers paying a small deposit into a bank. The inflation inherent in the system finally went out of control in 1926. With buyers failing to keep up payments, banks went **bust** and were quickly followed by everyone else. A **hurricane** devastated Miami the same year – the city's house-builders never thought to protect the structures against tropical storms – and an even worse hurricane in 1928 caused Lake Okeechobee to burst its banks and flood surrounding communities.

With the Florida land boom well and truly over, the **Wall Street Crash** in 1929 proceeded to make paupers of the millionaires, such as Henry Flagler and Sarasota's **John Ringling**, whose considerable investments had helped to shape the state, and who would later found the **Ringling Brothers Barnum and Bailey Circus**.

THE DEPRESSION AND WORLD WAR II

At the start of the Thirties, even the major railroads that had stimulated Florida's expansion were in receivership, and the state government only avoided bankruptcy with a constitutional escape clause. Due to the property crash, Florida had had a few extra years to adjust to grinding poverty before the whole country experienced the Depression, and a number of recovery measures – making the state more active in citizens' welfare – pre-empted the national New Deal legislation of President Roosevelt.

No single place was harder hit than **Key West**, which was not only suffering the Depression but hadn't been favored by the property boom either. With a population of 12,000, Key West was an incredible $5 million in debt, and had even lost its link to the mainland when the Overseas Railroad – running across the Florida Keys between Key West and Miami – was destroyed by the 1935 Labor Day hurricane.

What saved Key West, and indeed brought financial stability to all of Florida, was **World War II**. Once again, thousands of troops arrived to guard the coastline – off which there was an immense amount of German U-boat activity – while the flat inland areas made a perfect training venue for pilots. Empty tourist hotels provided ready-made barracks, and the soldiers – and their visiting families – got a taste of Florida that would bring many of them back.

In the immediate **postwar period**, the inability of the state to plan and provide for increased growth was resoundingly apparent, with public services – particularly in the field of education – woefully inadequate. Because of the massive profits being made through illegal gambling, corruption became endemic in public life. State governor **Fuller Warren**, implicated with the Al Capone crime syndicate in 1950, was by no means the only state official suspected of being in cahoots with criminals. A wave of attacks against blacks and Jews in 1951 caused Warren to speak out against the Ku Klux Klan, but the discovery that he himself had once been a Klan member only confirmed the poison flowing through the heart of Florida's political system.

A rare upbeat development was a continued commitment to the conservation measures introduced in the Broward era, with $2 million allocated to buying the land that, in 1947, became the **Everglades National Park**.

THE FIFTIES AND SIXTIES

Cattle, citrus and tourism continued to be the major components of Florida's economy as, in the ten years from 1950, the state soared from being the twentieth to the tenth most populous in the country, home to five million people. While its increased size raised Florida's profile in federal government, the demographic changes within the state – most dramatically the shift from rural life in the north to urban living in the South – went unacknowledged, and **reapportionment** of representation in state government became a critical issue. It was only resolved by the **1968 constitution**, which provided for automatic reapportionment in line with population changes.

The fervent desire for growth and the need to present a wholesome public image prevented the state's conservative-dominated assembly from fighting as hard as their counterparts in the other Southern states against **de-segregation**, following a ruling by the federal Supreme Court on the issue in 1956. Nonetheless, blacks continued to be banned from Miami Beach after dark and from swimming off the Palm Beach coast. In addition, they were subject to segregation in restaurants, buses, hotels, and schools – and barely represented at all in public office. As the **Civil Rights** movement gained strength during the early Sixties, bus boycotts and demonstrations took place in Tallahassee and Daytona Beach, and a march in St Augustine in 1964 resulted in the arrest of the movement's leader, Dr. Martin Luther King Jr. The success of the Civil Rights movement in ending legalized discrimination did little to affect the deeply entrenched racist attitudes among much of Florida's longer-established population. Most of the state's blacks still lived and worked in conditions that would have been intolerable to whites: a fact that, in part, accounted for the **Liberty City riot** in August 1968, which was the first of several violent uprisings in Miami's depressed areas.

The ideological shift in Florida's near-neighbor, **Cuba** – declared a socialist state by its leader Fidel Castro in 1961 – came sharply into focus with the 1962 **missile crisis**, which triggered a tense game of cat and mouse between the US and the USSR over Soviet missile bases on the island. After world war was averted, Florida became the base of the US government's covert anti-Castro operations. Many engaged in these activities were among the 300,000 **Cuban migrants** who had arrived following the Castro-led revolution. The Bay of Pigs fiasco in 1961 proved that there was to be no quick return to the homeland, and while not all of the new arrivals stayed in Florida, many went no further than Miami, where they were to totally change the social character – and eventually the power balance – of the city.

Another factor in Florida's expansion was the basing of the new civilian space administration, **NASA**, at the military long-range missile-testing site at Cape Canaveral. The all-out drive to land a man on the moon brought an enormous influx of space industry personnel in the early Sixties – quadrupling the population of the region soon to become known as the **Space Coast**.

Although it didn't open until 1971, **Walt Disney World** got off the drawing board in the mid-Sixties and was to have a terrific impact on the future of Florida. The state government bent over backwards to help the Disney Corporation turn a sizeable slice of central Florida into the biggest theme park complex ever known. Throughout its construction, debate raged over the commercial and ecological effects of such a major undertaking on the rest of the region. Undeterred, smaller businesses rushed to the area, eager to capitalize on the anticipated tourist influx, and the sleepy cow-town of **Orlando** suddenly found itself the hub of one of the state's fastest-growing population centers – soon to become one of the world's best-known holiday destinations.

CONTEMPORARY FLORIDA

The great commercial success of Walt Disney World, and a fortuitous set of circumstances – American fears of terrorism reducing foreign travel and price-wars between tour operators and airlines encouraging overseas visitors – have helped solidify Florida's place in the **international tourist market**. Directly or indirectly, one in five of the state's twelve million inhabitants now makes a living from tourism. Simultaneously, the general swing from heavy to **high-tech industries** has resulted in many American corporations forsaking their traditional northern bases in favor of Florida, bringing their white-collar workforces with them.

Behind the optimistic facade, however, lie many problems. Taxes kept low to stimulate growth have reduced funding for public services, leaving the apparently booming state with appalling levels of adult illiteracy, infant mortality and crime. Efforts to **raise taxes** during the late Eighties met incredible resistance and forced a U-turn by the state governor, Bob Martinez. A further cause for concern is the broadening **gap** between the relative liberalism of the big cities and the arch-conservatism of the bible-belt rural areas. While Miami is busy promoting its modernity and multicultural make-up (glossing over some severe inter-ethnic conflicts in doing so), the Ku Klux Klan holds picnics in the Panhandle, a children's storybook is removed from a north Florida school's reading list for containing the words "damn" and "bitch," and in Pensacola a doctor is shot dead by anti-abortion activists.

GUNS AND DRUGS

Contradictions are also apparent in efforts to reduce crime. In 1976, Florida became the first state to restore **the death penalty**, declaring it the ultimate deterrent to murder; yet the state's **gun laws** remain notoriously lax. Some districts impose a "cooling off" period of a few days while the background of a potential gun purchaser is checked, but in most, firearms can be bought over the counter on production of the flimsiest ID.

The multi-million-dollar **drug trade** active in the state shows few signs of abating. Geographically, Florida is highly convenient for the exporters of Latin America and estimates suggest that at least a quarter of the cocaine entering the US arrives through the state. In Miami, around ninety separate drug-law enforcement agencies are operative, but fear of corruption causes them to act alone and not pool information. Ironically, a recent switch of emphasis from capturing dealers to clamping down on **money-laundering** (the filtering of illegal profits through legitimate businesses) has begun to threaten many of Miami's financial institutions, built on – and it's an open secret – the drugs trade.

RACIAL ISSUES

President Clinton sought to gain support for the Democrats in Florida by involving himself in the Cuban situation. In 1994 it was decided that all Cubans trying to reach Florida would be interned at the US Navy's Guantanamo base in Cuba, though little thought was given to the fate of those refused entry. In 1995, the Cubans detained at Guantanamo were allowed into the US, but it was decreed that any future refugees would be returned to Cuba. This was a major policy shift that angered right-wing Cuban exiles. For the first time since Castro gained power, the US was officially saying that Cubans were not being persecuted en masse. It would be up to individuals to prove that they were in danger.

In 1996, in an attempt to appease right-wing elements of the Cuban exile community, Clinton agreed to accept the Helms-Burton law threatening sanctions on foreign businesses with interests in Cuba. Yet in so doing, he infuriated the governments of Canada, Britain, Mexico and other important US allies and trading partners. Because of this, Florida did not swing his way and vote Democrat in the November 1996 election.

VIOLENCE AGAINST TOURISTS

Repeated incidents of violence against European tourists, including the murders of German and British holidaymakers, have earned the state much adverse publicity. Governor Lawton Chiles (a liberal successor to Martinez, and elected against the odds in November 1990) responded in February 1993 by creating the Task Force on Tourist Safety. The task force launched pilot schemes in Miami and Orlando which entailed improved road signs (to show more clearly routes to major attractions), new tourist information centers at key arrival points, and an ending of the giveaway "Y" and "Z" plates on rental cars. Today, easy-to-see road signs emblazoned with a bright orange sun guide tourists through the confusing streets of Miami and toward the main highways, making it easier to navigate "Florida's Sun Route."

While the task force is a step forward, nobody seriously thinks that crime against the Florida tourist can ever be completely eradicated – the murder in 1996 of a Dutch tourist asking for directions at a Miami gas station is a reminder of this. State officials are swift to point out, however, that if European visitors heeded the routine safety precautions (outlined in Basics) that most Americans take for granted, the risks would be greatly lessened.

CONSERVATION

Increased protection of the state's **natural resources** has been a more positive feature of the last decade. Impressive amounts of land are under state control and, overall, wildlife is less threatened now than at any time since white settlers first arrived. Most spectacular of all has been the revival of the state's alligator population. On the downside, the Everglades – and its dependent animals – could still be destroyed by south Florida's ever-increasing need for drinking water.

HURRICANE ANDREW

In August 1992, **Hurricane Andrew** brought winds of 168mph tearing through the southern regions of Miami (blowing down the radar of the National Hurricane Center in the process). Although the hurricane was no surprise – scores of potential hurricanes develop off Florida's shores each year between June and November and are closely observed; most die out well before striking the coast – roofs were ripped off homes, supermarkets were gutted, 150,000 were left homeless or living in ruins, 230,000 more had no power supply, and the cost of damage was estimated at $30 billion.

Governor Chiles declared the stricken region a disaster area, deployed 1500 National Guardsmen to stem looting, and warned that Florida would be bankrupt if left to foot the bill alone. As criticism of the sluggishly paced and disorganized federal response to the emergency mounted, then president George Bush made two child-hugging tours of the devastated area, eventually deploying 20,000 marines and a naval convoy in what became the biggest relief operation ever mounted.

Even several years after the hurricane struck, signs of its handiwork are still apparent in the form of abandoned homes and destroyed businesses (for example, the Deering Estate along Old Cutler Road in Miami has never fully recovered, and still retains an eerie graveyard of stripped trees standing in memorial). Nevertheless, some good has emerged from the disaster – many parks have replaced uprooted trees with species endemic to Florida, which are much more likely to survive future hurricanes. The Fairchild Tropical Garden in Miami, which suffered a great blow by Andrew when many of its exotic and rare plants were ripped from their roots, has recovered with a vengeance, boasting new plant species and exhibits. It's there you can see a gigantic tree laying prone on its side, toppled by the hurricane but which continues to grow.

While older Floridians remembered the series of hurricanes that hit the state in the Twenties and Thirties, later arrivals had a tendency to play down the threat of hurricanes, with few people bothering to stock emergency provisions or take heed of evacuation warnings. Post-Andrew, however, this attitude has dramatically changed, and hurricane preparation events – which give tips on preparing for and surviving a hurricane – now attract very big crowds indeed.

NATURAL FLORIDA

The biggest surprise for most people in Florida is the abundance of undeveloped, natural areas throughout the state and the extraordinary variety of wildlife and vegetation within them. From a rare hawk that eats only snails to a vine-like fig that strangles other trees, natural Florida possesses plenty that you've probably never seen before, and which – due to drainage, pressures from the agricultural lobby, and the constant need for new housing – may not be on view for very much longer.

BACKGROUND

Many factors contribute to the unusual diversity of **ecosystems** found in Florida, the most obvious being **latitude**: the north of the state has vegetation common to temperate regions, which is quite distinct from the subtropical flora of the south. Another crucial element is **elevation**: while much of Florida is flat and low-lying, a change of a few inches in elevation drastically affects what grows, due in part to the enormous variety of soils.

THE ROLE OF FIRE

Florida has more thunderstorms than any other part of the US, and the resulting lightning frequently ignites **fires**. Many Florida plants have adapted to fire by developing thick bark or the ability to regenerate from stumps. Others, such as cabbage palmetto and sawgrass, protect their growth bud with a sheath of green leaves. Fire is necessary to keep a natural balance of plant species – human attempts to control naturally ignited fires have contributed to the changing composition of Florida's remaining wild lands.

Human intervention was desperately needed in July 1998, when Florida suffered one of its most severe summer droughts. In an instant, devastating wildfires roared out of control in Volusia County, and raged on a head-on course for downtown Daytona and the beaches. Over 140,000 acres of forested lands were destroyed – approximately ten percent of the land in Volusia County. The total loss attributed to the fires was estimated at $379 million. Weary firefighters from across the country came to fight the fires, and due to billowing smoke, a long stretch of I-95 was shut down. For the first time in history, the Daytona International Speedway canceled a major race because of the close proximity of the fires, and turned its massive steel structure into a temporary shelter for displaced residents. The good thing is that there were very few casualties; what's more, the destruction of the underbrush will in fact promote a healthy rejuvenation of the forest floor.

FORESTS AND WOODLAND

Forests and woodlands aren't the first thing people associate with Florida, but the state has an impressive assortment, ranging from the great tracts of upland pine common in the north to the mixed bag of tropical foliage found in the southern hammocks.

PINE FLATWOODS

Covering roughly half of Florida, **pine flatwoods** are most widespread on the southeastern coastal plain. These pine species – longleaf, slash and pond – rise tall and straight like telegraph poles. The Spanish once harvested products such as turpentine and rosin from Florida's flatwood pines, a practice that continued during US settlement, and some trees still bear the scars on their trunks. Pine flatwoods are airy and open, with abundant light filtering through the upper canopy of leaves, allowing thickets of shrubs such as saw palmetto, evergreen oaks, gallberry and fetterbrush to grow. **Inhabitants** of the pine flatwoods include white-tailed deer, cotton rats, brown-headed nuthatches, pine warblers, eastern diamondback rattlesnakes and oak toads. Although many of these creatures also inhabit other Florida ecosystems, the **fox squirrel** – a large and noisy character with a rusty tinge to its undercoat – is one of the few mammalian denizens more or less restricted to the pine flatwoods.

UPLAND PINE FORESTS

As the name suggests, **upland pine forests** – or high pinelands – are found on the rolling sand ridges and sandhills of northeastern Florida and the Panhandle; conditions that tend to keep upland pine forests dryer and therefore even more open than the flatwoods. Upland pine forests have a groundcover of wiregrass and an overstorey of (mostly) longleaf pine trees, which creates a park-like appearance. Redheaded woodpeckers, eastern bluebirds, Florida mice, pocket gophers (locally called "salamanders," a distortion of "sand mounder") and gopher tortoises (amiable creatures often sharing their burrows with gopher frogs) all make the high pine country their home. The latter two, together with scarab beetles, keep the forest healthy by mixing and aerating the soil. The now-endangered red-cockaded woodpecker is symbolic of old-growth upland pine forest; logging and repression of the natural fire process have contributed to its decline.

HAMMOCKS

Wildlife tends to be more abundant in hardwood **hammocks** than in the associated pine forests and prairies (see below). Hammocks consist of narrow bands of (non-pine) hardwoods growing transitionally between pinelands and lower, wetter vegetation. The make-up of hammocks varies across the state: in the south, they chiefly comprise tropical hardwoods (see the "South Florida Rocklands," below); in the north, they contain an overstory of oaks, magnolia and beech, with a few smaller plants – red-bellied woodpeckers, red-tailed and red-shouldered hawks and barred owls nest in them, and you can also find eastern wood rats, striped skunks and white-tailed deer.

SCRUB AND PRAIRIE

Scrub ecosystems once spread to the southern Rocky Mountains and northern Mexico, but climatic changes reduced their distribution and remnant stands are now found only in northern and central Florida. Like the high pines, scrub occurs in dry, hilly areas. The vegetation, which forms an impenetrable mass, consists of varied combinations of drought-adapted evergreen oaks, saw palmetto, Florida rosemary and/or sand pine. The **Florida bonamia**, a morning glory with pale blue funnel-shaped blossoms, is one of the most attractive plants of the scrub, which has more than a dozen plant species officially listed as endangered. Scrub also harbors some unique animals, including the Florida mouse, the Florida scrub lizard, the sand skink and the Florida scrub jay. The **scrub jay** has an unusual social system: pairs nest in co-operation with offspring of previous seasons, who help carry food to their younger siblings. Although not unique to scrub habitat, other inhabitants include black bear, white-tailed deer, bobcats and gopher tortoises.

Some of Florida's inland areas are covered by **prairie**, characterized by love grass, broomsedge and wiregrass – the best examples surround Lake Okeechobee. Settlers destroyed the bison that roamed here some two hundred years ago, but herds are now being reintroduced to some state parks. A more diminutive prairie denizen is the **burrowing owl**: most owls are active at night, but burrowing owls feed during the day and, equally unusually, live in underground dens and bow nervously when approached – earning them the nickname the "howdy owl." Eastern spotted skunks, cotton rats, black vultures, eastern meadowlarks and box turtles are a few other prairie denizens. Nine-banded **armadillos** are also found in prairie habitats and in any non-swampy terrain. Recent invaders from Texas, the armadillos usually forage at night, feeding on insects. Due to poor eyesight, they often fail to notice a human's approach until the last minute, when they will leap up and bound away noisily.

THE SOUTH FLORIDA ROCKLANDS

Elevated areas around the state's southern tip – in the Everglades and along the Florida Keys – support either pines or tropical hardwood hammocks on limestone outcrops collectively known as the **south Florida rocklands**. More jungle-like than the temperate hardwood forests found in northern Florida, the **tropical hardwood hammocks** of the south tend to occur as "tree islands" surrounded by sparser vegetation. Royal palm, pigeon plum, gumbo-limbo (one of the most beautiful of the tropical hammock trees, with a distinctive smooth red bark) and ferns form dense thickets within the hammocks. The **pine forests** of the south Florida rocklands largely consist of scraggly-looking slash pine. Wet prairies or mangroves surround the hammocks and pine forests.

EPIPHYTIC PLANTS

Tropical hammocks contain various forms of **epiphytic plants** – which use other plants for physical support but don't depend on them for nutrients. In southern Florida, epiphytes include orchids, ferns, bromeliads (**Spanish moss** is one of the most widespread bromeliads, hanging from tree branches throughout the state and forming the "canopy roads" in Tallahassee, see "The Panhandle"). Seemingly the most aggressive of epiphytes, **strangler figs**, after germinating in the canopy of trees such as palms, suffocate their host tree. They then send out aerial roots that eventually reach the soil and then tightly enlace the host, preventing growth of the trunk. Finally, the fig produces so many leaves that it chokes out the host's greenery and the host dies leaving only the fig.

OTHER PLANTS AND VERTEBRATES

The south Florida rocklands support over forty plants and a dozen vertebrates found nowhere else in the state. These include the crenulate lead plant, the Key tree cactus, the Florida mastiff bat, the Key deer and the Miami black-headed snake. More common residents include **butterflies and spiders** – the black and yellow yeliconia butterflies, with their long paddle-shaped wings and a distinctive gliding flight pattern, are particularly elegant. Butterflies need to practice careful navigation as hammocks are laced with the foot-long webs of the banana spider. Other wildlife species include sixty types of land snail, green tree frogs, green anoles, cardinals, opossums, raccoons and white-tailed deer. Most of these are native to the southeastern US, but a few West Indian bird species, such as the mangrove cuckoo, gray kingbird and white-crowned pigeon, have colonized the south Florida rocklands.

SWAMPS AND MARSHES

Although about half have been destroyed due to logging, peat removal, draining, or sewage outflow, swamps are still found all over Florida. Trees growing around swamps include pines, palms, cedars, oaks, black gum, willows and bald cypress. Particularly adapted to aquatic conditions, the bald cypress is ringed by knobby "knees," or modified roots, providing oxygen to the tree, which would otherwise suffocate in the wet soil. Epiphytic orchids and bromeliads are common on cypresses, especially in the southern part of the state. Florida's official state tree, the sabal palm, is another swamp/hammock plant: "heart of palm" is the gourmet's name for the vegetable cut from its insides and used in salads.

Florida swamps also have many species of **insectivorous plants**; sticky pads or liquid-filled funnels trap small insects, which are then digested by the nitrogen-hungry plant. Around the Apalachicola National Forest is the highest diversity of carnivorous plants in the world, among them pitcher plants, bladderworts and sundews. Other swamp-dwellers include dragonflies, snails, clams, fish, bird-voiced tree frogs, limpkins, ibis, wood ducks, beavers, raccoons and Florida panthers.

Wetlands with relatively few trees, **freshwater marshes** range from shallow wet prairies to deep-water cattail marshes. **The Everglades** form Florida's largest marsh, most of which is sawgrass. On higher ground with good soils, sawgrass (actually a sedge) grows densely; at lower elevations it's sparser, and often an algae mat covers the soil between its plants. Water beetles, tiny crustaceans such as amphipods, mosquitoes, crayfish, killifish, sunfish, gar, catfish, bullfrogs, herons, egrets, ibis, water rats, white-tailed deer and Florida panthers can all be found. With luck, you might see a **snail kite**: a brown or black mottled hawk with a very specialized diet, entirely dependent on large apple snails. Snail and snail kite numbers have drastically fallen following the draining of marshes for agriculture and flood control. So far, over sixty percent of the Everglades has been irreversibly drained.

WETLAND DENIZENS: ALLIGATORS AND WADING BIRDS

Alligators are one of the most widely known inhabitants of Florida's wetlands, lakes and rivers. Look for them on sunny mornings when they bask on logs or banks. If you hear thunder rumbling on a clear day, it may in fact be the bellow of territorial males. Alligators can reach ten feet in length and primarily prey on fish, turtles, birds, crayfish and crabs. Once overhunted for their hides and meat, alligators have made a strong comeback since protection was initiated in 1973; by 1987, Florida had up to half a million of them. They are not usually dangerous – only a handful of fatal attacks have been registered since 1973. Most at risk are people who swim at dusk and small children playing unattended near water. To many creatures, alligators are a life-saver: during the summer, when the marshes dry up, they use their snouts, legs and tails to enlarge existing pools, creating a refuge for themselves and for other aquatic species. In these "gator holes," garfish stack up like cordwood, snakes search for frogs, and otters and anhingas forage for fish.

Wading birds are conspicuous in the wetlands. Egrets, herons and ibis, usually clad in white or grey feathers, stalk frogs, mice and small fish. Turn-of-the-century plume-hunters decimated these birds to make fanciful hats, and during the last few decades habitat destruction has caused a ninety percent reduction in their numbers. Nonetheless, many are still visible in swamps, marshes and mangroves. Cattle egrets, invaders from South America, are a common sight on pastures, where they forage on insects disturbed by grazing livestock. Pink waders – roseate spoonbills and, to a much lesser extent, flamingoes – can also be found in southern Florida's wetlands.

LAKES, SPRINGS AND RIVERS

Florida has almost 8000 freshwater **lakes**. Game fish such as bass and bluegill are common, but the waters are too warm to support trout. Some native fish species are threatened by the introduction of the **walking catfish**, which has a specially adapted gill system enabling it to leave the water and take the fish equivalent of cross-country hikes. A native of India and Burma, the walking catfish was released into southern Florida canals in the early Sixties and within twenty years had "walked" across twenty counties, disturbing the indigenous food chain. A freeze eliminated a number of these exotic fish, though enough remain to cause concern.

Most Florida **springs** release cold fresh water, but some springs are warm and others emit sulfur, chloride or salt-laden waters. Homosassa Springs (see "The West Coast"), for example, has a high chloride content, making it attractive to both freshwater and marine species of fish.

Besides fish, Florida's extensive **river** system supports snails, freshwater mussels and crayfish. Southern river-dwellers also include the lovable **manatee**, or sea cow, which inhabits bays and shallow coastal waters. The only totally aquatic herbivorous mammal, manatees sometimes weigh almost a ton but only eat aquatic plants. Unable to tolerate cold conditions, manatees are partial to the warm water discharged by power plants, taking some of them as far north as North Carolina. In Florida during the winter, the large springs at Crystal River (see "The West Coast") attract manatees, some of which have become tame enough to allow divers to scratch their bellies. Although they have few natural enemies, manatees are on the decline, often due to powerboat propellers injuring their backs or heads when they feed at the surface.

THE COAST

There's a lot more than sunbathing taking place around Florida's **coast**. The sandy beaches provide a habitat for many species, not least sea turtles. Where there isn't sand, you'll find the fascinating mangrove forests, or wildlife-filled salt marshes and estuaries. Offshore, coral reefs provide yet another exotic ecosystem, and one of the more pleasurable to explore by snorkeling or diving.

SANDY BEACHES

Waves bring many interesting creatures onto Florida's **sandy beaches**, such as sponges, horseshoe crabs and the occasional sea horse. Florida's **shells** are justly famous – fig shells, moon snails, conches, whelks, olive shells, red and orange scallops, murex, cockles, pen and turban shells are a few of the many varieties. As you beachcomb, beware of stepping barefoot on purplish fragments of **man-of-war** tentacles: these jellyfish have no means of locomotion, and their floating, sail-like bodies often cause them to be washed ashore – their tentacles, which sometimes reach to sixty feet in length, can deliver a painful sting. More innocuous beach inhabitants include wintering birds such as black-bellied plovers and sanderlings, and nesting black skimmers.

Of the seven species of **sea turtle**, five nest on Florida's sandy beaches: green, loggerhead, leatherback, hawksbill and olive ridley. From February to August, the female turtles haul out at night, excavate a beachside hole and deposit a hundred-plus eggs. Not many of these will survive to adulthood: raccoons eat a lot of the eggs, and hatchlings are liable to be crushed by vehicles on the coastal highways when they become disoriented by their lights. Programs to hatch the eggs artificially have helped offset some of the losses. The best time to view sea turtles is during June – peak nesting time – with one of the park-ranger-led walks offered along the southern portion of the northeast coast (see Chapter Four, "The Northeast Coast").

MANGROVES

Found in brackish waters around the Florida Keys and the southwest coast, Florida has three species of **mangrove**. Unlike most plants, mangroves bear live young: the "seeds," or propagules, germinate while still on the tree; after dropping from the parent, the young propagule floats for weeks or months until it washes up on a suitable site, where its sprouted condition allows it to put out roots rapidly. Like bald cypress, mangroves have difficulty extracting oxygen from their muddy environs and solve this problem with extensive aerial roots, which either dangle finger-like from branches or twist outwards from the lower trunk. Various fish species, such as the mangrove snapper, depend on mangroves as a nursery; other **mangrove inhabitants** include frogs, crocodiles, brown pelicans, wood storks, roseate spoonbills, river otters, mink and raccoons.

SALT MARSHES AND ESTUARIES

Like the mangrove ecosystem, the **salt marsh and estuary** habitat provides a nursery for many fish species, which in turn fodder larger fish, herons, egrets and the occasional dolphin. **Crocodiles**, with narrower and more pointed snouts than alligators, are seldom sighted, and confined to salt water at the state's southernmost tip. In a few southern Florida salt marshes,

you might find a **great white heron**, a rare and handsome form of the more common great blue heron. Around Florida Bay, great white herons have learned to beg for fish from local residents, each of these massive birds "working" a particular neighborhood – striding from household to household demanding fish by rattling window blinds with their bills or issuing guttural croaks. A less appealing salt marsh denizen is the **mosquito**: unfortunately, the more damaging methods of mosquito control, such as impounding salt water or spraying DDT, have inflicted extensive harm on the fragile salt marshes and estuaries.

THE CORAL REEF

A long band of living **coral reef** frames Florida's southeastern corner. Living coral comes in many colors: star coral is green, elkhorn coral orange, and brain coral red. Each piece of coral is actually a colony of hundreds or thousands of small, soft animals called **polyps**, related to sea anemones and jellyfish. The polyps secrete limestone to form their hard outer skeletons, and at night extend their feathery tentacles to filter seawater for microscopic food. The filtering process, however, provides only a fraction of the coral's nutrition – most is produced via the photosynthesis of algae that live within the polyps' cells. In recent years, influxes of warmer water, possibly associated with global warming, have killed off large numbers of the algae cells. The half-starved polyp then often succumbs to disease, a phenomenon known as "bleaching." Although this has been observed throughout the Pacific, the damage in Florida has so far been moderate: the impact of the tourist industry on the reef has been more pronounced, though reef destruction for souvenirs is now banned.

Coral reefs are home to a kaleidoscopic variety of brightly colored fish – beau gregories, porkfish, parrot fish, blennies, grunts and wrasses – which swirl in dazzling schools or lurk between coral crevices. The **damselfish** is the farmer of the reef: after destroying a polyp patch, it feeds on the resultant algae growth, fiercely defending it from other fish. Sponges, feather-duster worms, sea fans, crabs, spiny lobsters, sea urchins and conches are among the thousands of other creatures resident in the coral reef.

FLORIDA ON FILM

The Silver Screen and the Sunshine State have one vital thing in common: escapism. Both on film and off, Florida has always represented the ultimate getaway. For nineteenth-century homesteaders, Cuban refugees, New York retirees, libido-laden college kids, or criminals on the lam, the state has always beckoned as some kind of paradise. Hollywood has also used Florida as an exotic backdrop for everything from light-hearted vacation flicks to black-hearted crime yarns, and the state has made the most of its movie-tinted charms. Henry Levin's phenomenally successful teen flick Where the Boys Are (1960), for instance, not only spawned a cinematic sub-genre, but also made Fort Lauderdale the country's top Spring Break resort. And Miami's rejuvenation in the Eighties can be attributed at least in part to the glamour imparted by filmmaker Michael Mann's TV series, Miami Vice – though whether the cantankerous residents of Seinfeld's Del Boca Vista will do the same for Florida retirement communities remains to be seen.

To immerse yourself in Florida's cinematic history, where images of palm trees, beaches and luxury hotels predominate, is to take a virtual vacation. And though there are plenty of mediocre Florida flicks (most of them sun-addled Spring Break romps or Elvis Presley showcases), there are many that convey the unique and varied qualities of the state. Here are forty of the best.

Ace Ventura, Pet Detective (Tom Shadyac, 1994). The film that launched Jim Carrey's thousand faces. Carrey stars as a bequiffed investigator on a quest to recover Snowflake, the Miami Dolphins' kidnapped mascot, on the eve of the Superbowl. The Miami Dolphins and their quarterback Dan Marino appear as themselves.

Aileen Wuornos: The Selling of a Serial Killer (Nick Broomfield, 1993). British documentarian Broomfield, in his inimitably fearless, in-your-face style, stumbles into a swamp of avarice and exploitation in his search for the true story of Aileen Wuornos, a woman convicted of murdering seven men on a Florida Interstate. That America's first female serial killer comes across as more sympathetic than most of the people around her makes this portrait of backwoods Florida all the more chilling.

The Bellboy (Jerry Lewis, 1960). This film was shot almost entirely within Miami Beach's ultra-kitsch pleasure palace *The Fontainebleau* (the same hotel where James Bond sunbathes at in the beginning of 1964's *Goldfinger*). Jerry Lewis, in his debut as writer-director, plays Stanley, the bellhop from hell, and cameos as vacationing movie star "Jerry Lewis" in one of the most site-specific movies ever made.

Beneath the 12 Mile Reef (Robert Webb, 1953). In this beautiful travelogue, Greek sponge fishermen from Tarpon Springs venture south to fish the "Glades" and tangle with the Anglo "Conchs" of Key West. Robert Wagner plays a young Greek Romeo named Adonis, who dares to dive the "12 mile reef" for his sponge-worthy Juliet.

The Birdcage (Mike Nichols, 1996). Nichols' Miami remake of *La Cage Aux Folles* makes playful use of South Beach's burgeoning gay scene, portraying the rejuvenated art deco playground as a bright paradise of pecs, thongs and drag queens. Impresario Armand (Robin Williams) and reigning Birdcage diva Albert (Nathan Lane) are happily cohabiting in kitsch heaven until the day Armand's son brings his ultra-conservative future in-laws to dinner.

Black Sunday (John Frankenheimer, 1976). Palestinian terrorists, with the aid of disgruntled Vietnam vet Bruce Dern, plan to wipe out 80,000 football fans, including President Jimmy Carter, in the Orange Bowl on Superbowl Sunday. Though the first half of the movie unfolds in Beirut and LA, the heart-stopping climax results in some fine aerial views of Miami.

Blood and Wine (Bob Rafelson, 1997). Jack Nicholson plays a dodgy Miami wine dealer with access to the cellars of Southern Florida's rich and famous. He enlists a wheezy expat safebreaker (Michael Caine), and a feisty Cuban nanny (Jennifer Lopez) in his scheme to snag a million-dollar necklace. When the jewels end up in the hands of his jilted wife (Judy Davis) and perpetually pissed-off stepson (Stephen Dorff) the action heads south to the Florida Keys.

Body Heat (Lawrence Kasdan, 1981). Filmed just south of Palm Beach in the small coastal town of Lake Worth, Kasdan's directorial debut makes the most of the sweaty potential of a southern Florida heatwave. Shady lawyer William Hurt falls for the charms of wealthy Kathleen Turner and plans to bump off her husband for the inheritance.

The Cocoanuts (Joseph Santley & Robert Florey, 1929). Set during Florida's real estate boom, the Marx Brothers' first film stars Groucho as an impecunious hotel proprietor attempting to keep his business afloat by auctioning off land (with the usual interference from Chico and Harpo) in Cocoanut Grove, "the Palm Beach of tomorrow." Groucho expounds on Florida's climate while standing in what is really a sand-filled studio lot.

Cocoon (Ron Howard, 1985). Even extra-terrestrials vacation in Florida. This sentimental, Spielbergesque fantasy centers around residents of a Florida retirement community who discover a local swimming pool with alien powers of rejuvenation. Nearly half a century after he danced with Betty Grable in *Moon Over Miami*, Don Ameche won a Best Supporting Actor Oscar for this film.

Distant Drums (Raoul Walsh, 1951). One of many films that have focused on Florida's Seminole Indians (the first was made by Vitagraph in 1906), *Distant Drums*, set in the midst of the Seminole Wars in 1840, stars Gary Cooper as a legendary Indian fighter who finds himself and his men trapped in the Everglades.

Cooper and his band encounter snakes, alligators, and hordes of Seminole braves as they attempt to reach dry land.

Dumbo (Ben Sharpsteen, 1941). In the opening sequence of this Disney animated classic there is a wonderful stork's-eye view of the entire state of Florida, where the circus has hunkered down for the winter. Though the show eventually goes on the road, this eyeful of Florida seems prescient considering Disney's role in the state some quarter of a century later.

Health (Robert Altman, 1980). Shot entirely at the Sunshine Center in St Petersburg, this barely released Altman flop satirizes the backstage shenanigans at a Florida health-and-nutrition convention. The film stars Glenda Jackson and Lauren Bacall, the latter of which plays an 83-year-old virgin.

The Heartbreak Kid (Elaine May, 1972). An underrated comic masterpiece written by Neil Simon, in which Charles Grodin marries a nice Jewish girl, and then, on the honeymoon drive down to Florida, starts to regret it. His doubts are compounded when goddess Cybil Shephard starts flirting with him on the beach while his sunburnt bride lies in bed.

A Hole in the Head (Frank Capra, 1959). Frank Sinatra plays an irresponsible Miami Beach hotel owner who has dreams of striking it rich by turning South Beach into "Disneyland." The breezy opening titles are pulled on airborne banners across the Miami Beach skyline.

Illtown (Nick Gomez, 1995). Depending on who you ask, Nick Gomez's film has been described as stylish, strange and ambitious or a pretentious mess. This mystical indie film features Tony Danza as a gay mob boss, and a gaggle of familiar indie stars (Michael Rapaport, Adam Trese, Lili Taylor and Kevin Corrigan) as an unlikely bunch of Miami drug dealers.

Key Largo (John Huston, 1948). Though shot entirely on Hollywood sets, Huston's tense crime melodrama about an army veteran (Humphrey Bogart) and a mob boss (Edward G. Robinson) barricaded in a Key Largo hotel during a major hurricane has the credible feel of a muggy summer in the Florida Keys.

Miami Blues (George Armitage, 1990). Adapted from Charles Willeford's fiction, this quirky crime story about a home-loving psychopath (Alec Baldwin), the naive hooker he shacks up with (Jennifer Jason Leigh), and the burnt-out homicide detective who's on their trail (Fred Ward), is set in a seedy back-street Miami that glitters with terrific characters, gritty performances, and delicious offbeat details.

Miami Rhapsody (David Frankel, 1995). Sarah Jessica Parker (kvetching like a female Woody Allen) weighs commitment against the marital dissatisfaction and compulsive infidelity of her extended family in an otherwise picture-perfect, upscale Miami: "I guess I look at marriage the same way I look at Miami: it's hot and it's stormy, and it's occasionally a little dangerous...but if it's really so awful why is there still so much traffic?"

Moon Over Miami (Walter Lang, 1941). Gold-digging, Texas-hamburger-stand waitress Betty Grable takes her sister and aunt to Miami, "where rich men are as plentiful as grapefruit, and millionaires hang from every palm tree." Grable has little trouble snagging herself a couple of ripe ones in this colorful, sappy musical comedy (the theme song "Oh Me, Oh Mi...ami!" sets the tone). On-location shooting took place in Winter Haven and Ocala, a few hundred miles north of Miami.

Night Moves (Arthur Penn, 1975). In one of the great metaphysical thrillers of the post-Watergate Seventies, Gene Hackman plays a weary LA private eye with marital problems who is hired to track down a young and underdressed Melanie Griffith in the Florida Keys.

92 In The Shade (Thomas McGuane, 1975). A nutty, laid-back comedy about rival fishing guides in Key West, starring a potpourri of Hollywood's greatest odd-balls: Peter Fonda, Harry Dean Stanton, Warren Oates, Burgess Meredith and William Hickey. Ripe with local color but somewhat lacking in affect, the film was based on Thomas McGuane's acclaimed novel of the same name.

Out of Sight (Steven Soderbergh, 1998). Flip-flopping between past and present and between a jazzy, sun-drenched Florida and a snow-peppered Detroit, Soderbergh's film is a hugely satisfying adaptation of Elmore Leonard's novel. The action is set in motion when George Clooney's urbane bankrobber tunnels out of a Pensacola penitentiary and into the life of Federal Marshall Jennifer Lopez.

The Palm Beach Story (Preston Sturges, 1942). In this madcap masterpiece, Claudette Colbert takes a train from Penn Station to Palm Beach ("the best place to get a divorce," a cabbie tells her) to free herself from her penniless dreamer of a husband and find herself a good millionaire to marry.

Palmetto (Volker Schlondorff, 1998). Woody Harrelson returns from jail to the Sarasota beach town of Palmetto and becomes Florida's number one patsy when a bleach-blonde Elisabeth Shue walks into his life and proposes a little fake kidnapping. Perfectly exploiting Florida's sultry charms, *Palmetto* is a somewhat cliched neo-noir, but has some satisfying twists and turns.

Porky's (Bob Clark, 1981). The *Citizen Kane* of randy teen movies, the notorious (and Canadian) *Porky's* is set in fictional Angel Beach near Fort Lauderdale in the mid Fifties. A group of high school guys with only one thing on their minds venture into Florida's backcountry in the hopes of getting laid at "Porky's," a licentious redneck bar.

Reap the Wild Wind (Cecil B. DeMille, 1942). A stirring account of skullduggery in the Florida Keys of the 1840s. Spunky Paulette Goddard vacillates between sea salt John Wayne and landlubber Ray Milland while trying to outwit pirates, gangs and a giant squid off the deadly coral reefs.

Revenge of the Creature (Jack Arnold, 1955). Transported comatose from the Upper Amazon, the Creature from the Black Lagoon is brought to Marineland's oceanarium to create the "greatest scientific stir since the explosion of the Atomic Bomb." He creates an even bigger stir when he cuts loose and heads for the beach, crashing a swing party at a seafront oyster house.

Ruby in Paradise (Victor Nunez, 1993). Ashley Judd plays Ruby, who leaves her home in the Tennessee mountains and hitches a ride south to taste life in the Florida Panhandle. Settling in Panama City, Ruby finds work in a tourist shop selling tacky souvenirs. She fends off the boss's son and finds herself along the way. The film was sensitively directed by Florida's own Victor Nunez, a true regional independent who has been making films in northern Florida since 1970.

Salesman (The Maysles Brothers, 1968). The second half of this brilliant and moving documentary follows four bible salesman to Opa-Locka on the outskirts of Miami. It's not a tale of beaches and luxury hotels, but rather low-rent apartments, cheap motels and the quiet desperation of four men trying to sell over-priced illustrated Bibles door-to-door.

Scarface (Brian De Palma, 1983). Small-time Cuban thug Tony Montana arrives in Miami during the 1980 Mariel boatlift and murders, bullies and snorts his way to the top of his profession, becoming Miami's most powerful drug lord. One of the great Florida movies, De Palma's seductive and shocking paean to excess and the perversion of the American Dream stars Al Pacino in a legendary, go-for-broke performance.

Seminole (Budd Boetticher, 1953). Set five years before *Distant Drums* (see above) and far more sympathetic to the Seminole's plight, Boetticher's Western stars Rock Hudson as a US Dragoon and Anthony Quinn as his half-breed childhood friend who has become the Seminole Chief Osceola. Attempting to claim even the swamps of Florida for white settlers, a power-hungry general sends a platoon into the Everglades to flush out the Seminole and drive them out west.

Some Like It Hot (Billy Wilder, 1959). Wilder's classic farce starts in 1929 in Chicago. Jazz musicians Tony Curtis and Jack Lemmon escape retribution for witnessing the St Valentine's Day massacre by disguising themselves as women and joining an all-girl jazz band on a train to Miami. Though *Some Like it Hot* could be a candidate for the best film ever set in Miami, it was actually shot at the *Hotel del Coronado* in San Diego.

Stranger than Paradise (Jim Jarmusch, 1984). Jarmusch's austere indie masterpiece about two laconic hipsters and their Hungarian cousin. The trio travels from snow-bound Ohio to a lifeless, out-of-season Florida. The film's Florida scenes consist of a cheap motel room and a deserted stretch of beach, proving the main characters' theory that everywhere starts to look the same after a while.

There's Something About Mary (The Farrelly Brothers, 1998). Years after a heinous pre-prom disaster (involving an unruly zipper), Rhode Island geek Ben Stiller tracks down Mary, the eponymous object of his affection, to her new home in Miami. Once there he finds he's not the only one suffering from obsessive tendencies. The Farrelly boys have created a hysterical, gross-out masterpiece.

Tony Rome (Gordon Douglas, 1967). Wise-cracking, hard-living private eye Frank Sinatra tangles with pushers, strippers, gold diggers and self-made millionaires on the wild side of Miami (the town his love interest Jill St John calls "Twenty miles of beach looking for a city"). The film is a run-of-the-mill detective yarn, but Frank was entertaining enough to warrant a sequel: *Lady in Cement*.

The Truman Show (Peter Weir, 1998). The picture-perfect, picket-fence community of Seahaven that Jim Carrey's Truman Burbank calls home turns out to be nothing more than a giant television studio, where Truman is watched every minute of the day in the world's longest-running soap opera. The false paradise of Seahaven is actually the real, but equally artificial, Florida Gulf Coast town of Seaside, a planned vacation community (built in 1981) that looks like it's stuck in the Fifties.

Ulee's Gold (Victor Nunez, 1997). Twenty-two years after *92 in the Shade*, Peter Fonda gave the best performance of his career as Florida beekeeper Ulee, a stoical Vietnam vet raising his granddaughters while his son is in jail. Florida auteur Nunez (*Ruby in Paradise*) knows and captures northern Florida better than any filmmaker, and despite a strained plot about a couple of ne'er do wells and a stash of money, this meditative, measured film is a triumph.

Wild Things (John McNaughton, 1997). A cartoonish, noir fantasy about handsome high school counselors, lubricious schoolgirls, and wealthy widows in a well-heeled community in the Everglades. Beautifully shot and played to the hilt by Matt Dillon, Kevin Bacon, Denise Richards and Neve Campbell, though it fails to live up to the promise of its campy set-up.

The Yearling (Clarence Brown, 1946). A Technicolor classic about a family struggling to eke out a living in the scrub country of northern Florida (in the vicinity of Lake George and Volusia) in 1878. Oscar-winner Claude Jarman Jr plays the son of Gregory Peck and Jane Wyman who adopts a mighty troublesome fawn. The film was shot on location and based on Florida scribe Marjorie Kinnan Rawling's Pulitzer Prize-winning novel of the same name.

BOOKS

Florida's perennial state of social and political flux has always promised rich material for historians and journalists eager to pin the place down. Rarely have they managed this, though the picture of the region's unpredictable evolution that emerges can make for compulsive reading. Many established fiction writers spend their winters in Florida, but few have convincingly portrayed its characters, climate and scenery. Those that have succeeded, however, have produced some of the most unique and gripping literature to emerge from any part of the US.

HISTORY

Edward N. Akin, *Flagler: Rockefeller Partner & Florida Baron*. Solid biography of the man whose Standard Oil fortune helped build Florida's first hotels and railroads.

Charles R. Ewen and John H. Hann, *Hernando de Soto among the Apalachee*. A history and description of the archeological site (located in downtown Tallahassee) believed to be a campsite used by Hernando de Soto in the sixteenth century.

Carl Hiaasen, *Team Rodent*. A native of Florida, Hiaasen has been a first-hand witness to Disney's domination of Orlando, and this book is a scathing attack on the entertainment conglomerate, exposing Disney for what Hiaasen thinks it is: evil. As he says in this book, "Disney is so good at being good that it manifests an

evil; so uniformly and courteous, so dependably clean and conscientious, so unfailingly entertaining that it's unreal, and therefore is an agent of pure wickedness." Like Hiaasen's fiction work (see below), a mix of sharp wit, informed research – and a lot of humor.

Stetson Kennedy, *The Klan Unmasked*. A riveting history of the Klan's activity in the post-World War Two era, including specific reference to Florida.

John M. Kirk, *José Marti*. A look at José Marti, the most powerful reactionary figure in Cuban resistance history.

Howard Kleinberg, *The Way We Were*. Oversized overview of Miami's history: colorful archival photos and text by a former editor-in-chief of the city's dominant newspaper, *The Miami News*.

Jerald T. Milanich, *Florida's Indians, from Ancient Times to the Present*. A comprehensive history spanning 12,000 years of Indian life in Florida.

Gary R. Mormino and George E. Pozzetta, *The Immigrant World of Ybor City*. Flavorful accounts of the Cuban, Italian and Spanish immigrants that built their lives around Ybor City's cigar industry at the turn of the century.

Helen Muir, *Miami, USA*. An insider's account of how Miami's first developers gave the place shape during the land boom of the Twenties.

John Rothchild, *Up for Grabs: A Trip Through Time and Space in the Sunshine State*. An irreverent look at Florida's checkered career as a vacation spa, tourist trap and haven for scheming ne'er-do-wells.

Charlton W. Tebeau, *A History of Florida*. The definitive academic tome, but not for casual reading.

Victor Andres Triay, *Fleeing Castro*. An emotional account of the plight of Cuba's children during the missile crisis. With their parents unable to attain visas, 14,048 children were smuggled from the island; many never saw their families again.

Garcilaso de la Vega, *The Florida of the Inca*. Comprehensive account of the sixteenth-century expedition led by Hernando de Soto through Florida's prairies, swamps and aboriginal settlements. Extremely turgid in parts, but overall an excellent insight into the period.

David C. Weeks, *Ringling.* An in-depth work chronicling the time spent in Florida by circus guru John Ringling.

Patsy West, *The Enduring Seminoles.* A history of Florida's Seminole Indians, who, by embracing tourism, found a means to keep their vibrant cultural identity alive.

Lawrence E. Will, *Swamp to Sugarbowl: Pioneer Days in Belle Glade.* A "cracker" account of early times in the state, written in first-person redneck vernacular. Variously oafish and offensive – but never dull.

NATURAL HISTORY

Mark Derr, *Some Kind of Paradise.* A cautionary history of Florida's penchant to mishandle its environmental assets, from spongers off the reefs to Miami's ruthless hotel contractors.

Marjory Stoneman Douglas, *The Everglades: River of Grass.* Concerned conservationist literature by one of the state's most respected historians, describing the nature and beauty of the Everglades from their beginnings. A superb work that contributed to the founding of the Everglades National Park.

Jon L. Dunn & Eirik A.T. Blom, *Field Guide to the Birds of North America, Second Ed.* The best country-wide guide, with plenty on Florida, and excellent illustrations throughout.

Harold R. Holt, *Lane's "A Birder's Guide to Florida."* Detailed accounts of when and where to find Florida's birds, including maps and seasonal charts. Aimed at the expert but excellent value for the novice bird-watcher.

Ronald L. Myers & John J. Ewel, *Ecosystems of Florida.* Technical yet highly readable treatise for the serious ecologist.

Joe Schafer and George Tanner, *Landscaping for Florida's Wildlife.* Step-by-step advice on how to replicate a sliver of Florida's wildlife in your own garden.

Glen Simmons with Laura Ogden, *Gladesmen.* Entertaining accounts of the "swamp rats": rugged men and women who made a living wrestling alligators and trekking the "Glades."

TRAVEL IMPRESSIONS

T. D. Allman, *Miami: City of the Future.* Excellent, incisive look at modern Miami, which becomes bogged down when going further back than *Miami Vice.*

William Bartram, *Travels.* The lively diary of an eighteenth-century naturalist rambling through the Deep South and on into Florida during the period of British rule. Outstanding accounts of the indigenous people and all kinds of wildlife.

Edna Buchanan, *The Corpse had a Familiar Face.* Sometimes sharp, often sensationalist account of the author's years spent pounding the crime beat for the *Miami Herald* – five thousand corpses and gore galore. The subsequent *Vice* is more of the same.

Joan Didion, *Miami* A riveting though ultimately unsatisfying voyage around the impenetrably complex and wildly passionate *el exilio* politics of Cuban Miami.

Lynn Geldof, *Cubans.* Passionate and rambling interviews with Cubans in Cuba and Miami, which confirm the tight bond between them.

Henry James, *The American Scene.* Interesting waffle from the celebrated novelist, including written portraits of St Augustine and Palm Beach as they thronged with wintering socialites at the turn of the century.

Norman Mailer, *Miami and the Siege of Chicago.* A rabid study of the American political conventions of 1968, the first part frothing over the Republican Party's shenanigans at Miami Beach when Nixon beat Reagan for the presidential ticket.

Roxanne Pulitzer, *The Prize Pulitzer: The Scandal that Rocked Palm Beach.* A small-town girl who married into the jet-set lifestyle of Palm Beach describes the mud-slinging in Florida's most moneyed community when she seeks a divorce.

David Rieff, *Going to Miami: Exiles, Tourists and Refugees in the New America.* An exploration of Miami through the minds of its conservative Cubans, its struggling black and Haitian communities, and its resentful Anglos – but with too many sexist musings to be credible.

Alexander Stuart, *Life on Mars.* "Paradise with a lobotomy" is how a friend of the author described Florida. This is an often amusing series of snap shots of both the empty lives led by the beautiful people of South Beach and the redneck "white trash" of up-state.

John Williams, *Into the Badlands: A Journey through the American Dream.* The author's trek across the US to interview the country's best crime writers begins in Miami, "the city that coke built", its compelling strangeness all too briefly revelled in.

ARCHITECTURE AND PHOTOGRAPHY

Todd Bertolaet, *Crescent Rivers*. Ansel Adamsesque photos of the dark, blackwater rivers that wind through Florida's Big Bend.

Barbara Baer Capitman, *Deco Delights*. A tour of Miami Beach's Art Deco buildings by the woman who championed their preservation, with definitive photography.

Laura Cerwinske, *Miami: Hot & Cool*. Coffee-table tome with text on high-style south Florida living and glowing, colour pics of Miami's beautiful homes and gardens. By the same author, *Tropical Deco: The Architecture & Design of Old Miami Beach* delivers a wealth of architectural detail.

Donald W. Curl, *Mizner's Florida: American Resort Architecture*. An assessment of the life, career and designs of Addison Mizner, the self-taught architect responsible for the "Bastard Spanish Moorish Romanesque Renaissance Bull Market Damn the Expense Style" structures of Palm Beach and Boca Raton.

Hap Hatton, *Tropical Splendor: An Architectural History of Florida*. A readable, informative and effectively illustrated account of the wild, weird and wonderful buildings that have graced and disgraced the state over the years.

Alva Johnston, *The Legendary Mizners*. A racy biography of Addison Mizner and his brother Wilson, telling how they wined, dined and married into the lifestyles of the rich and famous of the Twenties.

Gary Monroe, *Life in South Beach*. A slim volume of monochrome photos showing Miami Beach's South Beach before the restoration of the Art Deco district and the arrival of globetrotting trendies.

Nicholas N. Patricios, *Building Marvelous Miami*. Two-hundred-and-fifty photos document the architectural development of Florida's favorite city.

Woody Walters, *Visions of Florida*. Black-and-white photos, but ones which still convey the richness and beauty of Florida's terrain, from misty mornings in Tallahassee to shocks of lightning over the Everglades.

William Weber, *Florida Nature Photography*. A glossy, pictorial look at Florida's many state parks, recreation areas and nature preserves.

FICTION

Pat Booth, *Miami*. It had to happen: best-selling author uses the glitz-and-glamor of Miami's South Beach as a backdrop to a pot-boiling tale of seduction and desire.

Harry Crews, *Florida Frenzy*. A collection of tales relating macho outdoor pursuits like 'gator poaching and cockfighting. "[It] will hit you right between the eyes," says the *Chicago Tribune*.

Marjory Stoneman Douglas, *A River in Flood*. A collection of short stories (first published separately in the *Saturday Evening Post* in the Twenties and Thirties) that reflects on the many facets of Florida life: from hurricanes to cockfights. Today, at 108, Marjory Stoneman Douglas is the *grand dame* of Florida writers.

Edward Falco, *Winter in Florida*. Flawed but compulsive story of a cosseted New York boy seeking thrills on a central Florida horse farm.

Ernest Hemingway, *To Have and Have Not*. Hemingway lived and drank in Key West for years but set only this moderate tale in the town, describing the woes of fishermen brutalized by the Depression.

Carl Hiaasen, *Double Whammy*. Ferociously funny fishing thriller that brings together a classic collection of warped but believable Florida characters; among them a hermit-like ex-state governor, a cynical Cuban cop and a corrupt TV preacher. By the same author, *Skin Tight* explores the perils of unskilled plastic surgery in a Miami crawling with mutant hitmen, bought politicians and police on gangsters' payrolls, and *Native Tongue* delves into the murky goings-on behind the scenes at a Florida theme park.

Zora Neale Hurston, *Their Eyes Were Watching God*. Florida-born Hurston became one of the bright lights of the Harlem Renaissance in the Twenties. This novel describes the founding of Eatonville – her home town and the state's first all-black town – and the labourers' lot in Belle Glade at the time of the 1928 hurricane. Equally hard to put down are *Jonah's Gourd Vine* and the autobiography, *Dust Tracks on a Road*.

David A. Karfelt, *American Tropic*. Overblown saga of passion and power set during several key eras in Florida's history; just the job for idle hours on the beach.

Peter Matthiessen, *Killing Mister Watson*. Thoroughly researched story of the early days of white settlement in the Everglades. Slow-paced but a strong insight into the Florida frontier mentality.

Thomas McGuane, *Ninety-Two in the Shade*. A strange, hallucinatory search for identity by a young man of shifting mental states who aspires to become a Key West fishing guide – and whose family and friends are equally warped. The author also made the book into a film (see above). *Panama*, by the same writer, is also set in Key West.

Theodore Pratt, *The Barefoot Mailman*. A Forties account of the long-distance postman who kept the far-flung settlements of pioneer-period Florida in mail by hiking the many miles of beach between them.

Marjorie Kinnan Rawlings, *Short Stories*. A collection of 23 of Rawlings' most acclaimed short pieces, which draw heavily on Florida's natural surroundings for inspiration.

John Sayles, *Los Gusanos*. Absorbing, if long-winded novel set around the lives of Cuban exiles in Miami – written by a cult film director.

Edmund Skellings, *Collected Poems: 1958–1998*. A best-of collection of work by Florida's Poet Laureate. Of Skellings' poems, Norman Mailer says, "At their best, they shine like silver in the sun."

Daniel Vilmure, *Life in the Land of the Living*. Only the vigor of the writing lifts this purposeless story of two brothers rampaging through an unnamed Florida port town on a blisteringly hot Friday night.

CRIME FICTION

Edna Buchanan, *Nobody Lives Forever*. Tense, psycho-killer thriller played out on the mean streets of Miami. See also "Travel impressions."

Liza Cody, *Backhand*. London's finest female private investigator, Anna Lee, follows the clues from Kensington to the West Coast of Florida – highly entertaining.

James Hall, *Under Cover of Daylight; Squall Line; Hard Aground*. Taut thrillers with a cast of crazies that make the most of the edge-of-the-world landscapes of the Florida Keys.

Elmore Leonard, *Stick; La Brava; Gold Coast*. The pick of this highly recommended author's Florida-set thrillers, respectively detailing the rise of an opportunist black through the money, sex and drugs of Latino Miami; low-life on the seedy South Beach before the preservation of the Art Deco district; and the tribulations of a wealthy gangster-widow alone in a Fort Lauderdale mansion.

Charles Willeford, *Miami Blues*. Thanks to an uninspired film, the best-known but not the best of a highly recommended series starring Hoke Mosely, a cool and calculating, but very human, Miami cop. Superior titles in the series are *The Way We Die Now, Kiss Your Ass Goodbye* and *Sideswipe*.

COOKERY

Sue Mullin, *Nuevo Cubano Cooking*. Easy-to-follow instructions and mouth-watering photographs of recipes fusing traditional Cuban cooking with nouvelle cuisine.

Ferdie Pacheco and Luisita Sevilla Pacheco, *The Christmas Eve Cookbook*. A collection of over 200 holiday recipes and stories that illustrates the melting pot of immigrants that settled in Ybor City.

Steven Raichleu, *Miami Spice*. Latin American and Caribbean cooking meets Florida and the "Deep South," resulting in some of the tastiest dishes in America. Clear recipes and interesting background information.

Stay in touch with us!

ROUGH*NEWS* is Rough Guides' free newsletter.
In three issues a year we give you news, travel
issues, music reviews, readers' letters and the
latest dispatches from authors on the road.

I would like to receive ROUGH*NEWS*: please put me on your free mailing list.

NAME . . . .

ADDRESS . . . .

Please clip or photocopy and send to: Rough Guides, 62–70 Shorts Gardens, London WC2H 9AB,
England or Rough Guides, 375 Hudson Street, New York, NY 10014, USA.

Know Where You're Going?

Wherever you're headed, **Rough Guides** show you the way, on and off the beaten track. We give you the best places to stay and eat on your **budget**, plus all the inside background and info to make your **trip** a great experience.

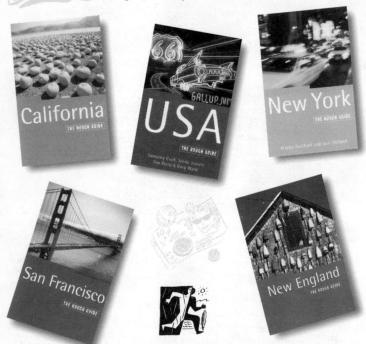

ROUGH GUIDES

Travel Guides to more than 100 destinations worldwide from **A**msterdam to **Z**imbabwe.

AT ALL BOOKSTORES • DISTRIBUTED BY PENGUIN

IF KNOWLEDGE IS POWER,
THIS ROUGH GUIDE IS A POCKET-SIZED BATTERING RAM

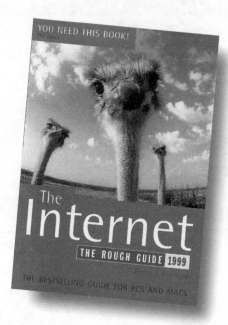

Written in plain English, with no hint of jargon, the Rough Guide to the Internet will make you an Internet guru in the shortest possible time. It cuts through the hype and makes all others look like nerdy textbooks

AT ALL BOOKSTORES • DISTRIBUTED BY PENGUIN

www.roughguides.com

Check out our Web site for unrivalled travel information on the Internet.
Plan ahead by accessing the full text of our major titles, make travel reservations and keep up to date with the latest news in the Traveller's Journal or by subscribing to our free newsletter ROUGH*NEWS* - packed with stories from Rough Guide writers.

HOSTELLING INTERNATIONAL
choose FLORIDA

MIAMI BEACH
ORLANDO/KISSIMMEE

Hostelling International–Miami Beach
is just two blocks from the ocean! Located in the Art Deco district of South Beach, this hostel is surrounded by night clubs, cafés and shops. The hostel is a hot spot, and a great way to experience South Florida!

Open 24 hours. Just $14-15 a night!
1438 Washington Ave., Miami Beach, FL 33139. For toll-free reservations within the U.S. call 1-800-379-CLAY. Telephone: 1-305-534-2988

Hostelling International–Orlando/Kissimmee Resort is just five miles from Walt Disney World, and the hostel offers inexpensive shuttle service to area attractions. While at the hostel, you can take a dip in the pool, enjoy a paddleboat ride on the lake, or have a barbecue in the picnic area. Check out the hostel's calender of exciting special programs and activities.

Open 24 hours. Just $16-18 a night!
4840 West Irlo Bronson Hwy, Kissimmee, FL 34746. For toll-free reservations within the U.S. call 1-800-909-4776, code 33. Telephone: 1-407-396-8282.

www.hiayh.org

The best hostels in the best places!

HOSTELLING
INTERNATIONAL

STANFORDS MAPS CHARTS BOOKS

Est.1852

World Travel starts at Stanfords

Maps, Travel Guides, Atlases, Charts
Mountaineering Maps and Books, Travel Writing
Travel Accessories, Globes & Instruments

Stanfords
12-14 Long Acre
Covent Garden
London
WC2E 9LP

Stanfords
at Campus Travel
52 Grosvenor Gardens
London
SW1W 0AG

Stanfords
at British Airways
156 Regent Street
London
W1R 5TA

Stanfords in Bristol
29 Corn Street
Bristol
BS1 1HT

International Mail Order Service
Tel: 0171 836 1321 **Fax**: 0171 836 0189

The World's Finest Map and Travel Bookshops

the perfect getaway vehicle

low-price holiday car rental.

rent a car from holiday autos and you'll give yourself real freedom to explore your holiday destination. with great-value, fully-inclusive rates in over 4,000 locations worldwide, wherever you're escaping to, we're there to make sure you get excellent prices and superb service.

what's more, you can book now with complete confidence. our £5 undercut* ensures that you are guaranteed the best value for money in holiday destinations right around the globe.

drive away with a great deal, call holiday autos now on **0990 300 400** and quote ref RG.

holiday autos miles ahead

*in the unlikely event that you should see a cheaper like for like pre-paid rental rate offered by any other independent uk car rental company before or after booking but prior to departure, holiday autos will undercut that price by a full £5. we truly believe we cannot be beaten on price.